BLOODY BREATHITT

BLOODY BREATHITT

Politics and Violence in the Appalachian South

T. R. C. Hutton

UNIVERSITY PRESS OF KENTUCKY

Scholarly publisher for the Commonwealth,
serving Bellarmine University, Berea College, Centre College of Kentucky,
Eastern Kentucky University, The Filson Historical Society, Georgetown College,
Kentucky Historical Society, Kentucky State University, Morehead State
University, Murray State University, Northern Kentucky University, Transylvania
University, University of Kentucky, University of Louisville, and Western
Kentucky University.
All rights reserved.

Editorial and Sales Offices: The University Press of Kentucky
663 South Limestone Street, Lexington, Kentucky 40508-4008
www.kentuckypress.com

17 16 15 14 13   5 4 3 2 1

Library of Congress Cataloging-in-Publication Data

Hutton, T. R. C.
  Bloody Breathitt : politics and violence in the Appalachian south / T. R. C.
Hutton.
      pages cm. — (New directions in Southern history)
  Includes bibliographical references and index.
  ISBN 978-0-8131-3646-2 (hardcover : alk. paper) -- ISBN 978-0-8131-4242-5
  — ISBN 978-0-8131-4243-2
  1. Breathitt County (Ky.)—History. 2. Breathitt County (Ky.)—Politics and
government. 3. Violence—Kentucky—Breathitt County—History. I. Title.
  F457.B85H87 2013
  976.9'19—dc23   2013010408

This book is printed on acid-free paper meeting the requirements of the
American National Standard for Permanence in Paper for Printed Library
Materials.

Manufactured in the United States of America.

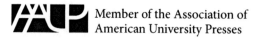 Member of the Association of
American University Presses

To my parents,
Bill and Cathy Hutton

Contents

PREFACE

When I first decided to write about Breathitt County, Kentucky, I expected I'd be writing a local study similar to most of the serious scholarship on Appalachia. What I discovered was a place where those in power needed violence in order to maintain their control, while those who refused to knuckle under to them saw violence as a tool themselves. These were flawed people, and even those who ended up on the "right side of history" got into that position by killing. Their stories were distorted by the language used to describe their actions without their verification. These are themes familiar to anyone who has studied Oliver Cromwell or Che Guevara.

In the half century after the Civil War Breathitt County was a violent place, but no more so than many other places in a particularly violent time period in a very violent country. I also discovered that different kinds of killing were damned or praised or tolerated according to the needs and wishes of powerful men.

Much of what went on in Breathitt County between the Civil War and World War I stands as an indictment of American exceptionalism. The United States of America maintains, at this writing, a republic with unparalleled longevity and stability. Americans should remember that this has required a tremendous amount of bloodshed. It also provides a commentary on how Americans separate past from present, here from there, and self from other. We like to admit our nation-state's violence while pushing it further back into the past than it actually was, separating (in Hannah Arendt's words) "heritage" from the "dead load" of atrocity. The history of the United States is full of atrocities and most of them Americans don't mind acknowledging, but without considering that their own past draws parallels with corners of the globe they consider less fortunate. (On that note, I apologize for any lapses into the jargons of anthropologists, political scientists, and others, but they serve the purpose of demonstrating that there are common currents of human activity that can be described without lapsing into lazy assumptions about progress and not progress.) When it comes to brutality, the United

States is hardly exceptional. The "savagery" of la Violencia in Colombia, or the Troubles in Northern Ireland, has happened in the United States, even if Americans consider themselves above such things. It's no wonder that what went on in Breathitt County was dismissed as so many "feuds."

From the moment I began my research I depended upon the support of others, especially an extraordinary publisher. The University Press of Kentucky's Anne Dean Watkins and Steve Wrinn are a skillful and patient editorial team. Their assistant Bailey Johnson helped me with technical details during the latter stages of my revising. Ashley Runyon and Mack McCormick helped me immensely during the early stages of promotion. Thanks also to Robin DuBlanc, an intricately perceptive copy editor. Bill Link, the New Directions in Southern History series coeditor, put me in contact with the press when my ideas for this book were in earliest bloom, and I still take that as a magnificent compliment. Finally, I appreciate Andy Slap and Bruce Stewart including my research in their anthologies published under the University Press of Kentucky banner.

Breathitt County, Kentucky, has its own dedicated native historians. Charles Hayes's kind permission to reproduce photos from his collection for this book is greatly appreciated. Stephen Bowling and Janie Griffith run the county's two public historical institutions, its library and its museum, respectively. They each provided me with matchless perspectives on how their county's citizens interpret their past. Sherry Lynn Baker is a thorough researcher and she shared some valuable materials with me while also helping confirm a number of vital factual details. Thanks also to Jerry Buck Deaton for doing the same. John Robertson, the webmaster for Historical County Lines (http://his.jrshelby.com/hcl/), helped me with the surprisingly formidable task of tracking down usable maps.

It is hard to imagine a state archive friendlier to a historian's needs than the Kentucky Department of Libraries and Archives in Frankfort. In nearly a dozen visits I always received help and advice from its staff. The state capital's Thomas D. Clark Center for Kentucky History was also useful. The staff at Berea College's library was especially attentive and a credit to the school's tradition of a student-run campus. Lastly, Dean Williams of Appalachian State University's William Leonard Eury Appalachian Collection has always supported my research immensely.

Bloody Breathitt began as a doctoral dissertation, and I owe much to those who supported me in its completion. David Carlton is a ready adviser, a meticulous reviewer, a constant resource for southern lore, and a friend. Richard Blackett, once he read part of my beginning chapters, was an early source of encouragement, and his dissertation seminars had a huge impact on later chapters. He and his wife, Cheryl, have welcomed me into their home many times. Dennis Dickerson, Larry Isaac, and Rowena Olegario are challenging intellects that provided important criticism. Although he was not on my committee, my MA adviser John A. Williams might as well have been since he set me on a certain path years earlier. The Vanderbilt University Department of History provided a young southernist with bed and board, and a generous amount of funding. The department's administrators, Jane Anderson, Brenda Hummel, and Heidi Welch, always helped me when I was in need.

I benefited from being surrounded by other young scholars who pushed me to excel. Tim Boyd shared with me an expatriated Briton's interest in the American South and its politics, and provided very important suggestions and criticisms. Countless conversations with Steven P. Miller deepened my thoughts on political culture and the importance of our work being relevant to the present though written about the past. Pete Kuryla provided an intellectual historian's perspective that motivated me to think beyond this book's most rudimentary purposes. I hope I was able to repay him, at least partially, by introducing him to the work of Christopher Lasch. Finally, Patrick Jackson was a knowledgeable sounding board while I was revising *Bloody Breathitt*. and, as my weight room partner, he never let a barbell fall on me and crush my face.

A historian's true home is the library, and Vanderbilt's Central Library provided me with a top-notch environment for reading, writing, and dawdling. Peter Brush is an excellent resource for history students, and Yolanda Campbell and Daisy Whitten were always helpful. The interlibrary loan staff, most notably Rachel Adams, tracked down the most obscure requests with what seemed like no effort. I could not have completed my revisions without help from Anne Bridges, the humanities librarian at the University of Tennessee's Hodges Library.

One of the best aspects of graduate-level research is becoming part of an international community of scholars. Professors Aaron Astor, Bruce Baker, John Burch, Bill Link, Sam McSeveney, Rob Weise, and Jason Yeatts have all been good enough to read chapters or portions of chapters and offer their ideas. Aaron Akey helped me track down a rare photograph. Robert Ireland, one of Kentucky's most important state historians, offered kind advice and clarification when it was asked of him. Jim Klotter and Altina Waller offered me encouragement when I told them I was following in their footsteps. The late George Graham was an intellectual inspirer nearly a decade ago when my research was at its very beginning. A special thanks goes to Steve Ash, Ernie Freeberg, and Bruce Wheeler for their advice on writing.

My parents, Bill and Cathy Hutton, provided decades of encouragement balanced with intellectual freedom. Childhood trips to museums fostered an early interest in American history and, growing up in the Hutton household, the past was never past. My grandparents Jim and Martha Clendenen were also especially supportive of all my goals.

This book is a product of my own work, but it is also a product of opportunity and infrastructure. Like other writers, I benefit from the leisure time provided by other peoples' labor. The chance to deal in ideas for a living came about because of the hard physical work of people, some still living and others passed, who worked for my family many years before I began higher education. George Cato, the Doss family, the Gentry family, the Ray family, Arch Skeens, the Surber family, the Thomas family, and the Wolfe family provided me with an education. I stand on the shoulders of the people who do the real work in this world, often without acknowledgment from the people who profit from it.

Introduction

"THE DARKEST AND BLOODIEST OF ALL THE DARK AND BLOODY FEUD COUNTIES"

The means used to achieve political goals are more often than not of greater relevance to the future world than the intended goals.
—Hannah Arendt, *On Violence* (1970)

This is a history of Breathitt County, Kentucky, in its first seven or so decades of existence, before and after it became known as Bloody Breathitt. I consider the county and its nickname two separate entities; Breathitt (pronounced "breath-it") County is a political unit, founded in 1839 in eastern Kentucky. "Bloody Breathitt," as I use it here, is a collection of factual and fanciful explanations for the county's history of violence, with broader implications for Kentucky, the South, and the United States. Breathitt County is a place that earned a singular reputation for killing between the Civil War and World War I; Bloody Breathitt is the accumulation of information and misinformation this reputation was made from.

In the early twentieth century Breathitt County was called "the darkest and bloodiest of all the dark and bloody feud counties," the first—and the last—Kentucky county associated with prolonged, reciprocal, vengeance-based personal or familial conflicts.[1] With that in mind, this book is also an attempt at explaining *feud,* a word Americans associate with history even though it has been used to defy and deny history in places like Breathitt County. This book is not about blood feuds. It is about acts of violence that were called blood feuds, and why this labeling is deceptive. I consider *feud* a vague expression, an element of what Wayne Lee calls "clouds of rhetoric" applied to various sorts of violent events in order to make their particulars less knowable.[2] It was one word, among many in the English language, used as an unclear or false description of homicide.[3] Above all, this book is about what one county's history reveals about how Americans think about killing.

Chapter Overview

Chapter 1 details Breathitt County's formation in sparsely populated eastern Kentucky, one of the last sections of the Appalachia Mountains to be permanently inhabited by whites.[4] The earliest settlers thrived raising unfenced livestock and hunting wild game until slaveholders and speculation-minded recent arrivals lobbied for the creation of a new county.[5] They then pared a Democratic county out of three consistently Whig (and later Republican) counties, establishing something very close to one-party rule. They named their new county for Kentucky's recently deceased Democratic governor, John Breathitt, and its county seat for Andrew Jackson, a president who despised the sort of rapacious capital/government connivances the new county represented.[6] The circumstances of Breathitt's very existence were a precondition for a crisis of legitimacy, a legitimacy questioned by its citizens and, eventually, by Americans looking in from the *outside world* (a phrase many observers used to intimate the supposed insularity of the county).[7]

It was a quiet affront to democracy, one that presaged the much larger crisis of legitimacy created by southern secession a little over two decades later.[8] Decades later, the Progressive Era's reformist nabobs could not believe that the banal mechanics of county government might inspire armed conflict, even as they criticized counties as a retrograde form of government.[9] What they failed to understand was the importance of local government, especially when larger institutions fell apart, as they did throughout Kentucky in 1861. After that, the question of legitimacy was applied to the diverse forms of violence witnessed in the county; some were found wanting (in the eyes of locals, the outside world, or both), while others, if carried out according to the wishes of white Kentuckians, were deemed legitimate.

When the Civil War began (as shown in chapter 2) Breathitt County was a Confederate beacon amid pro-Union counties. Poor mountaineers, both black and white, who had gained little from the county's formation, formed a long-lasting Unionist "stateless zone" within the county.[10] Thus began a narrative familiar to many parts of the border states, a "war between neighbors" in which personal relationships mingled with sectional politics. Whatever legitimacy the county's combatants claimed came from their blue or gray uniforms. Long after these uniforms became moth-eaten relics, the

Breathitt County in modern-day eastern Kentucky. (Richard Gilbreath, University of Kentucky Cartography Lab; based on a map created by Lindell Ormsbee)

war's political rupture remained, as did the blurred lines between soldier and civilian.

The county's circumstances in the 1860s and 1870s, as shown in chapter 3, reflected the rest of Kentucky, a non-Confederate state on the Solid South's fringes.[11] The state was not subject to presidential or congressional Reconstruction, and Confederate veterans were unhindered in maintaining a forceful counterrevolutionary control.[12] Breathitt County's biracial Unionist/ Republican minority fought back, creating the illusion of a contest between diametrically opposed equals. Considering the reunited American Republic's readiness to forget wartime politics, it was easy for Kentuckians to construe public violence as if it had strictly private meanings.[13] It was not happenstance that a southern Democrat coined the doleful sobriquet "Bloody Breathitt" in one of the bloodiest years of Reconstruction.[14]

Chapters 4 and 5 explain how the 1880s and 1890s were even bloodier than the Reconstruction years. As railroad tracks and corporate capital made their way to Breathitt County, there were plenty of exogenous sources of violence common to an entire region or nation-state. But the political nature of white intraracial ("white-on-white") conflicts was obscured by repeated references to endogenous causes: isolation from the outside world, poverty, lack of education, mania for revenge, obsession with kinship and racial vestigiality (Anglo-Saxon or Celtic "blood") in eastern Kentucky's "feud belt."[15] Kentuckians, in the mountains and beyond, maintained the flawed premise that economic advancement would bring an end to disorder. In these interpretations, violence simply "came natural."

These alleged endogenous traits had become the primary explanations for white intraracial violence by the time a political agitator named William Goebel was assassinated near the state capitol in 1900 (see chapter 6), leading to a similar public death in Jackson.[16] From the Civil War to the Progressive Era, all of Kentucky's convulsions were manifest in Bloody Breathitt. For that matter, it also embodied the decades of white-on-black bloodletting in other parts of the post-Reconstruction South even though most (but not all) victims there were white (as shown in later chapters, the subject of race reappeared in Bloody Breathitt countless times).

During official war or official peace, these were premeditated acts of *political* violence between Unionists and Rebels (and, subsequently, militarized Republicans and Democrats) in the most prosaic sense of the word and in a more far-reaching one; known acts of violence in Breathitt usually accompanied elections, and, when they did not, they still directly affected power relations in the body politic.[17] Breathitt County was subject to the contingencies of regionwide and nationwide trends—not least of these a civil war and the crisis of legitimacy that followed. However, "Bloody Breathitt" described an inherently violent place, defined by "irrationality generated by lack of information, randomness and unpredictability."[18] Violence "that arises in a modern context but will not fit the story of progress" is written off as a product of a "pre-modern culture" that conveniently casts no harsh light on the activities of powerful men.[19] And all of them men; women were not part of Kentucky's official political process until the passage of the Nineteenth Amendment, and were therefore neither victims nor assailants in violence centered on electoral politics. In fact, a few of the women who played significant roles in Bloody Breathitt were able to do so only because of their separation from the exclusively male realm(s) of politics and violence (including an enslaved woman who used gastronomical sabotage against Confederate soldiers, as told in chapter 2).

Inherency trumped contingency in most discussions of Bloody Breathitt, just as it usually has in most studies of violence in the American South. Wilbur J. Cash's inherent "savage ideal" has long competed with (among others) C. Vann Woodward's portrayal of a South undergoing changing contingencies of fortune and leadership. Neither interpretation has fully satisfied historians since places like South Carolina's "Bloody Edgefield" have produced an exceptional number of murders while still reflecting the South's regionwide contingencies.[20] Readers still seem to prefer sweeping explanations based upon inherency; one recent neomodernist global study of homicide attributed the American South's violent history to an absence of "the civilizing mission of government."[21] Perhaps the South has somehow preserved an "exceptional" culture given to pique and rapine. On the other hand, painstaking examinations of places like Breathitt County reveal a contested space where violence was deliberate, calculated, and connected with struggles for power; not, perhaps, unlike so many "trouble spots" all over the globe where political scientists, anthropologists, and historians have chosen to set aside Eurocentric, colonial assumptions about inherent violence and apply critical examination to the reasons people kill and die.

Nothing demonstrates this better than Breathitt County's typology of violence. Violence is not an inert substance. It has many different manifestations depending upon circumstances—a mugging and a carpet-bombing might both be deadly, but they are two very different events. In terms of quantities of injuries and deaths, Breathitt County was consistently violent, even by postbellum America's bloody standard. However, qualitatively, Bloody Breathitt contained "model-based" varieties of violence used all over the world.[22] First, during the antebellum decades, there was the violence endemic to a society with slaves. The county was a locus for guerrilla warfare during the Civil War (especially during the war's last two years), as were other slaveholding states. When southern communities were rent apart during Congressional Reconstruction, election-related rioting and insurrection were reproduced there as well. In the 1880s and 1890s Kentuckians reacted to the disorders of rapid economic change with lynching, legal capital punishment, and mass vigilantism.[23] Finally, when public assassination (like William Goebel's) became an international recurrence, it was employed in the streets of Jackson as well. From a broad comparative perspective, Bloody Breathitt represented nothing new under the sun.

Counterrevolutionary violence works best when the connection between means and ends is unclear, its motivations *depoliticized*, if not also its outcomes.[24] This was the role played by *feud,* a word (explored in depth in chapter 7) light in definition but heavy with implications—implications of things Americans consider familiar but foreign to their republic and its politics. The feud was a popular topic in the semihistorical fiction (William Shakespeare, Sir Walter Scott, Honoré de Balzac) that Victorian readers adored.[25] Anthropologists consider the feud an institutional conflict within "simple societies" where individuals, factions, families, or "clans" of equal standing supposedly engage in a relatively orchestrated exchange of fights or killings based on past enmities or injustices—a mutually recognized "pact of violence."[26] No state oversight is needed since horizontal reciprocity between peers suggests moral equivalency and eliminates victimhood (Prince Escalus in *Romeo and Juliet* steps in only when teenagers from the two feuding families commit suicide).[27]

In an American context the feud's intimations were far more important than any of its meanings. Perhaps its most important intimation involved time, the distinction between "now" and "then." It suggested a communal setting, the "pre-political realm of the oikos [the family] and the extra-political 'barbarian' world beyond the polis."[28] As popular as it was to say a century later, Victorian Americans did not believe that the personal was political; they also believed that the familial realm was to be kept apart from the public one. But they did acknowledge that their forbears believed otherwise, as did some unfortunate contemporaries they believed remained at the bottom of what Johannes Fabian has called a "temporal hierarchy": advanced societies often find it convenient to place their less-advanced neighbors in the past.[29] With white intraracial violence rampant in the decades after the Civil War (though never as widespread or politically significant as interracial white attacks on black southerners), the feud provided a grand device for tucking the violence of the present safely away in a fictive past. Southern conservatives used it to misdirect northern critics from the political nature of postwar chaos, convincing them that most—if not all—murders in isolated rural places were sui generis "ideology-free conflict[s]."[30] By Reconstruction's end many northerners had replaced their righteous anger with an acceptance of the South's "naturally" violent predisposition; the appearance of "racial instinct," according to historian Stephen Kantrowitz, trumped the reality of "counterrevolutionary conspiracy."[31] The feud helped Americans—northerners *and* southerners—write off, excuse, and forget atrocities, and helped preserve racial and economic inequality—even in a seemingly homogenous place like Breathitt County. It was always metaphorical but, if repeated enough times, metaphor often became illusory hyperbole. Its eventual indelible association with eastern Kentucky was a combination of political design, cultural happenstance, and deliberate obfuscation. By then, *feud* was a local description for one violent corner of a remarkably violent section of the United States. The fact that most victims were white was all that differentiated it from the rest of the South.

This is not to suggest that *feud* gained currency only in America. It was a very old concept in the Western world, albeit with premodern meanings that are almost as irresolute as its modern ones. As it was understood from Icelandic sagas or the sixteenth-century Mediterranean, the feud simply did not exist in the United States. As one anthropologist has noted, "Travelers, administrators and anthropologists . . . have in the main studiously avoided formulating an exact definition of what they mean by the word feud."[32] One medievalist has even expressed doubt as to whether it was ever a "particular mental category of dispute."[33] Perhaps "feud" has always been nothing more than narrative form applied to violence after the fact, hiding bloody political expediency behind themes of vengeance, kinship, and honor.

In the twenty-first-century Anglophone vernacular, *feud* has transited—like Hayden White's "trope"—from metaphor to irony; it now whimsically suggests killing that is beyond modern America's understanding or caring, violence that can be smirked at and "reserved for ironic treatment" in written accounts.[34] It suggests that the victims and perpetrators of violence are so distant in space or time (actually or virtually) *or* that their reasons for using violence are too arcane to investigate. For instance, isolationist congressman Hamilton Fish III spent five decades decrying Franklin Roosevelt's involvement in "ancient blood feuds" (that is, what most Americans knew as U.S. victory in World War II).[35] More recently, the feud is occasionally referenced in television dialogue when a shorthand for the brutal, antiquated, and/or primeval is needed (most notably on *The West Wing* and *30 Rock,* two programs known for their supercilious "blue state" viewer demographics).[36]

More than anything else, the feud represents an act of segregation, a segregation of violence from its purposes. Removing the politics from political violence is something states and nonstate actors practice as a matter of course; the feud was simply a means to that end. Even now, it performs roughly the same function, though with more implied derision. Whether in the past or the present, using simplistic, disdainful language for violent death is harmful.

Why Does Bloody Breathitt Matter?

Thanks to journalism, popular fiction, and theatrical adaptations, the feud in a southern/Appalachian/Kentucky milieu remains a familiar subject, encapsulating historical events that underwent a "transformation from history to folklore."[37] This misappropriation was partly due to an omission by consensus historians like Richard Hofstadter, who saw "a nation placidly evolving without serious disagreements," acknowledging only "legitimate" state violence.[38] At the end of the 1960s it was becoming clear that "legitimacy is in the eye of the beholder," and Hofstadter conceded that historians could no longer ignore political violence in their homeland even if it was "hard to cope with."[39] His Nixon-era admission coincided with a wealth of theoretical approaches to explaining political violence in a democracy.[40]

This new turn also coincided with the rise in the 1970s of Appalachian studies and the first serious attempts at examining the region's association with the feud.[41] Appalachian historians attached this association to themes of economic exploitation and underdevelopment brought on by the forced transition from agriculture to industrialization.[42] Feud violence, they found, was falsely attributed to "primordial explanations" for violence—definitively "illegitimate" within a wealthy nation-state (the Stanford *Encyclopedia of Philosophy* uses "a feud on the order of the Hatfields versus the McCoys" as a counterexample for its definition of "war"), the better to justify exploitation by a "dominant culture."[43] Most of Appalachian historiography has been defined by its preoccupation with dismantling (in the parlance of postcolonial studies) "hierarchies of place."[44]

I, too, try to set straight issues regarding Appalachia, most notably its place in southern political history. Nothing controverts Horace Kephart's spurious contention that preindustrial southern mountaineers "recognize[d] no social compact" better than their well-documented passion for the two-party system.[45] With this in mind, I share my forbears' interest in dispelling misconceptions about the region. However, I wish to do more than, as E. P. Thompson put it, rescue a population "from the enormous condescension of posterity" (a condescension that even the most multicultural-minded academics still cling to for some reason).[46] I see a portion of the mountain landscape where a "dominant culture" was present before corporations arrived, one that gained its power from the same confluence of class and race that defined southern politics.[47] I do not think that variations of the "internal colony" model effectively explain political violence. Kentucky mountaineers, at least the white male ones, were voting citizens of the American Republic (although many briefly cleaved to the Confederacy); in peace or in fighting, their citizenship motivated their political participation.

I also think that Bloody Breathitt, the feud, and all they entail are important for reasons that extend far beyond any one region. They are important because the language we use to talk about violence is important. The concept of the feud is only one euphemistic chimera, one palatable and familiar to nineteenth-century American tastes. Since then there have been others, such as the 1950s invention of "police action" in lieu of "war." Purposefully confusing language about killing, such as George Orwell identified in his essay "Politics and the English Language," continues to this day. My interest in Breathitt County began during Operation: Iraqi Freedom, when "terrorist," "militant," and "insurgent" were bandied about interchangeably, while mercenaries became "contractors," placing gunmen among the ranks of carpenters and electricians. Torture and imprisonment without trial were hidden behind perplexing phrases like "enhanced interrogation" and "extraordinary rendition."[48] All of that took place far from Kentucky. However, just like the word *feud*, this was language used to obscure, conceal, and lie in the service of, as Orwell put it, "the defense of the indefensible."[49] Violence is hegemonic, and so, too, are the words used to describe it.

There is political violence, and then there is the politics of interpreting violence. The school shooting phenomenon, especially Columbine High School in 1999 and Virginia Tech in 2007, along with a deranged gunman's near-fatal shooting of an Arizona congresswoman in 2011 and mass shootings in Colorado, Wisconsin, New York, and Connecticut in 2012, contributed to heated political arguments over "gun control" (a shooting rampage at Fort Hood, Texas, in 2009 was related to the "war on terror" and subsequently discussed in terms more related to geopolitics than to domestic policy) and reawakened debates over interpretation. While most of these crimes were not acts of "political violence" in the simplest sense of the phrase, they did spur political debate over the issue of "gun control." The common theme heard from the antiregulation side suggests that we live in social science's equivalent of a pre-Ptolemaic cosmos: acts that are "senseless," "tragic," or "irrational" cannot be counteracted because they passeth all understanding.[50] This reductionist "senseless violence" argument, used all over the world, is itself politically motivated and disingenuous but, since most people prefer not to contemplate carnage and mayhem, it is also believable and attractive.[51] What I show in later chapters is that these misleading lines of discourse have deep historical roots; it is how Breathitt County became Bloody Breathitt and it is how many homicides have gone unprevented or unpunished.

Firearm regulation aside, we cannot deny ourselves the ability to understand the most egregious acts of cruelty or the contexts that surround them.[52] Violence can be condemned without discouraging scholars from "exploring meaning, interpreting symbolic action and mapping the historical and social context of activities defined as violent."[53] Humans can understand human actions, and homicide is no exception. "[If] violence is whitewashed," wrote Jean Baudrillard, "history is whitewashed."[54] In the interest of preventing this whitewashing, lessons must be learned from violence: the more uncomfortable these lessons make us, the more likely they are to be valuable. In 1968 Martin Luther King Jr. called urban riots "the language of the unheard."[55] Perhaps other forms of violence can also be translated and read in the interest of understanding how a country that deems itself the greatest nation on earth continues to pose so many lethal threats to its citizenry.

1

"TO THEM, IT WAS NO-MAN'S LAND"

Before Breathitt Was Bloody

> Without hazarding any thing, I think, Sir, I may say, more of the happiness
> of this Commonwealth, depends upon the County Government under
> which we live, than upon the State or the United States' Government.
> —Alexander Campbell, delegate to Virginia's
> Second Constitutional Convention (1829)

As an old man, George Washington Noble recalled watching a "pitched battle" when he was a child in Breathitt County, Kentucky, in the 1850s. It was a semiofficial Court Day event, a hand-to-hand tussle for money and prestige between various communities' "champion fighters," referred to locally as "Tessy Boys."[1] As in a duel, the fights employed seconds to prevent foul play and to give a potential deadly free-for-all a measure of ritualized order; it was, after all, around the same time that another fight with no public supervision had ended in a fatal stabbing.[2] In Jackson, Breathitt's county seat, this display of fisticuffs added entertainment, and an aura of masculine brio, to a staid political and legal event, augmenting the more formal proceedings going on inside the courthouse. It was an inclusive activity, establishing democratic homosocial interactions between men from disparate neighborhoods across a very large county, gathering "high and low into deeply charged, face-to-face, ritualized encounters."[3] A rough, unruly, violent spectacle occurring during a public event that ensured civic order, the Tessy Boys' fight serves as an allegory for Breathitt County's social and political existence in the two decades before the Civil War. The incorporation of fighting into a state-ordained ritual like Court Day (an always-boisterous event in the antebellum South) mirrored the state's marginally successful attempt to bring stability to a chaotic environment.[4]

Antebellum Breathitt County was just another representation of southern society re-created in the Kentucky mountains. The Tessy Boys may have had a peculiar local name, but they were a pretty close facsimile to the semiorganized Court Day tussles that were then de rigueur throughout Kentucky and the other slave states.[5] Reading about Bloody Breathitt in 1905, one would have been falsely led to believe that it had always been a wooded preserve for antediluvian chaos. Once it had been named "Bloody Breathitt" in the 1870s this relatively peaceful stage of its history, Tessy Boys and all, was mostly forgotten.

Long before the homicides and mayhem for which it would later be known, antebellum Breathitt County did contain the potential for turmoil. The 1839 formation of Breathitt County in eastern Kentucky's Three Forks region (the drainage area of the Kentucky River's three tributaries) happened out of desire to bring a governmental and commercial order to an inert, untapped wilderness.[6] Well to the east of the old Wilderness Road (the main road between Virginia and central Kentucky that provided access to both for portions of southeastern Kentucky's mountains), it was one of the last areas of Kentucky with a permanent population. Breathitt County's creation was brought about by landowners who saw the area as a commodity rather than just a living space. It was a governmental entity, like other counties, but it was also a business venture carried out for personal, not public, gain. Moreover, it was a venture that ran counter to the interests of many of the preexistent population. This was meant to be a profitable order and, like many other such schemes of the nineteenth century, it had unforeseen outcomes.

"These people lived here in seclusion for several years; not knowing [of]what country or nation they were citizens"

The story of early Breathitt County is one of in-state sectionalism, an upland county founded according to mostly lowland interests. The enormously luxuriant rolling hills of the Bluegrass in north-central Kentucky, a cultivator's paradise where a facsimile of the Virginia plantation economy could be re-created, was the first section of any economic consequence for white settlers and their slaves.[7] "The [non-Indian] population of Kentucky until the separation from Virginia," wrote one early twentieth-century Kentucky historian, "was practically confined to the Bluegrass."[8] From there Kentuckians spread outward after 1792 statehood, south to the Green River Valley and westward to the tobacco-growing Pennyroyal and Jackson Purchase sections.

The Cumberland Plateau, the mountain range that covers most of eastern Kentucky, was always defined in contradistinction to the rest of the state, and it was a subject of little curiosity in the early Republic. In 1751 explorer Christopher Gist and his party probably became the first white men to see Breathitt County's future location when they passed through on their return from the Ohio Country.[9] "None of any particular note" is the only comment given for Kentucky's mountains in one 1815 atlas.[10] With the exception of longhunters and trappers, most first-generation Kentuckians considered the plateau little more than an impediment.[11] Settlers arrived only after lower-lying areas like the Bluegrass had become surveyed, taxed, and overcrowded beyond their satisfaction. Recognizing that theirs was a relatively new community, Kentucky mountaineers of the Civil War era still called the Bluegrass their state's "old settlements."[12]

In 1889 New England writer Charles Dudley Warner described Kentucky as divided into three distinct regions, "like Gaul," an oft-repeated allusion to Caesar's *Commentaries on the Gallic War*.[13] The dramatic contrast between the highlands and the central Bluegrass (the western third was eventually overshadowed or conflated with the central Bluegrass) popularized a more simplistic geographical commentary asserting "two Kentuckys" in place of Warner's three: one defined by the Bluegrass's agrarian wealth and the other by the highlands' hardscrabble deprivation.[14] This geographic metaphor came to influence Kentuckians' self-image. The patrician, commercially vigorous Bluegrass was obliged to share Kentucky's (inter)national image with the plebian, underdeveloped uplands, "polished blue grass civilization" eternally saddled with "the semi-barbarism of the mountains."[15] Residents of both sections eventually took this exaggerated stark contrast to heart. Breathitt County native E. L. Noble (George Noble's much younger cousin) portrayed his ancestors entering stateless "forest primeval worlds, rich in primeval glory and wealth of worlds now unknown to man. . . . These people lived here in seclusion for several years; not knowing [of] what country or nation they were citizens."[16]

Early travelers' accounts suggest that this was an old assumption, and one quickly challenged. In 1834 New Yorker Charles Fenno Hoffman was surprised to find highland Kentuckians "sing[ing] the praises of 'old Kaintuck' with as much fervor as the yeoman who rides over his thousand fat acres in the finest regions of Kentucky [that is, the Bluegrass]" despite their general "ignorance of the world."[17] Hoffman probably did not realize that his rustic hosts were likely themselves recent arrivals. Moreover, as unaware as eastern Kentuckians may have been of the "world" (which, to Knickerbocker Hoffman, was probably restricted to east of the Hudson River), they knew quite well who certified their contracts, counted their votes, and accepted their tax money. Early nineteenth-century eastern Kentucky was sparsely populated, but it was not the wilderness primeval "beyond the polis," as it was often portrayed.[18] As Durwood Dunn noted about Cades Cove, Tennessee, during the same period, "isolation was always relative."[19]

Isolation was relative, and also a problem partially solved by bringing government closer to home. For generations, Kentuckians who chose to settle in the mountains were forced to make a long trip westward to see or use any functions of government. Early state maps show tremendous counties covering vast amounts of land stretching far from their respective Bluegrass courthouse towns. In the Three Forks region extraordinary circumstances made it abundantly clear that a more available jurisprudence system was necessary. In 1805 conflict arose among cattlemen living between the middle and north forks. Steers belonging to the Strong and Callahan families strayed from a Virginia-bound cattle drive and destroyed crops belonging to one John Amis. Amis took revenge on his careless neighbors by somehow drowning a number of their cattle in the north fork. In retaliation, the Strongs and Callahans allegedly killed Amis's own livestock and assaulted his wife. Amis and his confederates struck back days later by firing on the offending party and shots were returned, with no immediate resolution to the fracas. The shooting eventually died down, and word reached the state capital, Frankfort, of what had gone on, but prosecution of the accused would be difficult, with Madison County's seat of government nearly a hundred miles from the Three Forks. The Kentucky General Assembly first formed Clay County out of Madison and two other counties in 1807, a landmass with fewer than six inhabitants per square mile.[20] If the state government's intention was to bring law and order to the area, it would seem that the effort was only partially successful; Amis was fatally shot while on the witness stand at Clay County's first court session.[21]

Typically, however, new mountain counties were founded because of everyday civic needs and desires. After a pioneer settlement turned into a multifamily village, those that saw a need for closer government—usually those with the most property—had only to gather a dozen or so signatures to form a new county. As tiny villages became county seats, petitioning "first families" gained tremendously, and enough of their new earnings trickled down to their neighbors to create a general agreement that county

Subbasins of the Kentucky River Basin

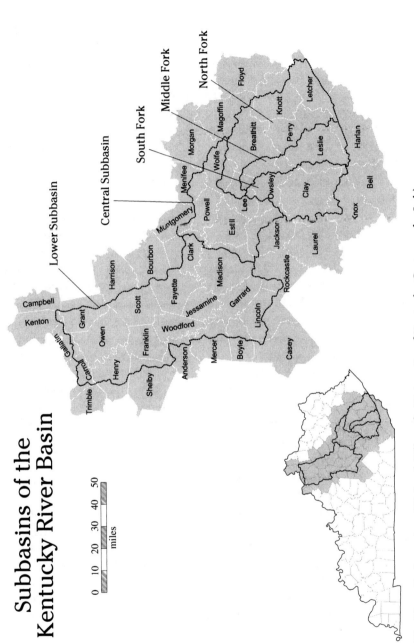

The Three Forks region. (Richard Gilbreath, University of Kentucky Cartography Lab)

formation was an unalloyed good.[22] In the spirit of pleasing voters, their requests were approved with alacrity. Drawing new county boundaries and the settling of subsequent border disputes became the Kentucky General Assembly's primary functions during the "frenzy of county-making" between 1806 and 1822.[23] Nor did it stop then; between 1822 and 1860 the number of counties in the state increased from 71 to 110, bringing courts closer to citizens while intensifying social and governmental parochialism. Nineteenth-century Kentuckians considered new counties a remedy for most, if not all, public ills.[24]

In these newer counties' infant years no immediate funds were available to build courthouses, so county and circuit court sessions had to be held in private homes. Clay, Perry, Breathitt, and perhaps most other counties in eastern Kentucky began this way, usually in the homes of the pioneer-descended "first families," whose primacy of settlement and wealth of land suggested a measure of disinterestedness.[25] Holding court in households was a seemingly innocuous arrangement that apparently attracted no complaints. However, as indebted Kentuckians came to realize after the Panic of 1819, patrician disinterestedness was fleeting—assuming it had ever existed at all.[26]

As the number of Kentucky counties increased, so did the general prevalence of county government, almost to the point of individual sovereignty. The powers of Kentucky county government in relation to the state were virtually "semi-federal" analogues to the state's balance of power with the federal government.[27] Under the state's second constitution (drafted in 1799), county courts had broad-reaching powers comprising not only the judicial but the legislative and executive branches as well, with few checks and balances between the three. Until Kentucky's third constitutional convention in 1849, most county offices were appointed by justices of the peace rather than elected, and justice positions themselves were often passed down as inheritance. Judges, sheriffs, and court clerks were consequently under the control of familiopolitical cliques for generations.[28] Justices and their clients could supervise election results, control local patronage, and use county funds for personal gain.[29] Since Kentucky state legislators often served simultaneously as justices back home, the oligarchic influence was felt in the General Assembly as well.[30] This all led to an early stagnation of political competition and an oft-permanent identification between county and party; in either the nineteenth or twentieth centuries, Kentucky had few "swing counties."[31]

Kentucky's incessant jurisdictional mitosis came with other unforeseen

Kentucky in 1800, 1820, and 1840. (Richard Gilbreath, University of
Kentucky Cartography Lab; based on a map created by Mark Lassagne
of GoldBug.com)

problems, particularly the decrease of county tax bases. County governments struggled to maintain revenue as land was chiseled away, often with little attendant legislative debate.[32] By the end of the 1850s, many of Kentucky's 110 counties no longer contained enough productivity to match their tax burdens. This "pauper county" problem, resulting in a state deficit of nearly $54 million, became a matter for comment in other states' press.[33] These pauper counties later became symbols of extreme parochialism, isolation, and poverty—as well as justification for conflating these three distinct problems.[34] Progressive Era political scientists attacked the county as a regressive, problem-ridden form of government and sought to replace it with more enlightened institutions.[35] But in the decades immediately before and after the Civil War, even the most reform minded had to accept what Thomas Jefferson had accepted decades before: counties produced poor government, but they were impossible to eliminate.[36]

In 1948 historian Charles Sydnor saw all of this as part of a larger nineteenth-century trend through which a southerner "naturally came to regard the county as having much and perhaps paramount importance among the governments to which he was subject."[37] But legal historian Robert Ireland has since suggested that both the eager propagation of counties and their potential for internal authoritarianism were distinctively Kentuckian.[38] More recently, John Alexander Williams concurred, saying that "no state carried the county government to greater extremes than Kentucky."[39] Cursory evidence bears this out, at least in terms of proliferation; the only two states with more counties are Georgia and Texas, two states far larger than Kentucky in land mass and population.

"The county always went Democratic"

The "Clay County Cattle War" was still spoken of in Breathitt County (and recited as a locally penned poem) at the nineteenth century's end.[40] But in comparison to Thomas Jefferson's nephews' slave murder in 1811 or the killing of Solomon Sharp fourteen years later, it never became a major chapter of Kentucky "dark and bloody ground" lore.[41] It did, however, illustrate a long-standing theme in the South's agrarian history: the conflicts of interest between cultivation and droving on land bereft of fences or definite ownership. Before the county frenzy the state had already become embroiled in a lengthy competition between settlers and speculators in which "almost every inch of Kentucky land was disputed."[42] After the Revolutionary War

Virginia had doled out most of what became Kentucky as grants for Continental army veterans, a latter-day version of the colonial headright system. Most veterans either sold their titles or never claimed them, and by 1800 the reward system had turned into a market dominated by fewer than twenty men, even as countless settlers occupied the land.[43] "The titles in Kentucky," an observer presciently foretold in 1816, "w[ill] be Disputed for a Centry to Come yet when it [i]s an old Settled Country."[44]

From this conflict emerged a political culture that inadvertently favored squatting, the landless farmer's only effective means of making a living without having to deal with the coercion of tenancy.[45] Landless Kentuckians used universal manhood suffrage to elect legislators who supported them, placing Kentucky "on the vanguard in recognizing the rights of the squatter."[46] Squatting may have violated property relations, some legislators argued, but it did so without challenging "the de jure distribution of property rights."[47] Unlike the speculators, who often failed to pay their taxes, squatters "attend[ed] to their own business" without lobbying or otherwise meddling in statehouse affairs.[48] In landowners' estimation, landlessness was synonymous with sloth, and repugnant to their sense of republican virtue, but their moral superiority was limited to their often-handicapped ability to prove their own legitimacy.[49]

This only lasted so long. Successful invocation of adverse possession turned squatters into landowners, while others migrated farther west. Under Henry Clay's Whiggish guidance, Kentucky legislators and judges came to look upon squatting more as a trespass than as inexpensive improvement of fallow land.[50] As Kentucky went from being the "first western state" with widespread landlessness to a southern state with widespread land ownership, "squatters' rights" eventually lost favor.[51]

In the mountains, however, squatting persisted longer than anywhere else in Kentucky.[52] There the squatter's presence was, if left otherwise unmolested, just as sustainable as "legitimate" land practices since landownership in preindustrial Appalachia often sowed the seeds of its own destruction.[53] For years the Three Forks served as a haven for this unenclosed way of life, one that almost equalized the conditions of the landed and the landless. Due to steep conditions that made grazing and cultivation more difficult than in the flatlands, both depended upon "forest farming" (a technique that combined marginal cultivation, the hunting of large and small game, and open-range grazing of livestock on titled *and* untitled land) and access to a "commons," unfenced and uncommodified open land.[54] Free-range grazing and long livestock drives, like the one that precipitated the Clay County Cattle War, were common throughout the nineteenth century.[55] Even the wealthiest farmer made a living in a manner very much like the landless who probably surreptitiously used his land. Simon Cockrell, a well-to-do slave-owning Three Forks farmer, was rich enough to act as his neighbors' creditor and sell his cattle as far away as Virginia's Shenandoah Valley in the 1840s. Though "worth an immense fortune" once its mineral riches were realized years after his death, his land "was regarded as of but little value" in his lifetime.[56] "Wealthy and arrogant" as he was, Cockrell "had no grass" and was obliged to graze his cattle on "cane and other winter forage" far beyond his own property boundaries.[57] That the ends of market-oriented farming like Cockrell's and those of others who simply "subsisted" were separate was unclear, since both relied on the same means.[58]

For the nineteenth century's first three decades, both property owners and the propertyless farmed and extracted for Bluegrass markets made accessible by the north fork—open to anyone with a log raft and a modicum of skill, the rivers were also a "commons" of sorts. Flatboat traffic from the very headwaters of the forks, reportedly common since the 1790s, gave the lie to the myth of eastern Kentucky's isolation from the *outside world.*[59] Three Forks farmers turned to market-based mining and forest extraction soon after their arrival.[60] Extraction may have surpassed agriculture as the Three Forks' primary exports by the 1830s, especially in the southern headwaters, where slave-powered salt-mining operations began in the late eighteenth century.[61] Cannel coal, a particularly valuable variety of the mineral, was common.[62] "Shallow pits" and "farmers' diggings" were sufficient for most early mining enterprises, although larger slave-labored enterprises were in operation at least as early as the 1830s.[63] In the long run, timber was an even greater asset to those interested in supplementing their farming. In 1835 flatboat crews felled and floated at least three thousand logs from the Three Forks to Bluegrass markets.[64] The other recorded products that Three Forks mountaineers shipped to the Bluegrass in the early nineteenth century—deer skins, furs, honey, and ginseng—demonstrate the way in which hunting and gathering contributed to the market economy (and reason to leave much of the common land "unimproved").[65]

The three tributaries were adequate for "frontier" transportation but, as the Three Forks region increased in population in the 1820s and 1830s, there came new demand for land transportation. In 1833 eastern Kentucky's leading merchant, Thomas Sewell, financed a new twenty-mile-long wagon road from Perry County's remote War Creek community north to the hamlet of Hazel Green.[66] Two years later, the state began financing navigational improvements on the north fork, and in 1837 a new road connecting Floyd County to the Bluegrass was completed.[67] With enterprises "prostrated" in other parts of the state by the Panic of 1837, farmers from the Bluegrass and other areas of eastern Kentucky were attracted to the area.[68] The Three Forks region was being "discovered" by both settlers and a revived speculative frenzy unmatched in Kentucky since the 1790s.[69] The area's new interconnectedness with the outside world was flamboyantly demonstrated in 1838 when a traveling circus arrived, treating locals to the incongruous sight of an elephant tromping through the oaks and poplars.[70]

Breathitt County became Kentucky's eighty ninth county a year after the elephant's visit, thanks to other recent arrivals.[71] After building a second home on the north fork of the Kentucky River, Simon Cockrell's son-in-law, Madison County native Jeremiah Weldon South, procured the delinquent Thomas Franklin grant, a parcel spanning more than 116,000 acres (just over 182 square miles) of mostly forested land lying between the Kentucky's north and middle forks.[72]

The area's timber was what originally attracted South, but it was a difficult resource to exploit in the near future. Plans for massive timber and coal extraction, a railroad's arrival—these were schemes for a vaguely envisioned speculative future. The untapped abundance of coal and timber was remarked upon twenty years after the first official surveys of Breathitt County's mineral wealth in the 1850s.[73] Eight years after South's death in 1888 well over half of the county's seven hundred square miles remained "unimproved," the "forest growth . . . almost untouched."[74]

The creation of a new county provided a much faster dividend for South's investment, attracting land buyers, potential tenants, and potential employees.[75] Most of all, it would increase his property values. With Cockrell's support, he canvassed the area with a petition, and in the winter of 1839 the least developed, least populated portions of Clay, Estill, and Perry counties were removed to form the new county.[76] Wealthy residents, most of them also recent arrivals, felt that "the [new] county in its undeveloped state offered inducements to men of enterprise to accumulate considerable money."[77]

Typically, new counties were formed around preexistent central settlements of one or more families. With Breathitt County this was not the case; it was a county formed without anything of a community that might constitute a town. Breathitt's founders were quick to fill this structural

Table 1. Improved and unimproved land in Breathitt and surrounding counties, 1850 and 1860

County	Families	Farms	Acres improved	Value of improved land (including implements) ($)	Acres unimproved	Improved land (%)	Average improved acres per family	Families with farms (%)
1850								
Breathitt	625	433	13,517	279,674	274,043	4.7	0.04	69.28
Clay	782	511	19,186	320,102	137,006	12.28	0.04	65.34
Estill	934	604	26,839	493,554	84,619	24	0.03	64.66
Owsley (1843)	588	484	14,887	369,148	226,241	6.1	0.03	82.31
Perry	500	396	14,145	233,263	279,673	4.8	0.03	79.2
1860								
Breathitt	824	471	18,093	458,647	226,518	7.9	0.04	57.16
Clay	1,005	596	27,590	518,417	227,306	12.1	0.03	59.3
Estill	2,133	558	40,828	992,961	106,868	38.2	0.05	26.16
Owsley	897	578	26,277	774,862	231,160	11.3	0.03	64.43
Perry	990	595	18,754	430,969	301,564	6	0.05	60.1

Sources: *Seventh Census of the United States, 1850; Eighth Census of the United States, 1860.*

Table 2. Agricultural and extractive production of Breathitt and surrounding counties, 1840

County	Coal (bushels)	Salt (bushels)	Lumber ($)	Other "products of the forest" (e.g., skins, ginseng) ($)	Sawmills/ Gristmills	Cattle	Corn (bushels)
Breathitt	21,017	70	0	1,617	1/9	3,517	91,185
Clay	88,950	106,000	5,230	2,745	6/29	6,321	153,140
Estill	98,525	0	2,457	1,135	5/27	5,118	296,697
Perry	0	7,000	0	14,889	1/34	6,001	88,070

Source: *Sixth Census of the United States, 1840.*

Jeremiah Weldon South, the "father of Breathitt County," circa 1878. South's ambitious real estate venture led to a cycle of bloodshed that lasted decades. (Courtesy of the Breathitt County Museum)

gap. Thomas Sewell's $1,000 sale of lots along the north fork, along with a reported ten-acre donation from Simon Cockrell, became the county seat, named Breathitt in 1839 and changed to Jackson in 1841 (when Jackson was incorporated in 1854, Sewell became its inaugural mayor). Jackson was adjacent to "the Panbowl," a narrow four-mile floodplain enclosed within a seven-mile bend in the north fork.[78] By 1855 Jackson's coal trade supplied "most of the ready cash circulating in the country."[79] Owing to Breathitt's commercial origins, it was a municipal rarity: an American county formed before any preexistent towns within its boundaries.

Jeremiah South brought with him a formidable Kentucky pedigree. His Maryland-born grandfather John South helped construct Boonesborough in 1779; he fought in the Continental army and then served in the Kentucky General Assembly's first sessions ten years after losing a son at the battle of Little Mountain in 1782. Jeremiah's father, Samuel, played a key role at Little Mountain as a boy, and later punctuated decades of Indian fighting with his own stint as state legislator (losing the house speaker post to a young Henry Clay by a single vote in 1807) and a brevet general's commission in the War of 1812. He later served as state treasurer for six years.[80] Although Jeremiah South came from outside the Three Forks region, many of the new county's locals were themselves newcomers, either from Virginia or the Bluegrass's "old settlements." They had little reason to think of him as an intruding comprador, especially after he and his brother Richard had both married Cockrell women, creating a definitive "first family."[81] Any propertied Kentuckian was a fellow, not a foreigner, especially a descendant of men who had helped seize the "dark and bloody ground" from the Wyandot and Shawnee nations.

Jeremiah South volunteered his canvassing services "without compensation," according to one resident, but he stood to gain much from forming a new county around his enormous estate, especially since his holdings amounted to roughly a third of the new county's landmass.[82] The formation of a new county seat placed de facto control over the county's government into South's hands and those of his cohorts—if nothing else, a handy arrangement at tax time.

With his new county established, South began building a local power base made up of mostly Bluegrass natives. As the primary petitioner for the county, South was able to name its first eleven justices of the peace, including himself.[83] Joined by his brothers John and Richard, Jeremiah had the latter appointed as Breathitt County's first sheriff (John, a lawyer who made a legal career representing heirs to the old Virginia grants, might have received his own appointment had he not died in 1838).[84] John Lewis Hargis and Simeon Bohannon, recent arrivals from Woodford County (a small Bluegrass county where a Virginia-style plantation economy took root), served as Breathitt County's first circuit court clerk and county clerk respectively, with Bohannon simultaneously serving as a justice of the peace and county commissioner.[85] One of the petition signatories, William Allen, hosted the county's first court session in his home.[86] He and Bohannon also served as two of Jackson's original town trustees.[87] The titular "father of Breathitt County" and his Bluegrass associates exhibited considerable control over their new political unit.[88]

South became the county's first state representative in 1840 and was elected to the state Senate three years later.[89] There he "favored [eastern Kentucky] even to the detriment of the state," and ended up "idolized by the mountain people."[90] His attempt at a military venture did not equal his record as a solon. In 1846 South organized Breathitt County's troop contribution to the Mexican War but failed to recruit enough men to earn a commission or martial glory (still, following the affectation enjoyed by wealthy white Kentuckians, he was remembered as "Colonel South"). Although he was unable to repeat his father's and grandfather's military records, his popularity remained undimmed and he was soon reelected to the General Assembly.[91]

Making Breathitt County benefited Jeremiah South and his new neighbors, at least the more well-heeled ones. The Three Forks region previously lacked what geographer Mary Beth Pudup has called an "indigenous vanguard class," a group of professionals skilled in the commercial ways of the "Bluegrass System."[92] Soon after he arrived, John Hargis hung out his shingle as the county's first attorney, a boon to many local farmers (and perhaps a bane to others); two more attorneys arrived soon afterward.[93] By 1848, Jackson boasted "one Methodist church, one Reformed church, two schools, five stores and groceries, two taverns, three lawyers, one doctor and five mechanical trades" as well as land values far higher than in neighboring counties.[94] In the early 1850s Hargis, South, and five of the county's other large-scale landholders became charter stockholders in the Lexington and Kentucky River Railroad Company, anticipating a future rail connection to the Bluegrass (a goal that did not come to fruition until after Hargis's and South's deaths).[95] South and his fellows were imposing a new middle-class discipline on the Three Forks region, bringing purpose to a place business-oriented Jacksonian Americans considered void and without form.[96] They became part of the "fifteen or thirty or forty people" empowered by forming a new county "not for the benefit of the people at large, but only for the benefit of people who were to be enriched by them"—or so charged a reformer ten years after South's death.[97] During his lifetime, however, the statesmanlike intentions of "the father of Breathitt County" remained unquestioned.

South's most permanent legacy was the creation of an unfailingly Democratic electorate. Breathitt County was carved from the three counties that composed the northeastern corner of the "Whig Gibraltar," Kentucky's southeastern quadrant where loyalty to Henry Clay's party was unfaltering.[98] In 1840 Breathitt County cast strong majorities for William Henry Harrison (by a nearly four to one margin) and Whig gubernatorial candidate Robert Letcher. Immediately thereafter Breathitt County began turning out Democratic majorities, a change that would seem inconsequential had it not happened so rapidly at a time when the Kentucky Democracy was failing.[99] Mountain Whigs survived their party's national downfall in the following decade, making Breathitt County's affiliation all the more peculiar and consequential. It was one of a very few dependable Democratic islands in what would later become eastern Kentucky's sea of Republicanism. "The county," George Noble recalled proudly, "always went Democratic."[100]

Breathitt County's switch in voting habits happened so abruptly as to suggest something other than shrewd politicking. Hargis and Bohannon, as the first clerks of the county court and circuit court respectively, could monitor party loyalty and possibly even manipulate election outcomes.[101] With his brother Richard as the first sheriff (and other fellow petitioners serving as the second and third), South was fully capable of using the carrot of patronage—and the stick of inconvenient summonses—to swell the Democratic vote.[102] In 1846 South, John Hargis, and their fellow Democrats orchestrated a petit coup by holding a meeting of the justices of the peace with only one of the two Whig members present (Thomas Sewell was the absent Whig). The Democrats filled the two Whig-held vacancies with their own selections, placing the county court completely under their control.[103] Whig governor William Owsley ignored Sewell's complaints of the Democrats' underhanded attempt to "get in power." In fact there was little that Owsley could have done and Sewell apparently did not press the matter any further.[104] His suspicions were justified; with Democrats in exclusive control over patronage and public works, the party's majority increased significantly for years.[105] Breathitt County's permanent association with the Democratic Party came to define practically every major event in its history.

For some of the county's "founding fathers," residency in their county was temporary. After his term as the first county clerk, Simeon Bohannon returned to the Bluegrass and kept his Breathitt County property as a summer home for his wife and daughters.[106] The Griffling brothers, one of Breathitt's "nice families," grew impatient waiting on the bread they had cast on the new county's waters and moved to Memphis after only three years.[107] Although he was a lifelong property owner in Breathitt County, South returned to the Bluegrass in the 1840s, leaving his son Andrew Jackson South in Breathitt County to manage local business (South fathered thirteen children, some of whom remained in or around Jackson until well after the Civil War).[108] Decades before national and international corporations took notice of eastern Kentucky's extractable wealth, South, Bohannon, Sewell (who moved west to Estill County in 1858), and others were initiating the much-maligned trend of absentee ownership.[109]

As "one of the controlling voices in the Democratic party in Kentucky," Jeremiah South was appointed state penitentiary superintendent and lessee (a position that "allowed a private citizen to incur the financial risks and reap the financial rewards of the penitentiary") in 1859.[110] As with Breathitt County's creation, his appointment revealed a constant collusion between government and private interests. The position meant personal control over all convict labor, ergo statewide control over internal improvements and a lifetime's supply of personal household servants.[111] During his first four-year term, he accumulated "an ample fortune, as the product of convict earnings," and his flagrant venality was later used as evidence in demands for prison reform in many states.[112] During a fifteen-year sentence for assisting runaway slaves, Methodist abolitionist Calvin Fairbank sustained some of his "thirty-five thousand stripes" under South's supervision. Still, the minister recalled South as having "more humanity . . . [and] less executiveness" than his cruel predecessor.[113]

His reputation outside of the prison walls was less qualified. South nurtured the relationships he had established in the General Assembly, supplying his political allies with "cheap boarding, cheap washing and free drinks," and giving out "curiously wrought walking sticks and cedar chests" to pet legislators.[114] When he died he was remembered as "perhaps, the most popular and influential man in all of Eastern Kentucky," even though he rarely returned from the Bluegrass in his last two decades.[115]

John Hargis, a Virginia native who had not come to Kentucky until the 1820s, had fewer Bluegrass connections and stayed in the county longer.[116] After starting his law practice he represented Breathitt in the state House of

Table 3. Presidential, gubernatorial, and congressional (U.S. House) elections in Breathitt County and its "birth" counties, 1828–1856

County	Democrat/ National Republican 1828 Pres.	Democrat/ National Republican 1832 Pres.	Democrat/ Whig 1836 Pres.	Democrat/ Whig 1836 Gub.	Democrat/ Whig 1840 Pres.	Democrat/ Whig 1840 Gub.	Democrat/ Whig 1843 Cong.	Democrat/ Whig 1844 Pres.	De
Breathitt	—	—	—	—	45 (D) 159 (W)	135 (D) 217 (W)	138 (D) 219 (W)	120 (D) 231 (W)	1! 25
Clay	58 (D) 348 (NR)	100 (D) 299 (NR)	153 (D) 202 (W)	136 (D) 356 (W)	91 (D) 438 (W)	141 (D) 447 (W)	102 (D) 443 (W)	92 (D) 335 (W)	2: 38
Estill	215 (D) 239 (NR)	227 (D) 311 (NR)	No returns	337 (D) 455 (W)	155 (D) 459 (W)	314 (D) 473 (W)	43 (D) 597 (W)	216 (D) 392 (W)	3: 44
Owsley	—	—	—	—	—	—	—	129 (D) 165 (W)	2. 15
Perry	59 (D) 100 (NR)	81 (D) 146 (NR)	83 (D) 172 (W)	134 (D) 165 (W)	45 (D) 185 (W)	159 (D) 266 (W)	144 (D) 154 (W)	84 (D) 113 (W)	14 24

Sources: *Tribune Almanac and Political Register, 1838*, 28; *1840*, 25–26; *1841*, 23–24; *1843*, 46; *1844*, 56; *1845*, 51; *1846*, 48; *1848*, 46; *1849*, 55; *1850*, 48; *1852*, 47; *1853*, 43; *1854*, 47; *1856*, 47; *1857*, 52; *1858*, 59; *1859*, 6.

Representatives, where he supported road construction and river improvement.[117] He unsuccessfully protested new counties' removal of territory from Breathitt County, and attempted to increase state funding for county common schools (in this he may have been more successful since the number of the county's school districts increased by nearly two-thirds during his time in office). Combs Academy, one of eastern Kentucky's first public coeducational high schools, opened in Jackson at the beginning of the Civil War.[118]

At Kentucky's 1849 constitutional convention, "the alpha and omega of his political career," delegate Hargis made Jacksonian appeals for electoral reform, local sovereignty, and rural supremacy.[119] Citing the "great danger to be apprehended from the influence [cities like Louisville] might exercise arising from the consolidation of wealth and numbers," he unsuccessfully attempted to prevent increases in urban representation.[120] Hargis also proposed term limits for sheriffs, opposed limiting county judge candidacy to lawyers and, remarkably, spoke out against Kentucky's most cherished political institution, *vive voce,* or voice voting.[121] Ballotless voting eased illiterate men's participation, but Hargis and others criticized it for allowing local elites to monitor and manipulate elections.[122] "I want my tenant to go and drop in his ballot without my knowledge of the man for whom it is given," he said during debate. "If they vote by ballot what landlord will know

rat/ g	Democrat/ Whig	Democrat/ Whig	Democrat/ Whig	Democrat/ Whig	Democrat/ Whig	Democrat/ Whig	Democrat/ Whig	Democrat/ American
5 g.	1847 Cong.	1848 Pres.	1848 Gub.	1849 Cong.	1851 Cong.	1852 Pres.	1853 Cong.	1856 Pres.
D) W)	158 (D) 382 (W)	143 (D) 151 (W)	120 (D) 278 (W)	126 (D) 401 (W)	0 (D) 369 (W)	96 (D) 234 (W)	223 (D) 373 (W)	112 (D) 502 (A)
D) W)	No Dem. candidate	125 (D) 377 (W)	229 (D) 416 (W)	321 (D) 351 (W)	330 (D) 348 (W)	185 (D) 278 (W)	271 (D) 398 (W)	369 (D) 421 (A)
D) W)	No Dem. candidate	238 (D) 485 (W)	381 (D) 490 (W)	391 (D) 377 (W)	325 (D) 466 (W)	322 (D) 358 (W)	410 (D) 565 (W)	474 (D) 543 (A)
D) W)	No Dem. candidate	248 (D) 330 (W)	268 (D) 270 (W)	256 (D) 294 (W)	241 (D) 315 (W)	294 (D) 326 (W)	178 (D) 476 (W)	335 (D) 401 (A)
D) W)	No Dem. candidate	No returns	177 (D) 192 (W)	291 (D) 392 (W)	149 (D) 220 (W)	77 (D) 130 (W)	121 (D) 257 (W)	173 (D) 295 (A)

Table 4. Tabulation of election results in Breathitt County and its "birth" counties, 1810–1860

County	No. Democratic majorities/ recorded elections	No. Nat. Rep., Whig, American, or opposition majorities/recorded elections
Breathitt	13/15 (86.6%)	2/15
Clay	3/19	16/19 (84.2%)
Estill	3/18	15/18 (83.3%)
Owsley (formed from part of Breathitt Co., 1843)	5/12	7/12 (58.3%)
Perry	6/18	12/18 (66.6%)

Sources: *Tribune Almanac and Political Register*, 1838, 28; *1840, 25–26; 1841, 23–24; 1843, 46; 1844, 56; 1845, 51; 1846, 48; 1848, 46; 1849, 55; 1850, 48; 1852, 47; 1853, 43; 1854, 47; 1856, 47; 1857, 52; 1858, 59; 1859, 56.*

anything about the vote of his tenant[?]" Since most of the other delegates owed their successes to this sort of knowledge, his plea for a secret ballot was ignored (by 1861 only Kentucky and Virginia still used vive voce).[123] Hargis also unsuccessfully proposed reducing the number of local electable offices such as county attorney, coroner, jailer, and "other little petty officers," preferring they be appointed by justices of the peace (this, too, was ignored since most other Democratic delegates favored expanding electoral authority).[124] With or without Hargis's suggestions (and mostly, it would seem, the latter), the new constitution ushered in his party's statewide resurgence. When it came to referendum in 1850, Whig citadel Clay County was the only county that rejected it.[125]

Hargis was absent due to illness for much of the convention and his contribution to the new constitution, and its vaunted expansion of *herrenvolk* democracy, remains ambiguous.[126] In contrast, his support for slavery was forthright and obvious. In a convention noted for being a referendum on slavery, Hargis stood as one of only a few representatives unambiguously in favor of an institution he believed was "sanctioned by the Bible."[127] Aware that men of the cloth had used the legislature as an abolitionist bully pulpit, he proposed a constitutional exclusion of "clergymen, priest or teacher of any religious persuasion, society, or sect" from serving as lawmakers.[128] Dreading an unmanageable free black population, he also proposed that all emancipated slaves be required to leave the state under penalty of reenslavement.[129]

Hargis's fear of free blacks reflected his Virginia and Bluegrass past more than it did Breathitt County slave life.[130] In the Three Forks whites outnumbered slaves by a tremendous margin, as they had since slaves were first brought to the area around 1800.[131] Jo, one of Jeremiah South's slaves, "with whom everyone in the county was acquainted," roved about as a hired messenger in the 1840s while "Yaller Bill," another South bondsman, was an acclaimed hunter.[132] Not far away, Clay County salt manufacturers broke state law by arming their slaves as members of biracial private militias.[133] Slave and free, black, white, and biracial, commingled liberally; free blacks lived in slave-owning households, and 1860's census listed more than a third of Breathitt County slaves as "mulatto."[134] Black and white were sometimes indistinguishable, particularly one "very pretty girl about 14 years old, well dressed with long golden ringlets, rosy cheeks and a fair complexion" who was sold "at a fancy price to a prominent bachelor lawyer" sometime in the 1840s.[135] As a slavery "perpetualist," or a voice for Negrophobia, John Hargis's views did not match his constituents' habits.[136]

Breathitt County's relationship to the peculiar institution demonstrates slavery's pervasive political influence in places where its economic impact was limited.[137] Slaves were an important investment for mountain farmers with low-valued landholdings; it was not unusual for masters to have slaves that were collectively worth more than the land they worked.[138] In the twenty years before the Civil War, Breathitt's slave population grew even as neighboring counties' numbers dwindled.[139] In a state with low numbers of slaves but widespread ownership, Jeremiah South, John Hargis, and Simeon Bohannon had little reason to see themselves differently than other Kentucky slaveholders.[140]

Still, slaveholders were only about 6 percent of the white population—a 6 percent that included all of the county's petitioners and almost all of the men who served as justices of the peace before 1860.[141] This disproportionality of interests between the governing minority and the governed majority was nothing unusual, and some Kentuckians sensed their own Slave Power conspiracy.[142] Antislavery activism had audiences in Kentucky until the late 1850s (albeit not without occasional violent reprisals), long after it was stifled in other slave states.[143] Outright abolitionism was rare, but frank distaste for bondage was palpable, especially in the mountains. James Sebastian, born a few months before Breathitt County was formed around him, despised "mixing, laboring and competing with slave labor" so much that he left for Illinois, returning to the Three Forks to fight for the Union in 1861.[144] Before young George Noble went off to join a Confederate unit that year, his father told him "that it was wrong to keep any human being in bondage."[145]

When Kentucky's flamboyant emancipationist Cassius M. Clay attempted a gubernatorial bid in 1851, Breathitt was one of a very few counties in which he commanded 5 percent or more of the vote. Heavily Democratic (by then) Breathitt was very different from the other nearby "Whig Gibraltar" counties that did so, including Breathitt's three "birth counties." Most were highly commercialized counties where slavery was a significant presence but not an overwhelming one. Finally, twelve of these counties (including all of the counties in the Three Forks watershed except for Breathitt) had hosted emancipationist or abolitionist gatherings shortly before 1851. That fifty Breathitt votes were cast for an unabashedly antislavery candidate in a county controlled and represented exclusively by slave owners reveals a conspicuous distaste for the local slaveocracy, a distaste only slightly more muted than what was seen in other sections of the mountains.[146] It was a sliver minority of the voting public, but Kentuckians learned how powerful minority opinion could be ten years later.

The distaste was measured six years later when an English abolitionist minister named William Ellaby Lincoln visited the county. After seeing American evangelist Charles Finney preach in his native London, Lincoln immigrated to Ohio's Oberlin College to dedicate his life to ending slavery.

County	Clay vote (%)	Black population in 1860 (%)	Whig majority	Known public antislavery activity
Breathitt	5.9	4.3	No	No
Butler	7.2	10	No	No
Clay	26.5	9.2	Yes	Yes
Edmondson	5.0	6.1	No	No
Estill	18.1	7.6	Yes	Yes
Fayette	5.1	47.3	Yes	Yes
Garrard	15.4	34.9	Yes	Yes
Jessamine	5.1	40.1	Yes	No
Knox	9.9	8.7	Yes	Yes
Laurel	7.3	3.4	Yes	Yes
Lincoln	6.9	33.7	Yes	Yes
Madison	35.2	35.9	Yes	Yes
Monroe	13.9	11	No	Yes
Ohio	8.7	10.8	No	No
Owsley	8.5	2.4	No	Yes
Perry	12.2	2.2	No	Yes
Pulaski	12.7	8	No	Yes
Rockcastle	19.4	7.4	Yes	No
Todd	6.8	42.3	Yes	No
Washington	7.1	24.8	No	No
Wayne	7.0	9.9	Yes	Yes
Whitely	13.2	2.9	Yes	No

Table 5. Counties returning greater than 5% for Cassius M. Clay for governor, 1851

Sources: *Tribune Almanac and Political Register, 1852*, 47; Mathias and Shannon, "Gubernatorial Politics in Kentucky," 271; Shannon and McQuown, *Presidential Politics in Kentucky*, 26.

In spring 1856 he left for Kentucky to offer his services to the Reverend John G. Fee, soon to be the founder of Berea College. Fee urged the young preacher to evangelize in Breathitt County and he agreed, beginning the excursion soon after. Along the way, Lincoln encountered resistance to his antislavery message until he arrived in Breathitt, where he was taken in by a sympathizer. Lincoln's unnamed host was "careful not to expose himself too much" since, as he said, local slaveholders were willing to defend their institution "even by mob violence."[147]

The two attended a revival meeting, where they heard a "colored preacher . . . whose sermon was a careful steer between the master & slave." In attendance were slaves, slave owners, and at least eleven men whom Lincoln found racially unidentifiable. The quiet abolitionist seated at his side asked Lincoln to play a strange game as the parishioners entered the meetinghouse. "Then in doubt, as to whether a man is colored or white, if white touch my right knee, if colored, my left," his friend told him. Unable to interpret the skin color of eleven of the men he saw, Lincoln was told that one of the men he had thought colored self-identified as white and "had killed 1 man and wounded another man who stuck to it, that [he] was colored." Lincoln's new friend was apparently trying to demonstrate the community's unique racial indistinctness, a population (in one local historian's phrasing) "considered part-black."[148] But the young Englishman was not prepared for the reality of racial mixing that he saw in front of him, attributing it to the men's "work outdoors in the sun and the wind."[149]

When Lincoln got behind the pulpit later that day, sheriff's deputies arrived to warn attending slaves away at gunpoint. During his exegesis of Jeremiah, the preacher realized that the same pistols were pointed in his direction from a front pew. He was able to shame the deputies into sheepishly lowering their guns during worship, but afterward some "young slaveholders" warned Lincoln that he would be shot if he did not leave quickly. As he made his way back to the reticent abolitionist's home (who had bowed out of going to Lincoln's service so as not to attract attention to himself), the deputies first feigned friendliness but then began shooting. Lincoln claimed later to have barely escaped with his life after his horse threw him from his saddle under fire.[150]

Lincoln's visit was the first, if not especially adroit, recorded challenge to slavery in Breathitt County. It showed that, as in other southern communities, protests against the slaveholding order were punished with violence. Also, the congregation of black, white, mulatto, slave, and free that he saw (but never understood) represented a "mixed" community that would later play a remarkable role during and after the Civil War. The ballot deviation of 1851 and the small show of abolitionist sympathies (as well as the violent effort to suppress it) also reveal antebellum Breathitt County's lack of a perfect white consensus—but hardly a serious challenge to Jeremiah South. He, John Hargis, and others established a slaveholder's rentier state, one that need not be well organized to be profitable. In its official institutions and formal political character, Breathitt County remained in the image of its "father."

But South's mastery over court did not translate into mastery over country. For the rest of his life, and for years after, squatters lived on his gigantic estate, hunting game, constructing cabins, sending livestock to mast, damming creeks, cutting timber, and mining coal.[151] Many of them probably occupied the land before South procured the delinquent title and considered themselves its rightful owners. Some even eventually received land patents that ignored the old Virginia grants, one of which was the basis for South's hardwood fortune.[152] He and his children learned the same lesson absorbed by so many absentee owners before and since: contractual ownership was often no match for direct knowledge of the terrain.[153] There were far too many people in the very large county who knew more about South's property—its creeks, coves, glades, timber, and coal seams—than he ever could, even with the most thorough land surveys. E. L. Noble described their viewpoint with his typical exaggeration: "To them, it was no-man's land."[154] The "true" land value could be exploited by South's uninvited guests over the years. The result of all of these factors was a long-standing stalemate between landed and landless.

This was a source of constant dismay for South, and numerous times he attempted to recoup his profits by placing felled timber under attachment in court. He also tried hiring some of his land's occupants to aggressively prevent trespassing. John Aikman (George Noble recalled him as "the bully of the mountains"), the South estate's "guard," exploited Jeremiah South's absence and eventually laid claim to a substantial mass of his property through adverse possession.[155] Aikman had the same problem with people he considered squatters, and he allegedly resorted to arson to get rid of them.[156] More than a quarter century after Jeremiah South's death, Breathitt County was said to still have the worst problem with overlapping land claims in all of Kentucky.[157] To complicate matters, the perpetuation of Jeremiah South's Democratic regime depended upon votes from men who brazenly violated his property. With vive voce, this was probably no secret.[158] South's authority as statesman and landholder was limited to his ability to exert authority over his own property and over local public institutions. Although the latter was fairly secure throughout the antebellum era, the former represented the innate illegitimacy of Breathitt County's very existence.

Breathitt County's creation was beneficial to men whose wealth was based on speculation and slaves who wanted greater access to courts and the sense of community and order they provided. These new boundaries were of little social consequence to families and individuals whose political, social, and economic relationships had been established before 1839. The new county's initiators could expect support from those who shared their interests, and hope for acquiescence from everyone else. The potential for conflict existed since the county's creation.

Still, the county had existed for three and a half decades before it was dubbed "Bloody Breathitt." The violence that inspired this moniker was a result of Breathitt County's role in the Civil War, a role Jeremiah South and his family engineered. Writing just before Breathitt County's centennial, E. L. Noble observed, "The Souths, while not feudists, seem to have done more to perpetuate feudal conditions in Breathitt than any family otherwise directly or indirectly connecting her history."[159]

2

"SUPPRESSING THE LATE REBELLION"

Guerrilla Fighting in a Loyal State

> As the nation was rent apart, so was the commonwealth; as the state so
> was the county; as the county, the neighborhood; as the neighborhood,
> the family; as the family, so brother and brother, father and son.
> —John Fox Jr., *The Little Shepherd of Kingdom Come* (1903)

> He has only one idea: the revolution; and he has broken with all the laws
> and codes of morals of the educated world. If he lives in it, pretending to
> be part of it, it is only to destroy it the more surely; everything in it must
> be equally hateful to him. He must be cold: he must be ready to die, he
> must train himself to bear torture, and he must be ready to kill in himself
> any sentiment, including that of honor, the moment it interferes with his
> purpose.
> His name remained a bugbear for decades.
> —Edmund Wilson, *To the Finland Station:*
> *A Study in the Writing and Acting of History* (1940)

Breathitt County native George Washington Noble became a lifelong be-
liever in divine portent when he was sixteen, not long before he joined the
Confederate infantry. One winter night in 1860 or 1861, he saw an enormous
comet in the winter sky. His father (no doubt informed by current events)
said that it was an omen of impending war between North and South.[1]
Months later, George felt called to defend his home from northern aggression, especially after hearing rumors that Yankees were "killing women
and children and carrying off the negroes" and Kentucky would soon be
occupied territory. After the Upper South's states seceded, most adult male
Kentuckians followed a path of least resistance, many taking their families

and slaves "to the hills" to "lay out" hostilities.[2] Others put aside their distaste for Abraham Lincoln and his party and joined the Union army. But Noble figured that the Confederate army "was just as good as the Northern Army" and, against his parents' wishes, joined a locally organized company in December. When Noble recalled his decision fifty years later, his reasoning remained succinct: "My grandfather came from the South, and I liked the Southern people the best."[3]

George Noble's Confederate service took him to Virginia, where he was captured and sent to a Maryland military prison until he was paroled and returned to Kentucky in 1864. His harshest moments of fear and sadness lay ahead of him even then. Although he initially feared a "foreign" army, he and other Breathitt Countians found that the greatest wartime dangers were not invaders but close neighbors—"Southern people" the young soldier knew personally.[4]

Years before Breathitt County was called Bloody Breathitt, its violent history began with the Civil War, its conditions determined by Kentucky's intricate internal sectionalism. To its north and east, between the Big Sandy River and the Kentucky River's northern fork, lay a pocket of pro-Confederate mountain Democracy. South and west of the county, between the Kentucky River's middle and south forks, the eastern edge of the old Whig Gibraltar, was the most consistently pro-Union area in all of Kentucky.[5] Like many wealthy Kentuckians, Breathitt's leaders supported the rebellion, and Breathitt County became a Confederate staging ground for attacks on nearby Unionist counties.

There were dissenters within the county; a defiant interracial martial polity "beyond the visible end of the spectrum" took up an intense offensive against their Confederate neighbors.[6] Theirs was a campaign against secession and slavery, but it was also an indictment against Breathitt County itself. Nearly surrounded by counties with Unionist leanings, and beset by its own internal divides, Breathitt became a nexus of guerrillaism: a collection of tactics that blurred the distinction between social relations and military strategy.[7] The intimacy between combatants, uniformed and otherwise, tempered the way in which they fought, amounting to what nineteenth-century Americans called a "social war."[8]

This was how the American Civil War was won and lost in many places, especially in the border South, although it was not a popular memory after the war. As the story of the "War between the States" was written after 1865, most Americans fancied a distinction between the guerrillaism in places like

Breathitt County and the larger "legitimate" war. The stories of veterans like George Noble were overshadowed by the more popular, more acceptable "stand-up war."[9] In the sparse historical record, warfare there took on the appearance of personal vendettas, property theft (in the guise of military confiscation), and terrorism. By Noble's own testimony, he fought for the South and he saw the Confederate cause as his own. But his home county's "local cleavage" fit poorly into the "master cleavage" Americans wished to remember.[10] For this reason, among others, Breathitt County's Civil War history was eventually depoliticized and absorbed within a narrative less associated with war than with feud.[11]

"A sublime spectacle of moral power"

In 1861 the birth state of Abraham Lincoln and Jefferson Davis had reason to distrust both sides of the national divide. Kentucky had one of the United States' largest slave-owning populations (but relatively few slaves), and many powerful Kentuckians wished to join their southern neighbors. They had few other practical motivations for abandoning the Union, and the federal government offered exceptional concessions to secure the state's loyalty.[12] Kentucky's Senator John J. Crittenden aspired to a mediator position, proposing a modicum of Henry Clay's 1820 Missouri Compromise just before Lincoln's inauguration.[13] After this failed, Kentuckians searched for other options as they watched the Union deteriorate. In May Southern Rights stalwart Governor Beriah Magoffin unhappily issued a proclamation of state neutrality.[14] The fact that southern sympathizers opposed this neutrality (while Unionists settled for it) did not bode well for the prospects of maintaining internal peace. Still, Kentuckians were optimistic that their state could be "a sublime spectacle of moral power" to inspire a speedy national reunion.[15] This lasted until Confederate forces entered the state in September 1861, prompting a decisive legislative declaration (over Governor Magoffin's veto) for the Union.[16] Eleven months later Magoffin resigned, leaving behind a mostly Unionist, and usually pro-Lincoln, coalition in control of the state.[17] In testament to his compromise's failure, each of Senator Crittenden's sons received an officer's commission, one in the Federal army, the other for the Confederacy.[18]

Nowhere else did state government show less leadership. Instead of inspiring national reunion, Kentucky's neutrality experiment allowed households and courthouses across the state to make their own decisions,

ranging from Unconditional Unionism to rebellion, with countless variations in between. On the whole, neutrality worked to Confederate advantage
since it made early Union recruitment difficult.[19] By 1862 "each individual
had by this time made his choice or was fast making up his mind" and "in
the meantime was fast arming himself," either as a recruit in a "regular"
military unit or as part of a less formal armed arrangement.[20] No other state
that hadn't seceded contributed more men to the Confederate army, while
ostensibly loyal sheriffs, judges, and other guardians of public trust "conducted themselves in ways approaching secession."[21] As a result, the Union
and the Confederacy each claimed Kentucky. More important, Kentuckians
claimed both the Union and the Confederacy.[22]

Slavery and preservation of the Union, the war's "master cleavage" issues, remained crucial to white Kentuckians, especially since so many of
them tried to save both. But once the fighting started, Kentucky's Civil War
played out as skirmishes fought over control of local government. As early
as December 1861 it had become clear which counties favored the South
and which ones favored the North. The "segmented sovereignty," the quasi-
federal balance of power between county and state Kentuckians held dear,
gave way to a "fragmented sovereignty" in which counties became themselves
smaller versions of states.[23] While these counties' representatives debated in
Frankfort, members of their electorate had already begun killing each other.

No group better defined Kentucky's disjointed Civil War experience
than the Home Guards, an organization that became a liberally defined
epithet for brutality toward civilians. In 1860 Kentucky established the State
Guard, a network of militias that remained only until most of its service-
men migrated south with their commander, Simon Bolivar Buckner, to join
the Confederate army.[24] Once the militias' collective pro-South character
became clear, the General Assembly authorized the more loosely organized
Home Guards, "wholly a defensive measure" but, unlike the State Guard,
tacitly Unionist.[25] Home Guards were mandated and armed by the state but,
reflecting the state's "little kingdoms," they were maintained under the aegis
of county judges and commanded by men who sometimes combined strategies of local defense with their own interests. For most of 1861 some Home
Guards kept up Kentucky's early Republic tradition of the apolitical militia;
Southern Rights men and loyalists patrolled together out of mutual fear of
slave insurrection.[26] When southern sympathizers withdrew, Home Guards
became local enforcers of Unionism, going as far as arresting state legislators
suspected of southern sympathies.[27] Like militias in other civil wars, they

were ultimately more political than military, bent upon local state building and unbuilding rather than vigilance against invaders.[28] In many places this meant excessive force against civilians and, in turn, a gradual corrosion of Unionist enthusiasm.[29] Home Guard oppression may have actually created a significant number of Kentucky rebels, but only late in the war when the larger rebellion was proving futile—thus giving Kentucky a unique kind of wartime misery. Months after the war's end, Governor Thomas Bramlette, having sacrificed all of his political fortunes to keep Kentucky in the Union, proclaimed the Home Guards a deplorable failure.[30] By the 1890s only the most steadfast defenders of Kentucky Unionism attempted to defend their memory against "gratuitous and unjust charges of perpetrating outrages."[31]

The means used by these militias ultimately delegitimized the ends for which they fought. "Home Guard" became synonymous with "bushwhacker," the nineteenth century's most damning epithet for wartime irregulars.[32] After the war, "Home Guard" mutated into an imprecise pejorative for men who supposedly took advantage of the war's chaos for personal gain and love of havoc, a lot despised by Unionists and Confederates alike for sullying their mutually "honorable" cause.[33] "Home Guard" became more a précis for the Upper South's guerrilla warfare than the name of an actual organization, a catchall affront to the legitimacy that Yankees and Rebels claimed during their joint process of reunion—a process that disingenuously discarded the entire war's political meaning.[34] The decidedly political Home Guards became depoliticized after the fact, reframed in decades of written war memory as brigands with minimal interest in either cause. This after they, and soldiers that were erroneously called Home Guards, arguably had a greater political impact on wartime Kentucky than did "legitimate" armies. Far away from Manassas and Appomattox, most of Kentucky's Civil War was a guerrilla war, especially in places like Breathitt County.

"What tyranny or what injury in any way has the State of Kentucky committed against you?"

Home Guards were stationed all over Kentucky, although some parts of the state required more enforced loyalty than did others. Western Kentucky had the most Confederate support, and an ersatz "rump" state capital was established in Russellville.[35] Mountainous eastern Kentucky was remembered, with some exaggeration, as the paragon of Union loyalty.[36] Between these areas, in the Bluegrass, Unionists and disunionists were "closely mixed," and wartime differences had to be treated as political bickering rather than martial opposition.[37] Leavening their support for the South with deference to their state's apparent majority, the Bluegrass's southern sympathizers held their tongues or resorted to a Fabian promotion of secession.[38]

Such was the case with state penitentiary supervisor and "strong southern rights man" Jeremiah W. South.[39] "Upon the inauguration of the Rebellion," recalled his then prisoner Calvin Fairbank, South was "in full sympathy with it" and made no effort to hide it.[40] For sixteen months after neutrality's end, he remained in one of the state's most powerful unelected offices. And South profited considerably since he monopolized prisoner labor, a commodity that became more and more dear as the war eroded slavery. In October 1861 the General Assembly granted him an emergency $5,000 loan "because of the troubles with which the country is now afflicted" that disrupted the penitentiary's exportation of hemp sackcloth.[41]

South may have continued to profit thus had he not worn his political heart so openly on his sleeve, even as the state government grew more resolutely Unionist. In March 1862 that body deemed South's associations and opinions liabilities and voted ninety to four to replace him with "a former Whig, Know-Nothing, and Union man" the following month.[42] South's expulsion deprived him of a large income and gratis labor, but it freed him to display his southern colors more publicly. Eleven months after his dismissal, South and other "active 'secesh,' and sympathizers with the rebellion" held a wildcat Democratic convention.[43] Federal soldiers dispelled the meeting, and even the most loyal of Kentucky Democrats were enraged by the disruption of peaceful assembly.[44] It was one of the first indications of Bluegrass Kentuckians' growing disillusionment with the war effort. Jeremiah South apparently played the rest of the war safe.

When he departed Breathitt County in the 1850s, Jeremiah South left behind him four adult sons, at least nine slaves, a coal mine, and one of the largest landholdings in Kentucky.[45] He also left behind a political apparatus prepared to lead his county toward secession and rebellion.[46] Secessionist handbills had circulated in the area since the 1860 elections, and early the next year, both of the county's attending legislators joined most Confederate sympathizers in voting against neutrality.[47] He also had a network of wealthy Democratic allies who controlled the county court. John Hargis's son Thomas was among the county's earliest Confederate recruits (his commission as captain in the Fifth Kentucky Infantry facilitated his eventual rise to become one of Kentucky's most respected Democratic jurists).[48]

South's brother Richard and four of his eight sons—Jerry, Barry, James, and Samuel (as well as three of his sons-in-law)—enlisted in the Confederate army. After he was wounded at the battle of Chickamauga, Samuel was field-promoted from private to colonel and awarded the Confederate Congress's medal of honor.[49] In November 1861 a Breathitt company arrived in Tennessee to muster into the Confederate First Kentucky Infantry.[50] The same month "groups of threes, fives and sevens, chiefly mounted, but many afoot" from Breathitt and other mountain counties descended upon Prestonsburg (Floyd County's county seat), eastern Kentucky's first "rallying point for the secessionists."[51] There the Confederacy's Fifth Kentucky was organized, one of the most poorly armed and outfitted infantry units in the southern military.[52]

The next year, in the summer of 1861, Jackson became the second such rallying point. Democratic county judge Edward Callahan "Red Ned" Strong, a descendant of some of the earliest Three Forks settlers and a slave owner of considerable means, joined Barry South in recruiting Confederate volunteers.[53] Over the following months at least 126 young men from Breathitt and surrounding counties were recruited to the Thirteenth Kentucky Cavalry, a hearty number for an area with ready opportunities to "lay out."[54] It seemed that most of Breathitt County's male citizenry, or at least those who left imprints on the public record, initially followed their county's "father."

After neutrality ended, Confederate Breathitt County stood out like the proverbial sore thumb in the otherwise heavily Unionist Three Forks. In November 1861 Colonel Leonidas Metcalfe came to the county to bring it back into the fold—though his expected arrival was interpreted as coercion and actually accelerated Confederate recruitment.[55] When he reached Jackson he found that the Rebels—at least the ones in uniform—had departed. Before leaving, he produced a proclamation imploring its citizens not to "take up arms against [their] fellow Kentuckians" and offering $100 to anyone who could explain "what right he had that the United States had taken from him."[56]

> Pause and reflect on such a course [supporting the rebellion], and ask yourselves why you must take up arms against your fellow Kentuckians—against your kin and the laws of your State. What law has Congress or the Legislature passed that oppresses you? What right did you ever have that has been taken away from you? What tyranny or what injury in any way has the State of Kentucky committed against you? What law has curtailed or even threatened your

Judge Edward Callahan "Red Ned" Strong, never a "feudist" but a long-lived member of Breathitt County's moneyed elite who helped define his home county for the outside world. (http://www.breathittcounty.com/RedNedStrong.html)

right to your slaves or all the rights you ever had in the Territories? Can any of you answer these simple questions? No, you cannot.[57]

The colonel couched his appeal in terms of civic kinship and state loyalty, with no mention of the Union or the Lincoln administration. It further addressed grievances many white Kentuckians shared while suggesting that the rest of the state had chosen to overlook them in the interest of unity. Clearly, concerns other than state fidelity had surpassed their interest in their home state.

Leonidas Metcalfe's wording suggests that he and many other border state loyalists did not fully understand their rebellious neighbors' motivations. Unionists and Rebels in the North and the South all used declarations of loyalty, either to the Union or to their respective states, to justify their actions even when those actions were really determined by political concerns like slavery. On the other hand, Confederate nationalism had a limited foothold in Kentucky, George Noble's sentimental remembrances of his southern grandfather notwithstanding.[58] And if Breathitt County answered the call out of a sense of white southerners' *communitas*, the same appeal was ignored by neighboring counties, Estill, Clay, Perry (the three counties from which Breathitt was formed twenty-two years before), and Owsley—let alone the vast majority of Kentuckians. There had to have been other factors at work. This was not a matter of loyalty to Kentucky or the United States or the South, but rather one of power.[59]

Slavery was "neither simple nor obvious" as the basis for most white southerners' wartime decisions, especially in the highlands where, one historian recently declared, it "exercised minimal influence over the decision of the mountaineers" who joined the "Southern cause."[60] A glance at eastern Kentucky demographics seems to bear this out; solidly Unionist Clay County's fortune-making salt mines used eastern Kentucky's largest slave population, while pro-Confederate Floyd and Morgan each had very few slaves.[61] In Breathitt County less than 2 percent of the white population lived in slave-owning households in 1860, while most of the county's forty-seven slave owners owned fewer than five slaves (roughly the average throughout Kentucky).[62]

Nevertheless, as was the case elsewhere in the mountain South, Breathitt County's "prominent landowners . . . owners of much live stock and fertile bottoms," tended to be the strongest Confederate sympathizers and supporters, and their ever-growing slave population (by 1850 Breathitt had a higher

Colonel Leonidas Metcalfe, the son of a former governor and the commander of the Unionist Seventh Kentucky Cavalry, believed that he could dissuade Breathitt County's rebels from revolting against their home state. His arrival in Jackson near the end of 1861 may have actually increased Confederate recruitment in eastern Kentucky. (Courtesy of Kalawakua Mayer)

Table 6. Slavery in Breathitt and surrounding counties, 1850

County	Slave-owners	Black slaves	Mulatto slaves	Free blacks	Free mulattoes
Breathitt	46	118	51	3	8
Floyd	42	110	39	0	59
Morgan	59	187	0	26	18
Owsley	41	114	22	7	15
Perry	33	85	32	1	8

Source: *Breathitt County Tax Books, 1861*, Kentucky Historical Society.

Table 7. Slavery in Breathitt and surrounding counties, 1860

County	Slave-owners	Black slaves	Mulatto slaves	Free blacks	Free mulattoes
Breathitt	46	115	75	7	19
Floyd	185	105	42	66	7
Morgan	53	115	55	58	23
Owsley	29	77	35	3	15
Perry	28	45	28	0	13

Source: *Breathitt County Tax Books, 1861*, Kentucky Historical Society.

enslaved percentage of its population than any of its contiguous neighbors) was one of their chief sources of wealth.[63] It is possible that Jeremiah South et al. were even more eager to defend slavery than their planter brethren in the Bluegrass—the latter, having grown queasy about being surrounded by a large population of potential insurrectionists, hastened slave exportation to the Deep South.[64] Wealthy from the fruits of human bondage but not frightened, mountain slave owners might have been less likely "to give up [their] slaves without a battle."[65] Moreover, many Breathitt County yeomen probably felt a common interest with their slaveholding neighbors, while even those with no aspirations to own slaves did not happily envision a future without slavery or were swayed through client-patron influence.[66] John Aikman, the South family's tenant who acted as their enforcer against squatter intrusions, went on to become Breathitt County's most fervent defender of the local Confederate cause at his patrons' behest.[67] It is likely that many others who answered the Confederate call were nudged in that direction because of economic arrangements with the Souths, the Hargises, and other slave owners, and Leonidas Metcalfe probably understood this.[68] As E. L. Noble noted, among those who "held to the Confederate wing" in Breathitt County, "slavery was asserting itself in a degree."[69]

Political party membership was probably an even greater enticement to rebellion than slavery was, especially since Kentucky was practically the last slave state with a modicum of two-party competition by 1861.[70] Even Democratic counties with few slaves like Breathitt, Floyd, and Morgan were categorically more likely to support the Confederacy, while Whig/opposition counties like Clay and the remainder of the Three Forks counties provided the most Federal volunteers (in terms of percentage).[71] In a postwar congressional hearing, a former Unionist testified that "the democratic party, in the State of Kentucky, and in the South, were much more rebellious in their notions and feelings than [their party's] platform would indicate."[72] But of course this was postwar assessment; Southern Rights Democrat John Breckinridge was a scion of old Kaintuck peerage, and so managed to win a large number of traditionally Whiggish counties in the 1860 presidential election (even though he narrowly lost the state to Tennessee neo-Whig John Bell). The number of Breckinridge votes was not necessarily proportionate to Confederate support (Breckinridge himself did not embrace the Confederacy until late in 1861).[73]

Slavery and party affiliation were only contributing factors to something almost approaching class consciousness.[74] In Breathitt County, tacit or active support for the Confederacy involved slavery, but was based more broadly upon support for the county itself—its Democratic regime but also, more important, its commercial significance. It was based upon how much one had benefited from the county's existence, the founding of Jackson, and the development Jeremiah South and his landed fellows had promised two decades earlier. Some families had benefited more than others, but in the instances in which kin were divided, economics trumped blood.[75] Land and slaves were property and, at least in Breathitt County, the Democratic Party was the party of the propertied—this in a county where nearly 40 percent of the population was, according one missionary's 1860 report, "destitute."[76] A sense of common goals and interests "happened" because of the opportunity of secession and the challenge of war.[77] Breathitt County's economically determined Confederatism was consistent with Kentucky war memory. In the minds of Kentucky's southern apologists, Unionism was nothing more than an envious means to the end of tearing down men like

Edward Strong and the South family. After the war, one regretful Bluegrass Union veteran remarked that "the Kentucky troops in the Confederate Army, being fewer in number and from the richer and more educated part of the state, were as a whole a finer body of men than the federal troops of the Commonwealth."[78] In Breathitt County and elsewhere, this "finer body" of propertied men held a remarkable degree of influence over most of their county's citizenry.

Table 8. Names found on both Confederate or Union military rolls and in 1861 *Breathitt County Tax Books*

Name	Wartime allegiance	Land wealth in 1861 ($)
Andrew Allen	Confederate	550
Ira Allen	Confederate	200
John Angel	Union	200
Levi Angel	Union	0
Nathan Arrowood	Union	0
Annanias Barnett	Union	0
George Belcher	Union	200
Elijah Bowling	Union	0
Edward Collinsworth	Confederate	100
Thomas Collinsworth	Confederate	0
William Crawford	Confederate	500
Jeremiah Davidson	Union	75
Edward Deaton	Union	100
George Deaton	Union	0
Joseph Deaton	Union	0
William Deaton	Union	0
Golden Flinchum	Union	0
Hiram Freeman	Union	0
James Freeman	Union	0
William Freeman	Union	0
William Gambill	Union	1,000
Henry Haddix	Confederate	0
Hiram Haddix	Confederate	200
William Haddix	Confederate	300
John Hall	Union	200

Table 8. Names found on both Confederate or Union military rolls and in 1861 *Breathitt County Tax Books* *(continued)*

Name	Wartime allegiance	Land wealth in 1861 ($)
William Harvey	Union	50
Alexander Herald	Union	500
Stephen Hogg	Confederate	0
Elisha Johnson	Union	225
James Johnson	Union	300
Jefferson Johnson	Union	0
Thomas Johnson	Union	350
Benjamin McIntosh	Union	150
Fugate McIntosh	Union	150
Henley McIntosh	Union	0
Nimrod McIntosh	Union	0
William McIntosh	Union	50
George Miller	Union	0
Hiram Miller	Confederate	0
Samuel Miller	Confederate	100
Booker Mullins	Confederate	100
Elias Noble	Confederate	0
John Noble	Confederate	200
Alexander Patrick	Confederate	1,500
John Riley Sr.	Union	50
John Riley Jr.	Union	0
Squire Riley	Union	0
Calloway Sebastian	Union	100
Lewis Sebastian	Union	0
Harden Sizemore	Union	0
Lewis Sizemore	Union	0
Irvine Spicer	Union	0
Edward Stamper	Union	50
Samuel Stidham	Union	0

Sources: *Breathitt County Tax Books, 1861*, Kentucky Historical Society; *War of the Rebellion*, series 1, col. 32 (1892), 433, 687; *Kentucky Adjutant General's Report*, 210–13; Wells, *1890 Special Veterans' Census for Eastern Kentucky.*

Table 9. Combs family members' names found on both Confederate or Union military rolls and in 1861 *Breathitt County Tax Books*

First name	Wartime allegiance	Land wealth in 1861 ($)
Alfred	Confederate	800
George	Confederate	400
Henderson	Confederate	160
Henry	Confederate	100
Jeremiah	Confederate	100
Mason	Union	0
Nicholas	Confederate	0
Seburn	Union	0
Tarlton Jr.	Union	0
William	Union	100
William B.	Confederate	100

Sources: *Breathitt County Tax Books, 1861*, Kentucky Historical Society; *War of the Rebellion*, series 1, vol. 32 (1892), 433, 687; *Kentucky Adjutant General's Report*, 210–13; Wells, *1890 Special Veterans' Census for Eastern Kentucky*.

Table 10. Jett family members' names found on both Confederate or Union military rolls and in 1861 *Breathitt County Tax Books*

First name	Wartime allegiance	Land wealth in 1861 ($)
Curtis	Union	4,600
Granville	Confederate	1,000

Sources: *Breathitt County Tax Books, 1861*, Kentucky Historical Society; *War of the Rebellion*, series 1, vol. 32 (1892), 433, 687; *Kentucky Adjutant General's Report*, 210–13; Wells, *1890 Special Veterans' Census for Eastern Kentucky*.

Table 11. Little family members' names found on both Confederate or Union military rolls and in 1861 *Breathitt County Tax Books*

First name	Wartime allegiance	Land wealth in 1861 ($)
Alfred	Union	0
Edward	Union	0
James	Confederate	300
John C.	Confederate	1,500
William B.	Union	0

Sources: *Breathitt County Tax Books, 1861*, Kentucky Historical Society; *War of the Rebellion*, series 1, vol. 32 (1892), 433, 687; *Kentucky Adjutant General's Report*, 210–13; Wells, *1890 Special Veterans' Census for Eastern Kentucky*.

Although he was the son of Kentucky's first anti-Jacksonian (that is, elected just before the controversial president's opposition coalesced into the Whig Party) governor, Colonel Metcalfe did not account for the influence of men like Jeremiah South and his Democratic cohort, although Brigadier General James Garfield discovered it for himself a few months later.[79] Describing a population he considered "very ignorant" (ignorant of what he did not say), the future president saw a mountain population "completely under the control of their party leaders" but failed to consider the possibility that mountaineers followed the leaders who best suited their interests.[80] Breathitt Confederates were those who shared the most with Jeremiah South: slavery, land wealth, and Democratic Party affiliation. The process that established the Three Forks region's only pro-Confederate county had begun in 1839.[81]

"Their policy is to organize these mountain counties against us"

In 1839 or in 1861, South's project had never been absolutely completed, and the substantial minority of Breathitt's Union loyalists reflected this. While some of this poorer segment of the population followed their more prosperous relatives in supporting the South, the very poorest men were the ones statistically most likely to favor Union loyalty. They found a leader in Edward Strong's cousin, Captain William Strong, the man who later personified everything "Bloody Breathitt" entailed. After he joined the Federal Sixth Kentucky Cavalry in September 1862, William Strong was transferred (under orders from General William Rosencrans) to the Fourteenth Kentucky Cavalry, a regiment recruited from the ultra-Unionist Whig Gibraltar counties and commanded by Estill County's Colonel Henry Clay Lilly.[82]

While his richer cousin embraced newer trends, William Strong's Unionism was based upon relationships that predated Breathitt County's existence. William Strong's home was near Crockettsville, a community near the Kentucky River's middle fork with greater social and commercial contact with heavily Unionist Perry County than with Jackson on the north fork (in fact, it had been part of Perry when Strong was born in 1825). It was, consequently, home to Breathitt County's only Union mustering grounds.[83] Perry County was home to two Unionist families with deep roots in the Three Forks region, William, Joseph, and John Eversole and Wiley and Thomas Amis, all officers in the Fourteenth Cavalry (in December 1861 the Eversole brothers and forty-five other Union soldiers defended the Eversole farm against a Rebel force nearly three times their number in what may have been

Captain William Strong, Breathitt County's leading Unionist and a constant enemy of the county's power structure. This photograph was made sometime during the Civil War. (Courtesy of Charles Hayes)

the Three Forks region's first skirmish).[84] Before they all joined the Federal army, the Strongs, Amises, and Eversoles shared a sense of community decades older than Breathitt County's apportionment from Perry.[85] Strong and the Amises' grandfathers had fought in the Clay County Cattle War six decades previous, while the Eversoles were sons of Perry County's "richest and strongest family."[86] As a testament to his family's persistence amid winds of change, Wiley Amis's farm lay atop the confluence of Breathitt, Perry, and (the most intensely Unionist of the three) Owsley counties by 1845.[87] To these children of the Three Forks' "first families," Confederate Breathitt County was an unwelcome aberration.

After Confederate forces were repelled at Perryville in October 1862, the Fourteenth Kentucky Cavalry was organized in preparation for future southern invasions. Within a year it had become abundantly clear that emergent Kentucky Confederatism was a far greater danger.[88] From then, the "Greasy Fourteenth" gained a reputation for crimes against Kentuckians of diminishing loyalties.[89] In March 1864 the Fourteenth was dismissed and Strong was commissioned as a company commander in the Three Forks Battalion—later nicknamed the Last Chance Battalion—one of thirteen State Guard units, an arrangement that signaled a change from "policing" the state to barefaced counterinsurgency (William and James Eversole were also company captains in the new unit, but the Amis brothers apparently were not).[90] With eight companies (most with more than eighty men each) under the command of Mexican War veteran Colonel Elisha Treadway, the Three Forks was the largest of these state battalions even though it patrolled one of Kentucky's most underpopulated areas.[91]

If the 1861 creation of Home Guards had made a "social war" in Kentucky more likely, the organization of the Three Forks (which was often misidentified as a Home Guard) and other units like it signaled an acceptance that a "social war" was well under way. After John Hunt Morgan launched his last Confederate foray in the summer of 1864, Federal general Stephen Burbridge (a Bluegrass native) tightened control over the entire state, summarily executing men identified as southern partisans and even arresting anti-Lincoln public speakers during the run-up to the presidential election. The new draconian measures only convinced Kentuckians of their preexistent suspicions of Federal malice, and former loyalists became Rebel guerrillas (not to mention Lincoln did not carry the state that November).[92] State troops like Treadway, Strong, and the Eversoles felt more empowered to seek out and punish rebellion even when it was not gray-clad. Their brutal "peer pressure" against their own neighbors was an effective weapon against disloyalty, but it also made future reconciliation much more difficult.[93] In 1864 Strong began, according to one descendant of pro-Confederates, "killing nearly every Southern citizen he found," an assessment that seems to have been exaggerated but only slightly. "The majority of the people [in Breathitt County] were Southern sympathizers," wrote the Democratic *Louisville Courier-Journal* more than ten years after the war's end, "and that made them legitimate game for the devil, who appeared in the person of Captain Bill Strong."[94] By the time he reentered civilian life in August 1865, "Captain Bill" had become "the most powerful man in Breathitt County"—albeit after being erroneously identified as one of the "insulting and barbarous" Home Guards.[95]

In class terms, Strong had more in common with his enemies than with most of his allies. He was a landowner of some substance (albeit with far smaller tracts than his wealthy cousin), and he also owned slaves as late as 1860.[96] William Strong did have personal reasons for opposing the South family. Jeremiah South's holding of the old Thomas Franklin Revolutionary grant threatened Strong's claim over land his father bought at the time of Breathitt County's founding (decades later, William Strong refuted the Franklin grant's veracity—as did many other local landowners).[97]

The Union rank and file had their own reasons for opposing the Confederacy. The Fourteenth Cavalry and the Three Forks Battalion attracted a cross-section of disenfranchised southerners, marginal landowners, tenants, squatters, and people of color, an alliance whose very existence threatened everything Confederate southerners sought to defend. Theirs was not an opposition based upon isolation and willful ignorance of the outside world, as mountain Unionism has been characterized, nor were they driven by premodern "traditional" modes of local economics.[98] These were men—all deplored by one Confederate officer as the most "bitter, prejudiced and ignorant" of mountain men—who had not benefited from Breathitt County's 1839 creation and, in fact, were simply following the Three Forks region's prevailing political trend.[99]

Nor were they strongly motivated by the mountain Unionist's alleged xenophobic fear of the African race.[100] Anecdotal evidence suggests that some of Breathitt County's black and mulatto population served as combatants.[101] One slave owned by a Breathitt Confederate partisan traveled to Perry County to warn John Eversole of an impending attack led by his master, while another "fleetfooted negro" warned Unionists of Confederate arrivals.[102] Mountain slaves and squatters used their shared "shadowy existence," a barely discernible presence in extant records, to their advantage.[103]

Shared commitment to the Union cause created a bizarre common interest between slaves and white farmers, even, in William Strong's case, white farmers who were themselves slave owners. Aside from "carr[ying] off" slaves on his raids against Confederate households, Strong also freed his own slaves early in the war and armed them, creating a small interracial alliance that confounded Breathitt Democrats for decades.[104] By virtue of his unique arrangement with his own slaves and other local people of color, Strong was remembered as the "special protector of [Breathitt County's] colored race" forty years after his death.[105] According to a story passed down in the Strong family, one of his female slaves (who may have been manumitted but still living in the Strong household) performed her own sort of domestic resistance when a Rebel raiding party came to the Strong home and demanded that she cook their breakfast.

> And so they told her to go ahead and cook for them and so she did. But this black woman, she fixed the bread up . . . instead of using milk or water to mix the meal with, she took [the flour] out behind the kitchen and urinated in this meal instead of using water. So she fixed this and mixed it up. So she went to the chicken house and got some eggs from under this old setting hen and they had little chickens formed in the eggs. She got them and took them and broke them up and stirred them all up together and fried these for the men. So they went ahead and ate and thought it was a pretty good meal.[106]

The woman was able to mete out her own form of punishment because of her innocuous role as cook, but she and other freedpeople probably depended upon William Strong during the war and for a long time after. Even as they fought side by side, and even though Strong risked his own life in his comrades-in-arms' interest, it was never a relationship of perfect equality. A former bondsman "who was with the Captain in all his wars" and resided in "the Strong neighborhood" in 1897 still deferred to "Mars Bill."[107] Slavery was definitively unegalitarian, but paramilitary vigilance was only slightly less so.

Two of William Strong's longtime associates, Henderson Kilburn and Hiram Freeman, represent his unusual black-white troupe. Historical records reveal little about Kilburn other than that he was a landless farmer at the beginning of the war, possibly on the South family's acreage.[108] He was from white mountain society's lowest stratum, one that probably cared little for either sides' overarching goals. In 1862 Kilburn was enlisted into the Confederate Fifth Kentucky Infantry but deserted after less than two months. After the war he claimed he had been "captured and taken in the rebel army" at gunpoint (his forced conscription was apparently not an isolated event; at least fourteen Confederate recruits from Breathitt County ended up in either the Fourteenth Kentucky or the Three Forks Battalion).[109] Kilburn defected to the Fourteenth Kentucky Cavalry in December 1862 and became a corporal in the Three Forks Battalion in early 1865.[110] A skilled sharpshooter, Kilburn was called Strong's "chief Lieutenant" and his deadly "right hand, right foot and right eye," killing an indefinite number of men between the war and his death in 1884.[111]

Hiram Freeman was part of the racially ambiguous population that had puzzled the Reverend William E. Lincoln before the war. Usually identified as a mulatto, Freeman negotiated multiple racial identities over the course of his life, including enlistment (along with his ostensibly white sons) in the officially all-white Fourteenth Kentucky Cavalry and Three Forks Battalion.[112] His father, George Spencer, was a former Virginia slave who adopted Freeman as his new surname when he settled in Clay County, Kentucky, after his manumission in 1812.[113] Like many other children of impoverished freedpeople, Hiram and his siblings ended up as indentures of apprenticeship when he was in his mid-teens. In 1836 he and his brother were apprenticed to one of William Strong's cousins to be "learnt the art and mystery of farming," while his younger sister was bonded to be trained as a seamstress. Two years later nineteen-year-old Hiram successfully challenged his and his siblings' bonds.[114] Freeman spent the next two decades raising a large family (his wife and children were listed as white in census records) and working as a farm laborer in what became southern Breathitt County the year after his release from indenture. Back in Clay County, his family lost their meager assets in the 1850s mounting legal defenses against trumped-up charges ranging from hog theft to fornication.[115] It was conditions like these that produced the quintessential nineteenth-century outlaw's antipathy toward law enforcement and, when Freeman enlisted as a U.S. soldier in 1862, he may well have done so as an act of rebellion rather than putting down rebellion. Though born free, Freeman's early life experiences taught him how tenuous freedom could be for a former slave's son in a society run by slave owners. Freeman was often seen armed in William Strong's company after the war, while also working on his former commander's farm.[116] Though Freeman was not as brutal as Kilburn, Breathitt County Democrats remembered him as "among the worst" of Breathitt's Unionists.[117]

Civil War side taking in Breathitt County, Kentucky, was a mingling of the peculiar and the mundane. Confederate recruitment was exceptionally successful considering it was in the most Unionist section of an unseceded state; but it would seem that most of the men were following local leaders in accordance with what they considered their economic interests. Unionist defiance in the county reflected the will of most of the Three Forks population, but it made for the strangest of soldierly bedfellows. Strong, the Eversoles, and the Amises shared a pioneer primacy; their inheritance was endangered by interloping speculative projects like Jeremiah South's. Strong's (manumitted) slaves had reason to support their former master, especially if his enemies were the official defenders of human bondage (even in a state where many slaveholders fought for the Union, arming one's slaves as William Strong did was otherwise unheard of, let alone whites serving militarily alongside free people of color). Hiram Freeman, although born free, was fighting the inequalities inherent in white supremacy, a fight he shared with the rest of Breathitt's colored population, free and enslaved. Henderson Kilburn and other squatters fought against the Souths' speculative interests and the coercion represented by forced enlistment.

Wartime service under Strong's command created a "small state" independent of the local state, heightening Strong's power as the squatters' "chieftain" and the "special protector of the colored race."[118] He produced a union of interests between blacks and poor whites, the sort of "radicalism" that many white southerners feared more than anything else. Just as was the case with the wealthy Eversoles, part of his leadership came from his socioeconomic position in southern Breathitt County, but it also came from his willingness to lead men in the most outrageous, sometimes heinous, acts deemed necessary for winning the war.[119] This was a combination pregnant with more implications than Breathitt County Democrats could stand after the Civil War.

"I knew the man I shot"

Breathitt County's Civil War presents a stark contrast with Americans' preferred memory, what Michael Fellman has called the "stand-up war with uniformed, flag-carrying massed troops charging one another in open combat."[120] Early in the war many Breathitt Confederates were sent to south-western Virginia, an area structurally crucial to the Confederacy's survival (unlike eastern Kentucky).[121] In their absence, "official" southern forces were busy in the Three Forks, oftentimes with the assistance of men who had never enlisted in any army. Publicly, General Humphrey Marshall was critical of ostentatious rapparees (like his comrade and fellow Kentuckian John Hunt Morgan) for the bad press they earned in the border states. Marshall real-ized that convincing the Kentucky public of Confederate legitimacy was an uphill battle, and he did not want his side equated with brigandage. Still, he sympathized with men who could not dedicate themselves to full-time soldiering duties, reasoning that "he who undergoes the task of gathering the corn from the fields and preparing it himself for bread finds little time for military maneuver."[122] Marshall also appreciated the local knowledge such men provided, and he quietly incorporated nonuniformed partisans who could tell him which households to assault.[123]

Morgan himself saw no need to molest friendly territory (recruitment was one reason for his sweep through the mountains). He and other Rebel commanders used Breathitt as a bivouac for launching attacks on nearby Unionist counties. Near the end of his months-long raid launched from east Tennessee, John Hunt Morgan claimed ownership of Unionist Estill County a few weeks before the battle of Perryville, declaring all its Home Guards "enemies of the government."[124] After "having driven off the families of the Union men in that vicinity," Confederate colonels Benjamin Caudill (the "Great Mountain Guerrilla Chieftain") and Andrew Jackson May, both eastern Kentucky natives, took temporary possession of Perry and Owsley counties the following January.[125] Clay County to the south, Owsley and Jackson counties to the west, all Unionist bastions, were targets for Breathitt-based raiders, mostly for the forced appropriation of livestock.[126] James W. Lindon, the county's sheriff, provided room, board, and intelligence for lo-cal Rebels.[127] The southern military presence in Breathitt was so pervasive that Confederate currency was in wide circulation.[128] The year 1863 began with Kentucky Unionism at its apex. In more populated areas of the state, practically all dissent against the strictest loyalty had been quelled, either through loyalty oaths or armed intimidation. But in one mountain county, enclosed within ostensibly pro-Union territory, the forces of secession were outperforming many of their comrades in the actual Confederacy.

In early 1863 John Eversole requested that a segment of the Fourteenth Cavalry be returned to the men's home counties, although records seem to indicate that Unionist "Home Guard" activity, probably under William Strong's command, had already commenced in Breathitt County.[129] Strong and his fellows set about reengineering his county using threats, thefts, and killings to make it more politically consistent with the rest of the Three Forks region. But, as a Confederate officer experienced in eastern Kentucky observed, Strong used a measure of brutality but also a fair amount of cajoling.

> Their policy is to organize these mountain counties against us. Taking advantage of our retreat from the State, they are trying to convince the people that we have given the State up. In this way they seduce many into their Home Guard organizations. They threaten others that they shall abandon the State unless they join them and take up arms against the South. In this way they are fast subjugating the people, and, if permitted to pursue their policy undisturbed until spring [1863], that whole country will be organized against us. They have adopted the wise policy of buying up our country, by paying, feeding, and clothing these soldiers and letting them remain in their native hills to hold them against us, and will succeed unless we checkmate them by a similar policy.[130]

During one raid he and his men "carried away" a slave belonging to a farmer named Jesse Spencer, and then "drove away most of Spencer's livestock, went into the house, split open the featherbeds with their knives, and poured jugs of 'sorghum' molasses into the 'Feather ticks.' Hams, middlings, and shoulders were taken from the smokehouse. They also destroyed what other property they could not take with them."[131] Strong understood soldiers' dependency upon civilians for provisions, intelligence, and succor, the relationship historian Stephen Ash has called the "communal nature of guerrillaism."[132] Food seized from passively aggressive civilians not only fed the raider and robbed his enemy but also demonstrated his political superiority (and, by extension, greater claim to political legitimacy) to his victim.[133]

When the courthouse in Jackson was destroyed by fire in 1863, it became clear that Breathitt would not remain unscathed.[134] By then, the county was "in a deranged and perhaps disorganized condition," and officers of the court saved whatever records they could and fled to the Bluegrass (as in antebellum days, Breathitt's officeholders were Bluegrass natives or else maintained property and business interests there). The county court clerk did not return even after the war's end.[135]

Later that year the Confederacy's fortunes changed for the worse after defeats at Gettysburg and Vicksburg in July 1863. It was time for Breathitt County Confederates to return home, and they used both legitimate and illegitimate means to return.[136] When the Confederate Fifth Kentucky Infantry was ordered south to augment Braxton Bragg's division in southeast Tennessee the following month, John Aikman and as many as a dozen other Breathitt County enlistees (along with other eastern Kentuckians) abandoned their company in Hansonville, Virginia. Desertions from other units peopled by Breathitt County volunteers were also common.[137] Edward Strong, by then a lieutenant in the same company, requested a leave of absence from his position as company quartermaster around the same time to have his family moved to safety. He later procured an appointment in Jackson, returning to the recruitment position he'd held at the war's beginning.[138] The midwar return of Breathitt's soldiers was a pivotal moment in the county's history. The rebels realized that their "master cleavage" had become a lost cause and that their priorities were at home.[139] Many of those who withdrew from the Fifth Kentucky began fighting a "parochialized" version of the war upon their return, a "people's war" that brought the battlefront to homes and farms.[140] Aikman, compelled by a desire to further the Confederate cause even after shirking its uniform, and also to protect the interests of his landlords' local regime, was known as one of the Three Forks region's toughest Confederates, his reputation strengthened by an apocryphal story: after he was shot in the back while fleeing Joseph Eversole's men, Aikman kept running, pausing only to spit out the lead ball which had traveled to his throat without killing him. He was quoted as saying the Unionists had fed him a "damned hot morsel."[141]

John Aikman probably knew the man who fired the shot he miraculously survived. Although disinterested observers often speak of guerrillas as nameless anonyms, within their embattled communities their identities are openly shared with friend and foe. After the war, men like William Strong and John Aikman spoke of their former adversaries by name, with meager reference to their respective political/military positions.[142] War within an enclosed community forced combatants to choose between the political and the personal, or somehow accommodate both. It was a condition of violent intimacy, "civil war in its most basic sense," though eclipsed by the prevailing North/South narrative.[143] War among intimately acquainted neighbors, relatives, and friends was a crucible for civil society, one in which all involved weighed the war's obligations against their memory of antebellum

During the Civil War and for years afterward, John Aikman went to violent extremes for the Confederate cause. (Courtesy of Charles Hayes)

peacetime. One Owsley County partisan left behind a succinct testimonial on the conditions involved: "I knew the man I shot. He had been a friend of mine but I knew we had to kill some of them or they would kill some of us and I had too good a bead on him to let him go."[144]

With the Three Forks region's northern half under Confederate control, Humphrey Marshall and Andrew Jackson South led "a guerilla band from Breathitt County" southwest to assault Owsley and Jackson, Kentucky's two most thoroughly Unionist counties, in the spring of 1863. Along the way they destroyed and ransacked more than forty "Union homesteads," but they were unsuccessful in finding any actual aggressors like William Strong.[145] Abijah Gilbert, a former state legislature who had helped prevent Kentucky's secession two years earlier, catalogued their destruction on and around his property.[146]

> Humphrey's men with the guerrilla band from Breathitt county, commenced coming into Jackson county, taking horses, cattle, and everything they could get hold of; came to Booneville, burned the jail, destroying the records in the Clerk's office, cut the books up, and scattered them through the streets; came to my house, took every horse and mule I had—numbering thirteen. . . . The Rebels then set fire to my house, burned everything I had, leaving my wife and children with nothing but the clothes they had on. Mine, I understand, was the seventeenth house they have burned on the route up as far as my place.

Gilbert was able to identify five of his attackers (he was unsure which of Jeremiah South's sons he had seen but certain that he had seen one of them). Having represented one of the state's most remote counties in the General Assembly, Gilbert understood the distance between his county's losses and the more storied war going on elsewhere. His description of the Three Forks Unionists' plight summarized the difficulty of choosing between the war's "master cleavage" and defending their homes in the equally dangerous "intimate" war at home.

> I have begged and plead hard with the [Union authorities] for help. One thing you know, and that is, the people here generally are so poor that they cannot get away, and if they could, how are they to subsist?

These counties that are suffering so much are the most loyal part of the state. Clay, Owesley [*sic*], and Jackson, which have furnished an average five hundred volunteers to the country, not one of whom is near enough to come to the rescue of their friends; they are all at Vicksburg, Murfreesboro [Tennessee], and other points out of the State.[147]

Civilian victimization by "[a] bunch of Democrats from Breathitt County" galvanized Owsley County, and it became the most Republican of Kentucky's counties forever after.[148] But, on a larger scale, raids of this sort damaged Kentuckians' faith in the war's larger goals by testing the resolve of Unionists with less dedication than Gilbert. At the same time the knowledge of their enemies' identities as citizens of neighboring communities had to be intensely demoralizing.

William Strong's style of combat was similar to the Breathitt Confederates' except that he attacked, plundered, and captured within his home county rather than in neighboring ones. Strong understood that war required regulation over civilian behavior. In one common tactic, he and his men would surround the home of a suspected "rebel scout" and demand the surrender of anyone who formerly served with Confederate forces or provided them with support.[149] Although many in Breathitt County saw nothing more than a human terror, one visiting Ohio Union officer wrote appreciably of Captain Strong's decisive role in eastern Kentucky.

John Gose and I, with a number of men have just returned from Breathitt County, where according to a prearrangement, we held a conference with Capt. Bill Strong. He and his Company of State Guards have charge of police duty in that County and he is certainly doing a wonderful work there. I asked one of our friends in Breathitt how Strong was getting along and he laughingly remarked that "he was killing rebels about as fast as they could bury them." I was much impressed with him as he seems to be a man of great determination and I predict that he will do a lot of good for the Union cause.[150]

The "rebels" that Strong killed for the Union cause were not always in uniform. Years after the war, a Democratic newspaper recorded the names of nineteen "private citizens" killed by Strong's "Home Guard."[151] George Noble recalled that Strong had shot a soldier named Miles Spurlock in the back while the young Confederate was at his home on winter furlough. Soon after, David Barnett, "an innocent man," in Noble's opinion, was summarily shot in his own home.[152] However, especially late in the war when the Federal army's harsher "Home Guard" tactics were unleashed and total warfare deemed necessary, this had become a detail less important than it once was.

"Intimacy" apparently worked in paradoxical ways for William Strong and George Noble. While the aforementioned Owsley County partisan was willing to overlook friendship in favor of partisanship, encounters between Strong and the young infantryman suggest that the reverse could just as easily take place. When Strong captured him late in the war, Noble secured a quick parole since the older man held the Noble family in high regard despite their leanings (it is just as likely that Strong released Noble because he saw little threat in the boy).[153] When Strong's brother John was captured in Owsley County and taken back to Jackson, Wiley Amis and their cousins Edward Strong and Wilson Callahan (the latter a "secret rebel" serving in Union forces) negotiated his release.[154] Months later, when John Strong was killed in ambush while on furlough (supposedly due to being mistaken for his brother), Noble regretted that his comrades had "killed the wrong man" instead of the terror of Breathitt County.[155] Still, when William Strong was attacked in Jackson after the war, it was George Noble he came to for protection.[156] "Intimate" war caused soldiers to perform unusual acts of cruelty or acts of kindness, and to trust their enemies in unguarded moments. After the war, veterans described their comrades and enemies in personal terms, belying the political reasons that had drawn them to choosing sides in the first place.

Young foot soldiers like George Noble were more likely to have mercy than Confederate commanders. The death of Jerry South Jr. at Strong's hand in February 1864 was especially horrible. South had a broken leg and was in hiding with a friendly family who agreed to return him to his home on a hastily constructed sled. On the way, Strong apprehended the party and shot the recumbent Rebel multiple times in front of South's wife.[157] Eleven months later, Strong killed his brother Andrew Jackson South at another civilian's home.[158] With that, Strong eliminated the Three Forks region's leading Rebel partisans, crippling the area's organized resistance months before the war's official end. The deaths of the sons of the "father of Breathitt County" decapitated Confederate Breathitt County.

And, for a time, it seriously crippled the Souths' party. Strong's bullying, and the absence of a large segment of the adult male population, provided Breathitt County's only defections from the Democratic Party in the nineteenth century. In 1863 only forty-seven men were willing to vote for the Democratic gubernatorial candidate, Charles Wickliffe, giving Union candidate Thomas Bramlette an overwhelming majority. Two years later the county polled a bizarre 212 to 17 majority in favor of the Union Party's candidate for state treasurer. Results from the 1864 presidential race might have shown drastic changes had they been recorded; Breathitt was one of nine Kentucky counties—eight of them in the mountains—that produced no returns in that election.[159] The dramatic sea change, unparalleled in any other surrounding county, could have been an indication of a Democratic electorate under the gun, or the "natural" results of elections with the South family's heavy hand removed. It was probably a measure of both.

Union victories did not guarantee Unionists' survival, nor did the official end of the war bring an end to fighting. John and Joseph Eversole were killed in the former's Perry County home twenty-three days after Appomattox.[160] Violence in southeastern Kentucky continued for months after that, even after the Three Forks Battalion disbanded in August. Strong's neighbors were less than willing to accept him in the role he apparently saw for himself: a victor in a war they had lost. Even the Breathitt County Rebels who acquiesced to U.S. citizenship after the war refused to grant Strong the legitimacy that came with being a soldier (his permanent title of "Captain Bill" notwithstanding); when Breathitt County citizens sued him after the war for the livestock he requisitioned, he always defended his actions as part of "suppressing the late rebellion."[161] As was true of many other white Unionist Kentuckians, especially the ones who went to the most violent extremes to fight secession and even to end slavery, Strong's atrocities (and his alleged atrocities) were depoliticized by those who described them.[162] Locally, he was often remembered as a Home Guard, a misnomer that was only technically untrue. He was also called a guerrilla, a term so subject to interpretation that it could have included almost every combatant in his home county. In the outside world he was better known as a "feudist." Always controversial and always influential, "Captain Bill" lived the rest of his life in Breathitt County, his name interchangeable with "Bloody Breathitt."

Guerrillaism turned out to be a double-edged sword for Breathitt County soldiers on both sides, just as it did for many other Kentuckians. It allowed men to fight for their flag of choice while remaining near their property, family, and their civilian life, the things that most southerners believed that they fought to defend in the first place. Yet it also heightened the likelihood that beloved civilians would be attacked in the process. Furthermore, men who fought as guerrillas, partisans, bushwhackers, or the like never had the chance to tell their story after the war. For one thing, their "small" wars were lost among the bipartisan din of triumphalism that defined the war memory's construction.[163] In fact, considering how many of them had attacked and killed people who knew them well, they had good reason to keep their mouths shut. Consequently, when their story was told, it was told by outside world observers who had little compunction against modifying the image according to the dictates of their "urban bias."[164]

The intimacy between Strong and his Confederate enemies like George Noble belied their stated purposes in taking up arms: defeating the rebellion and defending the "Southern people" respectively. Years later, when Breathitt County became known as Bloody Breathitt, commentators often mentioned the war's legacy in later violence there, but they scarcely considered the contingencies involved in a war fought between intimates.[165] Instead, the horrors of guerrillaism were attached to the county's supposedly inherent ferocity. "You mountaineers can't help it; you were born to it," a fictional soldier chided a cold-blooded "bushwhacker" in a 1900 Civil War novel. "What else could you expect from a man from Breathitt County, Kentucky?"[166]

"Previous to that time they knew nothing of pistols and bowie-knives"

After the Confederate surrender, Lieutenant General Nathan Bedford Forrest (who understood better than most the distinction between "regular" and "irregular" warfare) bid his troops farewell with a warning against "neighborhood feuds, personal animosities, and private differences" when they returned home.[167] Forrest knew that his troops were going back to communities torn apart by the war. He did not consider the distinction between war (political) and feud (personal) arbitrary, but he could certainly see how the former might cause the latter and how, when fought intimately within small spaces, the distinction between violence in war and violence after war might *become* arbitrary.[168] What Forrest did not acknowledge (if he realized it at all) was that, for many southerners, these supposedly small "private differences" back at the home front were the war itself. Although his CSA commission disqualified him from being a "guerrilla" per se (his performance was met with the approval of his general-in-chief, who notably disapproved of guerrillas), Forrest had pushed the envelope of "legitimate" violence more than almost any other general, Confederate or Federal.[169] But *feud* meant something smaller, strictly local, and far less consequential than the struggle for white supremacy he had just concluded. However careful the general was with his words, he was drawing a partition between the political and the communal, the large and the small, the important and the trivial.

Forrest unwittingly previsioned the intermingling of *feud* with *guerrilla* in years to come. *Feud* was a fine tool for stifling serious discussions of guerrilla warfare for a generation after the war. Men who had directly experienced the Civil War in places like Breathitt County recognized the political significance of later feud violence as an obvious fact (and, for that matter, were less likely than nonlocals to use *feud* as a descriptor). But to those peering into these places from the outside world, this sort of communal combat was unacceptable in the war memory and had to be made something other, even if it meant warping the facts. Nowhere else, save Missouri, was the course of the war more determined by irregular warfare. These gruesome tactics had been of utmost political importance to both sides, and perhaps for that very reason the memory of Kentucky guerrillaism was swiftly depoliticized, especially by historians who cleaved to the Lost Cause. Guerrillas were typically said to have "the name and uniform of either army" as nothing more than a fig leaf to camouflage their plundering.[170] "During 1864, there came upon Kentucky the scourge of guerrilla warfare, that constant accompaniment of war in all civilized lands," wrote one historian. "These bands of marauders wore today the uniform of the southern soldiers; tomorrow that of the Union forces. They belonged to neither army and brought reproach upon both. Made up in most cases of deserters from either army, they recognized no flag as their own and plundered alike the friends of the Union and the south."[171] Guerrillas were not only depoliticized but also placed in a past distant from the war memory. In 1926 E. Merton Coulter called Kentucky's guerrillas "mediaeval fighters" (echoing the associations with antiquity early twentieth-century writers made with Kentucky's "feudists") driven by "revenge and greed . . . motives that they, themselves, could torture into seeming honorable." "That the Kentucky guerrillas were acting under the orders of the Confederates," Coulter insisted, "is absurd."[172]

These were charges and dismissals often made, but rarely with evidence. In the historical record, even "marauders" with the most feeble connection to the "legitimate" war effort(s) never swapped sides and always plundered their political enemies—even Missouri's William Quantrill's worst atrocities were committed for the sake of political expediency.[173] Still, the apolitical guerrilla was a useful fiction after the war, and not only to Confederate sympathizers. With the United States bent upon postwar reunion, it was necessary that both causes, and their attendant gallant northern Virginia campaigns, overshadow the horrors that took place in the South's darker corners. The spirit of national reunion depersonalized the war, separating the opposing causes from the individuals who had fought for them—a difficult, or impossible, prospect in Breathitt County. However, its veterans were not those asked to establish the narrative.

As guerrillaism was separated from the war's history, so, too, was the mountain South. Eastern Kentucky's war was sundered from the "legitimate" one early on, when many northerners convinced themselves that all mountaineers in "the Switzerland of the South" were loyal Unionists.[174] The mountain South did indeed produce a large number of loyal dissenters. However, the myth of a solidly Unionist Appalachia, a myth that excluded Confederate Breathitt County and many other places, grossly oversimplified an intensely complex wartime situation. The roles of local elites like the South family and the function of counties during war were obscured by descriptions that favored a homogenous, unarticulated mountain population over considerations of economics and politics. It was a simplification that remained popular long after the war.[175]

Other distortions of the war in the mountains, especially in Kentucky, followed suit. Attempting to explain eastern Kentucky's barbaric wartime record carried out by men like William Strong and John Aikman, journalists credited the wartime mountaineers with an ersatz combination of patriotism and primeval innocence. But they were rarely credited as legitimate soldiers.

I am told that this lawlessness has only existed since the war; that before, the people, though ignorant of letters, were peaceful. . . . During the war the mountaineers were carrying on a civil war at home. The opposing parties were not soldiers, but bushwhackers. Some of the best citizens were run out of the country, and never returned. The majority were Unionists, and in all the mountain region of eastern Kentucky I passed through there are few to-day who are politically Democrats. In the war, home-guards were organized, and these were little better than vigilance committees for private revenge. Disorder began with this private and partly patriotic warfare. After the war, when the bushwhackers got back to their cabins, the animosities were kept up, though I fancy that politics was little or nothing to do with them now. The habit of reckless shooting, of taking justice into private hands, is no doubt a relic of the disorganization during the war.[176]

In a similar vein, another reported: "In the civil war this sturdy, honest people fought for the Union; previous to that time they knew nothing of pistols and bowie-knives. The local war between themselves and the guerrillas which raged at the time, first accustomed them to blood-shed; and the feuds then created by outrages perpetrated in the name of patriotism, endure even to the present day."[177] Their home state in political flux and their potential enemies so near, eastern Kentuckians made horrendously difficult decisions during the war. Their portrayal in postwar accounts utterly denied this.

Unable to fully explain the horrible acts that had taken place in the Kentucky mountains, other writers turned to a racial imagination. While the "hospitable, gentle-mannered" mountaineers who fought for the Union were of "English, Scotch-Irish and German origin," the "guerrilla companies which infested the country during the war" were a "second class of which there are only a few in the Kentucky mountains . . . a sallow, gypsy-like people, of unknown origin; idle, vicious, thoroughly conscienceless, and 'far more incorrigible' than either the Indian or the negro."[178] This was a particularly extreme (and unfounded) view since it suggested that there was some strange, as yet unseen, mountain race different from the supposedly "pure" Anglo-Saxon or Celtic blood the mountains were known for. Still, the castigation of a fictional "sallow, gypsy-like people" was not terribly unusual in its ultimate result of making the southern mountains somehow different from the South. Most preferred to have it both ways, hewing to the article of faith that feud was an inherency "transplanted from Scotland with the immigration of the first settlers" while acknowledging that "many of the Kentucky feuds . . . were born in the Civil War"—by the turn of the century, Americans wanted both to be true.[179] Finally, there was the view that the state's guerrilla warfare was a natural condition born "where family feuds had prevailed ever since the days of Daniel Boone or Cassius M. Clay."[180] The inconsistencies did not seem to trouble either northerners or southerners.

Breathitt County's war history was mostly lost amid the accepted generalizations about eastern Kentucky, except to Kentuckians. In Breathitt County's most detailed local history, Strong's troops, men like Hiram Freeman and Henderson Kilburn, became political tabulae rasae enslaved to his evil exploitation. "These men, in the main, had no opinion of their own,"

E. L. Noble wrote in the 1930s. "They were ignorant and savage, having no desires of their own; they desired only to be clothed and fed; thus they were fit subjects to execute what others desired done. They seemed void of conscience; knew nothing of the cause against which they fought."[181] Just as William Strong and his fellow Unionists refused to recognize Confederate Breathitt County's legitimacy, his soldiers' legitimacy was denied in turn.

Nineteenth-century Kentucky's most lauded academic, Nathaniel Shaler, concurred. Breathitt County's "mob outrages" and "blood feuds," said Shaler, were "the heritage of the Civil War." Like the others, Shaler curtailed the importance of politics in these later incidents by suggesting that later disputes gave veterans of both sides of the Civil War a common, apolitical enemy that they could unite against. "On the one side are arrayed those who fought in the two armies and their descendants," wrote Shaler, without providing an example. "On the other side, a clan of outlawish folk who belonged to neither side."[182] The war, it seemed, played a role in causing violence afterward, but Shaler did not accept anything other than the sort of apolitical white reunion that was taking place elsewhere between North and South, one in which "both sides were told that they were wrong and right."[183] In Shaler's telling, *feud* hurried the reunion.

Half-informed reports from the outside world were of little concern to the people who had been directly affected by the local war, especially while many of them were still dealing with the war's aftermath. Although he lived to a ripe old age, William Strong was forced to contend with old enemies and their successors for the rest of his life, a situation that was complicated by his continuing role as "chieftain" and "special protector," and his own irascible nature. He showed an unwillingness to accept anything other than the local regime change he had fought so hard for. While he managed to outlast the war by more than thirty years, his eventual death was not a peaceful one.

Jeremiah South, however, did not suffer loss of power or property because of the war. While his sons paid the ultimate price, South was able to remain aloof from the war's uglier side, remaining in the Bluegrass and commanding the actions of state government after the war.[184] Strong and South each survived the war, but not with equal laurels.

William Strong's "chieftain" status among the county's blacks and poor whites may have been what kept him safe from immediate reprisal after the war, but it was not without its own potential problems and was the cause of many tangible ones. Since this new "hidden" political arrangement was founded in war, codified through martial alliances, and did not benefit from peacetime state institutions, it continued to depend upon violence, or the threat of violence, for sustenance. However, as described in the following chapter, Strong and his former enemies made a frank effort to restore civil relations after the war. When he was once again involved in violence, it was because of the rift among Kentucky Unionists that formed during presidential Reconstruction—yet again, an exogenous conflict from the *outside world*.

Whatever Jeremiah South, his family, and other Rebels had fought for during the war rested only upon institutions within their own community, not that of the state or the nation. Managing to maintain a modicum of control over local pro-Confederate government within very pro-Union surroundings contributed to Breathitt County's political insularity, and perhaps made the stakes for control over its public institutions that much higher in the years after the war. And William Strong would continue to challenge that control. While the rest of the United States started a movement toward peaceful reconciliation between the sections, Bloody Breathitt had only concluded its first phase.

3

"THE WAR SPIRIT WAS HIGH"

Scenes from an Un-Reconstructed County

> Even though we are in full possession of the enemy's country, the conflict
> may break out again in the interior or through assistance from his allies.
> No doubt this may also happen after the peace, but this only shows that
> wars do not always contain the elements necessary for a complete decision
> and settlement.
>
> —Karl von Clausewitz, *On War* (1832)

By the end of 1865 Breathitt County had been thoroughly chastened for
rebelling against the United States. The harsh measures that Union captain
William Strong used against his own neighbors, and the wellspring of support
he had from Unionists in neighboring counties, ended what was probably
already a lost cause: a firm county-sized stronghold of rebellion within the
Kentucky mountains. Numerous defections to Union forces further indicted
the pro-southern elite's hold over the populace. The attempt to create a Confederate mountain outpost in a Union state was proven a failure.

The war's last twelve to eighteen months had been the bitterest, and
Strong and most of the Three Forks Battalion's companies remained in
uniform until three months after war's end. Throughout eastern Kentucky,
intermittent fighting continued well into 1866.[1] Still, by most accounts, sincere efforts to rebuild civil society by veterans of both armies proved their
shared willingness to parse the personal from the political.

Breathitt County's war was over, but the county earned its reputation for
inherent violence sometime later. In the 1860s and 1870s white Kentuckians revolted fiercely against the war's results, namely, the transformation
of slaves into citizens. The change hardly constituted a revolution in the

white-majority border state, but the white reaction in Kentucky was still comparable to the riots, raids, and bloodbaths that occurred farther south. White-on-white intraracial attacks may have actually been more common there than in perhaps any other southern state. "By 1865 Kentucky was in a rage because she had not seceded in 1861," one newspaperman recounted early in the twentieth century, "and she is scarcely in a good humor about it yet."[2] Decades later, C. Vann Woodward concurred: "Despite Kentucky's failure to secede and join the Confederacy, no state below the Ohio River presented a more solidly Confederate-Democratic front in the decade after Appomattox."[3]

Despite its supposed insularity from the outside world, Breathitt County was affected by the absence of Reconstruction in Kentucky. The violence that gave it the name Bloody Breathitt was symptomatic of the crisis of legitimacy suffered by a state that could not reconcile itself to the war's results, yet at the same time contained a minority insistent that Kentucky be remade with the Union's renewal. Both sides resorted to types of violence replicated all over the South.

Almost every "outrage" committed anywhere in the state was followed by the insistence of white Kentuckians (armed with their state's tacit loyalty to the Union) that their state's troubles had nothing to do with the obviously racial/political riots and massacres in places like Colfax, Louisiana, and Edgefield, South Carolina. The cultural South had a reputation for violence long before the political South rebelled, and white southerners often used the former as a smoke screen for the latter. *Feud,* a word for apolitical violence between equals, was useful for this purpose, especially when the victims of raids and lynchings happened to be white. In the end, the idea of Bloody Breathitt was only one manifestation of white Democrats' need to depoliticize the violence that helped them maintain control over Kentucky. Breathitt County helped their case since, unlike in most Reconstruction trouble spots, the Unionists ultimately appeared to be just as malicious as the former Rebels.

"These disturbances originated from private feuds"

As with all wars, the American Civil War's most dramatic political results became plain only after the fighting had stopped. This was particularly true in the most divided of border states. Although Kentucky remained officially loyal to the Union, many of its citizens felt that their loyalty to the United

States had been poorly rewarded. The Federal government's first and second Confiscation Acts, the presidential suspension of habeas corpus, and the Union army's manumission and arming of African Americans disillusioned otherwise loyal white Kentuckians and hardened their pro-Confederate neighbors' resolve (on the other hand, black Kentuckians were quick to claim new freedoms, especially through service in the U.S. Colored Troops; no other state save Louisiana contributed more recruits between 1863 and 1865).[4] Soon after that, the end of slavery and the prospect of black citizenship tore the state's Union Party asunder. Kentucky was the only southern state that did not revise its constitution to prohibit slavery (although the legislature passed a civil rights bill in 1866 that recognized the demise of the institution and repealed the state's antebellum slave codes).[5] Confederate veterans, reenfranchised almost immediately, combined with Southern Rights Democrats and moderate Unionists to form a dogged conservative majority that "clung to the decaying body of slavery" in the 1866 election.[6]

The last three years of Andrew Johnson's presidency were defined by an air of conservative remorse, and most white Kentuckians embraced him as their defender against congressional radicalism.[7] His break with Congress, and the lingering resentment over the Union Party's harsh measures against the former Rebels, turned Kentucky into a state of "belated Confederates."[8] Having refused to ratify the Thirteenth Amendment in 1865, the General Assembly went on to reject the Fourteenth and Fifteenth amendments as well, making Kentucky the last former slave state with black citizenship.[9] The death of aged Governor John Helm just five days after his September 1867 inauguration ushered Confederate-sympathizing John W. Stevenson into the office. "By a strange conjunction of circumstances," lamented one Unionist newspaperman, "what the rebels failed to do [in 1861], they freely realized in the year 1867."[10] Kentucky had gone from conservative Unionism to neo-Confederate Democracy within one election cycle.[11]

Even with Democratic/conservative dominance (or, as one Democrat put it, "three fourths of the wealth and all of the brains of the State"), Kentucky remained a two-party state.[12] The Unconditional Unionists were determined to follow through with their ambitious war aims beneath what one Democrat called "the hypocritical cry of Union."[13] As they became Republicans, mostly congregated in the mountains and the Ohio River cities, few were willing to self-apply the name "Radical."[14] Unlike in West Virginia and Missouri, they were never able to form a legislative majority and their congressional delegation was hardly a civil rights crusade.[15] In 1866 Unconditional Unionist congressman Lovell Rousseau punctuated his opposition to the Freedman's Bureau by severely caning an Iowa Republican (by the time Rousseau returned to Congress he had become a Democrat).[16] The bureau was removed from the state in 1869, three years before it disappeared elsewhere.[17]

The state's appointed positions were dispersed to Confederates soon after they gained elected offices. As a reward for keeping the Southern Rights faith since 1862, Jeremiah South was reinstated as penitentiary lessee in 1870. South's return to one of the most powerful offices in the state of Kentucky came about through a measure of political triangulation. J. Stoddard Johnston, the editor of Frankfort's anti-federal, anti-northern *Kentucky Yeoman,* was the only other contender for the post, and the General Assembly's Republican minority reluctantly threw their support to South, allowing the aging speculator to become even more influential than before (when he was reappointed yet again in 1874 he beat out a Confederate general and a colonel). When South had last held the position his leased inmates' gang labor had to compete with slavery. Upon his return South monopolized all compulsory labor in the state for road construction, river improvement, or anything at his discretion, and his new embarrassment of riches turned into scandalous abuses.[18]

His political capital rose exponentially until "nearly one third of the assemblymen in 1877–1878 were under his control as absolutely as were the convicts."[19] As the decade progressed, Kentucky's Grange and a number of workingmen's organizations came out against South's state-mandated catbird seat. Agrarian protest gave way to middle-class reform; the subject of free labor/convict labor competition was overshadowed by the penitentiary's atrocious conditions, especially after a Republican gubernatorial candidate called it Kentucky's "Black Hole of Calcutta." By 1879 even the Democrats could no longer ignore the subject, and they elected Luke Blackburn, a humanitarian physician (and Confederate general Sterling Price's onetime staff surgeon), as governor. Blackburn instituted a momentary zeal for reform that proved to be more than the sixty-nine-year-old Jeremiah South could bear, professionally or physically.[20] Under scrutiny for the first time since the war (and this time from his own party), he fell dead from a stroke while pleading his case on the Senate floor in 1880.[21] One of the largest funerals in Frankfort's history punctuated the end of de jure (if not de facto) profiteering in Kentucky's penal system.[22]

Jeremiah South's final years showed that public service in Kentucky could be an opportunist's game just as it had been when, as a younger man, he became "the father of Breathitt County." But Kentucky state government's greatest failure during the Reconstruction years was not the "legitimate" state violence of imprisonment or cloakroom corruption but rather the maintenance of law and order. In various counties "regulators" replaced state-mandated authorities, usually to enforce something of a continuing Confederate order in some localities.[23] "Skaggs' Men" terrorized Unionists and freedpeople in the southern Bluegrass's Marion and Boyle counties soon after the war, while "Rowzee's Band" did the same nearby until the early 1870s.[24] Their victims were of both colors, but black Kentuckians seemed to have taken the brunt. Between 1866 and 1870, sixty-seven black Kentuckians were lynched for alleged crimes (nineteen white Kentuckians were lynched during the same period)—and not only in racially diverse areas.[25] Between 1866 and 1870, one-fifth of the state's interracial lynchings were in the mountain counties, even though blacks made up less than 5 percent of most counties' populations.[26] Less than a year after the war's end, men in contiguous Floyd, Morgan, and Wolfe counties, three Confederate bastions, forcibly expelled federal tax collectors.[27] The Reverend John Fee's reestablishment of Madison County's biracial Berea College was impeded by midnight harassments in 1870. The "leading men" of Berea's neighboring black community were "taken from their beds, cruelly whipped, dragged over the flinty road . . . to deter them and friends from any attempt at political effort or influence."[28]

"The anti-negro feeling," remarked the Republican *New York Times* in 1870, "influences political action more in Kentucky than in Alabama," and in the former more than the latter, "it inspires demands for a reversal of the results of the war."[29] With "rebels in Kentucky" running rampant, Massachusetts Radical Republican senator Charles Sumner advocated placing Kentucky under federal military authority.[30] For reasons both political and constitutional, Sumner's suggestion was never enacted, although white Kentuckians considered a federal occupation an ever-present threat. All northern deprecations, like Sumner's, were dismissed as "radical falsehood."[31] When the Fifteenth Amendment brought black suffrage to Kentucky, white-on-black violence took on a more blatantly political motivation, especially in the Bluegrass, but even in sections where the black electorate was too small to challenge governmental white supremacy. At least thirty-six black Kentuckians were lynched in 1870 alone.[32] White regulators of varying collective names roamed the state with impunity until 1880, when two hundred men collectively surrendered to state authorities in Louisville.[33] By that point, their aims—the suppression of black citizenship and economic mobility, and the establishment of Confederate rule—had been well met.

Whatever went on after the war, white Kentuckians could always use their official wartime loyalty as a bona fide, and with few witnesses to these crimes willing to speak, motive for violence was not always patently obvious. Democrats could depoliticize their state's violence, reframe its reportage so that it did not seem so much resistance as it did undirected lawlessness. A month into his term in office, and then again two years later, Governor Stevenson dispatched the state militia to the southern Bluegrass, all the while disingenuously assuring the public that what were clearly paramilitary remnants of the late war was actually nothing more than apolitical vigilantism. "These disturbances originated from private feuds, or sprung from an impression in the minds of the 'regulators' that the laws were not sufficiently enforced; they do not owe their origin to any difference in political sentiment, and are wholly unconnected with antagonisms springing out of the late civil war."[34]

It was the first of many times that Kentucky governors would use the idea of feud to depoliticize the violence that rent their state apart for decades to come. *Feud* suggested violence with primordial causes in the distant past rather than current political events. More important, the word suggested a horizontal conflict between similar (white) people of equal means, lest anyone ask the identity of the initial (or only) aggressors or their politics. Stevenson may well have personally invented a new trope for the southern conservative apologist rhetorical arsenal. For years southern Democrats attributed violence against white Republicans to "family feuds," even when political motivations were obvious.[35] Feuds were understood to be between whites, except for the rare instances when it was useful for it be otherwise; case in point, "the ancient feud between the white man and the black man; a feud as old as Europe, Asia and Africa" that precipitated violent white reaction to black citizenship (to white conservatives, it was only a brief, dangerous moment during Reconstruction when the necessary horizontal equality existed between the races).[36] It was a lasting explanation, as shown by one historian's recent characterization of counterrevolutionary violence in Kentucky as an outcome of "local tribalism."[37] Inherent features like "inborn malevolence" and "tribalism" did not well describe the contingencies of a sectional war's remains.

Part of the reason that post-Confederate attackers' political motives were so easy to minimize was Kentucky's measure of extralegal Unionist militancy. Union Leagues and Loyal Leagues in other southern states demonstrated their potential for force more often than they actually used it and took up arms, with very few exceptions, only in self-defense.[38] In Kentucky they took a more aggressive tack in some areas, conjuring an illusion of even counterbalance between Kentucky's revolutionary and counterrevolutionary violences even when the latter typically had the greater advantage.[39] A "quasi-military" Union League chapter in Lexington and a secret society–style Loyal League in Louisville brought out the Republican vote through public shows of arms and strategic electioneering.[40] In mountain counties, Loyal League chapters intimidated Confederate veterans and Democrats during elections, bolstering the already-sturdy mountain Unionist/Republican turnout.[41] In the heavily pro-southern western edge of the state, Unionist vigilance committees were organized in 1865 to punish "men formerly identified with the rebellion" upon their return.[42] In 1870 and again in 1874, groups unironically labeled "Negro Ku Klux" supposedly harassed black Democrats.[43] Consequently, for more than a decade after the war, Democrats could gainsay Republican protests by citing documented persecutions of Confederate veterans. Attacks from either side were more often intraracial than those publicized in the Deep South, "white-on-white" (or, in the case of the dubious "Negro Ku Klux," "black-on-black"), while the common element of political violence in the Reconstruction era was the oppression of black southerners. Intraracial violence, even when its political motives were plain to contemporaries, was easily depoliticized.

The Ku Klux Klan, the definitive incarnation of southern political violence, appeared in Kentucky no later than 1868—at least three years before black enfranchisement came to the state.[44] Aside from Missouri, it was the only state outside of the former Confederacy where groups bearing the name appeared during the Reconstruction era.[45] The distinction between the Kentucky Klan and other preexistent paramilitary groups is imprecise, but this was not unique. All over the South the Klan "was less a formal organization than a rubric," a name and iconography that described disparate groups throughout the South who shared little more than a dedication to white supremacy, counterrevolution and, unfailingly, the Democratic Party as the means to those ends.[46] Democrats with reputable public faces considered them "allies not sought but accepted."[47] State and federal forces stationed in the former Confederacy eventually put an end to the organization with a "politics of force," but the Klan of un-Reconstructed Kentucky lasted longer there than that of any other state—as did its connections to the Kentucky Democracy.[48]

But even "the military arm of the Democratic Party" could be depoliticized, with conservatives often denying that the "genuine" Ku Klux Klan was responsible for political violence.[49] The Klan's own patriarch, Nathan Bedford Forrest, testified to Congress that the organization was for "self-protection" and "had no political purpose," despite evidence to the contrary.[50] Its reign of terror against black and white Republicans in Tennessee and the Deep South between 1868 and 1871 gave the lie to the general's testimony. However, the Klan's diffuse organization and its mysterious tactics made it quite possible for southerners and northerners to dismiss its importance, political or otherwise, or even to deny its very existence. By the beginning of the 1870s even some Republicans (primarily white northerners) had begun doubting the Klan was a serious danger to their southern comrades.[51]

Kentucky's relatively small black population, coupled with its de facto Unionism, gave Democrats a better measure of plausible deniability, room to insist that "Ku Klux outrages . . . common to the whole South" were "less serious in Kentucky than elsewhere" and "that politics had little to do with the operations of the Klan."[52] Other southern states' Klans were an unequivocally political response to northern tyranny (and accordingly had clear links to the southern Democratic Party), said *Louisville Courier-Journal* editor Henry Watterson (who, a former lieutenant under Forrest, claimed some authority on the subject).[53] As the white South's moderate voice, Watterson chided fellow Democrats for their "vacillation and want of celerity" in punishing wrongdoers.[54] But the *Courier-Journal* refused to grant its own state's record of violent crime the same significance. In Watterson's estimation, the Kentucky Klan "was not an outgrowth of civil war. Neither was it made up of ex-Confederate soldiers." Indeed, the editor insisted, Kentucky's pretenders to the Klan name embarrassed the "actual" organization. "One third bully and two-thirds whisky, a thorough coward and scoundrel, it disgraced the name of KuKlux when it assumed it."[55]

After his appointment to a U.S. Senate seat, former governor Stevenson followed suit, going to great rhetorical lengths to deny that any Klan, Kentucky's or elsewhere, was "a political organization."[56] Writing in 1875, a northern missionary who wished to defend Kentucky's continuing loyalty to the Republic despite its internal chaos echoed Governor Stevenson's language from eight years earlier, insisting that white intraracial violence "mistakenly attributed to the Ku Klux" was simply the outcome of "family feuds."[57] "There was nothing political in the organization, since as many ex-Union as ex-Confederate soldiers belonged to it," reasoned a former *Courier-Journal* correspondent—failing to account for the considerable number of white Kentucky Unionists who "defected" during the Johnson administration. The troubles he had recounted in the late 1860s "originated in family or neighborhood feuds" rather than the issues involved in Reconstruction.[58] Even Kentucky's leading Republican newspaper (an esteemed position with few contenders in the 1870s), usually in the habit of connecting all things harmful and disorderly to the Democratic Party, attributed all white intraracial bloodshed to "heated blood, family difficulties, old grudges, intoxication, and inborn malevolence" rather than organized reaction to postwar change.[59]

Believable or not, his denial set a precedent and constructed a useful device for conservatives. As late as 1888, years after the Klan "proper" was defunct and replaced by "whitecappers" (who, unlike their predecessors, originated north of the Ohio River), Watterson still insisted that the Klan of old "had little, if any, political significance and varied in its character according to the field of its operations." Of course, even more than a decade after Reconstruction's end, he felt it was "more than one could reasonably hope for to expect the truth from any Republican newspaper on such a subject."[60] Decades later, in his defense of Kentucky's conservative "readjustment," E. Merton Coulter attributed "ku kluxing," "feuding," and other postwar violence to "weakened respect for state authority" rather than attempts to affect or suppress political change.[61] Whenever white Kentuckians wished to deny their Reconstruction era injustices and atrocities, feud was perennial, but it was only one of a handful of words white Kentuckians used to deny that theirs was an embattled state.

Legislation that officially recognized political vigilantism as a punishable crime was delayed for years by debates over whether only the Klan was to be officially addressed in statute or if groups like the Loyal League should also be included.[62] The castrated peacekeeping law that was eventually passed allowed the governor to issue rewards for the arrest of members of groups that wore disguises in public and threatened local populations. White Kentuckians were disturbed by the imposition of martial law during the war. Accordingly, laws were passed that allowed Kentucky governors to dispatch the state militia only upon the request of a circuit court judge—this most judges did with hesitancy since it meant admitting their own powerlessness.[63] They did not compel local law enforcement to assist in warrants, an important omission since sheriffs and constables were often complicit in extralegal violence. Kentucky's counties remained "oligopolies of violence," each with its respective ability to enforce white supremacy and quell political dissent.[64] While this was an arrangement structurally identical to that enjoyed by antebellum oligarchs, it had become far more deadly after the Civil War.

"Although originating not long after the war, it was personal and not political"

As in Kentucky's other mountain counties, in Breathitt County the war's memory changed the political landscape for years afterward. Conservatives who wanted a facsimile of the antebellum order competed with those who either accepted the changes wrought by the war or those who worked to further these changes. Some of the old Jacksonian counties of eastern Kentucky were permanently changed, always after turning out Unionist/Republican majorities; others snapped elastically back to the Democracy. Still others abided somewhere between the two extremes.[65] Breathitt County was of the third group.

There were a number of years in which veterans of both sides of the war made a brave attempt at tense but peaceful coexistence. At least for a time, George Noble reasoned that "the true Union men . . . saved the Nation, and not the abolitionists," a variation on the reconciliatory depoliticization of the war's memory that lasted for decades in both North and South.[66] This, even after he and fellow Rebels were arrested for foraging livestock and food from Unionist neighbors in November 1865 after other Unionists had promised his parents they would "never law [sue or indict] any of us for what I did." When he was arrested he was taken to Perry County ("All the jails in the mountain counties were burned except that one") and locked away for a short time until his father posted bail. By that time Breathitt County judge David K. Butler (apparently one of the vicinity's only Union Democrats) knew to hire both Union *and* Confederate deputies—as well as to ignore their shared tendency to drink on duty.[67] Reconciliation was difficult but not impossible, and most of Breathitt County's veterans did not feel a need for vengeance. Even though political rifts remained, they endeavored not to let it remain personal—even after fighting their "intimate" civil war. "I do not call all democrats rebels," insisted a Breathitt Unionist in 1869, but this with an admission that the Democratic Party itself still represented disunion.[68]

Captain William Strong, recently decommissioned from the Three Forks Battalion, experienced his own combination of retribution and forgiveness. He, too, was sued by Breathitt County citizens for the livestock he had commandeered. Unlike Noble, he and other Three Forks veterans Wiley Amis,

Wilson Callahan, and Hiram Freeman could all testify that wartime acquisitions were carried out for the purpose of "suppressing the late rebellion" and had the lawsuits transferred to federal courts in Louisville.[69] In 1867's election for circuit court judge, Republicans in surrounding counties outvoted Breathitt's Democrats to elect former congressman William H. Randall, probably the first Kentucky jurist to admit Negro court testimony (before it became state law in 1872). Strong and other Unionists had an important ally in the "Radical" judge, and that balanced Strong's sometimes irascible behavior.[70] After assaulting one of his plaintiffs, Strong was sued for $500 for assault and battery. George Noble, one of the case's jurors, remembered how "the war spirit was high" in the courtroom and "it was pretty hard to enforce the civil law." Still, he persuaded the other jurors (including one "strong Rebel") to "soften the enemy rather than hardening him" by reducing the fine to $100. The defendant seemed to be somewhat willing to play along; after the trial Strong "treated" the jury at a Jackson grocery store that also served as a tavern. Seeing little threat from the young man he had once captured, Strong also returned Noble's favor by supporting his nomination for town constable.[71] Around the same time the captain, still wearing his dragoon's knee-high boots and two gun belts, surprised onlookers when he publicly extended his hand to a former enemy.[72] It seemed that anything done in public was saturated by the war's memory.

This did not mean all was forgiven. After the war Jeremiah South supposedly put a $500 bounty on Strong for the lives of his sons Andrew and Jerry. Strong was sleeping in a Jackson hotel when a knife-wielding assailant attacked him. Strong was able to grab the man's Bowie knife and repel the attack, but he remained cautious enough to ask others to stay with him when he lodged in Jackson overnight after that.[73] There was no proof that this would-be assassin had been doing South's bidding and, from then on, no more attempts on Strong's life of that type were attempted. Colonel South had his hands full in the Bluegrass for the remainder of his life, and Captain Strong went on to outlive him by nearly two decades.

William Strong maintained peaceful relations with his wealthy first cousin, former Confederate officer Edward C. Strong, who returned to the county judge's bench after David Butler.[74] As an estimable landowner himself, William Strong was able to mediate between the area's black and white poor and elites like his cousin. In fact, the self-described "Republican in principle" (who apparently eschewed the "Radical" label, unlike some compatriots) comported himself peaceably after the war, though with occasional sarcasm. Strong feigned mock deference, refusing to "drink before [his] landlord" after a Democrat of his own social and economic standing tried to cajole him with a dram of brandy.[75]

Strong did not protest when Breathitt County's ex-Confederates voted in 1868 even though the newly ratified Fourteenth Amendment forbade it.[76] Instead, he showed up at the polls to cast his own vote. He knew that within two years of his winning the war for the Union, he and the Unionists/ Republicans had become the minority, ruefully observing in 1869, "We have two parties in Breathitt County; occasionally they will run a democrat and then a rebel."[77] It was not the behavior of someone who supposedly tried to, according to E. L. Noble, "rid the county of all but republicans."[78]

Although he never made any public pronouncements on enfranchisement, as the "special protector of the colored race," he personally represented Breathitt County's greatest extreme of radicalism whether he meant to or not.[79] It is especially difficult to explain Strong's long-lasting association with Breathitt County's black minority, many of them former Strong family slaves. Though the association probably began as a wartime marriage of convenience, its longevity suggests that Strong's wartime experience molded his outlook on race and class; in the 1890s he was still considered the "feudal hero" of Breathitt County's landless and an "arch Republican" who, even in old age, refused to back down from confrontation.[80] Henderson Kilburn and Hiram Freeman remained loyal to Strong and bore arms on his behalf numerous times after the war. In turn, his Democratic adversaries grudgingly respected him as a formidable power broker. Postwar attempts at compromise between former enemies suggest that mountaineers in one of Kentucky's most war-torn counties recognized the complexities of life after war and were willing to react in ways other than overt retribution—at least, it seems, for the first few years.

This lasted until Kentucky Unionism was split asunder. Aside from Captain Strong, no Federal veteran had played a greater role in punishing Breathitt County's "secesh" majority than former Union lieutenant Wiley Amis. Still, according to Strong and other Republicans, Amis's loyalty during the war had been halfhearted. With Andrew Johnson's 1866 split with Congress, Amis "turned democratic" and, like most other white Kentucky Union veterans, "took the side of the President."[81] During the November 1868 elections Amis served as poll judge in Crockettsville, the county's most Republican precinct. Soon after voters gathered, he violated the neutrality of his post, first mocking the opposition's poverty and then threatening

Republicans with a club brought, he said, "to break radical heads." "Amis commenced the difficulty himself with me at the polls, and called me an old abolitionist," one Republican testified a few months later. "He asked me how I would like to vote with a nigger, and sit by them and smell of them. I told him that I had rather vote with a nigger, sit by him, smell of him, than to vote with a rebel, and smell of and sit by him, and this ended the discourse between us."[82]

When Amis saw "the damned radical" William Strong, he verbally menaced his former compatriot until Democratic and Republican bystanders began nervously unbuttoning their holsters. A blood spilling was forestalled at the last minute. "Amis . . . seeing what it would lead to, returned to his seat and the election went on." Amis's aims were partially met after "two or three good Union men left and did not vote." It came to light months later that "good Union people" as well as "cowardly Union men" had stayed home from the polls in other precincts.[83] With this coercion, and at least 138 ineligible Rebel votes counted countywide, Democrats carried Breathitt County and the entire eighth congressional district (although Ulysses Grant did quite well in many southeastern counties, his one-third of Breathitt County ballots was only slightly better than his poor showing in Kentucky overall).[84] In the end, Amis was inelegantly successful.

Wiley Amis's abuse of power became a matter of public record the next year when Republican congressional candidate Sydney Barnes vainly contested his loss to Democrat George M. Adams. Dozens of depositions from *Barnes vs. Adams* revealed poll cheating and coercion in every Breathitt precinct (as well as the district's seventeen other counties), apparently more so than in any other county under investigation.[85] It stood to reason that the eighth district's most hidebound Democratic county would go above and beyond the pale to support Adams. However, for the exact same reason, it was the county where graft and intimidation would have, theoretically, been least necessary. Even if Breathitt County was founded by followers of Jackson and an unbroken record of antebellum Democratic majority for nearly twenty years, re-creating this Democratic majority after the war required the same violence and intimidation utilized throughout the South. "A more determined democratic element" had regained the electoral advantage—but not without the threat of force.[86] In George Noble's mind, a man who still persisted in voting Republican did so only "to spite his neighbors."[87] Just as in the rest of Kentucky, "Redemption" came early in Breathitt County. And, just as elsewhere in Kentucky, Democrats employed an increasingly

Wiley Amis may have sympathized with the Confederacy even as he served as a Federal officer. Afterward he blamed his former compatriot William Strong for championing the war's most important result: black citizenship. (Courtesy of Sherry Lynn Baker via Ray Fox and Kash Eversole descendants)

popular term to depoliticize this use of force; during cross-examination Congressman-elect Adams asked a Republican witness if the Election Day affray might have been nothing more than "a very bitter personal feud." The witness did not attempt to insist otherwise.[88]

No sui generis dispute between mountaineers insulated from the outside world, Wiley Amis's outburst was one manifestation of a country watching its former slaves becoming citizens during an election that was essentially a national referendum on Reconstruction. The probability of black suffrage, even in a locality in which it would have a negligible electoral impact, was too much to risk. Wiley Amis's performance demonstrated his lack of confidence in his party's chances if unaided by violence. William Strong was Breathitt County's greatest advocate for black rights (granted, with little competition for that distinction) and the one most game to fight for it.

Under unspecified circumstances, Wiley Amis attempted to kill Strong the following winter. Strong did not immediately retaliate, but he began going armed.[89] Thus followed what became known as the "Strong-Amis feud," between Amis's "Black Stock" and Strong's "Red Strings."[90] The name "Black Stock" may well have been Amis's own ominous creation (he had announced them as his anti-Radical allies during the previous November's election) for himself, his brothers, his Union compatriot Wilson Callahan (apparently befitting, or despite, his position as the Crockettsville precinct's election "sheriff," Callahan maintained quiet during his friend Amis's disruptive behavior), and their friends—most likely including a number of Confederate veterans.[91]

"Red String," however, had currency elsewhere in the South. The "antiaristocratic" Red String (the name inspired by the book of Joshua), with origins probably in the North Carolina piedmont, was an enigmatic coterie of (mostly) white southern loyalists with connections to the better-known Loyal Leagues and "Heroes of America."[92] For years after the war, Red String denoted "the small farmers, tenants, laborers and rougher classes of the region," the Reconstruction South's *sansculottes*, more willing than most southern Republicans to expose the economic meanings hidden beneath the façade of skin color.[93] Despite their general obscurity, one North Carolina Klan klavern duly recognized them as an enemy organization "whose intention is to destroy the rights of the South, or of the States, or of the people, or to elevate the negro to a political equality with [themselves]" in 1871.[94] Unlike the Upper South's mostly conservative (especially in Kentucky) Republican organizations, Democrats considered the Red String an existential threat to white supremacy.[95]

Just as Ku Klux Klan lasted longer in Kentucky than in any other state, the Red String, its opposite number, did the same—at least in Breathitt County. Breathitt County's Red Strings were still a force of interracial dissent and subversion in the 1890s, long after the name had become an obscure footnote of Reconstruction elsewhere in the South.[96] And, after that, their class-based political culture outlasted the organization. As late as the New Deal, Breathitt County's landless still clung to the Republican Party, at least in local elections (of course, by then the local Democracy was still controlled by the wealthy).[97] More than seventy years after Strong's death, the name Red String remained in local memory, providing an obscure reminder that the Bloody Breathitt narrative was not just a bizarre local legend or a manifestation of eastern Kentucky's alleged feud phenomenon.[98] It was, in fact, part and parcel of a much larger struggle for control over the American South.

Details on what occurred between Strong, Amis, and their respective allies are scant and questionable, but it seems that fighting lasted sporadically until 1872 or 1873, when Strong finally "triumphed over his enemies and exterminated them."[99] In the summer of 1870 reports of "[a] sort of guerilla war" emerged from Breathitt County. "There are about thirty on each side," one South Carolina paper reported without attribution, "well armed, and on the lookout for each other."[100] The most detailed (and perhaps the least unreliable) sequence of events appeared in the *Lexington Herald*, but not until 1897, a few days after Strong's death: in spring 1870 Wiley Amis and his son John ambushed Strong as he was plowing. Strong took cover and returned fire, wounding John Amis in the legs. Wiley Amis waited until the following September (after his son had fully recovered) before attacking again, this time bringing a larger group of gunmen to lay siege to Strong's house. Hiram Freeman was wounded defending Strong's wife and children before Strong's young son Jim was able to slip away to Jackson to summon help. He returned with circuit court clerk Edward Marcum (William Strong's brother-in-law and his former lieutenant) and more than a dozen others, "nearly all of whom had fought under Cap. Strong" in the war. Marcum's group dispersed the Amises and rescued Strong. Strong appealed to Judge William Randall but was reportedly told that he would have to defend himself (future events suggest Randall used his courage economically). In October Strong gathered his forces together and confronted the superior-numbered Black Stock. All accounts agree that William Strong was the eventual victor after an indeterminable measure of blood was spilled. Wilson Callahan and at least three members of the Amis family were killed, after which Wiley and the other surviving Amises migrated to Kansas (he died in Arkansas, apparently from natural causes, in 1882).[101] However large or small the conflict was in comparison to regulator and Klan violence in other parts of the state, the "Strong-Amis feud" began and ended without state intercession. When someone found a souvenir coin identifying Wiley Amis as an officer in the Fourteenth Kentucky Cavalry in 1898, no one in Kentucky knew where to send it.[102]

What became known as the "Amis-Strong feud" was a manifestation of a conflict going on throughout the South in the late 1860s, one commenced by the breakdown between the federal government's executive and legislative branches. Closer to home, it reflected Kentucky's postwar Unionist fissure over black citizenship, the same rupture that produced Confederate supremacy from the 1870s until the early 1890s. In fact, it was most likely part of a larger concerted effort to punish white Unionism and destroy black freedom in eastern Kentucky. The Ku Klux Klan and other violent political organizations that undermined Union victory materialized in the mountains as soon as they did in the Bluegrass.[103] Their onslaught increased in 1870, the first year black Kentuckians cast votes.[104] In fall of that year, Klansmen killed nineteen Union veterans and other Republicans, "most of them white men," in Breathitt and three surrounding counties.[105] Estill County's state senator and local Democratic boss served as the head of a multicounty klavern in the early 1870s and led a barrage of torment against freedpeople who came to work in the county's iron industry (the Klan's authority in intensely Unionist Estill speaks to the intensity of "belated Confederate" sentiment Amis shared with other white Kentuckians).[106] When federal marshals and cavalrymen captured four wanted Klansmen in Estill and Clay counties in 1871, it was a federal victory rare enough to receive national media attention.[107] White mountaineers chose the Klan "rubric" because they saw connections between their own local conflicts and the larger struggle against black enfranchisement and federal authority going on all over the South.[108] Even moderate young Democrat George Noble became a Klan "vice-president" after serving as Jackson's town constable. The former was a position, Noble laconically recalled years later, that "gave a man great power over his neighbor."[109]

Rather than some bizarre, personally motivated abnormality contained within one remote county, the "Strong-Amis feud" was only one battle in an exogenous political war. This, however, is not how it was shared with the outside world. The Herald's and all other descriptions of the "feud" appeared in print many years later, all ignoring Amis's confrontation with Strong at the 1868 election. All highlighted the personal over the political while also calling into question their legitimacy as soldiers by emphasizing their sordid motivations for self-gain. They all blamed it on a personal disagreement over the apportionment of confiscated livestock in the last days of the war or shortly afterward. They also grouped the conflict with others that supposedly defined eastern Kentucky's feud phenomenon.[110] Owing to the fact that an earlier generation of Amises, Callahans, and Strongs had all been combatants in the Clay County Cattle War sixty years earlier, and considering that this more recent conflict was ostensibly started over livestock, it was widely assumed later on that this "feud" was nothing more than a continuation of ancient hatreds predating the Civil War (that descendants of both sides of the cattle war were allies during the Civil War was an unfortunate niggling detail).[111]

What makes the Amis-Strong conflict strange rather than familiar, if anything, was that it resulted in a bloody Unionist victory, the reverse of most reported southern violence circa 1870.[112] Yet, by being remembered as a feud, it was not remembered as a political victory for either side. The political propositions were roundly ignored and perhaps even suppressed, while the conflict's longevity was stretched to thirty-five years to give it proper feudal longevity.[113] "Although originating not long after the war," J. Stoddard Johnston protested too much in 1899, "it was personal and not political."[114] When the conflict's Civil War connections were conceded, it was in as confused and misconstrued a manner as possible; in 1909 a Kentucky newspaperman recalled Breathitt's "two Federal regiments," which "apparently endeavored to exterminate each other" for no discernible reason.[115] A few years later, another feud chronicler dubbed the "Strong-Amis feud" the first evidence that Breathitt County was "more fully imbued with the feudal spirit" than anywhere else in the Kentucky mountains.[116] It was a spirit that twentieth-century Kentuckians did not want to remember as associated with the state's internal divisions half a century prior. Just as it was used to depoliticize lingering violence immediately after the war, the feud remained useful in the 1910s for separating the nastiest memories from what had finally been deemed a "noble mutual experience that in the long run solidified the nation."[117] Short and picayune as it was, the "Strong-Amis feud" challenged this interpretation of the war and what came after it. It was better it be rendered apolitical folklore, if remembered at all.

William Strong avoided portraying himself as a postwar caudillo. In 1879 he told an interviewer that, after his service in the Fourteenth Kentucky

Cavalry (he omitted his service in the more notorious Three Forks Battalion), he had "returned home to live in peace" and had only gone after the Amises after other Breathitt County citizens had asked him to form a supposedly bipartisan militia to end their postwar depredations. Strong fervently denied that he was the "head of a belligerent faction ever since the war," even though he was associated with violence numerous times afterward.[118] Whether as a Unionist crusader or a "feudist," his reputation was permanently wedded to Bloody Breathitt.

"Too much attention to politics and not enough to corn"

A large part of the reason the "Strong-Amis feud" was easy to depoliticize was its lack of clear consequences. Strong's victory over the Black Stock did not stymie the Democratic reascendancy that was beginning in 1868. With decade's end came the expiration of the Fourteenth Amendment's ban on Confederates holding office (a ban scarcely enforced in Kentucky if the 1868 elections serve as evidence), a bolstering of the Democratic ticket, and the beginning of a long period of Confederate rule.[119] Something very much like the antebellum status quo returned, and Breathitt County returned to the speculative purposes for which it had been created.

With the South family absent and otherwise occupied in the Bluegrass, no one embodied their commercial spirit more than newly elected county judge Edward Strong.[120] In 1872 Kentucky's General Assembly authorized the county to increase the price of "vacant and unappropriated lands" in preparation for public sale.[121] After doing so, Judge Strong sold a tract of "wild lands" around Troublesome Creek (a large tributary to the north fork of the Kentucky River) to a land company from outside of the county, unintentionally drawing ire from local farmers, some of whom may have been Red Strings. Farming practices had not changed since before the war, and these "vacant and unappropriated" woods and pastures were still vital to the livelihood of squatters as well as landed farmers with adjacent property. When Judge Strong's surveyors arrived to draw boundaries near Troublesome Creek, an armed squad dissuaded them. This demonstration of armed force delayed further surveying of the area for years.[122] The "wild lands" remained wild regardless of who owned them.

Speculation was set back again the next year when the courthouse in Jackson burned to the ground, destroying extant land grants and calling into question virtually every land tenure in Breathitt County.[123] Those who laid claim to the old eighteenth-century land grants, most notably Jeremiah South and his heirs, were dealt a serious blow by the apparent arson, and they were forced to fight for their ownership claims in court for decades afterward.[124] On the other hand, the fire was a boon to those who most depended upon large expanses of unfenced, untitled land, those with little or no land—a population that had notably bucked the county leadership's pro-Confederate leanings in the previous decade.

As "republicans of the war element," William Strong and the Red Strings were implicated, but no indictments were passed down.[125] This was not the first time Breathitt County's courthouse had burned. When it had happened last, in 1864, courthouse fires in Kentucky were practically commonplace. They were not uncommon nine years later during the counterrevolutionary violence precipitating "Redemption," but by then they were more likely to be caused by sundry local crises of legitimacy; they could no longer be blamed on invaders from the outside world. "Republicans of the war element" or otherwise, anyone who had motive to destroy the locus of state at this late date was probably someone from within the county's borders.

The 1873 fire was a sign of discord, but 1874 proved to be the county's— and perhaps Kentucky's—most chaotic year since the war. White-on-black killings had increased since 1870, but August and September of 1874 constituted a crescendo of violence. August 1874 marked the first election cycle since the U.S. Senate's passage of what would become the 1875 Civil Rights Act. In a fevered combination of conservative alarm and new assertions of black rights, local violence erupted throughout Kentucky and the South, most notably a "terrible war between the whites and blacks" in the southern Bluegrass.[126] While newspapers gave Kentucky's disturbances due notice, the northern press was more keenly focused on Louisiana's White League revolt.[127]

William Strong's first public act of violence in years came soon after the tumultuous state elections, when a white man named David Flinchum allegedly murdered a Negro named William Hargis and was not prosecuted. With Hiram Freeman, Henderson Kilburn, and Freeman's sons William and Daniel, "Nigger Dick" Strong (a freedman said to have once belonged to Strong's father) and ten other unnamed men of both races, he performed what one newspaper termed a "coup d'état," taking possession of the newly rebuilt courthouse and its surroundings.[128] Strangely, Strong and the Red Strings seemed to have encountered little resistance, and there is no evidence of anyone in Jackson killed or injured, including Flinchum. By

1874's standard, it was relatively peaceful, a demonstration of the Unionists' refusal to recognize the legitimacy of the county's law enforcement and the men who ran it.

By mid-September rumors had spread to the Bluegrass that "outlaws, under the command of one Strong . . . have possession of the place and rule the county."[129] Within a few days reports claimed that "200 desperados" had barricaded themselves in Jackson's courthouse.[130] Unknown parties requested Governor Preston H. Leslie to send members of the militia to restore peace. Since his inauguration, Leslie had styled himself an active executive, but had since struggled with a legislature reluctant to punish or prevent mob violence.[131] Perhaps more than any other Kentucky governor of the period, Leslie acknowledged the "weakness [and] often venality of county law enforcement officials," even if most of those officials were his party mates, and he sympathized with citizens "who looked more and more to the authorities at Frankfort, instead of to the local authorities."[132] Still, he had been accused of personal hesitation in dealing with Klan violence, even after dispatching the state militia to two separate trouble spots in August 1874. Alarmed by the exaggerated reports, Leslie dispatched a militia company to Breathitt County and requested that Judge Randall suspend his other court dates in order to schedule a special session in Jackson that would allow no case continuances.[133] After false reports that the company had been attacked, Leslie anticipated further requests from Breathitt and sent four more companies. By the end of September more militiamen had been sent to Breathitt County than to any of the counties that had recently requested interventions.[134]

Strong and the Red Strings had relinquished control of the town and the courthouse before the militia arrived, and they subsequently disarmed without any recorded protest.[135] Beside the fact that they were far outnumbered by the militia, Strong and the Freemans were less reluctant to give up their arms knowing that the court was to be handed over to Judge Randall. Strong was not indicted for his attempted insurrection, and the Freemans, although indicted by a county magistrate in Crockettsville for delinquent murder accusations, were dismissed from trial due to a lack of witnesses for the prosecution.[136] Randall's early arrival may well have been Strong's actual goal.

Still, Strong's rebellion did not affect lasting change in Breathitt County. Judge Randall's leniency to the Red Strings may have been reported because, shortly after the beginning of the special court session, Governor Leslie

Judge William H. Randall's impressive record as a Reconstruction-era champion of civil rights did not help him bring peace to Breathitt County. (E. Polk Johnson, *A History of Kentucky and Kentuckians*)

instructed Randall to turn the court over to Breathitt County's Democratic county judge, James Back. In November Back indicted Strong and the Freemans for carrying concealed weapons, but all four men were found not guilty.[137] But Back did not attempt to reverse any of Randall's rulings, nor did he further pursue Strong and the Freemans for their earlier crimes. Randall's dismissal altered Leslie's original plans for the special court session. After Back was given control of the court, both criminal and civil cases were carried over to future court sessions, against Leslie's instructions.[138] No one was ever indicted for William Hargis's murder.

Strong's courthouse capture was motivated by Hargis's unpunished death, but there were other complicating factors that probably encouraged more farmers to support or join the Red Strings. It came amid Breathitt County's worst economic straits since the war, repercussions from the Panic of 1873 and a bizarre blight or storm that caused a localized corn famine.[139] Whatever his strategy, Strong's tactic in 1874 imitated an ongoing trend in the Reconstruction South. Court building usurpations were common in the 1870s although, unlike Strong's, the majority of recorded instances were carried out for counterrevolutionary purposes by groups like the Ku Klux Klan to prevent black participation in elections or jurisprudence. The Colfax Massacre in Grant Parish, Louisiana, in 1873, one of the single bloodiest events in southern history, began with a similar confrontation over a courthouse's physical custody.[140] Strong's forced occupation was quixotic and perhaps little more than symbolic but, like that of his political opposites in Colfax the previous year, it represented his refusal to accept what had become of his home county.

Strong's attempt at insurrection and the ensuing militia occupation and trials made national news, and the first public association between Breathitt County and feuds. The Republican *New York Times* lambasted Kentucky as a place where political disputes continued to slow the state's postwar development. Continuing political scuffles, the *Times* argued, were a natural outgrowth of the creation of "pauper counties," the result of partitioning counties into smaller and smaller units for electoral purposes while simultaneously creating smaller, poorer tax bases, "a Democratic luxury for which the remainder of the state must pay." The correspondent blamed the county's inhabitants for their troubles, not in the context of their being mountaineers but rather in their identity as white Kentuckians. "Too much attention to politics and not enough to corn," said the *Times* reporter, "has brought want to many households, even in this corn-producing region."[141]

A Republican newspaper in Cincinnati reacted to the governor's dispatch of the state militia by speculating that he did so only for fear that "frequent outbreaks in the South, especially at this time, will injure the prospects of Democratic candidates in the North at the approaching elections," or that this and other contemporary outbreaks would result in federal involvement. "This modern activity of Governor Leslie, after hesitating so long with the Ku Klux raiding within sight of his residence, it is said, is the result of his fear that Uncle Sam will suppress the lawlessness in the State if the governor is unable or unwilling to do such work."[142] Military Reconstruction was dwindling throughout the South, but the fear of its expansion to Kentucky was still tangible.

As they had since the 1860s, Kentucky Democrats used the concept of feud to parry these attacks. "The troubles in the county of Breathitt have been much exaggerated, especially by the radical press of Louisville and Cincinnati," said J. Stoddard Johnston's *Kentucky Yeoman*.[143] The courthouse capture was simply the "outgrowth of an old feud between two families of the county."[144] The *Yeoman*'s hated adversary, the Republican *Louisville Commercial*, also used familial language, but to implicate Breathitt County in an attack on Kentucky's planter elite. "Men who carry on a controversy of open violence for years always involve others in their difficulties, especially if they belong to the so-called 'respectable families,' families of 'high social position.' There is no more dangerous or delusive influence exercised in society than that of ungentlemanly gentlemen and families of mythical respectability, who strut about with a package of penitentiary morals hidden under silk and broadcloth."[145]

Of course neither of these explanations had the faintest association with Captain Strong's courthouse capture. Brushing Flinchum and Hargis aside, the *Yeoman* and other papers conflated the insurrection with a series of assaults, deadly and otherwise, leading up to July 1874. Although Strong was said to have taken part in this "Jett-Little feud," there is no proof of his participation as either aggressor or victim. Strong was not even subpoenaed as a witness in the resultant personal injury lawsuit.[146] It was better, however, for Strong's nakedly political crime to be cast within a contemporaneous apolitical conflict, one that played out (supposedly) in the fashion of an antebellum conte of southern intrigue. Bloody Breathitt was a plainly violent place in 1874, but distinguishing between different motivations and types of violence was to be discouraged.

Both of these Bluegrass newspapers' accounts demonstrated the strength that the language of the familial, and the intimation of there being some antebellum feud condition at work, held for their own antagonistic purposes. While the *Yeoman* used family to dissociate the incident from contemporary Ku Kluxing and such, the *Commercial* used the language of kinship to denounce what it saw as the harmful remnants of the South's ancien régime. Feuds, as they were understood in a nineteenth-century context, were a family-based phenomenon associated with the southern aristocracy.[147] The fact that the courthouse raid was not acted out by a family group, of the planter class or otherwise, was immaterial to either account; both served the papers' public agendas. In further coverage, the *Commercial* scolded the *Yeoman* for failing to compete with smaller "stiff Democratic paper[s]" in its coverage, implying that the *Yeoman* was insensitive to the state's problems with civil unrest.[148] Regardless of the actual details, Kentucky's most partisan members of the fourth estate saw Breathitt County as a foil for larger political purposes.

It became the task of Henry Watterson's *Louisville Courier-Journal* to diminish Breathitt County's political significance altogether. No newspaper dedicated more ink to Breathitt County in 1874, and no newspaper, consequently, ended up with a more varied, and puzzling, record of the year's events. The paper entitled one of its earliest articles on the incident "White and Negro Rioters in Breathitt," a headline that acknowledged the incident's similarity to contemporary, more blatantly race-based, crimes in other parts of the state.[149] However, in weeks to come the *Courier-Journal* became more intent on distancing Breathitt County from the rest of the state and, as was customary in its and other papers' treatment of their state during Reconstruction, depoliticizing violence. Rather than placing the county's disorder within a larger regional or statewide political context, the *Courier-Journal* highlighted the isolation of the "beautiful, wild semi-barbarian county."[150] The racially amorphous Freemans were first identified as "the terror of this county" since the Civil War but were scarcely given any other specific mention in the interest of diminishing the story's potential for racial significance.[151] After the state militia's arrival, the paper's coverage of Breathitt County dwindled until the only subject of interest was the militia's incidental day-to-day activities; the paper's final story dealt mainly with a baseball game, complete with box scores, played between two companies.[152] The seventy state troops remained another six weeks, apparently without incident, until the first week of December.[153]

As always, the *Courier-Journal* tried to maintain a middle ground between Kentucky's left and right flanks, befitting Henry Watterson's philosophy of North/South rapprochement. Other than placing implicit blame on the small number of people of color involved in the courthouse incident, Watterson's paper was less willing to make hay out of it than Republican newspapers but still willing to address the story to a greater extent than the *Yeoman*. Throughout the Reconstruction years, Henry Watterson's chief goal was to maintain his role as a leader among white southerners while simultaneously raising his state above the South's madding crowd (a balancing act he perfected), and by brushing Kentucky's violence under the rug and belittling black Kentuckians' role in their state without blatantly attacking them like other editors might choose to do (after all, race was the politically divisive issue of the day and—excepting his moment of anti-Hayes saber rattling in the winter of 1876–77—political divisiveness was to be avoided).[154] Explaining away troubles in an obscure, overwhelmingly white county far from the Bluegrass was hardly among his most daunting challenges, even following the ominous significance of white and black men cooperatively seizing a public building. Four years later, the paper misremembered the whole affair as "originat[ing] from family quarrels and feuds."[155]

"Neither the state nor the United States have done anything for Breathitt, and, in turn, Breathitt has 'done nothing for nobody'"

In the end, the Red Strings' 1874 show of force did not deter the county's Democrats and may well have hardened many voters' resolve against the former Unionists. In the 1876 presidential election, Breathitt County had its largest Democratic turnout in its history, no doubt encouraged by the continuance of local Klan activity.[156] But William Strong was given a new opportunity in 1878, when a newcomer challenged the local Democratic cabal. In 1875 a young Virginia lawyer named John Wesley Burnett moved to the county, joined the county bar, and made friends with then sheriff James Hagins and others in and around Jackson. Even though Burnett had a reputation for brashness (he was rumored to have come to Breathitt County to escape the repercussions of a duel he had won in Virginia), in the first three years after his arrival, he managed to remain aloof from Breathitt's internecine conflicts—until he decided on a bid for county judge.[157] Burnett was a Democrat; but as a political neophyte with no preexistent ties to the county, he was an interloper on the post-Confederate political scene. The Democratic committee nominated veteran jurist Edward Strong, and one prominent Democrat, county treasurer John Seldon Hargis, swore to spend $1,000 to prevent Burnett's election.[158] The weeks leading up to the August election were fraught with threats of violence, causing former county judge David Butler to withdraw from contention.[159] Though considered "lawless" by Democrats, William Strong influenced an angry Republican minority, particularly those provoked a few years earlier by Edward Strong's land sale. A brush fire that singed at least fourteen square miles of pasture in the northern part of the county the previous spring made the "wildlands" that the former judge wished to sell that much more vital to drovers.[160] Edward Strong sought out his cousin's endorsement through a third party, but William Strong instead endorsed Burnett and promised "to help protect him, no matter who molested him."[161] The young newcomer, the first electoral challenge to Breathitt County's Democratic rule in ten years, won the August election by eight votes.[162]

Before his election, Hagins had deputized Burnett to arrest Jerry Little (quite possibly the same Jerry Little involved in the "Jett-Little feud"). Burnett was said to have acted with particular brutality in carrying out the arrest, and after Little's subsequent acquittal, Little's family remained angry. When Little's uncle, Jason Little, was arrested for murdering his wife, newly elected Judge Burnett had him transferred more than one hundred miles away to Lexington.[163] Local Democrats interpreted the arrest and removal as politically motivated affronts or, just as likely, used the controversy as a stalking horse against Burnett.

Jason Little's return for trial during late November's circuit court session turned into a referendum on John Burnett's legitimacy as an elected judge. A confrontation between Civil War factions developed on Jackson's main thoroughfare before he could be removed from the jailhouse. On one side, a mob led by Confederate veterans John Aikman and Alfred Gambrel amassed, threatening to release Little. On the other, William Strong, Henderson Kilburn, Hiram Freeman, and Freeman's sons Daniel and William as well as a dozen other Red Strings who had come to town, according to Strong, to see that Burnett's (and circuit court judge William Randall's) court authority was respected.[164] As Randall instructed the grand jury, the two groups faced off down the street from the courthouse.

Verifiable stories of encounters between Aikman and Strong are scant, but many accounts of Bloody Breathitt said that they had been personal enemies since the war.[165] In 1873 Strong and seven other Union veterans testified against John Aikman in a murder trial. Five former Confederates testified in Aikman's defense and Aikman was subsequently acquitted.[166] While their enmity over the years may have been exaggerated, Aikman can be seen as Strong's opposite number in 1878: a feared Confederate veteran who did not consider the Civil War a closed matter and never showed particular concern for diktat or morality in demonstrating his displeasure. His connections to the Little family are unclear (most of the Littles had been Unionists), and it is likely that Aikman and others simply saw an opportunity to draw the Red Strings into the open.

After both groups had assembled near the courthouse, Daniel Freeman approached Aikman and demanded to know his intentions. Declaring he would "take a dead nigger," Aikman shot him. When William Freeman ran into the street to retrieve his brother Aikman shot him as well. Daniel died soon thereafter but William survived, even after lying in the street for a number of hours before any of the Red Strings were able to rescue him (William Strong later said he eventually died from his injuries).[167] At some point later in the day, a Red String named Wallace Maguire killed Tom Little, Jason Little's cousin who had joined with Aikman (William Strong later said that Tom Little had threatened to lead "two hundred Kuklux" from nearby Wolfe County).[168] With Aikman's group unable to free Jason Little, the day ended in Pyrrhic victory for the Red Strings.

Calm was temporarily restored after both groups retreated behind whatever cover was available. However, as Burnett was walking to the courthouse to convene court with Judge Randall the following day, Gambrel fatally shot him, prompting Randall to flee the county, only later sending word to Frankfort.[169] Even during the most horrible days of Reconstruction's crumbling into "Redemption," judges were rarely gunned down. Burnett's death represented a condition of local civil unrest far worse than anything reported in Kentucky at least since 1874. It was certainly a far greater emergency than that year's apparently bloodless courthouse coup that had prompted state intervention.

Yet a return of the militia was not an obvious proposition. Governor Leslie had run on a reform platform with an emphasis on bringing peace to Kentucky even while the rest of the South burned. During his term nearly $58,000 of state expenditures went into dispatching the State Guard to Breathitt and at least four other troubled counties.[170] His successor, Confederate veteran James McCreary, was of a more conservative bent, preferring that Kentucky's counties utilize their generous measures of allowed local sovereignty to take care of themselves.[171] When word of trouble drifted westward to Frankfort during the last week of November, McCreary initially dismissed the reports of rioting in Jackson as exaggerations. A county judge's homicide was not enough to persuade Governor McCreary to take action in Jackson, despite Judge Randall's constitutionally mandated request.

Executive complacency was not all that was at work. In 1877 Louisville hosted one manifestation of the Great Railroad Strike, the largest labor strike in American history, bringing commerce to a halt and causing massive property damage. City fathers were especially disturbed by a new cooperation the riot engendered between white and black workers. A few months later, emboldened immigrant laborers founded Louisville's first Workingmen's Party.[172] Fearful of future uprisings, the General Assembly revised Kentucky's militia law later in the year. In April 1878 the Louisville Legion, an urban militia unit not mustered since the close of the Mexican War, was revived and captained by both Confederate and Union veterans (although the former outnumbered the latter four to one).[173] The new sense of class antagonism provided an excellent opportunity for cheerful agreement between upwardly mobile Rebels and Yankees, and a grand step toward depoliticizing the war memory.[174]

Considerations of blue and gray notwithstanding, the new arrangement represented a stark divergence from the mentalities and strategies that had dominated Kentucky military life since the war. Most of the harm inflicted upon black and white Kentuckians since 1865 was meted out in rural areas, and it was there that Kentucky's militia had found itself most often until the mid-1870s. Since then, Klan and regulator violence had ebbed somewhat and white Kentuckians, particularly those of Henry Watterson's "New Departure" school of thought, were reluctant to believe that violence born of the war (at least when they were willing to admit said causation) could still bedevil the state. The Bluegrass urban middle class recognized that threats to civil order would now more likely emerge from cities, and it was deemed more important that Kentucky use its armed forces to protect commercial interests from further labor disruptions.[175] In 1874 William Strong's courthouse capture, not unlike the actions of White Leagues, Red Shirts, Pale Faces, and Knights of the White Carmelia farther south, made Jackson one among a number of trouble spots in Kentucky. In contrast, Breathitt County in 1878 did not appear to Governor McCreary and other urban Kentuckians to represent a continuation of old problems so much as an unfortunate distraction from newer ones. Too much acknowledgment of the politics behind Breathitt County rioting might have suggested otherwise. After all, Reconstruction was over, and it had never happened in Kentucky anyway.

The deluge of condemnations of the Jackson situation from northern newspapers was stinging. The Republican *New York Times,* almost as eager to wave the bloody shirt as it had been during the worst years of Reconstruction, reported that "not one man in 10 who commits murder in Kentucky is hanged."[176] "It may, perhaps, occur to Governor McCreary that it is disgraceful to have such scenes of violence and bloodshed enacted in a sovereign state of the Union," crowed the usually apolitical *New York Herald,* "but in any case the need of preserving the 'prominent citizens' of even so small a place as Jackson should move him to action. The State of the 'Mill Boy of the Slashes' [one of the late Henry Clay's nicknames] has no 'prominent citizens' to spare just now."[177] Conscious of criticism from the northern press as well as Kentucky's papers, and equally conscious of the ramifications of a public official's violent death, Governor McCreary reluctantly dispatched the Legion to Jackson in early December.[178]

Soon after the Legion's arrival, Judge Randall returned and court was reconvened, only to be interrupted by political maneuvering.[179] After Randall convicted Jason Little for his wife's murder, the Republican judge was removed from the bench and replaced by Louisville probate judge William Jackson to try the "conspirators" in John Burnett's death.[180] Randall's party affiliation, and his flight from the county a month earlier, made him too controversial for the more politically charged cases. Judge Jackson was a former Confederate brigadier general and a more acceptable presence among Breathitt Democrats.[181] An out-of-county jury convicted Alfred Gambrel for Burnett's murder, while Wallace Maguire, the only one of Strong's allies to be put on trial, was convicted for killing Tom Little.[182] Aikman had fled the county on the advice of a Klan collaborator but was later captured and convicted for conspiring to murder Burnett. He was, however, acquitted for killing Daniel Freeman.[183] Before his capture, the *Kentucky Yeoman* printed Aikman's letters accusing William Strong of using the chaotic situation for material gain.[184] The influential South family eventually interceded on Aikman's and Gambrel's behalf, and both were pardoned.[185] Breathitt County's old Democratic order was now truly restored, partly due to its own actions but not without help from the Kentucky state government.

Judge John Burnett's shooting death completely overshadowed those of his would-be defenders, William and Daniel Freeman, the biracial grandchildren of a slave. With this in mind, the shooting of the Freeman brothers looks quite familiar in the 1870s, people of color killed or injured amid a struggle for power by an all-white Democratic Party. As far away as Bloody

Breathitt was from the former Confederacy, its incentive for violence in November 1878 was essentially a southern one. The northern press, particularly Republican papers, seemed to recognize this.

This was why it was so important to Kentucky Democrats that the Freeman brothers' roles as aggressors and victims, the racial/political meanings behind Bloody Breathitt, be minimized. No one played a greater role in doing this than the *Louisville Courier-Journal.* In 1874, after William Strong's capture of the courthouse first caught the Louisville paper's attention, Henry Watterson's column space was still spent more on terror farther to the South (most notably Louisiana's White League riots), and news from Breathitt County was relatively commonplace. Since then, Watterson had personally stirred the sectional pot, calling for a Democratic march on Washington, DC, to support presidential candidate Samuel Tilden.[186] Even after reestablishing his New Departure stance, he and his editorial staff were still acutely sensitive to Kentucky's portrayal by the northern press. Initially, Watterson's task was defending Breathitt County—and, by extension, Kentucky—against their censure, particularly since phrases like "Kentucky KuKluxers" were bandied about in Pennsylvania. "These Kentucky KuKluxers are very much like the Mollie Maguires of this State," the *Philadelphia Inquirer* noted, "except that the latter were ignorant and poor, while the Kentucky knaves have had the benefit of education and are all in comfortable circumstances."[187] Before long, to counter this northern perspective, Watterson and other Democrats began a long series of propaganda harangues on Breathitt County to prove that its populace actually *was* as "ignorant and poor" as the Pennsylvania coalfield's Irish killers, and isolated far from the *real* Kentucky and the South.

For a while, this involved grudgingly admitting the politics involved, as when the "copperhead" Democratic *Cincinnati Enquirer* noted that Strong had been "a notorious home guard and bushwhacker during the war" (the *Courier-Journal* also mislabeled him as a Home Guard).[188] After the Louisville Legion was sent eastward, the Republican *Cincinnati Gazette* announced, "At the last State election [Breathitt] county was Democratic by a vote of nearly three to one."[189] The *Courier-Journal* defended Breathitt County against northern Republicans' hypocritical jabs of "race prejudice" and Ku Kluxing and blaming the county's "Loyal" (that is, Unionist) minority for causing the trouble.[190] When news arrived that many of the participants were of the same party of former Unionists that had captured the courthouse in 1874, Watterson countered the Ohio paper's insinuation with the subheading "Bad News for Deacon [Richard] Smith [the *Daily Gazette*'s editor]—the Mobs

Said to Be Loyal [Unionist] Bushwhackers." "The whole difficulty appears to be a Family Quarrel Among Republicans," he disingenuously reported, "who proved their loyalty during the war between the States by bushwhacking and murdering, and are now practicing among themselves."[191] The fact that the riot had multiracial participation did not mean it was racially motivated, reasoned the *Courier-Journal,* since Breathitt County's population included only thirty-one black men over the age of twenty-one. "Those figures are sufficient to convince even that truly good and pious man, Deacon Richard Smith that the present trouble is not one of races, though one of the killed and one of the wounded are negroes."[192] Watterson, determined that the latest riot was not to be pointed to as a persistence of rebellion in Kentucky, went to great lengths to see to it that the blame for the riot was placed upon the former Unionists while ignoring the fact that their adversaries were led by Confederate veterans.[193] It was they who had ambushed the county judge, but Watterson distorted the facts by saying that Burnett was killed due to "his being a Democrat."[194]

After other papers' interest in Breathitt County began to flag, the *Courier-Journal* changed its portrayal as the trials began, accentuating the county's physical isolation and its relationship to exogenous politics—while still defending it to a degree. "Neither the state nor the United States have done anything for Breathitt," the paper intoned, "and, in turn, Breathitt has 'done nothing for nobody.'"[195] The same correspondent concluded that he would "sooner live on the western plains and take the chance of being scalped by Sitting Bull, than to live in Breathitt County at the present time."[196] In early 1879, during the rioters' trials, the *Courier-Journal* began to sound less sympathetic toward Breathitt County while retaining a portrayal of the community as a country as foreign to the Bluegrass as possible. Rather than rising against the *New York Times*'s contention that the Ku Klux Klan "were gentle citizens compared with the desperadoes who infest the ravines and hills of Breathitt" (after it had once placed the Klan *in* Breathitt with no mention of topography), the *Courier-Journal* described Breathitt County as a savage environment with "meadows that were stripped of all pastoral suggestions" and "a land which did not overflow with honey and where civilization was but a puling strangled infant."[197] This change in tone followed soon after the revelation that (and, to the *Courier-Journal*'s credit, it was acknowledged) Confederates were the primary aggressors.

Shortly before this description was printed, a *Courier-Journal* correspondent interviewed William Strong and exonerated him as having acted in a purely defensive manner during the riot.[198] Although Strong had been named specifically in 1874's courthouse capture, the reporter did not press the matter, accepting Strong's insistence that he had kept the peace since Wiley Amis took flight years beforehand. But by doing so, the paper belied the political and sectional stance it had taken toward the situation just short weeks earlier. The "King Bee" of Breathitt County was no longer a radical Unionist, "a noted Federal freebooter," as the *Courier-Journal* had said weeks earlier, but a quasi-Scots "chieftain" with American Indian likenesses, albeit "sans horns, war paint and other paraphernalia."[199] "Instead of looking fierce as the lion in his native jungle, or the tiger in defense of her cub, his face was as calm as the surface of a sleeping lake and reminded me no more of war than do the innocent flowers of May. I felt considerably relieved when I shook hands with him and beheld that springtime smile upon his face, for my memory was just then quite vivid with recollection of the adverse criticisms I had indulged in toward the mountain Captain, and the smile dispelled the thought that he had come to chaw me up."[200] A few days after interview was published, the *Kentucky Yeoman* complained that the *Courier-Journal* had handled Strong too "delicately."[201] This was years before Stoddard Johnston learned the subtle craft of depoliticizing violence. In defanging William Strong, the more centrist paper was simply following the subterfuge it had used throughout the 1870s in most of its discussions of killings in Kentucky. Even if Strong was not the monster the correspondent had originally believed him to be (no doubt because of local Democrats' whispers), his image had gone from Union partisan to quasi-oriental exotic. Although he retained the title of "mountain Captain," by 1879 the partisanship that had led to his captain's commission in the previous decade was beginning to fade—thanks partly to papers like the *Courier-Journal*.

William Strong did not apparently try to counter this portrayal. He acknowledged his controversial position during the war but did not relate it to the 1878 election. He spoke of Burnett, his cousin Edward Strong, and others strictly by name, not by their political affiliation. Like other former guerrillas, Strong knew his enemies as local familiars before any of them chose different sides in the Civil War.[202] At odds with John Aikman for more than fifteen years by the time of the 1879 interview, the captain had no need to place anonymous epithets like "Rebel" on a rival whose genealogy he could probably describe in detail.

There were other reasons as well. Captain Strong's struggle had always been against people he knew intimately, either because of kinship or age-old familiarity. Strong's actions, both before this interview and afterward, demonstrated unambiguous Republican militancy. But when discussing matters with a representative from the outside world, especially a reporter for one of the United States' most important Democratic publications, it behooved him to be sketched as a colorful, apolitical rustic. He knew Kentucky's political tides had turned against him, and describing himself as a impenitent Union partisan would probably not help his interests.

Altina Waller has identified the *Louisville Courier-Journal*'s coverage of Breathitt County in 1878–79 as the media's initial "placement of feuding in the mountains."[203] Considering that the paper's coverage began with a different tone than that with which it ended, and taking into account coverage from other newspapers of differing political stripes, there is room for more elaboration on this point. Even when the fact that violence was born out of competition between political parties could not be denied, the significance of race could be. As the harsh memory of Reconstruction became more distant, even northern members of the media followed suit. One delusional northern newspaper went as far as to explain, without elaboration, "There is no distinction between races up in that country."[204] It was simpler and less troubling to tell this big lie than it would have been to discover why black and white mountaineers would take up arms together, especially with Reconstruction over. It was not long after that black involvement in Bloody Breathitt was forgotten.

In its place, Kentucky's flagship paper reified the otherness of what would later be called the "mountain whites." When, just after the Legion departed the mountains, reports of a courthouse riot in Perry County reached Louisville, Henry Watterson curtly remarked: "The people in the mountain counties need civilizing."[205] Watterson's assessment of the eastern half of the two Kentuckys did not explicitly employ the idea of feud, as he and other observers would later, to describe Breathitt County and its environs.[206] It did, however, demonstrate a commonly held determination to depoliticize a blatantly political problem in his state. Political and racial contingencies could be camouflaged by the mountain people's inherent savagery.

On its way home, the Louisville Legion was welcomed in Frankfort by a brass band and Governor McCreary. The relieved Democrat proclaimed the Legion an embodiment of the Second Amendment's well-regulated militia clause and commended their defense of the "good name and fame of Kentucky."[207] In his message to the Kentucky General Assembly later in 1879, McCreary declared, "No county is more orderly or peaceable than

Breathitt."[208] His pronouncement of success failed to acknowledge that, less than a month after the Louisville Legion withdrew from Jackson, Breathitt County's log jailhouse had been destroyed by a mob in apparent reaction to the convictions of Little, Gambrel, et al.[209] The following May a Confederate veteran named Andrew Carpenter was killed in ambush while working in his field.[210] One national publication judged Breathitt County's troubles to be the outcome of "an imperfect organization [resulting] from the practical isolation of the people, the unlettered authorities, and the absence of schools and moral example" as well as the lack of contact with "more advanced communities," a summation happily echoed in the Bluegrass's "advanced communities," which had only just begun to eye the mountains' untapped natural wealth.[211] Even as death and destruction continued in Breathitt County, Kentucky Democrats' apolitical interpretation of Bloody Breathitt had taken permanent hold. Within a few years it would determine how the United States thought of the supposedly all-white eastern Kentucky mountains and, by extension, southern Appalachia as a whole.

"A better, healthier public sentiment"

Andrew Carpenter's end marked a change in tactics for the Red Strings. Strong was never going to legitimately challenge his county's Democratic cabal. If the deaths that resulted from his support of Judge Burnett had proven anything, it was that his own public displays of force were of limited benefit; in the end, Kentucky's state government would always support his Democratic enemies. Still, unlike so many other southern Unionists who had already accepted Democratic "home rule," Strong refused to accede to those with whom he had fought for control of his county.

For this reason, William Strong stepped back to fighting a war of position, one paradoxically more bitterly violent than the war of maneuver he had tried since 1874. Gang occupations of the Jackson streets gave way to snipers skulking around secluded horse paths miles from the town. Between 1879 and 1884, at least nine men fell in "bushwhacker" killings attributed to Strong and the Red Strings. Strong's new practice guaranteed that, should he or his followers be indicted, witnesses and juries would fear being the next victims. Violence in Breathitt County was still as intimate as it had been during the Civil War. For the rest of his life Strong was wary of attacks but, for the most part, he strode around his home county without fear.

As horrible as this new state of affairs was, Captain Strong could always claim that, starting with the national rebellion he helped vanquish, his killing was always a response, not a drawing of first blood. He never tried to justify his actions, except perhaps in one apocryphal exchange published just after his death. "On one occasion a citizen of Breathitt county was sentenced to two years in the penitentiary for killing a man. He met Capt. Strong a few minutes after sentence had been passed and asked: 'How is it, Capt. Strong, that when I kill one man they send me to the penitentiary, and when you kill twenty men you are not even indicted?' The captain replied: 'I was right when I killed my men, and you were wrong.'"[212] Untold numbers of white southerners dissented against their respective communities during the war, and many continued to do so during the Reconstruction years. Few, however, were willing to commit warlike atrocities like Strong did (the bulk of historical scholarship insists Unionists were far more likely to be victims than aggressors). Fewer still kept up after white Democratic "home rule" was complete. It is difficult to imagine that William Strong would go to such great lengths if he did not believe in the righteousness of his actions.

Or that of the Red Strings. Another reason for Strong's lack of indictments was the plausible deniability his followers' loyalty afforded him. Henderson Kilburn, broadly estimated the deadliest Red String, supposedly carried out most, if not all, of these ambushes. In January 1884 he and a Negro teenager named Ben Strong (most likely a descendant of Strong family slaves) were arrested for the murder of a purported Klansman named William Thorp. Thorp, before dying, identified Kilburn as his killer but Ben Strong was named as an accomplice for hiding Kilburn and bringing him food. After their arraignment both men were kept in the jailhouse without bail to await the next circuit court session. Sometime after midnight on April 9, approximately fifty masked men, "very orderly in their proceedings" and "under a leader who directed every movement with precision and dispatch," gathered around the jail and forcibly extracted them. The pair was then hanged side by side from the courthouse portico, both bodies pinned with notes instructing that they not be removed for a day.[213] As always, the courthouse, the physical embodiment of the polis, was crucial to those who sought to bring about change, and to those who tried to prevent it. Just as William Strong's capture of the courthouse ten years earlier represented the Red Strings' attempt to reaffirm their wartime victory in Breathitt County, the lynching of Henderson Kilburn and Ben Strong in front of the same structure demonstrated that their crimes violated the commonweal and that deadly justice was meted out in a public setting.[214]

The murder of Judge Burnett and the lynchings nearly six years later showed that local Democrats had realized that their own brand of extralegal violence was necessary for the maintenance of their status quo. The double lynching was met with approval both in Breathitt County and in the outside world. Since arriving in Jackson a year earlier, Methodist missionary John J. Dickey had witnessed various small crimes supposedly brought about by alcohol and isolation and, in his judgment, this was no coincidence. After seeing the mob gather, he knew that their deaths reflected "the sentiment of the county" and "a better, healthier public sentiment" to come. Even though he was evidently unsure of their identities, Dickey assured himself that "these regulators [were] of the better class."[215] At least one Bluegrass editor agreed with Dickey. "The war in Breathitt County has ended," he said shortly after the lynching. "Circuit court is now in session and perfect peace prevails."[216]

Lynching, the "definitive metaphor for racial oppression," appeared in Breathitt County just as it began to increase in much of the rest of the South—and with the concomitant rituals and procedures associated with lynching for decades to come.[217] Its first recorded usage in Breathitt (the first two, according to the most comprehensive survey, of seven lynching victims in Kentucky that year) coincided with eastern Kentucky's becoming the generally accepted locale for feud violence.[218] White Kentuckians considered lynching a more orderly form of violence than anything feud suggested—in fact, this form of majoritarian violence that so many white Kentuckians looked upon with approval might yet have proven to be the cure for feuds and the outlawry they entailed (although some Democrats interpreted the lynching as a renewal of "the old feud").[219] The lynching of the two men at the county's seat of government indicated not only that their deaths were the will of the county's population but also that the lynching had been acted out in the interest of law and order, a law and order determined by the wealthier landowners who headed the local Democratic Party.[220] A highly ritualized, grisly performance, it was communal in one sense. But, like many other lynchings of the era, it was overtly political as well, since it was directed at those who had challenged the prevailing political party.[221]

And it apparently performed its intended function. The lynching of his most brutal compatriot and the black man who shared his surname marked the end of William Strong's aggression. After rumors circulated that he would avenge their deaths, Strong instead sent a request that their bodies be sent to him so that they could be "both buried in the same grave on his farm among their friends."[222] Until his death in 1897, Strong remained the "chieftain" of the county's squatters and the dwindling black population (Hiram Freeman and his surviving family apparently left the county not long after his sons' deaths). Still, Strong would no longer attempt insurrections, act as a public endorser or enforcer during elections, or order the assassinations of his political enemies. Friendship with legitimate authorities was in the past, too, after "staunch Democrat" Robert Riddell replaced William Randall as circuit court judge.[223] Any serious challenge to Democratic authority in Breathitt County, at least in the violent form that Strong preferred, had now come to an end. He was nearing sixty at the time of the lynching; his two youngest children—a ten-year-old son and a six-year-old daughter—still lived under his roof.[224] Even after his former cavalry commander Henry Clay Lilly was narrowly elected as a Republican circuit judge in 1886, Strong still lay low, and he continued to do so until the last months of his life.[225]

In most of its characteristics this lynching was an event inherent to its time and place. Captain William Strong fought the one-party rule that took over the South after Reconstruction came to an end—a rule that had a head start in his home state. Two members of his small fighting force perished in a way identical, almost in minute detail, to that of so many other black and white southerners who skirted its authority. However, the peculiar contingencies of life in Breathitt County gave this lynching its most unusual trait: the races of its victims. Cooperation between a young Negro and a violent white squatter, the very fruition of what white conservatives feared most, represented an obstruction to that commercial order, Breathitt County's own iteration of what would come to be known as the New South.[226] Neither that nor the broader phenomenon of lynching fit easily into the interpretation of violence suggested by feud. The 1884 lynching went on to be the most forgotten recorded incident of violence in Breathitt County's history.

Perhaps there were elements of feud in Strong and the Red Strings' ongoing assaults against Breathitt County Democrats. He was certainly faring better than southern Unionists who might have attempted what he was doing after Redemption. Perhaps in another part of the South he would not have survived his bold ventures of 1874 and 1878; and, since Strong had managed to carry out his quasi-guerrilla actions for so long afterward, did this mean there was some modicum of a horizontal conflict between equals? In a county with a small population, these were people who knew one another's identities quite well, and indeed there was surely some amount of personal enmity involved. Nevertheless, that he and the Red Strings were identified as "feudists" meant that the differences between them and other southern

Unionists were emphasized while their similarities were concealed. Considering the disorder developing in eastern Kentucky in the mid-1880s, his was only one group among many, a developing trend that white Kentuckians preferred be interpreted as, if not "feudal," then certainly as nonpolitical. "There is much talk of the outlaws in . . . Breathitt, and other counties of Eastern Kentucky, belonging to Democratic or Republican factions," wrote a western Kentucky Democrat in 1885. "This is all humbug, they are violators of law, and should be spoken of and dealt with as such."[227]

There was far more to the story than *feud* suggested, a complexity of postbellum politics in a border state combined with the endogenous intricacies of life in Breathitt County. It was in Kentucky Democrats' interest that this sort of complexity went unexplored. Relying on the idea of feuding performed their task quite effectively, especially as Breathitt County's economic potential came to the attention of the outside world.

4

"THE CIVILIZING AND CHRISTIANIZING EFFECTS OF MATERIAL IMPROVEMENT AND DEVELOPMENT"

Chaos was the law of nature; Order was the dream of man.
—Henry Adams, "The Grammar of Science," in
The Education of Henry Adams (1907)

On Christmas Day 1884, Louisville's *Courier-Journal* printed an unsigned letter from Breathitt County touting "the richest undeveloped timber, coal, and iron district in America." In the last three years "Northern parties" had bought nearly twenty-five thousand acres of forestland (Breathitt County's average land value was estimated at 92¢ per acre).[1] The long-anticipated Kentucky Union Railway Company (KU) had bought twenty times that amount in and around Breathitt County in order to link its coalfields to the Bluegrass and eventually create a transmontane connection to southwestern Virginia and, by extension, to the Chesapeake Bay.[2] A Harvard geologist offered his high expectations of the future rail line's capabilities in a KU promotional booklet.

> The line of the Kentucky Union Railway has . . . certain especial advantages over any other, in that it crosses the coal and iron belt at its widest part, and where there is the heaviest timber. . . . The distance from the eastern coal field to Louisville by this line would be *shorter than by any other*. . . . I believe it to be one of the most important roads for the mineral interests of Kentucky that can possibly be built. . . . The mountains of Kentucky, far from being a barrier to the passage of railways, constitute on the whole, a region more fitted for their passage than the Bluegrass Country.[3]

The KU's promoters predicted that theirs would be the Bluegrass's first direct access to "the only place in America where cannel coal can be successfully mined," connecting Kentucky's commercialized center with the Cumberland Gap by railway for the first time, making Jackson "a capital city" and Breathitt "a wealthier county than any in the bluegrass region."[4] Breathitt's future was looking up, and potential investors in Louisville or the Bluegrass were about to miss out.

Even this most booster-minded of communiqués was obliged to mention the county's checkered past, but only to announce its repentance. The chartering of a new school and the growth of Methodist and Presbyterian congregations demonstrated "marked change" in the "minds and purposes of our people":

> Our county people are not lacking in the qualities that have made mountain people famous in history, if their bottled-up energies in times past have found vent in partisan faction fights and neighborhood broils. With no communication with the outside world and no other way of working off superfluous steams, they must not be wholly blamed. They have had few opportunities for education of any kind. If their past annals have been more akin to those of the Highland Scotch and the boys of Tipperary, please believe that the days of local warfare are past, and nowhere will you find more quiet, earnest thought as to a great future than among some of the leaders of our county, which may yet pay more taxes into the State treasury than any two of the richest Bluegrass counties.[5]

The letter, presumably written by a Breathitt native, referenced Kentucky mountaineers' supposedly Celtic past and seclusion from the outside world with the same metaphors and comparisons used by local-color writers and home-mission workers.[6] The writer's clear intention was that the "bottled-up energies" and "superfluous steams" of his (or her?) less enlightened neighbors be channeled toward more profitable motives. With the Red Strings now at bay (the lynching of Henderson Kilburn and Ben Strong having taken place just seven months earlier), the political reasons for recent troubles were left unspoken, and for good reason, since potential Bluegrass financiers surely did not need to be reminded of the Civil War. The county's Democratic majority was sound, and prepared to guide commerce and advancement into its hills.

This pleading for investment and firm declaration of separating present from past were in keeping with the speculative strategy that had led to
Breathitt's founding forty-five years earlier. Jeremiah South and his associates had a vision of railroads and massive timber and coal extraction, but
these plans had not come to fruition in South's lifetime—instead, the county
had become known as an uncivilized containment of chaos (some of which
might have been avoided had South et al. not guided the county in favor of
the Confederacy).

Since 1874 the media discourse on Breathitt County violence was
intertwined with demands for industrial modernization. For sectional
and political reasons, the *New York Times* preferred to editorialize on
Breathitt County as a Kentucky problem rather than a mountain one: "All
her best citizens deplore and condemn the violence which has so long
disgraced her and made her seem deliberately barbarous. Kentucky is, as
everybody knows, a fine State, which needs development."[7] Bluegrass correspondents accompanying the state militia, however, saw things from a
different perspective. They exclaimed, as if entering some untouched terra
incognita, at the wealth of coal seams and virgin timber in what was, at
the time, the physically largest county in Kentucky.[8] The county had been
geologically surveyed decades earlier, and the findings had long been a
matter of public record. A sample of Breathitt cannel coal had won a gold
medal at Philadelphia's Centennial International Exposition in 1876.[9]
Though the Bluegrass had been collecting the Commonwealth's revenue
and casting its votes for years, now the county and its wealth were "discovered." Furthermore, the 1878 reawakening of Bloody Breathitt coincided
with Democrats' glacial acceptance of state-funded improvement of the
Kentucky River system—no doubt encouraged by coal prices soaring far
above "poor men's prices."[10] Articles stressed economic development's
utility in ending eastern Kentucky's lawless atmosphere—even by press-
men who traditionally balked at any and all government expenditure.
"The late disturbance in Breathitt county is only another argument in
favor of improving the navigation of the Kentucky river," the Bourbon
Democratic *Kentucky Yeoman* opined. "If we had good locks and dams,
it would be an easy matter to send troops from Lexington or Frankfort to
quell any unlawful outbreak in that remote quarter."[11] And in a later article,
the "insurrection against the civil authority" was blamed on "the further
want of the civilizing and Christianizing effects of material improvement
and development."[12] Even the *Courier-Journal* correspondent who said he

preferred taking his chances with Sitting Bull rather than living in Breathitt hoped that, with proper state funding, "the hills would reverberate with the sound of the woodman's ax and the whistle of the locomotive and steamboat, and employment would be given to thousands of men."[13] Just a few months before the Christmas Day letter, Harvard professor Nathaniel Shaler predicted "money, avarice, that master passion of the race, will subdue this archaic vice of violence."[14]

The newness of these discoveries was exaggerated to highlight Breathitt County's isolation from the polis of the Bluegrass. Nevertheless, there is little doubt that the publicity surrounding Judge Burnett's death and the resultant militia occupation of Jackson accelerated interest in Breathitt County's coal and timber. In 1885 an Ohio land speculator acquired sixty-seven thousand acres of timber and coal land and published an account of its potential wealth.[15] Echoing his report four years later, Charles Dudley Warner estimated that Breathitt County's untouched cannel coal seams "excel[led] the most celebrated coals of Great Britain, predicting it would "have a market all over the country when the railways reach it."[16] As always, plans for future development were leavened with promises of social uplift: "When railroads are built through these mountains civilization will reach the inhabitants, and the example of thrift and consequent profit will, no doubt, play its full part in inspiring a desire to indulge in habits of industry. Until then there is little chance of their improvement."[17] It was not supposed that railroads and "habits of industry" brought with them complications that could cause violence just as easily as prevent it.

"Free American citizens who break up courts, and shoot Judges, and carve their political opponents, would not be likely to tolerate missionaries"

Railroads and coal and timber companies could arrive only at a rate that was physically and economically feasible. Track laying from the Bluegrass to the Cumberland Plateau required tremendous expenditures for even the most well-heeled investment firms. To make matters worse, the KU's Louisville lawyers were so ignorant of their state's geography they confused "Breathitt" with "Bourbon," a Bluegrass county, when giving instructions to land surveyors.[18] As was the case in Breathitt County's first years of existence, capitalists' mastery of the local economy depended upon their relative knowledge of the place itself.

Before that could happen, Breathitt County's ill repute attracted what Appalachian scholars consider industrialization's scouts: outside evangelists. As of the late 1870s, eastern Kentucky became a favorite destination for missionaries who had given up on the uplift of the lowland South's freed-people, and may well have been the original target of eastern Kentucky's storied missions field.[19] "You will be astonished to learn that there is not a single church building in Breathitt county . . . not even at the county seat, not even a schoolhouse in that town," one missionary reported in 1883. "The true Sabbath is unknown, Sunday being a holiday spent in hunting, fishing, shooting-matches, logging, etc."[20] The eastern Kentucky mountains were "strongholds of cruelty and oppression" ripe to be "invaded" by Protestant enlightenment. Boasting of his recent conversions, one home missionary proclaimed that "people who had been kept under the power of darkness for a century past were brought to see the glorious dawn of a better day."[21] Four years later, it was still generally agreed that Breathitt County was "a type of all that was darkest and most God forsaken in the mountains of [Kentucky]."[22]

But Breathitt County had never been so heathen as it was sometimes claimed. Since the very earliest days of white settlement, the Three Forks region had a willing spirit of Christian belief, even though it was hindered by a weak flesh of few churches. The county's "native" Christian faith was the "Hardshell" or "Iron Jacket" Old Regulars, antinomian Baptists whose only access to corporate worship was the occasional camp meeting organized by an itinerant preacher.[23] Antebellum worship services were freewheeling. Occasionally, so recalled George Washington Noble, children initiated their own impromptu prayer meetings without adult guidance.[24] Charlatans were met with merciless skepticism. Once an unaffiliated faith healer named Jeremiah Lovelace the Prophet visited the county to publicly walk on water. He failed to perform his miracle only after some young "Doubting Thomases" removed the planks he had placed beneath the rushing river's surface, causing Lovelace's near drowning in front of an unsympathetic audience.[25]

Antebellum religious activity was not always so unorthodox. In the early 1840s wealthy farmer Simon Cockrell sponsored the ministry of "Raccoon John" Smith, an early preacher for the Disciples of Christ (also known as the Christian Church or, more generally, the "Campbellites" after the denomination's founders, Thomas and Alexander Campbell). Cockrell's son-in-law Jeremiah W. South and his family were associated with the

Bluegrass-centered denomination, and its arrival paralleled their role in connecting Breathitt County with the other side of the two Kentuckys.[26] But, lacking church buildings and permanent congregations, the Disciples were as limited to the occasional camp meeting as were the more decentralized Baptists. The 1878 Jackson courthouse riot made Breathitt County appear quite heathen, perhaps redeemable, perhaps not. In reaction to plans for New York missionary societies to send missions to Breathitt County (they reasoned that southern mountaineers' prior knowledge of English made their souls more winnable than those of Africans or Indians), the Republican *Cincinnati Gazette* scoffed: "Free American citizens who break up courts, and shoot Judges, and carve their political opponents, would not be likely to tolerate missionaries."[27]

Urban sneers could not deter the outpouring of interdenominational zeal flowing in all directions in the years following Reconstruction, especially for the least of these like Bloody Breathitt. While Breathitt County caught northern missionaries' eyes, Bluegrass evangelists had the most lasting impact upon the county. The anti-Calvinist "Mountain Evangelist" George Owen Barnes visited shortly after Judge Burnett's murder. Although he found one local boy to be "a young savage, as ignorant as a Hottentot," he was impressed by his Breathitt congregation's willingness to include Negroes in "a better looking crowd than the average of court crowds in the Bluegrass."[28] Barnes was enraptured when, at a camp meeting, the notorious John Aikman and other "desperate men . . . who had been at the centre of so many awful fights in Breathitt [came] to Jesus like little children."[29]

Barnes was succeeded by John Jay Dickey, a Methodist minister who initially passed through in 1882 out of "curiosity to see the people of Breathitt County because of the feuds."[30] He eventually decided to preach there and expand the county's meager public education. Finding no church buildings in Jackson, Dickey held services in the courthouse using a pipe organ Barnes had left behind.[31] With help from the KU's president and vice president, Dickey raised money for what was to become the Jackson Academy (later Lees College), Jackson's first attempt at schooling beyond the primary level.[32] In 1886 he augmented the new school with a two-thousand-volume county library, a rare civic treasure in the rural South, let alone the Kentucky mountains.[33]

Next came Presbyterian minister and physician Edward Guerrant in 1884. Guerrant had last visited the county two decades earlier as a Confederate lieutenant under Humphrey Marshall's command, at which time he had first developed a jaundiced eye toward the "bitter, prejudiced and ignorant" highlanders.[34] Parlaying old wartime acquaintances, he quickly established a congregation, and spent the next seven years attempting to wrest Breathitt County's religious life away from Dickey (the latter, it seemed, was unaware of there being any competition).[35] When Mormon elders arrived at century's end, their impact on local worship habits was negligible.[36]

Aside from their denominational differences, the contrasts between Guerrant and Dickey were marked. With an unconcealed prejudice toward mountain society that originated during his Confederate service, Guerrant fit the mold of missionaries who conflated "civilizing" with Gospel spreading. Either was cure for the Kentucky mountains' inherent proclivity toward deadly violence. His later writings display the common late nineteenth-century explanations of Appalachian otherness that combined racial determinism and spatial isolation. "The law is slow and lax in its administration, and so the people take it into their own hands," he explained after decades in the mission field. "There is some excuse for this; but the crying cause back of all this violence and bloodshed is the want of religion."[37] So, too, did he propagate other familiar tropes of preindustrial mountain life. "They are today the purest stock of Scotch-Irish and Anglo-Saxon races on the continent. For hundreds of years they have lived isolated from the outside world, with no foreign intermixture. I do not remember seeing a foreigner in the Cumberland mountains. They are not a degenerate people. They are a brave, independent, high-spirited people, whose poverty and location have isolated them from the advantages of education and religion. They have been simply passed by in the march of progress in this great age, because they were out of the way."[38] Guerrant was convinced that many, if not most, Kentucky mountaineers were "as utterly ignorant of the way of salvation as the heathen in China," and that his ministry was reaching previously untested territory.[39] Some mountaineers took issue with his arrogant assumption of their "want of the Gospel" previous to his arrival.[40] "We may be mighty ignorant back here," one of Breathitt County's "principal men" told another Presbyterian evangelist, "but we're not such fools as to not know who Jesus Christ is."[41] A few years later a local judge presented Dickey with a similar complaint. "We need no missionaries from the Blue Grass or from any other place . . . we know enough if we would only practice it. We have religion enough if we would only use it."[42] George Barnes, who had personal gripes with the more Calvinist segments of Knox's church, expressed annoyance at Presbyterians who claimed too much credit for "evangeliz[ing] dear old

George O. Barnes, the "Mountain Evangelist," was not the first preacher to preach the Gospel in Breathitt County. He was, however, apparently the first to arrive after the county became known as Bloody Breathitt. (Price, *Without Scrip or Purse*)

James J. Dickey, Methodist minister, educator, and newspaperman, tried harder than anyone to understand Bloody Breathitt. He spoke for other white Kentuckians when it came to distinguishing justifiable violence from chaos. (Courtesy of the Kentucky Wesleyan College Archives, Owensboro)

'Bloody Breathitt'" and predicted that haughtier preachers like Guerrant might turn tail should "some of [Barnes's] darling 'desperadoes' temporarily resume their abandoned habits."[43]

Dickey and Guerrant were both Bluegrass natives but, while his competitor portrayed Breathitt County as a far-flung exotic locale, Dickey expressed a kinship with most of the people he met—they were, after all, fellow white Kentuckians with plans to improve their state. Guerrant never seemed to have abandoned his image of a homogenous Anglo-Saxon mountain population, but Dickey recognized early on (just, in fact, after witnessing the lynching of Henderson Kilburn and Ben Strong) that his adopted community was led by a "better class" of white propertied men, and he fashioned his appeals for help in his enterprises in a way amenable to the Three Forks middle class and landed gentry.[44] Dickey welcomed local preachers (mostly lay ministers) to his pulpit for ecumenical services. Though he had initially thought

Former Confederate officer Reverend Edward O. Guerrant, whose wartime impressions of Breathitt County and his later ministries there shaped public opinion of eastern Kentucky: "The crying cause back of all this violence and bloodshed is the want of religion." (Courtesy of Aaron Akey)

Breathitt Countians to be "primitive" before his arrival, he never seemed to have wanted to radically change the environment in which he preached (his connections with the Kentucky Union Railroad notwithstanding). He dedicated countless hours to interviewing locals for information on their pioneer ancestors. He did not consider his new parishioners any sort of pure ethnic "stock" (no purer than his own, anyway), and insisted that "*environment* and not *heredity*" (Dickey's emphasis) was to blame for "the chasm between the people of the Blue Grass and the mountains."[45]

Denominational tensions in Bloody Breathitt never came to blows, and locals figured that "better times [were] sure to come."[46] Bluegrass observers approved of the Gospel's propagation, but they also appreciated the economic dividends of pacification. "The preacher in Breathitt saves ammunition to the State and saves money to the taxpayers while I doubt if all the missionaries who ever went to China have saved a dollar to anybody or cheated the devil out of a single almond-eyed Washee Washee man," wrote one Lexington commentator.[47] A correspondent from the Democratic *Hazel Green Herald* (the newspaper most local to Breathitt until the 1890s) concurred: "The preaching of Barnes . . . Guerrant, Dickey and others, has saved the State more money than the courts and all the military companies that have been sent among us," said one who thought the reforming influence of mountain evangelism should be rewarded with state revenue. "And a bad man changed from his evil ways by the gospel becomes an instrument of good instead of evil."[48] Further celebration was made of the conversions of "notable characters" like Aikman, Jerry Little, and one of William Strong's sons—although the senior Strong was not yet persuaded; Little reportedly offered Guerrant personal protection from the belligerent old captain ("the gospel of peace" having no need of bodyguards, the preacher demurred).[49] By 1886 it seemed that Breathitt had become one of "the quietest and most orderly counties in the Commonwealth."[50] As more credit was cast to the Gospel's civilizing effects and the promise of peace and railroads, fewer questions were asked as to what conflicts had made Breathitt bloody in the first place.

The Reverend Dickey shepherded church growth and public education and capped it off with another sort of civic engagement. In 1891 he leased the two-year old *Jackson Hustler*, Breathitt's first newspaper, founded by "a moral, enterprising young Kentuckian . . . whose father [had] vast landed interests" in the county.[51] Though he disliked the name "Hustler," it became his pulpit for preaching a prosperity gospel based upon prognostications of future wealth, owing to the good graces of "wealth and enterprise" that were beginning to take notice of the region's cannel coal. Like other boosters, Dickey suggested that his adopted home had only recently been "discovered"—even by its own inhabitants.

> Eastern Kentucky lay for almost one hundred years after the organization of the State a veritable terra incognita. Her mines of wealth and her illimitable forests were as completely unknown to the world as were the gold and silver of the Sierras and Rockies to the Apaches and Arapahoes. The old hunters roamed over these mountains after the wild game just as the red man did over Pike's Peak and the Black Hills, and equally as ignorant of the great possibilities around and beneath him. Wealth and enterprise have eyes that see. As soon as the commercial world learned of our great resources, experts were dispatched in haste to see if there was any truth in the reports that they had heard, and in every case the answer was, "the half has not been told."
>
> In no part of the United States is there such promise to the capitalist as this region to-day offers. Fortunes have been made and the development has only begun. The increase is biblical, "some thirty, some sixty and some a hundred fold."
>
> The capitalists are following the money gods to these mountain fastnesses and their devotion to this cause will be rewarded with thrones and kingdoms and scepters and crowns.[52]

This regalia—driven by Christianity, lucre, or both (like many Americans, Dickey saw little distance between the God of Abraham he professed and the "money gods" he prophesied)—would permanently alter the environmental factors that had created Bloody Breathitt. When he went to establish a new mission in London, Kentucky, in 1895, Dickey left behind a county that had become more interconnected with the urban centers of the Bluegrass while still retaining its internal political autonomy—prototypically Kentuckian.[53]

Still, "the civilizing and Christianizing effects of material improvement and development" did not heal the county's reputation, even as feud violence appeared in less remote places like northeastern Kentucky's Rowan County.[54] When news of multiple killings in Rowan's county seat reached the press, immediate reaction was to compare it to the recent "bloody internecine feuds of Breathitt."[55] In fact, Breathitt's new national attention as the center of the home-missions field may well have increased its notoriety as an inherently vicious place. Even as Dickey (who saw Breathitt's recent improvement as a positive example for other trouble spots like Rowan) and Guerrant built successful ministries, others considered Breathitt County too dangerous for even the most intrepid.[56] One American Missionary Association member warned, "Last fall a friend of ours had occasion to ride through the country; he was assured by the best citizens that it was not safe for a man to be on the [Jackson] streets after dark" (an outrageous circumstance in a community with "no foreign-born residents").[57] The *Hazel Green Herald* often sprang to its neighbor's defense, recognizing the subjectivity of "feud" as a descriptor of crime and often pointing out the contemporary rise in urban crime.[58] "For some years it has been, it seems, the mission of some of the Louisville daily papers to magnify any murder committed in one of the mountain counties, into a 'bloody faction or family feud' and their readers are treated to a most sensational account of an affair, but for its location, would only have been given as an ordinary bit of news. The ordinary killings in Louisville . . . if committed in any of the mountain counties would be heralded by the Louisville papers as 'mountain lawlessness.'"[59] Citing the recent construction of "two handsome church edifices and an elegant high school building" in 1885, the *Herald* declared, "Breathitt county is awakening to the fact that she does not deserve the malignant epithets which in the past have so frequently been bandied around and boosted by the press at large."[60] The paper faintly praised an 1886 political rally said to have numbered between six hundred and eight hundred men, where "everything passed off in the most perfect order."[61] Even after an Election Day stabbing a week later, the *Herald* insisted that "the fighting [was] not so bad as reported. Bloody Breathitt is not so bad, after all, when she gets justice."[62] When the courthouse burned to the ground two months after that, a Breathitt County correspondent did not draw the intuitive correlations with the 1873 courthouse burning but blandly reasoned that the fire had settled the long-debated question over building a new one.[63] Even in Bloody Breathitt fights could be isolated events, crimes could be punished, and accidents could happen.

"The Republican vote of Kentucky is made up very largely, if not almost entirely, of negroes and mountaineers"

If Breathitt County was improving itself under the tutelage of the Reverend Dickey and others like him, it was not recovering only from the county's local history. It was also rising above traits associated with the Kentucky mountains en masse. By 1880 Americans were coming to believe that "the eastern section of Kentucky [was] almost as foreign to the rest of the State as is Siberia to St. Petersburg."[64] A large part of this development came from popular depictions of upland white southerners that local-color writers were using to great effect in the last years of Reconstruction and afterward.[65] Not long after, the idea of the South's male "white savage," be he lowland or upland, became an increasingly useful device for convincing northern audiences that white-on-black interracial violence was "a fact of social life, almost a force of nature . . . cultural inheritance so deeply ingrained that it might as well be biologically rooted."[66] And there was also a growing nationwide disdain toward rural America North, South, East, or West; in the 1880s *hillbilly* was only one of many newly popular scornful names— *hayseed, rube, hick*—for the yeomanry.[67] The othering of eastern Kentucky was integral to Democrats' marginalizing of the state's Republican minority— a rhetorical process that "not only legitimized the state's Confederate identity but made it look like the preferable, more civilized one."[68] Despite electoral evidence to the contrary, eastern Kentucky was assumed to be a one-party section, the better to fence it off from the South's white mainstream (where white-on-black interracial violence was not necessarily defended but, in the "New Departure" mind, understandable).[69]

This was more exaggeration than outright falsehood. Kentucky mountaineers were just as attracted to the Republican Party as were upland southerners in other states.[70] Voting the same ticket as black southerners made them the target of Democratic derision just as in other southern states, although the charge was levied in slightly modified language. "The Republican vote of Kentucky is made up very largely, if not almost entirely, of negroes and mountaineers," wrote one Democrat in 1889. "As a Union soldier I was fond of the old chestnut about the mountains being cradles of liberty, because our volunteers in Kentucky were mostly recruited from these cradles. It is current belief that the mountains of Kentucky are cradles of illiteracy and lawlessness, and that deadly feuds are rife in these Republican strongholds."[71] For the novelist John Fox Jr., mountain Republicanism encapsulated eastern Kentucky's paradoxical domesticity and strangeness, and one-party rule was a theme common to most of his novels about eastern Kentucky.[72] By 1895 the conflation of Lincoln's party with mountain isolation and poverty was so complete a western Kentucky editor (who should have known better) counted unfalteringly Democratic Breathitt County among "four Republican pauper counties."[73] Democrats still had use for the exaggeration over the course of the following decade, such as when Senator Joseph Blackburn declared that "lawlessness in Kentucky is confined to the mountains," surmising (without elaboration) that "many years ago all the escaped convicts from the adjoining States fled into the mountains of Kentucky, and their descendants are now raising the devil."[74]

"Negroes and mountaineers" were two populations that white lowland Kentuckians had come to see as inferior or dangerous. They were not maligned equally; Senator Blackburn apparently did not count 1904's lynchings of at least two black men and one black woman within the confines of Kentucky's "lawlessness."[75] The mountain white was defined by, if nothing else, whiteness, and his vote was not taken away. However, it could be contained; in 1880 Kentucky's Democrat-controlled legislature gerrymandered a new congressional district circling most of the old Whig Gibraltar counties, effectively segregating most of the state's Republican electorate.[76] But they were both, nonetheless, maligned. Their shared membership in the hated Republican Party was a valuable weapon in the Democratic arsenal. The section's membership in the Republican Party, *any* political party, proved it to be a decidedly modern "participatory" political culture, even if observers from the Bluegrass or other parts of the outside world wanted it to be a "parochial" or "tribal" one. No other part of the American Republic has had its elected officials described by historians as "feudal lords" and "chieftains."[77] At the battle of New Orleans, the "Hunters of Kentucky" had represented the American Republic's "civic and archaic" backbone, "rustic citizen warriors" who mingled violence and egalitarianism to form a "virtuous militia" against imperial standing armies.[78] Two-thirds of a century later, however, Kentuckians who seemed to most resemble their ancestors were no longer venerated in the same way. The difference was that in the War of 1812, unlike the more recent war, all Kentuckians had been on the same side.

After southern conservatives introduced it as a tool of depoliticization during Reconstruction, *feud* became more specifically associated with the Kentucky mountains in the mid-1880s, largely because of various feud scenarios identified by the *Louisville Courier-Journal* and other newspapers. By the turn of the century, Kentucky's Democratic newspapers, even those in the mountains, derisively referred to their state's unfortunate "feud belt."[79] The feud belt's fictive designation established Republican eastern Kentucky as a political culture distinct from the American norm—even when the southern Democracy still carried with it the taint of Confederate recalcitrance.[80]

Henry Watterson's paper was liberal in its use of the word *feud,* applying it to isolated knife fights, brawls, and riots involving up to a dozen men, and to larger-scale affairs like the "Rowan County War." The only common denominator was that they were all white-on-white intraracial attacks and killings (ergo horizontal violence between equals) at a time when white-on-black interracial attacks and deaths were still very common in the state; between 1884 and 1886 at least a dozen black Kentuckians were lynched.[81]

Succinctly, the "feud belt" comprised a section of Kentucky that was supposedly homogenously Republican, a purposeful, long-lived oversimplification of mountain society.[82] It was useful to Democratic state authorities faced with inveigling the public and maintaining law and order even as Kentucky bucked the prevailing southern trend in gradually becoming a two-party state. This task fell most heavily on Governor Simon Bolivar Buckner, a former Confederate lieutenant general whose administration marked the end of unchallenged Confederate control over Kentucky's executive functions. Buckner's election in 1887 was narrow, and his record number of vetoes showed a diminished Democratic dominance.[83] Perhaps it is no coincidence that his administration played host to eastern Kentucky's most pronounced series of "feud" violence, mostly in counties lacking one-party dominance.[84] Early in his administration Buckner dealt with his state's most storied "feud," that of the Hatfield and McCoy families in Pike County, Kentucky, and Logan County, West Virginia. Buckner became embroiled in an extradition debacle with the neighboring state's governor and reluctantly sent a segment of the state militia to Pike County. Of all the well-known "Kentucky feuds," that of the Hatfields and McCoys had the least obvious ties to party politics. Still, Pike County lawyer and entrepreneur Perry Cline, who manipulated all parties involved without once firing a gun, was among Buckner's most faithful mountain allies. Both wealthy Democrats reaped benefits from the feud's outcome.[85] Decades later, the same area along the Kentucky–West Virginia border experienced a completely separate series of conflicts combining local politics with the fight between capital and industrial labor, and culminating in the "Matewan Massacre." Since it was an area already defined by the inherency suggested by "the feudin' Hatfields and McCoys," Americans in the outside world "turned a blind eye and a deaf ear" to the later events' contingencies.[86]

Not long after, unrest erupted in at least three contiguous counties in southeastern Kentucky. A conflict between a Three Forks Battalion officer's son and a newcomer in Perry County, both of them wealthy merchants, arose sometime in the mid-1880s and increased in notoriety as their hired gun-men fell.[87] Republican Joseph Eversole's private war with Democratic rival Fulton French supposedly originated in the former's efforts to protect local landowners from the machinations of land speculators.[88] As Perry County's poorer landowners' aggressive advocate, Eversole had a bit of a numerical advantage among its male, fighting-age citizens. To counter it, French sought out "thugs" from Breathitt County.[89] Jerry South III, the grandson of eastern Kentucky's most ambitious land speculation schemer to date, was among French's "lieutenants."[90] When he was finally brought to trial in 1895 for the various Perry County murders, French began a successful process toward acquittal by securing a change of venue to Breathitt in 1895.[91] By then, he had already resided there for six years, amassing property and strengthening ties to Jackson's Democratic elites. Less than a decade later, he was impli-cated—but never convicted—in more politically motivated homicides.[92] But not before his war with the Eversole faction had spilled into Breathitt, Knott, and Harlan counties, perhaps creating a more chaotic state of affairs than what had started in Perry.[93] The *Hazel Green Herald* disingenuously assured readers that "there are no politics involved, it being merely a personal feud that has extended until both parties have gathered up friends, who, previous to the quarrel, knew neither party."[94]

Around the same time, Harlan County's "Howard-Turner feud" erupted between a Republican gang and members of a Democratic courthouse ring who (according to one of the former) "wanted to be the supreme rulers of the universe" behind the guise of "Law & Order."[95] By the county judge's own admission, a seeming majority within the county either "openly espouse[d] their cause or quietly [lent] . . . aid, comfort or refuge" to the Republican outlaws Will Jennings and Wilson Howard (the judge attributed this to kin-ship—he did not address whatever grievances they had against him and his court).[96] Once Governor Buckner was convinced that local coal and timber operations were being impeded, he sent state troops, just as he had in Perry County.[97] The series of ambushes and skirmishes that comprised the 1889 conflict were roundly identified as actions within a "family feud," despite the large number of surnames involved. Also, the fact that the preexistent tension had flared into violence just after Fulton French had begun recruiting gun-men in the county went unexplored.[98] Eventually, most of the oral folklore regarding the events accepted the "trivial causes and tragic consequences" of the standard feud narrative without including exogenous details.[99] The actions of individuals, and their intentions, were hidden behind surnames.

Feud, as it was understood in the nineteenth-century lexicon, was a reciprocal form of controlled violence between equals, and all accounts of the early days of the "French-Eversole feud" seem to follow this model even if the "Howard-Turner feud" did not; it was something approximating gang warfare more than interpersonal revenge.[100] However, by late 1888, the combination of the two led to a murderous crime wave in at least three of the six counties in Kentucky's nineteenth judicial circuit. In the eighteen weeks between court sessions, circuit court judge H. C. Lilly reported to Governor Buckner, there had been five killings and eleven nonfatal shootings. Court could not be held until juries and attorneys were unafraid to attend court. Despite Lilly's supplications to send a segment of the State Guard (a month earlier Buckner had dispatched seventy militiamen to Perry County), Buckner refused to believe Breathitt contained "any organized opposition to the civil authorities," instead claming it suffered from "acts of individual lawlessness."[101]

> It is needless for me to say to you that in a Republic the employ-
> ment of the military arm in enforcing the law is of rare necessity,
> and the occasion for its use should not be doubtful propriety. The
> law invests the civil authorities with ample powers to enforce the
> observance of law, and expects those officers to exert their authority
> with reasonable diligence. When this is done there is seldom an oc-
> casion when the military force can be employed without detriment
> to the public interests and without bringing the civil authorities into
> discredit. When a people are taught that they are not themselves
> the most important factor in the conservation of order in society
> and that they must depend upon the exertion of extraneous force
> to preserve order amongst themselves, they have lost their title to
> self-government, and are fit subjects for a military despotism. I do
> not believe that any portion of this Commonwealth has reached
> that degree of political degradation.[102]

Lilly's petition was one of many. A state prosecutor and mountain lawyers (and at least one doctor) from all over the district, Democrats and Repub-licans, implored Buckner to send troops.[103] However, Buckner shared only Lilly's letters with the press, making it appear that the former Union colonel had lost his nerve. Democrats scourged the "worthless and cowardly" judge for his impotence in his circuit.[104] "The court has not been held and the blame rests upon the shoulders of this Republican judge, who will neither perform his official duties nor exchange with a Democratic judge, who offers to travel his circuit unguarded and clear the docket for him," the *Louisville Courier-Journal* intoned.[105] The following August, the county failed to report election results for the first time since the 1860s.[106] Even though Bloody Breathitt had received more attention in the past for disorders, in terms of sheer number of deaths and ensuing public disruption, the last few months of the 1880s constituted the county's worst period since the Civil War.

It was also the first time a governor rejected pleas for peacekeeping in the county. By the end of 1891 peace was restored, but only after Buckner had purposefully humiliated Judge Lilly. The judge's criminal docket (said to cover "357 acres" of paper by December 1891), which included nine murders and fifteen malicious shooting indictments, was delayed for months.[107] When Lilly ran for reelection in 1892 a young Democratic lawyer, David B. Redwine, soundly defeated him with the help of endorsements from the *Jackson Hustler* and the *Hazel Green Herald* (which had crossed party lines to endorse Lilly in 1886) and Lilly's own wounded reputation in his district's most Democratic county.[108]

Americans who read of troubles in southeastern Kentucky were no strangers to violence on their own soil. Since the Civil War, the reading public had become aware of counterrevolutionary violence against black southerners, the Great Plains "Indian wars," and the industrial class war escalating in various cities.[109] Killing by various means for power-related reasons was commonplace. The eastern Kentucky feud phenomenon appeared strange to the outside world because this violence could not be legitimized in terms that late nineteenth-century Anglo-Americans could easily understand. White northerners and southerners devised ways of finding legitimacy in the preservation of the American nation and/or white supremacy when dealing with the recent memory of the war. Even northerners who despised white southerners' defiance during Reconstruction understood that the latter were fighting for the preservation of a political status quo threatened by black citizenship.[110] Skirmishes with the Great Plains Indian nations were an expanding nation's culling of an obstinate, dying race; it was reasoned that, in such an immense struggle over power, killing was inevitable.[111] These were struggles that made sense according to postbellum America's understanding of political violence—they were the kinds of violence that were allowed in the Pax Americana, even if bereft of state sanction, because they forwarded Anglo-American projects.

Factional fighting between white Americans for outwardly obscure reasons in obscure places could not be easily attached to the available legitimacies: furthering white supremacy, nationalism, and ever-expanding commerce. Outside of these contexts, violence could not be politically motivated but could only be defined as primordial, inexplicable, and senseless—and, most important, acted out between equals within a perfectly homogenous environment.[112] Fighting *among* Anglo-Americans did not fit into this puzzle of legitimate violence. However, for those who benefited from this bloodshed, namely, Buckner and his Democratic Party mates, it was better not to address the particulars; "acts of individual lawlessness" could scarcely be traced to the ballot box. But, with or without Buckner, even the fisticuffs and knifings in many urban or rural communities were interpreted according to the dictates of *feud* when they happened in Breathitt County or nearby.[113]

Nearby was key; overshadowed by the Hatfield-McCoy, Howard-Turner, and French-Eversole feuds, Bloody Breathitt was bereft of media attention during the Buckner administration, even though the latter two situations affected the county (feud violence crossing county boundaries complicated and called into question significant parts of the feud narrative—particularly insularity from the outside world). As Altina Waller has noted, there must be core reasons for the contemporaneous "wars" so close to each other in eastern Kentucky, an allusive "common denominator." Waller pointed to a number of factors leading to mountain farmers' mounting poverty—ineffective farming techniques, partible inheritance, and other late nineteenth-century developments (new state regulations on hunting and fishing, heightened enforcement of federal revenue laws, land amassment by railroads and speculators)—that damaged eastern Kentucky's yeoman economy, bringing "forest farming" to a bitter, plodding end.[114]

These were contributing factors, especially since this sort of poverty created a male population desensitized and inured to violence. However, they cannot fully explain the mass violence seen in southeastern Kentucky in the late 1880s since there were plenty of counties that did *not* have analogous "feuds" during this time, counties undergoing the same economic hardships. What Harlan and Perry counties did not have (and what more stable mountain counties did have by 1885 or earlier) was either Republican or Democratic one-party dominance, and they were in a part of the state where wartime rivalries remained even after more than two decades. Intense examinations of political conditions in either county during the 1880s would probably reveal preexistent civil disorder exacerbated by Buckner's election (the relative calm in both counties after he left office suggests that something had changed).[115] Indeed, even though feuding was first associated with the Kentucky mountains a few years earlier, the concurrence of factional wars roughly between 1887 and 1890 was when the phenomenon was cemented in the American psyche. It fell to public servants like Judge H. C. Lilly to confront the complexities involved. The vast majority of the reading public elsewhere in Kentucky and the United States preferred simpler, anti-introspective explanations with uncritical, Whiggish solutions, "relics of antiquity . . . Rapidly Dying Out Before Civilization's Advance."[116]

"What a mighty revolution!"

After being overshadowed by its neighbors for a few years, Bloody Breathitt caught media notice in May 1889 when Edward Strong's teenaged granddaughter eloped with a Negro named Milton Richmond. A posse pursued the couple and Richmond was fatally riddled with bullets after he fired a shot at Strong, injuring the judge's hand. When the girl was returned home, her father tried to kill her and then himself before he was restrained.[117] What might otherwise have been only a local scandal in a community steeped in white supremacy (but, as described in previous chapters, also steeped in racial ambiguity) somehow reached the national wire service, most likely because "Judge Strong was a participant in the Breathitt war."[118]

After this scandal, the press renewed its interest in novel accounts of Breathitt's primitiveness, isolation, or general strangeness. Often facts fell prey to expectations. In 1890 the *Chicago Tribune* selected a drunken shooting in a Jackson "blind tiger" (a common enough case of tavern manslaughter in an era of high alcohol consumption), whimsically predicting it would be the beginning of "a new feud."[119] Other papers across the country reported on the affray as well, except that in these other versions, it had happened at either a religious revival or a suicidal teenager's funeral (the more detailed articles suggested the latter). Further violence did not ensue, prompting a Georgia editor to express disappointment.[120] When, later that month, "a negro preacher named Pennington" was shot to death in Jackson's streets over a stolen pair of trousers, the incident was not so widely disseminated.[121]

The Reverend James Dickey and other Jackson nabobs refused to let the troubles of 1888–89 dim their booster spirit, especially as the KU came closer and closer. After nearly three years of track laying (an enterprise said to have employed more than two thousand men), a spur connected northern Breathitt County with Beattyville (Lee County's booming county seat at the confluence of the Kentucky River's three forks) in 1890.[122] By this point the ambitious plan to connect the Bluegrass to Virginia had been forgotten. Still, the connection of Kentucky's "darkest and most God forsaken" county to Lexington was considered an incredible transformation. "What a mighty revolution!" Reverend Dickey proclaimed in the *Hustler*. "Go to Beattyville by rail and steam boat in about two hours where formerly it required a day's hard riding on horse back."[123] Despite local gripes over the requisite hike in property taxes, the *Hustler* insisted that the KU would save the county $40,000 per year.[124] And fewer landowners had need to worry, anyway; as the rails approached, faraway firms purchased gigantic individual hardwood trees and vast expanses of forested land, in some cases at astounding prices of $10 an acre ($1 an acre having been a recent rate).[125] The best was yet to come; in 1893 this new connection to the outside world was commemorated with another display of Breathitt County cannel coal at yet another international industrial fair, this time the Chicago's World Exhibition.[126]

Traffic on Jackson's original conduit to the Bluegrass, the Kentucky River's north fork, continued under new conditions. The river was no longer the freely accessed egalitarian watercourse it had once been. In 1876 Judge Edward Strong cofounded the Troublesome Creek Boom Company, a firm established to invest in a boom across the tributary for the acquisition and marketing of logs felled farther upstream. The charter allowed for the crossing of logs owned by those outside of the company, but it also provided an impediment to squatters' rafting traffic by recognizing only the passage of legally owned timber.[127] In 1882 Republican congressman John D. White had secured $75,000 of federal funding for a lock and dam farther downstream at Beattyville (White was a native of Clay County, where large-scale industrial development had first begun in eastern Kentucky). Opened in 1886, it was the most expansive river improvement to date, but a mixed blessing since the dam created artificial rapids that endangered flatboats.[128] However, this did not deter venture capitalists. By the mid-1890s, timber companies (some leasing railroad land and others buying their own) monopolized river passage, constructing log booms to control the movement of timber and clogging the north fork with far more logs than it had ever floated before.[129] What had once been the free domain of yeomen and squatters was becoming the possession of corporations and holding companies. For the first time, wage labor was imposed upon a large segment of Breathitt

County's male population. One journalist noted the organization of the new transportation system.

> Cheaper as the boom system is than the rafting, the cost seems a big item when put into figures. The construction of pockets, etc., for a two and one-half mile boom, in Breathitt County, for instance, came to eight thousand dollars recently.
>
> The work is sometimes fast and furious, as when logs are going by at the rate of from fifty to ninety a minute. Sometimes the men are obliged to work for two or three days and nights at a time, only the excitement of the work sustaining them. Their food during such an ordeal is taken by "jerks and snatches," and lucky is the "sorter" who is excused for a cat nap.[130]

The sorters who now worked for these corporations were probably the sons of men who had felled their own logs only a few years earlier.

Occasional timber piracy on company-owned land showed that the old freebooting economy persisted to a small extent, but with little sympathy from the law-and-order, business-friendly *Hustler*.[131] On the same pages the paper also printed the speeches of Henry George and his acolyte John W. Kramer condemning the evils of land speculation.[132] Dickey may well have been oblivious to the irony of reprinting criticism of land speculation in a county that had been founded for that sole purpose—not to speak of his simultaneous defense of corporate property. By 1891 the county was no longer under the thrall of the men who had created it and, with Gilded Age policies in full swing, the old ideal of disinterested government they had once violated had become moot.

Times had changed, and class lines between white Kentuckians had become more distinct than ever before. Soon after finally reaching the northern edge of Breathitt County, the KU fell months behind on paying track layers and local loggers who had sold it timber. In response, "ignorant mountaineers" tore up tracks, derailed cars, cut down telegraph poles, and destroyed bridges and culverts, inflicting up to $50,000 worth of damage less than a month after Dickey's declaration of revolution.[133] The wildcat strike was an astonishing collaboration between yeomen and wage laborers (though only one of many Kentucky railroad strikes in the last two decades of the nineteenth century), and it caught the attention of papers from Virginia to Texas and Kansas, while the *Hustler* and the *Hazel Green Herald* neglected to mention it.[134] The mass sabotage preceded a broad agitation among mountain workers. Early the next month railroad men and lumberyard workers went on strike in Whitley and Rockcastle counties near the Tennessee line; within months a massive workingmen's fight against convict labor in Kentucky and Tennessee had begun.[135] Closer to home, however, the situation revealed more about the KU's weakness than it did class antagonism. The railroad lost backing and fell into court-ordered receivership before it reached Jackson that summer.[136] Even after it was reestablished as the Lexington & Eastern (L&E) in 1894, the railroad could not afford further extension.[137] Although the wealth of bituminous and cannel coal was touted over and over again throughout the 1890s, even the ever-growing Louisville & Nashville (L&N) octopus did not eye the L&E and Breathitt County with any serious consideration until a few years into the twentieth century.[138] Still, connection to the small metropolis of Lexington by any railway was indeed a welcomed "revolution." Within two years of the railroad's arrival, Jackson was considered (but eventually rejected) for the site of a new federal district court, a consideration that would have been unimaginable just a few years earlier.[139] "Law is more rigidly enforced than at any time since the civil war," boasted the *Hustler* at the end of 1891. "The completion of the railroad has brought us in contact with the outside world."[140] Within the next ten years Jackson's population increased by 1,100 percent.[141]

Breathitt County, especially Jackson, remained a disorderly place, but most agreed that the nature of local chaos had changed since the railroad's arrival. Alcohol, a nationally popular scapegoat, was a popular replacement for primordial explanations of violence. In 1873 Breathitt became the first of many Kentucky counties to enact a "local option" ban on all sales of alcohol, an ordinance that proved ineffectual, as it did all over the state.[142] Whiskey sales continued unabated, and political mass meetings were always the best settings for tippling. Dickey's *Hustler* was as much a Methodist organ as it was a Democratic one, and the editor/preacher blamed both parties for turning conventions and rallies into debaucheries. "These meetings are usually more of a howling mob than of a dignified gathering of patriots. Liquor is king on these occasions and the candidates usually furnish the liquor. We look forward to the time when candidates will not dare use such vile means to secure nomination. We believe it is coming. Political meetings should be conducted with as much decorum as religious ones. The highest interests of the people are involved. May God hasten better times."[143] Local ordinance or not, eastern Kentucky remained a major producer of unbounded spirits, and the new arrival of miners, loggers, and railroad men gave nearby distillers an insatiable clientele.[144] This gave the *Hazel Green Herald* a source of blame for violence that was increasingly popular among investment-minded flatlanders, while also having a reason to praise Jackson's increasingly efficient law enforcement, after the town's 1890 incorporation necessitated appointing a constable and a police judge.[145] The Democratic paper was torn between defending political allies in the neighboring county and conceding that Breathitt County did indeed seem to be a repository for mayhem. But the ambitious townspeople of the less notorious Wolfe County saw that their fortunes would soon be connected to those of their rowdier neighbor, so ameliorating Breathitt County's image was in everybody's best commercial interest.

It was a difficult task as, through the 1890s, Jackson and its county occasionally proved to be an untamable beast. As Jackson's population soared, demand increased to reverse Breathitt's local option and issue liquor licenses. In the pages of the *Hustler* Dickey remained adamantly in favor of continued prohibition until a Saturday night in May 1893 when saboteurs dynamited his office, destroying the printing press and "distributing type all over town." A collection was taken and, by the end of the summer, the *Hustler* renewed printing, advocating convict labor and greater scrutiny of candidates for public office. Two men, one of them Jeremiah South III (a grandson of the "father of Breathitt County"), were indicted for the destruction.[146] If licensure had any public following before, it was now associated with "that lawless element which once gave Breathitt County such unenviable notoriety."[147] Local option was vindicated, but "blind tigers" persisted.

As the county's population grew, so did juries' willingness to punish homicides. For years reform-minded Kentuckians had blamed the timidity of the courts for their state's record of white intraracial homicide. Their dissatisfaction fed the white fervor for lynching, as it did elsewhere, but it also increased demand for the state-mandated death penalty; in 1892 an unprecedented ten men (six black, four white) were executed in six Kentucky counties.[148] Breathitt's citizens, many of them recently arrived from other parts of the state, also saw active law enforcement as the key to putting Bloody Breathitt to rest. The spring court term of 1895 produced an avalanche of guilty verdicts—including three murder convictions—evidence that "Breathitt" might "no longer be the synonym for crime." It also gave lowland Kentuckians a chance to self-congratulate for the good influence railroad connections to the outside world had on the county. "The good citizens of Breathitt are determined that murder and lawlessness shall cease in that county," one Bluegrass editor crowed after one of the sentences was passed down.[149] "The county," another agreed, "seems to be inclined to wipe out its black record of such long standing."[150]

This new fervor for justice led to the famed public execution of Thomas "Bad Tom" Smith, the only legal hanging in Breathitt County's history. Branded a "feudist," Smith could more accurately be termed a ne'er-do-well willing to kill for money. Smith had been Fulton French's primary assassin in Perry County, and he exemplified a growing population that warlords like French could easily exploit: rootless, profligate men under forty, victimized by recent economic developments that pushed them away from yeomanry and toward drunkenness, gambling, and whoring.[151] His first five admitted murders, all ending in acquittals or mistrials, had been at the wealthy French's direction. When he shot Dr. John Rader during an argument over a shared paramour in the winter of 1895, he had no patron, and he was no longer shooting for a faction that much of Breathitt seemed to sympathize with (for that matter, the death of the recently arrived Rader meant the loss of a physician in a growing town with measly medical resources). No longer part of a "feud," Smith was on his own, and he received a death sentence.[152]

While incarcerated, Smith feigned illness and unsuccessfully planned escape as his attorney fruitlessly appealed his sentence.[153] But when it came time for his execution in late June, his gallows performance was the essence of meekness and resignation, a model of the repentant condemned convict, and a personification of the roguish county that was now enacting a cleansing justice in the form of his death sentence.[154] With an estimated four thousand men, women, and children swelling Jackson's streets, Smith was baptized in the north fork a few hours before he ascended the scaffold (reporters noted the presence of Captain William Strong, John Aikman, Jerry Little, and other famed rogues). He tearfully embraced his sister, sang hymns to the crowd, confessed his life of murder and other sins, and implored all assembled to forgive their neighbors as Smith hoped to be forgiven.[155] Confessing guilt, he also claimed victimhood to the archetypal Victorian rake's progress.

> My last words on earth to you are to take warning from my fate. Bad whiskey and bad women have brought me where I am. I hope you ladies will take no umbrage at this, for I have told you the God's truth. To you, little children, who were the first to be blessed by Jesus, I will give this warning: Don't drink whiskey and don't do as I have

Done. I want everybody in this vast crowd who does not wish to do the things that I have done, and to put themselves in the place I now occupy, to hold their hands.[156]

It was a presentation that mingled elements of the sacred and the profane, proclaiming Christian justice and redemption while also reaffirming the state's moral authority (befittingly, a rail-delivered one hundred gallons of Lexington whiskey was immediately sent back, lest the solemn hanging's wholesome atmosphere be spoiled).[157] Of all Bloody Breathitt's storied killings, this one had the most witnesses and, by virtue of state sanction, the greatest blessings of legitimacy. Even, perhaps, more so than most public hangings; defying tradition, Sheriff Breck Combs did not bother to conceal his identity when he pulled the lever that opened the trapdoor beneath Smith's shackled feet.

Breathitt County's first (and it would turn out to be the last) legal hanging was cast as a triumph of state-sanctioned violence over feuds and all their antiquated connotations.[158] It was the culmination of forces set in motion on Christmas Day in 1884, when an anonymous epistler requested assistance and investment in the *Louisville Courier-Journal*; next came missionaries and rail traffic and, finally, state-approved capital punishment. "In Breathitt county, which by many people is considered to be beyond the pale of civilization," the Democratic *Hartford Herald* remarked a few days before Smith's death, "the day of reckoning which will mark an era in the history of Eastern Kentucky is near at hand."[159] Or, as a Missouri newspaper interpreted it: "Jackson built a school house and a railroad reached the town recently, and the ringing of the school bell and the whistle of the locomotive were the signals that told the hill country that the murdering days were over."[160] By demonstrating that violence could be used to punish crime rather than commit it, Breathitt County ingratiated itself to the *outside world*. In the past, violent death had been a divider, but now it was a uniter. Bad Tom Smith had been a "feudist," but as part of an affair in another county, and it was probably a relief to many that the crime of passion for which he was hanged was unconnected to past power struggles. Unlike so many killings before it, Bad Tom Smith's execution was a civically consensual, apolitical killing. Almost no one questioned it as a legitimate form of violence.[161] And, if it was to bring about an unprecedented peace accompanied by the riches of industrial growth, it reaffirmed the legitimacy of the local state (which, no doubt, many Kentuckians had come to doubt).

The same could not be said for the double lynching eleven years past. It is little surprise that Smith's hanging is a buoyant bit of Kentucky folklore, while Henderson Kilburn's and Ben Strong's are largely forgotten (the *Louisville Courier-Journal* erroneously called Smith "the first man ever hanged in Breathitt County").[162] One Kentucky Democrat inadvertently echoed the Reverend J. J. Dickey's affirmation from eleven years past. "Whatever mistakes may have been made in the way of enforcing the law in the past, let us forget, and see to it that a healthy public sentiment is so openly expressed that it brings about a rigid enforcement of the law in the future."[163] For all of these reasons, paradoxical as they may have been, Smith made an exemplary sacrificial lamb, a final propitiation for Bloody Breathitt's communal sins.

For a short time it seemed as if the act of atonement had worked. Then, a little more than a year later, came the arrests of former Breathitt sheriff William Bryant and his mistress after they absconded to Arkansas with embezzled county funds.[164] Crime in Breathitt County had graduated to a form less sanguinary and atrocious and more avaricious and scandalous. It could only mean progress.

5

DEATH OF A FEUDAL HERO

Here beyond men's judgments all covenants were brittle.
—Cormac McCarthy, *Blood Meridian; or,*
The Evening Redness in the West (1985)

After Jeremiah South's death in 1880, his family experienced a number of setbacks. Barry, his most enterprising son, replaced him as penitentiary executive but, like his father, ran afoul of the reformers who sought to humanize Kentucky's appalling penal system.[1] Barry South's 1887 bid for state treasurer was trounced in the Democratic primary just months before he lost thousands of dollars of uninsured property in a Frankfort warehouse fire.[2] His elder brother, Confederate congressional medal honoree Colonel Samuel South, died the next year, while their nephew Jerry South III fell into a life of crime and dissolution.[3] One of the few adult Souths still living in Breathitt County by the 1890s, Jerry was involved with the French-Eversole feud, and the dynamiting of the *Jackson Hustler* office (it was later revealed that he wanted to destroy the Reverend J. J. Dickey's paper because he was "strongly opposed to evangelists coming into Eastern Kentucky"). He was shot to death in 1896 while arguing over the spoils of a fish-poaching operation. His accused assailants were acquitted on a technicality.[4]

It was an ignoble decline for a family that had once been on the make. Any number of factors might be blamed for the Souths' dwindling prosperity, and most of them related to land ownership in an industrial age.[5] They had never been able to properly exploit the vast Breathitt County acreage that had appreciated in value since their patriarch first purchased the land and arranged for the county's creation. Poor surveying kept farmers and speculators from making unimpeachable claims to ownership, especially when faced with well-lawyered timber and coal companies. As enormous parcels of Breathitt County land were sold in the 1890s, prices soared and state-recognized property demarcation became truly vital. The long-standing confusion of boundaries was no long tolerable.

An acceleration of litigation ensued, as Barry South and others tried to defend their holdings. For years after his father's death, other claimants challenged him for what was left of his inheritance as he tried to prevent unknown parties—the hunters and marginal drovers, Breathitt County's "wood denizens"—from felling what he considered his timber. As those who aspired to legitimate land ownership came upon hard times, they thrived on absentee-owned land for indefinite years until they were discovered and driven off.[6] In 1894 Barry South told a federal judge that he and his coheirs had not been able to "invade" their Breathitt County property for twenty years because of a "lawless and desperate" population of squatters who were hostile to surveyors and unwilling to provide depositions. What was left of the old Thomas Franklin Revolutionary grant was far more land than even a family of means could survey or surveil. So it remained the domain of men "who built houses and eked out a bare existence," armed with superior knowledge of its landscape, its coal seams, and its phenomenally valuable hardwood.[7] The landless never need worry about becoming land poor; railroads and large-scale extractors could also afford to bide their time. Barry South could not.

Of course many of these "wood denizens"—or their fathers—had also been on the opposite side of the Civil War from Barry South and his brothers. This may have mattered less if they were not still led by one Captain William Strong, "one of the most notorious men in the state" even as late as 1894. Strong maintained his hidden sylvan martial state on and around his farm in the southern part of the county. Although he was no longer a challenge to Breathitt's post-Confederate Democracy, he still served as the county's disfranchised and defiant, poor whites, and a small number of former slaves. In describing Strong, the South-sympathetic *Hazel Green Herald* trotted out all the specious feud associations it had always complained of when they appeared in newspapers from outside the mountains, including the ever-popular medieval analogy. "Strong is a sort of feudal hero," it read, "exercising over his own neighbors a greater power than ever did landed baron in the days of night-errantry." It was claimed (no doubt to raise the federal judge's hackles) that Strong was also the guardian of an unknown number of whiskey stills, and he had supposedly planned to immolate a revenue agent a few years before. Perhaps a far greater slander, the *Herald* suggested that Strong was to blame for John Burnett's death in 1878, even though it was public record that Strong had been the young judge's main defender (this sort of fact reversal being among the tasks *feud* performed best).[8] That Strong had fought to restore the Union years earlier was left unmentioned. From the *Herald*'s perspective, he was a villainous version of Robin Hood.

Also unmentioned was Strong's own claim to a large segment of the same land. In 1891 he and his nephew obtained a grant for 190 acres he claimed through "continuous, notorious and adverse possession."[9] Unlike the Souths, Strong had lived in the vicinity the entire time, depending upon its resources for livelihood and knowing it firsthand in ways simple contractual ownership could not provide.[10] It is little wonder that, since the war, the bond between him and the landless remained, even if he was a "legitimate" landowner. As had always been the case in the Three Forks, landed farmers and their unpropertied neighbors had ways of life that were deceptively similar. *Ownership* was not the latter's enemy so much as was the *absentee ownership* of speculators and corporations. His legal defense of his own adverse possession was also a defense of a threatened way of life.

William Strong's leadership among the "wood denizens" and his un-repentant Union partisanship were intertwined. But the old man's mildly subversive existence in the 1890s was a pale reminder of his brazen past. His willingness to go the peaceful route to civil law courts suggested that he had renounced his past aggression, as did his recent decision to begin attending church with his wife. His twilight years would have remained so, were it not for the reemergence of the Ku Klux Klan in Breathitt County, a development Strong refused to ignore.

As always, Bloody Breathitt's mass violence was symptomatic not of isolation but rather of statewide trends, most notably the challenge to Democratic one-party rule. The forty-eight homicides in the summer of 1896 indicated not a concerted counterrevolutionary revolt but a tension roiling all over the South. Even though white supremacy was never truly threatened in Kentucky, growing Republican successes, such as William O. Bradley's election as governor in 1895, were equated with "Negro domina-tion" by proxy.[11] A record-high turnout gave William McKinley a 142-vote advantage over William Jennings Bryan; a Republican presidential candi-date carried the state for the first time in its history.[12] The results triggered months of mob rule and "whitecapping," a vigilante tendency that appeared in various corners of rural America during the Gilded Age. In December at least six men, three white and three black, died in Kentucky's worst one-month lynching pogrom since 1870. The spate of violence continued well into the winter, inspiring Governor Bradley's demand for Kentucky's first antilynching legislation in spring 1897.[13] Even Democrats conceded that "inflammatory speeches" made "by the men who stumped the State for Mr. Bryan" were to blame.[14]

After "Bad Tom" Smith's 1895 execution there followed an agitation against whiskey and immorality in the Three Forks region. Unlike in most 1890s whitecapping situations, moonshiners were the targets rather than their constituency, often producing grassroots imitations of the growing temperance movement. In May 1896, fifty rifle-armed "women whitecappers" smashed a moonshiner's still and barrels in neighboring Knott County.[15] One Breathitt grand jury assembled in summer 1896 included five Baptist preachers whose indictments were "making the way of transgressors hard."[16] Bloody Breathitt, it seemed, was expunging its own sins through both legal and extralegal means.[17]

While whitecappers emulated the Klan's tactics in the 1890s, most did so without explicitly adopting the Klan identity (to many former Unionists and other white southern Republicans, the Reconstruction era's Klan was politically unacceptable even if its tactics were deemed necessary to maintain local interpretations of orderliness).[18] In southeastern Kentucky, however, the Klan name of old was still used, particularly by the "band of regulators patterned somewhat after the old Ku-Klux Klan," made up mostly of newcomers "who had come into Breathitt since the advent of the railroad," all the while maintaining the old organization's implicit link with the Democratic Party.[19] Even after men of "prominence" were arrested for ku-kluxing in Jackson, and even after citizens of both parties were outraged when a child was shot during one of their raids, the new "modern Kuklux" persisted.[20]

In response, William Strong gathered his Red Strings. Just as in the 1870s, the Red Strings were branded "the lawless element," purportedly counting "nearly all of the illicit whisky sellers and moonshiners of the mountain country" among their ranks.[21] This was probably more an exaggeration than falsehood; the Red Strings had never been numerically large but it is likely that many of those that remained by Strong's side were involved in "blockading." Still, there was more at work in the winter of 1896–97 than just vigilantism and organized crime. The fact that both sides readopted the old Reconstruction-era names, *Kuklux* and *Red String*, showed that they saw their differences as part of a much older battle, a malevolent element of the two-party system that had survived since the 1870s. While the former represented a distinct memory (reawoken less than six years later when novelist Thomas Dixon published the first of his Klan-glorifying trilogy of novels), the more obscure Red Strings were largely forgotten, especially since most mountain Unionists had been long since cowed by the Lost Cause.[22] The nomenclatures were especially significant in an aberrantly Democratic, formerly pro-Confederate, mountain county with a seemingly exceptional history of violence. When the seventy-two-year-old Strong "denounced [the Kuklux] in unmeasured terms" in 1896, he was condemning the same element—if not the same individuals—he had fought since the Civil War.[23]

In December 1896 the Breathitt Kuklux killed Thomas Barnett, the brother of a reputed moonshiner and Red String.[24] The "copperhead" Democratic *Cincinnati Enquirer*, a paper that had often taken a sympathetic stance toward white southern conservatives, called Breathitt's Kuklux "an organization principally of responsible men, who were weary of the continued deviltry throughout that section."[25] Vague reports of violence followed over the next few weeks until moonshiners killed a Democratic deputy federal marshal named William Byrd.[26] Byrd had been popular in Jackson, and his friends had to be dissuaded from lynching the two suspects (one of whom died from measles while in custody) before their trial.[27] The crime was never traced to Captain Strong, but the shooting death of a material witness in the surviving defendant's trial, and then an attempted shooting and a store arson, were all blamed on the Red Strings.[28]

William Strong next accused Edward Callahan of being the Kuklux ringleader.[29] Callahan was the son or grandson of Strong's former Union army compatriot, the alleged "secret rebel" Wilson Callahan who was killed during the Strong-Amis feud thirty years past. Unlike most of William Strong's more relentless enemies, Callahan was not from Jackson or the area around the county seat. He lived in Crockettsville in southern Breathitt County, the hamlet that had served as a Union mustering ground in 1862. Callahan was one of the wealthiest men in that less developed area and the owner of the only mercantile outside of Jackson. He was chairman of the county's Democratic central committee, an influential Democratic presence in a part of the county that Strong had otherwise controlled during the 1860s and 1870s.[30] By naming Callahan, Strong was asserting the Kuklux's union with Breathitt's old political order, as opposed to it being made up entirely of new arrivals, as was reported. Callahan never denied the accusation but he apparently did not welcome the attention.

In April 1897 Democratic county judge C. B. Day issued warrants

Edward Callahan, purported Ku Klux Klan leader and sheriff. (Courtesy of Charles Hayes)

against Callahan and Strong and arranged a public rapprochement in Jackson. Perhaps expecting a street confrontation as in 1878, Callahan and Strong each arrived with more than two dozen armed men. However, the two leaders peaceably appeared before Judge Day and assured him that they harbored no personal animosities. Day apparently did not admonish them for arriving with their small armies; rather than addressing their respective Kuklux and Red String leadership roles, and the larger significance these roles might have reflected, the judge accepted their assurances of peace and adjourned court. Their late conflict was considered an elevated personal grievance, and so an orchestrated handshake was assumed to be the end of the matter.[31] Mass violence was averted, but without any acknowledgment of the larger problems that the continuing presence of the Red Strings and the Kuklux represented.

And neither side seemed to have a problem with this. The same week of Strong's and Callahan's appearance before Judge Day, the former's claim to a large portion of the Thomas Franklin grant was upheld, assuring his family's financial future.[32] While he was in Jackson, a Lexington & Eastern Railroad employee invited him to the Grand Army of the Republic encampment that was to be held the second week of May, and Strong made plans to attend.[33] If his "feudal" status had overshadowed his military service, recognition at the fraternal organization's meeting would soon put it right. Strong told a Cincinnati journalist that "he was at peace with all the world, and hoped his declining years would be free from strife."[34]

On a Sunday morning less than three weeks later, Strong was found shot to death under his mule's carcass on a roadside ten miles south of Jackson. His wounds and evidence found nearby suggested that he had been waylaid by at least three gunmen hidden by a jury-rigged "blind." After he and his mount were shot from afar, according to later reports, members of the killing party approached his body and shot him several times more. Strong had grasped his pistol but had not managed to pull it from his holster before he expired. His young grandson, found screaming nearby, was unable to identify any of his killers.[35]

In recognition of Strong's controversial role in a nationally infamous county, newspapers all over Kentucky and beyond recorded the circumstances of his death. Wire copies from Louisville, Lexington, and Cincinnati papers announcing Strong's death were reproduced from Boston to Sacramento. A negotiation between differing interpretations of William Strong's colorful record ensued. "Capt. William Strong, the greatest mountain fighter in Eastern Kentucky, died with his boots on today, after successfully dodging bullets for twenty-five years," the *Lexington Herald* announced the following day.[36] It and other newspapers maintained his depiction as a "mountain fighter" or "feudist," also detailing his Federal service (the *Boston Globe* opining that his "Confederate Neighbors Did Their Worst") and its connections to his later travails.[37] Strong's expansive *Louisville Courier-Journal* obituary detailed his war record as a Unionist and Republican as well as his more recent opposition to the Ku Klux Klan and the ensuing trouble he faced against Edward Callahan—although with some confusions in chronology.

> It seems that shortly after the war, and after Capt Strong had gone to work to pay for his home, the Ku Klux began to terrorize the community. It was generally conceded that the clan was composed chiefly of young men who were not old enough to enter the army at the breaking out of hostilities between the States, but who had grown up with a deep-seated prejudice against the Unionists. Capt. Strong was considered a leader among the ex-Federal soldiers and a strong Republican. He was outspoken against the depredations of the Ku Klux, and is credited with having organized an anti-Ku Klux party, which did much toward putting down the clan.[38]

The *Courier-Journal* omitted what the "strong Republican" had done in the 1870s. His audacious publicized actions, the attempted courthouse capture in 1874, and his defense of young Judge Burnett four years later were left unmentioned. The same newspaper that, in 1878, had branded Strong a "Loyal [Unionist] Whangdoodle" who exhibited the "Wonderful Effect of the Firing on Fort Sumter" poignantly lamented the passing of an aged "mountain fighter" who was "one of the most *picturesque* characters in Breathitt County."[39] Nor did the paper express outrage, surprise, or approval that an organization not heard from for years was active in eastern Kentucky; "Red String" was roundly treated as a sui generis Breathitt County peculiarity.[40] The Strong-Amis feud of the 1860s was given lengthy attention in all of Strong's obituaries, but it was treated as a strictly property-based conflict and suggested to be the original event that led to his death, even though Wiley Amis and the rest of his family were long since departed. Oddly, although it had reported his pact with Callahan weeks earlier, Wolfe County's *Hazel Green Herald* did not report his death.[41]

The *Cincinnati Commercial-Tribune* printed a description of Strong's life and death that differed little from the *Courier-Journal*'s except for a slightly lengthier account of his military service. The Ohio paper told of Strong's service in the Fourteenth Kentucky Cavalry and later the Three Forks Battalion, but skirted the fact that this service had involved terrorizing Breathitt County (by this time the myth of eastern Kentucky's exclusively Unionist leanings was well entrenched). Strong was portrayed as quite popular among "the most powerful and influential citizens of Breathitt" regardless of his politics.[42] The *New York Times* left out any mention of Strong's political affiliations but repeated a prediction that "Strong's friends . . . will never rest until his murder is avenged," thereby casting his killing as part of an interpersonal feud rather than a factional conflict with origins in wartime politics.[43]

When William Strong captured the Breathitt County courthouse and traded bullets with Confederate veterans on the streets of Jackson, these same newspapers had been nominally willing (as shown in the preceding chapter) to use him and his actions as grist for their own political ends. But since the 1870s, the widely circulated newspapers of cities far from the Three Forks region had abandoned their more obvious sectional and political biases and "claimed to be independent of party dictation."[44] To varying degrees they had abandoned party loyalty for human interest. Had Kentucky's more partisan broadsheets, the dogged party organs printed in almost every county seat (like Wolfe County's *Herald*), taken a greater interest, the full implications of his death might have been explored further. As it stood, "Union partisan" and "feudist" were not necessarily mutually exclusive, but the latter was the more satisfyingly colorful and closer to what readers were acclimated to hearing about the Kentucky mountains. And in 1897, no one in Kentucky or anywhere else wanted to acknowledge that there remained deadly political breaches left over from the Civil War.

The more that was said of the captain's past, the less was speculated of who was behind his murder. No one apparently called foul when Bradley announced a $300 reward for the capture of Strong's murderer(s) two weeks after his death (the following July the governor offered $250 for the capture of Thomas Barnett's killer).[45] It was initially assumed that his death resulted from the Kuklux–Red String conflict of late, but suspicion also fell on John Aikman, an enemy of Strong's since the war.[46] Aikman implicated Callahan while other "leading men of the 'Kuklux'" disavowed any knowledge of the slayers' identities.[47] Callahan had been in Frankfort at the time of the shooting and denied involvement, mentioning only that Strong "had many enemies in the country around Jackson."[48] Neither he nor Aikman were ever prosecuted.[49]

Much of the publicity surrounding Captain Strong's death acknowledged his bizarre political role in a place where the two-party system had remained somewhat militarized. It is also fairly remarkable that practically no journalists contextualized Strong's death explicitly within the more recent "feud" violence in southeastern Kentucky. But Strong was to be remembered more as a "feudal hero" than a "strong Republican." When the newspapers of Louisville, Cincinnati, and New York had first taken notice of Strong in the 1870s, the memory of the war was pervasive, but the idea of the primitive mountain South was in its infancy. Then, *feud* was only a word used to depoliticize white intraracial violence at a time when it was commonplace in the South. Since that time, the "feuds" of Rowan, Perry, Harlan, and other counties had since been established in the public consciousness as horizontal conflicts fueled by the barbarism and primordial vengeance of the mountain white, rather than as issues of local state power. The conflation of these trends with mountain Republicanism (compounded by the party's diminished status in the South after the end of Reconstruction) further minimized the role of party politics in these fights. The ensuing attention of evangelists and their bestial portrayals of Kentucky mountaineers encouraged this communal interpretation. Although his own war making predated this reification of the "two Kentuckys," Strong's memory fell victim to this mass depoliticization, his most overtly political acts of violence forgotten and veiled by his personal and allegedly familial ones. He died exactly one day before the state Senate's passage of the antilynching law that Governor William Bradley had demanded, but no one related this to Strong's death or to the lynching of his Red Strings almost exactly thirteen years beforehand.[50] These were deemed different kinds of violence.

Most of all, William Strong and his role in Bloody Breathitt were propelled into the past. In the interest of demonstrating that feud violence was not a product of Kentucky's present, the recent killing (or its motivations) were placed as far back in time as possible by both Breathitt County natives and newspapers from the *outside world*. Fourteen months later, John Aikman insisted that Strong's death was a very late retaliation for the late-1860s dispute between Strong and Wilson Callahan that involved the latter's, and Wiley Amis's, defections to the Democratic Party (Aikman, having no association with these former Unionists, told this story probably as a claim of innocence).[51] Aikman took for granted that the younger Callahan would, as a matter of course, avenge his grandfather at this late date. He did not address the question of why, had this been purely a matter of familial revenge, Callahan had not killed Strong years earlier.

Some spoke of Strong in language that sent him back even further. What may have been a misspelling on the part of the *Courier-Journal* is nonetheless telling: *clan,* a word Americans would have associated with extended families and Scottish warlords of past centuries (a decidedly parochial time and place) was used in place of *klan,* which, in contrast, referred directly to a recent crisis of legitimacy in the American South.[52] Within six years, when violence in Breathitt County had yet again gained national interest, the events that had led to Strong's shooting had become collectively known as the "Strong-Callahan feud."[53] Similarly, a history of Breathitt County produced by the Works Projects Administration's Writers' Project described Callahan's source of authority as "a paternal rule, in the rustic style of a Scotch clan chieftain."[54] Granted, these were only analogies, but they were analogies repeated so often that they ultimately overshadowed the actual events and their attendant political implications. The aberrational late persistence of the Ku Klux Klan in Breathitt County, its Red String enemies, and the fact that these groups founded during the South's internecine political wars in the 1860s and 1870s somehow remained in one isolated corner of Kentucky were all but forgotten. With the passing of a generation, the causes that men once killed and died for were becoming as distant and archaic as those of some ancestral Jacobite.

Even if the Strong-Callahan feud was personal, it was also political by virtue of the respective past and present roles of the men who took part in it. Strategically, the "bushwhacking" of Strong in 1897 was little different than the double lynching of Henderson Kilburn and Ben Strong thirteen years earlier. By the time of his death, Democratic control over the county was in no electoral danger, and the old Republican patriarch had far less authority than he had in the 1870s. The county's African American population had dwindled and his role as "special protector of the colored race in Breathitt" did not garner him even a small measure of local support.[55] What little political legitimacy he might have once held was gone. Even if Strong had ceased his belligerence, he and the Red Strings represented the county's past, a past that stood in the way of its continuing economic development. The pocket of guerrilla defiance he established during the Civil War could not be tolerated as Breathitt County became a more influential part of Kentucky and the New South.

Moreover, William Strong was not to be remembered as a kind of political leader but rather a premodern curiosity. A feudal chieftain had to be a thing of distant history, in fact as well as name. With Strong dead, the use of mass violence as had been employed by the Red Strings and the Ku Klux Klan in past years was no longer necessary. After Breathitt's grand jury indicted sixteen men for "ku-kluxing" in the summer of 1897, both groups apparently dissipated.[56] Groups that openly went by the name were no longer heard from—at least until the 1910s and 1920s, when a new national version of the Klan emerged.[57] The internal crisis of legitimacy that they represented had been resolved; political violence in Breathitt County had not come to an end, but it would no longer be dressed in emblems of the past.

Strong had enough enemies for Edward Callahan to avoid being implicated. But, given their history of political differences and mutual antagonism, Callahan was believed to be the one who had dispatched the last remaining threat to Democratic rule in the county (at least among threats that drew their power from a gun barrel), and this reputation added to his political stock considerably.[58] Callahan would go on to further damage his home county's reputation while also becoming one of eastern Kentucky's most invincible politicians.

And even if Strong had not been so great a threat to Callahan in those later years, the former's death had a symbolic significance, a demarcation between Breathitt County's dark feudal past and its bright future that also worked in Callahan's favor. When Strong's nephew James B. Marcum later accused the ascendant Democrat of complicity in his uncle's death, Callahan could have responded like a "feudist," vowing personal vengeance for sullied honor and reputation. Instead, he upbraided Marcum for "keeping up the old trouble."[59]

But the county's next political debacle, one that placed it under unprecedented national scrutiny, produced a new complex turn toward violence that could not be tucked so neatly into the past. Even after the death of Bloody Breathitt's "feudal hero," the county's most famous killings were yet to come.

6

"THERE HAS ALWAYS BEEN THE BITTEREST POLITICAL FEELING IN THE COUNTY"

A Courthouse Ring in the Age of Assassination

> So it should be noted that when he seizes a state the new ruler must determine all the injuries that he will need to inflict. He must inflict them once for all, and not have to renew them every day, and in that way he will be able to set men's minds at rest and win them over to him when he confers his benefits. Whoever acts otherwise, either through timidity or misjudgment, is always forced to have the knife ready in his hand and he can never depend on his subjects because they, suffering fresh and continuous violence, can never feel secure with regard to him. Violence must be inflicted once and for all; people will then forget what it tastes like and so be less resentful. . . .
>
> And it is to be observed, men are either to be flattered and indulged or utterly destroyed—because for small offences they do usually revenge themselves, but for great ones they cannot—so that injury is to be done in such a manner as not to fear any revenge.
>
> —Niccolò Machiavelli, *The Prince* (1532)

"Republicanism," Henry Watterson envisioned in late 1888, "is simply an epidemic. Like Federalism, cholera, Know-Nothingism and yellow fever, when it has run its course, it will pass away."[1] It was an oddly sanguine appraisal of incumbent Grover Cleveland's recent electoral defeat (Benjamin Harrison had narrowly lost the popular vote while winning the Electoral College) and Republican congressional gains. Marse Henry's lifelong raison d'être was to rally his party, even in hard times. Nevertheless, it was a peculiar time to predict the Grand Old Party's imminent demise, even from the northernmost edge of the Solid South.

As far as Kentucky's near future went, Watterson was not so much overly optimistic as he was absolutely wrong. The 1888 death of vive voce and the adoption of a secret ballot benefited Republicans all over the state as well as the western counties' tobacco-belt Populist insurgency.[2] Just as it had once been caught between North and South, Kentucky was again wedged between the state's agrarian past and its industrial future—an advantageous position for Republicans. In 1895 (the first year the secret ballot was used statewide) they captured the state's House of Representatives and elected William O. Bradley, "the Kentuckian who broke the 'Solid South,'" its first Republican governor.[3] As they watched the rest of the South circle the wagons of Jim Crow, Democrats were appalled by what they called Bradley's "mongrel ideas of mixed schools and similar vicious principles."[4] His plea to repeal the state's "separate coach law" was met with white jeers (and the aforementioned chaos of 1896), and his summoning of militia to Frankfort during a prolonged legislative conflict angered both factions.[5] Even after such heavy-handedness, Bradley's party slowly flourished as Democrats "left the party in its hour of need."[6] William McKinley's razor-thin 142-vote advantage over William Jennings Bryan, and the appointment of the state's first Republican U.S. senator, amounted to "a bitter morsel in the mouth of Kentucky Democracy."[7] "It's goodbye solid South," a western Kentucky Democrat lamented as Bryan's defeat was confirmed.[8]

Even with vigorous, honest, two-party competition, Democrats refused to accept Bradley's legitimacy, especially given his vetoes of any and all regulation over the Louisville & Nashville (L&N) "Railway Emperor" and its ever-increasing freight prices.[9] Distrust of Bradley and the L&N fueled the career of one of the South's most unlikely firebrand politicians, Democrat William Goebel.[10] The Pennsylvania-born Union army veteran's son, a watchmaker's apprentice turned lawyer, represented the urban minority of a rural state still electing Confederate veterans as governors (a wizened James McCreary returned to the office in 1911 after a thirty-two-year intermission).[11] For a time, "control by the conservative well-to-do, aristocratic, ex-Confederates of the [Democratic] party was passing," while politicians like Goebel, "more demagogic, more radical, more willing to please tenant farmers and labor were taking control" in many southern states.[12] What set him apart from a Comer, Blease, Aycock, or Vardaman was his express openness to black voters (most of whom received him coolly).[13] Goebel confronted not only

Would-be governor William Goebel. Goebel's firebrand gubernatorial run in 1899 divided Kentucky's Democratic Party and brought the state to the brink of civil war. His assassination in 1900 reunited his party and reinitiated the state's status quo. (http://history.ky.gov/governors.php?pageid=27&sectionid=8)

the unwelcome Republicans but also the wing of his own party controlled by industrialized planters like the L&N's chief lobbyist, Confederate doyen Basil Duke.[14] Working from within their own party, Goebel became the first real threat to members of Kentucky's Bourbonocracy since the days when they had counted people among their commodities.

William Goebel compounded his controversy by his embrace of violence. He mastered Kentucky's vaunted art of killing in 1895, when an armed banker confronted him over an unflattering article Goebel had penned. Goebel responded with a bullet to the banker's head and was later acquitted on grounds of self-defense. Many accounts mistakenly interpreted the shooting as a duel, although there was no previous planning for the encounter and the banker never pulled his own gun, a scenario that hardly qualified as the traditional (and, by this time, sharply declining) white southern ritual.[15] When arsonists burned tollbooths to protest high turnpike fees, the young state senator expressed sympathy for their aims, giving conservative legislators further reason to associate him with lawlessness.[16]

Nothing he did outside of the state capitol could surpass the controversy surrounding what became known as the Goebel election law. In 1898 Goebel (who was by this time senate pro tem) proposed a reform bill to centralize election management, a measure that would theoretically strengthen his party while simultaneously diminishing the power of county courts, most of which were Democratically controlled.[17] Republicans considered it a disenfranchising "Force Bill," while many prominent Democrats opposed it on principle, but it passed over Bradley's veto in 1898.[18]

Goebel's nomination for governor the following year was widely attributed to the Democratic state convention chair, Breathitt County's "ardent Democrat of the Jeffersonian school" Judge David B. Redwine.[19] A dark horse of the mountains, Redwine had few binding relationships and was not a member of one of the state's great dynastic political families like the Clays or the Breckinridges. His origins were relatively obscure even within his own impoverished, remote court circuit (where he had been accused of "boodle" and assisting in local election fixing since early in his judicial career).[20] Perhaps most important, his residency in one of the only Democratic stalwarts in a heavily Republican section brought with it a certain pariah status; anyone outside of eastern Kentucky who had heard of it since 1878 associated it with nothing more than the irrational violence and depravity implied by feuds.[21] As the political drama was recounted over the following years, particularly from Republican memory, the young judge (whose 1892 rout over H. C. Lilly surprised many mountaineers even after the latter's embarrassment over Breathitt County) was better remembered as being from "'bloody' Breathitt."[22] For years it was suggested that only a "mountain henchman" was intrepid enough to stare down a hostile convention floor.[23]

The Democrats' infamously rowdy "Music Hall Convention" of June 1899 was nationally known as a meeting of Kentucky's dregs brought to act as delegates. Riverfront roustabouts and gamblers mingled with policemen, firemen, and ward heelers as incessant brass band music, inebriated raucousness, and a constant threat of riot prevailed on the convention floor.[24] Ignoring physical threats, Chairman Redwine insisted on a dizzying flurry of roll call votes and refused to adjourn until Goebel's other conventioneers could negotiate a firm majority. He managed enough aplomb to remain onstage beating time with his walking stick to some angry delegates' impromptu rendition of "We'll Hang Jeff Davis from a Sour Apple Tree" with "Redwine" substituted for "Jeff Davis."[25] Throughout, Breathitt County's James "Big Jim" Hargis was "one of the main manipulators," cajoling delegates and supposedly threatening Redwine with bodily harm when he considered leaving the lectern for his own safety.[26] Redwine "apparently desired the world to surrender on its knees," recalled a disgruntled Republican memoirist. "Parliamentary usages formed no part of his code. He was not there for

From the chaotic 1899 Democratic convention in Louisville to the murders on the streets of Jackson in 1902 and 1903, Judge David B. Redwine was always near the center of controversy while always managing to walk between the raindrops. (Courtesy of the University of Louisville Law Library Collection)

the convention to direct, but to direct the convention. There was but one man he obeyed, but one man he served, and that man was William Goebel. Him he served with all the fidelity with which a slave serves his master."[27] The twenty-sixth ballot produced a nomination for Goebel and nationwide outrage; Republicans saw correlations between Goebel and the specter of anarchy, while some Democrats reproved the Goebel election law as an attack on "home rule."[28] David B. Redwine's reputation (and, to a lesser extent, James Hargis's) was indelibly connected to Goebel's contentious nomination, and for years Redwine was anathema among Republicans. Goebel himself coyly disregarded his role at the convention.[29] "I want to know if Judge Redwine really was for me," Goebel said at a whistle-stop in Jackson. "They say he was but I want to know."[30]

Nomination in hand, candidate Goebel scarcely mentioned his Republican opponent, Attorney General William S. Taylor, by name. "There are only two candidates for governor of Kentucky," he announced a month before the election. "There are more than that number who pretend to be candidates, but the only real candidates are the Louisville Company [the L&N] and the person who addresses you."[31] His election law, by far his most outrageous legacy, was repugnant to "Honest-election" Democrats who nominated former governor John Y. Brown as their candidate at a separate convention.[32] Even with William Jennings Bryan's support, and a reluctant late endorsement from Watterson's *Louisville Courier-Journal* (Goebel's meteoric rise coincided with an alarmingly rapid drop in subscriptions, apparently revealing some fairly disturbing writing on the wall), Goebel's divisiveness led to his apparent narrow defeat.[33] The new election review board—Goebel's own notorious handiwork—found in William Taylor's favor.[34]

Goebel conceded shortly before Taylor's December inauguration, but Democrats (including "Honest-election" men) accused Republicans of fraudulent ballots and poll intimidation.[35] Invigorated by this newfound support, Goebel rescinded his concession and returned to Frankfort in January to question more than one-third of the state's counties' returns. The Democrat-controlled legislature selected a committee made up of nine fellow party members (including James Hargis), one Republican, and one Populist to review the evidence as armed Democrats patrolled Frankfort's streets.[36] The Republicans retaliated by summoning more than a thousand armed men from the eleventh congressional district, the district Democrats had gerrymandered around the upland "Whig Gibraltar" counties.[37] The L&N volunteered its rolling stock to transport the Republican montagnards to Frankfort gratis except for (according to one horrified Democrat) each having a "pistol to get a free pass."[38] "The roughest crowd ever gotten together in the mountains" came mainly from three southeastern foothill counties, Knox, Laurel, and Whitley, but Democrats described their origins less specifically, the better to emphasize eastern Kentucky's preexistent primitive image.[39] One Democrat hoped the "invasion of hill billies from the Eleventh

Cartoon depiction of a mountain Republican occupying Frankfort in January 1900. The cartoon was published just days before William Goebel was fatally shot. Tucked into the mountaineer's gun belt is a carte blanche pardon from Republican governor-elect William Taylor. (*Louisville Courier-Journal*, January 27, 1900)

district" would disperse with the unusually cold January weather (most did depart, except for approximately 175 of the most dedicated), while the *Louisville Courier-Journal* warned, "If a single Democrat is harmed the guilt will be upon the Republican leaders and not the ignorant men" the party had "corralled in this little city."[40] Only a few Bluegrass Republicans defended the mountaineers gathered to "protect their liberties."[41]

On the morning of January 30 a hidden rifleman shot Goebel as he and two Democratic friends walked by the statehouse.[42] He was carried back to his hotel as premature rumors of his death spread, and armed men prevented the election committee from entering the capitol. Without knowing Goebel's condition, the committee announced a party-line decision in his favor without publicizing the exact numbers of the returns. Governor Taylor took this as an act of sedition and dismissed the General Assembly with instructions to reassemble in Laurel County. Only the Republican legislators complied, while the others assembled in the hotel where Goebel lay dying and ratified the election committee's decision.[43] While being fed oysters and succumbing to a fatal case of pneumonia, Goebel twice took the oath of office from two friendly judges.[44] Even as Taylor presided over a rump General Assembly in the eleventh district, Democrats declared his recumbent opponent the state's thirty-fourth governor.

Goebel's death three days later did not settle matters. Democrats had become incensed with the possibility that Taylor had directed Goebel's assassination through the "ignorant and uncouth" troop of "Republican mountaineers."[45] One Kentucky Democrat combined his suspicion with the preexistent eastern Kentucky feud lore.

> The outside world does not know the Kentucky mountaineers, one of whom shot Goebel. They differ from any other mountaineers on earth. They don't know how to do like other beings. If you give one the lie he doesn't smack your face like you or I might do, but draws and shoots. They have been raised that way and know no other law. Now, these men are attracted to Frankfort. They could not see the merits of the case, if there were any. All they could see was that one man was keeping up the excitement.
>
> They regarded Goebel merely as a man in their way, and, as they have always done, they rid their path of him. There was no fanatical sentiment or even hatred, as with Booth when he shot Lincoln. They merely said he is in our way; he must get out of it.[46]

Apparently no one, not even Republicans, publicly entertained the possibility that Goebel may have been laid low by a fellow Democrat.[47] After sixteen initial indictments, Republican secretary of state Caleb Powers and two other mountain Republicans were convicted of his murder.[48] A jury "made up entirely of Democrats" sentenced Powers to life imprisonment, but years of politically charged trials and appeals eventually led to pardons for all three men (all but one by the state's next Republican governor, Augustus Willson).[49] Two years after his release, the eleventh district voted Powers into Congress.[50]

Would-be governor Taylor fled to Indiana, where the Republican governor gave him a lifetime asylum (Taylor established a law practice in Indianapolis and never returned to Kentucky).[51] After a series of court battles (the U.S. Supreme Court demurred from hearing the case), Goebel's running mate J. C. W. Beckham ended up governor.[52] Perhaps seeing the wages of transgression in Goebel's death, Beckham avoided his mentor's controversial reforms and made sure the election law was repealed during a special legislative session in the late summer of 1900. He also became a firm friend of the L&N.[53]

Kentucky's 1899 gubernatorial election and the litany of ensuing events created an unparalleled crisis of legitimacy, almost "plunging a state into civil war."[54] His death, however, healed a chronic fracture that had been expanding in the Kentucky Democracy since the 1880s. Even Democrats who had once hated Goebel frequently conjured up the "martyr to [the party's] cause," and his memory became "the bloody shirt of Kentucky politics" for nearly a decade.[55] The assassination's aftermath provided Democrats with yet another impetus to conjure *feud* in eastern Kentucky. Sedate Laurel County became "the center of the so-called feud district," while the men who came to Frankfort became "regular mountain feudists."[56] The supposed gunman in the Goebel killing, Jim Howard, was said to have agreed to act as sniper in exchange for a pardon for a previous murder charge (this came to light after the sum of all Democrat-imagined fiends, a mulatto "feudist" named "Tallow Dick" Combs, briefly fell under suspicion as the possible trigger-man).[57] Even the *Hazel Green Herald,* a mountain paper that had good reason not to sully its own section, held to the party line, while defenses of the mountains were few and far between among timid lowland Republicans.[58] Whereas once a "feudist" was someone who fought for apolitical revenge against an equal, intimate enemy, now he was a raw brute whose violence could be directed by higher powers. Goebel's death, compounded with eastern Kentucky's wars and rumors of wars, allowed Democrats to make *feud* mean whatever they wanted it to mean.[59] In the process, all of eastern Kentucky was pilloried as never before.

The Goebel affair and the supposed dangers posed by Kentucky mountaineers were entwined for years, providing a means for Kentuckians and other Americans to reconcile (or confuse) political and communal uses of violence and draw boundaries between the two Kentuckys. Novelist John Fox Jr. (for whom the Kentucky mountain feud was a recurrent leitmotif) made a fictionalized retelling of the Goebel affair, and its effects on a fanciful family feud, the subject of *The Heart of the Hills* (1912). His use of *feud* was different than that of the Democratic press in 1900, as were his purposes. Rather than claiming that Goebel had died due to the inherent "feudal" tendencies of his slayer, Fox devised a plot in which two families who had fought each other for untold generations finally united in opposition to "the autocrat" in Frankfort; the feud was prepolitical, and political involvement brought its end. After most of his stories had patronized eastern Kentucky for its violence and resistance to change, Fox meant for *The Heart of the Hills* to be a redeeming portrayal.[60] However, like most of his previous writing, it upheld the supposed political chasm between the two Kentuckys, a purely Republican mountain region as the exception to white Democratic Kentucky's rule. It changed few minds and, for the most part, reaffirmed the otherness of the "mountain white."

What he omitted was the role mountain Democrats had played in Goebel's candidacy. Judge David Redwine's name would always be attached to Goebel's rise to power, but his and James Hargis's origins as mountaineers was discussed with decreasing frequency for the next few years until Bloody Breathitt yet again gained national attention. The notion of "feud" worked better if eastern Kentucky's two-party reality was eclipsed by "mountain feudists, cowardly assassination and things like that, which have become so closely associated with Republican government in Kentucky."[61] Exceptions to that hard-and-fast rule were rarely discussed and, as subsequent events would show, were suppressed when Kentucky Democrats saw fit.

"Breathitt's debut into political circles in her long robes of state"

James Hargis's arch role in Kentucky politics began only after his mastery of his home county and his collaboration in building a quintessential Gilded Age courthouse ring. A few months after his nemesis William Strong's 1897 death, Edward Callahan, chairman of the county's Democratic Party, came to odds with Hargis over selection of nominees for county school superintendent (a position with immense power over the allotment of local spoils). After Callahan's favorite seemed to win the initial canvass by six votes, Hargis's man somehow won the party committee's endorsement. Still comfortable in using force to meet his ends (even after Breathitt's Ku Klux had apparently dissolved), Callahan led an armed party into the courthouse, captured the ballot box, and recanvassed the returns, not surprisingly finding in his own candidate's favor. Hargis knew that he was in no position to confront Callahan directly, so he contacted the chairman of the state party organization, who promptly recognized Hargis as the new county party chairman.[62] Callahan was removed as chairman (though he was restored to the position within a year).[63] Hargis had led a coup by responding to violence with an appeal to higher authorities, a clear indication that bureaucratic modernity was surmounting Breathitt County's history of "rifle rule."[64]

Callahan was a product of the Three Forks region's settler stock, related by blood or marriage to many of the "first families." James Hargis was a great-nephew of John Hargis, one of the Bluegrass Democrats who had helped engineer the county's creation in 1839 (his father had briefly served as a state senator). His first cousin was a former state appeals judge, one of the state's most influential career politicians.[65] To turn-of-the-century local-color writers, the growing intraparty dispute between the Hargis and Callahan factions could have been interpreted as the flowering of conflict between two of Breathitt County's oldest "clans." But this was not to be the case. Callahan and Hargis (along with circuit court judge David B. Redwine) soon entered into a political partnership based upon their shared interests as merchants (Hargis in Jackson, Callahan in Crockettsville) and a desire to maintain Democratic supremacy.[66] Their respective relationships to Breathitt County and its history were key to their alliance's success. "Hargis still sat high in the councils of his party, while Callahan," wrote a Cincinnati newspaperman a generation after the pair's salad years, "always the lesser light, kept his fingers gripped upon county affairs."[67]

As a former Klan chief, Callahan bridged the gap between postwar mass violence and legitimate political action. Hargis and Callahan had been young children during the Civil War, and they had little interest in exhuming the county's old mayhem. With a Republican in the governor's mansion, their mostly Democratic (the gold standard debate had swelled Breathitt's Republican ranks slightly, as had in-migration from other mountain counties)

Camera-shy James Hargis posed for few photographs, and the reading public outside of Breathitt County had to rely on artists' renderings to know what the mysterious county judge looked like. (Courtesy of the Breathitt County Museum)

home county's political stock was high in the last five years of the nineteenth century.[68] In 1895 Republicans had made a preelection boast that Breathitt would be theirs, but it had not come to pass.[69] In 1899 Hargis became the first Breathitt County resident appointed to his party's state central committee, a position that gave him patronage power over his entire congressional district and a voice in the party's highest echelons.[70] The Hargis-Callahan partnership (with Redwine as a fellow traveler) was recalled as "Breathitt's debut into political circles in her long robes of state."[71]

The partnership also coincided with William Goebel's rise, and they saw to it that Breathitt County supported him.[72] The Goebel platform potentially benefited them economically and politically. James Hargis had only one other mercantile competitor in Jackson, while Callahan's store in Crockettsville, far from the closest railroad tracks, was the only store for miles.[73] Both men had numerous coal and timber investments but, next to the behemoth holding companies and corporations of the day, they were still small businessmen. Like most southern merchants they favored Goebel's brand of trust busting.[74] The relatively small Lexington & Eastern Railroad had made Jackson a boomtown, and Goebel's attacks upon the much larger L&N probably appealed to Hargis and Callahan (and very possibly the vast majority of Breathitt County voters as well), since any reduction or regulation of the larger railroad kept freight rates amenable to local gentry. Any enemy of the L&N octopus was obliged to be an ally to Breathitt County's men of means; even a Democrat accused of turning his party over to "Anarchists, Socialists and Populiste" could support the local status quo.[75]

However, the Goebel election law may have been their primary enticement. The law established a state board of election commissioners as well as corresponding boards in each county. With a Democratic majority in the General Assembly and the consequent Democratic control over the majority of county boards, Callahan and Hargis could conceivably maintain their party's power within Breathitt County indefinitely, perhaps without continuing to make their county notorious for gunshots. Their connections to William Goebel and the methods that had been used to win the county for him dictated that a perpetual air of controversy would follow them both.

A mass meeting in the summer of 1899 produced a "a healthy rebuke to McKinleyism, Hannaism [a reference to William McKinley's campaign manager Mark Hanna], and the Phillipineism" in the next year's presidential race as well as a supposedly unanimous show of support for Goebel, but the entrance of "fair election Democrat" John Y. Brown represented a more conservative option, especially for Breathitt County's Confederate veterans.[76] "Old line Democrat" county judge J. Wise Hagins endorsed Brown and accused Hargis and Callahan of fraud at every opportunity after the Music Hall Convention.[77] It was the first gubernatorial election in which mountain Democratic votes could not be disregarded; Goebel's majority in the most famously Democratic mountain county was deemed crucial.[78]

Repeating a smaller version of his gambit from two years earlier, Callahan hired armed men to guard the most heavily Republican precinct's ballot box and repel Republican election inspectors during the November polling. An armed gang of "Goebel desperadoes" then interrupted the final count, firing pistols in the air, driving all the Republicans from the courthouse and then procuring the ballot box. Even in precincts where Republican inspectors were allowed to remain, all of the accompanying Democrats favored Goebel, with none present for Brown (who, in such a heavily Democratic county, may well have been the greater threat to Goebel). According to the state Republican campaign chairman's accusations, 400 Breathitt ballots

Jackson, Kentucky, circa 1903, where calculated political violence hid beneath the gui

were counterfeit. With "bulldozing never seen in Breathitt County before," Goebel won the county with 756 votes.[79]

"Every Republican knows that Redwine is the Circuit Judge and that the Sheriff is a Goebel man," Jackson's Republican election commissioner lamented while visiting Lexington a week after the election. "If a Republican resisted any sort of an attack he would be punished to the full limit of the law—if he were killed his murderer would be acquitted. What are you going to do about it?"[80] "The Republicans are at the mercy of the Breathitt county Goebel men and they are even afraid to protest," the New York Sun reported, "as it would mean in many instances certain death."[81] After the election, the only other counties that reported similarly "severe" tactics to secure the Goebel vote were those with large cities where ward organizations made

ımtown raucousness (as well as the town's "feudal" history). (Courtesy of Charles Hayes)

fraud more common and expected.[82] With the "strong Republican" William Strong dead for nearly three years, there was no one to match to the Democrats' extralegal electioneering. Whatever embarrassment Breathitt County's violence might have caused Bluegrass Democrats was outweighed by the advantage of having a Democratic bastion in the mountains that remained enigmatic (at least one out-of-state editor refused to believe mountain Democrats even existed and refuted Republican claims of wrongdoing thus).[83] Governors were still required to await the request of a circuit judge for the militia to be summoned; even if Governor Bradley saw fit to do so, Judge Redwine was hardly inclined to make the petition, since the "bulldozing" benefited his gubernatorial endorsee. Breathitt County, long known for its singular record of violence, had become simply another piece of evidence for the statewide crisis of legitimacy, the most overtly forceful example of "the Goebel methods."[84] As always, Bloody Breathitt was left to its own devices.

"There is no politics in the law"

Once Democrats reunited around Goebel's martyrdom, there was no demand for indictment, except in places where the "Goebel methods" had the most immediate local effects. In 1901 Hargis and Callahan ran for county judge and sheriff respectively to cement the hold on Breathitt County's government that they had already established as party heads. It was too much for many of their party mates. As popular as he was with many local Democrats, Callahan had a difficult time escaping his past "feudist" reputation, and his candidacy brought with it controversies other than his and Hargis's Goebel connections. Dissident Democrats imitated the recent anti-Democrat southern strategy, forming a fusion with Republicans.[85]

The fusion was organized by Jackson's Democratic town marshal Jim Cockrell and attorney James Buchanan Marcum, one of the election inspectors harassed by the "Hargis-Callahan Goebellites" in 1899.[86] Despite his namesake, Marcum was a rising star among Kentucky Republicans, an affiliation inherited from his Three Forks Battalion veteran father Edward, and Edward's brother-in-law-in-arms Captain William Strong. During the 1890s James Marcum made an unsuccessful run for Congress (and later appellate judge) while representing his controversial uncle in court throughout as the older man asserted his legal possession over thousands of timbered acres.[87] Though cut from the same political cloth as his uncle, Marcum was not a crusading "war element" Republican.[88] A U.S. commissioner (appointed by Benjamin Harrison), university trustee, and counsel for the L&E, he had more in common with Republicans who championed the gold standard and the "McKinley Tariff," while addressing the "Negro Question" as seldom as possible.[89] Rather than crouching in a fortified woodland hermitage with squatters and former slaves, he lived in a white clapboard house in Jackson and had a Democratic law partner, following Atlanta editor Henry Grady's entreaty to "put business in place of politics."[90]

Whatever his kinship or professional affiliations, no one could associate thoroughly modern Marcum with his uncle's so-called feudal origins in "night-errantry."[91] The closest Marcum came to being involved with "feudists" was acting as counsel for Joseph Eversole's faction after the French-Eversole feud (he later represented Bad Tom Smith, Fulton French's primary gunman,

Unlike his uncle William Strong, James Buchanan Marcum challenged his county's Democratic ringleaders through peaceful means. His 1903 assassination became Bloody Breathitt's most infamous killing. (Courtesy of Charles Hayes)

in his murder trial) as well as his uncle's wartime nemesis, John Aikman.[92] He did not harbor ancient hatreds, but he was angered by his recent opponents' dearth of fair play. Democrats had carried Marcum's home county for most of his life, but their need for violence was an exposed weakness. Moreover, his challenge to the Hargis courthouse constituted a fight between one of Kentucky's most influential Republicans against one of its most powerful Democrats—this in a county that, a few years earlier, had been a sparsely populated backwater ignored for everything except its nationally known proclivity for violence.

With or without Marcum's credentials, the fusionist campaign was an abortive effort from the beginning. Repudiations of the Democratic Party could not work, and denouncement of the local party leaders could do only so much. Former county judge Wise Hagins released an anti-Hargis circular preposterously accusing him of supporting Republican candidates since the 1880s, jibes Hargis easily dismissed by invoking Goebel and William Jennings Bryan.[93] In rebuttal, Hargis accused Hagins of approving the Goebel assassination, implying not only bad moral character but, more important, disloyalty (earning Hagins comparisons to Judas Iscariot and Benedict Arnold in the Hargis-friendly *Hazel Green Herald*).[94] Hargis then retained Marcum's law partner, O. H. Pollard.[95] In 1901's fall elections, the fusionists captured every local office except for county attorney and county judge. Hargis, the "alleged chief conspirator," retained his bench, but only after weathering the first electoral "just rebuke" against Breathitt Democrats in decades.[96]

Callahan's victory was slightly less sure. After Callahan won the office by a mere sixteen votes, his opponent contested the outcome, prompting Judge Redwine to declare the election void.[97] Once in office, Judge James Hargis created an uproar by appointing Callahan acting sheriff until a new election could be held. Callahan's right to the office was challenged in the Kentucky State Court of Appeals in 1903 (which sustained Hargis's and Redwine's decisions). By then, Callahan had been serving as sheriff for nearly two years, hiring his and Hargis's choice of deputies and amassing influence.[98] Even during Jeremiah South's lifetime, so much power had not been contained in so few hands in Breathitt County.

Sometime in early 1902, a verbal altercation in Marcum and Pollard's law office led to drawn pistols between them, Hargis, and Callahan. Shooting was avoided, but the police judge (an unstated fusionist supporter) issued a warrant for all four of them. Hargis refused to appear in police court and instead surrendered to a county magistrate he trusted. To allay future confrontations, Marcum moved the case be dismissed, but not before Jim Cockrell and his brother Tom (who was also his deputy) attempted to serve Hargis warrants in the courthouse, leading to another unholstering.[99] Within judge's chamber walls and law offices, the mutual threat of violence was sufficient to maintain self-restraint and an uneasy stalemate, albeit a stalemate that did not stifle Hargis's and Callahan's power. A few weeks later Tom Cockrell confronted Hargis's younger brother Ben at a whiskey wholesaler's. The two young men initiated a roomwide gunfight, and each was seriously injured. Cockrell recovered under the care of his "guardian" (the Cockrells were both in their twenties and orphans), Dr. Braxton D. Cox. Ben Hargis died in Judge Hargis's home a day later.[100]

Ben Hargis's death was nothing unusual in its setting: an intensely masculine, alcohol-drenched environment replete with concealed weapons.[101] Jackson, a small county seat turned coal and timber boomtown, was undergoing a rapid change in its population and character, as were so many other industrializing towns, and it was well acknowledged that this was a new sort of exogenous violence, even in a county with a nasty past. "These killings recall some old-time days when Breathitt was foremost as a bloody ground; there is a difference between those days and the present," a Jackson resident wrote to the *Hazel Green Herald*. "Feuds between factions, which were long and almost unending, were the causes of so many killings then, but recently there were no feuds, but owing to the resulting influence of so many 'blind tigers' existing in this county. This does not speak for the general morality of the county, nor for the will of the people, but owing to the lack of execution of the law, such is being carried on."[102] Even if current violence could not be ignored, there was still a need to parse past from present. What the outside world once considered primitively quaint and picturesque was becoming a danger to prosperity and civic morality.[103] Ben Hargis's end was an outcome of social ills common to intemperate communities all over the United States.

James Hargis saw it differently or, at least, he wanted the world to believe he did. Utilizing Breathitt County's past history, real and imagined, Judge Hargis pasted together a number of incidents from recent history with local genealogy to portray his brother's death as part of an ongoing, years-old feud. In 1895 his other brother, John Hargis, had tried to intimidate a black voter on Election Day. Jerry Cardwell, the Republican candidate for Jackson town marshal, came to the voter's defense and then earned John Hargis's further hatred by winning the election.[104] The two met again the following year aboard an L&E passenger car en route to Jackson when Cardwell was working as the railroad's "special detective" (probably a temporary title inspired by the L&E's unease over statewide bloodletting during the McKinley-Bryan presidential race). Under unclear circumstances, Cardwell confronted the unruly Hargis and the men exchanged gunfire, leaving Hargis fatally wounded.[105] Cardwell was convicted of manslaughter, only to be pardoned by Governor William Bradley (since the first melee happened during the election in which the Republican Bradley was elected, this would have infuriated the surviving Hargises all the more).[106]

Like many other white Kentuckians, James Hargis probably felt victimized by the Republican Party. Cardwell's shooting of John Hargis had no connection to later events, other than his kinship to men Judge Hargis considered enemies by 1902—and even that connection was circuitous. Jerry Cardwell's brother was the police judge Hargis had refused to appear before, while Dr. Braxton Cox was married to Cardwell's sister. Jerry Cardwell himself had not been involved in the ongoing post-Goebel commotion but that did not matter since feuds hid individuals behind their "clans." Feuds had been associated with Bloody Breathitt since James Hargis's youth, and he knew how to use the concept to his own ends; if he retaliated, or if his political enemies began to fall mysteriously, Hargis could hide behind his own surname and his loss of two brothers, claiming to be embattled. The declaration of a new feud in Bloody Breathitt would not be met with much skepticism. And it contributed to factual errors in the papers, including moving John Hargis's death from 1896 to 1902 so that it fit better into his brother's feud narrative.[107] For years, Bloody Breathitt had had *feud* imposed upon it from the outside world. Now, at least one Breathitt native had found a way to use this contrived narrative to his advantage. By establishing that his family was besieged, he justified any future violence directed at his enemies as retribution, while simultaneously obscuring its political import. Even if Judge Hargis was implicated, an indictment would be unlikely (let alone a conviction), and his motives would remain unclear—in a time and place where "disentangling murder from assassination" was difficult.[108] Even though he might be ridiculed as a "feudist," Hargis would still retain power.

Braxton Cox's shooting death the following April seemed to verify this feud's existence.[109] After a late-night telephoned request for a house call turned out to be a false alarm, Cox was walking home on Jackson's main thoroughfare when he was riddled with buckshot.[110] No witnesses ever came forward, but it was rumored that the fatal blast had come from either the

The midnight shooting death of Dr. Braxton Cox initiated a new era of violent death in Jackson, one that reflected Breathitt County's recent changes. (Courtesy of Charles Hayes)

courthouse or Judge Hargis's livery stables. Cox's eighty-year-old mother-in-law, secure in her age and sex, was the only Jackson resident willing to publicly accuse Judge Hargis.[111] Apparently, no one ever expressed suspicion that the initial telephone caller was a conspirator.

James Cockrell's murder that July attracted far more attention.[112] This was a midday shooting, and it was widely acknowledged that the rifle shots had come from a second-story courthouse window (the schematic similarities to William Goebel's killing were palpable). Only days before, he had exchanged gunfire with Curtis Jett, one of Edward Callahan's deputies, in a hotel dining room, and he was preparing to leave Jackson to avoid more fights.[113] Cockrell was trundled onto an L&E railroad car and transported to a Lexington hospital, as notice of his imminent arrival was telegraphed ahead.[114] Before he expired from five bullet wounds the next day, the press had already placed his impending death within a feud narrative that swapped facts for plot coherence. One paper announced the young town marshal was the latest "Breathitt County feuds" casualty, and faintly praised him as "superior in every way to Thomas Cockrell, his brother" (whose killing of Ben Hargis was implicitly blamed for beginning the chain of events that had led to the older Cockrell's imminent demise). An evening edition interchangeably called Ben Hargis Judge James Hargis's son and brother, foreshadowing future media errors.[115] The fact that Ben Hargis was killed via reciprocal-fire manslaughter, while Cox's and Cockrell's deaths were obviously premeditated assassination-style first-degree murders, was not addressed. Once the series of deaths was branded (no later than July 1902) the "Hargis and Cockrell feud," it was far less likely that such nuances would be acknowledged.[116] Judge Hargis's insistence had done its work.

As circumstantial evidence built against James Hargis and Edward Callahan, their motive(s) became a subject of statewide speculation. Initially, the revenge motif seemed more likely than calculated elimination of political opponents, especially in light of the armed altercation between a Cockrell and a Hargis that had preceded another Cockrell's murder. The Republican *Lexington Leader,* the paper that had produced a stirring account of Cockrell's death the day before, was strangely unaware of Cockrell's role in the fusionist campaign. "One of the strangest features in connection with the feud is that while it originated in a political contest, and was increased by the killing of Ben Hargis by Tom Cockrell, both factions are Democrats, so that whatever political feeling exists in the feud it is all on one side and in one party."[117] Instead, it was suggested that James Cockrell had been disposed of so that his brother, awaiting trial for murder in another county, would be utterly defenseless. While the Cockrells had been successful in securing a change of venue, Governor J. C. W. Beckham had assigned Judge Hargis's Bluegrass cousin and fellow Democratic State Committee member, Thomas Hargis, as special judge.[118] Thomas Cockrell, the *Leader* predicted, was "to be left to the tender mercies of his enemies who are now said to be in control of the legal machinery of the county." As in past interpretations of feud violence in eastern Kentucky, Cockrell's death was headlined as only "Another Dark Chapter Added to Bloody Breathitt's Terrible Record That Savors of Middle Age Barbarism."[119]

Wolfe County's Democratic *Hazel Green Herald* reported its neighbor's tribulations with a typical combination of local defensiveness and regional solidarity, but with Breathitt County held at arm's length. During the weeks leading up to Thomas Cockrell's trial, it criticized other papers' factual errors in "the Hargis-Cockrell feud in Breathitt."[120] Shortly after James Cockrell was killed, the paper criticized the *Leader*'s (and other "outsiders'") sudden interest in Jackson's internal affairs. Breathitt County's citizens were having an endogenous "hell of their own," and "people outside the immediate trouble do not know the cause of any of the parties involved, save as retailed to them, and are apt, therefore, to misjudge." Without explicitly announcing a feud, the *Herald* assured readers that the troubles were strictly a "family affair."[121] But weeks later, when Hazel Green was selected as Tom Cockrell's change of venue (which Redwine attempted to block), the *Herald* editor crowed that a trial "out of the range of the 'feud belt'" would put an end to the sordid events.[122] Judge Hargis was never implicated personally. No doubt noting that heightened exposure of Breathitt County would damage his administration, he stated that he and his adherents "were never in any feud" and elected to abort his pursuit of Tom Cockrell's conviction a month after James Cockrell's death (Tom Cockrell was acquitted).[123] No one asked Hargis why the three homicide victims happened to all be fusionists. The political elements of the story were already fading.

The existence, or denial, of an ongoing "family feud" was not enough to misdirect all Kentuckians, especially Republicans who remembered the Breathitt judges' role in the Goebel campaign. After Judge Hargis withdrew from Tom Cockrell's prosecution, the *Lexington Leader* kept up its assault, using William Goebel's memory as a rhetorical weapon. "There never would have been an hour during the entire trouble when the Circuit Court could not have controlled the situation absolutely, if [Redwine] had injected into it one-hundredth part of the zeal shown on the occasion of the foul assassination of Mr. Goebel at Frankfort when the state was taxed $100,000 and every piece of its constabulary was set in motion to run down the assassins."[124] A few months later, the paper again exhumed Goebel in connection to Breathitt's judges: "Breathitt county is today the political stink hole of Kentucky, and elections there are nothing more than licensed orgies of brutality and crime. Judge Redwine was the chairman of Goebel's Music Hall Convention and Judge Hargis was one of the master spirits of the Goebelites on the floor and, under their absolute sway Breathitt County is today the best exemplification of the horrors of Goebelism to be found in the Commonwealth of Kentucky."[125] Only the newspapers that had bitterly opposed Goebel three years earlier called for further investigation of Cox's and Cockrell's murders.[126]

After James Marcum alerted the *Leader* of the death threats he had received since Dr. Cox's death, the Republican paper enhanced its attack, printing letters from Marcum, Hargis, and Callahan but allowing Marcum the lion's share of column space. He produced an affidavit signed by one of his criminal case clients, Mose Feltner, claiming that Judge Hargis and Sheriff Callahan had once offered him money to kill Marcum (Feltner had a lengthy criminal record and little apparent compunction against trigger pulling).[127] Marcum's claims were reprinted all over the state, while the *Leader* proclaimed that "murder [in Breathitt County] has been used systematically as a means of intimidation" and that "the processes of the court have a terror only for innocent men."[128]

Hargis and Callahan both responded bitterly, claiming that Marcum had lied for incomprehensible reasons. Hargis cited his own record of shutting down blind tigers as evidence of his county's lack of troubles.[129] Callahan was more candid, acknowledging that Marcum might have reason to be alarmed after the unsolved shooting deaths of "two prominent men." As sheriff, Callahan had to own up to the county's civil disorder, but he was quick to deny that it was anything but undirected disorder, and certainly not a "conspiracy."[130] Marcum responded by expressing fear that Callahan's deputies, Curtis Jett and Tom White, were out to kill him. He also accused Callahan of involvement in the murder of his uncle, William Strong, in 1897.[131]

Marcum and the *Leader*'s most damning accusation was that Breathitt's courthouse ring was protected by Democrats all over the state. "[Hargis and Callahan] have men employed, newspaper correspondents, to misrepresent the facts," Marcum asserted, "and Hargis is now trying to arouse political prejudices in order to secure the sympathy of the Democratic press. There is no politics in the law. It was made for all parties and should be obeyed by all, even the 'leading Democrats in Eastern Kentucky.'"[132] Hargis directed Breathitt County's grand jury to indict Marcum for criminal libel, silencing Marcum for the next seven months (the charges were eventually dismissed).[133] The year 1903 began with an apparent détente, but with Marcum going into self-imposed isolation.

In May 1903 Marcum was shot and killed in the doorway of the Breathitt County courthouse.[134] A bullet entered his back, apparently fired from inside the building, and a second one was emptied into his head, apparently at very close range, after he had fallen.[135] For months he had left his home only in the company of women or while carrying his infant son—his own portable "domestic sphere" was an effective deterrent.[136] This noontime foray was said to be his first walk by the courthouse in adult male company since 1902. By dying violently after publicly implicating the courthouse ring, Marcum almost succeeded in his goal: demonstrating that what the United States knew as the "Hargis-Cockrell feud" was not a horizontal "family affair" but instead the outgrowth of a statewide struggle for legitimacy that Kentucky had dealt with for years. The daytime murder of such a prominent figure proved to be the beginning of the end for Jackson's courthouse ring. Still, James Marcum's death was forever after misunderstood as part of a feud narrative.

"This is only one of many similar feuds which have disgraced the State"

James Marcum's murder was the most widely publicized "feudal" death in years. Most of the fatalities in the French-Eversole feud and the Rowan County War (or, for that matter, the deaths of Judge Burnett in 1878 and William Strong in 1897) were men unknown outside their respective communities. But this mountain attorney was a leader in Kentucky's Republican Party, an officer of the federal government, a corporate representative, and the very incarnation of his section's recent advancement. His death presented a conundrum for Bluegrass Kentuckians who had previously interpreted the eastern third's feud phenomenon as a sui generis product of isolation or racial (Anglo-Saxon or Celtic) peculiarity. His ally Tom Cockrell's assertion that Marcum "was never implicated in any feud" motivated many to consider his death an accident of sorts.[137] An editorial in the *Louisville Courier-Journal* printed soon after his death illustrates the turn in interpretation of what many Kentuckians considered a familiar occurrence presented by the Hargis-Cockrell feud's latest death.

> The feud which took Mr. Marcum's life has caused, it is said, no less than forty deaths in the last two years. This would be an astounding statement to any one who was a stranger to these mountain vendettas. But this is only one of many similar feuds which have disgraced the State and will continue to disgrace it until the State shows a more resolute purpose and power to uphold the law.
>
> These feuds have too often been looked upon as romantic episodes of primitive life in our backwoods. That is entirely too charitable a view to take of them. There is nothing romantic or manly

about them. Originating in some trivial quarrel, they continue for generations of cowardice, treachery and assassination. The murders which are their outcome are not even committed man to man, in the open, but almost invariably are perpetrated after patient lying-in-wait and ambush extending over months and years.[138]

The editorial provided a succinct description of Kentucky's endemic feud violence as it was understood nationally: series of violent acts employing ambush-style homicides (as the same paper had described the death of William Goebel) taking place deep in the mountains, caused by disagreements of an unknown or unimportant nature, producing an undetermined number of deaths, and lasting over the course of generations by a mutual motivation of vengeance (the editorial notably omitted the family or "clan" as the basis for feud factionalism). But the ways in which the Hargis-Cockrell feud did not fit into this previously formed mold, namely, its chronological brevity and fairly clear political motivations, were generally ignored. The "forty deaths" was a melding of Jackson's new industrial age harum-scarum and its older postbellum reputation.

Marcum's assassination stood out from both, and the men who had engaged him in an editorial-page war of words a few months earlier had clear motive. Judge Hargis's best tactic was a continuation of feud-related rhetoric, with himself cast as indignant victim (it was not hard to do with his opposition keeping silent, as Hagins and other fusionists were doing). The previous year he had cast James Cockrell's death within a larger feud narrative that acknowledged enmity between his family (but not necessarily himself) and the Cockrells. Now, Hargis called Marcum one of a number of "Republican leaders" who had "endeavored to run [Hargis] out of the county." But Hargis still insisted that this was a communal, multigenerational conflict motivated by old, bitter memory, not current party matters. When Hargis was a boy, the judge told one journalist, Marcum's uncle William Strong had raided the Hargis farm, leaving him and his siblings hungry and shoeless.[139] Marcum, he said, had since been "reared in an atmosphere of feuds" and that there was "not a *family* in Breathitt county some one of whose members has not been slain by Marcum *blood*" (my emphasis).[140] Their local Civil War experience was so defined by intimacy, with the stories of visceral suffering that entailed, that its politics need not be addressed. Breathitt County's violent past was putty in Hargis's hands.

The *Lexington Leader* remained the only major Kentucky paper eager to examine the killings of 1902 through a political lens, placing Marcum's death specifically within the lineage of Cox's and Cockrell's, referencing Marcum's accusations from the previous November.[141] Republicans had endured more than three years of abuse for their assumed complicity in William Goebel's death. Now that one of their own had fallen in a similar manner, they were quick to find the beams in their Democratic accusers' eyes. Maysville's *Public Ledger* minced no words a month after Marcum's death. "When it comes to real-simon-pure-unadulterated18-karat-brand-burned-in-the-barrel feudocracy, the good old rock-ribbed Democratic county of Breathitt can give any 'Republican mountain county' hearts and spades and beat it to never-come-back."[142] "Amidst the newspaper illustrations and accounts of the 'War in Breathitt,' it should not be forgotten that Breathitt is one of the staunch Democratic counties of Kentucky. All its local officers are Democrats, and the Circuit Judge is a Goebel of Democracy."[143] Even though the circumstances of these "political and feud murders" could not fully challenge the more popular explanation for mountain violence, it did at least temporarily call into question the assumption that eastern Kentucky was a "barbarians' world beyond the polis."[144]

Some Republicans even accused "the State Democratic machine" of finding "the Hargis outlaws" useful.[145] "While the business men of Kentucky are trying to build up," said one, "the politicians are doing their best to pull down."[146] Feuds existed in the mountains, blasted a Lexington Republican, but a feud proper was motivated by honor or revenge, not material gain. "Time will make a splendid civilization in the mountains of Kentucky, and the feud will be eradicated as it was in Scotland. As for that Breathitt county business—there is the filth of lucre in that, blood shed for money, not for revenge. That is disgraceful, and the mountains will not put up with it."[147] A Republican insistence that contingent/political violence was taking place did not negate the inherent/communal explanations for violence that Americans of all political stripes had been absorbing and believing since the 1880s.

The Republicans' Goebel/Marcum comparisons were hardly flawless. "The assassination of Marcum was coldly planned in a business way—not in the heat of excitement," reasoned one Republican. "Mr. Goebel was shot at the Statehouse door during a period of unsurpassed excitement and tension, and nobody actually saw the man who fired the shot. The case as to Marcum was much simpler than as to Goebel." Perhaps, he opined, "the Democratic Machine [was] in the official saddle seeking to hide the facts and save the Democratic party," but it was beyond spurious and unfounded to say Marcum's killing was any more "coldly planned" than Goebel's.[148] In trying to prove the true nature of Bloody Breathitt's most renowned crime, Republicans balked at admitting that political violence was a tool available to both parties. Pro-Hargis Democrats could still wave Goebel's bloody shirt in their faces.

Of course most Democrats preferred that Breathitt County's killings be considered "lawlessness" unrelated to party politics.[149] Even Democratic papers that had no interest in using the language of feuding insisted on at least acknowledging that, since "murder is murder," politics aside, Marcum's slaying "was as bad as the murder of Goebel," while another disingenuously praised Breathitt County's "Democratic officials" for "using every effort to bring the guilty to justice," unlike when Goebel "was assassinated on the capital grounds under Republican rule."[150] Hypocrisy, they said, was thick within any and all Republican censures of Hargis et al., and had Kentucky Democrats rushed to the defense of their malefactors as Republicans had done for Goebel's accused murderers?[151] "There is not a Democratic paper in Kentucky that has stood back from denouncing the feuds and assassins of Breathitt county on account of the political aspect of the case. How different is the picture from that of the assassination of Wm. Goebel, when every cross-roads organ of the Republican party in Kentucky either openly or tacitly excused or defended his murderers."[152] While Republicans had hindered Caleb Powers's and Jim Howard's prosecutions, the Democratic press, in contrast, could now claim to be "on the forefront" of nonpartisan justice for Marcum, "the Republican son of Breathitt."[153] Democratic admissions of "the political aspect of the case" were exceptionally rare. At least one Democrat doubted that Marcum's killer "had any politics."[154]

Louisville's *Courier-Journal* continued its generation-old practice of balancing mild party loyalty with an attempt to mollify everyone with apolitical descriptions of violence. "Officers of the law and courts of justice" did not direct the actions of "assassins and anarchists," but were instead cowed by them.[155] The "law officers . . . of the so-called county of Breathitt," were not so much vicious as inept.[156] Well aware of the ever-present danger of libel charges, most other newspapers throughout Kentucky were careful to treat Breathitt County's violence as the local authorities' sins of omission rather than their directed violence. In a state with little central oversight over county affairs, Hargis and Callahan could withstand these insults while maintaining their tremendous amount of power. As commentators all over Kentucky yammered on, the judge and the sheriff remained in their lofty positions in Jackson. During May 1903, it was often said that the identities of Marcum's (and Cox's and Cockrell's) killer(s) were widely known, and that fears of reprisals kept the populace silent.

It took someone from outside the political sphere to expose the crimes of James Hargis and Edward Callahan. James Marcum's widow, Abrelia Hurst Marcum, wasted no time accusing Hargis and Callahan for her husband's death, not only implicating Hargis's "clan" in her husband's homicide but broadly blaming "the administration of Judge Hargis" for leading to a general atmosphere of lawlessness.[157]

> Judge Hargis and the whole state knows that there have been thirty-eight homicides in Breathitt county during his administration as county judge. What attempt has been made by him as the highest official in the county to have the laws enforced? When he became county judge about two years ago there was no more peaceful county in Kentucky. Our people walked the streets at night in the pursuit of their vocations with absolute safety and no thought of danger.
>
> Today business men who can are leaving. Our citizens do not dare to express their opinion for fear of assassination. Citizens dare not leave their homes at night for fear of being the mark of men who are immune from punishment. Every man whose life's blood has stained the soil of Breathitt county during Judge Hargis's administration of law has bit the dust at the hands of some adherent of their clan, or his identity remains unknown and no strenuous effort has been made to find him.[158]

Although Marcum interchangeably blamed Hargis for crimes of malice and of negligence, she notably blamed the entirety of Breathitt County's violence on him, with no reference to past troubles. If Breathitt County was presently a place where violence was tolerated, it was contingent upon individuals currently in positions of power, not because of the brutal inherencies suggested by the decades-old nickname Bloody Breathitt.

As a woman and expectant mother (she gave birth the following September), Abrelia Marcum was practically immune to the violence used on the streets of Jackson. Brutality toward women, especially spousal abuse, was not unheard of in Breathitt County any more than elsewhere else in the United States (an uxoricide arrest began the confrontation that led to the death of Judge Burnett in 1878). But deadly violence with clearly political purposes

In a time and place in which men were afraid to accuse the Hargis courthouse of murder, only a woman, Abrelia Marcum (pictured with her children), could expose the courthouse ring's misdeeds. (*Washington Times*, October 20, 1907)

(that is, the vast majority of Bloody Breathitt's most notorious events) could not be directed at women since they were not recognized as political actors. Even the most ruthless men kept violence, especially politically motivated violence, as far from women as possible. James Marcum's successful tactic of shielding himself with women and children in the weeks before his assassination demonstrated the sacredness of the "separate sphere."[159] Far from being a motivation for violence, as the narrative of feuds suggested, the women and children that represented family were obstructions to violence. Just as Dr. Braxton Cox's elderly mother-in-law felt free to speak out against the courthouse ring, Abrelia Marcum was able to do the same. She represented to Breathitt County men communal institutions that had not often been violated by the county's decades-old cycle of violence.[160]

Even though she was protected from her husband's fate, her words could do only so much to implicate the men in power. Just after Governor Beckham offered a $500 reward for James Marcum's murderer, Curtis Jett was indicted.[161] Jett hired Judge Hargis's business partner Fulton French as his attorney, and went to lengths to see that he was tried in Breathitt County (soon after, deputy Tom White was indicted as well).[162] Edward Callahan recused himself from his role in summoning witnesses for the trial, and he and Hargis took a very public role in supporting Jett and White's defense.[163] They and French engaged in an apparent effort to prevent Jett and White from plea-bargaining and implicating them all in a larger conspiracy. Jett was an agent of the county court, but that was minimized somewhat by the rumor that he and James Marcum had "quarreled" publicly shortly before the latter's death, a rumor that emphasized personal enmity over political calculation.[164]

Suspecting that the trial would prove to be politically charged, and chagrined by growing criticism of his relationship with the Hargis courthouse, Governor Beckham sent the state militia to Jackson.[165] Beckham announced that the "situation" in Jackson "has been exaggerated" and he was hesitant to send more members of the militia to fortify the ones already sent. Less than four weeks later, the militia unit was ordered back to the Bluegrass to prevent a potential lynching during a highly publicized murder trial of three black men.[166]

As national attention surrounded Jett and White's trial, *Harper's Weekly* attacked Breathitt County as an example of a larger problem. "These assassinations in Kentucky are attributed by some observers to the system of county politics in Kentucky," it announced. "The struggle for the county

Deputies Tom White (left) and Curtis Jett (right) under guard after their arrest for murder. Even though they were officers of the county court, it was difficult to prove that Judge Hargis or Sheriff Callahan had directed them to kill. (Courtesy of Charles Hayes)

offices is so intense that rival politicians and their partisans are led to murder to attain their ends, and assassination is further fostered by the spirit of the vendetta which prevails in the mountainous regions of the State."[167] A fire that destroyed a hotel belonging to a witness for the prosecution during the trial prompted members of both political parties to concur.[168] Yet circuit court judge Redwine remained aloof from implication. When the trial in Jackson ended with a hung jury (with Redwine on the bench), the *Hazel Green Herald* surmised it could only mean an end to the "holy alliance of Hargis & Redwine" (Redwine retired from the circuit bench later that summer).[169] A change of venue to a presumably neutral county resulted in life sentences for both Jett and White.[170] Jett was later found guilty of murdering James Cockrell and sentenced to death, but the sentence was reversed in 1905.[171]

Jett's and White's convictions convinced many that justice had been served, and for the rest of 1903, Breathitt's courthouse bosses were free from scrutiny. Throughout it all, Hargis's position in Kentucky's Democratic central committee remained safe. Shortly after Jett and White's change of venue, Democrats feted him at a banquet in Lexington.[172] Governor J. C. W. Beckham's embarrassment was harder to hide. Hargis's boast that he could get anyone pardoned was enough to make many Kentuckians suspicious, and Beckham's (he had issued a record number of pardons in his first five months in office) subsequent pardoning of Tom White seemed to confirm this, as did Curtis Jett when he secured a Beckham pardon for an unrelated crime.[173] Questions about Beckham's connections to the Hargis courthouse emerged days after Marcum's death, and the governor was forced to address the unhappy county at the beginning of his 1903 reelection campaign.[174] With rote references to Goebel's death at Republican hands, Beckham countered that Governor Bradley had issued far more pardons, and cited accused conspirator James Howard (from his prison cell Howard angrily accused Beckham of using him to "distract the public gaze from [Beckham's] conduct, his political pardons, his trades and unholy alliances").[175] Beckham accused Kentucky Republicans of making "political capital" out of the Breathitt murders, while applauding Democratic papers for condemning them apolitically.[176] The governor also parried with northern critics over the relative quantity of violence in his own state compared to theirs. "The calling into service of the entire national guard of one of the northern states to suppress a strike, where hundreds may be slain, does not attract one-half the notice as does the use of one company of Kentucky militia in aiding some Circuit court in trial of a criminal."[177] As the summer months passed, the Breathitt County issue did not go away. At the official opening of the Democratic state campaign, Beckham declared,

> That the Democratic officials have done everything in their power to put an end to the troubles in Breathitt County no one disputes. They were purely local, and not half as serious as the feudal outbreak in Clay County during the [Bradley] administration. If the Republicans had shown the same desire to punish the assassins of William Goebel that the Democrats did to punish Marcum's assassins, both crimes would now be avenged. Let the past be forgotten, and let us stand together henceforth shoulder to shoulder as Democrats, with our hearts full of devotion for the welfare of our State and Nation.[178]

Beckham's address had multiple insinuations. Even many of his own party mates may not have been convinced that Breathitt County's killings were rooted only in local conflicts. Breathitt County's violence had to be, as had always been the case in other eastern locales (especially where Republicans ruled), purely internal and without any greater significance or implication. In addition, his reference to an analogous "feud" situation in Republican Clay County during a Republican administration negated whatever attempts Republicans might make to pillory his party for sanctioning violence. Breathitt County's recent assassinations and the "Clay County War" were, by virtue of their placement in the state's (supposedly Republican) primitive mountains, cut from the same cloth, even if they had grown from two separate conflicts and under different regimes.[179] Even if local party affiliations were the origin of violence, they were based upon small differences between decidedly local politicians and their henchmen, with no relation to larger issues faced by the state or national parties.

Beckham echoed the *Courier-Journal*'s tone in portraying Breathitt County after the 1878 riot. Against the threat of northern/Republican censure it was to be carefully defended. But when addressing the issue to an audience within the state, it was more advantageous to rhetorically place the mountains outside of Kentucky and outside of the present. Implicitly, this suggested that these feuds were hardly political at all, but rather primeval products of their mountain environment and far into "the past," which was better "forgotten." "Purely local" "feudal outbreak[s]" could be easily dismissed, especially when individuals with direct connections to the governor's office were left unmentioned.

Beckham's November victory indicated that sacrificing the reputation of eastern Kentucky (at least when done to a Kentucky audience) was an effective Democratic tool. Safely back in office, Beckham repeated these claims in his annual address the following January. This time he did not try to excise Kentucky's highlands from the rest of the state but did repeat his critique of urban crime up north. "Irresponsible romances" had inflated Breathitt County's conditions. "It is not an exaggeration to say that there was not a day during the past year that human life was not safe in Kentucky, even in Breathitt County, than it is any night upon the streets of Chicago or New York, from the sanguinary columns of whose voracious journals the people have been told day after day of the awful condition of lawlessness and crime in Kentucky."[180] Of course this was easy to say long after the assassinations had ended.

By the time of Jett's and White's convictions the county had received more critical inspection "than any other section of the world," revealing a small chink in the courthouse ring's armor.[181] Henry Watterson's *Courier-*

Journal declared what many already believed, that the two young deputies were simply "pawns" under the sway of higher authorities, and that Hargis, Callahan, and Redwine would be implicated in the future (although, at the time, Watterson refrained from naming names).[182] The sheriff and judges did not fire back but, sensitive to complaints about their operating behind closed doors, they began making more public appearances like Jackson's Salvation Army street performances.[183] J. Wise Hagins, now almost alone in his concerted effort to fight the courthouse ring, felt safe enough to publish an anti-Hargis paper, the *Breathitt County News,* that fall. He endorsed a Republican for sheriff over Hargis and Callahan's "Midnight Ticket," so named because the Democrats' six-man nomination committee met "in a lonely hall, long after honest yeomanry of the county had retired . . . in the company of the bats, owls and midnight marauders."[184] In November Edward Callahan won reelection over the Republicans' "Law and Order Ticket" despite Hagins's continuing attacks (Hagins later impotently blamed the state militia for fixing the election in Callahan's favor).[185] By the end of 1903 it appeared that the Marcum murder had far less of an impact on Breathitt County's political status quo than many had suspected months earlier. The Hargis-Cockrell feud that spawned it was all but forgotten for the time being. The Hargis-Callahan courthouse ring was popular among Bluegrass Democrats and, in Breathitt, it still inspired enough public fear that popularity was becoming unnecessary. Still, it is notable that public assassinations had apparently come to an end.

James Hargis's role in one of the most expansive pieces of Jim Crow legislation in American history proved how well regarded he remained among the Democratic patriciate. In January 1904, Carl B. Day, newly elected state representative for Breathitt and two other counties (and Hargis's nephew), introduced a bill to prohibit integrated educational facilities in all private institutions (Kentucky's public education system was already constitutionally segregated).[186] The bill's sole target was Berea College, the only integrated school in the former slave states, which Kentucky Democrats wanted to "send to Ohio or some other Negro equality State."[187] Day's inspiration, so the story went, was his disgust at seeing two different-complexioned female Berea students exchange a sisterly kiss at a train station.[188] He was also hitching his star to the white southern outcry over Theodore Roosevelt's White House luncheon with Booker T. Washington.[189] Perhaps "in the absence of any other," Kentucky Democrats wished to "make negro equality . . . the issue" to defeat "Rooseveltism" in 1904.[190] Day conjured the specters of social equality and miscegenation, and averred that "co education . . . would ultimately lead to a downfall of the nation."[191] He produced a petition signed by Kentuckians living near Berea who considered the school "an open defiance of the organic law."[192] He also implied the bill was a platform of reunion for a party that had become dispersed and dissolute. "The Democratic party in our State stands almost as a unit on the race question, and I do not believe there is a Democrat in either branch of the legislature who would be willing to go back to his white constituents and say: 'I voted against a bill which prohibited white and negro children from going to school together.'"[193]

Those constituents' approval of Day's House Bill No. 25 was confirmed, not only by its seventy-three to five passage in the House but also by its five dissenters' (all from eastern Kentucky districts) electoral defeats the following November. The bill became law the following summer when the Senate passed it.[194] Although Hargis's name had become synonymous with "feudism" during the past year, he and Redwine attended the closed session of the statehouse's educational committee (representatives from Berea College were excluded) to express their support as well as that of their "section." The press did not portray Judge Hargis's presence at the capitol as peculiar or deleterious to the bill's potential passage. In fact, many attributed its popularity to his endorsement.[195]

Indignant liberals blamed the "Day Law" on the whole South; others accused the state of Kentucky or Breathitt County for producing it. One unversed author, ignorant of Carl Day's mountain roots, decried "the other two thirds of the State" for imposing upon eastern Kentucky a needless inoculation against race mixing, and even favorably compared Berea to Breathitt County's own Jackson Academy.[196] In good Progressive fashion, other critics conflated iniquity with backwardness. One member of Berea's board of trustees blamed the "notorious" Breathitt County itself while another attacked Day as "that polished and cultured statesman from Breathitt County—Bloody Breathitt—who is not sure whether Shakespeare was the discoverer of America or the inventor of a new kind of breakfast food."[197] The imprecise attribution of the county's violence to "ignorance" worked equally well for its apparent production of state-mandated race hatred but failed to acknowledge the Day Law's overwhelming popularity among other white Kentuckians. For that matter, it also failed to acknowledge Bloody Breathitt's authoritative position in Kentucky's Democratic Party.

Many black Kentuckians blamed Berea's president William Frost more than they did the state's Democrats since his interest in educating "mountain whites" overshadowed his interest in teaching co-racial classrooms. For his part, Frost was careful not to blame personally any Kentucky legislators "compelled . . . to satisfy the rougher element among their supporters."[198] One had told him that he had put aside misgivings and voted yea or else be obliged to "discuss the Nigger question in every political speech as long as I live."[199] Rather, Frost spread the blame broadly across the "Bourbon movement which had extended over the whole South." "To understand the South," he wrote to northern benefactors, "we must remember that the Southern States have never had a really democratic government and that the majority of the people of the South have no comprehension of what fairness, equality, and republican institutions really are."[200]

In the years after the Day Law's June 1904 passage, various commentators blamed its unprecedented enforcement of segregation on Carl Day's egregious personal racism or his personal vendetta toward Berea College.[201] Day's proposal to prevent "the contamination of the white children of Kentucky," and Hargis's and Redwine's endorsement thereof, was undoubtedly a product of an enduring popular belief in white supremacy, even in a place with few blacks.[202] Their espousal of forced segregation reflected a local party apparatus as dedicated to white supremacy as any other Democratic courthouse clique in Kentucky. Hardly anyone questioned why a representative from the overwhelmingly white Three Forks region took such a great interest in segregation. Also, no one commented on Day's other bill, one that allowed timberland owners to deny others "rights of way over adjoining lands, for the purpose of securing an outlet to water or to market."[203] It was meant to be the final nail in the coffin for the past century's free-ranging mountain economy, and it came as little surprise from the pen of a lawmaker from "one of the wealthiest and most prominent [families] socially and in business in the mountain section" who was "prominently identified with the commercial and timber interests of Breathitt County."[204] As was typical of New South ordinances, racial concerns cast a haze over economic ones. The complex relationship between the seemingly all-white county and the maligned statute was also saved from widespread scrutiny. Most observers with close knowledge of the college and the state considered the Day Law more a cynical political maneuver than a sincere attack on integration. One defender of co-racial education avowed that, aside from its being "evidence of the negrophobia which is sweeping over the South," it was just as likely "a political move [by Hargis and Day] to win the favor of those who desire to keep the colored people in subjection, and also of those who dislike Berea's work for the education of mountain Republicans."[205] An unnamed writer associated with Berea concurred, blaming Day, "Judge Hargis, Redwine, and other notorious characters" from the "bloody county" for trying to "win notoriety and favor with the masses by doing something which would be understood as an attack on the colored man."[206] The Day Law represented Breathitt County's continuing importance as a Democratic bulwark within the Republican mountains, a function that was perhaps not as damaged by the Marcum assassination as some may have assumed. Although Hargis had been the source of violent scandal, it showed that he and the Breathitt Democrats were their party's exemplars. While it may have redeemed him in the eyes of his fellow party members, it may have instead demonstrated that he was never in need of atonement. "Whether it be just or not," the *Lexington Herald* charged, "those members of the Legislature who vote for this bill will be held to approve of what has occurred in Breathitt during the past six years."[207]

Embittered by the wound its hometown institution had sustained, the Republican *Berea Citizen* groused that the formation of a new judicial district "for the sake of enthroning the famous Judge Hargis" was next on the General Assembly's agenda (Redwine had said that a new gerrymandered district would "eliminate feudal warfare").[208] The redistricting passed four days later, ensuring absolute Democratic control over the circuit courts of Breathitt and two other counties.[209] Carl Day, already ailing when he introduced his bill, died from inflammatory rheumatism in April 1904, just shy of his twenty-ninth birthday.[210] Since he had served as a legislator so briefly, the ban on co-racial education was his only legacy. After Berea was found guilty of violating the Day Law a few months later, its student body remained all white for the next forty-six years.[211] Though Day did not live to see it in action, his bill had at least some of its intended effects a month beforehand: an expansion of power for the Hargis courthouse.

"Every Goebel Democrat in this county is hot for us"

Soon after Hargis's Frankfort appearance, Abrelia Marcum brought suit against him, his brother Alexander Hargis, Edward Callahan, and B. F. French for $100,000.[212] By attacking Hargis et al. in a civil case outside of Breathitt County, Marcum hoped to avoid the politically concerned juries Hargis and Callahan had manipulated in the past. Hargis used his party affiliation in his defense, delaying proceedings by branding the trial judge a biased political enemy. "As leader of the Democratic forces of Breathitt County," Hargis had denounced the judge's bid for the state court of appeals bench years earlier. "Existing and continued state of hostile feeling," he said, was grounds for dismissal.[213] Hargis's motion was denied, and he and Callahan were eventually found to be culpable for James Marcum's death, but the plaintiff was unable to connect French and Alexander Hargis to the crime (although both were charged with contempt of court for arranging to bribe witnesses for the prosecution and to spirit at least one out of state). Mrs. Marcum's tort strategy was only a partial success, barely damaging her targets' power and awarding her only $8,000 (with interest accrued, the award eventually amounted to $11,000).[214] During the trial Breathitt's Democratic central committee saluted Edward Callahan's "executive ability and services to the party" by unanimously reappointing him its chairman.[215]

Nevertheless, it was the beginning of the end for the Hargis courthouse. The civil suit broadcast the details of the killings of 1902 and 1903 as never before. The next month a Lexington grand jury indicted Hargis, Callahan, and a number of confederates for Jim Cockrell's murder (although shot in Jackson, he had died in Lexington's jurisdiction).[216] The indictment represented an unraveling of Hargis's earlier framing of Cockrell's death within a feud story. In 1902 many Lexingtonians had volunteered for "arbitration in the Breathitt county feud," but by 1905 the suggestion of mutual reciprocity between two families was seeming false; what they now saw was a series of unsolved murders. Fayette County's circuit court judge proclaimed that a trial of Hargis and the others was based upon "the serious charges made against the civil government of Breathitt county" rather than the accused individuals.[217] Wise Hagins's Republican/Fusionist *Breathitt County News* lauded the indictment as "a revelation to the outside world" of what residents of Jackson had known for years.[218]

There were revelations to come, but the criminal trials that followed over the next two years produced more embarrassment than justice. Hargis, Callahan, and their associates were tried for involvement in three homicides, producing no convictions. With a massive number of testimonies against him, Hargis managed a hung jury, and then an acquittal, for Cockrell's murder by challenging the Fayette County court's right to try him for a crime committed in another county (a defense based upon Kentucky's age-old belief in county sovereignty).[219] His trial in Lee County for James Marcum's murder was an even greater prosecutorial disaster the following year. After he signed an affidavit implicating Hargis and Callahan, Curtis Jett refused to testify that he had been hired to kill Marcum, instead attributing his actions to his own drunkenness (this he did while apparently inebriated on the witness stand). He swore to the jury (said to be packed with Democrats) that Marcum had been his personal "bitter enemy," approximating classic feud behavior.[220] Hargis and Callahan were again acquitted in less than a week, this time by a Beckham-appointed judge known for his "unwavering allegiance to the Democratic Party."[221] Finally, the trial for the murder of Braxton Cox, held in northeast Kentucky's "inaccessible and surrounded by wilderness" (and heavily Democratic) Elliott County in 1907, was dismissed before it had even commenced after the prosecution's key witnesses never materialized.[222] In the meantime, Judge Hargis was allowed to await trial shooting marbles in the grass outside the jailhouse.[223]

Most spectators agreed that justice was being miscarried. The "uncrowned Czars of Eastern Kentucky" said a *New York Times* correspondent, were able to "maintain an army of retainers and dependents, as did the great feudal lords of the middle ages," so avoiding a murder conviction was a simple task.[224] But the reporter's medieval metaphor belied the real force at work: Kentucky's Democratic Party. Nowhere was this more openly exhibited than the Lexington trials. "Men . . . no more loyal Democrats than I," lamented the prosecutor, "whose friend I have been all my life, have turned their backs upon me, because, in my capacity as an officer of the law, I have dared to prosecute James Hargis."[225] Wise Hagins detected "something rotten in the execution of the laws of Kentucky" and traced it to the Democratic "State House gang."[226] While Edward Callahan was incarcerated, a Lexington merchant treated him to "50 quarts of whisky and about 50 boxes of cigars a two bushel tub of apples and case of beer all free," to serve "at least 3000" well-wishers who visited his cell. Callahan assured one of his tenants of the local support he, Hargis, and the others enjoyed while on trial in Lexington. "The Fayette County Democrats are Red hot for us they want to fight for us too. Every Goebel Democrat in this county is hot for us."[227]

Breathitt County's old status as "the best exemplification of the horrors of Goebelism" was well remembered.[228] For years before he was elected its sheriff, Callahan displayed a willingness to employ violence for Democratic victories. More than five years after Goebel's death, Bluegrass Democrats still recognized Callahan's forceful role in their most difficult campaign. With William Goebel's "bloody shirt" still on display in Kentucky politics, the hospitality shown to the imprisoned Callahan vindicated his actions and placed him on a higher pedestal than "mountain feudist." Indeed, however

Bloody Breathitt was framed within the imprecise parameters of feuding, it all came back to William Goebel.

Despite Callahan's popularity among Bluegrass Democrats, the murder trials proved to be the beginning of the end for his and Hargis's political careers. During their trials Wise Hagins had time to revitalize the Breathitt County fusionists, supporting only one Republican and a raft of anti-Hargis Democrats, lest "the Hargis followers . . . slegmatize it as a republican measure."[229] While Hargis awaited trial for the Cox murder, he was defeated by more than seven hundred votes, even as Democrats gained in local and district elections all over the state (Callahan was not on the ballot, although his proxy entrant for sheriff was also soundly defeated).[230] Hargis unsuccessfully contested the election before falling ill.[231] "No longer can [Hargis] claim to represent the State administration," announced one Democrat. "No longer can his adherents boast that they control the pardoning power; no longer can he and Callahan prostitute the offices of County Judge and Sheriff for the protection of assassins and the persecution of their enemies."[232] Absent intimidation and violence, the Breathitt courthouse ring's foundation was brittle.

The revolt, however, was against the violent past, not necessarily the Democratic Party. Kentucky Democrats used the opportunity to cast out inner demons—and to demonize other party malefactors. "The ticket which will be declared elected in Louisville is no more a Democratic ticket than was the Hargis ticket in Breathitt," reasoned the *Lexington Herald*. "It simply masqueraded under the name of Democracy, and if those who controlled it lived in a Republican state and a Republican city they would be Republicans. They are a type of men who claim the name and sieze the organization of the dominant party in the state in which they happen to live."[233] The *Herald* used Hargis's defeat to defend its party while reaffirming that the party's statewide advantage was a natural condition. Knowing his place, Wise Hagins concurred, calling the Hargis ticket "in no true sense a Democratic ticket, simply using the name because they had control of the Democratic organization."[234] By intimation, any Kentucky Democrats who had assisted or approved of the Breathitt courthouse ring were exonerated.

Hargis's statewide power continued to crumble even as juries and judges absolved him in court. In October 1906, six men elected to the Democratic state central committee accused Hargis of arbitrarily denying them membership.[235] The next month, with support from a Breathitt majority, Kentucky's tenth congressional district elected its first Republican representative since the 1890s.[236] Bluegrass Democrats, who suffered not at all from Bloody Breathitt shootings, were "red hot" with approval for the "Hargis-Callahan regime." However, Breathitt County's voters saw no gain from ongoing bloodshed in their streets, and for a time they revolted by voting Republican. The most dramatic injury was when William Howard Taft carried the county in 1908's presidential election, Breathitt's first non-Democratic presidential majority since William Henry Harrison's 1840 victory—and the last one for exactly a century. The county's traditional party identity had not changed, but its most recent political leaders were chastened by the largest voter turnout (just over 92 percent) in the county's history.[237]

Even as Kentucky Democrats distanced themselves from Breathitt County, the murders of Bloody Breathitt still had statewide ramifications. As details of the various crimes came to light, Republicans charged the governor with joining Breathitt's "assassination chiefs" to further "Gobelism, Redwineism and Hargisism," and imposing "many indignities on Breathitt County's peaceful majority" since 1900.[238] In 1907 the "stinking bung-hole" of "Hargis-Beckhamism" helped narrow the Democrats' legislative majority and give Kentucky its second Republican governor.[239] When Beckham attempted to run for U.S. Senate a year later, four Democrats bolted and helped make William O. Bradley Kentucky's second Republican U.S. senator. Beckham's political wounds caused by his Breathitt connections were temporary, and he became Kentucky's first popularly elected U.S. senator six years later.[240] Kentucky never rejoined the Solid South (the state elected two more Republican U.S. senators and three Republican governors before World War II), but Democrats retained a manifest advantage for most of the twentieth century, especially on the local level (the Whig Gibraltar counties remaining a notable exception). It was scarcely noted that, as in the Solid South, this advantage came about through intimidation and murder. The more scarcely the better, said the state's politicians; Augustus Willson, Kentucky's second Republican governor who knew that "the one hope of Republican success [was] in Democratic support," came to office promising "to eliminate the discussion of the Goebel murder trials and the Breathitt county feud cases."[241]

Later candidates for Breathitt County public offices had to be clear as to what kind of Democrats they were, even after their party had recovered. "I want to say in the beginning before stating my platform that I have not now, or ever have had, any connection in any manner whatever with any of the so-called Breathitt county feuds, Kuklux or Red String bands, or any other secret organization that would mar the peace and happiness of an American citizen," a candidate for school superintendent vowed in 1908.[242] It was a plague on both of Bloody Breathitt's political houses, and it failed to acknowledge that the most recent violence had been a one-sided, nonreciprocal affair; it had been more than ten years since Breathitt Republicans had fired guns, at least for political purposes—and even then it had never been they who controlled any governmental office. Now, revolutionary and counterrevolutionary violences were both renounced, but the assumptions that comprised *feud*, its insistence of moral equivalency between the two, were affirmed. Further, as Kentucky Democrats disavowed Callahan and (especially) Hargis, they also distanced their party from the violence that had been used in its furtherance. Even with the Hargis courthouse removed, young men fled the county to avoid getting "mixed up in the feud troubles."[243] Yet again, Bloody Breathitt was depoliticized.

Ensuing events went even further to suggest that, even if there was no ongoing feud in Breathitt County, the place seemed to be fraught with a preternatural penchant for violence. During Judge Hargis's trials, his oldest son, Beech, began bristling up the crest of his youth, often disappearing from Jackson only to be later retrieved besotted from Lexington brothels and Cincinnati jails.[244] Enraged by Beech's most recent highly publicized escapade, the disgraced former judge beat his son almost to the point of unconsciousness in February 1908.[245] A few days later Beech came to his father's store and shot him to death, and then attempted suicide by swallowing morphine. Judge Hargis's death at his son's hand appeared a "natural sequel" to recent events—patricide, after all, seemed a likely component of a "family feud."[246] It could also be seen as a reproduction of a historical truism: children of powerful, corrupt men often inherit a capacity for committing horrible acts, but without their fathers' cunning and restraint.

On trial for murder, Beech Hargis was represented by his father's old ally David Redwine and, surprisingly, Senator-elect William Bradley. It was difficult to avoid a life of sin, they argued, with a father who turned the home into "the rendezvous of a band of murderers," and in this light, the younger Hargis had acted in self-defense.[247] The bipartisan legal team also charged the Republican judge with political prejudice, leading to a second trial in which their young client was convicted and sentenced to life in prison.[248] After he was paroled in 1916, he left to join the Canadian army and was never heard from again.[249]

After his former partner's death, Edward Callahan gradually withdrew

Beech Hargis shot Judge James Hargis to death and then tried to use his father's ill fame to get an acquittal on grounds of self-defense. Judge Hargis's funeral was well attended even after the crumbling of his political empire and the bad reputation he had revisited upon his home county. By dying at his own son's hand, the judge punctuated the façade of kinship over politics he had used years beforehand; the phrase *family feud* suggested that the intricacies of Bloody Breathitt need not be explored too deeply. (Courtesy of Charles Hayes)

from politics, but not without first being implicated in Breathitt County's worst election-related riot since 1878 (Republican governor Willson responded, less reluctantly than his Democratic predecessors, with yet another militia occupation of Jackson in 1909). David Redwine, unsullied by recent history, returned to the circuit bench as Breathitt returned to the "Democratic column" and "back to Hargisism," but Callahan felt his life in danger.[250] Over the next few years he grew increasingly paranoid, avoiding Jackson and building a protective bunker around his Crockettsville home (he was sometimes seen running frantically between there and his nearby store). On the seventh anniversary of James Marcum's assassination, a hidden rifleman fired at Callahan as he stood at a window in his house, wounding him in the groin.[251] When John Fox Jr. visited him forty days later, the author found him in comfortable convalescence, wearing a pair of bullet-punctured trousers. Asked if he thought it wise to leave Crockettsville, he insisted that "they would say I was a coward" were he to leave his home and business interests.[252] A little over a year later, however, he put his home up for sale and prepared to leave the county to "escape assassination."[253]

Callahan never got around to moving. On the ninth anniversary, May 3, 1912, a rifle shot fired in precisely the same manner killed Callahan just as he was concluding a telephone conversation with his old adversary Wise Hagins. His shooting death seemed to confirm the existence of ongoing, permanent "feudal warfare" in Bloody Breathitt regardless of the county's recent advancements; the telephone, the "most useful invention of modern times," which gave his "feud-ridden county" the "opportunity of communicating with the outside world," played a role in Callahan's murder, just as it had in Dr. Braxton Cox's death (which Callahan may have directed) a decade before.[254] While the timing of Callahan's murder suggested a motive of revenge for Marcum's death, the "noted feudist" had amassed too many enemies, both personal and political, for there to be a definite motive or suspect.[255] As much as he had lived by the sword, most of the blood he had spilled was for the tangible modern goals of power and party. Still, one obituary ridiculously attributed Callahan's crimes to "the old feud spirit of his ancestors."[256] The more evidence accrued showing the political nature of Bloody Breathitt, the more writers seemed bound and determined to say otherwise.

The same could be said for other men connected to the Hargis court-house ring, although most came to ends unrelated to it. After opening a Lexington tavern named the Mountaineer, Tom Cockrell lived peacefully for a few years until he was killed in a railroad accident in 1908.[257] Judge David Redwine, always on the periphery of controversy, managed a peaceful passing and a posthumous reputation untarnished by feud. Even his role in the Music Hall Convention was largely forgotten.[258] Fulton French, who was probably personally responsible for more murders than any other single person in Kentucky, succumbed to asthma "in his chair" in 1915.[259] Mose Feltner was killed by a federal revenue officer in 1916. His only role in the Hargis-Cockrell feud had been trying to prevent further killing by announcing Judge Hargis's culpability; nonetheless, he was eulogized as a "noted feudist."[260] After Curtis Jett's release from prison he published a Christian *bekenntnis* about the deliverance of a "one time feudist" and became an evangelist.[261] He later divided his time between the Bluegrass and the eastern coalfields, alternating between preaching Methodism and acting as a strikebreaking "gun thug" in Harlan County. After two divorces and a denominational swap to Baptism, he died in 1946 at the improbably ripe old age of seventy-seven.[262] Abrelia Marcum remarried and eventually left Kentucky for Chattanooga, Tennessee, where she died in 1953.

"If such a state of affairs constitutes a 'feud,' it is, as regards active participation, a solitaire game"

Political consequences for politically motivated homicides: all of the horrible events contained within the Hargis-Cockrell feud had the potential to challenge most early twentieth-century Americans' preconceptions about eastern Kentucky. During Jett's and White's trials, a Louisvillian insisted to a New York newspaper that, despite most newspapers' "editorials, squibs and cartoons," there was "no family feud in Breathitt" but instead "one powerful, bold, bad man, served by minions and ruffians among them officers of the law, who lords it over his neighbors in the fashion of a mediaeval baron."[263] As a home-missions campaigner observed a few years later, Judge Hargis "was neither poor nor ignorant, and had had no little contact with public affairs in the larger world of men."[264] Feuding, it seemed, did not quite describe a machine politician's dispassionate use of underling-wielded deadly force to eliminate electoral and legal challengers. There seemed to be something else, something far more modern, at work.

In its extended coverage of Abrelia Marcum's 1904 lawsuit, Louisville's *Courier-Journal* wrote detailed local genealogy describing the manner in which almost everyone involved in the Hargis-Cockrell feud—Marcums, Hargises, Callahans and (in spirit), Strongs—was related by blood or by marriage, suggesting a kinship-based narrative going back to the pioneer generations. "Factional strife in Breathitt County is equivalent to family dissension. Internal warfare is waged not against aliens, but against one's own flesh and blood. The kinship of the people whose names have been prominently mentioned in connection with the troubles here is very close in instances, and it appears links of blood relation ought to tend to bind them together."[265] Owing as always to its policy of New Departure moderation, Henry Watterson's flagship could admit both premodern "feudal" behavior and the political motives that were quite clear to many Kentuckians as equal dynamics in the disreputable county.

The following month the same paper printed what amounted to a mixed concession to its familial explanation, although it did not phrase it as such, acknowledging what Republican newspapers had long insisted: a definitive political element to the county's troubles based upon its peculiarly Democratic voting history. "As a rule, the Kentucky mountain counties are Republican, but Breathitt is unique in that, almost without exception, it has ever been found in the Democratic column. There has always been the bitterest political feeling in the county, and politics has been more or less directly responsible for every one of the feuds, and is to-day the cause of the terrible state of affairs there."[266] As always, Watterson felt that he—and Kentucky—could have it both ways.

But this most summative and accurate of media statements about Bloody Breathitt was lost amid the barrage of more flamboyant feud interpretations. By including the events of the Hargis-Cockrell feud into the longer lineage of "feuding" in the county, the origins of the most recent troubles in Bloody Breathitt were completely forgotten. Unlike in past years easy answers were not more attractive to observers of particular political opinions. Assassinations that encapsulated the statewide furor over William Goebel were ultimately nothing more than "the human nature's daily feud."[267] Accordingly, any and all news from Breathitt County was related in some way to the existence of an extant feud; relying on wire reports, the *Chicago Tribune* reported a random knifing at a fiddle show outside of Jackson as "feud" related.[268] When Judge Hargis's nephew Matt Crawford was shot in 1910 his death was blithely recounted as part of "a feud which has long been carried on in Breathitt County," even though Crawford had no part in his uncle's political wranglings.[269] Perhaps the most dramatic explication of the familial concealing the political appeared in a 1917 law review article in which James Marcum was characterized as a family, rather than an individual.[270] "The Hargis-Cockrell feud was like nearly all the other mountain feuds," Lewis Franklin Johnson thoughtlessly wrote in one of the first book-length efforts to catalogue Kentucky's mountain feud phenomenon. "It was a family difficulty."[271] For many reasons this was the more attractive reading. The feud narrative required kinship and historical longevity as its driving forces, even if these themes were not borne out by facts. Even though the murders James Hargis directed eventually cost him his political office (the prize that had motivated murder in the first place), his strategy of casting Cox's and Cockrell's deaths within the context of an ongoing family feud was an overwhelming success.

The gunshots that killed Hargis, Callahan, and Feltner were the effect of any number of factors that helped to portray Breathitt County and eastern Kentucky as an environment of directionless "lawlessness." With the possible exception of Callahan's ambush (carried out in a fashion strikingly reminiscent of William Strong's end, which Callahan was suspected to have directed fifteen years earlier), their deaths were not directly related to the feud that caused the three most famous murders of 1902 and 1903. In the course of a history of extrapolitical lawlessness, the huge amount of support from Kentucky Democrats for the Hargis courthouse ring was conveniently forgotten. Even John Fox Jr., who contributed to eastern Kentucky's renown for familial vengeance more than virtually any writer of fiction or nonfiction, was obliged to recognize a broader (but still quite parochial) political motif at the heart of Breathitt County's ill-gotten fame. "The outside world couldn't very well omit Breathitt when it made law, and Breathitt accepted the gift with gratitude so far at least as it should serve the personal purpose of the man who held the law in the hollow of his hand. Not that there are not bitter complaints of lawlessness in Breathitt, and stern upholders of the law. There are: but I observed that the bitterest and the sternest were not allied with the party that happens just now to be in power."[272] Late in 1903, during the brief lull in public interest in Breathitt County that followed the convictions of Curtis Jett and Tom White, one of the bluntest accounts of recent troubles was composed, although probably not published.

> For several months the gaze of the public press had been turned almost daily upon the little mountain town of Jackson, Kentucky, the county seat of "Bloody Breathitt" County the scene during the previous year of three assassinations of increasing boldness and atrocity, and occurring within a 100 steps of the business centre of the town. In the many newspaper accounts of the tragedies the word "feud" has been almost universally employed to denote the state of affairs in Jackson. "Feud" is a choice word for picturesque, romantic, and unique effects. It has a pleasant medieval sound, a distinct flavor of the antique, but in this instance it is misleading. An acquaintance of several years with the town and the people, including all these prominently connected with recent events in Jackson, leads me to think it necessary to look for other motives than those usually supposed to actuate participants in a family feud.
>
> The three men who were assassinated were, it is true, in certain legal and business relationships to one another; but there was not

among them any tie of blood so close as that subsisting between one of the victims of assassination and the man who according to the testimony of an eyewitness shot him deliberately from a well-selected hiding place. Personal feeling entered into the situation, as it must, but as will appear in the sequel political motives have been to all appearance at least as strong in their influence. And the so-called "other side" has not, so far as I am informed, fired a shot or attempted to fire a shot. If such a state of affairs constitutes a "feud," it is, as regards active participation, a solitaire game.

The author concluded that, instead of being part of a feud proper (if such a thing existed), the three men's deaths were part of "a conspiracy on the part of those in official power to accomplish criminal ends."[273] This assessment was not rare or unprecedented; other observations on the deaths of Cox, Cockrell, and Marcum, especially those of the *Lexington Leader,* had expanded upon the political motivations surrounding their deaths and had tended to agree that the deaths on Jackson's streets were indeed a nonhorizontal "solitary game" carried out by men in power and unanswered by those they wished to eliminate.

The author fully acknowledged that the "family feud" was an existent social phenomenon and probably would not have denied that Breathitt County had experienced true feuds in the past. But the murders of 1902 and 1903, it seemed, were something different. The clear irrelevance of kinship and isolation in the affair removed the vital element of this form of institutionalized violence. Wise Hagins expanded on this argument four years later. "Our people are not feudists," Hagins insisted. "If there had been any feudal blood in our people it surely would have cropped out during these four years struggles in the courts, but not a hand had been raised to violence" since Hargis and Callahan had first been put on trial.[274] Hagins knew better than almost anyone that what went on in Jackson's streets was scarcely a *feud* (in later years he often preceded the word with the phrase "so-called").[275] But even he was not prepared to believe that feuding was not an actual thing, and one endemic to Kentucky's mountain whites.

Perhaps most important, the newly vital commercial center was only "90 miles by rail from the center of the 'Bluegrass,'" an observation of Breathitt County's loss of isolation. Feuds were an antiquated occurrence with no place in thriving Jackson, a town "by no means wholly outside the pale of civilization and progress."[276] Indeed, it was difficult to blame isolation for crimes in such an unisolated place. This recent rash of killings, with clear political motivations, was a product of newer trends and a variety of violence that seemed more at home in such a progressive, modern setting. Assassination, it seemed, was a different animal than feuding.

"It is rare indeed, that one of these assassins and anarchists is brought to punishment"

In February 1900 William Randolph Hearst's *New York Journal* printed a prophetic quatrain by Ambrose Bierce alluding to William Goebel's recent demise.

> The bullet that pierced Goebel's breast
> Can not be found in all the West;
> Good reason, it is speeding here
> To stretch McKinley on his bier."[277]

Hearst was one of President William McKinley's sharpest detractors and, when self-styled anarchist Leon Czolgosz fatally wounded McKinley nineteen months later, rumors flew that a clipping of Bierce's poem had been found in the assassin's pocket. Bierce swore that he had never meant for his stanzas to be taken as a veiled threat; his intent was to alert readers of the dangers posed by "foreign elements" who espoused Georges Sorel's deadly "propaganda of the deed"; in Italy, France, and Spain the public deaths of a king, an empress, and two presidents between 1894 and 1898 (and in the United States, before long, McKinley) revealed the emergence of a new style of industrial age political violence.[278] Bierce had placed William Goebel's assassination within what he saw as a shock of the new, not as an outcome of inherent racial or cultural tendencies.

His analogy was made in vain, especially after McKinley's death; Kentucky Republicans, firmly entrenched within the two-party system, were legitimate, beyond the reproach reserved for anarchists, even when they apparently employed anarchist tactics.[279] Accordingly, violence was granted with, or stripped of, legitimacy according to the politics of the groups or individuals that wielded it. "President McKinley was assassinated by an anarchist whose act had no political significance," William Jennings Bryan remarked on his old opponent, while "the Goebel assassination was purely a political act."[280] Henry Watterson concurred: "Goebel was shot down for a purpose, for a price, while the noble life of McKinley was sacrificed to the wanton fury of a fiend."[281] As clouded as the Goebel assassination was by the narrative of feud, it still was rated as more politically legitimate than anarchism.

When Kentuckians were alarmed by James Marcum's murder in front of Jackson's courthouse three years later, similarities with this new, insidiously foreign method of political violence were already widely recognized. Guerrilla warfare during the Civil War was carried out throughout the state with no measure of uniformity and often according to the whims of local military leaders with tenuous ties to the Union and Confederate causes. It was based upon material wartime goals: the weakening of the local state and the punishment of civilians with oppositional loyalties. The mass violence of the Reconstruction years were, with the exception of the symbolically charged act of lynching, without elaborate orchestration. Furthermore, these parochial acts of violence were generally aimed at victims whose political or social significance was, outside of their immediate communities, obscure. Like most violence during and after wars, it was among intimates.

In contrast, assassinations in Frankfort and Breathitt County had broader implications. They replaced the deadly intimacy of the Civil War and Reconstruction years with violent anonymity. Goebel was killed in the morning while walking through Kentucky's capitol grounds. While the assassin's identity was never proven beyond doubt, it was widely known that the rifle shot came from the second-story window of the State House, a building "tenanted by Republicans exclusively."[282] Goebel's end was meant to publicly demonstrate his illegitimacy as (had he ever had the chance to assume the office) governor-elect.[283] It was orchestrated so as to seem the will of the state, even though it was evidently only that of one political party's leaders. It was an undeniably political act loaded with symbolism.

The murders of Braxton Cox, James Cockrell, and James Marcum took place under remarkably similar circumstances, particularly the latter two. Dr. Cox was killed in the dead of night with a close-range shotgun blast in an area of Jackson close to both the courthouse and James Hargis's commercial property (some newspaper accounts erroneously said that Cox was leaving a church service when he was shot).[284] Cockrell and Marcum were killed by gunshots aimed from the Breathitt County courthouse in broad daylight in front of numerous witnesses (Judge Hargis and Sheriff Callahan were in the general proximity, their presence sending a silent message).[285] The town marshal and the lawyer were part of Breathitt's fusionist uprising, so their eradication was more public and flamboyant than Cox's; but all three men were killed within the physically small "assassination center of Jackson," a patch of earth that was nearly as heavy with meaning as Frankfort's capitol grounds.[286]

When Marcum's uncle William Strong attacked his neighbors during the Civil War he did so under the authority of the Union army, but he was at no more of an advantage than his Confederate enemies since so many locals had decided to renounce the Union's local legitimacy—neither side saw fit to disguise themselves in any way. When he overtook the courthouse on the same street in 1874, or when he faced down former Confederates to defend the newly elected county judge in 1878, the "ownership" of this symbol and repository of the local state was still under dispute. But as political life in Breathitt County became more complex and less parochialized, a greater measure of surreptitiousness was deemed necessary. Curtis Jett and other courthouse ring assassins carried out their appointments from hidden places within the building, sending an implicit message of whose will commissioned the slayings. Whereas once the courthouse had been the prize to be captured or destroyed, it was now a physical tool for counterrevolutionary violence. The new style of killing warranted a more contemporary vocabulary in Kentucky's flagship paper. "It is rare indeed, that one of these assassins and anarchists is brought to punishment," the *Louisville Courier-Journal* complained just days after Marcum's death.[287] The conspirators behind William Goebel's death and the conspirators in Breathitt County's assassinations were probably unaware of continental anarchism's ideological underpinnings. But their deadly handiwork nevertheless utilized "the propaganda of the deed." And it was a far cry from anything implied by feuds. As easy as it may have been to include the "Hargis and Cockrell feud" with Bloody Breathitt's past, the differences in method outweighed the similarities.

This new strategy reflected Judge Hargis's political modus operandi. Since the Music Hall Convention, Hargis's statewide political strength had been bolstered by a healthy measure of stealth, and Hargis tended to avoid public settings—even in Jackson—and decline interview requests (in 1902 Hargis had a Louisville reporter threatened by "toughs," and a few years later threatened a visiting playwright who planned to write a dramatic account of Jackson's assassinations).[288] Before his first indictment in 1904 he had avoided newspaper photographers, and during one of the ensuing trials even entered the camera-free safety of the courtroom with a quilt over his head (he later reluctantly posed for a photographer).[289]

Being Bloody Breathitt's mysterious faceless judge brought with it a measure of power, but that was coming to an end. It was not the use of directed violence itself that brought about Hargis's downfall, but rather the unexpected publicity attracted by the deaths of Cox, Cockrell, and (to the greatest extent) Marcum.

As these killings gained national attention, they overshadowed one of the most vicious acts of violence in Breathitt County's history. During Abrelia Marcum's lawsuit against Hargis and his co-conspirators a white man living in Frozen Creek (a community nine miles from Jackson) invited a group of Negroes to his home with the promise of free liquor. When they arrived the host opened fire in an apparent attempt to exterminate the lot, killing one of them.[290] The crime was reported in two local papers, neither of which attempted to contextualize the racially motivated killing within a larger narrative of lawlessness or white supremacy—let alone feuding. A story of interracial mass murder did not support the larger description of a place defined by white intraracial violence. Worse, it challenged the delineation that Bluegrass elites, Democratic or Republican, preferred to have drawn between their own section and the mountains (white violence against black Kentuckians was still a common occurrence; between William Strong's and James Marcum's deaths at least twenty-nine Kentuckians were lynched).[291] White-on-white assassination was easy to make strange, while white-on-black massacres were all too familiar in 1904 and they did fit into the narratives composed about Bloody Breathitt. It was the kind of violence that Kentuckians preferred go unspoken, and the story was unnoticed.

Breathitt County's assassinations and the ensuing trials of the accused were known to have broader implications when they took place. The political significance of violence in the county was emphasized most broadly by the Republicans who despised the island of mountain Democracy and its continuity with the hated Goebel legacy. But the Cox, Cockrell, and Marcum homicides were usually included within the older "Bloody Breathitt" narrative of violence, a cycle of convincingly inherent, communal violence devoid of politics. *Feud* endured as the dominant descriptor because of the influence of Democratic elites outside of the county, elites who, like their brethren farther south, profited from violence even as they distanced themselves from it.

Breathitt County's violence was depoliticized also by an American culture that legitimized or delegitimized violent acts according to parameters of race, class, geography, and history, parameters that could not easily include eastern Kentucky. Even with "mainstream" political violence a recent memory, the prevalence of the feud narrative in explaining white intraracial violence determined how Breathitt County was to be interpreted by its own citizens and by others from the *outside world*.

7

"The Feudal Wars of Eastern Kentucky Will No Doubt Be Utilized in Coming Years by Writers of Fiction"

Reading and Writing Bloody Breathitt

> "When I use a word," Humpty Dumpty said, in rather a scornful tone, "it means just what I choose it to mean—neither more nor less."
> —Lewis Carroll, *Through the Looking Glass, and What Alice Found There* (1871)

> When the legend becomes fact, print the legend!
> —Maxwell Scott, character in the cinematic adaptation of *The Man Who Shot Liberty Valance* (1962)

In 1898 the Reverend John J. Dickey interviewed Edward Callahan "Red Ned" Strong to find out what the elderly Breathitt County native knew (or had heard) about his grandfather's role in the "Clay County Cattle War" between 1805 and 1807. The violent events that comprised the cattle war had begun and ended just over ninety years earlier, but Strong felt it had a much longer longevity. Not only, insisted the retired judge, had it somehow led to the Strong-Amis feud that involved his cousin William in the 1860s but, even at century's end, "the effects of the [cattle] war have not ceased to this day."[1] Other interviews with Breathitt County's older citizens corroborated his opinion, although none explained the continuity between the cattle war and more recent troubles. In local folklore, the Clay County Cattle War was the first salvo of Bloody Breathitt.

The connection contains a measure of logic. The cattle war was the earliest known violent conflict since whites first settled the Three Forks region, and it involved family names—Strongs, Amises, Callahans—that later became notorious.[2] Their descendants shed each other's blood later on: How could the combination of family names and deadly violence be a coincidence? The premise that Breathitt County was an inherently violent place (and residents like Judge Strong seemed to have accepted this) required that violence have an antediluvian heritage—or, at least, Jeffersonian origins before any living person's memory. The cattle war was an interpersonal, reciprocal dispute between equals in an isolated, semi-wilderness setting with no material implications beyond the direct experience of its participants; for all intents and purposes, it was a feud, albeit a short one. Strong was simply reapplying the most basic elements of the feud narrative to more recent events in his home county, a place already considered "the storm centre of the feud troubles of the State."[3] The old judge's privileging of ancient continuity over historical and political contingencies may have just been an aged mountaineer's desire for something unchanging in an otherwise rapidly shifting world. And Dickey may have encouraged him; many of the preacher's oral histories were done "in an effort to determine why [people in Breathitt County] were always fighting each other."[4] It was a durable and satisfying idea; in 2002, when election-related violence reemerged in the "fabled Kentucky hills," the *New York Times* traced "feuding" back to the cattle war's "poisonous precedent."[5] A perfunctory scan of the historical record suggests this continuity.

In a close examination, however, this does not hold up. Between 1807 and 1861 the territory that became Breathitt County did not experience any recorded local strife that resulted in multiple deaths or paramilitary factionalism (or, for that matter, familial "feuds"). When the Civil War started, Strongs and Amises found a common cause fighting Confederate forces (Edward Strong himself chose to fight *for* the Confederacy) even though their forefathers had opposed one another sixty years before. William Strong and Wiley Amis did not bear arms against each other until 1868, and then it was for the same political reasons that divided Kentucky Unionists during Reconstruction, not age-old kin hatred. The commonality of surnames in the respective conflicts spoke not to a continuity of conflict but instead to the paucity of new blood in a place with large families but small overall population.

In any case, it was in Judge Strong's interest to make this case. Men like Edward Strong, a Democrat, a Confederate veteran, and a longtime member of Breathitt's commercial elite, wanted this—needed this—to be true because it was they who had caused most of the post–Civil War violence, directly or indirectly. Bearing a last name that he knew would always be associated with "feudalism" but possessed of a relatively unblemished personal reputation, he had good reason to portray "Bloody Breathitt" as a saga older than his own adulthood. His infamous cousin was now dead and, despite having himself once been identified as "a participant in the Breathitt war," Judge Strong had always managed to stand apart from the events he had lived through (the murder of his younger cousin James Marcum was still five years in the future).[6] By extending the provenance of Breathitt County's troubles backward to a time long before the Civil War, Edward Strong and his peers remained blameless even if it meant portraying his home as a vessel for the alpine version of the southern "white savage."[7] It was a story not unlike the one President McKinley was using even as the Reverend Dickey conducted the 1898 interview: diminishing the politics of "sectional feeling" to bring northern and southern whites together in mutual support for the war against Spain.[8] Edward Strong's apolitical interpretation of his home county's history was a political act, whether he meant it to be or not.

It was an interpretation of Breathitt County's history that already had a massive following. Conceptually, blood feuds predated Bloody Breathitt and even the Clay County Cattle War. A feud, as an actual event or a literary subject, was familiar to nineteenth-century Americans through their knowledge of European history and even more readily via their most beloved novels and dramas—products of the nineteenth century's "culture industry." Because of its rootedness in (semi)historical fiction rather than history, the feud had a tenuous, perhaps nonexistent, connection to the "sedimentary existence" of modernity.[9] It did not ask to be taken seriously, and it stopped questions from being asked, questions such as "Who was the aggressor?" "Who was the victim?" "How were lives affected"? Moreover, like a fight started over so many free-ranging steers, feuds' points of origin were always arcane, petty, and of no importance to anyone aside from the two involved parties. It suggested neutralization via reciprocation, and through neutralization came moral equivalency (how many people believe that the Capulets were right and the Montagues were wrong or vice versa?). It allowed audiences to view violence nonchalantly and refrain from asking questions about justice. *Feud* conveyed familiar but unspecific images representing something irrevocably rooted in the past and only accidentally thrust upon the present, not unlike Edward Strong's interpretation of his county's history. At some point in the nineteenth century, applying the concept of feud to real-life conflicts made these traits a sine qua non. Rather than face the internal problems that had caused political violence in Breathitt County, the rest of Kentucky, the South, and the United States, Americans relied upon the relatively easy answers provided by the idea of feuds. Eventually, so did the citizens of Breathitt County.

"People who live lonely lives and have few neighbors"

Perhaps not surprisingly, the word *feud* "made a comparatively late appearance" in the English lexicon and is "of unsolved etymology."[10] The *Oxford English Dictionary* records its appearance in relation to enmity and violence no earlier than the thirteenth century.[11] At least as late as the 1820s, scholars of medieval legal history used *feud* interchangeably with *fief*, a word for land tenure, not ritualistic bloodshed.[12] By the time Noah Webster got around to providing his own American definition, it was requisitely treated as a vestigial British concept, "irrelevant or impossible" in an American context and, almost by definition, "consigned to the past."[13]

Nineteenth-century Americans deemed the blood feud a social mechanism carried out through pathos but motivated by ethos—at least the obscure ethos of certain erstwhile societies. Its tendency toward reciprocity for wrongs done to an individual or group were carried out in the conservative interest of maintaining a mutually accommodating status quo.[14] Neither insurrectionary nor counterinsurrectionary, blood feuds were motivated by "strong feelings of justice and moral order" that traversed the possibility of chaos presented by a weak state.[15] Nineteenth-century sociologists Émile Durkheim and Max Weber each considered the blood feud a phenomenon exclusive to less developed societies. But Durkheim did not give violence as much credit for sustaining social order as did Weber. For Weber, the arrangements involved in a blood feud comprised a prototypical state; Durkheim instead cast the blood feud in a condition of prepolitical statelessness.[16] Despite their divergent interpretations of feuds, there was a clear consensus: it was a specific kind of retributive violence with no direct relationship to modernity, and was only acceptable (if at all) in societies that had not achieved the occidental world's level of social and political rationalization.[17]

But most Civil War–era Americans got their blood feuds from novels and plays rather than encyclopedia or history books. Proper storybook feuds contained abrupt, impetuous acts of brutality instigated by hot blood and passion, not circuitous, studied schemes devised by politicians or generals and carried out by henchmen or soldiers. As *Romeo and Juliet's* opening scene demonstrates, underlings could act as violent proxies for their masters, but they did so for the same purposes of defending honor rather than over issues of state power. Fictional feuds, almost by definition, were more farcical than catastrophic at their points of departure, like Lilliput's factional division over breaking eggs. Their narratives invariably cautioned the listener as to the triviality and frivolity of the feud's point of origin as well the needlessness of the ensuing violence. Questions of justice or injustice were not addressed, lest one party seem too much the protagonist. Both sides must be at fault so that, through the equanimity of mutual violence, *neither* was at fault. Therefore, *feud* came to represent conflicts whose genesis was unworthy of serious inquiry.

Verona's doomed lovers and their feuding clans were more than familiar to Shakespeare-obsessed Americans. But more recent writers also played a major hand in popularizing the theme. Novelist Sir Walter Scott used feud motifs, skirting the boundary between myth and political history in late medieval Scotland; Scott always made a clear-cut distinction between the contingent/exogenous struggle against English oppression and the inherent/endogenous Highland feuds, the latter always originating "in some quarrel of little importance."[18] Notably, Scott's most avid readers were white southerners, and his indirect influence on their mores and behavior was a subject of snickering commentary on their society's belligerent inclinations. "Sir Walter had so large a hand in making Southern character, as it existed before the war, that he is in great measure responsible for the war," Mark Twain quipped shortly before the release of *Huckleberry Finn* (1884), a novel featuring one of the most noted feud narratives in American letters.[19]

Scott's seventeenth-century Scotland was most antebellum Americans' point of reference for feuds, but by midcentury, Sicily and Corsica became equally well known for reciprocal "clan" violence.[20] *Vendetta*, a more recent, Italian import to the English vocabulary, and one more explicitly specific to revenge, became almost synonymous with *feud*, and in Corsica the practice's rudiments were recorded in supposedly unbroken forms since the sixteenth century (with suggestions that it actually stretched back at least three centuries before that). In "regions not easily accessible to culture" used by Italian city-states and Ottomans as tokens of empire, vendettas were understandable outcomes of political stresses, according to one sympathetic Prussian. "In a state of nature, and in a society rent asunder by prevailing war and insecurity, the family becomes a state in itself; its members cleave fast to each other; if one is injured, the entire little state is wronged. The family exercises justice only through itself, and the form this exercise takes, is revenge."[21] Most readers looking at the island from the outside world, however, preferred to think of the inherency suggested by the "primitive character" that "survived so many obsolete institutions" of government imposed by other nations over the centuries.[22] It was a simpler explanation.

The Mediterranean model allowed Anglo-Americans to transfer their feud discourse from a temporal other (that is, their own British past) to a geographic, cultural other that persisted into the present. In the mid-eighteenth century, Corsica had formed a republic but was then bloodlessly absorbed by France, a consoling demonstration to sentimental Euro-Americans that political and economic change did not necessarily destroy sturdy folkways.[23] This provided a historical correlation with the South that was probably not lost on hopeful postbellum industrialists. After the Civil War the North viewed the white South, lowland or highland, as civilization's outskirt, just as Corsica was to Europe. White southerners were a fiercely democratic people who could be easily integrated into a larger economy. But most, if not all, accounts of Corsican or southern feuds failed to delve into the material causes of conflict, demonstrating a preference for them to be shrouded in obscurity rather than be brought to the light of day. There was sufficient evidence to show that these feuds did not involve only kinship, but it was a concession that observers made reluctantly.[24] When the 1878 courthouse riot on the streets of Jackson, Kentucky, prompted the *New York Times* to name the state "the Corsica of America," the editorial growled that "the Kentucky vendetta is worse than that of Corsica, since it includes not near relatives merely, but remote kindred and friends of the parties involved, and is carried on more openly and defiantly."[25] The differences between Kentucky and Corsica could not make the two different, but instead only make the former "worse." In any case, the Corsican metaphor required little elaboration.

Narrators of American "feuds," Jeffrey Guy Johnson has succinctly observed, "have shown little obligation to veracity even when claiming to tell the truth."[26] The interpretation of feud violence among American scholars and lay readers suffered from a liberal conflation of history, current events, and fiction. When the idea of feud violence came to be applied within the United States' confines, it was to describe events that were "not a discrete social practice with an accepted form, defined historical origins, or customary rules" as were their British or European analogues.[27] If nonfictional feuds took place in America, they did so in a new, strange manner in which no one ever declared an "official" customary condition of mutual enmity and attack. In all correctness, the feud in America was little more than an analogy or metaphor. Still, the word persisted.

Some of the first uses of *feud* to describe factual deadly violence in North America came from a decidedly non-European subject: white descriptions of Native Americans in the era of removal. During an 1832 trip west of the Mississippi, Washington Irving complained of how difficult it was "to get at the right story" as to the origins of "these feuds between the White & red man."[28] Some years after Cherokee relocation to the Indian Territory, the Polk administration became alarmed by what appeared to be the continuation of preexistent blood feuds among a native population thought to be pacified and "civilized."[29] In fact, *feud* scarcely described the reality: a nation thrown into civil war by the conditions of forced removal and competition for power over its new domain. Once Cherokee emissaries arrived in Washington in 1846 to appeal for a brokered peace, it should have been abundantly clear that this was a political fight caused by new exogenously imposed conditions (that is, the previous decade's federally enforced exile), not the exercising of old hatreds. A Confederate officer's description of their Civil War partisanship sixteen years later ("the [most] serious feud ever existing among the Cherokee Indians") suggested that their demonstration was not well remembered.[30] Even if the Cherokee Nation was ruptured by civil war as the United States was, the narrative of feud suggested that it was, nevertheless, not part of the "proper" war from a white perspective.

Reports of blood feuds among the Cherokee provided a precursor to the strange fusion of racial determinism and southernness that would be used to explain feuds among the "pure" Anglo-Saxon/Celtic mountain whites decades later, and it inspired the same debates over "native" populations' innate depravity versus ability to assimilate.[31] The association stuck even after American varieties of feuding had become associated exclusively with eastern Kentucky, where ostensibly Anglo-Saxon "fighters of the fiercest kind" killed without compunction because of the "Indian blood in their veins."[32]

This, however, was not the prevalent racial association. Whiteness in its purest form (a valuable nineteenth-century commodity) was a more popular link to feuds, and familial feuds were said to be most common among a lowland South's aristocracy "resigned to [violence's] necessity."[33] The lack

of any "strong extra-familial institutions," such as a state that effectively monopolized legitimate violence, augmented the social significance of kinship
beyond the normal boundaries of civil society.[34] Even when the divergence
began over "manifestations of public life," it always ultimately shrunk "to
the sphere of the family."[35] As Bertram Wyatt-Brown observed in *Southern
Honor*, prolonged violent feuds between individuals or families often prevented the more ordered practice of dueling; duels were a procedural safety
valve for masculine passions, while feuds seemed to be passion unfettered.[36]
This may be why such protracted conflicts appear in the historical record
only through a glass darkly. Most accounts of Old South feuds, in fiction
(more often) or nonfiction, were published in the North after "the fomenters
of the great southern feud" [that is, the Civil War] were finally "out of sight
and out of mind." All, like Twain, used the narrative of feud to underscore
the obsolescence of white southern society.[37]

Real-life occurrences that resembled the feud narrative were rare, such
as when novelist William Faulkner's great-grandfather William C. Falkner
began a personal vendetta against an entire family in 1849. Falkner's feud
with this Hindman family seemed to be an outgrowth of his status anxiety
(he began initially stabbing and shooting after he blackballed a newcomer
from a Mississippi temperance club) as he rose through the ranks of local
society, with the Hindmans opposing his ascension at every turn. The "feuds"
in which he took part were probably not ritualized and given to particular
codes of behavior, but were called *feuds* only because of the length of time
Falkner dedicated to his various fracases and because he earned the hatred
of multiple males in the same family. More than likely, Falkner was simply a
belligerent who attracted others like him. After he became "one of the richest
men in his county," a former business partner killed him, *sans façons*, in 1889.[38]

Most southern feuds were understood to be between entire families
and, through fact or embellishment, they followed the European model of
ordered equal reciprocity over long periods of time. In 1863 a Union soldier
observed an ongoing "family feud . . . quite 'Corsican' in its character" between neighboring Tennessee families even as the Chattanooga campaign
was fought around them.[39] The end of a twenty-one-year "domestic war"
in eastern Tennessee's Carter County (begun "about a very trifling affair")
ended in 1867 when the last male members of the respective families shot
each other to death on the streets of the county seat (the possibility that this
might somehow relate to the dozens of other white intraracial homicides all
over eastern Tennessee that year was not suggested).[40]

Scott, Honoré de Balzac, and other authors of feud narratives fascinated antebellum American readers, but the theme took on added significance after Appomattox. A feud was an "ideology-free conflict between evenly matched families," a perfect allegory to white northerners and southerners bent upon reuniting their nation-state and separating past from present without dealing with the political issues (race and slavery) that precipitated the war.[41] But even before the novels that fixed feuding indelibly on the American scene, namely, George Washington Cable's *The Grandissimes: A Story of Creole Life* (1880) and Twain's *Huckleberry Finn,* the language of *feud* had already entered into the debate over Reconstruction. The "actual" Darnell-Watson feud Mark Twain reported in his 1883 *Life on the Mississippi* (and the basis for the feud between the Grangerfords and Shepherdons in the next year's *Huckleberry Finn*) began at an undisclosed time over "a horse or a cow" between two well-fixed families on the Kentucky-Tennessee border near the Mississippi River (Twain also used a pretend blood feud between white southern belligerents in the unfinished *Simon Wheeler, Detective*).[42] Recalling his hearing of the family feud before the war. Twain proclaimed that in "no part of the South has the vendetta flourished more briskly, or held out longer between warring families" than in the Mississippi backwaters.[43] Befitting his jaundiced eye toward white southern society (and toward Sir Walter Scott), Twain made the bond between honor and deadly violence a lampoon, but one derived more from Shakespeare than from verifiable southern history.[44]

During the 1870s war of words between northern and southern newspapers, *feud* took on an unprecedented hyperbolic dimension. For southern conservatives, as demonstrated in an earlier chapter, it framed violence without any racial (therefore political) significance. It denoted locally endogenous causes for violence, suggesting that it would be appreciated if the North minded its own business.[45] The North, on the other hand, could use a southern feud to exemplify not only white southerners' irredeemable affinity for needless violence, but also the region's continuing sustenance of a useless, premodern aristocracy fed upon the labor of others and, consequently, self-destructive.[46] In both cases, the narrative of feud focused on the rock-ribbed inherencies of culture rather than the plastic contingencies of politics. It served the purposes of northern Republicans as they began giving up on the South and, therefore, inadvertently empowered white southerners as well.

As long as feuds seemed to be a habit of the white southern gentry— purely communal and fought over personal or local trivialities, strictly horizontal (as well as inherent to a society given to honor-based violence), and not concentrated in one discrete area of the region—hardly any criticism was projected in their direction. As indicated by the *New York Times*'s 1872 prediction of an oncoming "good old fashioned southern feud" in Virginia, they were rare enough to be thought of more as quaint than threatening even as southern Republicans were harassed and killed throughout the former Confederacy.[47] The concept of feud was instrumental for discouraged northern idealists expressing their cynicism and disillusionment after Reconstruction's failure. In 1883 former Radical Republican Carl Schurz included white-on-white "family feuds" among the categories of directionless violence he knew to be rampant after Reconstruction's end. It was a condemnation of the white South but one without racial or political significance; more than anything else it suggested Schurz's rejection of his own past zeal.[48] The *Nation* kept the radical faith for years after Schurz abandoned it, denouncing the southern Democracy at every turn, yet nevertheless deduced in 1879 that violence in the rebellious states was "not a Democratic disease simply" and that even if "every Southern white voted the Republican ticket . . . there would still be plenty of outrages and assaults and batteries." Southern politics, it said, was afflicted not by race hatred and aristocratic rule but rather "by the family feuds which fill up the time and thoughts of people who live lonely lives and have few neighbors."[49] That this was a variation on the same excuse for violence used by southern conservatives since 1865 was unmentioned. Schurz and *Nation* editors had lost any stomach for their postwar fight to reform the rebellious states. The idea of feuds helped them continue to criticize the white South while simultaneously disguising their resignation.

Homicide, North and South (1880), a state-by-state quantitative comparison of violent deaths compiled by Cincinnati journalist Horace V. Redfield, is best known for exposing the post-Reconstruction South's bloody record (many southern states each numbered the same total of killings as up to eight northern states in a year).[50] Redfield's book was also one of the most authoritative pronouncements on white southerners' inherent appetite for deadly vengeance, regardless of the recent war or other exogenous conditions. Environmental factors were not to blame, Redfield surmised, since expatriated southerners carried it with them even when they left the former war zone—as in Illinois's "bloody Williamson" County, where "a feud among families or factions of the peculiar southern type" carried out "by population from the old slave States" and "originat[ing] among the [white] population of Southern antecedents . . . was carried on in the Southern shot-gun style." The only difference was that, it being a northern state, "the 'feud' was suppressed, murder was punished," eventually leaving Williamson "as quiet and orderly as any county in Illinois."[51]

Redfield's Illinois anecdote was consistent with his larger program of depoliticizing southern violence. As a southern correspondent for the *Cincinnati Commercial,* Redfield was keenly aware of the difference between political and extrapolitical violence, especially after witnessing Alabama Democrats' vicious reaction to 1874's proposed federal civil rights act.[52] While South Carolina's blatantly political Red Shirts and Louisiana's White League (as well as the countless Ku Klux Klan blocs across the southern states) seemed to have supplanted the older style of communal violence, white southerners' "natural" proclivity for bloodletting still seethed beneath national attention. Redfield seemed to concentrate solely on white intraracial assaults at a time when white-on-black interracial killing was more prevalent. In the same vein, he even dismissed white intraracial attacks on southern Republicans. "Although there have been many political murders in the Southern States, yet the great majority of homicides," said Redfield, "have no more connection with politics than has petit larceny in New York."[53] This included South Carolina's knife fights and arsons, but oddly not as part of its "great political excitement" of 1876.[54] As correspondent for the Queen City's conservative Republican daily (as opposed to the radical *Gazette*), Redfield had reason to underestimate "grossly exaggerated accounts of [white-on-black] 'outrages'" and depoliticize those that defied complete dismissal.[55] His thesis demanded that white southerners be ferocious with or without politics—thus he could curse the white South without appearing to be a defender of the maligned black electorate. In less than two decades South Carolina's "Pitchfork Ben" Tillman was using a very similar argument to vindicate lynching.[56]

"The point of honor, as something to fight about, has pretty well disappeared in Anglo-Saxon countries"

Around the time *Homicide, North and South* was published, Kentucky's apparent special relationship to feuding was becoming nationally known. However, its reputation for armed interfamilial antagonism can be traced back to before the war. In 1854 a roguish son of a Mississippi planter published a florid account of his cousin Dr. Hezekiah Evans's thirty-year grudge with his neighbors, the Hill family (one of whom was a rival physician) in the Bluegrass's Garrard County. A Hill attacked Evans for abusing a leased slave in 1829—or so the story went. Years later, the neighbor's son, Dr. Oliver Perry Hill, publicly criticized Evans for being a subpar "steam doctor," and a series of confrontations between Evans, Hill's yeoman cousins, and the "rabble" economically attached to both families cost nine lives.[57] The conflict demonstrated simmering class tensions among Bluegrass whites (after Oliver Hill turned down Evans's challenge to a duel, Evans considered the other Hills too far beneath his notice to invite into the ritual) as well as a clash of egos involving medical professionalization.

Other than the sycophantic author's praising Evans as "a genuine son of Erin," ethnicity was not made an issue.[58] Still, the author self-consciously attempted to frame the story within a European past. The Mississippian, a veteran of the Peruvian navy, originally wanted to write it as a "Spanish romance," the better to display his knowledge of his favorite language. Even in a nonfiction format that described real, recent events in an American/southern setting, the blood feud was still a product of the Old World; even an American author trying to vindicate his real-life kinsmen wanted to treat it as a novel (Evans's reputation meant more to him than his young cousin's linguistic skills, and he insisted it be written in English).[59]

Once the locus of the feud narrative was moved from the lowland South to eastern Kentucky (and, by extension, the southern highlands in toto) during the 1880s, continuity with a European past had become more regression than romance.[60] It also triggered the question of whether Kentucky's "feud belt" was due to something inherent in Kentucky society (the oft-cited "pauper counties" problem being a likely culprit) or to various conditions found in southern Appalachia within Kentucky and beyond.[61] By the turn of the century the latter interpretation was becoming more popular, with or without documentation; one writer obtusely suggested that unreported feuds must also exist in North Carolina and Tennessee, but Kentucky's came to light only because of that state's superior ability to stop them through militia force of arms.[62] For most of the twentieth century practically any narrative of violence set in any part of Appalachia was explained as a feud (for instance, Ralph Stanley's prologue description of a Tennessean's revenge murder recounted in his recording of "Hills of Roan County").[63] In the 1930s New Deal caseworkers pointed to the very absence of feuds in North Carolina's westernmost Swain County as a sign of federal-initiated progress. Nothing of the sort had ever taken place there "except in the imagination of writers."[64] But that was beside the point; the narrative of feuds provided New Dealers with a useful counterpoint.

However, this viewpoint went against prevailing evidence and proved unconvincing. The inherency of feuding to eastern Kentucky, or at least a tendency toward factional white intraracial violence scarcely seen elsewhere, was hard to deny. If *feud* were Kentuckian, defined by containment within a state's boundaries, it would imply acknowledgment of its political associations. Basing *feud* upon its mountain environment did the exact opposite. Eastern Kentucky became "a synechdoche for all the southern uplands."[65] In the process there followed a tremendous amount of confusion and misinformation.

Kinship remained the established raison d'être once feuding was decided to be a fixture of the Kentucky mountains rather than the lowland plantations, but with a significant change in syntax. The old antebellum variety of "family feud" could be interfamilial (between either fictive or biological family groups) or intrafamilial (within one family; as Wyatt-Brown mentions in *Southern Honor,* it was popular for the latter sort to be portrayed as being between brothers).[66] In contrast, Kentucky mountain feuds were understood to be ultra-factional with very clear kin-based delineations, taking place between two familial groups who might be related by marriage but suffering no identity crisis as to which side they are on—thus making kinship an even greater motivational factor for killing.[67] Presumably, killing became more about eliminating an enemy than about preserving one's honor, thereby allowing the anonymous (as the *Louisville Courier-Journal* phrased it when William Goebel was shot) "mountain method of ambush" to replace the more publicly acceptable custom of dueling.[68] But most important, their alleged aboriginal predilection with kinship conjured an image of "'tribes' stuck in the 'Middle ages,'" placing mountaineers on a lower rung of a "temporal hierarchy" than the mass of Anglo-America.[69] It was this conceptual turn that helped to validate William Frost's oxymoronic "contemporary ancestors" title for Kentucky mountaineers.[70]

Frost's semifamous quote highlights the trait the lowland feudist and the mountain feudist did share, a special obsession among post-Reconstruction Anglo-Americans, feuds notwithstanding: whiteness. During the advent of scientific racism and the attendant "cult of Anglo-Saxonism," elaborations of whiteness relied upon a shaky combination of biology, anthropology, and history.[71] From the 1870s until well into the twentieth century, discussions of feuding in the Kentucky mountains included constant citation of the Anglo-Saxon bloodlines or culture (the two were scarcely distinguished from each other), insistence upon preservation of old behaviors through this continuity, and frequent medieval analogies. In a society bent upon white supremacy, one pervaded by interracial violence against nonwhite minorities, absolute whiteness made these Kentucky/mountain feuds appear horizontal and communal. The constant paeans to "the purest Anglo-Saxon stock in all the United States" gave their "pure" existence a measure of scientific authority.[72] The myth of feudists' absolute whiteness was imperative to this construction. Their citizenship in the American Republic became secondary to their alleged anthropological traits.

But there were inconsistencies. Many scholars of race were sure that the inherent traits that allowed the greatest of the Nordic races to fill the earth and subdue it could not include violence unmandated by state or commerce. "The point of honor, as something to fight about, has pretty well disappeared in Anglo-Saxon countries," observed a 1918–19 *Harvard Law Review* article on international law.[73] If Anglo-Saxons ruled the world, how could they also be primitive, even if they were "contemporary ancestors"? Kentucky's mountain whites were so currish, reasoned eugenicist Madison Grant, that there had to be "other hereditary forces at work there as yet little understood."[74] Anthropologist Emma Connelly's aforementioned imagined "sallow, gypsy-like people . . . 'far more incorrigible' than either the Indian or the negro" (a population whose existence was very difficult to prove) living next door to the "purest Anglo-Saxon stock in all the United States" (which was, in contrast, impossible to disprove) was not popular, but it demonstrates Connelly's own difficulty reconciling the orthodoxy of Anglo-Saxon ascendancy with the mountain whites' wartime bushwhacking and feuding that followed.[75] Scholars, especially those who were white Kentuckians and southerners, did not want to be any less racially pure than their more rustic neighbors, but they certainly could not share their regressive tendencies. Consequently, Anglo-Saxonism could not tell the whole story, and so not all racial explanations of feud behavior were the same. Anglo-Saxon determinism was hoisted upon its own shaky petard.

What if, then, Kentucky's mountain whites were not quite pure Anglo-Saxon but rather Celtic, a racial designator only subtly inferior (although it was a subtlety not lost on firm disciples of racial science)?[76] Applying "pure" Celtic, Scottish, or "Scots-Irish" (sometimes "Scotch-Irish") to the mountain feudist could set the unevolved "mountain white" apart from the mass of the Anglo-Saxon race while preserving his indispensable whiteness. Even if Anglo-Saxon Americans of the New England variety had given up old forms of violence, nineteenth-century feuds had a famous precursor among "the

Scotch Highlanders a century ago—the likelihood that most residents of the Kentucky mountains were primarily descendants of Scottish lowlanders was a detail minor enough to ignore.[77] Language that nineteenth-century Americans associated with Sir Walter Scott's odes (such as the aforementioned "clan") was often accompanied by exaggerations of recent feuds' historical longevities and obfuscations of their origins, suggesting that the practice continued from Old World to New, "the feud instinct being transplanted with the blood."[78] Feuding, if not racially determined, could also be interpreted as a bygone custom that somehow "survived to the present day."[79] "The feud is an inheritance," wrote one journalist in 1901. "There were feuds before the war and it is not a wild fancy that the Kentucky mountain feud takes root in Scotland."[80] Without noting that the recent decades' rash of feud violence was made up of separate conflicts all contained within one state, one journalist took the generalization further in 1912, claiming, "Actually, they are all one feud, and all are products of the old Highland clan spirit."[81]

Allusions to medieval Scotland could also be an allegorical disciplining of the feud phenomenon even when writers did not claim there was a direct connection. One southern commentator reasoned that, since "feudal troubles . . . of the Scotch type involved but little loss of life and less of property," they were relatively harmless and, most important, cast no reflection on statewide, regional, or national political conditions.[82] Except when these mountain Scots escaped the mountains (at least in fiction); in John Fox Jr.'s fictionalization of the mountain Republicans' 1900 Frankfort occupation was an "invasion from those black hills led by the spirit of the Picts and Scots of old . . . aided by and abetted by the . . . best element of the Blue-grass."[83] These metaphors were convincing enough for later Kentucky historians, who remembered Rowan and Breathitt counties' modern, constitutionally ordained judges and sheriffs as "chieftains" and "feudal lords."[84]

Celtic determinism proved to be more enduring than Anglo-Saxonism, and it remains popular in the twenty-first century, emerging as "highland games" and Scottish novelty stores in the southern tourist economy as well as within organized white supremacy.[85] Historians continue to casually find undetailed connections across "vast temporal and physical expanses" between post–Civil War "family feuds" and the Scotland or Ulster of previous centuries.[86] Nevertheless, when it came to the feud narrative, the Celtic mountain white served the same purposes as the Anglo-Saxon one: the depoliticization of feud violence by thrusting the modern mountain white back to the sceptered isle and far back into (as Eric Hobsbawm put it) "an ancient past beyond effective historical continuity, either by semi-fiction . . . or by forgery."[87] In the final analysis, it was not so much about ethnicity or race as it was about time. Collecting all of the reported Kentucky county wars into "one feud . . . products of the old Highland clan spirit" took each out of its respective context and belied the local cleavages that motivated men to take up arms. Even though evidence that "the family feuds of Kentucky . . . seem[ed] peculiar to families bearing Scottish names" was limited, at best, to anecdote, it proved believable and an effective means of depoliticizing *feud*.[88]

The Scottish/Celtic inherency theory stripped these conflicts of whatever modern political import that would have been plain had specific facts been publicized. Ethnicity or race were not only ends but also means to providing a place of detachment between eastern Kentucky's "survival of Elizabethan days" and Bluegrass Kentuckians, or between the former and the mass of Anglo-Americans.[89]

Ethnocentric explanations of feud narratives do not match with the historical record of Breathitt County and eastern Kentucky in the nineteenth century. The surnames associated with the Clay County Cattle War, Strong (English and Irish), Callahan (Irish), Eversole (German), and Amis (Huguenot French) reveal a population hardly diverse by twenty-first-century standards, but certainly not homogenous (the Freeman family's Afro-white biraciality suggests even more complications—not to mention a generous contribution of Native American genes). And by the time eastern Kentucky became associated with feuding, these ethnic identities had become quite meaningless. Early mountain settlers intermarried across pedigree lines with alacrity in the 1700s, and their Civil War–generation descendants carried bloodlines and folkways that spanned nations and (in many cases) continents.[90] The obsession with "pure" Anglo-Saxon or Celtic inheritance was a vapid fetish. Still, with outside observers like Frost and Connelly setting the standard of interpretation, the actual heritage of the "mountain whites," as well as their actual history, was less important than the racial politics of the day. People looking at eastern Kentucky saw what they wanted to see.

Interpretations of feud violence could not be fully explained by race, even by a generation that considered race the transcendent determinant of human affairs. In 1889 Charles Dudley Warner suggested that the origins of the "race of American mountaineers occupying the country from western North Carolina to eastern Kentucky" was "in doubt" and that their "lawlessness" was nothing inherent to their makeup but just a "relic of the disorganization during the war" (but even if the war started troubles the writer was fairly sure that "politics has little or nothing to do with them now").[91] In *Blue Grass and Rhododendron: Outdoors in Old Kentucky* (1901), John Fox Jr. relates that a Kentucky mountaineer told him that before the Civil War anyone would have been "druv outen the country" for drawing knives and guns in public (the more public manifestation of what was considered feudlike violence). By the present, however, "now hit's dirk an Winchester all the time," a change the interviewee attributed to the war's introduction of easy killing.[92] Sometimes semblances of political/contingency elucidations of mountain life provided a modest challenge to the communal/inherency/racial ones.

For that concern, a discourse of frontier and isolation was needed, the post-Reconstruction imagining of the "two Kentuckys," a division based more upon space and imagined time than race. "Less than a hundred miles divide[d] the *habitat* of these wildly different types. Their origin was the same, for their forefathers came West over the Wilderness Road," wrote one feud chronicler. "The slipping of a linch pin in the mountains kept here and there a family up among the crags, and they remained there nursing their primitive superstitions and hatreds. Their brothers moved on down to the blue grass, became educated and wore broadcloth."[93] As shown in chapter 1, eastern Kentucky was part of "New Appalachia," settled relatively late, prompting mountaineers to refer to the Bluegrass as their state's "old settlements."[94] But for the feud to be properly distanced historically, this ineffaceable fact had to be obscured or ignored.

It took a British historical journal to finally proclaim in 1952, "The figure of the feuding Hillman . . . is a phenomenon of modern America rather than of pioneer times" (but considering that the same article was subtitled "the scene of family feuds as fierce as any fought, before the Union of the Crowns, on the Anglo-Scottish border," the tone of temporal confusion was still present).[95] And this was only briefly after fellow Briton Arnold Toynbee had declared that Kentucky's "mountain people . . . acquired civilization and then lost it," a viewpoint that avoided the issue of temporal hierarchies altogether while still echoing the same implications. For his part, Toynbee saw Appalachian Kentucky as more Celtic than Anglo-Saxon.[96]

"We've been cartooned for the world with a fearsome, half-contemptuous slap on the back"

Picts and Scots aside, John Fox Jr. did not always think of the Kentucky feud phenomenon as something wedged in a frozen past. In *The Heart of the Hills*

(1912), the novelist suggested that historical change could affect a (fictional) feud's boundaries of conduct. What had once been an honor-based family affair, the Hawn-Honeycutt feud, eventually took on the taint of the outside world and its politics after both families began to see better days financially.

> As old Jason Hawn and old Aaron Honeycutt had retired from the leadership, and little Jason and little Aaron had been out of the hills, leadership naturally was assumed by these two business rivals, who revived the old hostility between the factions, but gave vent to it in a secret, underhanded way that disgusted not only old Jason but even old Aaron as well. For now and then a hired Hawn would drop a Honeycutt from the bushes and a hired Honeycutt would drop a Hawn. There was, said old Jason with an oath of contempt, no manhood left in the feud. No principal went gunning for a principal—no hired assassin for another of his kind.[97]

The egalitarian "manhood," the primal force that gave the mountain whites their native animus and had once defined the ritualized blood feud, had been polluted by a less valorous form of combat that involved the employment of hired underlings. Not only was the original Hawn-Honeycutt feud apolitical but it was antithetical to politics. Politics, and the violence that it involved, supplanted the communal conflict that the two families had kept going in their locale until forced to deal with the outside world. Now that the feud had resumed, however, it had lost its "manhood" by taking on hierarchies (that is, politics) on each side.

Later in the novel Fox Jr. returned to "manhood" in a soliloquy by Colonel Pendleton, an elderly Bluegrass *patrón* who mentors a young Jason Hawn Jr. while he attends stately Centre College. On his deathbed the colonel confesses Kentucky's sins committed between the 1860s and 1910s:

> The war started us downhill, but we might have done better—I know I might. The earth was too rich—it made life too easy. The horse, the bottle of whiskey, and the plug of tobacco were all too easily the best—and the pistol all too ready. We've been cartooned for the world with a fearsome, half-contemptuous slap on the back. Our living has been made out of luxuries. Agriculturally, socially, politically, we have gone wrong, and but for the American sense of humor the State would be in a just, nation-wide contempt. The

John Fox Jr. peppered his fiction with references to Breathitt County and once interviewed its infamous former sheriff Edward Callahan. His fictional portrayals of eastern Kentucky probably determined Americans' reading of violence in the county more than any newspaper articles. (Courtesy of the Library of Congress, Prints & Photographs Division, Bain Collection, LC-DIG-ggbain-03385)

Ku-Klux, the burning of toll-gates, the Goebel troubles, and the night-rider are all links in the same chain of lawlessness, and but for the first others might not have been. But we are, in spite of all this, a law-abiding people, and the old manhood of the State is still here. Don't forget that—*the old manhood is here.*[98]

Fox Jr. temporarily sets the "two Kentuckys" motif aside, suggesting that all of the ugly incidents and types of violence witnessed in the state since before feuding was in flower developed from the same decadent source. But the images conjured were related more to the antebellum Bluegrass, and Colonel Pendleton noticeably left feuding off of his list. These other forms of violence were openly insurrectionary or (in the case of the Ku Klux Klan) politically motivated vigilantism. Feuding and its "manhood," he implied, was apolitically horizontal and, accordingly, a vestige of a Kentucky *before* it went "downhill," a vestige that hearkened back to the old undivided consensus white Kentuckians—and perhaps all white southerners—once shared.

Louisville poet Madison Cawein, "the Keats of Kentucky," apparently agreed, at least in terms of placing feuds in the past. Between 1887 and 1914 he acknowledged all the recent horrors in verse, and in "Ku Klux," "The Lynchers," and "The Feud," they received their due. While the first two vividly depict the terrors their titles evoke, "The Feud" only describes a dilapidated bullet-riddled cabin, an archeological site bearing proof of a long-ago attack. Lynch mobs were current, but feuds were an event from an irredeemable past even when the shooting continued into the present.[99]

Journalist Charles Mutzenburg, second only to John Fox Jr. as a popular interpreter of feud violence, used the same anecdotes from Kentucky's recent history to protect the mountaineers from self-righteous condemnation. All of Kentucky's violent embarrassments, in Mutzenburg's view, were from the same source; the "lack of confidence of the people in their courts" conveyed a public atmosphere still suffering from the postbellum crisis of legitimacy. However, violence that was seen as "feudal" did not affect women and children, or impede commerce, as did other outrages.[100] Compared to this hateful violence, communal feudists did not upset the status quo beyond their wooded environs.

We believe it germane to the matter under discussion to add that not only feuds, but mobs and the like, are, and ever have been, the direct outgrowth of a lack of confidence of the people in their courts. The shameful nightrider outrages in the western part of Kentucky a few years ago, in a section which had boasted of a civilization superior by far to that of the mountaineers, where schools and churches are to be met with at every corner, were the outcome, so it is claimed, of the failure of the law to deal sternly with the lawless tobacco trust, the "original wrongdoer" in the noted tobacco war. If this were true, if this justified the destruction by incendiaries of millions of dollars' worth of property, brutal whippings, the indiscriminate slaughter of entire families without regard to age or sex, the butchery of little children (for aiding the tobacco trust, no doubt) then, indeed, is the mountaineer feudist also innocent of wrongdoing; more so, for he, at least, never made war upon suckling infants, nor have women suffered harm, except in one or two instances. Nor is the cultured Blue Grass citizen free to censure him, when he calls to mind the outrages of the toll-gate raids, or takes into account the numerous lynching bees, proceedings from which the mountaineers have always been *practically* [my emphasis] free.[101]

The fact that Kentucky's last purported "feud" climaxed with the assassination of a well-known political figure (James B. Marcum) was left unmentioned; it did not suit Mutzenburg's thesis.

While Fox Jr. and Mutzenburg established eastern Kentucky as the home of the feud phenomenology, they were only following the lead of countless newspaper stories. Small-circulation Kentucky papers displayed party stripes until well into the twentieth century and, as revealed in preceding chapters, their interpretations of commotions in the eastern third of the state were usually guided by their loyalties (especially before 1880 when the feud narrative served as a political diversion for southern conservatives). But editorial party devotion was a dying trend when national interest in the Kentucky feud was growing. Flourishing national news conglomerates favored human interest and sensationalism over party line toeing. By the middle of the 1890s the scandalous and the grotesque had become the currency of widely read publications as they divested themselves of their old party identities.[102] As a result, the party associations that made up most Kentucky feuds were scarcely addressed. A parochial "political rivalry" could be casually included within a list of trivial quarrels over "a horse trade, a gate left open and trespassing cattle, the shooting of a dog . . . or a difficulty over a boundary fence," according to Ellen Semple.[103] Journalists led scholars like Semple and William G. Frost to favor explanations of feuds that dealt with race and spatial isolation. By the beginning of the twentieth century the Kentucky/mountain feudist was considered a social type invariably formed by a combination of geography, breeding, and medieval qualities.

> In the mountain counties of [Kentucky's] eastern border, where the rugged and untaught minds are dominated by a crude and savage idea of the meaning of honor, the deadly vendetta still rages, and no one can say when it will cease. So long as the mountain defiles remain uninvaded by the emigrant; so long as their mountain sides intimidate the prospective railroad line; and above all, so long as their wild, barbaric blood remains uncrossed by a gentler strain—just so long will their internecine wars prevail. For here men are governed by a medieval idea of right and wrong, and each man's mind is his own court and judge. He acknowledges no other, and by it are his actions governed. And when it has led him to wanton slaughter, as it often does, the endless stretches of forest-clad mountains afford a refuge which it is impossible to lay bare. But it is a rare thing that the slayer of his kind seeks the shelter of the hills. When his enemy is done to death, the victor goes home and tells his friends, and the clansmen gather on either side, as they did in the days of Roderick Dhu [a character from Sir Walter Scott's six-canto narrative poem *The Lady of the Lake*].[104]

Bluegrass optimists had once expected that the civilizing influences of church, dam, bank, and steel track would bring peace to Kentucky's more restless counties. But by 1900 "men had fallen dead by feudists' bullets on the doorsteps of the churches" and the arrival of railroads had not ceased the killings.[105] The mountain whites' feudal habits were beginning to appear something irredeemably inherent. In what could have been one of the most open admissions that feud violence might have some internal political import, activist John C. Campbell wrote that the "name commonly applied to the feud in Kentucky is 'war,' and the principle upon which it was carried out was the principle of warfare—to do as much harm to the enemy as possible while incurring the least risk oneself."[106] This description was a far cry from the classical feud's ritualistic practice. But instead of crafting a commentary on how feud had been applied to eastern Kentucky arbitrarily by exogenous observers, Campbell intended for the war analogy to be only an illustration of the hypothetical mountain feudist's ruthlessness as well as his arrogance in applying the air of legitimacy attendant to war onto his own personal vendettas. However, Campbell inadvertently acknowledged that there had been something at work in eastern Kentucky that did not fit well into the Old World's feud template.

By the time of Campbell's writing the associations of *feud* were making a transition from the Old World to North America. What need did twentieth-century Americans have for Montagues and Capulets (especially as the number of American Shakespearean productions declined) when they had McCoys and Hatfields at their disposal? The "Hatfield-McCoy feud" began to "fire the public imagination" at the end of the 1880s, although the public generally had little interest in the facts surrounding it.[107] Long before it became an American English idiom, it was identified as an absurd fight between "Chatfields and McLoys" in Virginia. Between 1878 and 1888 ten men and two children were killed in a series of Election Day confrontations, ambushes, and an arson in the Tug River Valley community straddling the Kentucky–West Virginia border. The feud's most widely publicized deaths coincided with the French-Eversole feud and the Rowan County War, and might have been lost among eastern Kentucky's 1880s feud propagation had it not been for New York reporter T. C. Crawford, who made Hatfield-McCoy the newly discovered mountain phenomenon's epitome. It went on to become the only feud manifestation that the American reading public remembered by name—albeit in simplified, distorted form. Historian Altina Waller believes that Crawford (along with one other reporter) "probably had more to do with the development of the hillbilly stereotype than any other individuals."[108]

In choosing this particular atrocity over others, Crawford permanently established how Americans defined feud.[109] His rendering was popular as a broad illumination of white intraracial violence in the United States, as were versions of the Hatfield-McCoy feud that followed in print and eventually on film.[110] Its origins were murky enough (originally reported as one white family's absurd attempt to enslave another, it was eventually reported as beginning after a lawsuit filed over a stolen sow) that it was commonly believed that the feud lasted generations rather than a more modest twelve years; the entirety of the violence took place in one of the most remote areas of the Cumberland Plateau; and, in the style of Edmond Rostand's play *Les romanesques* (1894), it ended with a supposedly forbidden romance between the combatants' children.[111] The story had charisma that the Rowan County

War or the French-Eversole feud lacked because it combined aesthetic elements of European romanticism with frontier color in a satisfying manner. Although it pleased readers not to know its beginnings (or to marvel at how petty they were), it did have an exciting middle and a satisfying end. Above all, it was entertaining, at least as Crawford and his imitators told it.

Perhaps most important, the Hatfields' conflict with the McCoys, in its factual and fictional versions, was less offensive than others because of its communal rather than political theme. The homicides involved were committed either as impulse or in revenge, befitting a Corsican vendetta. The feud was between families and factions of modest means and did not indict men in high places (even after an extradition conflict between West Virginia and Kentucky, no politicians were unduly embarrassed by the whole thing).[112] It was unmistakably horizontal and devoid of class significance, thus sustaining the popular notion of the egalitarian mountain white. It had no definite connection to intimate hostilities created by the war, and therefore did not challenge the promise of a national reunion based upon whiteness. Well into the twentieth century, long after Progressive Era racial determinism faded, it was still believable that the feud had roots in the British Isles; beneath a 1982 article commemorating the centennial of the feud's cessation, the county seat newspaper in the Hatfields' and McCoys' old territory (now Mingo County, West Virginia) expressively printed images of both families' supposed coats of arms.[113] Even after books that strove to treat these "feudists" as historical people were published (notably, Otis Rice's *The Hatfields and McCoys* [1982] and Altina Waller's *Feud* [1988]), most Americans still prefer the event's more primordial explanations. It could easily be written off as the product of a strange aboriginal culture rooted in the past rather than an outgrowth of the affairs of state. As close as it was in time and space to Bloody Breathitt, the Hatfield-McCoy feud was everything that Breathitt was not, thus making it far more popular and almost inspiring. "Hatfields and McCoys" had lasting power as an American idiom, even though eastern Kentucky's most demoralizing episodes of feud violence, the Clay County War and the Hargis-Cockrell feud, were yet to come and would eventually be forgotten on a national scale. In American memory it was the feud's extrapolitical apotheosis.

As Altina Waller has shown, the Hatfields, McCoys, and people of other surnames who were directly involved in their conflict rarely got the opportunity to tell their own story but were reticent when they did (especially the latter; a 1975 televised drama called *The Hatfields and McCoys* called

every historically based character either "Hatfield" or "McCoy" lest historical fact confuse the pat dramatic dialectic). The majority of interpretations
of Kentucky's feud violence between the 1870s and 1900s did indeed come
from the city-dwelling journalists and industrialists who were products of,
simply put, a "dominant culture."[114] The Hatfield-McCoy feud's mythologi-
cal arrangement was fundamentally a hegemonic device to make way for
economic exploitation in the Tug River Valley. Along the way, it inadvertently told an oversimplified story about "mountain whites," irrespective of
their relationship to violence. Feuds and "Hatfields and McCoys" became
emblems for things with nothing at all to do with their actual historical or
linguistic meanings.

As "Hatfields and McCoys" made the transition from human-interest
story to idiom, it produced the broader popular culture "hillbilly" image as
a cultural codicil.[115] By the 1930s, the ever-bearded feudist, native to some
unnamed mountain locale, appeared in popular media with little or no
contextual elaboration needed—it was something Americans simply knew.
These characters were so detached from their intended audience's points of
cultural reference that they approached surrealism, the realm of cartooning
rather than literature or dramaturgy. Their prevalence in pre–World War II
cartoons, both still and animated, gave them a surreal, timeless quality that
further detached mountaineers from objective reality (Paul Webb's *Esquire*
drawings are considered the characterization's true quintessence before the
more famous Li'l Abner Yokum and Snuffy Smith—both mountaineer cari-
catures but not necessarily feudists—premiered).[116] "Hatfields and McCoys,"
a bloody anecdote from nineteenth-century history, had become material
for the funny papers in approximately the same half century's time a similar
thing happened for "cowboys and Indians."

Academics have also blithely employed the feud trope for their own
purposes, purposefully or inadvertently, with uncritical abandon. A historian
of southern violence wrote in the 1980s that "isolated mountain people"
in the years after the Civil War "had no notion of cultural pluralism or
moral relativism—only right and wrong," suggesting that spatial removal
from metropolitan areas resulted in a lack of nuanced attitudes toward
relationships of power (one wonders how great other nineteenth-century
Americans' perceptions of such decidedly twentieth-century concepts were
in comparison).[117]

In a mid-1990s political science monograph, nineteenth-century white
intraracial violence in Kentucky provided a primordial explanation for a

very current political trend. "Because of Kentucky's history of dueling and feuds, its penchant for self-reliance, and its isolation, one would not be surprised to find that 95 percent of rural Kentucky households are armed; about half of the males in those areas, it is estimated, carry guns either on their person or in their vehicles. Given such powerful attitudes, it is also not surprising that the Kentucky General Assembly, strenuously lobbied by the National Rifle Association (NRA), in 1984 prohibited Kentucky localities from regulating the distribution of firearms."[118] By placing the origins of their supposed "powerful attitudes" about gun ownership into a past "beyond the polis" suggested by dueling and feuds, opposition to gun control was invalidated as acceptable political behavior (for that matter, the NRA's lobbying power in the legislature was conflated with a popular affinity for guns as a causal factor, thus rendering the argument inconsistent and confused). This cast the gun control debate as a hierarchical relationship between a knowledgeable, benevolent urban elite and a rural populace ignorant of modern norms and obsessed with an unfortunate past defined by "regressive political tendencies."[119] Although Breathitt County was not individually mentioned, its history of since-depoliticized violence was integral in delegitimizing the ideology of late twentieth-century Kentuckians as well as distorting the temporal distance between the age of "dueling and feuds" and the late twentieth century's "culture wars."

In another scholarly engagement with the rural working class, an anthropologist studying gender and labor relations in western North Carolina used *feud* in a more nuanced fashion in a published moment of confession. The scene described a family quarrel over a matter of racial and regional identity politics (and involved the use of a racial epithet) that ended with one subject reminding another that their living in "the South" ultimately stifled the debate. "I have been loathe to offer this vignette because it presents mountain whites as ignorant, hate-mongering, and racist—*a partial truth which invokes the Hatfields and McCoys* [my emphasis]. Failing to note instances such as these, however, I unwittingly construct Appalachia as egalitarian, bucolic, and *white* [Anglin's emphasis], echoes again of the local schema. It is equally important to note that this moment of virulent racism did not go unchallenged, but was refracted and relocated in the debate between Hazel and her father [Anglin's subjects]."[120] The vignette reflected an issue probably very common to researchers who harbor sympathy for their subjects. But the language the author used to reveal this is more telling than was probably intended. "Hatfields and McCoys," the phrase that

Americans use interchangeably with "feud," was offhandedly linked with the "ignorant, hate-mongering, and racist" even though the ethnographic sketch in question had nothing to do with a familial vendetta or, for that matter, any act of violence. The anthropologist used the familiar surname pair as a surrogate for some mudsill of white American existence that could only be spoken of in the fictive form of mythologized historical figures and that is, unlike her previously idealized subjects, undeserving of her sympathy or "help." It would seem that *feud*, or its synonyms, suggests not only a format for primordial violence but a racial and cultural presence that tests the limits of scholars' belief in multiculturalism and "cultural pluralism or moral relativism."

More recently, *feud* had a particularly egregious mishandling in Malcolm Gladwell's best-selling *Outliers: The Story of Success* (2008). In trying to trace the variety of unstudied factors that contribute to various types of human "success," Gladwell appropriated Harlan County's Howard-Turner feud of the 1880s as an example of the omnipresence of "cultural legacies."[121] In doing so, he displayed as "little obligation to [historical] veracity" as J. Stoddard Johnston, John Fox Jr., T. C. Crawford, or any of the other local-color writers who interpreted eastern Kentucky's history of white intraracial violence for their own ends.[122] As detailed in an earlier chapter, the so-called Howard-Turner feud not only involved men of more than two surnames, it had far more to do with one county's two-party system than familial hatred.[123] In Gladwell's telling, Harlan County was "a remote and strange place, unknown by the larger society around it," founded in 1819 by "eight immigrant families from the northern regions of the British Isles."[124] He then skipped ahead many years to the obscure livestock-related feud origins (in the 1880s) without mentioning any other specific dates, the better to demonstrate its primordialism. The "Scotch-Irish," "steeped in violence" in the Old World, brought their proclivities with them to Appalachia but, although Gladwell argued that "one of the world's most ferocious cultures of honor" took root throughout the southern highlands, he neglected to explain why the four feuds he named all happened within one discrete corner of Kentucky rather than all over Appalachia (or, for that matter, any parts of the United States with substantial "Scotch-Irish" populations but no history of notable violence).[125]

Gladwell's use of Harlan County, Kentucky, shows that cultural continuities and social inherencies still hold popular currency when it comes to explaining human behavior. To demonstrate this he quotes historian David

Hackett Fischer (for whom the feud phenomenon was only part of a larger ahistorical thesis on British inherency and primordialism) and journalist John Ed Pearce, while leaving out the more thorough work of Altina Waller, Kathleen Blee, and Dwight Billings. In fact, it would seem that Gladwell selected the relatively obscure Howard-Turner feud in order to avoid their books due to their dedication to detail and emphasis on contingency and historical context—attributes that do not support Gladwell's point. The origins of the "feudists'" dialogue he uses is uncited. *Outliers* was a humble middlebrow suggestion that, although continuities provide satisfying answers, change does happen, and therefore contingency should receive more attention. Gladwell's chapter on Harlan County suggests precisely the opposite. His selection of the Howard-Turner feud and his employment of apocryphal sources rather than more thorough ones comprised a purposeful, gratuitous disservice to understanding violence.[126]

Gladwell's poor handling of feuds has deep roots, namely, an abiding refusal among educated people to acknowledge complexity within what they hold to be "simple societies."[127] During the worst days of troubles in Rowan, Perry, Harlan, Pike, or Breathitt counties (or any number of other smaller incidents the Gilded Age press labeled a "feud"), the number of newspaper correspondents was always low. Reportage of events often gave way to innuendo and unfounded assumptions. Throughout the nineteenth century discussions of feuds had always been more associated with fancy than with fact, but this was when the concept was almost purely within the fantasy. When *feud* was applied to factual violent deaths during Reconstruction and afterward, it meant the belittlement of killing.

This was partly a timeworn war correspondent's syndrome, an urban outsider's tendency to "explain violence as a product of marginality and relative deprivation, or even [evoke] simple theories of violence as a phenomenon of the frontier."[128] Attributing violence to environmental "otherness" ("They are simply not like us") has always been easier than delving into bare facts, especially when men with guns stand in front of these bare facts. But the refusal of writers to strive to find the origins of feud violence is also a tool for delegitimizing its practitioners and even its victims, as is the primeval social atmosphere suggested by kinship, temporality, and the various other attributes applied to eastern Kentucky by the *outside world*.

Breathitt County, the place that John Fox Jr. considered the Kentucky/mountain feud's alpha and omega, was not interpreted exclusively by the outside world.[129] "Bloody Breathitt" was recorded and created according to a combination of the wants and needs of outsiders as well as those of the county's own inhabitants. But the end results were analogous to that of the Hatfield-McCoy feud or the Harlan County War. In due course, it was decided to be in virtually everyone's interests for the causality of political divisions to be subordinated to the language of feud.

"A killing in Breathitt always seems to be big news"

In Jackson, Kentucky, the news of 1891's peace between the Hatfields and McCoys was received as it was everywhere else: a telegraphed half column in the newspaper with references to the Middle Ages, gross exaggerations of the conflict's length and death toll, and a general oversimplification of the facts. "The Hatfield-McCoy feud which has lasted nearly twenty years, and caused the death of 100 persons [in] Logan county W. Va., and Pike county Ky., has at last ended. Like the 'War of the Roses' it was terminated by a marriage. A truce was proclaimed, a Hatfield married a Miss McCoy, a peace congress was call and terms amicable to both parties were agreed upon. Thus ends one of the most bloody feudal wars of modern times not equaled in ferocity and fatality, perhaps, by the wars of the Scottish High-landers." John J. Dickey received the news with foreboding. Noting the recent heightened national attention on eastern Kentucky as a whole, Dickey dourly predicted that fact and fancy would become intermingled in written accounts of his adopted section's "feuds." "The feudal wars of Eastern Kentucky will no doubt be utilized in coming years by writers of fiction," read a *Jackson Hustler* editorial. "It is in this form, perhaps, they will go down to poster-ity as no historian feels like chronicling the naked facts, and incorporating them into local history. Already two novels have been written to celebrate the deeds of the Hatfields and McCoys."[130]

The missionary journalist's concerns reflected a passion for historical accuracy that shone through the oral histories that filled hundreds of pages in his immense diary. Breathitt County was home not to one iconic famous feud but to a series of marginally well-known spates of lawlessness dating back to the war, making the truthful recording of its past a task so byzantine as to be almost impossible. Since his arrival Dickey had touted the county's improvements over other eastern Kentucky trouble spots and protested what he considered unfair media misrepresentations.[131] He had tried to be fair to Breathitt County in his own recording of its "naked facts," and he was concerned that other writers would not. And he was correct; eastern

Kentucky feud narratives almost always subordinated facts to colorful façade, and descriptions of events in Bloody Breathitt were no exception. A little over twenty years after Dickey made his prediction, one daft author placed "a family feud between the McCoys and the Hatfields" in Breathitt County.[132]

The Hatfield-McCoy feud's end coincided with the Kentucky Union Railroad's arrival in Breathitt County. The railroad's eminence in the lives of Jackson's residents represented an opportunity not afforded to the residents of the more isolated Tug River Valley to the northeast. It offered Breathitt an opportunity to divest itself of an image that dated back to the 1870s. If white intraracial violence was a product of isolation and "family feuds," as had been said for years, the railroad was a sure cure. But just over a decade later, when James Marcum's death reoriented national attention toward the county again, this assumption was disproven. "The Breathitt County feuds," wrote the *Courier-Journal* soon after Marcum's murder, "furnish a contradiction to the old adage that wherever newspapers, railroads, and colleges penetrate feuds are vanquished."[133] Bloody Breathitt seemed to embody the conception of feud, while also negating its most popular assumptions.

The same newspaper had begun Bloody Breathitt's definition more than twenty-four years before, when the Kentucky militia's Jackson occupation gained national press attention. But this was long before Bloody Breathitt became familiar to Americans outside Kentucky. The mountain Kentuckians' alleged need for civilizing in the winter of 1878–79 (as detailed in a previous chapter) established what would become the feud belt's essential premise. When Breathitt County once again received widespread media scrutiny, the mold for its interpretation had already been set in other eastern Kentucky counties. Because of the "feuds" of the 1880s and 1890s, it was arguable that Breathitt's experience was an example of a greater whole. But Bloody Breathitt's creation came about with contributions from a diverse, often conflicting array of forces, not all of whom agreed upon how the strange county should be defined. To an observer from the outside world with no prior knowledge of the county's history or politics, it was an eastern Kentucky county little different than most others, beset by a racial or cultural tendency toward communal violence irrespective of county boundaries.

But at the same time, there was also an impulse to make Breathitt seem strange even among its neighbors and within eastern Kentucky's larger feud mythos, a viewpoint more likely to be espoused by the mountain white's self-proclaimed defenders. Whenever the "outbreak of another feud in 'bloody Breathitt'" was reported, "the world infer[ed] that battle, murder, and sudden death are commonplaces in Appalachia," travel writer Horace Kephart complained from his North Carolina hermitage in 1913.[134] Relatively orderly feuds were carried out in surrounding counties, opined a fictional character in 1922, "not laywaying and ambushing and sech, like in Breathitt, whar the wrong man gets kilt often as not."[135]

But Bloody Breathitt's seemingly inherent violence did not encourage greater attention to be paid to possible political causes. The conception of "Bloody Breathitt" was very different than the Hatfield-McCoy feud or any of the other feuds or "wars" that were reported in other eastern Kentucky counties. A feud was an event, or a series of events, with a beginning (albeit an often obscure or unimportant one) and an ending. To a degree, it was determined by clear contingency. But for there to be a series of relatively self-contained feuds within the confines of one county, as was the case with Breathitt, violence would have to be a permanent product of the terrain rather than of human agency, and therefore inherent in the culture for reasons beyond direct comprehension; Harlan County, Kentucky's renaming as "bloody Harlan" during the coal strike violence of the 1930s was a product of a similar rhetorical turn.[136] This was why the persistence of the Hargis-Cockrell feud was exaggerated and said to continue "despite the fact that most of its actors have been laid low by bullets."[137] By suggesting that the late feud lasted past the deaths of most of the political actors who acted as instigators or victims, *feud* was suggested to be a localized ontology of violence rather than a historically finite event or series of events. Whether Bloody Breathitt was part of the feud belt or singularly perverse, its violent history was decidedly inherent, irrespective of what went on in the outside world. No matter what was revealed about the political stratagem that led to James Marcum's murder, it was ever after considered something as intrinsic to a place as flora and fauna.

After the Hargis-Cockrell feud, the international feud analogies continued in the press, forecasting that "Breathitt" was on its way to argot status. "The feuds of Breathitt County and of the mountains," concluded one activist, grew out of the "code of morals which belong to the old Scotch Highlanders."[138] Newspapers in Frankfort and Chicago agreed that the events of 1902 through 1908 rivaled "the worst stories that have come out of Corsica and Sicily."[139] Sources that acknowledged political impetus used temporal exaggerations to make the feud's electoral origins seem more distant in time than they actually were. Even when the "official position and political influence" of modern politicians was recognized, they were still considered only aggravating factors in "feud wars" that had "raged since the Kentucky mountains were first settled by white men," or at least were "older than [the] War."[140] A children's novel published less than six years after James Hargis's death (and a year before Sheriff Callahan's) recounted the feud lasting "for generations" after "some election for a county judge."[141] "The Breathitt folks live in the Eighteenth century; you might almost say in the Seventeenth," said the *New York Sun* via telegraph from Jackson in 1903. "They have not changed much since the Revolution" and "know little and care less about the opinions of the world beyond the mountains."[142] Republican Kentucky newspapers, usually less willing to separate Bloody Breathitt from the state's political present than the Democratic opposition, still could not resist comparing the Hargis courthouse's corruption to the conditions of the "the middle ages."[143] In the interest of being au courant, Louisville's *Evening Post* ran cartoons associating Bloody Breathitt with Russia's ongoing invasion of Manchuria as well as the recent slaughter of Bessarabian Jews.[144] Breathitt County existed in the United States of the present, but it was easier to dismiss its implications if it was placed as far away in space and time as possible— nowhere served that purpose better than tsarist Russia.

WHY NEWS FROM BREATHITT IS SCARCE

(Left and opposite) In 1903, Louisville's *Evening Post* lampooned Breathitt County's murders in several zany cartoons, some making snide comparisons with contemporary events abroad. (*Louisville Evening Post*, May 13 and 29, 1903)

PROBABLY THE CAUSE OF YESTERDAY'S ATTACK.

Breathitt County Mountaineer: "Well, well, these Russians are beating me to it. I'll have to do something!"

After 1903, "Breathitt," bloody or unmodified, briefly became a glib metaphor. After the grisly murder of Serbia's King Alexander I (involving disembowelment followed by defenestration) just weeks after James Marcum's death, a *Life* editor compared it to "habits in Breathitt" (a Chicago newspaperman compared Alexander's successor King Peter I's chances of assassination to that of a Breathitt County prosecuting attorney).[145] A Memphis newspaper included "Breathitt County fandangos" in a list of civilization's woes Arctic explorer Frederick Cook had left behind him.[146]

In the humor magazine *Puck,* a grizzled westerner named "Tarantula Tom" told about "Crimson Gulch," a rowdy mining camp left pacified after "a feller come along from Breathitt county, Kentucky, an' we felt so much like amateurs that the boys all quit tryin' to show off."[147] Seven years later the same magazine hoped "some beneficent, heedless, rakehelly, irresponsible, light-hearted cyclone, earthquake, avalanche, conflagration, tidal wave, comet, pestilence, or plague would arise and smite, overwhelm, wipe out, submerge, consume, chew-up-and-spit-out, devour, emasculate, or destroy" Breathitt County and other recent trouble areas.[148] In a reverse of the old Mediterranean metaphor, a character in an American novel about Sicily exclaimed that the island's vendetta habit was "worse than Breathitt County, Kentucky," with no further explication needed.[149] When a Virginia court-house massacre made national news in 1912, one commentator branded it "an echo of the Breathitt County feud."[150]

Fictional accounts of mountain feuds in the first decades of the twentieth century also exploited the recent memory of the Hargis-Cockrell feud. A settlement schoolteacher's fictional memoir used the town of Jackson and Breathitt County as its model and began the story line briefly after the cessation of a recent prolonged fracas between town politicians.[151] The surnames Jett (as in Curtis Jett) and Valentine (the first name of one of the more famous Hatfields) were used as character names in a feud novel set in the story-bound town of Leeston.[152]

Although fascinated by Breathitt County, John Fox Jr. never used it as a setting for one of his novels (he tended to avoid using explicitly real places for such), but the county was mentioned as a neighboring locale in two short stories and a novel (he used Marcum as a character's name in one novel).[153] His primary concern was establishing feud violence as something innate to the experience of the mountain white, not just a series of events between two families or factions. For that reason, the violent streets of Jackson and the bushwhacker-rife woods that surrounded it made for better subject matter than the finite vendettas of other Kentucky counties. In order to be interesting, feuds had to have historical (or ahistorical) longevity, and even though the length of other feuds was exaggerated for dramatic effect, Fox Jr.'s interest in authenticity led him to what he considered an inherently violent territory rather than simply a place that had played host to a feud or two. The inherency of violence came to replace the historical facts of feuds in the memory of Bloody Breathitt and the rest of eastern Kentucky.

By the 1920s the only nationally available account of the Hargis-Cockrell feud that announced the facts of the conflict and made explicit use of full names (particularly Judge Hargis's and Sheriff Callahan's role in organizing James Marcum's death of at the hands of Curtis Jett and Tom White) was a folk song of dubious composition. As late as 1920 song collectors discovered that Breathitt County's native balladeers were reluctant to sing it, and its eventual musicological "recovery" took place in Texas a few years later. Though recorded numerous times, it never became a folk standard even when it was targeted at a "mainstream" audience; pop composer Johnny Mercer's recording of "The Murder of J. B. Markham" was met with little response, violent or otherwise, in 1937.[154]

By the high years of the New Deal, it was no longer politically advantageous for Breathitt County to be set off from the rest of Kentucky or the United States; instead it was brought into the same efforts at incorporation as the rest of the South. In the years that had passed since Edward Callahan's shooting death (often considered the end of the "feudal era"), the county had become a prime target of reform efforts bent upon hookworm eradication, flood prevention, and other types of uplift.[155] These Progressive efforts often restated eastern Kentucky's long-standing reputation for isolation and deprivation for which feud violence had been blamed since the 1870s, but as the notorious Breathitt County came to be seen as one mountain county suffering from the same social and infrastructural ills as many others, its individual fame waned. In the 1930s the county was a frequent subject for photographer Marion Post Walcott as she collected the Farm Security Administration's visual data.[156] Rather than taking pictures of aging "feudists," Walcott focused upon muddy roads and parched cornfields, images that made Breathitt County part of a larger regional whole rather than singling it out. In 1936 one pair of educators acknowledged the deleterious effects that Breathitt County's being defined by the outside world had on its well-being: "the epithets which role so easily off the tongue—a 'Kentucky feud,' a 'hillbilly song,' 'poor whites,' and that telltale appellation which so many of the inhabitants would like to live down, 'Bloody Breathitt.' It is through these stock phrases that some of us have come to know this part of the South."[157] Given the need for cooperation between local elites and federal arrivals, politics was not acknowledged as the root cause of the county's past horrors. An indictment of the Democratic Party of the past might have seemed like an indictment of present Democrats, especially considering that, save for a brief period after the Hargis-Callahan regime's end, they had ruled the county perpetually (and, by the 1930s, "controlled everything").[158] And, in any case, a society disadvantaged on "the scale of cultural and social values" (a more advanced sociological version of "contemporary ancestors") could not be blamed, considering that "in these days there is hardly any people competent to judge another."[159] It was now time for the county to reenter the rest of the region, even if it meant being part of what President Franklin Roosevelt would call "the Nation's number one economic problem."[160]

Feuds were now an event thankfully stuck in the past and absent in a county with access to federal aid and centralized planning. But as Breathitt County was the historical home of the feud country, its past of factional violence could not be completely forgotten, especially considering that its rate of violent crime was still relatively high as late as 1940. "Even though the county may have one or two well-broadcasted murders every year—for a killing in Breathitt always seems to be big news—educational facilities, better roads, in short, greater contact with modern forces have corroded the feudal spirit," said one 1941 local history published by the Works Progress Administration. Feuds were understandable in their day because of environmental factors beyond the control of the mountain pioneer. The "hilly country where ridges and creeks tended to mark off one clan and its supporting faction from another, and where Mother nature was hostile and niggardly" contributed to the development of "feudal ties between men." To observers from the outside world, common criminal violence was even less legitimate than feuds, but recent unnamed troubles, readers were reassured, had "not assumed the proportions of a feud."[161] Even if Breathitt Countians supposedly retained a customarily nonchalant attitude toward murder, "life was cheap" now because "the hills were stripped, the timber business expired, floods washed the topsoil off the farms."[162] Violence in Bloody Breathitt was no longer a product of the residents' temporal dissonance from the Bluegrass and the rest of the outside world but was now the outcome of very current economic problems. Although crime had supplanted feud, violence of either sort was still useful. More than ten years later, even the county's reputation for "unrestrained lawlessness" was, by itself, admissible evidence in a corporation's 1953 lawsuit against a striking labor union.[163]

Long after John Fox Jr.'s death, Breathitt County garnered at least one more fictional sketch in two of James Jones's World War II novels. In his debut, *From Here to Eternity* (1951), Jones featured Sergeant Fatso Judson, Schofield Barracks' sadistic stockade guard who is mentioned in passing as having Breathitt County origins. Judson is eventually punished for his cruelty to prisoners when he is killed by Private Robert E. Lee Prewitt (himself from

Harlan County, a locale with far more notoriety than Breathitt by 1951; a third character is similarly from Hazard, Kentucky).[164] A "small, thin, Breathitt County Kentucky boy" named Private Witt was prominent in Jones's *The Thin Red Line* (1962), this time in a combat setting. Like Prewitt, Witt is an exceptional fighter (with shades of Alvin York, gaining his flawless sharpshooting from having "shot squirrel all of his life") and ceaselessly loyal to his comrades. He shared the same independence and antinomian worldview attributed to various Fox Jr. protagonists, although, unlike them, Witt could never assimilate to the forces of modernity (in this case the army's self-defeating chain of command during the battle of Guadalcanal). "He was free, white and twenty-one," in Jones's description, "and had never taken no shit off nobody and never would, and as the prospect of action got closer and closer he could feel himself tightening all up inside with excitement, exactly like he used to do in the [nonhistorical] coal strikes back in Bloody Breathitt."[165] Judson, Witt, and Jones's other eastern Kentucky soldiers shared an inherent aptitude for violence, while Breathitt was only one place-name among many; as a fictional character's casually mentioned place of birth in an early 1960s novel, Breathitt County had joined "Harlan" and "Hazard" as synonyms for labor struggle rather than feud, the prefix "bloody" assumed to be from the famously deadly coalfield battles for unionization. For Jones (a native of southern Illinois), Bloody Breathitt represented a segment of the American population living in the twentieth century against its will and able to exist in the unwelcome present only because of its valuable (at least in a time of war) propensity for hurting and killing.

By the time the War on Poverty was initiated, Breathitt County was an oft-advertised exemplary of Appalachia's unsolved economic problems. When Kentucky's red-baiting Republican governor Louis Nunn vetoed federal Office of Economic Opportunity (OEO) funds for a Jackson-based development council in 1969, the ensuing war of words became the "Nunn-Howell feud" (so named for the council's Democratic chairwoman Treva Turner Howell).[166] Newly hired OEO assistant Dick Cheney went to Breathitt County to investigate and found none of the irregularities Nunn (who had been southern campaign chairman for Cheney's boss, Richard Nixon, in 1968) had alleged. The upheaval discomfited Nixon and OEO chief Donald Rumsfeld, and tousled the president's "southern strategy." More important, it shortened the life of the OEO; complaints of Howell's corruption (which neither J. Edgar Hoover nor John Ehrlichman could uncover) gave Nixon an excuse to dissolve the program after his reelection. The "Feud in the

Hills," as *Time* magazine called it (echoing the *Louisville Courier-Journal's* "Breathitt Feud" headline) was a crippling blow to the Great Society as well as another embarrassment for Breathitt County—caused, once again, by local machine politics (Howell's Turner forbears began amassing influence in Breathitt not many years after the end came to the Hargis courthouse, though more incrementally and with less dependence upon counterrevolutionary murder).[167] As always, the feud narrative (or, as Rumsfeld minimized the kerfuffle forty-two years later, "an old-fashioned Southern political blood feud") added its emblematic element of deception, suggesting the elite parties' victimless warring when, in fact, the victims were the Breathitt citizens the OEO had benefited.[168]

From John Fox Jr.'s Progressive Era novels to Donald Rumsfeld's 2011 apologia, Bloody Breathitt was largely the creation of outside observers who were heedless or ignorant of the exigencies of life in the county, be it the violence of the past or the poverty of the present. Breathitt County seemed to be one exemplar of the larger eastern Kentucky feud phenomenon but, at the same time, seemed to stand out from the others as well. In Cincinnati newspaper editor Harold Coates's *Stories of Kentucky Feuds* (1942), "true and accurate descriptions of the various Kentucky Feuds" (an anthology of stories published individually in pamphlet form in the 1920s), three of the twelve vignettes were dedicated to Breathitt, from William Strong's 1874 courthouse capture to the death of Edward Callahan in 1912.[169] Rather than protesting, twentieth-century Breathitt Countians avoided discussions of conflicts over power, and instead tried to place violence as far into the past as possible. They, too, contributed to the mythology of Bloody Breathitt.

"We know that, from the first, the wilderness was their teacher"

Judge James Hargis was quite successful in using the cover of feud to protect himself from criminal conviction, and was probably unbothered by his subsequent magazine portrayal as a "Middle Ages character" a few months before his death.[170] A large part of his success depended upon how ingrained the feud narrative already was in eastern Kentucky, so ingrained that even his greatest detractor, the *Breathitt County News,* casually described "feuds" in other mountain counties while Hargis was still in office.[171] Those from Breathitt County who were able to make their voices heard, mainly Jackson's commercially interested elite, echoed the language of the outside world, and the four-letter word was not avoided once it was widely popular.

For one thing, they believed in race and all it entailed. Language employing the racial politics of the day was just as popular in Breathitt County as it was among the anthropologists and local-color writers. The aforementioned booster who anonymously begged for the Bluegrass's investment in 1884 attributed past violence to the Scots and the Irish.[172] Breathitt's Anglo-Saxon families presented such a numerical fight against "race suicide," the *Courier-Journal* snarked in 1904, that "President Roosevelt's heart would be gladdened by a sight of Jackson" (Roosevelt was a well-known proponent of Nordic monumentalism).[173] Once word of their unadulterated, superior Anglo-Saxon blood was a widely known fact, white Kentuckians in and around the county clung fiercely to the ethnic badge that they probably had never doubted was theirs in the first place, even if it did implicitly suggest an innate tendency toward modern savagery. Upon reading of a 1905 lecture that suggested that the "Kentucky mountaineer" was the progeny of Indians and "white slaves" (the lecturer presumably meant seventeenth-century indentured servants), a Perry county resident protested:

> There is not one family out of a thousand of the present inhabitants of the Cumberlands whose parentage may be traced either to the Indians or to those white slaves who had been freed by the Virginia planters. They are descendants of families who had been prominent in the Revolutionary struggles, and those people have known almost no intermingling of other blood from the time of their immigration to the present. The allegation that these bold, generous, hospitable, strong-minded neighbors about us in Breathitt, Perry and Leslie counties are a new class of humanity and descendants of Indians and white Virginia slaves is a slander which we repel.[174]

As the national debate over the teaching of evolution was building steam in 1922, a *Breathitt County News* editor fired off a similar salvo when his county's state representative cast the deciding vote to strike down an anti-Darwinism bill.[175] "The professors at the state university [in Lexington] may believe they are descended from apes and baboons, but let it be known that the good people of Breathitt are pure Anglo-Saxon."[176] Racially conscious Breathitt Countians were as aware as other white southerners that whiteness dealt as much, and perhaps more, with material and social attainment as it did with skin color. For a place and a people increasingly economically marginalized, and vilified in the media as something culturally or even biologically different than the white southerners they had once been, racial validation was crucial.

Backtalk from Breathitt came in other forms as well. Louis Pilcher's *The Story of Jackson City* (1914), the last in a series of promotional publications promoting eastern Kentucky towns, became Bloody Breathitt's most all-inclusive written defense. Pilcher, a self-styled "literary free lance" from Lexington, wrote as if he were a Breathitt County native, peppering "brief biographies of prominent citizens" with ingratiating trivia about Jackson.[177] For Pilcher, the story of "Bloody Breathitt" had already been told in fictional form and the more fictional it was, the better. "If the reader is seeking any light or information on the feuds of Breathitt County," he warned, "this book will be a disappointment for I want to go back to the 'City of Sudden Death' [a nickname for Jackson], and I don't like to write about feuds anyway." Because, after all, "feuds and pistol toting are so vulgar and low flung."[178] Pilcher hoped that literary interest in Kentucky's feuds would soon die down, lest it pollute young minds. "Just contemplate what a terrible nightmare such a book [collecting all of Kentucky's feud stories] would produce on the plastic minds of the youth of Kentucky; a veritable chamber of horrors."[179] Jackson, the "inspiration of the new Kentucky," had eliminated feuds through progressive social engineering: de facto zoning that kept disorder confined within spatial boundaries and class designators. The absence of licensed saloons helped to keep the peace, and the civically maintained enclosure of "Snake Valley," the sin district along the river, kept the town quiet enough to require "only one policeman and but little for him to do except collect city taxes and electric light bills."[180]

Even if violence that took the feud form was in the past, Pilcher stood by his belief in the racial determinism that caused it. Although he shared others' belief in Kentucky's "purest Anglo-Saxon stock," Pilcher put a greater emphasis on the sociology of race and saw the less adulterated eastern portion of the "two Kentuckys" as America's last great white hope.[181] "It is a well-known fact in sociology of Kentucky and the South that the Afro-American race has for long been the 'escape valve' in morality and immorality—there also being another division, unmorality. In certain sections of Kentucky—notably in the eastern part—the absence of Negroes has laid the heavy toll upon the white race, and hence there is more white immorality than in communities where Negroes abound, Central Kentucky and many Southern States having a greater number of Negroes than Caucassians."[182] "We [eastern Kentuckians] will not stand for miscegenation," wrote Pilcher.

"It is said that in Louisville and Indianapolis, Cincinnati and Chicago, that many depraved and degenerate white women have Negro husbands."[183]

But pure eastern Kentuckians' massive childbirth rates guaranteed the unassisted survival of whiteness. "When fathers count their progeny from eight to a dozen, race-suicide is out of the question and the crusade for eugenics makes the healthy bucks that snuff the mountain air, smile in derision when the name is defined. It belongs to hot-house civilization and degenerating, neurotic practices" (he did not know that, less than ten years later, Breathitt County would have its own interracial cooperation committee and a $7,000 schoolhouse dedicated to colored education).[184] Just as when Hiram Freeman and his sons opposed Breathitt County's Democrats in the 1870s, black mountaineers were not to be mentioned. In 1912, with the prospect of "race-suicide" on many Americans' minds, their invisibility was more crucial than ever in a place assumed to be racially uncontaminated.

The county's nonwhite minority did not fit the outside world's image of Bloody Breathitt as did the white "healthy bucks" who were natural "fighting men . . . big, powerful fellows [and] men of courage and fine marksmen; sometimes ignorant, wary and good shots, like the Boers."[185] And entrance into politics was eastern Kentucky's chief means of harnessing this natural energy and aiming it toward useful purposes. "It is a fact in criminology of the mountains that the 'tough customers' are frequently reformed and become good citizens by elevating them to offices, and so there is no end of Deputy Sheriffs and Constables and Deputy Constables in Breathitt, Perry and Letcher Counties. It has had a salutary effect in many instances I hear and frequently Sheriffs, Jailers, County Attorneys and County Judges are 'reformed' bad men elevated to offices of dignity and power."[186] Even with Judge Hargis and Sheriff Callahan gone, most of the men who had been peripherally involved in their courthouse ring were still alive, and Pilcher was careful to spin their colorful pasts in as flattering a style as possible. More important, however, it was vital that political office be these "bad men's" redemption. Pilcher framed the recent past's problems as a social system worthy of envy.

Pilcher's interpretation of eastern Kentucky's "fighting spirit," and by implication the history of the feud, confirmed popular ideas about masculinity and the environmental construction of American humanity. His employment of the feud concept divorced violence from actual events, making it instead an abstract product of an inherent white mountain *Volksgeist* that stood as a model for all white Americans. Life in the Kentucky mountains was a

Rooseveltian "strenuous life" all to itself and, combined with the people's unsullied Anglo-Saxonism, provided a cure for the urban North's enervating industrial life and ethnic pollution. *Feud* was now a useful artifact, one with a rakish façade and no mention of injustice; Pilcher never mentioned the widow Abrelia Marcum Tucker, remarried and still living in Jackson (though he erroneously identified her late husband as "Judge Marcum"), even though he did reference Callahan and Hargis. Actual death and suffering, the (in Hannah Arendt's phrasing) "dead load which by itself time will bury in oblivion," could be forgotten, replaced by a mountain "heritage" that toughened its descendants without causing any real harm.[187] Ultimately, *The Story of Jackson City* was little different than the anthropological and fictional portrayals of eastern Kentucky produced by writers from the outside world.

Men who had actually participated in violence did not take Pilcher's booster role, but instead personalized Bloody Breathitt. None had more to say about this than Curtis Jett. By his own admission "as vile a sinner as ever came down the pike," Jett was famously converted to Christianity while serving time at the Frankfort Reformatory (where, in an odd echo of his former employer's role in William Goebel's campaign, he challenged one of the convicted conspirators in Goebel's death for the Penitentiary Christian Endeavor Society's presidency).[188] To help "put down Kaiserism," he organized an in-prison Red Cross fund-raising effort after the United States' entrance into World War I. Despite Abrelia Tucker's efforts, he won an early release, thanks to his conversion testimonial and a one-prisoner crusade to have pool tables removed from the state penitentiary. He then began a new life as an evangelist.[189]

Jett's story of his evil path that led to the assassinations of 1902 and 1903 was a pat combination of nature and nurture, explaining Bloody Breathitt and his own role as a "feudist." Now happily a Bluegrass resident, Jett confirmed many of the assumptions held regarding the section of his birth; his upbringing was nominally Christian but "weak along spiritual lines," while his own love of "strong drink," "pistol toting," and cigarette smoking were learned from his "typical mountaineer" father and a "drunkard" neighbor.[190] During his childhood in Breathitt County, he discovered that "every one in that section had an axe to grind," and he and his impressionable young friends "were ambitious when we became men to become leaders of such a click, to take our chance in the mountain battles and some day to carry revolvers and Winchesters with notches cut to indicate the number of enemies we had outwitted and gotten the drop on."[191] Leaving Bloody Breathitt for incarceration in the more advanced Bluegrass, where he discovered a love of God, patriotism, and personal industry (as the penitentiary's horticulturalist), was an integral part of Jett's salvation. In Jett's telling, the mountains were a natural training ground for violence, especially for an eager pupil such as himself. The exodus of an "old wild dog of the mountains" from "his former mountain days" was a spiritual journey but it was a geographical journey as well, confirming that Jett's former sinfulness and eastern Kentucky were firmly entwined.[192] Appropriately, after his release he attended seminary at Edward Guerrant's Asbury College.[193]

In *From Prison to Pulpit: Life of Curtis Jett* (1919), Jett depoliticized the feuds of his childhood. He noted the fighting between William Strong's Red Strings and Edward Callahan's Ku Klux in the 1890s (which he referred to it as the "Strong-Callahan feud"). By the end of his incarceration in 1919, he had absorbed enough written and spoken feud lore involving honor and Anglo/Celtic determinism to make it part of his description.

> Many of the leaders of the feuds were men of good circumstances and of fine intelligence. They were kind and courteous to their friends, but they came from a race of people beyond the sea who, for centuries, had not looked to the courts for protection, but had taken their affairs into their own hands. With them it was perfectly honorable to defend themselves and take the life of any they suspected of having ill will toward them. The leaders of the mountain feuds were something like the old Scottish Chieftains who gathered their clans about them and fought their misunderstandings to a finish.[194]

His retelling of his own participation in the Hargis-Cockrell feud was circumspectly apolitical, dwelling more on remembrances of his own personal failings than on the circumstances that brought him to be one of Sheriff Callahan's deputies.

> There was much animosity and ill feeling which culminated in several deaths on both sides of the feud. So far as any part I may have had in these unfortunate affairs is concerned that has been thoroughly threshed out in the civil and criminal courts of the State, and I could not add anything which would involve anyone who has not already been involved in the courts. I did not participate in these for any price or cause except for the love of my people and the unfortunate

spirit of revenge in my own heart. A merciful God has granted my forgiveness which I feel toward all men and believe it would be unwise for me to enter into any further discussion of the matters.[195]

Throughout his book, filled with his poems and his own and others' verifications of his redemption, he never once mentioned James Hargis or the men he was convicted of killing, nor his then role as deputy sheriff. His "love of [his] people" and "unfortunate spirit of revenge" gave a personal and communal basis to his behavior when he had been a killer, and implicitly placed his actions within a much longer narrative of inherent violence. "The feud" Jett had participated in was now an organic thing all to itself, devoid of factual details.

Another son of "typical mountaineers" who parlayed his connection to Bloody Breathitt into an evangelical style employed feud in a way that Jett could not. Wolfe County native Charles "Bulldog Charlie" Wireman, fifteen years Jett's junior, echoed his illustration of a rowdy, undisciplined, and armed adolescence. He credited Bluegrass Kentuckians with bringing a more enlightened Christianity to the "purest Anglo Saxon blood to be found on the American Continent." Even though he had once served as a deputy sheriff, his career had no discernible connection to political struggles or any conflict deemed organized into a feud proper. Yet Bloody Breathitt was still available to him as a foil for his own story of salvation although, as of 1950, Wireman's readers were more familiar with the Hatfield-McCoy feud, and he began his book with it rather than with anything that had happened to him personally.[196]

Feud, as long as it was in a distant enough past, was a useful memory, especially in conversion narratives that depend upon a stark division between a wicked past and a virtuous present. Accounts of Bloody Breathitt written outside of the county were not as consistent in employing this stark division; it depended upon whether or not the storyteller wished to portray a space that was inherently violent or progressively developed (by the passage of time or the contingency of positive exogenous forces) to a point where violence no longer took place, at least in an archaic "medieval" form like a blood feud. In contrast, local accounts like those of Pilcher, Jett, and Wireman left violent inherency in the past, but for different purposes. However, what they shared was a commitment to sustaining Bloody Breathitt's memory as the site of an undeniably horizontal dispute or series of disputes, one defined by revenge and lawlessness rather than struggles over public power. For the last generation to have witnessed or taken part in Breathitt County's feuds, the specifics of the past were best left in the past. If there were "deaths on both sides of the feud," as Jett concluded, then no one was denied justice by this omission. The possibility that this might not be the case was left roundly unconsidered.

Later generations of people from Breathitt County also showed a need to separate past from present. In the 1930s Breathitt County high school students, assigned to collect family oral histories, accepted their county's violent past with the adolescent's temporal detachment. Two students' grandfathers, now happy to freely discuss the Hargis-Cockrell feud (and possibly the 1908 election riot that followed the subsequent Republican victories) openly described their struggle's political nature as well as evidence that the famous courthouse assassinations were only part of a larger effort on Hargis's and Callahan's part. "I had six brothers until one of my brothers Jim was murdered on the middle fork in the Hargis and Callahan battle," one reported to his grandchild. "I was lucky to get out alive but me and Fletch never was even wounded during the time we were fighting. The Callahans were trying to run the county and who ever tried to get ahead of them they meraly shot them down and that was all. But they had a job trying to run us out."[197] Another student whose grandfather had died before his or her birth reported that "before [his death] a fuge came up between several parties and it was over politics."[198] Another elaborated, "It begun in 1902, and lasted until 1907, and after this period Breathitt county, was called bloody Breathitt. We people of Breathitt should be thankful for what our forefathers has done for us."[199]

Depression-era teenagers had no reason to shy away from admitting the political causality of a past generation's violence, since it bore no reflection upon their own lives. To them, turn-of-the-century elections were practically as distant as seventeenth-century Scottish chieftains, and there was no need to create a temporal façade or apply a teenager's ironic detachment. The misspelling "fuge" suggests a relative unfamiliarity with the word. However, another student, who was asked to comment on more recent violent crime, felt inclined to comment on what he or she considered the county's distant past, particularly a communal "state of nature" that preceded politics. "We know that, from the first, the wilderness was their teacher and they obtained a kind of education which fitted them for a life in the rough, for it was gained through actual experience with their environment."[200]

Even though these high school students were presumably natives of Breathitt County and only a generation removed from the county's last nationally reported account of egregious violence, their descriptions of crime and violence within their home territory employ the same language of foreignness used by "outsiders" since the 1870s. To say that "the wilderness was [the students' for-bears'] teacher" denied the historical nearness of violence in Breathitt County, placing it further back in history to a pioneer past. None of the students claimed any direct knowledge or experience in violence of any sort, let alone attempted to defend their home county against the mockery and criticism that it had long endured. With access to the enlightenment of national incorporation provided by New Deal programs, these students were now outside of the experience that had made Bloody Breathitt, and at least one refused to lay claim to it without invoking a nostalgic "wilderness" past. As Breathitt natives they had unique insights but, as was the case with most American teenagers in the 1930s, their local knowledge was mitigated by mass culture.

"The dirty old Breathitt County courthouse still stands"

In 1978, eighty-one-year-old Breathitt County native Harlan Strong ex-pressed a similar resolve to remember Bloody Breathitt as a past enormously different from the present, and expressed mild reverence for the lost strenu-ousness of his childhood. "The horse and buggy days, they're past and gone. Now it's automobile and airplane and stuff like that. The Bible said they'd go weaker and wiser. People are certainly getting wiser but they're weaker. They're weaker in strength and wiser in knowledge. This day and time a kid 15 years old, I'd say twelve years old knows as much as I did when I was 25. That's the truth. They see so much and know so much. That's right. A lot of it is worthless, but still they know it."[201] The late nineteenth-century violence that Harlan Strong was aware of, probably from popular rather than personal memory, was far away and factually confused. He knew of the factional align-ments designated by the "Red Strings" and "Ku Klux," although he offered no elaboration on the larger Reconstruction-era contexts of these two names. He also erroneously recollected the 1884 lynching of Henderson Kilburn and Ben Strong as occurring in his lifetime (according to his own disclosure, Harlan Strong would have been born about 1896). He also seemed to recall knowing "Bill Strong," who "belonged to what was called the Rebel and Yankee army," even though the real-life Bill Strong had been killed in 1897.[202] When asked to explain Bloody Breathitt's origins, Harlan Strong reaffirmed the primordial foundations of a frontier society that many people both in and outside of the county had summoned up in the twentieth century, but augmented this by allusions to prevailing technological change. "The only difference now than back then is there's just more people now. That's why people can see so much more because they're more people and there's more to talk about. But they did just as bad in the early days when I was raised up as they're doing right now. There just weren't so many people. Mohegan law back in them days. An eye for an eye. A tooth for a tooth. If you shoot me, I'll shoot you. They abide by the law now. Sure do."[203] "Mohegan law" ascribed the past with qualities that 1970s white Americans associated with Native Americans, who (like feuding mountain whites) were cognitively tucked safely within a distant earlier historical period. A metaphor involving a savage Indian-related past, coupled with the biblical analogy of violent reciprocation, confirmed Bloody Breathitt's persistence as a place and time of communal violence. The death of Native American nations and that of feuds could both be looked back upon as inevitable, since those looking back from a modern present could scarcely imagine it otherwise.[204]

But Harlan Strong's "prosthetic memory" of a lynching that took place before his birth, and others, demonstrates the continuity of a vague memory of political conflict.[205] The ostensibly nonsensical "Rebel and Yankee army," even if it suggested Harlan Strong's ignorance of the Civil War, illustrated the political confusion of the era; as a member of the Yankee army, William Strong had indeed been a rebel within Confederate Breathitt County.[206] A memory of the Red Strings and Ku Klux Klan confirmed the political foundations of the violence that took place before his childhood. Long after its characteristic events, Bloody Breathitt was still a usable past, and one that did not require the same level of conscious subterfuge and omission that Louis Pilcher had employed sixty-four years before. Nevertheless, as always, the causes for violence, the motivations for half-remembered killings, remained somewhere between hazy and absent. Meanwhile, the feud narrative, with or without the violence, was permanently wedded to Breathitt County.

Were it not for one oral history project sponsored by the *New York Times* (the northern newspaper that had once seemed reluctant to place feuds in the mountains rather than the state of Kentucky), Harlan Strong's individual memory of Bloody Breathitt would have remained unspoken and unrecorded. The project had been inspired by a renewed interest in eastern Kentucky in the late 1950s based on the national recognition of Appalachian poverty. Allusions to Bloody Breathitt remained a useful tool for illustrating the region's underdevelopment. During congressional hearings for the proposed creation of the Area Redevelopment Administration (ARA) in 1959, a Louisville paper's article on Breathitt County was used as evidence for the section's dire need for federal sponsorship.[207]

This is the land of legends, the mountain country of eastern Kentucky where a century of time is thought to have somehow got lost. Blood feuds, moonshining, child brides, place names like Hell-for-Sartain, Shoulderblade—the stuff for a thousand tales. They were not all fictional.

The dirty old Breathitt County courthouse still stands, the place where [James] Cockrell and J. B. Marcum were shot down in cold blood in the incredible Hargis-Cockrell feud that claimed upwards of fifty lives before it ran its course a half century ago. This courthouse was recently condemned, an act that serves as well as a symbol of the gradual passing of the life of the legends. Society is in transition [in Breathitt County], it is desperately trying to catch up with the 20th century.[208]

The "stuff for a thousand tales" had been the subject of fiction for so long that, by the 1950s, it was reasonable to assume that nineteenth-century history had become more "legendary" than factual. Men killing other men for now-murky reasons had been replaced by the more recent memories of the battle of Blair Mountain and "bloody Harlan," conflicts that could be more readily understood, and hardly denied, especially with John Lewis's then hearty United Mine Workers of America around as a reminder.[209]

Battles between coal companies and unions had now overshadowed previous atrocities. Less iconic stories from the mountains were even more shrouded in doubt. Cockrell and Marcum were victims' names remembered only by a dedicated student of Kentucky history, but they could still be used to prove a point. For a structure associated with one of these medieval feuds, the symbol of local state authority that had been at the center of sporadic killings for years, to still be standing was an affront to progress, proof that Breathitt County and the region needed federal assistance to "catch up with the 20th century." The dilapidated courthouse stood for a time of partisanship and had no place in an era of consensus and prosperity. It was the only remainder of a past that had mostly passed on to legendary status, an especially ugly reminder in that it connected the feud to an emblem of state power. For Breathitt County to achieve the legitimacy of being truly part of Kentucky and the American Republic, the "symbol of the gradual passing of the life of the legends" had to go.

EPILOGUE

When we say that Americans are lawless, we usually mean that they are
less conscious than other peoples of the august majesty of the institution
of the State as it stands behind the objective government of men and laws
which we see.

—Randolph Bourne, "Unfinished Fragment on the State
(Winter, 1918)," in *Untimely Papers* (1919)

The offending old building was eventually torn down and replaced by the
structure that serves as Breathitt County's court building at this writing
(designed by a Lexington architectural firm—fitting, since the men from
the relatively distant Bluegrass city had long claimed a shepherding role in
Jackson).[1] But the source of its infamy was not completely erased. In the
twenty-first century a marker near Breathitt County's present courthouse in
Jackson marks the spot of James Marcum's "feudal" death. Not everyone in
Breathitt County wanted history to be relegated to "legend." Even if no one
wished to recount the political details, these events, after all, did happen.

But a larger marker nearby commemorates the county's other celebrated
distinction: its contribution to military service in World War I. Breathitt men
had always contributed to American wars, and evidence almost suggests they
began preparations for war in Europe years before the rest of the country. As
early as 1914, Jackson's army recruiting station had "more enlistments than at
any station south of the Ohio River."[2] When the United States entered into the
largest war in human history three years later, Breathitt County's volunteers
exceeded its 182-man quota. As a result, no draft notices were issued. It was
not the only county to hold that distinction but, for one reason or another,
the county—and "her patriotic ex-feudists"—caught national attention.[3]

From one perspective, the tremendous outpouring of Breathitt volunteers was political; an ever-Democratic county rallying to a Democratic
president's call to make the world "safe for democracy." From another, it was
the masculine "fighting spirit" that journalist Louis Pilcher had touted a few

The "feud" marker in Jackson near the present-day courthouse. (Courtesy of Charles Hayes)

years earlier, evidenced by Breathitt-native Sergeant Willie Sandlin's single-handed bayoneting of twenty-four German soldiers at Bois de Forges, France, in 1918 (which earned him the Congressional Medal of Honor).[4] From yet another, it was a patriotism born of the county's natural environment. "The charge of ignorance to which they have been subjected for years is proved libelous by their knowledge of the European situation," the *Christian Science Monitor* rhapsodized. "They are natural democrats. They are natural foes of aristocracy and autocracy."[5] Finally, the remarkable record of volunteers may have just as easily revealed a supposition familiar in all American wars: a young male population with few prospects and a collective eagerness to leave their rural home.

In any case, this new distinction was widely celebrated. The history of intraracial white violence that had segregated Breathitt County from the United States was now balanced by a "sturdy Americanism" that incorpo-

Breathitt County's World War I Memorial. (Courtesy of Charles Hayes)

rated it into the whole, a call to duty from an exogenous source to replace its damaged and unusable endogenous identity.[6] "All honor to Breathitt county, long known to the world as 'Bloody Breathitt'!" western Kentucky's *Hartford Republican* announced in 1917. "All honor to the men there who, though they may sometimes have been guilty of mountain feuds and have sometimes fought with unpardonable fury, have heard the call of civilization to protect the women and children!"[7] "Thus," cheered another Kentuckian a year later, "does the outlaw mountain county of Kentucky vindicate herself in the eyes of the world, mocking those who would shame her with a record more fanciful than true."[8] The "fanciful" agreed; "We've killed too many of our own folks," a short story character lamented. "Now this war gives us a chance to show the outside world that there's more good than bad in us; that we can leave off fighting each other and use our lead on the Germans."[9]

The subtext that lurked beneath the praise was that Breathitt County was a vessel of inherent violence that could now be harnessed by the outside world. When "the strange land and peculiar people" of the Kentucky mountains had been "discovered" nearly a half century earlier, their suspected tendency toward killing had been glorified as the prime mover of the American Revolution and westward expansion. Since then, however, present-day violence had cooled Progressive Era Americans' nostalgia for past violence, and Bloody Breathitt had instead become symptomatic of a social problem that defied education, industrialization, or planning.[10] In 1917 the problem had become a solution. The contingencies that had caused so much killing in Breathitt were still ignored, perhaps more than ever.

Though the county's marked volunteerism for the "call of civilization" involved more killing and dying, it would now be for a cause that Bloody Breathitt could share with the rest of the United States. Unlike *feud*, the legitimacy of the "War to End All Wars" was a national article of faith. The common use of deadly force had once demonized Breathitt County. When carried out in the name of patriotism, however, deadly force was the key to its redemption.

NOTES

Abbreviations

AAC	*Appleton's Annual Cyclopaedia and Register of Important Events*
ACN	*Adair County News* (Columbia, KY)
AGACK	*Acts of the General Assembly of the Commonwealth of Kentucky*
AOHP	*The New York Times Oral History Project:* The Appalachian Oral History Project of Alice Lloyd College, Appalachian State University, Emory and Henry College, and Lees Junior College, Kelly Library, Emory & Henry College, Emory, VA
BCN	*Breathitt County News* (Jackson, KY)
CDT	*Chicago Daily Tribune*
CSSUS	*Congressional Serial Set*
FRA	*Frankfort Roundabout*
HGH	*Hazel Green* (KY) *Herald*
HLSCA	Hutchins Library Special Collections & Archives, Berea College, Berea, KY
HMC	*Hickman* (KY) *Courier*
HVK	*Hopkinsville Kentuckian*
JJDD	*John J. Dickey Diary,* Margaret I. King Library Special Collections and Archives, University of Kentucky, Lexington
KAGR	*Kentucky Adjutant General's Report: Confederate Kentucky Volunteers, 1861–1865* (Frankfort, KY: State Journal, 1915)
KDLA	Kentucky Department of Libraries and Archives, Frankfort
KHJ	*Kentucky House Journal*
KHS	Martin F. Schmidt Research Library and Special Collections, Kentucky Historical Society, Frankfort
KLR	*Kentucky Law Reporter*
KLSCA	Margaret I. King Library Special Collections and Archives, University of Kentucky, Lexington
KPD	*Kentucky Public Documents*
KSJ	*Kentucky Senate Journal*
KTY	*Kentucky [Tri-Weekly] Yeoman* (Frankfort)
LCJ	*Louisville Courier-Journal*
LEP	*Louisville Evening Post*

LRA	*Lawyers' Reports Annotated*
MPL	*Maysville* (KY) *Public Ledger*
MSA	*Mt. Sterling* (KY) *Advocate*
MVB	*Maysville* (KY) *Bulletin*
MVS	*Mount Vernon* (KY) *Signal*
NYS	*New York Sun*
NYT	*New York Times*
RDPCRCSK	*Report of the Debates and Proceedings of the Convention for the Revision of the Constitution of the State of Kentucky, 1849* (Frankfort, KY: A. G. Hodges, 1849)
SIJ	*Semi-Weekly Interior Journal* (Stanford, KY)
SWR	*The Southwestern Reporter, Containing All the Current Decisions of the Supreme Courts of Missouri, Arkansas, and Tennessee, Court of Appeals of Kentucky, and Supreme Court, Court of Criminal Appeals, and Courts of Civil Appeals in Texas*
TAPR	*Tribune Almanac and Political Register*
WPA	Workers of the Writers' Program of the Works Projects Administration in the State of Kentucky

Introduction

1. Kirby, *Selected Articles on Criminal Justice,* 101. See also Waller, "Feuding in Appalachia," 354–55, 364–66.

2. Lee, *Crowds and Soldiers in Revolutionary North Carolina,* 3.

3. James A. Smallwood has made a similar argument about Texas's Sutton-Taylor feud in the Reconstruction era: "Billed as a great feud by many writers, the Sutton-Taylor affair was anything but, for the word 'feud' suggests that two individuals had personal grudges to settle or that two families had differences wherein there was no real right or wrong. Black and white faded to nebulous gray: There was only personality clashes." Smallwood, *The Feud That Wasn't,* xviii (quote), 181–82.

4. Salstrom, "The Agricultural Origins of Economic Dependency," xvii.

5. Richard B. Drake, *A History of Appalachia,* 59–79; Perkins, *Border Life,* 84–85; Perrin, Battle, and Kniffin, *Kentucky,* 59.

6. McFaul, *The Politics of Jacksonian Finance,* 172–74; Feller, *The Jacksonian Promise,* 162–75. See also Otto, "The Decline of Forest Farming in Southern Appalachia," 18–27.

7. Legitimacy "reflects the vitality of the underlying consensus which endows the state and its officers with whatever authority and power they actually possess, not by virtue of legality, but by the reality of the respect which the citizens pay to the institutions and behavior norms. Legitimacy is earned by the ability of those who conduct the power of the state to represent and reflect a broad consensus." Nieburg, *Political Violence,* 54. See also Dahl, *Political Oppositions in Western Democracies,* particularly 348–402.

The phrase *outside world* appears in various contexts whenever authors have need of contrast between a remote, insular settlement/community/population and the "general" population. In an Appalachian context it is typically used to convey the popular trope of geographical or cultural isolation. See, for instance, Levi W. Powell, *Who Are These Mountain People?* 7. For the best deconstruction of Appalachian isolation, both physical and discursive, see Hsiung, *Two Worlds in the Tennessee Mountains,* especially 1–17, 69–98, 186–88.

8. As historians uncover more and more evidence of southern resistance to secession and the Confederacy, a clearer picture is forming of secession and the formation of the Confederacy as political projects that may have sought basis in the consent of the (white male) governed, but failed to do so. It is quite possible that "the South" lost the Civil War because too few southerners supported its cause. Later chapters reference this new wealth of literature on southern anti-Confederatism. For a broad approach to the Confederacy's crisis of democratic legitimacy, see McCurry, *Confederate Reckoning,* 38–84; Freehling, *The South vs. the South,* 141–73. See also Inscoe, introduction, 1–5.

9. Ogg and Ray, *Introduction to American Government,* 732. See also Gilbertson, *The County;* Beard, *Readings in American Government and Politics,* 556–66; Forman, *Advanced Civics,* 195–202; "Lobbyists and Legislatures," 197.

10. James C. Scott, *Seeing Like a State,* 187.

11. Many histories of the postbellum South as a region have excluded Kentucky, primarily because most historical conceptions of the section are based upon the states of the Old Confederacy. However, as demonstrated most prominently by the state's inclusion in C. Vann Woodward's *Origins of the New South,* much of Kentucky's history was determined by its similarities to, and (albeit complicated) relationship with, the South as a whole before and after the Civil War, especially in terms of politics and economic traits. The legacy of slavery, inherited from the beginnings of its statehood, is principal among many reasons Kentucky should be considered a southern state. For Kentucky state histories that make the state's southern identity evident, see Tallant, *Evil Necessity,* 103–4; Harrison and Klotter, *A New History of Kentucky,* 181–82; Penny M. Miller, *Kentucky Politics and Government,* 54–56.

12. Violence, when used to meet political ends, can be either revolutionary (attempting to affect change through the overcoming of a present regime or adverse consequences) or, often in response, antirevolutionary (violence enacted, usually by the state or an agent of the state in order to prevent changes that may be or seem detrimental to the status quo). Counterrevolutionary violence is acknowledged as part of American history but discussions of political violence have tended to minimize its presence since it has only rarely appeared in state-sanctioned form and is typically relegated to fringe movements unrelated to state rule such as the Ku Klux Klan (even though the Klan's original nineteenth-century manifestation had direct links to the southern Democratic Party). Suzanne Ogden, "Inoculation against Terrorism in China," 245; Mendel, *Essential Works of Marxism,* 535.

For the connections between the 1860s–70s Ku Klux Klan and the southern Demo-
cratic Party, see Zuczek, *State of Rebellion*, 51–62; Grantham, *The Life and Death of the
Solid South*, 33; Bloom, *Class, Race, and the Civil Rights Movement*, 32–33; Trelease,
White Terror, xvi–xvii; Foner, *Reconstruction*, 425.

For southern political violence outside of warfare, see Markovitz, *Legacies of Lynching*; Barnes, *Who Killed John Clayton?* Barnes differentiates "political" violence from
"racial" violence in a manner that I do not imitate here. This book also defines "political
violence" only in its counterrevolutionary capacity even though it is conceivable that,
in the course of the South's history, violence has been used to effect change as well as to
prevent it. See also Brundage, *Lynching in the New South*.

13. This is not unlike the means by which Reconstruction-era white southerners
described other forms of political violence in nonpolitical language. See Parsons, "Klan
Skepticism and Denial in Reconstruction-Era Public Discourse"; and Fairclough, "'Scalawags,' Southern Honor, and the Lost Cause." See also Owens, "Distinctions, Distinctions,"
32; Lee, *Crowds and Soldiers in Revolutionary North Carolina*, 1–9.

14. *KTY*, October 1, 1874.

15. Ireland, *Little Kingdoms*, 72–78; Waller, *Feud*, 6–8. These endogenous explanations for violence in rural places are only part of a larger global trend, particularly as
used in imperialist or postcolonial rhetoric for justifying the exploitation (via forced
modernization) of non-Western places. See Vahabi, *The Political Economy of Destructive
Power*, 44–47; Van Young, *The Other Rebellion*, 400–401; Chalmers Johnson, *Revolutionary Change*, 129–32; Kalyvas, *The Logic of Violence in Civil War*, 72–80, 331.

16. Gordon McKinney, *Southern Mountain Republicans*, 91–96, 198–99.

17. Nieburg defines political violence as "acts of disruption, destruction, injury
whose purpose, choice of targets or victims, surrounding circumstances, implementation,
and/or effects . . . tend to modify the behavior of others in a bargaining situation that
consequences for the social system" (*Political Violence*, 13); Foner, *Reconstruction*, 430.

18. Vahabi, *The Political Economy of Destructive Power*, xi. See also Fearon and
Laitin, "Ethnicity, Insurgency, and Civil War," 75–90. Although the two are "almost
always intertwined and hard to disentangle," inherency and contingency describe two
"antithetical" causal environments for the occurrence of violence. The former suggests
omnipresent conditions that make violence likely while the latter involve those that
are "not understood without special explanation, happening outside the boundaries of
likelihood." Both are given to a great measure of subjectivity based upon the perceptions
of observing "authorities." Eckstein, "Theoretical Approaches to Explaining Collective
Political Violence," 138–42 (139 quote). Political scientists and anthropologists who study
places torn by mass violence have, in recent years, tended to look upon explanations that
favor inherency with a skeptical eye. Violence that takes place because of contingencies such as war, famine, or political oppression can be written off as the offspring of a
society that is inexplicably inherently violent without need for further explanation. See
Deas, "Violent Exchanges."

19. Mamdani, "Making Sense of Political Violence in Postcolonial Africa," 72. See also Blok, *Honour and Violence,* 112–13.

20. The negotiation between inherency and contingency has been at the center of most historical approaches to violence in the American South. Some of the most lauded examinations of white southerners' uses and interpretations of violence limited their respective examinations to the years before the Civil War (i.e., the "Old South"). These studies limited themselves to white southerners, albeit with the understanding that antebellum modes of violence contributed to a racial status quo based upon white supremacy and black slavery. Therefore, while cultural qualities dictated inherent (usually white male) southern attitudes toward violence beforehand, the contingency of the war, it is implied, brought an abrupt end to the society that sustained these qualities.

While not suggesting that the war was a unique precedent for killing in the South, others have tended to attach the issue of violence to the political discord that followed it, most notably involving white resistance to black emancipation and citizenship, and focus primarily on "white-on-black" interracial violence. Postwar "white-on-white" intraracial violence, a subject that has gotten less scholarly attention, has been said to have differed from Old South to New. C. Vann Woodward identified the New South's "gunplay, knifing, manslaughter, and murder" as the successor to the Old South's more ordered "traditional expression of violence," the "code duello." W. J. Cash's *The Mind of the South,* the work that is otherwise credited with placing the greatest emphasis on the continuity of traits in southern history, recognized a change in the frequency of southern violence and the types of violence used after the Civil War. To Cash, what had once been an expression of frontier individualism became a means of enforcing conformity to a "savage ideal" among white southerners and reactionary fear of black increases in power (adamant in keeping up the portrayal of trait continuity into his own time, Cash dismissed this difference as a "contradiction [that] is not so great as it sounds at the first hearing").

If inherency suggests the continuity of traits irrespective of political change brought about by war and statecraft, it would seem that neither it nor the interpretation based upon contingency has become absolutely dominant in southern historiography. See Franklin, *The Militant South;* Bruce, *Violence and Culture in the Antebellum South;* Wyatt-Brown, *Honor and Violence in the Old South;* Wyatt-Brown, *Southern Honor* (originally published in 1982); Lemann, *Redemption;* Vandal, *Rethinking Southern Violence;* Nieman, *Black Freedom/White Violence;* Herbert Shapiro, *White Violence and Black Response;* Rable, *But There Was No Peace;* Woodward, *Origins of the New South,* 158; Cash, *The Mind of the South,* 114–23, 138–41 (quotes 115, 138).

For other works that assert nonpolitical currents stretching from before the war to after in shaping southern violence, see Hackney, "Southern Violence" and "Southern Violence," in Graham and Gurr, *Violence in America,* 393–410; Gastil, "Homicide and a Regional Culture of Violence," 412–27; Albert C. Smith, "'Southern Violence' Reconsidered," 527–64; Ayers, *Vengeance and Justice;* John Hammond Moore, *Carnival of Blood.*

Recently, one historian has suggested that during Reconstruction, "traditional honor killing" (i.e., communal/inherent violence) and political violence (political/contingent) became "intertwined," and that neither extreme is fully satisfactory for explaining postbellum white intraracial violence (Fairclough, "'Scalawags,' Southern Honor, and the Lost Cause," 826).

As a Deep South community, Edgefield, South Carolina, was typically allowed to be interpreted, for better or worse, as an exemplar of the South as a whole (and, therefore, part of the outside world, at least on a regional basis). However, it is generally acknowledged that, from Reconstruction until the twentieth century, Edgefield's history of violence outdid the rest of the state, perhaps because there the political stakes were especially high for both black and white South Carolinians. Burton, *In My Father's House Are Many Mansions*, 4–6; Brown, *Strain of Violence*, 67–90; Ford, "Origins of the Edgefield Tradition," 328–48.

21. Pinker, *The Better Angels of Our Nature*, 98–99. Most of Pinker's observations about southern violence are based upon experiments in behavioral psychology performed by Richard Nisbett and Dov Cohen that demonstrate a heightened tendency toward honor-based behavior among male college students from the American South in the late twentieth century. Nisbett and Cohen, *Culture of Honor*.

22. Tilly, *The Politics of Collective Violence*, 18.

23. Brundage, *Lynching in the New South*, 17–48.

24. Americans are loath to admit political violence between their own shores. However, Anglophone scholars have produced a bumper crop of literature on the concept of depoliticized political violence in the developing world; Elaine Thomas, "Muting Inter-ethnic Conflict in Post-imperial Britain," 436–39; Beardsworth, *Derrida and the Political*, 95; Cohen, "Crime and Politics," 242–46; Feldman, *Formations of Violence*, 259; Schlichte, "State Formation and the Economy of Intra-state Wars," 27–44; Savenije and Van der Borgh, "Youth Gangs, Social Exclusion and the Transformation of Violence in El Salvador," 155–71; Edwards, "The People's Sovereignty and the Law," 11, 28n; Wendy Brown, *Regulating Aversion*, 13–24. Of these, not all use the term *depoliticization*. They do discuss the portrayal of political violence as something outside of the political realm as it is understood by Western observers.

It should be noted that I do not use *depoliticization* in the same way Joel Williamson uses it to describe the disfranchisement of black southerners in the late nineteenth century. *The Crucible of Race*, 224–58.

25. Jeffrey Guy Johnson, "Feud, Society, Family," 24–53.

26. Quoted from Khan, "Speaking Violence," 106–7; Abner Cohen, *Two-Dimensional Man*, 89. See also Das, "Sexual Violence, Discursive Formations, and the State," 422; and Conteh-Morgan, *Collective Political Violence*, 87–88. Since one of my main precepts in this project is the subjectivity with which *feud* is used to describe violence, I do not offer an a priori definition of the word. However, objectively existent feuds, as they are portrayed by historians and anthropologists, are defined by their strictly horizontal realm

of conflict (i.e., between "equals") and by their origination from "small differences" that have little to no bearing on transcendent issues of ideology or state power. Historians and anthropologists habitually use the word *feud* exclusively for conflicts between individuals or groups of equal standing. This is demonstrated most pointedly in studies of societies in which factional violence became, or has become, institutionalized and accepted as a normal course of action on a strictly horizontal basis. Furthermore, it seems that scholars are more comfortable with speaking of feuds in a setting defined by spatial, cultural, or (perhaps most important) temporal distance. See Michael S. Drake, *Problematics of Military Power,* 81–84; William Ian Miller, *Bloodtaking and Peacemaking,* 179–220; Lamley, "Lineage Feuding," 71, 99, 367 (quote). See also James C. Scott, "Corruption, Machine Politics and Political Change," 1146n.

27. For horizontal relationships of violence, see Heidbuchel, *The West Papua Conflict in Indonesia,* 142–52, 161–88, 400–401; Kalyvas, *The Logic of Violence in Civil War,* 330, 370.

28. Keane, *Violence and Democracy,* 38–39. The concept of communal, as opposed to political, violence comes from the field of subaltern studies and has, since the 1990s, been used to describe incidents of religious and ethnic violence in the Indian subcontinent. Singh, *Communal Violence;* Kaur, "Mythology of Communal Violence," 23. See also Pandey, *Routine Violence;* Kalyvas, *The Logic of Violence in Civil War,* 71–72. Another examination of violent geographical spaces uses "direct violence" and "cultural violence" to make a similar distinction. MacGregor and Correa, "Rejoinder to the Theory of Structural Violence," 52. See also Cynthia Brown and Karim, *Playing the "Communal Card,"* vii.

29. Fabian, *Time and the Other,* 11–21, 75–79, 81–82 (I am grateful to Helmut Smith for introducing me to this important book). For another description of the same anthropological phenomenon, see Torgovnick, *Gone Primitive,* 8–9, 18–19.

30. Jeffrey Guy Johnson, "Feud, Society, Family," 52.

31. Kantrowitz, *Ben Tillman and the Reconstruction of White Supremacy,* 8 (quote)–9, 308–9. See also Friedman, *The White Savage.*

32. Black-Michaud, *Cohesive Force,* 1.

33. Hudson, "Feud, Vengeance and Violence in England," 33, 48.

34. Hayden White, *Metahistory,* 36–38; Jeffrey Guy Johnson, "Feud, Society, Family," 42.

35. (Carmel, NY) *Putnam County Courier,* January 8, 1937; Fish, *Tragic Deception,* xxv.

36. Television references to a feud, historical or fictional, convey an inability to conform to modern norms of behavior and therefore a diminished right to exist in the modern world and an irredeemable role as an outsider (and, notably, always a *white* outsider). For instance, a fictional presidential adviser's frustrated observation on the Israeli-Palestinian conflict in a 2004 *West Wing* episode: "It's *tribal,* it can't be solved, *it's Hatfield and McCoy* [my emphasis] and there is no end." In 2008 a cellular phone com-

mercial portrayed a nuclear Hatfield family (oddly housed in an expensive-looking cul-de-sac neighborhood) calling an end to their feud with the McCoys because of finally being able to reach them by cellular phone (calling to mind the late nineteenth-century hope that communication and technology would end feud violence). The song "Shenandoah" plays lightly and what appear to be daguerreotypes hang on the wall in the background, subtly evoking a past century. But the product advertised in the commercial and the teenager and his parents are undeniably products of the twenty-first century, dressed in the costume of the suburban upper middle class. The punch line: "Who will we feud with now?" (A follow-up commercial depicted the Montagues and Capulets reconciling for similar reasons but they, in contrast, were still in Elizabethan garb, unlike American feudists trapped forever in a literary past—but armed with cellular phones.) Even amid the trappings of twenty-first century consumerism the pathological urge endures. In the same year, a character in the sitcom *30 Rock*, an unsophisticated naïf typically portrayed as an overly religious refugee from superannuated southern poverty (and called a "hillbilly" by other characters) declared that before his move to the big city he had "promised my mother that if I ran into any Mackenzies, I would kill them." The quip suggests that this feud is ongoing and permanent and potentially enactable outside its place of origin. Moreover, even though a possible act of violence is referenced, it is for purposes archaic and primitive and therefore not to be taken seriously by a sophisticated urban audience.

A more recent series based on stories by crime novelist Elmore Leonard, *Justified*, has revisited the theme of the feud. Set in a heavily baroque "alternate South" version of Harlan County, Kentucky, a 2011 story line depicted the renewal of a waning blood feud between men whose ancestors first came to blows over rival distillery interests during Prohibition. It is quite possibly the first popular media representation of a Kentucky feud with no association with the nineteenth century. See *NYT*, January 5, 2012.

In 2012 cable television's History Channel broadcast a six-hour theatrical miniseries about the Hatfield and McCoy feud with a relative dedication to factual accuracy. During the airing the program's sponsor, Government Employees Insurance Company, aired a farcical commercial about a latent twenty-first-century Cro-Magnon acting as a human resources executive trying to mediate an alleged dispute between descendants of the Hatfield and McCoy families. As an abiding vestige of the past himself, the "caveman" is unable to accept that the two coworkers have their families' conflict behind them and become friends. "Hatfields and McCoys" remained a pathetically risible name for deadly violence but, unlike in the earlier commercials mentioned, descendants are allowed to put their past behind them.

37. Waller, *Feud*, 249.

38. Foner, "The Education of Richard Hofstadter," 597. For legitimate violence and the state, see Max Weber, "Politics as a Vocation," in *From Max Weber*, 78.

39. Foner, *Reconstruction*, 346 (quote); Hofstadter, "Reflections on Violence in the United States," 4 (quote); David S. Brown, *Richard Hofstadter*, 214–18. Altina Waller criticizes Hofstadter's relative inattention to feud violence. Waller, *Feud*, 6–7.

40. Gurr, *Why Men Rebel,* 13; Skolnick, *The Politics of Protest;* Nieburg, *Political Violence;* Rubenstein, *Rebels in Eden;* Havens, Leiden, and Schmitt, *The Politics of Assassination;* Graham and Rudoy, *Violence;* Short and Wolfgang, *Collective Violence;* Graham and Gurr, *Violence in America.*

41. A thorough effort at revisionist treatments of the history of the Appalachian region and its image had its beginnings with Henry Shapiro's *Appalachia on Our Mind: The Southern Mountains and Mountaineers in the American Consciousness, 1870-1920.* For a brief description and critique of 1970s Appalachian studies, see Cunningham, "Appalachian Studies among the Posts," 377–86.

The idea of white southerners in the Appalachians, particularly eastern Kentucky, being different from whites of the lowland South, culturally or otherwise, is most concisely exemplified by William G. Frost, "Our Contemporary Ancestors in the Southern Mountains," 311.

42. Gordon McKinney, "Industrialization and Violence in Appalachia in the 1890's," 131–44; Klotter, "Feuds in Appalachia," 290–317; Waller, *Feud;* Waller, "Feuding in Appalachia," 347–76; Billings and Blee, *The Road to Poverty;* Billings and Blee, "Where 'Bloodshed Is a Pastime': Mountain Feuds and Appalachian Stereotyping," in Billings, Norman, and Ledford, *Confronting Appalachian Stereotypes,* 119–37.

For histories that inspired these interpretations of Appalachian history, see Wiebe, *The Search for Order;* Trachtenburg, *The Incorporation of America;* Thelen, *Paths of Resistance.* For a very good summation of Appalachian history's "revisionist" generation, see Banker, *Appalachians All,* 2–5.

43. Orend, "War"; Orend, *War and International Justice,* 7 (quote); Henry Shapiro, *Appalachia on Our Mind,* 102–7. Like descriptions of "feuds," primordial explanations of violence "[invoke] the centuries of 'accumulated hatreds' between 'nations' with primordial origins. . . . The argument suggests that the illiberal politics of identity, with its claims of collective exclusivity, and tendencies toward xenophobia and intolerance are more natural to human societies than liberal politics of interest." Primordial explanations are more widely referred to as reports of *communal* violence, acts of destruction that represent an "outside threat" originating "outside the social frame." Communal violence is action that takes place without the authority, or beyond the supervision, of the modern state and, consequently, beyond its responsibility as well. It is believed to be "the product of 'deep-seated hatreds' or 'ancient animosities'" that "[take] on the appearance of a natural phenomenon which outsiders have no right to condemn and no hope to prevent" or is portrayed as such so that "presiding governments" can distance themselves from blame. Communal violence originates over issues that have nothing to do with the modern state and therefore do not offer a viable censure of its ability to rule, and for that reason cannot be deemed political by the state's standards or those of metropolitan observers. Emotional descriptors like "hatred" and temporal descriptors like "ancient" suggest that violence taking place in the present has very little to do with the "real" present as it is seen by outside observers. Beverly Crawford, "The Causes of

Cultural Conflict," 10–13 (quote 10–11). See also Laitin, *Nations, States, and Violence,* 26–27. For "dominant culture," see Waller, "Feuding in Appalachia," 370.

44. Ching and Creed, "Recognizing Rusticity," 14.

45. Kephart, *Our Southern Highlanders,* 309. Andrew L. Slap has recently made a similar point about politics in Appalachia. See Slap, "Introduction: Appalachia, 1865–1900," 16–17.

46. E. P. Thompson, *Making of the English Working Class,* 12.

47. The "classical" model of revisionist Appalachian history tends to, at the risk of exaggeration, treat case study localities as relatively inert bodies that were and are acted upon, exploited, and changed from outside, typically by the late nineteenth-century arrival of railroads and large-scale extractive industries. In these works, conflicts that took the form of anything from feuds to labor-related violence were attributed solely to these types of familiar "imperialist" events. Recently, a small number of monographs have delved into the economic and political activities of Appalachian communities before the period of incorporation and discovered a series of societies given to vigorous internal activity and hardly isolated from the outside world. In these "postrevisionist" studies, communities in what came to be known as Appalachia generated their own origins of conflict, often from early in the history of white settlement. Wiese, *Grasping at Independence;* Burch, *Owsley County;* Bailey, *Matewan before the Massacre.*

48. The echoes of the feud narrative were made even more explicit during the build-up to the invasion of Iraq when President George W. Bush identified Saddam Hussein as someone "who tried to kill my dad [former president George Herbert Walker Bush] at one time." By invoking kinship and a son's duty to right a wrong committed against a father, Bush gained popular sympathy for the war he was preparing to fight by (if only momentarily), suggesting an attack on Iraq might have apolitical, visceral purposes to which all Americans with families might relate. The "redemptive narrative" of familial vengeance helped deflect doubt over the paucity of evidence justifying the impending invasion's actual geopolitical purpose: the prevention of Iraq's use of "weapons of mass destruction." Jeff Zeleny, "For Bush, Joy of Capture Muted at the End," *NYT,* December 30, 2006; McAdams, "Redemptive Narratives in the Life and the Presidency of George W. Bush," 150.

49. Orwell, "Politics and the English Language," 173.

50. A good example of this spurious argument is Tobin, "Why Nothing Can Be Done about Shootings."

51. Mamdani, "Making Sense of Political Violence in Postcolonial Africa," 72.

52. In this sense I concur with David Nirenburg's attempt to "find sense in horrors" despite criticisms that attempts to do so "trivialize or minimize the violence that is its subject matter." I believe that a close examination of violence performs the opposite function. Nirenburg, *Communities of Violence,* 16–17.

53. Blok, *Honour and Violence,* 112–13.

54. Baudrillard, *The Transparency of Evil,* 45.

55. Warren, *King Came Preaching,* 196.

1. "To them, it was no-man's land"

1. George Washington Noble (hereafter G. W. Noble), *Behold He Cometh in the Clouds*, 5. The "Tessy Boy" fights were only one version of a Court Day custom in many southern localities. Franklin, *The Militant South*, 37.

2. Simple fisticuffs, a less drastic form of combat than armed dueling, nevertheless served a similar purpose in that the ordered undertaking of a "battle" ensured that disputes were settled in the public eye and according to community parameters; Gorn, "'Gouge and Bite,'" 18–43; William Barney, *The Road to Secession*, 157; Ireland, "Homicide in Nineteenth Century Kentucky," 142–43. For the fatal knife fight between Arch Augh and J. B. Combs in Breathitt County, see *Daily Ohio Statesman*, April 25, 1857.

3. Quoted from Waldstreicher, "Rites of Rebellion, Rites of Assent," 41.

4. Noble's description of the Tessy Boy fights suggests an exhibition somewhat more regulated and sedate than some others on record. For descriptions of Court Day violence in Kentucky, directed and undirected, see Ireland, *Little Kingdoms*, 90–100.

5. Tapp and Klotter, *Kentucky*, 110.

6. The "Three Forks region" refers to the area of land draining into the Kentucky River's north, middle, and south forks within the following counties (in order of formation): Clay, Estill, Perry, Breathitt, Owsley, Letcher, Powell, Wolfe, with parts of Knott and Rockcastle included. Verhoeff, *The Kentucky Mountains*, 6; *Nineteenth Biennial Report of the Bureau of Agriculture Labor and Statistics*, 43; Billings and Blee, *The Road to Poverty*, 28; Kleber, Clark, and Harrison, *The Kentucky Encyclopedia*, 204.

7. Wall, "'A richer land never seen yet,'" 139–40; Verhoeff, *Kentucky River Navigation*, 131n.

8. Ibid., 42.

9. Johnston, *First Explorations of Kentucky*, 154n.

10. G. A. Thompson, *The Geographical and Historical Dictionary of America and the West Indies*, 12.

11. Verhoeff, *Kentucky River Navigation*, 141; Salstrom, "The Agricultural Origins of Economic Dependency," xvii (quote).

12. William Davis and Swentnor, *Bluegrass Confederate*, 251 (quote); Friend, *Kentucke's Frontiers*, 223–25.

13. Warner, *Studies in the South and West*, 359.

14. James Lane Allen, "Through Cumberland Gap on Horseback," 50; Henry Shapiro, *Appalachia on Our Mind*, 26–29.

15. *Philadelphia Inquirer*, September 18, 1889. The Bluegrass's productive superiority to all other parts of the state remained a constant throughout Kentucky's agrarian history. The gross disparity between sections impeded the state's ability to make commonly beneficial state policies. See Clark, *Agrarian Kentucky*.

16. E. L. Noble, *Bloody Breathitt*, 1:40, 81; Samuel Wilson Collection, KLSCA.

17. Charles Fenno Hoffman, *A Winter in the West*, 199–200.

18. Keane, *Violence and Democracy*, 38–39.

19. Dunn, *Cades Cove*, 145.

20. Verhoeff, *Kentucky River Navigation*, 133. The territory that Clay County covered in 1807 became most of what is, at this writing, nine other counties.

21. Interviews with Sarah Baker, Preston Campbell, Mrs. Candell, Andrew Combs, Harry Eversole, William Eversole, T. T. Garrard, William L. Hurst, Matilda Duff Lewis, James L. Moore, and E. C. Strong, *JJDD*, reel 3, pp. 2126–27, 2182, 2271–72, 2322, 2365–66, 2406–10, 2419–25, 2430–32, 2436, 2444, 2460–63, 2544; Strong Family Papers, 86, Breathitt County Public Library; Jess D. Wilson, *A Latter Day Look at Kentucky Feuds*, 44–48; Rolff, *Strong Family of Virginia and Other Southern States*, 86–87; DenBoer and Long, *Kentucky*, 117; Owings, *The Amis Family*, 79; Billings and Blee, *The Road to Poverty*, 107–8.

22. *Wheeling Register*, March 9, 1897; *KSJ, 1839*, 377; Billings and Blee, *The Road to Poverty*, 110; Trimble, *Recollections of Breathitt*, 8.

23. Scalf, *Kentucky's Last Frontier*, 194 (quote); Ireland, *Little Kingdoms*, 1–2, 6–7; Webster, "The Spatial Reorganization of the Local State," 66–67.

24. The trend continued after the war as well; between 1865 and the early twentieth century ten more counties were added. At this writing, Kentucky has the third most counties of any state. Shannon and McQuown, *Presidential Politics in Kentucky*, 2; James Rood Robertson (ed.), *Petitions of the Early Inhabitants of Kentucky to the General Assembly of Virginia*, 84, 89, 107–8, 114, 117, 130, 141. For the profligacy with which nineteenth-century Kentucky expanded its number of counties, see Ireland, *Little Kingdoms*, 2.

25. Interview with Judge Dickerson, March 9, 1898, *JJDD*, reel 2, pp. 2170–71; Pudup, "Land before Coal," 5, 161; Jess D. Wilson, *The Sugar Pond and the Fritter Tree*, 48; Trimble, *Recollections of Breathitt*, 8. For the significance of disinterestedness in republican ideology and practice, see Gordon Wood, "Interests and Disinterestedness in the Making of the Constitution," 69–109.

26. In the first half of the 1820s, Kentucky's General Assembly's attempts to prevent foreclosures were blocked by a conservative court of appeals that sided with voracious creditors. The legislature bit off more than it could chew when it attempted to establish a debtor-friendly "New Court," rending the electorate between it and the "Old Court," thereby creating a dire constitutional crisis. In the elections of 1825 and 1826, the Old Court faction retook control, but only after many future Jacksonians had become disillusioned by the judiciary's siding with lucre. Friend, *Along the Maysville Road*, 235–36. For a different take on the Old Court/New Court battle, see Ramage and Watkins, *Kentucky Rising*, 86–88; *KSJ, 1839*, 377; Billings and Blee, *The Road to Poverty*, 109–10; Trimble, *Recollections of Breathitt*, 8.

27. Sydnor, *The Development of Southern Sectionalism*, 39–40.

28. Billings and Blee, *The Road to Poverty*; Pudup, "Land before Coal"; Burch, *Owsley County*; Wiese, *Grasping at Independence*; Preston, *The Civil War in the Big Sandy Valley of Kentucky*.

29. Ireland, "Aristocrats All," 368–69, 382–83.

30. Ireland, "The Place of the Justice of the Peace in the Legislature and Party System of Kentucky," 206–7.

31. Ireland, *The County Courts in Antebellum Kentucky,* 7–10, 12–15, 74–76.

32. Ireland, *Little Kingdoms,* 5–6, 124–32, 152.

33. *Charleston Mercury,* December 5, 1859.

34. "Assassination in Kentucky," 778.

35. Progressives considered county government antiquated and corrupt, in contrast to the ongoing contemporary civic reform and centralized planning on local and national levels. If county government was not banal, it was, even worse, antiquated and corrupt in contrast to the contemporary civic reform and centralized planning ongoing on local and national levels during the Progressive Era. "County government is the most backward of all our political units," the National Municipal League announced in the early 1920s, "the most neglected by the public, the most boss-ridden, the least efficiently organized and most corrupt and incompetent, and, by reason of constitutional complications, the most difficult to reform." Quoted in Ogg and Ray, *Introduction to American Government,* 732. See also Beard, *Readings in American Government and Politics,* 556–66; Forman, *Advanced Civics,* 195–202; "Lobbyists and Legislatures," 197. For a secondary assessment of the Progressive attack on the county (and its long-lasting scholarly legacy), see Menzel, introduction, 4–10.

36. Sydnor, *The Development of Southern Sectionalism,* 42, 285.

37. Ibid., 38. Robert C. McMath Jr. concurs with Sydnor: "For most nineteenth century southerners, 'The Government' and 'The County' were almost synonymous terms. The seat of the county court also became a center of trade and, to a lesser extent, of organized social life." However, McMath modifies the thesis in saying that, aside from being communities, nineteenth-century southern counties also "*contained* communities." "Community, Region, and Hegemony in the Nineteenth-Century South," 285.

38. Ireland, *Little Kingdoms,* 1, 33.

39. Williams, *Appalachia,* 136.

40. *JJDD,* reel 3, pp. 2272, 2322, 2419–25.

41. "Dark and bloody ground" was an appropriation from Cherokee chief Dragging Canoe's description of a sanguinary history since his nation had contended with the Shawnee for mastery of the region long before white settlement. The phrase was popularized by John Filson's *The Discovery, Settlement and Present State of Kentucke* (1784) and reapplied to various violent events in Kentucky's subsequent history. The phrase's intimation is of a territory inherently violent regardless of who occupied it. Slotkin, *Regeneration through Violence,* 268–312.

42. Quote from Watlington, *The Partisan Spirit,* 16. Aron, "Pioneers and Profiteers," 181.

43. Dunaway, "Speculators and Settler Capitalists," 54; Coulter, "Early Frontier Democracy in the First Kentucky Constitution," 665; Perkins, *Border Life,* 126, 147; Gates, "Tenants of the Log Cabin," 5; Verhoeff, *Kentucky River Navigation,* 130, 130–31n.

44. Dunaway, "Speculators and Settler Capitalists," 61.

45. Aron, "Pioneers and Profiteers," 181.

46. Kentucky's 1792 constitution was the second state constitution (after Vermont) to have no property requirements for voting or running for public office. Other states followed suit early in the next century. Wooster, *Politicians, Planters and Plain Folk,* 13. In the 1820s and 1830s, state legislation consistently favored occupiers' rights to the disadvantage of Virginia grant claimants. While one pro-squatter Kentucky law was struck down by the U.S. Supreme Court in 1823, it upheld a similar law nine years later; Ireland, *The Kentucky State Constitution,* 211. For other preemption legislation, see Kulikoff, *The Agrarian Origins of American Capitalism,* 81–83; Ramage, "The Green River Pioneers," 184 (quote), 190.

47. James C. Scott, *Weapons of the Weak,* 32. See also Aron, *How the West Was Lost,* 150–52; Dupre, "Ambivalent Capitalists on the Cotton Frontier," 225–26; S. Bolton, *Territorial Ambition,* 72–76; Kulikoff, *The Agrarian Origins of American Capitalism,* 77–90.

48. Ramage, "The Green River Pioneers," 184, 190.

49. "Without legal claim to land and often without permission to live where they did, the very poor seemed the greatest threat to the ideal of 'work & be rich.' Their alleged avoidance of work fundamentally clashed with the industry of persons determined to carve a profitable existence out of the West." Friend, *Along the Maysville Road,* 110–11. This sentiment was shared by planters farther south for decades, especially after preemption laws came to be viewed as a threat to southern land values. In describing class differences in the antebellum South, Alabaman Robert Hundley described squatters as "useless to themselves and the rest of mankind." D. R. Hundley, *Social Relations in Our Southern States,* 119.

50. Although Clay had begun his career with firm support from landless Kentuckians, his "American System" looked askance at the rights of the unpropertied and he tended to support speculator interests, especially as they came under attack from Andrew Jackson. By the mid-1800s, Kentuckians followed suit with other southern states in opposing federal homestead acts. *Register of Debates in Congress,* 24th Cong., 1st sess., March 31, 1836, 1029. During the later years of Clay's congressional ascendancy, federal land policy, which ostensibly granted the right of preemption in 1841, favored only settlers who were able to purchase lands they were to occupy in the near future. Aron, *How the West Was Lost,* 199; Picht, "The American Squatter and Federal Land Policy," 72–83; Feller, *The Public Lands in Jacksonian Politics,* 77–79.

51. The availability of land west of the Mississippi River could only threaten the value of southern real estate. When the last antebellum federal preemption bill was struck down by Congress in 1859, southeastern Kentucky's U.S. House representative, John Elliott, joined most other southern congressmen in opposing it. Congressmen representing New Appalachia realized (apparently correctly) that the opening of western lands would lead to the decrease of already marginal land values in their districts. *TAPR, 1859,* 23, 58; Salstrom, *Appalachia's Path to Dependency,* 22–23.

52. Although it is difficult to trace accurately because of its inherent invisibility among public records, the continuation of squatting can be demonstrated somewhat accurately by identifying specific surnames registered as landless over the course of multiple decades. One survey of antebellum Appalachia suggests that landlessness was often intergenerational, with families that had arrived west of the Alleghenies without land in 1800 still without land in 1860. Dunaway, "Speculators and Settler Capitalists," 83. Dunaway insists that "there was no such thing as 'free' land or 'squatters' rights" in antebellum Appalachia (86). This statement pertains only to the contractual ownership of land and not the "ownership" brought about by occupation and applied labor that was the original legal and moral basis of preemption. While there may have been nothing resembling squatters' rights in most of the southern states by the eve of the Civil War, that does not mean that many people did not enjoy access to open land and perhaps profit from it as much as a farmer with "legitimate" ownership. Anecdotal accounts show that in Breathitt County farmers without documentation of land ownership operated with relative impunity until the early twentieth century.

53. Families of the nineteenth-century Cumberland Plateau were forced to deal with two factors that turned land inheritance into a process of increasing poverty: a dearth of arable land coupled with one of the highest birth rates in the United States. This condition was exacerbated by the practice of "partible inheritance" in which land was equally distributed to all eligible heirs (or all male heirs). As a result, familial land-holdings became smaller over the course of generations. While landless farmers would have suffered from the increase in population along with their landed neighbors, partible inheritance had little impact on people with no land to inherit. In fact, the shrinking of individual landholdings may have made squatting seem more attractive. Salstrom, *Appalachia's Path to Dependency*, xxv, 22–23, 53–55; Wiese, *Grasping at Independence*, 261–80; Waller, *Feud*, 21–22, 58–59; Williams, *Appalachia*, 153–54; John Sherwood Lewis, "Becoming Appalachia," 115–19.

54. Ronald Lewis, *Transforming the Appalachian Countryside*, 27–28. For the inherent condition of inequality involved in land commodification in Appalachia, see Billings and Blee, *The Road to Poverty*, 36–39. Billings and Blee suggest that Kentucky mountaineers saw little problem in accepting land as a saleable commodity. For an opposing viewpoint on this subject (pointing out the cultural barriers to land commodification), see Batteau, "Mosbys and Broomsedge," 457–63. Both of these explanations of land commodification in New Appalachia take into account only land "known" by its owner and the legal and social implications of that knowledge. While this was the case for many landowners, the prevalence of absentee ownership had the effect of giving unauthorized land users greater knowledge of the land than its official owners. This chapter submits that direct knowledge of and engagement with land were indirect forms of "ownership" that, while not legally recognized, nevertheless served squatters' economic and perhaps moral purposes.

The portrayal of "peasant" societies as communities that perpetually work toward common goals has been criticized as a situation in which "scholars tended to idealize and homogenize the peasant community, constructing it as a seamless universe in which all agreed on how to define the moral economy and on what parts of the old world they sought to regain. Internal dissension, exploitation, or violence, no matter how important to the operation or definition of the community, tended to disappear from view." In his "post-revisionist" study of the political economy of nineteenth- and early twentieth-century Floyd County, Kentucky, Robert Wiese calls this tendency "household localism" and contends that mountain yeomen of practically all possible financial situations were careful not to enter into arrangements that benefited anyone outside their immediate families. There is little reason to believe that eastern Kentucky's landless would have behaved much differently from their landed neighbors in this respect. Wiese, *Grasping at Independence*, 11–13, 59–60. For a recent critique of the drawing of a stark distinction between "nonmarket and market-based societies" (using water rights in the American West as its case study), see Arnold, "Rethinking Moral Economy," 85–95; Mallon, *Peasant and Nation*, 64.

55. The raising of free-range livestock presented a challenge to private property just as it did in other parts of America. Sources that address the conflict between cultivation and droving in other parts of the South are Hahn, *The Roots of Southern Populism*, 239–68; R. Ben Brown, "Free Men and Free Pigs," 117–37; Walpole, "The Closing of the Open Range in Watauga County, N.C.," 320–35; Verhoeff, *Kentucky River Navigation*, 146.

56. Trimble, *Recollections of Breathitt*, 5.

57. Quotes from Scalf, *Kentucky's Last Frontier*, 158, and Trimble, *Recollections of Breathitt*, 17; *LCJ*, June 3, 1904.

58. The distinction between the two has been of special importance to historians of Appalachia who disagree as to what degree the region's economy was based upon a larger market before the Civil War. Market relations are perhaps more difficult to trace in such terrain than would be the case in, for instance, the contemporary lowland South; however, this does not convince all historians that Appalachia was not the "target" of capitalistic enterprises from very early on after white occupation. For descriptions of the two "extremes" of this argument (and others that fall in between), see Blethen and Wood, "The Appalachian Frontier and the Southern Frontier," 36–47.

59. Flat-bottomed "push boats" were the primary vehicle of eastern Kentucky's logging industry before the arrival of railroads and did not immediately disappear afterward, remaining common well into the twentieth century. Ellis, *The Kentucky River*, 53–80; Trimble, *Recollections of Breathitt*, 11.

60. Breathitt County native and historian E. L. Noble recollected a local fable from what he fancifully called "the medieval history of Eastern Kentucky" about a man who, sometime before the county's partitioning, traded "an entire creek of land, some two to three thousand acres" for a rifle. The moral of the story, Noble explained, was that while "the man buying the gun today [the 1930s] is looked on as an imbecile . . . in fact [at that time in history] he made the best bargain." While the deed to the land brought with it the potential for wealth, this was wealth that involved the application of arduous labor:

the plowing of rough ground and fencing of crops, the tending of livestock, the hiring of possibly undependable help, not to mention the burden of paying property taxes. In contrast, ownership of the rifle, compounded with unfettered access to all the territory one was willing to traverse, made one "heir to all the game that roamed the woods in a thousand valleys, or on a thousand hills." Noble added that "a fish hook in those days was more valuable than a common farm." E. L. Noble, *Bloody Breathitt*, 1:13, 28–29.

61. Tyrel G. Moore, "Economic Development in Appalachian Kentucky," 222–34; Ellis, *The Kentucky River*, 56, 68, 73–74.

62. Cannel is primarily a surface coal, and could be easily surface-mined without deep shaft digging, making early coal mining a simple winter vocation for farmers. The mining of cannel coal in the nineteenth century was statistically safer than bituminous mining due to a lessened need for blasting. Hower, "'Uncertain and Treacherous,'" 312.

63. Banks, "The Emergence of a Capitalistic Labor Market in Eastern Kentucky," 191; Hoffman, *A Winter in the West*, 184–85; WPA, *In the Land of Breathitt*, 18–19; Verhoeff, *Kentucky River Navigation*, 171n.

64. *KSJ, 1835*, 39 (appendix); Verhoeff, *Kentucky River Navigation*, 174–75.

65. Lewis Collins, *Historical Sketches of Kentucky*, 210–11; Trimble, *Recollections of Breathitt*, 10. See also Ripley and Dana, *The New American Cyclopaedia*, 659; Verhoeff, *Kentucky River Navigation*, 141–42.

66. Perrin, Battle, and Kniffin, *Kentucky*, 776; Trimble, *Recollections of Breathitt*, 10–11; Mathias, *Incidents and Experiences*, 22.

67. WPA, *In the Land of Breathitt*, 29; "Report of Board of Internal Improvement," *KSJ, 1839*, 38; Verhoeff, *Kentucky River Navigation*, 23–30; Trimble, *Recollections of Breathitt*, 1.

68. Mathias, *Incidents and Experiences*, 22.

69. Harry Watson, *Jacksonian Politics and Community Conflict*, 160–61; Robbins, "Preemption," 343–45; McFaul, *The Politics of Jacksonian Finance*, 172–74.

70. Trimble, *Recollections of Breathitt*, 1–2, 8.

71. Lewis Collins, *Historical Sketches of Kentucky*, 95.

72. The Thomas Franklin grant had been sold for taxes numerous times before South's purchase. *Stewart Kentucky Herald*, August 13, 1799; *Western Monitor*, September 22, 1815; *Morse v. South et al.*, Circuit Court D of Kentucky, April 15, 1897, in *The Federal Reporter*, 80:206–18; Jillson, *The Kentucky Land Grants*, 173; *Old Kentucky Entries and Deeds*, 101, 449; E. L. Noble, *Bloody Breathitt*, 2:51–52.

73. Owen, *Fourth Report of the Geological Survey in Kentucky*, 94–96, 351, 357, 362, 367, 369, 372, 417, 419, 420; MacFarlane, *Coal-Regions of America*, 346.

74. In 1888 the state geological survey listed Breathitt County with just under 389 square miles of forest land, one of the state's largest acreages at a time in which forest reserves were said to be running drastically low. *LCJ*, June 17, 1889; Haskel and Smith, *A Complete Descriptive and Statistical Gazetteer of the United States of America*, 78; Davie, *Kentucky*, 273; Trimble, *Recollections of Breathitt*, 8 (quote).

75. WPA, *In the Land of Breathitt,* 49; Ireland, *Little Kingdoms,* 2; Trimble, *Recollections of Breathitt,* 9.

76. *KHJ, 1839,* 426; Trimble, *Recollections of Breathitt,* 9; Clements, *History of the First Regiment of Infantry,* 147.

77. Trimble, *Recollections of Breathitt,* 11.

78. *AGACK, December, 1838* (Frankfort: A. G. Hodges, 1839), 144–45; and *AGACK, December 1853–March, 1854* (Frankfort: A. G. Hodges, 1854), 2:527; Trimble, *Recollections of Breathitt,* 9–10; WPA, *In the Land of Breathitt,* 84; Conti, "The Cultural Role of Local Elites in the Kentucky Mountains," 54; Ellis, *The Kentucky River,* 113.

79. Quoted in Verhoeff, *Kentucky River Navigation,* 175.

80. During his time on the General Assembly as representative from Madison County, Samuel South would have represented the sparsely populated area of the Three Forks region that his son later purchased. "Samuel South Letter, 1825," microfilm roll 82-0026, Clift folder 884, KHS; *Stewart Kentucky Herald,* August 11, 1801; *Western Monitor,* August 9, 1817; *Maysville Eagle,* February 6, 1818; Lewis Collins and Collins, *Collins' Historical Sketches of Kentucky,* 2:179; George Robertson, *Scrap Book on Law and Politics,* 2; John Frost, *Heroes and Hunters of the West,* 147; Wilder, *Kentucky Soldiers of the War of 1812,* 240; Hume, "The Hume Genealogy," 110–11; James Rood Robertson, *Petitions of the Early Inhabitants of Kentucky to the General Assembly of Virginia,* 51; Quisenberry, *Kentucky in the War of 1812,* 29, 110; Belue, *The Hunters of Kentucky,* 292–93n.

81. Dunaway, *The First American Frontier,* 311.

82. *Morse v. South et al.,* Circuit Court D of Kentucky, April 15, 1897, *The Federal Reporter,* 80:217; Trimble, *Recollections of Breathitt,* 9 (quote). After Owsley County was created in 1843, partially carved out of Breathitt County, South's holdings amounted to more than 37 percent of land owned in Breathitt County and, by 1860, over a quarter of the county's land mass. *Annual Report of the Auditor of Public Accounts of the State of Kentucky,* 47.

83. *KSJ, 1839,* 377.

84. Trimble, *Recollections of Breathitt,* 9; *KSJ, 1839,* 309, 320, 343, 377. The office of sheriff put one in charge of all county-level tax collection and bond execution, thereby placing the financial well-being of an entire county within the discretion of one individual; William B. Allen, *Kentucky Officer's Guide and Legal Hand-book,* 201–3.

85. *KPD: Reports Communicated to Both Branches of the Legislature of Kentucky at the December Session, 1840* (Frankfort: A. G. Hodges, 1840), 154–55; *KSJ, 1838,* 377–78; Trimble, *Recollections of Breathitt,* 8.

86. *AGACK: December, 1838* (Frankfort: A. G. Hodges, 1839), 144; Trimble, *Recollections of Breathitt,* 10.

87. *AGACK: December Session, 1844* (Frankfort: A. G. Hodges, 1845), 197–98.

88. Jeremiah Weldon South was referred to as the "father of Breathitt County" in his later years and especially after his death in 1880. *LCJ,* July 27, 1877, February 10, 1880; Trimble, *Recollections of Breathitt,* 9. For South's influence in Kentucky government,

see Ayers, *Vengeance and Justice,* 195; Lowell H. Harrison, *Kentucky's Governors,* 65; Robert Gunn Crawford, "A History of the Kentucky Penitentiary System," 29; Ireland, *Little Kingdoms,* 2.

89. *Mt. Sterling Sentinel-Democrat,* April 14, 1880; Hume, "The Hume Genealogy," 110.

90. Robert Gunn Crawford, "A History of the Kentucky Penitentiary System," 29; *Mt. Sterling Sentinel-Democrat,* April 14, 1880.

91. *FRA,* April 17, 1880; Mathias, *Incidents and Experiences,* 31, 156; Hume, "The Hume Genealogy," 110. For Kentucky support for the Mexican War, see Ramage and Watkins, *Kentucky Rising,* 170–86.

92. Pudup, "Land before Coal," 127. Pudup's conception of class in nineteenth-century eastern Kentucky depends upon E. P. Thompson's dictum that class is defined not only by economic relationships but is also formed according to the dictates of very specific historical contexts. Essentially, class relations in eastern Kentucky were defined according to the parameters of the immediate vicinity, involving factors such as land ownership, profession, and kinship that may not have corresponded directly to other parts of Kentucky, the Upper South, or the United States as a whole. E. P. Thompson, *Making of the English Working Class,* 11.

The "Bluegrass System" was the forerunner of Henry Clay's "American System" that favored a society led by planters and merchants. The creation of Breathitt County was one of many manifestations of the Bluegrass System transported to the mountains. Friend, *Kentucke's Frontiers,* 218–19; Aron, *How the West Was Lost,* 124–49.

93. "List of Lawyers in Kentucky," 416; interview with William L. Hurst, October 27, 1898, *JJDD,* 2453.

94. Lewis Collins, *Historical Sketches of Kentucky,* 210–11.

95. *AGACK: November Session, 1851* (Frankfort: A. G. Hodges, 1852), 728.

96. *Discipline* is the act Michel Foucault used to describe the treatment and manipulation of the body in the modern age. I use the term analogically since it is general yet not overly imprecise in describing the manipulation of bodies (or in this case a body of land and a body politic) in ways not limited to the physical, political, and economic but combining elements of all three. Breathitt County's creation involved a holistic attempt to combine contractual ownership with the establishment of a corresponding political and administrative unit. The level of control involved in such an undertaking (made structurally possible by the freedom granted to individuals in nineteenth-century Kentucky to almost single-handedly "create" a county) can be well described as "an uninterrupted, constant coercion, supervising the processes of the activity rather than its result and it is exercised according to a codification that partitions as closely as possible time, space, movement." Foucault, *Discipline and Punish,* 137. For analogous examples of the Foucauldian concept of discipline applied to a modern "managed nature," see Oliver, "The Thames Embankment and the Disciplining of Nature in Modernity," 227–38; Peluso and Vandergeest, "Genealogies of the Political Forest and Customary Rights in Indonesia, Malaysia, and Thailand," 761–812.

97. It was the occasion of Kentucky's 1890 constitutional convention where delegates resolved to make county making more difficult. The new rule was tested in 1904 when the legislature voted to form a new county, Beckham County (after the names "Hardscrabble" and "Goebel" were rejected), but a lawsuit charging that the county was too small for the parameters drawn out by the constitution prompted the new county to be dissolved. It was not until 1912 that another county, McCreary County, was formed, to become the state's 120th, and last, county. Birchfield, "Beckham County," 60–70; *Official Report of the Proceedings and Debates in the Convention,* 395 (quote). (I am grateful to John R. Burch for directing me to this quote.) For further convention debates on county government, also see 328–29, 333, 358, 368–69, 391, 399, 403–4. For a thorough analysis of the problems associated with Kentucky county government addressed at the 1890 convention, see Webster, "The Spatial Reorganization of the Local State," 71–80; Ireland, *Little Kingdoms,* 143.

98. Wallace B. Turner, "Kentucky Politics in the 1850's," 132; Mathias and Shannon, "Gubernatorial Politics in Kentucky," 248. Those who gained their wealth from new roads and easy credit favored Clay's American System, while poorer elements voted Whig in areas where Democratic slaveholders dominated elections. Kentuckians of many societal strata had thrown their support to the Whigs and, as was the case in most southern communities, they created relatively homogenous party loyalties in their respective communities (loyalties that usually extended to the county level). Harry Watson, *Jacksonian Politics and Community Conflict,* 220, 304; Volz, "Party, State and Nation," 29–34; Ronald Lewis, *Transforming the Appalachian Countryside,* 65–68. Historians of the nineteenth-century American South who consider political parties to be tools of the elite, as well as historians who deem them true vehicles of mass opinion, all recognize the Whig Party's special formidability in the upland South, particularly in eastern Kentucky. Billings and Blee, *The Road to Poverty,* 109; Holt, *The Rise and Fall of the American Whig Party,* 34–35, 116; Degler, *The Other South,* 109–10; James S. Brown, *Beech Creek,* 7–8.

99. (Columbus) *Ohio Statesman,* December 2, 1840; *Boston Daily Atlas,* November 27, 1844; *New York Herald,* December 15, 1845, November 11, 1848. Until majorities began casting votes for Unionists during the Civil War (perhaps due to violent coercion), Breathitt County's electorate produced majorities for the Democratic Party for all offices, legislative and executive, on the state and federal levels. *TAPR, 1838,* 28; *1840,* 25–26; *1841,* 23–24; *1843,* 46; *1844,* 56; *1845,* 51; *1846,* 48; *1848,* 46; *1849,* 55; *1850,* 48; *1852,* 47; *1853,* 43; *1854,* 47; *1856,* 47; *1857,* 52; *1858,* 59; *1859,* 56.

Eastern Kentucky counties exhibit party loyalties that (if Whig, Know-Nothing, Opposition, and Republican tickets can be uneasily lumped together) span centuries. Breathitt County's Democratic deviation from its Whig neighbors is especially significant considering the tendency of county electorates in the Three Forks region to follow the political lead of the counties out of which they were partitioned. Floyd and Morgan counties, older counties situated to Breathitt County's north and east nineteenth-century boundaries, exhibited the same staunch loyalty to the Democratic Party throughout the nineteenth century and, like Breathitt, held pro-Confederate leanings during the Civil War. Intuitively, this might indicate that Breathitt County's political socialization came from economic and social ties between these counties. However, the similarities may be misleading. Aside from the waterways that drained into the three forks of the Kentucky River, Breathitt County's only other major transportation conduits across county boundaries was a state road that connected the county with Clay, Perry (counties that lost territory to the former's formation), and Owsley (a newer county to which portions of Breathitt County were lost), counties that were all traditionally Whig. Before 1850, there were no mapped roads between Breathitt and its similarly Democratic neighbors, suggesting that such physical ties of socialization might have been relatively minimal and giving further credence to Jeremiah South's personal influence on the electorate. *Albany Argus,* April 13, 1843; *Statutes at Large and Treaties of the United States of America,* 128; Tallant, *Evil Necessity,* 136–37; Conti, "Mountain Metamorphoses," 186. Ernest Collins, "Political Behavior in Breathitt, Knott, Perry and Leslie Counties," 41; Tyrel G. Moore, "Economic Development in Appalachian Kentucky," 224; Copeland, "Where Were the Kentucky Unionists and Secessionists?" 350–51; Mathias and Shannon, "Gubernatorial Politics in Kentucky," 263, 265, 267, 269; Tapp and Klotter, *Kentucky,* 7; Volz, "Party, State and Nation," 19–26, 69–70; Wallace B. Turner, "Kentucky Politics in the 1850's," 123–24.

100. G. W. Noble, *Behold He Cometh in the Clouds,* 158.

101. Trimble, *Recollections of Breathitt,* 10; William B. Allen, *Kentucky Officer's Guide and Legal Hand-book,* 201–3; Ireland, *Little Kingdoms,* 45–46, 124–32.

102. *KSJ, 1838,* 378; *1839,* 377; *1843,* 42.

103. Shaffner, *The Kentucky State Register for the Year 1847,* 53. Apparently this sort of maneuver was common in Kentucky during the later Jacksonian years and used by both parties (although, according to Robert Ireland's research on the subject, the majority of recorded county coups were instigated by Democrats). As Kentucky moved further away from the party of Jackson on a statewide level, local squires were attempting to maintain the duchies, and one-party "rump sessions" were frequent. Ireland, "Aristocrats All," 375–77; Ireland, *The County Courts in Antebellum Kentucky,* 65–72.

104. Papers of Governor William Owsley, box 4, folder 72, KDLA. Judging by the nature of letters sent to the governor's office in 1846, Governor Owsley had his hands full with other matters. A year earlier a member of one of Clay County's most prominent families had been jailed for murder and Owsley was obliged to send the state militia to Manchester to ensure that a mob did not attack the Clay County jail. Soon after this matter had abated, Owsley's attention was taken up by popular rumblings of war against Mexico. Governor's Letter Box, microfilm roll 993680, KDLA; Laver, *Citizens More Than Soldiers,* 54–56.

105. *Kentucky Library Commission Fourth Biennial Report,* 56; Shackleford and Weinberg, *Our Appalachia,* 40–43; *America at the Polls.*

106. *KSJ, 1839,* 377; G. W. Noble, *Behold He Cometh in the Clouds,* 8; Trimble, *Recollections of Breathitt,* 18.

107. Trimble, *Recollections of Breathitt*, 11.

108. *Eighth Census of the United States, 1860*, KHS; Woodson, "My Recollections of Frankfort," 204. South's other sons may have kept a residence there as well but were not recorded as living in Breathitt County but rather in Madison County.

109. South's and Bohannon's return to the Bluegrass is consistent with Wilma Dunaway's assertion that absentee ownership was common in antebellum Appalachia (although it has traditionally been associated with Gilded Age corporate ownership). Dunaway, *The First American Frontier*, 56–57. For Sewell's 1858 departure, see Perrin, Battle and Kniffin, *Kentucky*, 776.

110. Quoted from Robert Gunn Crawford, "A History of the Kentucky Penitentiary System," 29. See also Sneed, *A Report on the History and Mode of Management of the Kentucky Penitentiary*, 553–54; *AGACK: January 17–April 5, 1861* (Frankfort: Jno. B. Major, 1861), 22; *The National Almanac and Annual Record for the Year 1863*, 463; *KHJ, 1876*, 630–31; *Report of the Special Committee on the Penitentiary to the Senate of Kentucky, February 26, 1880*, 3–82; *KPD, 1881*, 55–56; Fairbank, *Rev. Calvin Fairbank during Slavery Times*, 129; Wallace B. Turner, "Kentucky Politics in the 1850's," 139. Parenthetical quote from Ayers, *Vengeance and Justice*, 68.

111. "Lessee" was a new state-mandated position when South took it (although the arrangement Kentucky's state government made with another Bluegrass investor was different only in particular details) and one that exemplified the Whiggish complicity of private and public interests rampant in antebellum Kentucky government. By the 1850s Kentucky was one of five slave states that used a variation on this arrangement to utilize prisoner labor. As lessee, South received direct personal income from convict labor after his initial $12,000 investment after being appointed. Until the end of his term, South was "complete and authoritative ruler of the prisoners." After emancipation, and the subsequently amplified dependence upon convict labor for public works, the position (which South retained except for a brief period during the war) was even more influential and supposedly carried with it more power than that of the governor in influencing state government. Ayers, *Vengeance and Justice*, 195; Lowell H. Harrison, *Kentucky's Governors*, 65. For an account of South using convict labor in his Frankfort home, see *FRA*, February 14, 1880; Robert Gunn Crawford, "A History of the Kentucky Penitentiary System," 6–7, 19–23 (quote 7).

112. Wines and Dwight, *Report on the Prisons and Reformatories of the United States and Canada*, 260; Robert Gunn Crawford, "A History of the Kentucky Penitentiary System," 6–7, 19–29; Ireland, *Little Kingdoms*, 82–83.

113. Norman Barton Wood, *The White Side of a Black Subject*, 216; Fairbank, *Rev. Calvin Fairbank during Slavery Times*, 129.

114. *LCJ*, July 27, 1877, February 10, 1880; Baird, *Luke Pryor Blackburn*, 81.

115. Robert Gunn Crawford, "A History of the Kentucky Penitentiary System," 29.

116. McAfee, *Kentucky Politicians*, 74; *Breckinridge News*, May 14, 1879; Trimble, *Recollections of Breathitt*, 12.

117. *KHJ, 1856,* 391, 476; McAfee, *Kentucky Politicians,* 74; Otto, "The Decline of Forest Farming in Southern Appalachia," 21–22; Verhoeff, *The Kentucky Mountains,* 100.

118. *KHJ, 1850,* 203; *1856,* 472; *1858,* 473, 545, 639, 649, 661; *AGACK, 1861* (Frankfort: John B. Major, 1861–63), 48–49; Rice, "History of Education in Breathitt County, Kentucky," 51; WPA, *In the Land of Breathitt,* 104.

119. *HGH,* April 7, 1886.

120. *RDPCRSK,* 396–97, 523–24, 560 (quote). Hargis's stand for rural supremacy was defeated as other conventioneers allocated new districting to Kentucky's largest city. While this may have slightly diminished "country" dominance over Kentucky, it increased the Democratic electorate, just as Whig opponents predicted that it would. This apparently did not interest Hargis. Volz, "Party, State and Nation," 79–81.

121. *RDPCRSK,* 299–300.

122. Bensel, *The American Ballot Box in the Mid-Nineteenth Century,* 56–57; Ireland, "Aristocrats All," 368. The secret ballot was instituted for the state in the original 1792 constitution but its 1799 replacement established vive voce as standard in Kentucky for a century. For the role of vive voce as a method of social control and an advantage to eastern Kentucky elites, see *Annals of the American Academy of Political and Social Science* 25, no. 1 (1905): 125; Waller, *Feud,* 26; Billings and Blee, *The Road to Poverty,* 106, 374.

123. It is just as likely that Hargis wanted to eliminate illiterates voting. Knowing that he was in the minority, Hargis apparently did not push the issue and submitted his own draft of a proposed constitution that allowed for vive voce. Kentucky did not eliminate it until the 1880s. *RDPCRSK,* 43, 336; Tracy Campbell, *Deliver the Vote,* 17, 97.

124. *RDPCRSK,* 362.

125. Volz, "Party, State and Nation," 82.

126. *RDPCRSK,* 362. While the 1849 constitution was supposedly an improvement over its 1799 predecessor (in terms of expanding democracy), many historians agree that its most lasting legacy was a killing blow to the Kentucky Whig Party (a result that Hargis no doubt approved of) and, as a result, the weakening of vigorous two-party competition experienced throughout the South in the 1850s. For a critical approach to Kentucky's 1849 constitution, see Mathias, "Kentucky's Third Constitution," 18.

127. Although the convention ended with new constitutional support for slavery, it had begun with more than fourteen thousand votes for emancipationist delegates. Only two openly antislavery delegates ended up at the convention, but their presence ensured that slavery dominated debate for most of the proceedings. The convention ended with one of the strongest proslavery constitutions in the United States. Bowman, "Kentucky's 'Athens of the West,'" 56; Ramage and Watkins, *Kentucky Rising,* 272–73.

128. *RDPCRSK,* 43. Presbyterian minister and dauphin of one of Kentucky's most lauded families, Robert J. Breckinridge served in Kentucky's General Assembly in the 1820s, resigning in anger after his pleas for gradual emancipation legislation were roundly rebuffed. Lowell H. Harrison. *The Antislavery Movement in Kentucky,* 40–41; Klotter, "Central Kentucky's 'Athens of the West,'" 23.

129. *RDPCRCSK*, 42–43, 560. In his history of the state in the Civil War era, E. Merton Coulter claimed that Kentuckians held fast to slavery for constitutional rather than economic reasons and supported its continuance out of fear of a free black population. One result of the new state constitution was a seeming "settling" of the slavery issue. While debate over the institution had previously been vigorous, after the new constitution's passage public argument became permanently stifled. Coulter, *The Civil War and Readjustment in Kentucky*, 7–8; Tallant, *Evil Necessity*, 159.

130. Hargis may have been influenced by the previous year's reportedly white-led escape attempted by dozens of slaves from three Bluegrass counties. Tallant, *Evil Necessity*, 146.

131. Interview with Edward C. Strong, July 21, 1898, *JJDD*, reel 3, p. 2422. Nat Turner's revolt alarmed Kentuckians to such a degree that in 1833 the state instituted a slave anti-importation law. The law, popular among all but the wealthiest of planters, remained on the books until it was repealed during the negotiations leading up to the 1849 constitutional convention. Harrold, *Border War*, 6; Ford, *Deliver Us from Evil*, 385–86.

132. Trimble, *Recollections of Breathitt*, 5.

133. Billings and Blee, *The Road to Poverty*, 120–21, 125, 213; Friend, *Kentucke's Frontiers*, 194–95.

134. *Breathitt County Slave Schedules, 1860*, KHS; For the importance of relationships between slaves and free blacks as resistance networks, see Hahn, *A Nation under Our Feet*, 57–61.

135. Before the sale, one white teenage boy asked the fair-skinned slave's mistress (thinking her the slave's mother), and mutual embarrassment ensued. Trimble, *Recollections of Breathitt*, 8–9. Such white-appearanced female slaves were particularly popular as "fancy girls" sold at Kentucky slave auctions. Gerald L. Smith, "Slavery and Abolition in Kentucky," 84–85; Lucas, *A History of Blacks in Kentucky*, 86.

136. For "perpetualism" in Kentucky, see Harrold, *Border War*, 51.

137. Due to the small numbers involved, slavery's place in New Appalachia has generally not been a popular historical subject. Historians have begun to study slavery in southern Appalachia in recent years, but have tended to look to areas farther south (notably western North Carolina, northern Georgia, and Alabama), areas in which slavery was marginal compared to the lowlands but not numerically negligible as it was in eastern Kentucky and northwestern Virginia. The only book-length works that have studied slavery as an institution common throughout New Appalachia are Dunaway's *Slavery in the American Mountain South* and *The African-American Family in Slavery and Emancipation*. But although Dunaway acknowledges slavery in the mountainous Upper South, most of her data are gleaned from sources pertaining to Appalachia's extension into the Deep South states where slavery was more economically viable and slave owners had an even firmer hold over state and local government than in the Upper South.

138. David Chandler, the owner of one of the county's largest chattel holdings in 1861, owned a total of thirteen slaves valued at $5,500 yet valued his seven-hundred acre farm at only $2,000. *Breathitt County Tax Books, 1861*, KHS.

139. Ernest Collins, "Political Behavior in Breathitt, Knott, Perry and Leslie Counties," 40–41.

140. Hardly exceptional, Kentucky is only one good example of a condition common throughout the South: most slave owners (comprising roughly one-third of the white southern population) owned fewer than ten slaves. The owner of five slaves living in a locality with minimal slave ownership would have nevertheless felt a kinship of economic interest with other slave owners more than with slaveless neighbors. Breathitt County's largest slaveholding in 1861 was only fifteen, while most of the county's thirty-five slave owners owned fewer than five. In the same year, only seventy Kentuckians owned more than fifty slaves. *Breathitt County Tax Books, 1861,* KHS; Harrold, *Border War,* 6; Ernest Collins, "Political Behavior in Breathitt, Knott, Perry and Leslie Counties," 9, 13; Sprague, "The Kentucky Pocket Plantation," 69; Owsley, *Plain Folk of the Old South,* 8–9.

141. *Breathitt County Slave Schedules, 1840, 1850, 1860,* KHS; Shaffner, *The Kentucky State Register for the Year 1847,* 53; interview with Edward C. Strong, July 21, 1898, *JJDD,* reel 3, p. 2422; Lewis Collins, *Historical Sketches of Kentucky,* 260–61; Ernest Collins, "Political Behavior in Breathitt, Knott, Perry and Leslie Counties," 9, 40–41. As a comparison, Woodford County held Kentucky's largest proportional slave population during the last two decades before the Civil War. For a numerical comparison of slavery between southeastern Kentucky and other parts of the state, see Lucas, *A History of Blacks in Kentucky,* xx.

142. Oakes, *The Ruling Race,* 144.

143. Harrold, "Violence and Nonviolence in Kentucky Abolitionism," 16–17.

144. Perrin, Battle, and Kniffin, *Kentucky,* 973.

145. G. W. Noble, *Behold He Cometh in the Clouds,* 8.

146. In Breathitt County Clay carried 5.9 percent of the vote, a percentage that amounted to fewer than fifty votes. The estimation of the number of votes this would have comprised depends upon Breathitt County's having a potential vote of 761 in the following year's presidential election. *TAPR, 1852,* 47; Mathias and Shannon, "Gubernatorial Politics in Kentucky," 271; Shannon and McQuown, *Presidential Politics in Kentucky,* 26. Eighteen counties contributed larger percentages of their respective votes to Clay than did Breathitt, with Clay's native Madison County contributing the highest at 35.2 percent. Of these eighteen, all but four had slave populations proportionally larger than that of Breathitt (and most were considerably larger). These four, Laurel, Owsley, Perry, and Whitley counties, were all in the Three Forks region south of Breathitt County, suggesting that within the slave economy generated by iron and salt mining slavery was not universally accepted. Also, twelve of these counties (including all of the counties in the Three Forks region except for Breathitt) had hosted emancipationist or abolitionist gatherings shortly before 1851, revealing at least a small ferment of native antislavery sentiment and resultant impetus for an emancipationist voting base. Clay's relative success in these counties was also partly due to his Whig past as well as to the intraparty divisions over the issue of slavery and the Democratic Party's ability

to attract both slaveless yeomen and large-scale planters. Clay accordingly claimed the credit for the ensuing Whig defeat and declared it evidence of slavery's intractability in Kentucky. In contrast, the counties in which Clay had his poorest showings were ones in which slavery was either a large part of the economy (the northern Bluegrass and the plantation-heavy "Jackson Purchase" area to the far west) or ones where slavery was relatively "out of sight and out of mind" (such as the eastern counties bordering Virginia), most of which were typically Democratic counties. Mathias and Shannon, "Gubernatorial Politics in Kentucky," 273; Smiley, *The Lion of White Hall*, 43, 147; Lucas, *A History of Blacks in Kentucky*, xx; Tallant, *Evil Necessity*, 249; Billings and Blee, *The Road to Poverty*, 60; Volz, "Party, State and Nation," 98–100.

147. "William Lincoln to Bro. [William G.] Frost," October 18, 1909, William E. Lincoln Papers, Founders and Founding Collection, HLSCA. William E. Lincoln, manuscript: "Wellington Rescue"; "Personal Reminiscences with an Account of the Rescue of the Negro Slave," 1915, Palmer Collection, Western Reserve Historical Society Library.

148. Luntz, *Forgotten Turmoil*, 36.

149. In fact, considering that he maintained this interpretation in 1909, he was not ready for it as an old man either. "William Lincoln to Bro. [William G.] Frost," William E. Lincoln Papers, Founders and Founding Collection, HLSCA.

150. Ibid.; Brandt, *The Town That Started the Civil War*, 8–12 (quotes 11).

151. In 1846 approximately half of Breathitt County's heads of household reported having no land, this while South owned more than one-third of the county's acreage. *Breathitt County Tax Books, 1846*, KHS.

152. HGH, May 10, 1894; *Miller v. South &c.*, Kentucky Court of Appeals, filed September 16, 1890, *KLR*, vol. 12, no. 1 (July 1, 1890), 351–52; *Morse v. South et al.*, Circuit Court D of Kentucky, April 15, 1897, *The Federal Reporter*, 80:207–8; *Sizemore &c. v. Trimble, &c.*, Kentucky Court of Appeals, May, 4, 1904, *KLR*, vol. 26, no. 1 (July 1, 1904), 8–10; E. L. Noble, *Bloody Breathitt*, 2:51–52.

153. As was the case with the Sussex "Blacks," the organized poachers of the royal forests in Hanoverian England; the land's sheer physicality, especially unimproved forest, places the advantage of physical *possession* (in contrast to legal ownership) in the hands of the unauthorized inhabitants who have the greater knowledge of the topography. E. P. Thompson, *Whigs and Hunters*, 240. See also James C. Scott, *Seeing Like a State*, 11–52.

154. E. L. Noble, *Bloody Breathitt*, 1:40.

155. *H. F. Davis & Co. v. Sizemore et al.*, Court of Appeals of Kentucky, December 20, 1918, *SWR*, vol. 207 (January 22–February 12, 1919), 17; *SWR*, vol. 37 (1896–97), 260; *Aikman v. South et al.*, Court of Appeals of Kentucky, October 31, 1906, *SWR*, vol. 97 (1906–7), 5; G. W. Noble, *Behold He Cometh in the Clouds*, 158.

156. *Aikman v. Commonwealth*, filed March 17, 1892, *KLR*, vol. 13 (July 1, 1891–June 15, 1892), 894–96.

157. BCN, March 16, 1906.

158. Planters farther to the south who chafed at having to fence their crops for protec-

tion from drovers while depending on these same drovers' votes suffered an analogous problem. Hahn, "The Yeomanry of the Nonplantation South," 40.

159. E. L. Noble, *Bloody Breathitt*, 2:44.

2. "Suppressing the late rebellion"

1. G. W. Noble, *Behold He Cometh in the Clouds*, 7. The 1858 sighting of Donati's Comet was followed by others in 1860 and 1861. All three were said to foretell an impending war, just as others before and since were popularly interpreted as premonitions of impending strife. S. A. Mitchell, "The Return of Halley's Comet," 443.

2. G. W. Noble, *Behold He Cometh in the Clouds*, 7. Unless one had the most fervent political or sectional convictions for either side, most men of fighting age saw no benefit to actively supporting either side in the escalating conflict, except in the defense of their own families and communities. Freehling, *The South vs. the South*, 69.

3. G. W. Noble, *Behold He Cometh in the Clouds*, 8, 30, 50.

4. The "classical" portrayal of wartime Appalachia has asserted that southern mountaineers were consistently against slave interests and consequently supported Federal authorities during the war, even against the efforts of their respective state governments and the Confederacy as a whole. This interpretation of Civil War–era Appalachia was dominant until the 1970s, when historians began to recognize that the southern Appalachians were a place of considerable wartime division and that slavery was only one factor among many that motivated mountaineers. Literature from recent decades has consistently shown the Appalachian Civil War as defined by internal dissension and close-quartered fighting. Noe, "'Deadening Color and Colder Horror,'" 67–68. Historians of the Civil War in Appalachia have been more willing to abandon the traditional military history approach to the war and embrace a social history that attempts to explain how the war affected localities and how individuals made personal decisions to join, support, or ignore the opposing armies. For other "revisionist" accounts of Civil War–era Appalachia, see Sarris, *A Separate Civil War*; McKnight, *The Civil War in Appalachian Kentucky and Virginia*; Gordon McKinney, "The Civil War and Reconstruction"; Martin Crawford, *Ashe County's Civil War*; Inscoe and McKinney, *The Heart of Confederate Appalachia*; Susan G. Hall, *Appalachian Ohio and the Civil War, 1862–1863*; O'Brien, *Mountain Partisans*; Noe and Wilson, *The Civil War in Appalachia*; Paludan, *Victims*; Shaffer, *Clash of Loyalties*; Trotter, *Bushwhackers*. Although the historiography on the mountain South in the Civil War is diverse, Appalachia's wartime exceptionalism, or at least its challenge to the dominant paradigms of Civil War history, remain common themes in many of these histories. The majority of these books (with McKnight's and Shaffer's being important exceptions) are dedicated to areas within the Confederacy's official political boundaries.

5. Preston, *The Civil War in the Big Sandy Valley of Kentucky*, 5, 14–24.

6. Quoted from James C. Scott, *Domination and the Arts of Resistance*, 183.

7. *War of the Rebellion*, series 1, vol. 32 (1892), 433, 687. *Guerrilla* suffers from a

poverty of definition in modern discourse, and it was defined almost as loosely in the nineteenth century. During the U.S. Civil War, *guerrilla* was often interchanged with *partisan* (positive connotation), *bushwhacker* (damning), and *irregular* (somewhat neutral), among others. The only common denominators were the practice of engaging enemies in a manner considered "irregular" by the standards of the time and a proclivity for defending or attacking specific communities (possibly to the detriment of broader goals). I would add that, in many cases, an integral element in guerrillaism was combatants' mutual knowledge of identity, be it personal, familial, or political. Geiger, *Financial Fraud and Guerilla Violence in Missouri's Civil War*, 103–6; Sutherland, *A Savage Conflict*, xi–xiii. See also Robert Mackey, *The Uncivil War*, 6–10. For "guerrillaism," see Ash, *When the Yankees Came*, 47–75.

8. *KPD: Annual Report of the Superintendent of Public Instruction of Kentucky*, 36; Sutherland, *A Savage Conflict*, 14. "Social war" was used often in describing the condition of fighting within communities. Previous to the 1860s the phrase *social war* generally referred to the war fought within the Athenian Empire in the third century B.C.; like *feud*, it was a concept nineteenth-century Americans considered temporally foreign, if not culturally alien.

9. Fellman, *Inside War*, 23.

10. A civil war's "master cleavage" describes "ideological, ethnic, religious, or class" issues that seem to motivate violence by both sides within one war's setting (e.g., the American Civil War's master cleavage[s] was/were the national debate over slavery and the southern states' subsequent secession from the Union). Within this overarching political context smaller conflicts arise, many with only tenuous connections to the "larger" national issues. It is possible for these smaller conflicts to supersede the official war goals and perhaps even disrupt them, to the point where "the national is often subverted by the local." Kalyvas, *The Logic of Violence in Civil War*, 364–76 (quote).

11. Recent literature on what has been popularly labeled eastern Kentucky's "feud" violence has tended to dissociate the war's legacy from later instances of factional brutality. The revisionist interpretations of "feud" violence (Waller's *Feud* and Billings and Blee's *The Road to Poverty*) detract from the Civil War's importance in influencing later violence. While Billings and Blee fail to give the war significant mention (perhaps considering that their setting, Clay County, was thoroughly Unionist), Waller asserts that the war probably played a small role in the Hatfield-McCoy feud, since extramartial hostilities did not emerge between the factions until more then a decade after the war's cessation. However, Waller concedes that the same issues that had determined allegiance in the Tug River Valley in the 1860s were still present when the "feud" emerged years later. Lacy Ford's review of Waller takes issue with this ambiguity. Waller, *Feud*, 18, 194–95; Ford, review of *Feud*, 726; Coulter, *The Civil War and Readjustment in Kentucky*, 57–80.

12. Coulter, *The Civil War and Readjustment in Kentucky*, 57–80; Paludan, *A People's Contest*, 200; Sutherland, *A Savage Conflict*, 37–40. In fact, the strength of Kentucky's two-party system in the 1850s may have been the key to its failure to secede and/or join

the Confederacy. See Gary R. Matthews, "Beleaguered Loyalties," 9–24; Volz, "Party, State and Nation," 477–81.

13. Astor, "Rebels on the Border," 60–61, 72, 112–13; Lowell H. Harrison, *The Civil War in Kentucky*, 8.

14. Astor, "Rebels on the Border," 65–66, 89–90, 94–102; Volz, "Party, State and Nation," 448–51.

15. Quote from *KSJ, 1861* (special called session), 20; Crofts, *Reluctant Confederates*, 355; Shortridge, "Kentucky Neutrality in 1861," 285–87; Simkins, *The South, Old and New*, 135; Coulter, *The Civil War and Readjustment in Kentucky*, 50–51.

16. Frank Moore and Everett, *The Rebellion Record*, 29–31, 129; Thomas C. Mackey, "Not a Pariah, but a Keystone," 25–45; Wooster, *The Secession Conventions of the South*, 206–22; Coulter, *The Civil War and Readjustment in Kentucky*, 35–57; Edward C. Smith, *The Borderland in the Civil War*, 1–39, WPA, *Military History of Kentucky*, 147; McQuown and Shannon, *Presidential Politics in Kentucky*, 36.

17. Astor, "Rebels on the Border," 318n; Coulter, *The Civil War and Readjustment in Kentucky*, 142–44.

18. Klotter and Klotter, *A Concise History of Kentucky*, 111; Paludan, *A People's Contest*, 26.

19. Preston, *The Civil War in the Big Sandy Valley of Kentucky*, 23.

20. Coulter, *The Civil War and Readjustment in Kentucky*, 88.

21. Using the most updated estimates, a recent Kentucky history estimates that between sixty-six thousand and seventy-six thousand white Kentuckians fought for the Union, while between twenty-five thousand and forty thousand fought for the Confederacy. Marshall, *Creating a Confederate Kentucky*, 20; Ireland, *Little Kingdoms*, 60 (quote).

22. The abundance of personalized war memoirs written by Kentuckians on both sides speaks to the lack of consensus in the state and the need for participants to define the war individually; it is little wonder that this was the state where so much of a political conflict (war) was spoken of as an interpersonal dispute (feud). See Dallam, *A Union Woman in Civil War Kentucky;* William Davis and Swentnor, *Bluegrass Confederate;* Chapman, *Ten Months in the "Orphan Brigade"; Diary of Brigadier-General Marcus J. Wright;* Young, *Reminiscences of a Soldier of the Orphan Brigade;* Jackman, *Diary of a Confederate Soldier;* Mosgrove, *Kentucky Cavaliers in Dixie.* It should be noted that many, if not most, wartime memoirs written by Kentuckians dealt with experiences outside Kentucky. Even though the accounts are personalized, they tend to stress their participation in the larger war effort rather than the discord within the state.

23. The "War between the States" motif, a condition in which delineations of "segmented authority" are purportedly clearly drawn, makes the American Civil War seemingly unique among civil wars of the last three centuries since secession created what were virtual definitive boundaries between the war's oppositional forces. However, in the Three Forks region, and communities throughout the South whose wartime stories have only begun to be told, the war was fought "intimately" within communities, suggesting

that this civil war was perhaps more similar to others than may have been previously suspected. Ash, *When the Yankees Came,* 125. For "fragmented authorities" and "segmented authorities," see Kalyvas, *The Logic of Violence in Civil War,* 83, 88–89, 330–63.

24. Simon, "Lincoln, Grant, and Kentucky in 1861," 6; Astor, "Rebels on the Border," 119.

25. *KSJ, 1861* (special called session), 24 (quote); Speed, Pirtle, and Kelly, *The Union Regiments of Kentucky,* 696–98; Sutherland, *A Savage Conflict,* 37–38; Shortridge, "Kentucky Neutrality in 1861," 299; Tapp and Klotter, *Kentucky,* 6; Coulter, *The Civil War and Readjustment in Kentucky,* 87–91; Astor, "Rebels on the Border," 100, 309n.

26. Rhyne, "Rehearsal for Redemption," 44; Mathias, *Incidents and Experiences,* 74–75; Laver, *Citizens More Than Soldiers,* 66–97.

27. Perrin, Battle, and Kniffin, *Kentucky,* 357; Kirwan, *Johnny Green of the Orphan Brigade,* 8–10; Coulter, *The Civil War and Readjustment in Kentucky,* 147; WPA, *Military History of Kentucky,* 166.

28. The means by which a militia becomes "a political rather than a military institution" is explained in Kalyvas, *The Logic of Violence in Civil War,* 107–9.

29. WPA, *Military History of Kentucky,* 240.

30. *Lexington Observer and Reporter,* December 9, 1865.

31. Speed, Pirtle, and Kelly, *The Union Regiments of Kentucky,* 697.

32. William Davis and Swentnor, *Bluegrass Confederate,* 245, 252. For the linguistic distinctions between *bushwhackers, guerrillas,* and *partisans* as they were understood in the nineteenth century, see Mackey, *The Uncivil War,* 6–10.

33. Speed, Pirtle, and Kelly, *The Union Regiments of Kentucky,* 697; WPA, *Military History of Kentucky,* 240.

34. Blight, *Race and Reunion,* 53, 212–16, 382–91.

35. Lowell H. Harrison, "The Government of Confederate Kentucky," 84–89, 93–97; Astor, "Rebels on the Border," 71.

36. Historians have successfully debunked the myth of stolidly Unionist southern Appalachia, revealing a far more complex array of factors that contributed to the formation of divergent allegiances in the mountains. Civil wars create combatants, but they do not dictate that they fight uniformly and for uniform causes. Southern Appalachia's Civil War experience was more like that of the majority of the modern era's civil wars in which the larger war actually played host to a "mosaic of discrete miniwars," many of which had only peripheral connections to the "master cleavage" (in the case of the United States, secession) that initiated a state of war. For these phrases and their significance in describing civil war, see Berkeley, *The Graves Are Not Yet Full;* Marshall, *Creating a Confederate Kentucky,* 151, 9–18, 111–16.

37. Rockenbach, "'The Weeds and the Flowers Are Closely Mixed,'" 3.

38. Volz, "Party, State and Nation," 467.

39. G. W. Noble, *Behold He Cometh in the Clouds,* 57.

40. Fairbank, *Rev. Calvin Fairbank during Slavery Times,* 129.

41. *KHJ, 1861,* 327.

42. *KSJ, 1861,* 555; Rockenbach, "'The Weeds and the Flowers Are Closely Mixed,"'1–2; Robert Gunn Crawford, "A History of the Kentucky Penitentiary System," 24, 29.

43. Quote from Tomes and Smith, *The War with the South,* 54; *Congressional Globe,* vol. 54, part 2 (February 21, 1863): 1161–62.

44. Coulter, *The Civil War and Readjustment in Kentucky,* 171–72.

45. Owen, *Fourth Report of the Kentucky Geological Survey in Kentucky,* 351.

46. Brian McKnight's history of the Civil War in the "central Appalachian divide" suggests that mountaineers were capricious in their loyalties and unwilling to provide firm support for either side. Having produced an unambiguous military history, McKnight does not take strong account of the role of local government or violent political agency outside the parameters of official military units or units of peripheral officiality. I contend that under the direction of local elites, eastern Kentucky's male population, white and black, exhibited a distinct interest in the war's outcome (or at least its local outcome) and thus participated actively, although not always within the confines of regular military forces. McKnight, *The Civil War in Appalachian Kentucky and Virginia,* 3–5, 109–13.

47. *Wisconsin Daily Patriot,* November 19, 1860; Wooster, *The Secession Conventions of the South,* 206; Scalf, *Kentucky's Last Frontier,* 500; Volz, "Party, State and Nation," 449–51, 500.

48. *Hartford Herald,* April 30, 1879; McAfee, *Kentucky Politicians,* 74–75; Doolan, "The Court of Appeals of Kentucky," 463.

49. Brockman, *History of the Hume, Kennedy and Brockman Families,* 43; Hume, "The Hume Genealogy," 110; Walden, *Remembering Kentucky's Confederates,* 29; Kleber, Clark, and Harrison, *The Kentucky Encyclopedia,* 541.

50. Ed Porter Thompson, *History of the Orphan Brigade,* 700–704.

51. "Campaign Sketches No. 3," 179; Scalf, *Kentucky's Last Frontier,* 281 (quote); Preston, *The Civil War in the Big Sandy Valley of Kentucky,* 23, 30–31.

52. Perry, *Jack May's War,* 1–5, 13–14; Ed Porter Thompson, *History of the First Kentucky Brigade,* 753, 755–56; Preston, *The Civil War in the Big Sandy Valley of Kentucky,* 65.

53. Ed Porter Thompson, *History of the Orphan Brigade,* 701; Walden, *Remembering Kentucky's Confederates,* 29; Rolff, *Strong Family of Virginia and Other Southern States,* 106–7.

54. *War of the Rebellion,* series 1, vol. 32 (1892), 433, 687; Clements, *History of the First Regiment of Infantry,* 147; *KAGR,* 210–13.

55. G. W. Noble, *Behold He Cometh in the Clouds,* 8.

56. *Cincinnati Press,* November 8, 1861.

57. *New York Herald,* November 24, 1861.

58. Although nationalism does not fully explain Confederate loyalty in a Union state, Noble's testimonial suggests its contribution in conditions in which it was not previously part of the political or cultural atmosphere. "Nationalism is contingent; its creation is a

process. It is not a substance available to a people in a certain premeasured amount; it is rather a dynamic of ideas and social realities that can, under the proper circumstances, unite and legitimate a people in what they regard as reasoned public action. Such a view of nationalism, moreover, underlines the political nature of the undertaking, directing attention to the social groups seeking to establish their own corporate ideals and purposes as the essence of group self-definition." Faust, *The Creation of Confederate Nationalism*, 1–21 (quote 6); Martin Crawford, *Ashe County's Civil War*, 121–24.

59. Christopher Phillips has said that the Civil War–era "border experience," in contrast to the attempts at Confederate nationalism farther south, "fits best within the political . . . rather than the cultural realm." "'The Chrysalis State,'" 160.

60. Degler, *The Other South*, 122 (quote); McKnight, *The Civil War in Appalachian Kentucky and Virginia*, 17. For similar views, see McKenzie, *Lincolnites and Rebels*, 6; Fowler, *Mountaineers in Gray*, 20, 26; Groce, *Mountain Rebels*, 70; Martin Crawford, *Ashe County's Civil War*, 132; Waller, *Feud*, 31.

61. Breathitt, Floyd, and Morgan counties were peculiar in being "Confederate in sympathy" compared to most counties in eastern Kentucky. Tapp and Klotter, *Kentucky*, 7; John Britton Wells, *10th Kentucky Cavalry*, 4–6. Floyd County was the home of one of Kentucky's Confederate senators, John Milton Elliott. "Campaign Sketches No. 3," 179; *KAGR*, 1:210–13.

62. The typical Kentucky slave owner, like the majority of slave owners throughout the South, owned fewer than ten slaves. In 1860 only seventy Kentuckians owned more than fifty slaves. Sprague, "The Kentucky Pocket Plantation," 69; *Breathitt County Tax Books, 1861*, KHS.

63. Herbert W. Spencer, "Captain Bill's January Raid"; Inscoe, *Mountain Masters*, 9–10. In 1850 these contiguous counties were Floyd, Morgan, Owsley, and Perry. Goodrich, *A Pictorial Geography of the World*, 233–43; Ernest Collins, "Political Behavior in Breathitt, Knott, Perry and Leslie Counties," 9, 13; *Breathitt County Tax Books, 1861*, KHS.

64. Tallant, *Evil Necessity*, 91–100; Barnett, "Virginians Moving West," 244; Coulter, *The Civil War and Readjustment in Kentucky*, 6–8.

65. Ernest Collins, "Political Behavior in Breathitt, Knott, Perry and Leslie Counties," 41 (quote).

66. For the patron-client relationships and martial violence, see Schmidt et al., *Friends, Followers and Factions*, xxxii–xxxiii. White southern mountaineers, within and outside the seceded states, agreed with their lowland fellows that the alleged northern threat to slavery was an equal threat to all property and autonomy. Aside from this, even in a place like Breathitt County where black and white mingled freely, the white fear of a free black population was probably also a factor as it always was in the South (especially the Upper South). See Inscoe, *Mountain Masters*, 9–10, 123–30.

67. E. L. Noble, *Bloody Breathitt*, 2:50–52; *Breathitt County Tax Books, 1861*, KHS.

68. Dunaway, *African-American Family*, 10.

69. E. L. Noble, *Bloody Breathitt*, 2:5.

70. Waldrep, "Rank and File Voters and the Coming of the Civil War," 70–71; Coulter, *The Civil War and Readjustment in Kentucky*, 440–47; Volz "Party, State and Nation," 1–8, 469–81.

71. This suggests that southeastern Kentucky was consistent with the rest of the state, since cursory analysis of Kentucky's sectional divides on the 1861 neutrality vote reveals a consistent correlation between Democracy and antineutrality. The same areas that had supported Henry Clay and his Whigs during the party's salad days tended to favor neutrality in 1861 and contributed the greater amount of Union support after Kentucky's official participation in the war. Counties that had continued Democratic leanings since the 1820s opposed neutrality and accordingly provided the larger numbers of Confederate volunteers over the next four years after the state's early attempt at neutrality was revealed as a clear failure. Fox, "The Southern Mountaineer," 389; Rossiter, *Parties and Politics in America*, 85–86; Preston, *The Civil War in the Big Sandy Valley of Kentucky*, 20–23. For similar data from other slave states (with relatively similar conclusions), see Trelease, "Who Were the Scalawags?" 445–68.

72. *Barnes vs. Adams, CSS*, vol. 1432, no. 2, 41st Cong., 2nd sess., H. Misc. Doc. 13, p. 216; Coulter, "Some Reasons for Kentucky's Position in the Civil War," 50–52; Volz, "Party, State and Nation," 500.

73. Astor, "Rebels on the Border," 47–48, 71, 74–75, 117–18; Shannon and Mc-Quown, *Presidential Politics in Kentucky*, 32–38.

74. Relatively few histories of the U.S. Civil War have used white southern class concerns to explain wartime Unionism in the southern states (in fact, only recently has the subject of southern Unionism been broadly explored). For four exceptions, see Degler, *The Other South*; Escott, *Many Excellent People*; Durrill, *War of Another Kind*; and Current, *Lincoln's Loyalists*. For a complex examination of the changing relationships of "aristocrats," yeomen, and poor whites in the occupied South, see Ash, *When the Yankees Came*, 170–94.

75. Most Breathitt County surnames were found exclusively on either Union or Confederate recruitment rolls, showing that kinship played a significant role in picking sides—brothers and cousins often stuck together. But the small number of surnames found on both sides, when compared to 1861 tax records, suggests that economic considerations often trumped familial ones. *Breathitt County Tax Books, 1861*, KHS; *War of the Rebellion*, series 1, vol. 32 (1892), 433, 687; *KAGR*, 1:210–13; Charles C. Wells, *1890 Special Veterans' Census for Eastern Kentucky*.

76. *Forty-fourth Annual Report of the American Bible Society*, 67.

77. In E. P. Thompson's understanding, class is not so much a thing as it is an event, a historical phenomenon that occurs when people "as a result of common experiences (inherited or shared), feel and articulate the identity of their interests as between themselves, and as against other men whose interests are different from (and usually opposed to) theirs." Viewed as a continentwide conflict, the American Civil War hardly appears as a war between classes. However, within one divided community with no definite

attachment to either North or South, class formation (at least for a historically finite length of time) is a useful heuristic for understanding what made some men fight for the North and some men fight for the South, and why some attempted (unsuccessfully) to avoid the war altogether. E. P. Thompson. *The Making of the English Working Class*, 9.

78. WPA, *Military History of Kentucky*, 240.

79. This is a bit of an irony considering Governor Thomas Metcalfe's clash with Andrew Jackson in 1830. National Republican Thomas Metcalfe was elected as Kentucky's tenth governor in 1828. He was a firm defender of publicly funded internal improvements, a trait that gave him natural distance from President Jackson's policies disdaining same. Jackson's veto of a federal bill funding a road between Lexington and the Ohio River during Metcalfe's term marked the beginning of Jacksonian decline in most (but not all) Kentucky politics. Ramage and Watkins, *Kentucky Rising*, 26–27, 90–92; Friend, *Along the Maysville Road*, 256–72.

80. Surprised by the amount of Confederate support he found in eastern Kentucky in early 1862, Colonel James Garfield advocated loyalty oaths for these heads of party, hoping that lead rams would change the flocks' direction. *War of the Rebellion*, series 1, vol. 10, part 2, p. 68; G. W. Noble, *Behold He Cometh in the Clouds*, 13–14.

81. Robert Gunn Crawford, "A History of the Kentucky Penitentiary System," 29.

82. *Barnes vs. Adams, CSS*, vol. 1432, no. 2, 41st Cong., 2nd sess., H. Misc. Doc. 13, pp. 195, 199; *KAGR*, 1:388; interview with William B. Eversole, January 15, 1898, *JJDD*, reel 2, p. 2146; Speed, Pirtle, and Kelly, *The Union Regiments of Kentucky*, 251–59; *The Union Army*, 356.

83. As of 1847, it had the only post office outside of the county seat. It was close enough to towns in other counties for regular commerce so residents of the community and its surroundings had only to visit Jackson on court days. Twenty years after the war, there was a failed proposal to make it county seat for a new county. *MVB*, January 24, 1884; *SIJ*, January 25, 1884; *KAGR*, 2:786–87; *The Kentucky State Gazetteer and Business Directory for 1879–1880*, microfilm reel S92-68, p. 133, KLSCA; Rolff, *Strong Family of Virginia and Other Southern States*, 91, 93–94.

84. Speed, Pirtle, and Kelly, *The Union Regiments of Kentucky*, 257–58; *Cincinnati Press*, December 28, 1861; *Richmond Climax*, August 31, 1898.

85. Although Strong's grandfather had opposed members of the Amis family decades before during the brief but violent Clay County Cattle War, this apparently had little bearing on his willingness to join forces with members of the family during the war, further suggesting that, just as family loyalty was only one among multiple factors that influenced wartime loyalties, past familial enmities were put aside in the interest of mutual political interests. Nevertheless, those who wished to lessen the war's apparent impact on mountain society preferred to begin the story of Bloody Breathitt with the miniscule cattle war rather than the American Civil War. Therefore, when William Strong ran afoul of Wiley Amis after the war (as will be shown in the following chapter), their ensuing "feud" was attributed to a conflict that began and ended before their births

rather than the political rift that formed between them in their own lifetimes. G. W. Noble, *Behold He Cometh in the Clouds*, 30; Pudup, "Land before Coal," 292; interview with Anderson Combs, April 26, 1898, *JJDD*, reel 3, pp. 2267–73; E. L. Noble, *Bloody Breathitt*, 2:37; Strong Family Papers, Breathitt County Public Library; U.S. War Department, *Official Army Register of the Volunteer Force of the United States Army*, 1236; Perrin, Battle, and Kniffin, *Kentucky*, 728.

86. *Bismarck Daily Tribune*, October 18, 1894.

87. *AGACK: Passed at December Session, 1845* (Frankfort: A. G. Hodges, 1846), 16.

88. E. Polk Johnson, *A History of Kentucky and Kentuckians*, 368; Sutherland, *A Savage Conflict*, 220.

89. Clements, *History of the First Regiment of Infantry*, 148.

90. Although a local account that was generally sympathetic to Strong's enemies suggested that he had deserted the Fourteenth Kentucky Cavalry, records show that Strong was given official authorized leave from the unit. His official connection to the Three Forks Battalion bears this out as well. This is an important distinction since many of his actions in the latter part of the war that inspired much of his reputation as a brigand, murderer, and "feudist" were performed under the auspices of the Federal government. Suggestions that Strong had deserted the Union army were one of many attempts to depoliticize his memory. *Barnes vs. Adams, CSS*, vol. 1432, no. 2, 41st Cong., 2nd sess., H. Misc. Doc. 13, pp. 195, 199, 630; *SIJ*, February 16, 1892; *HMC*, April 1, 1892; *KHJ, 1876*, 1199; *KAGR*, 1:388–89; G. W. Noble, *Behold He Cometh in the Clouds*, 23–24.

The Three Forks Battalion was one of ten battalions within the "1st Regiment of Capital Guards" created by the Kentucky legislature in January 1864, and authorized by Secretary of War Edwin Stanton the following May, to suppress the state's internal "guerrilla evil" once major invasions from the south had trailed off. *Barnes vs. Adams, CSS*, vol. 1432, no. 2, 41st Cong., 2nd sess., H. Misc. Doc. 13, pp. 195, 202, 630, 646–47; G. W. Noble, *Behold He Cometh in the Clouds*, 23; *KAGR*, 1:388–89; Charles C. Wells, *1890 Special Veterans' Census for Eastern Kentucky*, 52, 228; *JJDD*, reel 92, p. 2146; *The Union Army*, 360; Burch, *Owsley County*, 36.

91. *Annual Report of the Auditor of the State of Kentucky*, 191; *AGACK: Passed at December Session, 1865* (Frankfort: A. G. Hodges, 1865), 272; Speed, Pirtle, and Kelly, *The Union Regiments of Kentucky*, 693; *The Union Army*, 360; Coulter and Connelley, *History of Kentucky*, 4:276; Burch, *Owsley County*, 36.

92. Sutherland, *A Savage Conflict*, 222–24; Ramage and Watkins, *Kentucky Rising*, 317–24; Coulter, *The Civil War and Readjustment in Kentucky*, 184–88, 228–38.

93. For "peer pressure" as an analogy for the intimacy of guerrillaism, see Kilcullen, *The Accidental Guerrilla*, 201.

94. *LCJ*, December 3, 1878.

95. Quote from "H. Hawkins, Colonel Fifth Kentucky Regiment [Confederate] to Provisional Governor R. Hawes, November 23, 1862," in *War of the Rebellion*, series

1, vol. 20, part 2, *CSS*, issue 2575 (1889), 451; Burch, *Owsley County*, 36; E. L. Noble, *Bloody Breathitt*, 2:5–6 (quote).

96. *Breathitt County Slave Schedules, 1860*, KHS; *Breathitt County Tax Books, 1861*, KHS.

97. *Morse v. South et al.*, Circuit Court D of Kentucky, April 15, 1897, *The Federal Reporter*, 80:208–9.

98. Ronald Lewis, *Transforming the Appalachian Countryside*, 27–28. The assumption that belief in "tradition" is shorthand for resistance against market economics as a determinant of border state loyalties during the Civil War is found in Thelen, *Paths of Resistance*, 59–62. See also Martin Crawford, *Ashe County's Civil War*, 125–33.

99. William Davis and Swentnor, *Bluegrass Confederate*, 246.

100. "Unionist Highlanders" were said by one historian to have "disliked Negroes as well as slavery." Paludan, *Victims*, 59.

101. Slave assistance to regular Unionists was not unheard of in other parts of the South. See McCurry, *Confederate Reckoning*, 290; Jenkins and Stauffer, *The State of Jones*, 88–90; Storey, "'I'd Rather Go to Hell,'" 70–82; William Davis and Swentnor, *Bluegrass Confederate*, 254.

102. G. W. Noble, *Behold He Cometh in the Clouds*, 9; William Davis and Swentnor, *Bluegrass Confederate*, 461, 464. This "treachery" apparently did not surprise mountain native George Noble. The mobile nature of mountain agricultural labor afforded slaves a freedom of movement and lack of surveillance, two things rarely enjoyed by slaves in the plantation South. See Sprague, "The Kentucky Pocket Plantation," 77–79, 84. The county's 1860 slave schedules reveal a large number of manumitted slaves living alongside those still in bondage, further contributing to their physical mobility and the covert conveyance of information. By 1860, more than half of Breathitt County's slave-owning households were also home to manumitted slaves. *Breathitt County Slave Schedules, 1860*, KHS. For the importance of relationships between slaves and free blacks as resistance networks, see Hahn, *A Nation under Our Feet*, 57–61.

103. Williams, *Appalachia*, 109–10.

104. At least one former Strong slave, Sam Strong, "who was with the Captain in all his wars," was still part of this arrangement at the time of William Strong's death in 1897. *Lexington Herald*, May 11, 1897. William Strong's decades-long bond with his former slaves and their families was indeed unique. However, there is documentation of Unionist slaveholders in other parts of the South employing their chattel as spies and saboteurs against Rebel neighbors. See Storey, *Loyalty and Loss*, 140–51; Herbert W. Spencer, "Captain Bill's January Raid."

105. E. L. Noble, *Bloody Breathitt*, 2:56; WPA, *In the Land of Breathitt*, 59.

106. Interview with Samuel Strong Jr., July 1973, AOHP, no. 280, pp. 2–3.

107. *Lexington Herald*, May 11, 1897.

108. *Breathitt County Tax Books, 1861*, KHS.

109. *Barnes vs. Adams*, *CSS*, vol. 1432, no. 2, 41st Cong., 2nd sess., H. Misc. Doc. 13, pp. 172, 202, 630.

110. Ibid., 172, 202; *KAGR*, 1:388; Charles C. Wells, *1890 Special Veterans' Census for Eastern Kentucky*, 223, 228; Kilburn and McIntosh Family Files, Breathitt County Public Library; *KAGR*, 1:388; Speed, Pirtle, and Kelly, *The Union Regiments of Kentucky*, 257. The act of switching sides was not unheard of, especially in the mountains. However, in most recorded cases, enrollment in either Union or Confederate forces involved the draft but was not as coercive as it supposedly was in Kilburn's case. Williams, *Appalachia*, 163.

111. E. L. Noble, *Bloody Breathitt*, 2:56, 82.

112. Lincoln, "Memoir," 13, William E. Lincoln Papers, Founders and Founding Collection, HLSCA. Freeman was a Breathitt County surname long associated with biraciality or racial ambiguity. Years after Hiram dropped off the historical record, a nephew or grandson named Henry Freeman was identified as a "half-breed negro" who, because he "always associated with white people," was typically identified as white in and around Jackson. *Lexington Herald*, April 23, 1907. For Freeman's military service, see *KAGR*, 1:388; Speed, Pirtle, and Kelly, *The Union Regiments of Kentucky*, 257; Charles C. Wells, *1890 Special Veterans' Census for Eastern Kentucky*, 239.

113. Sharfstein, *The Invisible Line*, 43–44; Manual Ray Spencer, *The Descendants of Joseph Spencer*, 325.

114. *Freeman v. Strong and Others*, Appeal from Circuit Court, Clay County, April 20, 1838, Records of the Court of Appeals of Kentucky, KDLA. Among the nineteenth-century Kentucky county's most coercive constitutional powers was the ability to assign orphaned minors into forced apprenticeships, a practice that was used most often with free blacks. Poor children, black and white, were commonly bound to farmers and artisans to learn the "art and mystery" of various trades. Hollingsworth, "'Mrs. Boone, I presume?'" 128n.

115. Sharfstein, *The Invisible Line*, 51.

116. *Ninth Census of the United States, 1870*, KHS.

117. G. W. Noble, *Behold He Cometh in the Clouds*, 55.

118. Phillip Gosse, *The History of Piracy*, 1–2; E. L. Noble, *Bloody Breathitt*, 2:56; WPA, *In the Land of Breathitt*, 59.

119. Strong benefited from a sociopolitical dynamic common to all civil wars, in which command positions are extended to the individuals most willing to commit violent acts. Kalyvas, *The Logic of Violence in Civil War*, 57–58.

120. Fellman, *Inside War*, 23.

121. After the possibility of forcibly swaying Kentucky toward the Confederacy proved to be a lost cause after 1862, most of the state's pro-Confederate resources were concentrated around the Virginia-Tennessee line in the interest of protecting the mines of Saltville, Virginia, and the vital Virginia-Tennessee Railroad from federal capture. Ramsey, *The Raid*, 147–54.

122. "Marshall to General S. Cooper, January 20, 1862," in *War of the Rebellion*, vol. 17, p. 53 (quote); Burch, *Owsley County*, 37.

123. Sutherland, *A Savage Conflict*, 155–56.

124. "To the People of Estelle and Adjoining Counties," broadside, John Hunt Morgan Papers, 1840–1870, 1890, Southern Historical Collection, Wilson Library, University of North Carolina. See also *Louisville Daily Journal*, January 29, 1863. Morgan had visited Breathitt County at least as early as 1856 to retrieve a lost horse. *Lexington Leader,* October 7, 1958; Bull, "Writings on Kentucky History, 1958," 241.

125. *Louisville Daily Journal,* January 29, 1863; *Abingdon Virginian,* July 3, 1863 (quote).

126. McKnight, *The Civil War in Appalachian Kentucky and Virginia,* 225–26; Jess D. Wilson, *When They Hanged the Fiddler,* 75; Preston, *The Civil War in the Big Sandy Valley of Kentucky,* 24. Jackson County, located just west of the Three Forks region, was the only county in the state said not to have produced a single Confederate recruit while being drained of "every male under sixty years of age, and over fifteen" for the Union. On the western edge of the Cumberland Plateau, Jackson County nevertheless became an oft-cited piece of evidence for southern mountain Unionism. It trailed only neighboring Owsley County in the percentage of its military-age population recruited by Federal forces and contributed 25 percent of its votes to Lincoln in the 1860 presidential election, by far the highest county-level margin for Lincoln in the state. In 1864 it was the only Kentucky county Lincoln managed to carry. *TAPR, 1867,* 59; Fox, "The Southern Mountaineer," 389; Rossiter, *Parties and Politics in America,* 85–86; *Louisville Daily Journal,* April 20, 1863; Storke, *A Complete History of the Great American Rebellion,* 1575–76; Dalton, "Brig. General Humphrey Marshall," 192.

127. *Barnes vs. Adams, CSS,* vol. 1432, no. 2, 41st Cong., 2nd sess., H. Misc. Doc. 13, p. 172.

128. Interview with Wood Lyttle, April 13, 1898, *JJDD,* reel 2, pp. 2242–43; G. W. Noble, *Behold He Cometh in the Clouds,* 14.

129. Sutherland, *A Savage Conflict,* 159–60.

130. "H. Hawkins, Colonel Fifth Kentucky Regiment [Confederate] to Provisional Governor R. Hawes, November 23, 1862," 451.

131. Herbert W. Spencer, "Captain Bill's January Raid."

132. Ash, *When the Yankees Came,* 64. In guerrilla settings, civilian populations, even those with little or no direct connection to fighting forces, act as a "support system" for partisans in providing provisions, intelligence, or refuge. Wickham-Crowley, "Terror and Guerrilla Warfare in Latin America," 225.

133. Vahabi, *The Political Economy of Destructive Power,* 69–70.

134. Though the crime was blamed on "rebel outlaws," implying a pro-Confederate act, the county's Confederate identity was well established and notorious, enough so that it could well have been perpetrated by Unionist Kentuckians. *AGACK, 1864* (Frankfort: Wm. E. Hughes, 1864), 365–66.

135. *Haddix, adm'r, vs Chambers & Little, April 26, 1868,* in W. P. D. Bush, reporter, *Reports of Selected Civil and Criminal Cases decided in the Court of Appeals of Kentucky,* 172–73.

136. As has been the case in many other wars, desertion during the American Civil War was a communal phenomenon. Confederate units with large numbers of soldiers from the same community were more prone to desertion than units made up of men recruited from disparate areas. Bearman, "Desertion as Localism," 340.

137. *Barnes vs. Adams, CSS,* vol. 1432, no. 2, 41st Cong., 2nd sess., H. Misc. Doc. 13, pp. 199–202, 204–6, 211–18, 645–48.

138. *KAGR,* 210–13; Strong Family Papers, 82, Breathitt County Public Library. Thomas Hargis notably stayed with the Fifth Infantry. He received a captain's commission and was captured four times. After the war he returned to Kentucky but did not resettle in Breathitt County. McAfee, *Kentucky Politicians,* 74–75.

139. Kalyvas, *The Logic of Violence in Civil War,* 382–87.

140. The "parochialization" of civil war takes place when extensions of a national conflict are acted out in an enclosed location. Local issues come to take precedence over national ones as the basis for conflict such that there is a "shift in meaning from the *great* to the *little* tradition" (my emphasis). Aikman's patrons, the South family, retained their national concerns in fighting for the Confederacy, namely, the upholding of "southern rights," but they were equally concerned with maintaining order and a modicum of political uniformity within their county. Although Aikman continued to fight under the Souths' leadership (or at least the leadership of Jerry South Jr.), his return to wage a more localized war against individuals with whom he was probably socially acquainted prior to the war represented a means by which local interests (i.e., the political and economic primacy of his patrons, the South family) came to eclipse abstractions like "southern rights" espoused by the patrons themselves. See James C. Scott, "Protest and Profanation," 220–22. For "people's war," see Cooling, "A People's War," 117–18.

141. G. W. Noble, *Behold He Cometh in the Clouds,* 59; E. L. Noble, *Bloody Breathitt,* 2:14–15 (quote).

142. Fellman, *Inside War,* 254.

143. Kalyvas, *The Logic of Violence in Civil War,* 83, 330–36; Ash, *When the Yankees Came,* 125 (quote).

144. Jess D. Wilson, *When They Hanged the Fiddler,* 75–76.

145. *Lexington Observer and Reporter,* April 18, 1863; *Louisville Journal,* April 20, 1863; Dalton, "Brig. General Humphrey Marshall," 192; Perry, *Jack May's War,* 63–65.

146. Lewis Collins, *Historical Sketches of Kentucky,* 673; Burch, *Owsley County,* 35.

147. *Washington National Republican,* April 27, 1863; Thos. L. Wilson, *Sufferings Endured for a Free Government,* 98–100. Storke and Brockett, *A Complete History of the Great American Rebellion,* 1575–76.

148. Jess D. Wilson, *When They Hanged the Fiddler,* 75.

149. G. W. Noble, *Behold He Cometh in the Clouds,* 32. *Scout,* in wartime parlance, described an unenlisted partisan. It was a term just vague enough for Strong to use to justify attacking civilians he suspected of subversive activity. Sutherland, *A Savage Conflict,* xi.

150. Henry C. Hurst to William L. Hurst, March 2, 1865, in Hurst, *Hursts of Shenandoah,* 102.

151. *KTY,* December 22, 1878.

152. Whether or not Barnett's purported innocence alluded to his being nonpartisan or nonmilitary was not revealed. G. W. Noble, *Behold He Cometh in the Clouds,* 32, 78.

153. Noble's age and the minimal threat he represented may also have weighed upon Strong's decision. Ibid., 35–36.

154. Said a Confederate veteran of the "secret rebel" Wilson Callahan: "He always told me he was a mighty good rebel; and whilst I was in the rebel army he gave me all the information he could. He would tell me where the Union forces were, and how many, and directed me how to manage." After the war, according to a "common rumor in the country . . . [Wiley Amis] was writing backwards and forwards to the rebels whilst he was a lieutenant in the Union army." Considering his postwar politics, his (as will be covered in the following chapter) collusion with Wilson Callahan, and his eventual violent break with his former ally William Strong, it is highly possible that Amis was himself a "secret rebel." On the other hand, as shown in the following chapter, Amis's postwar change in politics was also influenced by his disillusionment over the results of Union victory, a disillusionment shared by many Kentucky Unionists. *Barnes vs. Adams, CSS,* vol. 1432, no. 2, 41st Cong., 2nd sess., H. Misc. Doc. 13, pp. 169 (quote), 191, 195, 198.

155. G. W. Noble, *Behold He Cometh in the Clouds,* 54 (quote); Rolff, *Strong Family of Virginia and Other Southern States,* 96.

156. G. W. Noble, *Behold He Cometh in the Clouds,* 84.

157. *Barnes vs. Adams, CSS,* vol. 1432, no. 2, 41st Cong., 2nd sess., H. Misc. Doc. 13, p. 200; *KTY,* January 7, 1879; *Trimble et al. v. Spicer et al.,* October 17, 1900, Court of Appeals of Kentucky, *SWR,* vol. 58 (August 6–December 3, 1900), 579; Strong Family Papers, 111, Breathitt County Public Library; Ed Porter Thompson, *History of the Orphan Brigade,* 746; Herbert W. Spencer, "Captain Bill's January Raid"; McKnight, *The Civil War in Appalachian Kentucky and Virginia,* 225–26.

158. G. W. Noble, *Behold He Cometh in the Clouds,* 62; Rolff, *Strong Family of Virginia and Other Southern States,* 111.

159. Only 95 men voted in favor of Bramlette out of a total 142 votes counted, a fraction of the usual voter turnout in the county but more than enough to give the Union candidate a considerable majority. Over the next two years of the war, the small number of extant returns suggests that Democratic ballots were virtually forbidden from being cast. *TAPR, 1862,* 61; *1863,* 60; *1864,* 59; *1866,* 59; *1867,* 57; Ernest Collins, "Political Behavior in Breathitt, Knott, Perry and Leslie Counties," 63.

160. *Barnes vs. Adams, CSS,* vol. 1432, no. 2, 41st Cong., 2nd sess., H. Misc. Doc. 13, p. 195; interview with William B. Eversole, January 15, 1898, *JJDD,* reel 2, p. 2145; G. W. Noble, *Behold He Cometh in the Clouds,* 53–54.

161. *Wm. M. Combs agst. Capt. William Strong, Wiley Amis and Other Defendants, 1867–1869; Wm. M. Combs agst. Hiram Freeman and Jason Little, 1867–1869; William Strong Sr. vs. Wilson Callahan & comp.*, May 15, 1867, Breathitt County Circuit Court Records, KDLA.

162. Rhyne, "Rehearsal for Redemption," 180–95.

163. Blight, *Race and Reunion,* 381–83.

164. Kalyvas, *The Logic of Violence in Civil War,* 38–48.

165. Rolt-Wheeler, *The Boy with the U.S. Census,* 23; Lewis Franklin Johnson, *Famous Kentucky Tragedies and Trials,* 320; Clements, *History of the First Regiment of Infantry,* 147; Haney, *The Mountain People of Kentucky,* 77.

166. Altsheler, *In Circling Camps,* 125.

167. Foote, *The Civil War,* 1002.

168. Kalyvas, *The Logic of Violence in Civil War,* 21, 71.

169. As subjective as definitions of guerrillaism may be, the prevailing ideas in military science at the time of the Civil War considered Forrest's tactics those of a "partisan" rather than a guerrilla. This was a distinction made not by virtue of Forrest's style of fighting but by his formal relationship to the Confederate war machine; Geiger, *Financial Fraud and Guerilla Violence in Missouri's Civil War,* 103–4.

170. Lewis Collins and Collins, *Collins' Historical Sketches of Kentucky,* 110.

171. E. Polk Johnson, *A History of Kentucky and Kentuckians,* 368.

172. Coulter, *The Civil War and Readjustment in Kentucky,* 228–29. Coulter did, however, consider the possibility that the Confederate high command did not look upon guerrillas "with any great degree of aversion."

173. Stiles, *Jesse James,* 81–82, 95–97.

174. Lord, *The Effect of Secession upon the Commercial Relations between the North and South,* 75–76. During the Deep South's secession in the winter of 1861, another author predicted that mountaineers would stall the Upper South from following suit. "Their interests are more directly opposed than those between the Cotton States and the extreme North, because the wide distance that separates the latter renders them independent of each other, while the Cotton States are seeking, by every possible means, to drag all the Slave States with them, for the purpose of compelling them to share their burdens, and of giving greater strength and dignity to their cause." "Southern Aids to the North," 242. This was only partially true. The Bluegrass, the section of the state with the largest number of slaves and slaveholders, had spotty interest in secession. In fact, it was the section of the state that produced the most vocal spokesmen (including Senator Crittenden) for trying to compromise: combining the continuance of slavery with the preservation of the Union. For an example of a historical verification of this exaggeration, see Robert L. Kincaid, "Lincoln Allegiance in the Southern Appalachians," 164–79.

175. This image was important for comfortable reconciliation between the sections as well as the expansion of (as will be discussed more broadly in a later chapter) the postwar discourse on the region's supposed Anglo-Saxon purity. Silber, *The Romance*

of Reunion, 143–47; Noe, "'Deadened Color and Colder Horror,'" 77–80; Batteau, *The Invention of Appalachia,* 77.

176. Warner, "Comments on Kentucky," 263. See also E. L. Noble, *Bloody Breathitt,* 1:270–71.

177. Emma M. Connelly, *The Story of Kentucky,* 268.

178. Ibid., 266–67.

179. Spaulding, *The Men of the Mountains,* 47.

180. Brooks, "Back to Dixie, a Hard Trip," 58.

181. E. L. Noble, *Bloody Breathitt,* 2:11.

182. Shaler, *Kentucky,* 405.

183. Hoffer, *The Caning of Charles Sumner,* 133.

184. As will be detailed in the following chapter, after Kentucky's Unionists had lost control over state government, Jeremiah South was reappointed as penitentiary lessee and remained in that position until just prior to his death in 1880. Rockenbach, "'The Weeds and the Flowers Are Closely Mixed,'" 1–2; Robert Gunn Crawford, "A History of the Kentucky Penitentiary System," 24, 29.

3. "The war spirit was high"

1. As Brian McKnight has made clear, the finality represented by the surrender at Appomattox was of limited significance in eastern Kentucky. Although news of the Confederacy's defeat spread quickly, there was no assurance that fighting would end in an area where ties to both sides were often tenuous. McKnight, *The Civil War in Appalachian Kentucky and Virginia,* 231–34.

2. Stealey, *Twenty Years in the Press Gallery,* 208.

3. Woodward, *Origins of the New South,* 6. E. Merton Coulter's *The Civil War and Readjustment in Kentucky,* the classic yet dated history of the state during the 1860s and 1870s, maintains the essentially pro-Confederate, white supremacist character of Kentucky politics during Reconstruction and suggests that the state's failure to join other states in secession was essentially a mistake that did not reflect the general will of white Kentuckians. Liberal historians, reacting to Coulter's neo-Confederate sympathies, later downplayed Kentucky's postwar conservatism. Ross Webb's revisionist *Kentucky in the Reconstruction Era* explains the state's lack of cooperation with postwar federal policies as resistance to unwelcome federal authority rather than genuine adherence to the Lost Cause. Thomas Connelly ("Neo-Confederatism or Power Vacuum") also deemphasized the importance of race and the Confederate memory in the years following the war; after 1865 Kentuckians were supposedly more caught up in sectional competition over internal resources and railroad construction than in issues relating to the recent war. By the mid-1870s the "New Departure" school of political thought, favored by the state's development-minded Democrats, had led the state into an era of relative prosperity unmatched by the rest of the South due to greater cooperation with northern interests. In Connelly's interpretation, as a state Kentucky was therefore detached

from the ravages of Reconstruction disorder. Considering Coulter's overt Confederate sympathies, both Webb's and Connelly's revisions are understandable. But by taking a more local approach, and one that does not depend as heavily upon evidence from the Bluegrass as a supposed "Kentucky writ large," historians have more recently described a Kentucky countryside rife with counterrevolutionary violence against both blacks and white Unionists, suggesting that Kentucky's postwar Confederate sympathies have been underestimated since Coulter's time. Rhyne, "'We Are Mobed and Beat'"; Crane, "'The Rebels Are Bold, Defiant, and Unscrupulous in Their Dementions of All Men.'" See also Marshall, *Creating a Confederate Kentucky*, 55–80.

4. Marshall, *Creating a Confederate Kentucky*, 20.

5. Slavery was eventually outlawed in the state's 1890 constitution. Wright, *Racial Violence in Kentucky*, 27.

6. Foner, *Reconstruction*, 37.

7. Coulter, *The Civil War and Readjustment in Kentucky*, 199–200.

8. Astor, "Rebels on the Border," 10–16, 255–56.

9. Patrick A. Lewis, "The Democratic Partisan Militia and the Black Peril," 145–47; Berlin et al., "The Destruction of Slavery, 1861–1865," 4, 66–67, 73–74, 173–74; Coulter, *The Civil War and Readjustment in Kentucky*, 258–61, 316, 420–23; Ross Webb, "Kentucky," 27.

10. Quoted in Tapp and Klotter, *Kentucky*, 22. Since then, historians have placed Kentucky's political turn slightly earlier. As conservative historian E. Merton Coulter semifamously wrote in 1926, the state seemingly "seceded in 1865" (*The Civil War and Readjustment in Kentucky*, 334). See also Ireland, *Little Kingdoms*, 53.

11. Astor, "Rebels on the Border," 143–44.

12. *LCJ*, December 25, 1868, quoted in Prichard, "Popular Political Movements in Kentucky," 7.

13. *KTY*, December 2, 1865.

14. Ibid.; Tapp and Klotter, *Kentucky*, 10–14; Curry, *Radicalism, Racism, and Party Realignment*. On the other hand, E. Merton Coulter makes the questionable claim that the true Republican Party was not established in Kentucky until 1871, when the party's conservative faction wrested control from radicals. This does not take away from the fact that both factions, under one name or another, had existed in the state since 1865 (and, arguably, even before then under the name "Unconditional Unionists"). Coulter, *The Civil War and Readjustment in Kentucky*, 272–86, 433–34.

15. Astor, "Rebels on the Border," 255–56, 266–67, 271–75.

16. Marshall, "'The Rebel Spirit in Kentucky,'" 64.

17. At its inception the Freedmen's Bureau was limited to the rebellious states. But passage of the Thirteenth Amendment was followed by recognition of the need for the bureau in Kentucky as well. The relatively small African American population in Kentucky and its resultant impact upon the electorate was also a hindrance to the

organization. *House Executive Document,* no. 11, 39th Cong., 1st sess., p. 31, Ireland, *Little Kingdoms,* 70.

18. Robert Gunn Crawford, "A History of the Kentucky Penitentiary System," 29.

19. *LCJ,* February 10, 1880.

20. *Legislative Document No. 18,* 9–82; *KSJ, 1880,* 39–47; *AAC* 4 (1886): 539–40; Tapp, "Three Decades of Kentucky Politics," 197–206; Baird, *Luke Pryor Blackburn,* 78 (quote); Ireland, *Little Kingdoms,* 82–83.

21. *FRA,* April 17, 1880; *HMC,* April 23, 1880; Baird, *Luke Pryor Blackburn,* 86–88.

22. The most dramatic change was the adoption of a salaried warden to replace the graft-ridden lessee position. Robert Gunn Crawford, "A History of the Kentucky Penitentiary System," 59–62, 122–25, 130; Tapp and Klotter, *Kentucky,* 178–82; Baird, *Luke Pryor Blackburn,* 88.

23. Astor, "Rebels on the Border," 162–70.

24. *Nation,* November 1, 1866; *AAC* 3 (1869): 421–22; Dubois, *Black Reconstruction in America,* 568; Astor, "Rebels on the Border," 9, 162, 218–19, 280–81; Coulter, *The Civil War and Readjustment in Kentucky,* 359, 361; Ross Webb, *Kentucky in the Reconstruction Era,* 25.

25. From the 1870s until the 1920s, Kentucky had more white lynching victims than any state east of the Mississippi River. Wright, *Racial Violence in Kentucky,* 307–11. See also Rhyne, "'We Are Mobed and Beat'"; Crane, "'The Rebels Are Bold, Defiant, and Unscrupulous in Their Dementions of All Men'"; Przybyszewski, "The Dissents of John Marshall Harlan I," 154–55; Coulter, *The Civil War and Readjustment in Kentucky,* 359, 361; Marshall, *Creating a Confederate Kentucky,* 59.

26. Dunaway, *African-American Family,* 247.

27. McKnight, *Contested Borderland,* 229.

28. J. W. Alvord to General O. O. Howard, January 29, 31, 1870, in Alvord, *Letters from the South,* 39.

29. *NYT,* November 12, 1870. While this may have been intentionally hyperbolic, many historical studies show a record of Reconstruction-era oppression on par with the Deep South, even though the stakes for conservative whites (i.e., the prospect of Negro political domination) were considerably lower. See Pem Davidson Buck, *Worked to the Bone;* Wright, *Racial Violence in Kentucky;* Victor B. Howard, *Black Liberation in Kentucky;* Lucas. *A History of Blacks in Kentucky.*

30. *Cincinnati Commercial,* May 31, 1867; Sumner, *Charles Sumner,* 200–202; Coulter, *The Civil War and Readjustment in Kentucky,* 334.

31. *McConnelsville Conservative,* January 20, 1871.

32. Kentucky's August 1870 elections were the first statewide balloting in which black men participated. Patrick A. Lewis, "The Democratic Partisan Militia and the Black Peril," 148. In his study of lynching, George C. Wright discovered that one-third of Kentucky's recorded lynchings happened between 1865 and 1875, preceding the national numerical peak by nearly two decades. The state's experience with the phenomenon suggests

a heightened correlation between lynching and counterrevolutionary attacks on black citizenship (when lynching became far more widespread in the post-Reconstruction South, after black southerners were roundly denied the ballot, victims were most often men accused of murder or rape). Wright, *Racial Violence in Kentucky,* 8, 309–11.

33. *AAC* 3 (1867): 422; Emma M. Connelly, *The Story of Kentucky,* 258–59, 317–21.

34. Lewis Collins and Collins, *Collins' Historical Sketches of Kentucky,* 183–84.

35. Foner, *Reconstruction,* 434. One 1872 testimony to a joint congressional committee illustrates the clear extrapolitical value of the concept of feud and one example of its being used to make the political appear communal. A congressman asked a Cleveland County, North Carolina, resident to explain a series of affrays between two planter brothers he had witnessed in recent months. The witness answered that, even though one brother was a Republican and one a Democrat and their enmity had begun with the close of the war, it was impossible to determine whether their rupture was related to the local "bad feeling" between the parties or was "merely a family feud" (the witness indicated that he considered the latter more likely). It was admitted that the Republican brother had been attacked by a body of men in a clear attempt to dispatch a dissident scalawag, but the witness repeated his invocation of "family feud" twice more. *Testimony Taken by the Joint Select Committee to Inquire into the Condition of Affairs in the Late Insurrectionary States,* 306–7. See also Fleming, *Documentary History of Reconstruction,* 690–93; *Louisiana Affairs,* 384.

36. Thorpe, *The Constitutional History of the United States,* 323.

37. Cooling, "After the Horror," 357.

38. Hahn, *A Nation under our Feet,* 280–82; Rable, *But There Was No Peace,* 85–86.

39. Tapp, "Three Decades of Kentucky Politics," 12–13.

40. Albert Deane Richardson and Hanby, *The Secret Service,* 168; Thomas Louis Owen, "The Formative Years of Kentucky's Republican Party," 63.

41. *KTY,* March 17, 1871.

42. Ibid., January 2, 1866.

43. *LCJ,* October 9, 1874; Patrick A. Lewis, "The Democratic Partisan Militia and the Black Peril," 150–51.

44. (Columbia, SC) *Phoenix,* March 26, 1868; J. W. Alvord to General O. O. Howard, January 29, 31, 1870, in Alvord, *Letters from the South,* 37–39; *AAC* 10 (1871): 426–27; Rable, *But There Was No Peace,* 93; Tapp and Klotter, *Kentucky,* 8–10, 49–50, 381–85; Foner, *Reconstruction,* 428.

45. Patrick A. Lewis, "The Democratic Partisan Militia and the Black Peril," 146–49; Astor, "Rebels on the Border," 221.

46. *Testimony Taken by the Joint Select Committee to Inquire into the Condition of Affairs in the Late Insurrectionary States,* 1278; *NYT,* August 25, December 10, 1871, April 18, August 11, 1873; Fitzgerald, "Extralegal Violence and the Planter Class," 155–68; Hahn, *A Nation under our Feet,* 267 (quote); Trelease, *White Terror,* 51; Foner, *Reconstruction,* 425.

47. Coulter, quoted in Tapp and Klotter, *Kentucky*, 381. For more on unspoken complicity between the Klan and southern Democrats, see Perman, *The Road to Redemption*, 34–36, 63–64; Zuczek, *State of Rebellion*, 51–62.

48. *HGH*, May 20, 1897; *LCJ*, May 10, 1897; *NYT*, September 13, 1897; Severance, *Tennessee's Radical Army*, xi; Rable, *But There Was No Peace*, 111; Patrick A. Lewis, "The Democratic Partisan Militia and the Black Peril," 147–50; Luntz, *Forgotten Turmoil*, 20–64; Wright, *Racial Violence in Kentucky*, 19; Ireland, *Little Kingdoms*, 85–89; Trelease, *White Terror*, 89. The Ku Klux Klan's appearance in Breathitt County in the 1890s, at a time when it was virtually nonexistent anywhere else, is covered in a later chapter.

49. *NYT*, September 10, 1874; Rable, *But There Was No Peace*, 70 (quote), 95 (quote). For the relationship between the Democratic Party and the Ku Klux Klan of the 1860s and 1870s, see Tracy Campbell, *Deliver the Vote*, 58–59; Foner, *Reconstruction*, 343–45, 427–42; Trelease, *White Terror*, 283–84n; Astor, "Rebels on the Border," 265–66.

50. Blight, *Race and Reunion*, 122 (quote); Trelease, *White Terror*, 49–50.

51. Parsons, "Klan Skepticism and Denial in Reconstruction-Era Public Discourse," 68–71.

52. "Notes on Kentucky and Tennessee," 134; Shaler, *Kentucky*, 369. See also *LCJ*, August 13, 1870; Coulter, *The Civil War and Readjustment in Kentucky*, 361.

53. Henry Watterson was the chief advocate of the southern Democracy's "New Departure" sect, one that "advocated relinquishing any sectional animosities and racial conservatism that might hinder business and counseled acceptance of the Reconstruction amendments." Anne E. Marshall, *Creating a Confederate Kentucky*, 52 (quote)–54.

54. *LCJ*, August 13, 1870. For Watterson's conciliatory tone during and after Reconstruction, see Gaston, *The New South Creed*, 92–99; Sullivan, "Louisville and Her Southern Alliance," 239–64.

55. *LCJ*, March 14, December 2, 1870. See also Friedman, *The White Savage*, 40. Watterson's opposition to the "Bourbons" of his party was based upon his moderate public pronouncements on race, one of the primary planks of his paper's "New Departure" platform. However, as a conservative often mistaken for a progressive by white editors farther south, Watterson often preferred that the less said about race the better, especially before the cessation of Reconstruction. Woodward, *Origins of the New South*, 6; Osthaus, *Partisans of the Southern Press*, 152–54; Anne E. Marshall, *Creating a Confederate Kentucky*, 69–71.

56. *AAC* 11 (1872): 174.

57. Wheatley, "Correspondence," 26.

58. Merrill, "The Invisible Empire," 199.

59. *Louisville Commercial*, June 15, 1870.

60. *LCJ*, December 17, 1888.

61. Coulter, *The Civil War and Readjustment in Kentucky*, 365.

62. Ibid., 364; Anne E. Marshall, *Creating a Confederate Kentucky*, 68.

63. *NYT*, December 15, 1878; Ireland, *Little Kingdoms*, 85–86.

64. Schulte-Bockholt, *The Politics of Organized Crime and the Organized Crime of Politics*, 201–4. For Max Weber's definition of the state as an organization or body that holds a "monopoly of legitimate use of physical force within a given territory," see *From Max Weber*, 78–79.

65. Preston, *The Civil War in the Big Sandy Valley of Kentucky*, 86–91.

66. G. W. Noble, *Behold He Cometh in the Clouds*, 50; Blight, *Race and Reunion*, 53–54, 215–16, 382–83.

67. G. W. Noble, *Behold He Cometh in the Clouds*, 80–81.

68. *Barnes vs. Adams, CSS*, vol. 1432, no. 2, 41st Cong., 2nd sess., H. Misc. Doc. 13, p. 191.

69. *Wm. M. Combs agst. Capt. William Strong, Wiley Amis and Other Defendants, 1867–1869*; *Wm. M. Combs agst. Hiram Freeman and Jason Little, 1867–1869*; *William Strong Sr. vs. Wilson Callahan & comp.*, May 15, 1867, Breathitt County Circuit Court Records, KDLA.

70. *Barnes vs. Adams, CSS*, vol. 1432, no. 2, 41st Cong., 2nd sess., H. Misc. Doc. 13, pp. 20, 24, 58, 60, 66, 74, 80, 85, 87–89, 101, 110, 135, 165, 167, 223, 240, 292, 541, 569, 644, 647; Lewis Collins and Collins, *Collins' Historical Sketches of Kentucky*, 214; Hardy, "Some Kentucky Lawyers of the Past and Present," 310; interview with Judge Dickerson, March 9, 1898, *JJDD*, reel 2, p. 2172; Zachariah Frederick Smith, *The History of Kentucky*, 773–74 (quote), 802; *Review of the Financial and Political History of the State of Kentucky*, 16, 17; Decker and Jones, *Knox County Kentucky History*, 143; Hood, "For the Union," 204–5, 208–12, 214–15; Victor B. Howard, *Black Liberation in Kentucky*, 56–57, 147; E. Polk Johnson, *A History of Kentucky and Kentuckians*, 768; Perrin, Battle, and Kniffin, *Kentucky*, 957–58; Speed, Pirtle, and Kelly, *The Union Regiments of Kentucky*, 84; Gordon McKinney, *Southern Mountain Republicans*, 54.

71. G. W. Noble, *Behold He Cometh in the Clouds*, 83–84 (quote), 92.

72. Interview with Samuel Strong Jr., July 1973, AOHP, no. 280, p. 4.

73. G. W. Noble, *Behold He Cometh in the Clouds*, 84.

74. *LCJ*, January 16, 1879.

75. Ibid.

76. *Barnes vs. Adams, CSS*, vol. 1432, no. 2, 41st Cong., 2nd sess., H. Misc. Doc. 13, pp. 8–9, 18, 170.

77. Ibid., 196.

78. E. L. Noble, *Bloody Breathitt*, 2:18.

79. Ibid., 2:56; WPA, *In the Land of Breathitt*, 59.

80. *HGH*, May 10, 1894; *Lexington Herald*, May 2, 1897. James McPherson has suggested that martial participation has a politicizing effect, prompting many soldiers to conflate their initial individual or communal reasons for fighting with the war's larger calling. Strong never testified as to his opinions on the Civil War's "big picture," but the war clearly established him as a leader (in James C. Scott's phrasing, "beyond the visible end of the spectrum") among Breathitt County's black and white poor. It is doubtful

that he would have come to this position without serving in the Union army. James McPherson, *For Cause and Comrades;* Scott, *Domination and the Arts of Resistance,* 183. For a similar argument, also see Eugen Weber, *Peasants into Frenchmen.*

81. E. L. Noble, *Bloody Breathitt,* 2:7; *Barnes vs. Adams, CSS,* vol. 1432, no. 2, 41st Cong., 2nd sess., H. Misc. Doc. 13, p. 193.

82. *Barnes vs. Adams, CSS,* vol. 1432, no. 2, 41st Cong., 2nd sess., H. Misc. Doc. 13, pp. 192–93, 196.

83. Ibid., 192 (quote), 196.

84. Ibid., 18. Grant carried 25.5 percent of Kentucky's votes; Shannon and Mc-Quown, *Presidential Politics in Kentucky,* 42–44.

85. *Barnes vs. Adams, CSS,* vol. 1432, no. 2, 41st Cong., 2nd sess., H. Misc. Doc. 13, pp. 1–22; Tapp and Klotter, *Kentucky,* 21.

86. Poll results show that Democratic majorities in Breathitt County elections were permanently restored as of 1867. *TAPR, 1869,* 83; *1870,* 60; *1871,* 65; *1872,* 71; *1873,* 60; *1875,* 91. Quote from E. L. Noble, *Bloody Breathitt,* 2:26–27.

87. G. W. Noble, *Behold He Cometh in the Clouds,* 104.

88. *Barnes vs. Adams, CSS,* vol. 1432, no. 2, 41st Cong., 2nd sess., H. Misc. Doc. 13, p. 194.

89. Ibid., 194.

90. Ibid., 196. For other accounts of William Strong and his militants being described as "Red Strings," see *LCJ,* December 5, 1878, May 10, 1897; *Hopkinsville Kentuckian,* May 11, 1897; *NYT,* May 10, September 13, 1897; *Columbus Enquirer,* September 14, 1897; *Lexington Herald,* September 15, 1897; *Washington Times,* August 17, 1902; *BCN,* September 11, 1908; interview with Ebb Herald, 1973, No. 139, p. 5; interview with Harlan Strong, 1978, AOHP, nos. 279, 355, pp. 20–21; Luntz, *Forgotten Turmoil,* 58–59.

91. *Barnes vs. Adams, CSS,* vol. 1432, no. 2, 41st Cong., 2nd sess., H. Misc. Doc. 13, p. 169.

92. The "red string" used by members as a discreet emblem of membership hearkened to the biblical account of the Israelites' secret infiltration of Jericho and the red cord their collaborator, the harlot Rahab, displayed in her window to save her from slaughter. In North Carolina Red String members were said to display a small red thread on their lapel. There is no indication that Breathitt County's did the same.

For more general descriptions of the group's larger activities during the Civil War and Reconstruction (particularly in North Carolina), see *NYT,* April 29, 1867, March 11, 1871, January 31, 1882; *New York Herald,* October 6, 1867; "Midnight Gathering of a 'Red String League,'" 115; *New Hampshire Sentinel,* March 16, 1871; *Galveston News,* July 31, 1872; *Chicago Inter-Ocean,* October 1, 1880; *Raleigh News and Observer,* July 27, August 25, 1882; Fleming, *Documentary History of Reconstruction,* 334, 354; Brinsley Matthews and Pearson, *Mōnon Ou,* 39; Edward King, *The Great South,* 493; Van Noppen, *The South,* 351; Baggett, *The Scalawags,* 91 (quote); Durrill, "Political Legitimacy and Local Courts," 577–602; Scott Reynolds Nelson, *Iron Confederacies,* 102–3, 207; Scott

Reynolds Nelson, "Red Strings and Half Brothers," 37–53; Honey, "The War within the Confederacy," 55–71; Noe, "Red String Scare," 301–22; Escott, *Many Excellent People,* 64; Ellis, "The Bingham Family," 14; Auman and Scarboro, "The Heroes of America in Civil War North Carolina," 327–63; Trelease, *White Terror,* 338.

93. Van Noppen, *The South,* 351.

94. Fleming, *Documentary History of Reconstruction,* 354.

95. *Raleigh News and Observer,* July 27, August 25, 1882.

96. *Lexington Herald,* May 11, 1897.

97. Interview with Melvin Profitt, August 11, 1975, AOHP, no. 164, pp. 6–7.

98. Interviews with Ebb Herald, 1973, and Harlan Strong, 1978, AOHP, nos. 279, 355, pp. 20–21.

99. *Louisville Commercial,* December 8, 1878.

100. *Columbia Phoenix,* July 13, 1870.

101. *KTY,* December 22, 1878; *LCJ,* January 16, 1879; interview with John Aikman, July 20, 1898, *JJDD,* reel 3, pp. 2412–13; *Boston Globe,* May 10, 1897; "A Kentucky Vendetta," 3; Rolff, *Strong Family of Virginia and Other Southern States,* 93; Davison, *Davi(d)son,* 6. Callahan family history suggests that Wilson Callahan was killed by Hiram Freeman's son William and William Strong's son Flint around the same time. http://www.kykinfolk.com/breathitt/databases/edwardcallahan_mahalabrock/d3.htm (viewed March 1, 2011).

102. *Richmond Climax,* August 31, 1898.

103. Victor B. Howard, *Black Liberation in Kentucky,* 178.

104. Patrick A. Lewis, "The Democratic Partisan Militia and the Black Peril," 146–49.

105. *Louisville Commercial,* December 28, 1870 (quote); *McConnelsville Conservative,* January 20, 1871.

106. *LCJ,* July 23–25, 1871. The Klan's control over Estill County demonstrates how dramatically many previously loyal white Kentuckians became seriously aggrieved toward the federal government directly after the war. During the war Estill had been among the most pro-Union counties in the state. But in later years labor difficulties brought about by the entrance of cheap freedman labor in the county's iron mines brought about a political sea change and a fierce local attempt to rid the county of its black minority. Dunaway, *African-American Family,* 247–48; Gordon McKinney, *Southern Mountain Republicans,* 55; Trelease, *White Terror,* 316.

107. *NYT,* August 25, 1871; Trelease, *White Terror,* 316.

108. Even for white southerners who had no involvement in the Klan's original incarnations, the organization nevertheless "provid[ed] a model that other groups emulated." The costume, iconography, and reputation of the Ku Klux Klan carried enough resonance among white southerners to be sustained even within movements that had little or nothing to do with enforcing white supremacy. The original program initiated by the Klan became conflated with numerous other causes. Holmes, "Moonshining and Collective Violence," 592–93; Ireland, *Little Kingdoms,* 73–76.

109. G. W. Noble, *Behold He Cometh in the Clouds*, 179.

110. *NYS*, May 2, 1897; *Lexington Herald*, May 2, 1897; interview with John Aikman, July 20, 1898, *JJDD*, reel 3, pp. 2412–13; interview with Edward Callahan Strong, July 21, 1898, *JJDD*, reel 3, pp. 2424–25; *Washington Times*, August 17, 1902; Lewis Franklin Johnson, *Famous Kentucky Tragedies and Trials*, 320; Vanatta, "On the Trail of a Mystery," 18; Haney, *The Mountain People of Kentucky*, 77; Clements, *History of the First Regiment of Infantry*, 147–48; Day, *Bloody Ground*, 126; Lawrence Sidney Thompson, *Kentucky Tradition*, 98; Billings and Blee, *The Road to Poverty*, 375; Pearce, *Days of Darkness*, 124. This discrepancy may have been due to a confusion of names. In 1867 Strong's pro-Confederate uncle, also named William Strong (possibly Edward Callahan Strong's father), sued Wiley Amis and Wilson Callahan for compensation for wartime confiscations (unlike his nephew, the senior Strong was actively pro-Confederate). *William Strong Sr. vs. Wilson Callahan & comp.*, May 15, 1867, Breathitt County Circuit Court Records, KDLA; *Barnes vs. Adams*, CSS, vol. 1432, no. 2, 41st Cong., 2nd sess., H. Misc. Doc. 13, p. 196.

111. Interview with Edward C. Strong, July 21, 1898, *JJDD*, reel 3, p. 2424; Pearce, *Days of Darkness*, 124; Billings and Blee, *The Road to Poverty*, 375.

112. In that year there were thirty-six reported lynching deaths in Kentucky, three reported as carried out for voting the Republican ticket. Wright, *Racial Violence in Kentucky*, 309–11.

113. "Kentucky's Vendettas," 259; Vanatta, "On the Trail of a Mystery," 18.

114. Johnston, "Romance and Tragedy of Kentucky Feuds," 554.

115. *Winchester News*, February 24, 1909.

116. Lewis Franklin Johnson, *Famous Kentucky Tragedies and Trials*, 320.

117. Blight, *Race and Reunion*, 383.

118. *LCJ*, January 6, 1879.

119. Anne E. Marshall, *Creating a Confederate Kentucky*, 40–54.

120. In an interview conducted by the Works Progress Administration's Federal Writers' Program, an elderly cousin of the judge humorously warned that if Edward Strong's grave were disturbed, his ghost would return and "have mortgages on everything in Breathitt County." Interview with William Haddix, 1938, Federal Writers' Project (interviewer: Margaret Bishop), http://www.breathittcounty.com/BreathittWeb2/THaddix.html (viewed December 19, 2008).

121. *KHJ, 1871*, 438.

122. *Morse v. South et al.*, Circuit Court D of Kentucky, April 15, 1897, *The Federal Reporter*, 80:206–18; *HGH*, May 10, 1894; G. W. Noble, *Behold He Cometh in the Clouds*, 177.

123. E. L. Noble, *Bloody Breathitt*, 2:26 (quote); *AGACK: Regular Session, 1877–1878* (Frankfort: S. I. M. Major, 1878), 1:145; *KHJ, 1878, 932*; *Morse v. South et al.*, Circuit Court D of Kentucky, April 15, 1897, *The Federal Reporter*, 80:208.

124. *Morse v. South et al.*, Circuit Court D of Kentucky, April 15, 1897, *The Federal*

Reporter, 80:208. Later in the 1870s Kentucky's General Assembly passed an adverse possession law, making the legal recognition of old land titles even more difficult than it was already. Claimants who held the old eighteenth-century land grants like the one Jeremiah South had based his claim upon were saddled with a greater burden of proof in verifying ownership of land occupied or improved by alleged squatters. *The General Statutes of Kentucky,* 180–81.

125. E. L. Noble, *Bloody Breathitt,* 2:26.

126. *New York Tribune,* August 1, September 30, 1874; *LCJ,* August 26, September 7, 16, 1874; *CDT,* September 9, 1874; *NYT,* August 6, 8, 12, 14–15, 23, 25–26, 29, 30, September 6, 10, 15, 28, October 12, 26, 1874; *KTY,* September 22, 1874; "Notes on Kentucky and Tennessee," 148; James McPherson, "Abolitionists and the Civil Rights Act of 1875," 507–8; Wyatt-Brown, "The Civil Rights Act of 1875," 769–70; Rable, *But There Was No Peace,* 120; Perman, *The Road to Redemption,* 138–41; Gudridge, "Privileges and Permissions," 120.

In 1874 a Republican party boss in the Bluegrass town of Lancaster armed a number of local African American men in an effort to capture the Garrard County courthouse during a hotly contested election (local Democrats engaged the group in a weeklong gunfight, prompting the arrival of federal troops from nearby Fort Dick Robinson). After initially reporting a "terrible war between the whites and blacks" during the Lancaster riot, the *Commercial* assured readers that the riot was not between whites and blacks but that "the connection of blacks in the affair is purely from their friendship for the contesting parties" (this of course omitted the fact that Kennedy's Democratic factions included only white men). When Lancaster's 1874 election riot was recounted in the twentieth century, it had become the "Kennedy-Sellers feud," and personal enmity between the two party leaders was accentuated over their political differences. *NYT,* August 26, 1873, August 33–24, September 1, 1874; *LCJ,* August 20–24, 1874; *CDT,* November 4, 1874; *Louisville Commercial,* August 22, 1874; Coates, *Stories of Kentucky Feuds,* 239–58; Gordon McKinney, *Southern Mountain Republicans,* 54–55.

127. *NYT,* August 20, September, 2, 4–5, 10, 12–13 15–18, 21, 23–26, 29, 1874; *CDT,* August 5, September, 5, 10, 15–18, 21, 25, 28, 1874; Vandal, *Rethinking Southern Violence,* 84–85.

128. *Chicago Inter-Ocean,* September 19, 1874; *LCJ,* September 28, 1874 (quote); *NYT,* December 7, 1878.

129. *NYT,* September 15, 1874.

130. Ibid., September 19, 1874.

131. Ibid., February 10, 1874; *Louisville Commercial,* October 31, 1874; Tapp and Klotter, *Kentucky,* 124–28.

132. Tapp, "Three Decades of Kentucky Politics," 106 (quote); Trelease, *White Terror,* 317. Leslie had supposedly bought an entire flatboat's load of Breathitt County coal in return for its being "worked up" by a local canvasser. Leslie had made the promise flippantly but, when the mountaineer showed up in Frankfort with far more coal than

Leslie wanted, the newly elected governor was obliged to fulfill his promise. *SIJ,* April 11, 1882.

133. *Louisville Commercial,* September 20, October 1, 13, 1874; *Cincinnati Daily Gazette,* September 25, 1874; *NYT,* September 28, 1874.

134. *LCJ,* September 16, 19, 1874; "Fayette Hewitt to His Excellency, Hon. Jas. B. McCreary," "Legislative Document No. 14: QuarterMaster General's Report, December 31, 1875," *KPD,* vol. 3. (Frankfort: E. H. Porter, 1879), 5; Wright, *Racial Violence in Kentucky,* 31.

135. *LCJ,* September 28–29, 1874; *NYT,* December 7, 1878; Ingmire, *Breathitt County, Kentucky Death Records,* 18.

136. *LCJ,* October 9, 1874.

137. *Comm. vs. Freeman and others,* November 19–21, 1874, Breathitt County Circuit Court Records, box 4, bundle 1, KDLA.

138. *LCJ,* September 28, October 6, 1874.

139. George Noble described it: "In August, 1874, the same year, a storm came and blew all the corn flat to the ground when it was in roasting ears, and it made about one-third of a crop. The same fall the squirrels came through the country in great droves. They would swim the streams and eat the corn all along. They were travelling toward the Cumberland Mountains. They were thick all along the public road and in the mountains. I saw that there was a famine on hand in the country." G. W. Noble, *Behold He Cometh in the Clouds,* 150.

Using evidence from Breathitt County's county court minutes from 1874, Altina Waller connects Strong's 1874 attack on the courthouse to the county's financial crisis, which was tied to the exoneration of some taxpayers' debts, tax support for an approaching railroad, and a lawsuit against absentee landowners. Simmering war-born tensions between Democrats and Republicans, however, are not considered. Although the county's declining economy (a decline that began the previous year during the nationwide Panic of 1873) probably exacerbated the Red Strings' ire, newspaper accounts of Strong's attack written by reporters who followed the state militia to Jackson agree that it was in reaction to William Hargis's murder. Also, accounts of the affray from Democratic and Republican newspapers reveal that both recognized the party-based animosity in Breathitt County. Waller, "Feuding in Appalachia," 365.

140. Foner, *Reconstruction,* 437; Higginbotham, *Shades of Freedom,* 88; Hubbs, *Guarding Greensboro,* 215–16; Lemann, *Redemption,* 6–7; Lane, *The Day Freedom Died,* 22.

141. *NYT,* September 26, 1874.

142. *Cincinnati Daily Gazette,* September 25, 1874; *NYT,* September 28, 1874.

143. Woodward, *Origins of the New South,* 6.

144. *KTY,* September 22, 1874.

145. *Louisville Commercial,* September 26, 1874. For the *Commercial's* role as one of Kentucky's only Republican newspapers in the 1870s, see Summers, *The Press Gang, Newspapers and Politics,* 209.

146. In July 1874 Jeremiah (or Jerry) Little engaged in a street fight with James Cockrell, Hiram Jett, and John Jett. Though Little reportedly killed John and seriously wounded Hiram, he too was wounded, and that fall (after regular courts had resumed following William Strong's capture of the courthouse), Little sued Hiram Jett for $2,000 in damages for shooting him, leaving the former "incapable of hard labor." The jury awarded him $280. Newspapers identified Little as the aggressor and reported the affray as part of a "family feud" without exploring its origins any further. *Jeremiah Little vs. Hiram Jett and James Cockerill*, September 1874–June, 1877, Breathitt County Circuit Court Records, KDLA; *Philadelphia Inquirer*, July 24, 1874; *New Orleans Times*, July 24, 1874; *HGH*, February 2, 1887; Clements, *History of the First Regiment of Infantry*, 148; Lewis Franklin Johnson, *Famous Kentucky Tragedies and Trials*, 321; Waller, "Feuding in Appalachia," 355.

147. Wyatt-Brown, *Southern Honor*, 352.

148. *Louisville Commercial*, September 26, 1874.

149. *LCJ*, September 28, October 6, 1874; Waller, "Feuding in Appalachia," 364. At times the word *riot* is employed but with an understanding of the limitations this term brings with it. Although it is easily defined as violent or unruly action carried out by a group of three or more individuals, this does not account for the various nuances that could distinguish a riot from a mob or any other word describing a violent concerted effort. At best, *riot* is "an imprecise term for describing popular actions," but it is difficult to imagine a more descriptive word in many cases. E. P. Thompson, "The Moral Economy of the English Crowd in the Eighteenth Century," 107.

150. *LCJ*, September 29, 1874.

151. Ibid., October 6, 1874.

152. Ibid., October 17, 1874.

153. "Fayette Hewitt to His Excellency, Hon. Jas. B. McCreary," 5.

154. Anne E. Marshall, *Creating a Confederate Kentucky*, 50–54, 68–73, 98.

155. *LCJ*, December 16, 1878.

156. As in the rest of the United States, voter turnout was particularly high in Kentucky in the race between Hayes and Tilden. In 1876 the state had the highest number of votes cast (proportional to population) for a presidential election since 1844. Breathitt County went Democratic with a 70.1 percent majority, with 72.6 percent of potential votes cast. Shannon and McQuown, *Presidential Politics in Kentucky*, 45, 47.

157. Altina Waller has suggested that before his election, Judge Burnett had "obvious ties" to the Bluegrass-based Kentucky Union Railroad which, as will be examined in the following chapter, began amassing land in Breathitt County starting in the 1870s. I have found no evidence of Burnett's connections to it or any other railroad and, considering that he was from Virginia rather than the Bluegrass, this is unlikely. However, Judge William Randall was a member of the railroad's board of directors when it was chartered, as were George M. Adams and Sydney Barnes. Waller, "Feuding in Appalachia," 365–67; *The Kentucky Union Railway Company*, 65.

158. *LCJ,* December 5, January 6, 1879; *Louisville Commercial,* December 8, 1878.

159. *Louisville Commercial,* December 8, 1878; G. W. Noble, *Behold He Cometh in the Clouds,* 177.

160. "Crystals," 5.

161. *LCJ,* January 16, 1879.

162. Ibid., November 30, December 1, 19, 1878, January 16, 1879; *Louisville Commercial,* December 8, 1878; *Cincinnati Daily Gazette,* December 2, 1878.

163. *LCJ,* December 1, 19, 1878; *KTY,* February 1, 1879.

164. *Cincinnati Daily Gazette,* December 2, 3, 1878.

165. *Lexington Herald,* May 11, 1897.

166. *Commonwealth of Kentucky vs. John Aikman,* June 12, 1873, Breathitt County Circuit Court Minutes, box 4, bundle 1, Public Records Division, KDLA.

167. *LCJ,* November 30, 1878, January 6, 1879; *Chicago Inter-Ocean,* December 5, 21, 1878; *Hartford Herald,* December 11, 1878; "Report of Second Lieut. A. C. Speed, concerning a Detachment under his Command, from January 1, 1879, to January 24, 1879, Acting as Cavalry at Jackson, Breathitt County, Kentucky," in *Legislative Document No. 1,* 24.

168. *LCJ,* December 19, 26, 1878, January 6, 16, 1879; *Louisville Commercial,* February 1, 24, 1879; WPA, *In the Land of Breathitt,* 64–65.

169. *The Commonwealth of Kentucky against J. C. B. Allen et al.,* Breathitt County Circuit Court, September Special Term, 1878–79, Breathitt County Circuit Court Records, KDLA; *LCJ,* November 30, December 1, 19, 24, 1878; *Chicago Inter-Ocean,* December 2, 21, 1878; *Cincinnati Daily Gazette,* December 2, 3, 1878; *Hartford Herald,* December 11, 1878; G. W. Noble, *Behold He Cometh in the Clouds,* 185–86.

170. "Fayette Hewitt to His Excellency, Hon. Jas. B. McCreary," 5.

171. Tapp, "Three Decades of Kentucky Politics," 134–35; Ramage and Watkins, *Kentucky Rising,* 342–43.

172. Dacus, *Annals of the Great Strikes in the United States,* 430–34; Weaver, "Louisville's Labor Disturbance," 179–83; Tapp and Klotter, *Kentucky,* 310–11; Steven J. Hoffman, "Looking North," 105–35; Sullivan, "Louisville and Her Southern Alliance," 290–95; Tapp, "Three Decades of Kentucky Politics," 156–58.

173. "J. M. Wright to His Excellency Governor James B. McCreary," "Legislative Document No. 1: Adjutant General's Report, June 15, 1879," *KPD,* vol. 3 (Frankfort: E. H. Porter, 1879), 3; WPA, *Military History of Kentucky,* 257.

174. Anne E. Marshall, *Creating a Confederate Kentucky,* 96–98; Sullivan, "Louisville and Her Southern Alliance," 292–93.

175. Kentucky's transition from military surveillance of its hinterlands to a more urban-based military presence parallels the federal government's pivotal post-Reconstruction transition from using military coercion as a tool for solving "the southern question" to protecting northern capitalist interests through strikebreaking. Foner, *Reconstruction,* 583–86. For New Departure Democrats, see Perman, *The Road to Redemption,* 58–86, 149–77; Prichard, "Popular Political Movements in Kentucky," 9–31.

176. *NYT,* December 2, 1878.

177. *New York Herald,* December 3, 1878. For Henry Clay's nickname, see Ramage and Watkins, *Kentucky Rising,* 18.

178. *LCJ,* December 3, 5, 8, 1878; *Cincinnati Enquirer,* December 11, 14, 1878; "J. M. Wright to His Excellency Governor James B. McCreary," 3–5.

179. *Hartford Herald,* January 8, 1879.

180. *NYT,* January 31, 1879; *KTY,* February 1, 1879; G. W. Noble, *Behold He Cometh in the Clouds,* 185–86.

181. Johnston, "Romance and Tragedy of Kentucky Feuds," 554.

182. *Louisville Commercial,* February 1, 24, 1879; *KTY,* February 25, 27, 1879.

183. *Chicago Inter-Ocean,* November 26, 1879; "Report of Second Lieut. A. C. Speed, concerning a Detachment under his Command, from January 1, 1879, to January 24, 1879, Acting as Cavalry at Jackson, Breathitt County, Kentucky," in *Legislative Document No. 1,* 24–26; G. W. Noble, *Behold He Cometh in the Clouds,* 186.

184. *KWY,* February 6, 1879.

185. E.L. Noble, *Bloody Breathitt,* 2:34.

186. Anne E. Marshall, *Creating a Confederate Kentucky,* 72–73.

187. *Philadelphia Inquirer,* December 23, 1878.

188. *Cincinnati Enquirer,* December 6, 1878; *LCJ,* December 1, 1878. See also Waller, "Feuding in Appalachia," 365–66.

189. *Cincinnati Daily Gazette,* December 2, 1878.

190. *Cincinnati Commercial,* December 1, 8, 1878; *Cincinnati Daily Gazette,* December 2, 1878; *LCJ,* December 3, 5, 8, 1878; *NYT,* December 7, 1878.

191. *LCJ,* December 3, 1878.

192. Ibid., December 5, 1878.

193. Ibid., December 3, 5, 1878.

194. Ibid.

195. The same article highlighted the county's poverty: "The worldly goods of these five or six thousand people do not much exceed in value those of so many Indians on a government reservation. Under such a state of life society must approximate a primitive condition, and if the Bluegrass counties are inclined to turn up their noses at it we beg them to count up their own killings and remember that none of us are any better than we ought to be. I am informed that a baker's dozen will cover the number of men killed in personal difficulties in this county since the war and many a more favored county can discount that with a single year's crop, and get ahead of Breathitt as much in 'stiffs' as they do in cereals." *LCJ,* December 5, 1878.

196. Ibid., December 24, 1878.

197. Ibid., January 26, 1879; *NYT,* January 26, 1879.

198. *LCJ,* January 16, 1879.

199. Ibid., December 19, 1878.

200. Ibid., January 6, 1879.

201. *KTY,* January 18, 1879.

202. Fellman, *Inside War,* 254; Kalyvas, *The Logic of Violence in Civil War,* 330–33.

203. Waller, "Feuding in Appalachia," 353–56 (quote), 364–66.

204. *New York Herald,* November 30, 1878. The *Herald*'s assertion that the Freemans enjoyed equality in Breathitt County was unusual in its time, but reflects larger assumptions about the mountain South's misbegotten placement in a region generally defined by a black presence. For Breathitt County to be properly depoliticized, it had to be completely dissociated from racial difference, the primary cleavage in postwar southern society that defined the region's politics. For an elaboration on Appalachian "racial innocence" in fictional contrast to "the biracial character of the rest of the South," see Inscoe, "The Racial 'Innocence' of Appalachia," 85–97 (quote 89).

205. *LCJ,* March 26, 1879.

206. Between 1874 and 1895 the *Louisville Courier-Journal,* with Watterson still at the helm, identified forty-one violent conflicts as "feuds" in thirty-one different Kentucky counties throughout the state. Waller, "Feuding in Appalachia," 353, 354, 357–58.

207. *KTY,* February 25, 27, 1879.

208. Tapp and Klotter, *Kentucky,* 499.

209. *Breckinridge News,* March 26, 1879; *Washington Post,* March 21, 1879.

210. *NYT,* May 27, 1879.

211. *AAC* (1879): 540–541.

212. *Washington Times,* May 10, 1897.

213. *JJDD,* entry, April 9, 1884, reel 1, pp. 285–86; *Cleveland Herald,* April 16, 1884; *MVB,* April 18, 1884; *SIJ,* April 18, 1884 (quote); *HMC,* April 25, 1884; E. L. Noble, *Bloody Breathitt,* 2:71–77; WPA, *In the Land of Breathitt,* 74–75. A highly erroneous account of an attack on the Breathitt County jailhouse, one that ended with a heroic jailer holding off the mob, was printed in the *NYT,* April 25, 1884; *Baltimore Sun,* April 26, 1884.

214. In the nineteenth and twentieth centuries aspiring lynch mobs could not escape their own knowledge of the difference between the legitimate "ritual of the courthouse" and their own questionable legitimacy as arbiters of justice. In order that their vigilantism have at least a symbolic aura of legitimacy, the courthouse's physical structure, or the "courthouse square" common to many southern county seats, was often used as a setting for victims' hanging, immolation, or both. The larger the lynch mob, it seemed, the greater the importance that the victim's (or victims') death(s) take place in this most consecrated of centralized public spaces. Brundage, *Lynching in the New South,* 257 (quote); Ifill, *On the Courthouse Lawn,* xiii–xix, 7–23; Dray, *At the Hands of Persons Unknown,* 30; Madison, *A Lynching in the Heartland,* 1–2; Piepmeier, *Out in Public,* 141.

215. Entry, April 9, 1884, *JJDD,* reel 1, p. 286. For Dickey's fears of racial equality in Kentucky's future, see Tapp and Klotter, *Kentucky,* 92–93.

216. *MVB,* April 23, 1884.

217. Hangings in front of courthouses, bodies affixed with notes proscribing how long they were to remain on public display: Breathitt County's 1884 lynch mob followed

a template that, by the 1890s, created the impression that "their members had attended formal schools on procedures." Joel Williamson, The *Crucible of Race*, 185; Amy Louise Wood, *Lynching and Spectacle*, 5 (quote); Apel, *Imagery of Lynching*, 23; Ayers, *The Promise of the New South*, 156; Wright, *Racial Violence in Kentucky*, 7–8.

218. Wright, *Racial Violence in Kentucky*, 314.

219. *MVB*, April 18, 1884.

220. Brundage, *Lynching in the New South*; Kaufman-Osborn, "Capital Punishment as Legal Lynching?" 32–33; Waldrep, "Word and Deed," 239–43.

221. For the "communal" interpretation of southern lynching, see Jacquelyn Dowd Hall, *Revolt against Chivalry*, 145; Trudier Harris, *Exorcising Blackness*, 1–23. For empirical accounts of lynching with clear political motives, see Baker, *This Mob Will Surely Take My Life*.

222. *Cleveland Herald*, April 16, 1884; *MVB*, April 18, 1884. Although Kilburn's body was taken to William Strong's farm after his request, Ben Strong's uncle claimed his body before he could be transported, and Strong was apparently buried elsewhere. *JJDD*, entry, April 10, 1884, reel 1, pp. 286–87 (quote).

223. *MVB*, May 29, July 10, 1884; Perrin, Battle, and Kniffin, *Kentucky*, 957–58, 964 (quote), 973.

224. Rolff, *Strong Family of Virginia and Other Southern States*, 94.

225. *HGH*, July 7, 14, 1886; *SIJ*, August 24, 1886.

226. See Hahn, "Hunting, Fishing and Foraging," 55–57; Hahn, *A Nation under our Feet*, 185–98; Fitzgerald, *The Union League Movement in the Deep South*.

227. *HMC*, July 31, 1885.

4. "The civilizing and Christianizing effects of material improvement and development"

1. *Bourbon News*, April 28, 1882 (quote), April 3, 1883; *FRA*, January 6, 1883; *LCJ*, December 25, 1884.

2. *Hickman Courier*, July 16, 1880; *Bourbon News*, April 10, 1883; *SIJ*, January 15, 1884; *LCJ*, December 25, 1884; *The Virginias* 5, no. 2 (1884): 21; *MVB*, July 21, 1887; Allison, *The City of Louisville and a Glimpse of Kentucky*, 32; Warner, "Comments on Kentucky," 263; *Manual of the Railroads of the United States*, 670; Verhoeff, *Kentucky River Navigation*, 118; E. L. Noble, *Bloody Breathitt*, 1:41.

3. *The Kentucky Union Railway Company*, 4–5.

4. *Bourbon News*, March 6, April 10, 1883; *LCJ*, December 25, 1884; *HGH*, April 22, 1885.

5. *LCJ*, December 25, 1884.

6. As will be addressed in a later chapter, racial interpretations of feud violence abounded from the 1880s until well into the twentieth century. The widespread belief that the Kentucky mountains maintained a repository of "pure" Anglo-Saxon blood were balanced with other accounts that made mountaineers out to be purely "Celtic."

7. *NYT*, December 26, 1878. This article was written before the rash of violence in other parts of Kentucky, and the "best citizens" were still considered white southerners rather than innately violent "mountain whites" in the minds of the metropolitan media.

8. *Hartford Herald*, February 6, 1884.

9. *Executive Documents of the House of Representatives for the Second Session of the Forty-Ninth Congress*, lv, 610; Henry Weinholt to J. P. McGaughey, March 27, 1887, in *General Assembly of the Knights of Labor of America*, 1604.

10. *FRA*, November 8, 22 (quote), 1879; Tapp, "Three Decades of Kentucky Politics," 154–56, 206–8.

11. *KTY*, December 3, 1878.

12. Ibid., December 17, 1878.

13. *LCJ*, December 19, 1878.

14. Shaler, *Kentucky*, 406.

15. *Description of a Tract of Timber, Coal, and Agricultural Land.*

16. Warner, "Comments on Kentucky," 264. See also *HGH*, July 22, 1885, June 15, 1887.

17. *Wisconsin State Journal*, September 4, 1885.

18. "Alex P. Humphrey and John Boyle to J. W. Gaulbert, Esq., April 17, 1889" and "R. M. Jones to Kentucky Union Land Company, May 27, 1889," Kentucky Union Land Company Records, box 1, folder 2, KLSCA.

19. Following the research of Henry Shapiro, scholars of Appalachian history have long pointed to the role that evangelical home missions in the southern mountains played in establishing Appalachia as a distinct place and its inhabitants as a "peculiar people." Gilded Age evangelicals tended to conflate Christianity with modernization, thereby ignoring the possibility that much of apparently unchurched Appalachia (particularly underdeveloped "New Appalachia") was lacking in Christian influence. See Friend, *Kentucke's Frontiers*, 165–66; McCauley, *Appalachian Mountain Religion*, 9, 392–93; Whisnant, *All That Is Native and Fine*, 8–10; Klotter, "The Black South and White Appalachia," 832–49; Henry Shapiro, *Appalachia on Our Mind*, ix–xiv.

20. "Heathen Mountaineers in Kentucky," 2.

21. McKee, "Invading the Kentucky Mountains," 2.

22. "Editorial Notes," 205.

23. Breathitt County Old Regulars were part of the New Salem Association of United Baptists, founded in 1825. Callahan, *Work and Faith in the Kentucky Coal Fields*, 24–27; "Heathen in Our Own Country," 121; McCauley, *Appalachian Mountain Religion*, 90–100; E. L. Noble, *Bloody Breathitt*, 1:19; Trimble, *Recollections of Breathitt*, 3. Old Regular Baptists were noted for their belief in congregational autonomy and their decentralization, combined with the infrequency of regular church meetings, made the mountain denomination appear weak and disorganized. However, the extant records of one Breathitt County congregation reveal detailed record keeping and abundant tithe collection. Quicksand, Kentucky, Regular Baptist Church records, 1858–98, microfilm roll 1, KLSCA.

24. G. W. Noble, *Behold He Cometh in the Clouds*, 1–2.

25. Trimble, *Recollections of Breathitt*, 19–20.

26. Sparks, *Raccoon John Smith*, 425; Trimble, *Recollections of Breathitt*, 11, 15, 20–21; Scalf, *Kentucky's Last Frontier*, 272–75.

27. *Cincinnati Daily Gazette*, December 4, 1878.

28. *NYT*, December 16, 1882; Price, *Without Scrip or Purse*, 178–268 (quote 199–200); *JJDD*, undated entry, reel 1, p. 104; Scalf, *Kentucky's Last Frontier*, 264–72; Waller, *Feud*, 162.

29. Price, *Without Scrip or Purse*, 203.

30. *JJDD*, undated entry, reel 1, p. 90; *HGH*, May 6, July 1, 1885.

31. *JJDD*, undated entry, reel 1, p. 104; G. W. Noble, *Behold He Cometh in the Clouds*, 206.

32. *Bourbon News*, June 26, July 20, July 31, 1883; *MVB*, July 30, 1883; *AGACK* (Frankfort: M. Major, 1884), 1:756–58; *Independent*, August 16, 1883; *HGH*, January 13, 1886; *MVB*, November 20, 1886; "Jackson, in the Kentucky Mountains," 2; G. W. Noble, *Behold He Cometh in the Clouds*, 206.

33. *MVB*, May 10, 1886.

34. Whisnant, *All That Is Native and Fine*, 37–38; William Davis and Swentnor, *Bluegrass Confederate*, 246 (quote).

35. *HGH*, September 8, 22, 1886; *MVB*, October 9, 1886, August 23, 1887; Huddle, "Soul Winner," 50, 53–54; Congleton, "The Jackson Academy and the Quest for Presbyterian Ascendency in Breathitt County," 160–61, 164, 166, 168–70.

36. *Spout Spring Times*, May 8, 1897.

37. Guerrant, *The Galax Gatherers*, 154.

38. Quoted in McAllister and Guerrant, *Edward O. Guerrant*, 91. See also Guerrant, *The Galax Gatherers*, 46–48, 98, 152–56, 157–60; Whisnant, *All That Is Native and Fine*, 37–41.

39. Quoted in Link, *The Paradox of Southern Progressivism*, 84.

40. *HGH*, October 7, 1885.

41. "Editorial Notes," 205–6.

42. *JJDD*, entry, June 8, 1898, reel 2, p. 2479.

43. *SIJ*, November 8, 1887 (quote); Waller, *Feud*, 162.

44. *JJDD*, entry, April 9, 1884, reel 1, p. 286; Huddle, "Soul Winner," 58–60.

45. "I read an article in Harper's magazine for June 1887 tonight, from the pen of John Mason Brown, in the Kentucky Pioneer's in which he says, 'The fair name of the State they founded has sometimes been tarnished by violence and lawlessness and at times has come upon many for the wickedness of very few. But he who will very carefully search out the history of her population and the antecedents of Kentucky wrong doers will discover in them a class different in blood from their pioneers. He will find that the too frequent homicides of certain neighborhoods have an origin (wholly) entirely different, drawn from an originally immoral class, and justifying the law of hereditary. But

in those areas where the original and true pionners made their lodgement and held it, the stamp of their qualities may still be observed, modified by the lapse of years but the same in essentials; the badges of a martial, hospitable, truthful and self reliant people.'

"I am sure that this imputation can be removed from our mountain people and God helping me, will do it. I know that it is *environment* and not *heredity* that has made the chasm between the people of the Blue Grass and the mountains. This I can prove by tracing the geneology of these people and I will do it if it requires the rest of my life. My first and greatest desire is to change their environment and thereby change their character but while I am doing this I can write their 'simple annals' and show to posterity that Kentuckians have a common ancestry without regard to 'areas' they occupy." Entry, December 21, 1895, *JJDD*, reel 1, pp. 1594–95.

46. *HGH*, July 1, 1885.

47. Ibid., August 5, 1885.

48. Ibid., September 16, 1885. The *Hazel Green Herald* first put type to press in March 1885 under publisher Spencer Cooper, a Union veteran and Bluegrass Democrat. Over the following years, the *Herald* became eastern Kentucky's most prominent Democratic newspaper. In the 1890s the *Herald* veered in favor of Populism, providing the People's Party with a rare mountain following. G. W. Noble, *Behold He Cometh in the Clouds,* 306; Tapp and Klotter, *Kentucky,* 323.

49. *HGH*, May 6, 1885; *MSA*, February 26, 1901.

50. *HGH*, September 22, 1886.

51. *JJDD*, entry, November 22, 1888, reel 1, p. 1185; *Richmond Climax,* January 9, 23, August 7, 1889; *MVB,* February 18, 1889, July 24, 1890, October 9, November 20, 1891.

52. *Jackson Hustler,* quoted in *MVB,* December 10, 1890.

53. *MVB,* July 30, 1895.

54. Of all the large-scale white intraracial conflicts counted among the "Kentucky feuds," the "Martin-Tolliver feud," (also known as the "Rowan County War") originated far afield from where most Kentuckians considered their state's mountainous "feud belt." Rowan County, situated in the hilly northeast quadrant of the state, was commercially vibrant, with a spur of the immense Chesapeake & Ohio Railroad and relatively simple access to the market of the greater Ohio Valley. Accusations of vote tampering in 1884 resulted in a series of riots pitting the followers of the county's Republican and Democratic ringleaders. Rowan's Republican leadership was made up of a business-minded middle class with interest in increasing the economic presence of "outside" investment. Amid the economic giddiness of the 1880s, John Martin, a frequent Republican candidate for various offices, was forced to contend with a Democratic challenge from Craig Tolliver, a recent arrival from a less developed, heavily Democratic mountain county. The Democrats led by Tolliver were mostly a ragtag group of young disadvantaged men whose economic autonomy was threatened by Martin's railroad-friendly Republicans.

Fearful of civil unrest but eager to cut another chink in the mountainous Republican stronghold, the Democratically controlled state capital allowed the Tolliver faction to terrorize Rowan County's electorate for months before acting. When Democratic governor J. Proctor Knott finally intervened, it was as a mediator rather than an executive enforcer of peace. The *New York Times* complained that Knott "treated the ruffians with all the consideration due from one great nation to another. He had ambassadors appointed by each of the contending factions, received them in Louisville, and after two pleasant 'conferences' with the murderers induced them to sign a treaty of peace, and sent them home with his thanks" (*NYT*, June 27, 1887). As Altina Waller has pointed out, Rowan County was not a particularly isolated part of eastern Kentucky; it's portrayal as a feud involved stretching the "feud belt" some ways from the mountains in order that it might be included within an increasingly popular media heuristic (Waller, "Feuding in Appalachia," 358). This was of special importance if the marriage between geography and white intraracial violence were to be sustained; the Rowan County War was probably the single bloodiest affair in Kentucky since the Civil War. "Letters to the [Mt. Sterling, Kentucky] *Sentinel-Democrat* pertaining to the Rowan County Feud and Other Matters," 1885–86, KLSCA; *HGH*, April 8, 1885; *NYT*, December 11, 1884, July 6, 8, 11, 1885, August 10, 1886; *AAC* 15 (1891): 474; *BCN*, November 20, 1903; Ireland, *Little Kingdoms*, 72–74; Klotter, "Feuds in Appalachia," 298–99.

Writing of the Martin-Tolliver feud in the first decade of the twentieth century, a Kentucky state militia veteran recalled that "the trouble in the beginning was somewhat connected with politics, but afterwards assumed the form of organized brigandage." MacPherson, "The Louisville Legion," 9.

55. *SIJ*, March 20 (quote), 1885; *HGH*, April 8, 1885.

56. *HGH*, July 15, 1885.

57. Myers, "The Mountain Whites of the South," 19.

58. G. W. Noble, *Behold He Cometh in the Clouds*, 306; Tapp and Klotter, *Kentucky*, 323.

59. *HGH*, December 23, 1885.

60. Ibid., March 11, 1885.

61. Ibid., August 4, 1886.

62. Ibid., August 18, 1886.

63. *SIJ*, October 15, 1886; *HGH*, October 13, 1886. See also *JJDD*, entry, October 24, 1886, reel 1.

64. *Omaha Herald*, March 20, 1880.

65. Harkins, *Hillbilly*, 40–45.

66. Kantrowitz, *Ben Tillman and the Reconstruction of White Supremacy*, 8–9, 273–308 (quote 9).

67. Lears, *Rebirth of a Nation*, 134; Ayers, *Promise of the New South*, 213.

68. Anne E. Marshall, *Creating a Confederate Kentucky*, 111–32 (quote).

69. In the late 1880s, a travel writer remarked that "in all the mountain region of eastern Kentucky I passed through there are few to-day who are politically Democrats." Decades later, an early twentieth-century visitor who shared the contemporary belief

in the strict distinction between the "mountain white" and lowland white southerners noted that eastern Kentucky's "staunch adherence" to the Republican Party was so well established that "topography has defined the mountain section as one of the political divisions of the State by a kind of common law of both political parties in their conventions and in common parlance." Warner, "Comments on Kentucky," 264; Semple, "The Anglo-Saxons of the Kentucky Mountains," 611–12.

Warner and Semple were influenced by local-color writer Will Wallace Harney. Harney did not seriously address mountain politics, but his 1873 article has been credited with beginning the literary movement that established the southern Appalachians as a place distinct from the South and the United States as a whole. Harney, "A Strange Land and a Peculiar People," 429–38.

70. As detailed in previous chapters, the strength of the antebellum Whig Party had translated into adamant Unionism in most eastern Kentucky counties during the Civil War and provided a fertile field for the growth of the Republican Party afterward, especially when candidates were willing to ignore the national platform's emphasis on civil rights for African Americans. Aside from the business-minded Republican coteries in urban areas, by 1900 the party had become almost exclusively peopled by increasingly disfranchised African Americans and white mountain men. After Kentucky's postwar readjustment, the party found the same source of growth as it did in other economically comparable pockets of the South. For many poor whites (and eastern Kentucky was consistently the state's poorest area) the Republican Party offered a clear alternative to the Bourbonism that overtook the Democratic Party after Reconstruction. Gordon McKinney, *Southern Mountain Republicans,* 50–54, 63, 68–69; Ireland, *Little Kingdoms,* 44–45; Richard B. Drake, *A History of Appalachia,* 160–62; Snay, "Freedom and Progress," 100–114; Samuel Webb, *Two-Party Politics in the One-Party South;* Samuel Webb, "From Independents to Populists to Progressive Republicans," 734–36; Hyman, *The Anti-Redeemers,* 43, 117–18, 182–86, 217–18.

71. Letter to the editor from "Mugwump."

72. Fox Jr. expressed this politically enmeshed abnormality in *The Heart of the Hills* (1913), his last best-selling novel. The protagonist and narrator was a plucky young mountain boy who (typical of leading characters in most of his books) prospers by embracing the education afforded to him by the "outside world" (i.e., the ever progressive but largely Democratic Bluegrass) without rejecting his alpine manliness. The young man, now college educated but still a ruggedly masculine Anglo-Saxon, witnessed the beginnings of a political intrigue that threatened to tear Kentucky apart while also heightening his section's electoral importance. He "knew that at home Republicans ran against Republicans for all offices, and now he learned that his own mountains were the Gibraltar of that party, and that the lines of its fortifications ran from the Big Sandy [River], three hundred miles by public roads, to the line of Tennessee." In the process, "in spite of the mountaineer's Blue-grass allies," the young mountaineer hero "had come to believe that there was a state conspiracy to rob his own people of their rights." Fox,

The Heart of the Hills, 203, 206. I am grateful to Bill Hutton for making me aware of this novel. For another analysis of Fox Jr.'s thematic use of mountain Republicanism, see Anne E. Marshall, *Creating a Confederate Kentucky,* 123–31.

73. *Hartford Herald,* February 27, 1895. In 1900 a Washington, DC, editor made a similar educated mistake. Knowing that eastern Kentucky was "completely Republican," he figured that Breathitt County was "the last place in the world to look for any attempt to obstruct Republican balloting," despite evidence to the contrary. *Washington Times,* November 10, 1900.

74. Quoted in *Berea Citizen,* September 24, 1903.

75. Wright, *Racial Violence in Kentucky,* 320.

76. Gordon McKinney, *Southern Mountain Republicans,* 119; Shannon and Mc-Quown, *Presidential Politics in Kentucky,* 71.

77. Clark, *Kentucky, Land of Contrast,* 208–9. In "participant political cultures" citizenship defines social relations and the relationship between individuals and the state and, by extension, the citizen expects the state to serve as a means to preserve, or gain, popular expectations. In opposition, the area of Kentucky that was increasingly referred to as the "feud belt" constituted a "parochial" political culture in which there is an absence of specialization among political roles. Parochial cultures are associated with "tribal" government, political bodies that American citizens generally associated with either their own distant European past or members of races deemed inferior, most notably Africans or Native Americans. For a full contrast between participatory and parochial political cultures, see Almond, "Comparative Political Systems," 396–97; Almond and Verba, *The Civic Culture,* 17–20.

Since its mid-twentieth-century inception, "political culture" has come under tremendous criticism for its conceptual amorphousness and its utility in allowing cultural historians to "evade certain classic considerations of political life, namely, power, and who exercises it" and for "repeat[ing] social history's earlier slighting of power and policy dimensions." For this reason, the phrase should be used with care when dealing with violent political conditions since, as Harry Eckstein has remarked, the existence of political cultures suggests a measure of continuity while violence is irrevocably associated with "drastic political change." I disagree with this only slightly since Eckstein considers violence only within revolutionary usages without addressing counterrevolutionary state violence. However, the concept's problematic nature should be noted. "Political culture" is used here only within the precise boundaries in which it was originally formulated: a means of understanding individual or group political actions in atmospheres within which basic understandings of "ideology" are not strictly delineated. Political culture covers the "vaguer and more implicit orientations" of political action that ideology cannot explain. For a critique of political culture from which the earlier quotes are taken, see Formisano, "The Concept of Political Culture," 395. For political culture and violence, see Eckstein, "A Culturalist Theory of Political Change," 790–92, 797.

78. Pocock, *The Machiavellian Moment,* 536.

79. *National Geographic*, February 14, 1894, 632; *Lexington Herald*, December 16, 1900; *HGH*, August 28, 1902. See also *Kansas City Journal*, May 3, 1903; *NYT*, May 30, 1903; *MSA*, July 1, 1903; Barton, "The Church Militant in the Feud Belt," 351–52; *Decatur Daily News*, March 14, 1910, March 24, 1912; Charles Neville Buck, *The Call of the Cumberlands*, 102; Davenport, *Primitive Traits in Religious Revivals*, 305.

80. White mountaineers' Republican loyalty represented to northerners an uncommon patriotism that would be instrumental to sectional reconciliation. But accepting these southern mountaineers as part of the (northern) American political mainstream was difficult when they were simultaneously being portrayed as strange, primitive, and "vastly out of step, culturally and economically, with the progressive trends of industrializing and urbanizing nineteenth-century America." After white northern self-consciousness about national reunification waned, the significance of mountain Republicanism remained. Eastern Kentucky was proof of "the geological distribution of politics," but it was a distribution based partly on empirical fact but also upon speculation, faulty anthropology, and colorful mythology. Billings, Pudup, and Waller, "Taking Exception with Exceptionalism," 1; Coulter and Connelley, *History of Kentucky*, 2:1047; Anne E. Marshall, *Creating a Confederate Kentucky*, 119–23; Silber, *The Romance of Reunion*, 145–46.

81. The *Courier-Journal* identified thirty-one different "feuds" in various parts of Kentucky between 1882 and 1893. Waller, "Feuding in Appalachia," 355–61. See also Batteau, *The Invention of Appalachia*, 76–79; Henry Shapiro, *Appalachia on Our Mind* ix, 63; John A. Williams, *Appalachia*, 192; Anne E. Marshall, *Creating a Confederate Kentucky*, 127–32; Wright, *Racial Violence in Kentucky*, 314.

82. For the late nineteenth-century cultural explanations for feud violence, see Batteau, *The Invention of Appalachia*, 76–79; Henry Shapiro, *Appalachia on Our Mind* ix, 63; John A. Williams, *Appalachia*, 192.

83. Governor-elect Buckner defeated Republican William O. Bradley in 1887 by 16,197 votes, the smallest Democratic margin of victory in a gubernatorial election since the Civil War. Stickles, *Simon Bolivar Buckner*, 336–44; Tapp and Klotter, *Kentucky*, 234–36, 246.

84. Stickles, *Simon Bolivar Buckner*, 348–55.

85. Waller, *Feud*, 162–63, 174–81, 194–210.

86. Bailey, *Matewan before the Massacre*, 238–39.

87. "J. P. Marrs et al to His excellency S. B. Buckner, undated," "B. W. Combs et al to Governor Buckner and General Hill, November 14, 1888," "W. W. Baker to G. M. Adams, November 16, 1888," "G. B. Brandon to Governor Buckner, November 18, 1888," "J. B. White et al to His Excellency S. B. Buckner, December 4, 1888," Governor's Correspondence, November–December, 1888, box 1, folders 18–19, KDLA; "Captain J. M. Sohan to Governor S. B. Buckner, November 14, 1888," "Legislative Document No. 17: Adjutant General's Report for the Year 1889," *KPD*, vol. 4 (Frankfort: E. Polk Johnson, 1889), 7, 36–56; *HMC*, June 18, September 3, 1886; *SIJ*, June 11, July 27, 1886, December

24, 1889, October 10, 1893; *MVB*, August 26, December 8, 1886, April 18, 1887, November 6, 1888, November 13, 1889, May 16, 1892, September 27, October 17, 1894; *HGH*, August 4, September 15, 22, November 24, 1886, May 15, 1891, September 27, 1894, January 3, August 22, 1895, May 14, 1896; *Hartford Republican*, December 14, 1894; *NYT*, July 31, 1886, November 16, 1886, November 10, 1890; *Joseph Atkins et al., Appts., v. Commonwealth of Kentucky*, January 10, 1896, *LRA, 1896*, 32:108–13.

88. Harry Caudill, *Their's Be the Power*, 178. See also Pearce, *Days of Darkness*, 77.

89. *MVB*, November 13, 1889; *HGH*, May 21, 1896; Ireland, *Little Kingdoms*, 76–77.

90. *HGH*, May 21, 1896; various letters, Governor's Correspondence, November–December, 1888, box 1, folder 18, KDLA.

91. *SIJ*, September 24, 1895; *MSA*, September 24, 1895; *Richmond Climax*, September 25, 1895; *HGH*, December 19, 1895; *Lexington Herald*, January 25, May 26, 1896.

92. *MVB*, November 13, 1889; *MSA*, July 1, 1902; *Hartford Republican*, February 26, 1904.

93. "James S. Mahan et al to his Excellency Simon B. Buckner, Governor of the Commonwealth of Ky., November 26, 1888," "J. B. White et al to His Excellency S. B. Buckner, December 4, 1888," Governor's Correspondence, December 1888, box 1, folder 19, KDLA.

94. *HGH*, November 24, 1886.

95. "Will Jennings to Governor S. B. Buckner (Wilson R. Howard cosigned)" (no date but postmarked September 1, 1889), Governor's Correspondence, March–April 1889, box 2, folder 34, KDLA.

96. "Wilson Lewis to Governor Buckner, July 24, 1889," Governor's Correspondence, March–April 1889, box 2, folder, 31, KDLA.

97. "T. S. Ward to Governor S. B. Buckner, July 22, 1889," "Alex A. Arthut to Governor Buckner, July 23rd, 1889," "Wilson Lewis to Governor Buckner, July 24, 1889," "J. K. Bailey to Governor Buckner, August 4, 1889," "Will Jennings to Governor S. B. Buckner (Wilson R. Howard cosigned), postmarked September 1, 1889," Governor's Correspondence, March–April 1889, box 2, folders, 31, 34, KDLA.

98. *HMC*, October 8, 1886; *SIJ*, August 9, 13, 1889; *Pittsburgh Dispatch*, August 7, 1889; *Richmond Climax*, September 4, 1889; *LCJ*, September 23, 1889; *AAC* 14 (1889): 487; "Commonwealth of Barbarians," 295–97; Tapp and Klotter, *Kentucky*, 395–96; Waller, *Feud*, 80.

99. Portelli, *They Say in Harlan County*, 58–63 (quote 59).

100. *Richmond Climax*, November 28, 1888; Otterbein, *Feuding and Warfare*, 236.

101. "S. B. Buckner to Hon. H. C. Lilly, December 14, 1888," "Adjutant General's Report for the Year 1889," *KPD*, vol. 4 (Frankfort: E. Polk Johnson, 1889), 7, 58 (quote); *MVB*, November 6, 1888; *NYS*, December 16, 1888; *Richmond Climax*, January 9, 1889; Ireland, *Little Kingdoms*, 85–86.

102. *KPD*, vol. 4, no. 17 (1889), 58 (quote), 64; "Simon Buckner to H. C. Lilly, Febru-

ary 8, 1889," Sheriff Jeptha Watts to his Excellency S. B. Buckner, March 26, 1889, Governor's Correspondence, March–April 1889, box 2, folder 24, KDLA; *MVB*, December 11, 1888; *Hartford Herald*, January 9, 1889; *SIJ*, July 25, 1890; G. W. Noble, *Behold He Cometh in the Clouds*, 211.

103. "James S. Mahan et al to his Excellency Simon B. Buckner, Governor of the Commonwealth of Ky., November 26, 1888," "J. B. White et al to His Excellency S. B. Buckner, December 4, 1888," Governor's Correspondence, November–December 1888, box 1, folders 18, 19, KDLA; Sandra Lee Barney, *Authorized to Heal*, 22–23.

104. *SIJ*, July 25, 1890.

105. *Hartford Herald*, January 9, 1889.

106. In the August 1889 election for state treasurer, Breathitt County was apparently the only county in the state not to report. *MVB*, September 5, 1889.

107. *Richmond Climax*, September 3, 1890; *MVB*, December 9, 1891 (quote).

108. *HGH*, July 7, 14, 1886, October 7, 21, 1892; *MSA*, October 25, 1892; *MVB*, November 19, 1892.

109. Carl S. Smith, *Urban Disorder and the Shape of Belief*, 86, 90, 163, 172.

110. David Blight divides these postwar rationalizations among whites in the North and South as the "reconciliationist" and "white supremacist" visions, both of which worked toward national reconciliation by depoliticizing the Civil War's memory. While reconciliationists might recoil in horror at the murders of black southerners as a means, they could understand the white South's intended ends. Blight, *Race and Reunion*, 2.

111. Heather Cox Richardson, *West from Appomattox*, 36–37, 76–77, 116.

112. Despite its being a "meaningful social action" laden with interpretive possibilities, violence is often treated as "an unchanging 'natural' fact" that defies characterization or study. By being taken out of the political realm and placed within the context of geographical or racial determinism (i.e., "natural"), feud violence became "senseless" but only in the ways that it was defined by people with no direct experience with it. Blok, *Honour and Violence*, 112–13 (quote).

113. *Richmond Climax*, September 17, 1890; *MVB*, January 23, 1891.

114. Waller, *Feud*, 37–52, 98–101.

115. In their study of Clay County, the site of the later Garrard-Baker-White feud, Dwight Billings and Kathleen Blee note a break in stalemate between county and state government initiated by the election of Kentucky's first Republican governor. Billings and Blee, *The Road to Poverty*, 299.

116. *Columbus Enquirer*, November 4, 1892.

117. *CDT*, May 12, 1889; *Richmond Climax*, May 22, 1889. See also *CDT*, April 8, 1895.

118. *Richmond Climax*, May 22, 1889.

119. *CDT*, September 14, 1890 (quote); *Philadelphia Inquirer*, September 14, 29, 1890; *Wheeling Register*, September 14, 1890.

120. *Macon Telegraph*, September 19, 1890.

121. *SIJ*, September 26, 1890.

122. *Ninth Report of the Railroad Commissioners of Kentucky*, 27; *MVB*, November 13, 1888; *SIJ*, June 20, 1890; G. W. Noble, *Behold He Cometh in the Clouds*, 217.

123. *Jackson Hustler*, April 3, 1891.

124. *MVB*, November 20, 1891; *HGH*, January 29, 1892.

125. *HGH*, June 15, 1887; *SIJ*, October 14, 1887; *Richmond Climax*, January 23, 1889; *MVB*, February 18, 1889; *MSA*, November 17, 1891.

126. Handy, *The Official Directory of the World's Columbian Exposition*, 715.

127. *AGACK, Regular Session, Begun 31 December, 1875* (Frankfort: James A. Hodges, 1876), 2:285–87. One large fork of Troublesome had been declared navigable in 1871, making the building of dams, booms, seining nets, and household mills on it punishable by law. *KHJ, 1871*, 981–82.

128. Burch, *Owsley County, Kentucky*, 41–43.

129. *FRA*, April 25, 1891, Verhoeff, *Kentucky River Navigation*, 110–12, 205–6.

130. "The Timber Boom," 279.

131. "A man is as much a thief who steals the saw logs of a rich corporation as the one who enters a church by night and bears away the Bible or the communion service. That men should be guilty of this crime and yet ask to be considered respectable, is a marvel of impudence and effrontery. The law can not be too rigidly enforced against violators of law of any kind, and especially should it be done when the principal industry of this great country is so effected." *Jackson Hustler*, April 17 (quote), May 3, 24, 1891.

132. "How speculative rent checks production may be seen not only in the valuable land withheld from use, but in the paroxysms of industrial depressions which, originating in the speculative advance in land values, propagate themselves over the whole civilized world everywhere paralyzing industry and causing more waste and probably more suffering than would a general war. Taxation which would take rent for public uses would prevent this, while if land were taxed to anything near its rental value, no one could hold land that he is not using and, consequently, land not in use would be thrown open to those who would use it. Settlement would be closer and, consequently, labor and capital would be able to produce much more with the same exertion." Reprinted in ibid., April 3, 1891.

133. *MSA*, April 21, 1891; *Alexandria Gazette*, April 21, 1891; *Knoxville Journal*, April 22, 1891; *Columbus Enquirer*, April 22, 1891; *Roanoke Times*, April 22, 1891; *Wichita Eagle*, April 23, 1891; *Dallas Morning News*, April 29, 1891 (quote); *Big Stone Post*, May 1, 1891.

134. Between 1880 and 1900 there were at least 140 strikes in Louisville alone, most over companies' failure to maintain wages. With small lines crossing the state's more rural areas, it is likely that work stoppages were even more common but left unreported because of smaller newspapers' unwillingness to report bad news about local economic conditions. Tapp and Klotter, *Kentucky*, 311.

135. *NYS*, May 2, 1891; *SIJ*, May 15, 1891; *Hickman Courier*, September 11, 1891; Karin A. Shapiro, *A New South Rebellion*, 139–72.

136. *Columbia Finance & Trust Co. v. Kentucky Union Ry. Co. et al.*, Circuit Court of Appeals, 6th Circuit, February 5, 1894, *The Federal Reporter*, 60:794–803; *SIJ*, May 15, 1891; *Big Stone Post*, May 15, 1891; *MVB*, July 17, 1891; *NYT*, November 29, 1892; *SIJ*, August 8, 1893; *HGH*, September 13, 1894; *MPL*, January 23, 1894; *Wall Street Journal*, February 12, 1891, March 12, 1894; George Copland to Joseph T. Tucker, September 12, 1900, Kentucky Union Land Company Records, box 1, folder 5, KLSCA.

137. *MPL*, October 15, 1894; *SIJ*, October 16, 1894; *MVB*, October 17, 1894; Verhoeff, *Kentucky River Navigation*, 119; Herr, *Louisville and Nashville Railroad*, 183–84.

138. The L&N eventually purchased the entirety of L&E stock in 1909. Klein, *History of the Louisville and Nashville Railroad*, 401–3; Herr, *Louisville and Nashville Railroad*, 184–88.

139. *CSS*, vol. 347, no. 4, 25th Cong., 3rd sess., H. Doc., p. 139.

140. Quoted in *MVB*, December 3, 1891.

141. D. H. Davis, "Urban Development in the Kentucky Mountains," 95.

142. *Louisville Commercial*, December 8, 1878; *Cincinnati Daily Gazette*, December 9, 1878; *MVB*, July 13, 1885. Despite the weakness of the regulation, a majority of counties followed suit; by 1908, 94 of the state's 119 counties were dry. Jutkins, *Handbook of Prohibition*, 166; "The Amazing Progress of Temperance in Kentucky," 23; *Gambill v. Commonwealth*, February 16, 1911, *Kentucky Reports*, vol. 25 (December 1, 1910–February 1, 1911), 312–14; Woodward, *Origins of the New South*, 390; Ayers, *Promise of the New South*, 178. For the local attribution of violence to alcohol consumption, see *HGH*, November 4, 30, 1891, May 14, 21, 1896.

143. *HGH*, September 2 (quote), 23, 1892.

144. The levying of the first postbellum whiskey tax was a source of social and legal disruption in the Kentucky mountains and the uplands of other states farther south. The distillation of homemade liquor had endured since the Jefferson administration; whiskey making was especially important to farmers with limited access to acreage and wagon roads since corn was more valuable (as well as more easily transportable) in distilled liquid form than it was by the bushel. Southern mountaineers considered the 1867 tax law a violation of their commercial rights and went to great efforts to resist federal efforts toward regulation. Large-scale organization of outlaw distillers, sometimes in numbers that encompassed whole communities, was used to resist and expel federal revenue enforcement. "Blockaders" found enough of a common cause within their trade to form organized groups, often numbering in the dozens, to guard production sites, repel revenue agents, and punish informants. Between 1870 and 1900, "moonshining" was probably more prevalent in Kentucky than it was anywhere else outside of the former Confederacy. Federal revenue agents began coming to Breathitt County in search of illegal distillers as early as 1882. *SIJ*, December 8, 1882, February 9, 1883; *Bourbon News*, February 20, 1883; Holmes, "Moonshining and Collective Violence," 593–95; Bensel, *Yankee Leviathan*, 378. For mass organization of moonshiners in Breathitt County and elsewhere in eastern Kentucky, see "Letter from the Secretary

of War in Relation to the Papers in the Claim of George Williams, March 8, 1880," *CSS*, vol. 24, no. 4, 46th Cong., 2nd sess., H. Doc., pp. 83–84; *NYT*, July 7, 1871, March 13, 1881, July 15, 1886; *HGH*, July 14, 1886.

145. "The moral and religious atmosphere of Jackson is wonderfully improving, due greatly to the vigilance of the police authorities and the hasty execution of the law against the guilty. The police court is presided over by C. X. Bowling, with Charley T. Byrd, a Wolfe County man, for city prosecutor. The 'blind tiger' cannot thrive here, and other evidences of evil are conspicuously absent." "The late grand jury of Breathitt is also to be commended for the noble week's work it has just recorded in history. One hundred and seventy-five indictments were returned against all offenses known in the calendar of crime, and all indications point to a good omen for Breathitt County." *HGH*, June 19, 1899. For Jackson's incorporation, see *AGACK* (Frankfort: E. Polk Johnson, 1890), 1:846–59. See also *Richmond Climax*, March 20, 1895.

146. *MSA*, May 30, 1893; *MVB*, June 1 (quote), 6, 1893; *SIJ*, June 9, 1893.

147. *MVB*, June 6, 1893.

148. Wright, *Racial Violence in Kentucky*, 326.

149. *SIJ*, April 9, 1895.

150. *MPL*, April 11, 1895.

151. *NYS*, December 16, 1888; *HGH*, May 23, 1895; G. W. Noble, *Behold He Cometh in the Clouds*, 257; Waller, *Feud*, 95–97. Smith's preexecution confessions led to French's indictment the following fall. *MSA*, September 24, 1895; *SIJ*, September 24, 1895; *HGH*, September 26, 1895; *Lexington Herald*, May 26, 1896; *Richmond Climax*, June 3, 1896.

152. Catherine McQuinn, the woman at the center of Smith and Rader's quarrel, was convicted as an accomplice to Rader's murder but pardoned in 1897 after new evidence suggested her innocence. *HGH*, February 14, March 21, 1895; *MPL*, March 14, 16, 18, 1895, November 30, 1897; *SIJ*, March 15, 1895; *MVB*, June 1, 22, 1895; *Hartford Herald*, June 26, 1895; *HVK*, March 19, June 28, 1895, December 3, 1897; *FRA*, June 29, 1895; E. L. Noble, *Bloody Breathitt*, 2:101–13.

153. *HGH*, April 11, May 30, June 20, 1895; *HVK*, May 7, 31, June 25, 1895; *MSA*, May 7, June 25, 1895; *SIJ*, May 7, 31, June 18, 25, 1895; *Richmond Climax*, May 22, June 19, 1895; *Knoxville Journal*, June 1, 24, 1895; *MVB*, June 1, 22, 1895; *Hartford Herald*, June 26, 1895.

154. *Kansas City Star*, June 28, 1895; *FRA*, June 29, 1895; *Hickman Courier*, June 28, July 5, 1895; *HVK*, June 28, July 2, 1895; *Knoxville Journal*, June 29, 1895; *MPL*, June 29, 1895; *MVB*, June 29, 1895; *MSA*, July 2, 1895; *SIJ*, July 2, 1895; *HGH*, July 4, 1895.

155. *HVK*, June 28, 1895; *SIJ*, July 2, 1895; *HGH*, July 4, 1895; *Hickman Courier*, July 5, 1895; Charles Hayes, *The Hanging of "Bad Tom" Smith*; William Leonard Eury Appalachian Collection, Carol Grotnes Belk Library & Information Commons, Appalachian State University. For similar, almost textbook, prehanging performances, see Amy Louise Wood, *Lynching and Spectacle*, 39.

156. *LCJ*, June 30, 1895.

157. *MPL,* June 29, 1895. "Public executions in early America were pageants designed to reinforce the moral order of the community and express the ineffable force of law, carefully staged dramas devised to impart an array of lessons to an audience brought forth and transfixed by the promise of violent death: the state shall punish vice; religious authorities shall ensure that the moral order be reestablished; the offender with his death shall atone for his sins against man and God. If everything went according to script, the criminal would see the error of his ways and warn the spectators to never tread his awful path." Schoenbachler, *Murder and Madness,* 202. See also Amy Louise Wood, *Lynching and Spectacle,* 19–44 (particularly 38–41).

158. *HVK,* June 25, 1895.

159. *Hartford Herald,* June 26, 1895.

160. *Kansas City Star,* August 15, 1895.

161. Charles C. Moore, the Voltairesque editor of Lexington's *Blue-grass Blade,* disagreed with the buoyant assessment of Smith's public death, especially after publicized violence was reborn in Bloody Breathitt in 1902: "Kentucky papers printed that excursion trains were run to Jackson, Ky., to witness the hanging of 'Bad Tom Smith' and that there were numbers of pregnant women in the brutal mob that witnessed the criminal dangling at the end of a rope. The conditions of affairs at Jackson, Ky., today prove the brutalizing influence of such scenes. If hanging prevents or deters the criminal classes from murder, why do our authorities deem it best to conduct them in private, as is becoming general now?" *Blue-grass Blade,* August 10, 1902.

162. *LCJ,* June 28, 1895. "Bad Tom" Smith's hanging and his improvident life that led to it remain subjects of discussion in the twenty-first century. Aside from his being a frequent topic on Kentucky genealogical Web sites, Smith's execution was memorialized in an eponymously titled song by the Lexington band Blind Corn Liquor Pickers in 2004. More recently, a Cincinnati microbrewery commemorated Smith's memory with a Bad Tom Ale.

163. *MSA,* July 2, 1895.

164. *HVK,* October 23, 1896; *Knoxville Journal,* November 24, 1896; *Lexington Herald,* October 15, 22, 25, November 26, December 1, 1896; *Mt. Sterling Democrat,* December 8, 1896.

5. Death of a Feudal Hero

1. *HMC,* October 3, 1884, February 5, 1886; *SIJ,* January 29, 1886; *HGH,* February 3, 1886; *FRA,* September 17, 1892.

2. *HGH,* February 16, May 18, 1887; *Richmond Climax,* August 31, 1887.

3. *SIJ,* January 25, 1889; Ed Porter Thompson, *History of the First Kentucky Brigade,* 704.

4. *Lexington Herald,* May 18, 1896; *SIJ,* May 19, 1896; *Richmond Climax,* May 20, November 11, 1896.

5. Waller, *Feud,* 37–41, 152–55, 204–5.

6. *FRA*, February 18, 1893; *Miller v. South &c.*, Kentucky Court of Appeals, filed September 16, 1890, *KLR*, vol. 12, no. 1 (July 1, 1890), 351–52; *Morse v. South et al.* Circuit Court D of Kentucky, April 15, 1897, *The Federal Reporter*, 80:207–8; *H. F. Davis & Co. v. Sizemore et al.*, Court of Appeals of Kentucky, December 20, 1918, *SWR*, vol. 207 (January 22–February 12, 1919), 17; *SWR*, vol. 37 (1896–97), 260; *Aikman v. South et al.*, Court of Appeals of Kentucky, October 31, 1906, *SWR*, vol. 97 (1906–7), 5. Writing in the 1930s when squatters were still being found on titled land in Breathitt County, E. L. Noble used the nomenclature "wood denizens" interchangeably with "squatter," suggesting not only Breathitt County squatters' affinity for unimproved, wooded land but also their foreignness to the mainstream of local society suggested by their apparent unwillingness to seek out legally recognized land tenure. E. L. Noble, *Bloody Breathitt*, 2:58.

7. *HGH*, May 10, 1894.

8. Ibid.

9. *Morse v. South et al.*, Circuit Court D of Kentucky, April 15, 1897, *The Federal Reporter*, 80:206–18; *Strong et al. v. Kentucky River Hardwood Co. et al.; Morse et al. v. Same*, Court of Appeals of Kentucky, November 12, 1920, *SWR*, vol. 225 (December 15, 1920–January 26, 1921), 359.

10. *The Mine, Quarry and Metallurgical Record of the United States, Canada and Mexico*, 476.

11. *MPL*, March 30, 1896; Wiltz, "The 1895 Election," 118, 124; Wright, *Racial Violence in Kentucky*, 131–32; Vandal, *Rethinking Southern Violence*, 197–98.

12. This was with just under 446,000 ballots counted (over 100,000 more than in the previous presidential race). *NYT*, December 28, 1896; *CDT*, November 28, 1896; *TAPR, 1896*, 238; *1897*, 241; Shannon and McQuown, *Presidential Politics in Kentucky*, 67–73.

13. *Hartford Herald*, January 6, 1897. A 1902 amendment weakened the law after Bradley left office. Wright, *Racial Violence in Kentucky*, 177–83, 310–19.

14. *CDT*, December 29, 1896 (quote); *MVB*, November 17, 1896; *HVK*, November 20, 1896; *Crittenden Press*, January 7, 1897; *Paducah Sun*, March 29, 1897; *Hartford Republican*, October 15, 1897.

15. *Lexington Herald*, May 22, 1896. Later that year "a gang of female white cappers" attacked a woman in Pike County. *SIJ*, October 6, 1896.

16. *SIJ*, June 16, 1896.

17. *WKY*, December 17, 1878.

18. With fairly perceptible resemblances to the Ku Klux Klan, which had withered in the previous decade, groups identified as whitecappers first appeared in the late 1880s in Indiana. Whitecappers lacked the Klan's specific iconography, ritualism, and affiliation with southern Democrats. In terms of tactics, however, "[whitecapping] seems to have been an important link between the first and second Ku Klux Klans." Quote from Gurr, *Violence in America*, 39. See also *LCJ*, December 17, 1888; *Lexington Herald*, January 19, 1896; Crozier, *The White-Caps*; Palmer, "Discordant Music," 5–62; Link, *The Paradox of Southern Progressivism*, 62, 312; Holmes, "Whitecapping," 165–85;

330 Notes to Pages 144–147

Holmes, "Moonshining and Collective Violence," 593–95; Brundage, *Lynching in the New South,* 24–25, 17–48.

19. *SIJ,* May 5, December 1, 11, 1896; *HVK,* December 18, 1896; *MPL,* December 22, 1896, March 8, August 10, 1897; *CDT,* December 29, 1896; *Lexington Herald,* January 25, May 2 (quote), 1897; *MVB,* January 26, 1897; *Wheeling Register,* March 9 (quote), 1897; *LCJ,* May 10, 1897; *Cincinnati Commercial-Tribune,* May 10, 1897; *Spout Spring Times,* August 14, 1897; *Richmond Climax,* August 18, 1897; *Crittenden Press,* August 19, 1897; interview with Harlan Strong, 1978, AOHP, no. 279, pp. 20–21; Luntz, *Forgotten Turmoil,* 61–62. The purported appearance of Klan organizations in conjunction with new railroad construction is consistent with the Ku Klux Klan's growth in the Carolinas during its Reconstruction heyday. See Scott Reynolds Nelson, *Iron Confederacies,* 72–94, 106–14, 126–38.

20. *MPL,* August 20, 1896 (quote); *SIJ,* December 1 (quote), 11, 1896.

21. *HVK,* December 18, 1896; *Lexington Herald,* January 25, 1897 (quote).

22. Sarris, *A Separate Civil War,* 166–80.

23. *Kansas City Journal,* May 10, 1897 (quote); interview with Ebb Herald, AOHP, no. 279, p. 2.

24. *Lexington Herald,* December 15, 1896, January 25, July 31, 1897; *SIJ,* December 22, 1896; *HVK,* December 18, 1896; *SIJ,* December 22, 1896, March 12, 1897; *Paducah Sun,* March 11, 1897; *Cincinnati Commercial-Tribune,* May 10, 1897.

25. *Lexington Herald,* January 25, 1897.

26. Byrd's murder was quickly politicized, the better to tarnish Republican governor William Bradley. The summer beforehand, a drunken Byrd had catcalled Bradley during a campaign speech. In a story reminiscent of Henry II and Thomas Becket, a rumor circulated that Bradley promised to pardon anyone who might kill Byrd in the future, and Byrd's credulous future killers took it to heart. *Lexington Leader,* January 15, 1897; *MPL,* January 16, 18, February 16, 1897; *SIJ,* January 19, 22, 1897; *HVK,* January 19, March 2, 1897; *Richmond Climax,* January 20, 1897; *MVB,* January 26, 1897; *MSA,* February 23, April 6, 1897; *Spout Spring Times,* April 10, 1897; Guerrant, *The Galax Gatherers,* 97–98.

27. *NYS,* January 18, 1897; *MPL,* January 18, 22, February 22, 1897; *Richmond Climax,* January 20, February 24, 1897; *SIJ,* January 22, 1897; *Lexington Herald,* February 22, 1897; *HVK,* March 2, 1897; *Paducah Sun,* March 11, 1897; *MSA,* April 6, 1897.

28. *NYT,* March 9, 1897; *Paducah Sun,* March 11, 1897; *SIJ,* March 12, 1897; *Richmond Climax,* April 7, 1897; *LCJ,* May 10, 1897.

29. *Lexington Herald,* September 15, 1897.

30. *The Kentucky State Gazetteer and Business Directory for 1879–1880,* microfilm reel #S92-68, pp. 214–15, KLSCA; *Cincinnati Commercial-Tribune,* May 10, 1897; *SIJ,* September 17, 1897.

31. *NYS,* April 16, May 2, 1897; *SIJ,* April 20, 1897; *HGH,* April 22, 1897; *Lexington Leader,* May 9, 1897; *Cincinnati Commercial-Tribune,* May 10, 1897; *Washington Evening Times,* March 14, 1901.

32. *Morse v. South et al.,* Circuit Court D of Kentucky, April 15, 1897, *The Federal Reporter,* 80:207–8.

33. *Lexington Herald,* May 10, 1897.

34. *Cincinnati Commercial-Tribune,* May 10, 1897.

35. *Lexington Herald,* May 2, 10–11, 1897; *Lexington Leader,* May 10, 1897; *NYS,* May 10–11, 1897; *Boston Globe,* May 10, 1897; *Washington Times,* May 10, 1897; *HVK,* May 11, 1897; *SIJ,* May 11, 18, 1897; *LCJ,* May 12, 1897; *Earlington Bee,* May 13, 1897; *Spout Spring Times,* May 15, June 12, 1897; interview with Henry Duff, July 22, 1898, *JJDD,* reel 2, pp. 2428–29; *Strong et al. v. Kentucky River Hardwood Co. et al; Morse et al. v. Same,* Court of Appeals of Kentucky, November 12, 1920, *SWR,* vol. 225 (December 15, 1920–January 26, 1921), 359–60; Kash, "Feud Days in Breathitt County," 343; interview with Ebb Herald, AOHP, no. 279, p. 3; Rolff, *Strong Family of Virginia and Other Southern States,* 93–94.

36. *Lexington Herald,* May 10, 1897.

37. *Boston Globe,* May 10, 1897.

38. *LCJ,* May 10, 1897.

39. Ibid., December 3, 1878, May 10, 1897. The *Courier-Journal* did not completely ignore the political significance of Strong's career as a "feudal chieftain." However, the newspaper's admission of Strong as a political actor after a fashion was not particularly remarkable considering that the struggles that Strong had taken part in probably would have seemed more quaint than controversial to most readers at such a late date as 1897. See also *Cincinnati Commercial,* May 10, 1897.

40. *LCJ,* May 12, 1897.

41. The *Jackson Hustler* probably did, but there are no extant issues from 1897.

42. *Cincinnati Commercial-Tribune,* May 10, 1897.

43. *NYT,* May 10, 1897.

44. Baldasty, *The Commercialization of News in the Nineteenth Century,* 139.

45. *Lexington Herald,* May 27, July 31, 1897; *MPL,* July 31, 1897; *HVK,* August 3, 1897.

46. *Lexington Herald,* May 11, 1897; interview with Ebb Herald, AOHP, no. 279, p. 3.

47. *LCJ,* May 12, 1897; interview with John Akeman [Aikman], July 20, 1898, *JJDD,* reel 2, pp. 2412–13.

48. *Lexington Leader,* May 10, 1897.

49. *SIJ,* May 24, 1912.

50. Wright, *Racial Violence in Kentucky ,* 180–81.

51. Aikman: "Ned Callahan and Capt. Strong compromised [reprised?] their troubles in Jackson and in a few days Strong was killed. Their excuse for that way of doing was that Capt. Strong did the same way with the Amises. He, Al [?] and John Amis and old Wilson Callahan agreed to go home and go to work and he would not trouble them. In two days he had them killed at least it was only a few days. Old Wiley, Tom, Ause and Bob Amis bundled up and left at once. I don't think any of the Strong

men were killed. I do not remember that any besides these were killed on the Amis side. The war lasted over a year. Strong kept his men around him. The others did not have the means to support their men in a body as Strong had." Interview with John Aikman, July 20, 1898, *JJDD*, reel 2, pp. 2412–13. See also Rolff, *Strong Family of Virginia and Other Southern States*, 93.

52. The use of the word *clan* as a reminder of specific historical events in past centuries is not the only way in which the press removed Breathitt County and, by extension, eastern Kentucky, from the present. The allusion to kinship in describing Breathitt County's violent politics is telling. Kinship, by modern definitions, is a social designator firmly rooted in societies that existed (or exist) in the past since modern society replaces familial bonds with administrative or bureaucratic forms of rationalization. The application of kinship therefore is "fraught with temporal connotations" especially after anthropologists of the nineteenth and twentieth centuries used degrees of kinship to construct "temporal scales" (by which societies could be judged as paradoxically existing in the past or present). Fabian, *Time and the Other*, 75–76.

53. *LCJ*, May 5, 1903; Clements, *History of the First Regiment of Infantry*, 148–49.

54. WPA, *In the Land of Breathitt*, 71.

55. During the 1890s Strong's ties to Breathitt County's African American population seemed to have diminished. A possible reason for this is that, after 1870, the already tiny segment of the population had shrunk steadily. Hiram Freeman and his family had left Breathitt County sometime in the 1880s, and by the late 1890s the Red Strings had apparently become an exclusively white group. However, at least a few of the Strong family's former slaves and their descendants lived on or near William Strong's property. *Lexington Herald*, May 11, 1897; Ernest Collins, "Political Behavior in Breathitt, Knott, Perry and Leslie Counties," 10.

56. *Spout Spring Times*, June 12, 26, 1897.

57. If the organization refounded in Georgia by William J. Simmons in 1915 eventually included a local klavern in Breathitt County, it is very possible that it may have had a greater measure of continuance from the nineteenth century than almost any other klan-hosting locality due to the latter's phenomenal longevity. For historical comparisons and contrasts between the two versions of the organization, see Wade, *The Fiery Cross*.

58. Aside from John Aikman, all of the men that Strong's family suspected of being his slayer, Abner Baker, Asbury Spicer, and John Smith, were Edward Callahan's employees or Democratic associates (and possibly Klan members). John Smith would later be implicated in another murderous scheme involving Callahan. *Begley v. Commonwealth*, Court of Appeals of Kentucky, February 19, 1901, *SWR*, vol. 60 (January 21–March 18, 1901), 847–49; Strong Family Papers, 93–94, Breathitt County Public Library; *LCJ*, May 10, 1897; *Cincinnati Commercial Tribune*, May 10, 1897; *NYT*, January 12, 1907; Rolff, *Strong Family of Virginia and Other Southern States*, 93–94.

59. *Lexington Leader*, November 12, 1902.

6. "There has always been the bitterest political feeling in the county"

1. *LCJ*, December 24, 1888.

2. While the new constitution reaffirmed ballot voting, a law had already been passed two years before the convention eliminating vive voce in elections for state office. *LCJ*, January 14, 1888; *MVS*, March 16, 1900; *Hickman Courier*, September 11, 1891; Scalf, *Kentucky's Last Frontier*, 370–71.

Agrarian protest against corporate ascendancy emerged just as divisions between Bourbons and New Departure Democrats were beginning to heal in the late 1870s. Populists were able to take a large chunk out of the Democratic electorate until many Democrats began heisting their platform, espousing railroad regulation and silver coinage. This, however, was too late to prevent Republicans from taking advantage of these divisions. Kinkead, *A History of Kentucky*, 216 18; Thomas J. Brown, "The Roots of Bluegrass Insurgency," 231–41; Klotter, *William Goebel*, 11–12; Tapp, "Three Decades of Kentucky Politics," 212–16; Bland, "Populism in Kentucky," 140; Lowell Harrison, *Kentucky's Governors*, 103–6; Thomas Louis Owen, "The Formative Years of Kentucky's Republican Party," 165.

3. *Earlington Bee*, November 7, 1895; *MPL*, November 9, 1895 (quote); *Richmond Climax*, October 9, 1895; Kinkead, *A History of Kentucky*, 216–17; Wiltz, "The 1895 Election," 133.

4. *HGH*, September 19, 1895 (quote); Woodward, *Origins of the New South*, 29.

5. *MPL*, March 30, 1896; *Paducah Sun*, October 7, 1898; Pearce, *Divide and Dissent*, 16–17; Wright, *A History of Blacks in Kentucky*, 70–76, 90–91; Bland, "Populism in Kentucky," 109; Tapp and Klotter, *Kentucky*, 369; Lowell Harrison, *Kentucky's Governors*, 168–79.

6. *HVK*, March 17, 1896.

7. McKinley won Kentucky by a mere 142 votes. *TAPR, 1896*, 238; *1897*, 241; Powers, "My Own Story," 265 (quote); Harpine, *From the Front Porch to the Front Page*, 179; Woodward, *Origins of the New South*, 288. Kentucky's first Republican U.S. senator was elected in 1897. Gordon McKinney, *Southern Mountain Republicans*, 198; Lowell Harrison, *Kentucky's Governors*, 108; Klotter, *William Goebel*, 24–25.

8. *Paducah Sun*, November 30, 1896.

9. *Breckinridge News*, March 2, 1898. Bradley came to office just in time for the South's widespread first wave of demand for railroad legislation. Grantham, *Southern Progressivism*, 145–52. Suspicion toward the L&N began in 1887 when the railroad unsuccessfully lobbied for the abolition of Kentucky's regulatory railroad commission, a lobbying effort accompanied by a well-known measure of bribery. Although the Kentucky House passed the L&N's proposal, it was defeated in the Senate. However, anti-L&N Kentuckians did not consider this a permanent victory and continued to attack the railroad as a conspirator in statewide graft. *KSJ, 1893* (vol. 3), pp. 3909, 3929, 3949; Gary Robert Matthews and Ramage, *Basil Wilson Duke*, 265; Clark, "The People,

William Goebel, and the Kentucky Railroads," 48; *LCJ*, January 19, 1888, quoted in Woodward, *Origins of the New South*, 7; Bland, "Populism in Kentucky," 4.

10. Even though the earlier respective popularities of the Greenback Party, Grange, Farmer's Alliance, Colored Farmer's Alliance, and Agricultural Wheel resulted in enthusiasm for Populism in the state (especially the tobacco-growing west), the history of Kentucky's People's Party was relatively brief. The Republicans' 1895 gubernatorial victory alarmed Kentucky Democrats enough that they followed the national trend in absorbing the Populist platform, after which "the People's Party itself wither[ed] away." However, under Goebel's leadership, "Populism became more than a party in Kentucky; it became a style." Conti, "Mountain Metamorphoses," 185–86; Thomas J. Brown, "The Roots of Bluegrass Insurgency," 241.

11. This problem was exacerbated by his rivalry with fellow Democrat "blue-blooded, ex-Confederate soldier" W. J. Stone. To add further weight to the war memory's contribution to the controversy, Goebel's two primary Democratic detractors were two of the state's most highly regarded Confederate veterans: W. C. P Breckinridge and Henry Watterson (although the latter eventually cautiously endorsed him). Clark, "The People, William Goebel, and the Kentucky Railroads," 37; Klotter, *William Goebel*, 47–49.

Despite, or perhaps because, of his age, McCreary was said to have "established the most progressive record of any chief executive in Kentucky up to that time." Burckel, "From Beckham to McCreary," 305.

12. Tapp, "Three Decades of Kentucky Politics," 451 (quote); Hahn, *The Roots of Southern Populism*, 176–82, 279–87; Grantham, *Southern Progressivism*, 147–49; Ayers, *Promise of the New South*, 409–17; Woodward, *Origins of the New South*, 374–79.

13. Unlike most Kentucky Democrats, Goebel welcomed black men's votes, which made up about one-seventh of the state's electorate. However, his dedication to separate but equal disenchanted most black power brokers. Wright, *A History of Blacks in Kentucky*, 93–94; Tapp and Klotter, *Kentucky*, 410; Ayers, *Promise of the New South*, 413.

14. Klein, *History of the Louisville and Nashville Railroad*, 382–83.

15. *NYT*, April 12, 13, 1895; "Kentucky's Political Anarchy," 126. The manner in which Goebel dispatched his street-side antagonist adds credence to C. Vann Woodward's contention that the public "shooting on sight" had supplanted the traditional duel as the primary method of white intraracial violence after Reconstruction, especially since Goebel apparently did not respond to a "customary challenge to a duel" by the L&N's lobbyist Basil Duke a few years later. Had he done so, he would have been disqualified from ever taking the oath as governor since, by 1900, Kentucky's constitution forbade anyone who had ever participated in a duel in any capacity from assuming the office. "Executive Order #I," February 3, 1900, Papers of J. C. W. Beckham, Special Reports and Studies (Goebel Incident), box 1, folder 8, bundle 11, KDLA; Gary Robert Matthews and Ramage, *Basil Wilson Duke*, 277; Woodward, *Origins of the New South*, 158, 160, 378.

16. *SIJ*, October 20, December 1, 1896; *NYT*, December 7, 1896; *Paducah Sun*, February 27, 1897; *Earlington Bee*, March 18, 1897; *Bourbon News*, March 19, 1897; *MVB*,

March 19, 1897; *Lexington Herald,* April 9, 1897; *AAC* (1896): 375; (1897): 437; (1898): 356; Klotter, *William Goebel,* 22; Tapp, "Three Decades of Kentucky Politics," 352–60.

17. *Lexington Herald,* February 19, 23, 1898; *MPL,* April 16, 1898; Bolin, *Bossism and Reform in a Southern City,* 26–29; Tapp and Klotter, *Kentucky,* 356.

18. As a product of Kentucky's ancient inclination toward county autonomy, election officers were chosen by county courts, meaning that ballot boxes were subject to the whims and wishes of county judges, clerks, and sheriffs. If multiple parties were to be represented in the boxes' management, it was solely up to local courts to do so. Goebel's bill took this authority away from local officials and placed it in the hands of a commission chosen by the General Assembly. Succinctly, the directors of local elections would be chosen without the permission of the local court, a potentially problematic situation in cases in which county courts were under the control of a different party than happened to currently hold the majority in the General Assembly. While the most immediate effect of this law was to place elections in all counties (including those controlled by Republicans) under the management of the then Democratically controlled legislature, Goebel insisted that his election bill was a remedy for the alleged corruption that resulted in William Bradley's election and the L&N's continuing influence. *Lexington Herald,* February 27, March 1, 2, 10, 11, 12, 13; *NYT,* March 5, 1898; *Columbus Enquirer,* March 12, 1898; *KSJ, 1898,* 1022, 1145; *AAC* (1899): 356; *Hartford Republican,* October 5, 1900; Klotter, *William Goebel,* 46–47.

19. *MVB,* June 22, 1899; *SIJ,* June 23, 1899; *HVK,* June 23, 1899; *Lexington Herald,* June 27, 1899; *Hartford Republican,* June 30, 1899; *CDT,* December 4, 1899; Hughes, Schaefer, and Williams, *That Kentucky Campaign,* 16–42; Levin, *The Lawyers and Lawmakers of Kentucky,* 556 (quote); Klotter, *William Goebel,* 57.

20. *HGH,* November 10, 1886; interview with David Redwine, July 18, 1898, *JJDD,* reel 2, p. 2538. In Redwine's time, accusations of collecting "boodle" were more salacious innuendo than they were allegations of betraying the public trust. Whether or not Redwine was guilty of buying votes, it was more the rule than the exception in the 1880s. Summers, *Party Games,* 91–106.

21. The first book-length account of the Goebel affair (written from a Goebel-friendly perspective at that), published within less than a year of Goebel's death, introduced Redwine as being from Breathitt County with no need for a fuller explanation. Hughes, Schaefer, and Williams, *That Kentucky Campaign,* 34.

22. For instance, Powers, *My Own Story,* 86; Levin, *The Lawyers and Lawmakers of Kentucky,* 556; Gordon McKinney, *Southern Mountain Republicans,* 195.

23. *Hartford Republican,* June 30, 1899.

24. Hughes, Schaefer, and Williams, *That Kentucky Campaign,* 46–48; Tapp and Klotter, *Kentucky,* 418–22.

25. Hughes, Schaefer, and Williams, *That Kentucky Campaign,* 34; Powers, *My Own Story,* 86.

26. *Lexington Herald,* July 11, 1899; *Lexington Leader,* November 14, 1902; *LCJ,*

February 6, 1908; Clark, *Kentucky: Land of Contrast*, 209 (quote). James Hargis was the son of former Breathitt County treasurer and (briefly) state senator John Seldon Hargis.

27. Powers, *My Own Story*, 80.

28. *Lexington Herald*, June 28, 29, 30, July, 1, 2, 3, 1899; *Louisville Dispatch*, August 27 (quote), 1899; *Lexington Herald*, November 18, 1899. See also Fenton, *Politics in the Border States*, 41–44.

29. *HVK*, September 19, 22, 1899; *MVS*, October 13, 1899.

30. Hughes, Schaefer, and Williams, *That Kentucky Campaign*, 108.

31. *LCJ*, October 17, 1899.

32. *NYT*, June 24, 1899; *AAC* (1899): 409.

33. *Lexington Herald*, September 11, 1899; *NYT*, October 15, 1899; Henry Loomis Nelson, "The Kentucky 'Boss's' Desperate Campaign," 1083; Tracy Campbell, *The Politics of Despair*, 33–36; Powers, *My Own Story*, 56, 58–59, 89–97, 120–23; Tapp, "Three Decades of Kentucky Politics," 446.

34. *Lowell Harrison*, "Taylor, William Sylvester," *870*.

35. *KHJ, 1900*, 46–52; *KSJ, 1900*, 60–66.

36. Hughes, Schaefer, and Williams, *That Kentucky Campaign*, 145; Clements, *History of the First Regiment of Infantry*, 119; Klotter, *William Goebel*, 95.

37. When Kentucky's Democrat-majority General Assembly "conced[ed] the mountain counties to the Republicans" in 1890, they created an "oversized" congressional district containing territories formerly controlled by different Republican bosses. The intended effect was that these preexistent machines would come into conflict, further weakening and isolating the Republicans. As demonstrated by the eventual election of William Bradley as governor and steady Republican legislative gains elsewhere, the strategy was not flawless. *MVB*, March 20, 1890, December 4, 1899, January 31, 1900; *MSA*, December 5, 1899; *Hartford Herald*, December 6, 1899; *LCJ*, January 26, 31, 1900; *Washington Times*, February 2, 1900; *MVS*, February 2, 1900; *Caleb Powers, Appt., v. Commonwealth of Kentucky*, Kentucky Court of Appeals, *LRA*, 53:258–60; Gordon McKinney, *Southern Mountain Republicans*, 119, 167–76 ("conceding" on 168); Shannon and McQuown, *Presidential Politics in Kentucky*, 71.

38. *Hartford Herald*, December 6, 1899; *LCJ*, January 26, 1900 (quote).

39. *LCJ*, January 26 (quote), 1900; *MSA*, March 27, 1900; *Richmond Climax*, March 28, 1900; *HMC*, March 30, 1900; *Crittenden Press*, July 19, 1900.

40. *LCJ*, January 26, 1900; *HVK*, January 30, 1900.

41. *Lexington Herald*, January 26, 1900.

42. *LCJ*, January 31, 1900.

43. *Blue-grass Blade*, February 11, 1900.

44. *HVK*, February 2, 1900; *Washington Times*, February 2, 1900; *William S. Taylor and John Marshall, Plffs. In Err. v. J. C. W. Beckham, Drt. Err.*, U.S. Supreme Court (argued April 30 and May 1, 1900), *Supreme Court Reporter, Cases Argued and Determined in the United States Supreme Court, October Term, 1899*, vol. 20 (November 1899–July

1900), 895; "Executive Order #I," February 3, 1900, Papers of J. C. W. Beckham, Special Reports and Studies (Goebel Incident), box 1, folder 8, bundles 9, 12, KDLA; Tapp and Klotter, *Kentucky,* 450.

45. *ACN,* February 14, 1900.

46. *Washington Times,* February 2, 1900.

47. In 1912 James Gilbert, a Helena, Arkansas, sheriff's deputy formerly of Breathitt County, confessed to being the triggerman in Goebel's death twelve years earlier. Gilbert's confession was made with his last dying breath after a gunfight. His confession was apparently not investigated. *Washington Herald,* February 16, 1912; *MSA,* February 21, 1912.

48. Proclamation of Governor Beckham, Governor's Correspondence, Papers of Gov. J. C. W. Beckham, box 1, folder 1, bundle 16, KDLA; *Howard v. Commonwealth, Kentucky Reports,* vol. 18, part 1 (April 1904), 2–18; Powers, *My Own Story,* 122–23.

49. *Breckinridge News,* December 18, 1918.

50. *AAC* (1899): 409; *Berea Citizen,* April 29, 1909.

51. *SIJ,* March 27, 1900; *Hartford Herald,* April 4, 1900; *Hartford Republican,* April 13, 1900; *MVS,* May 18, 25, 1900; *MSA,* May 29, 1900; *Bourbon News,* June 1, 1900; Klotter, *William Goebel,* 113–14.

52. Beckham had taken the oath of lieutenant governor at the same time the dying Goebel took the governor's oath. He took the oath as governor the following day just after Goebel's passing. *William S. Taylor and John Marshall, Plffs. In Err. v. J .C. W. Beckham, Drt. Err.,* U.S. Supreme Court (argued April 30 and May 1, 1900), *Supreme Court Reporter, Cases Argued and Determined in the United States Supreme Court, October Term, 1899,* vol. 20 (November 1899–July 1900), 1187–1212; "Executive Order #I," February 3, 1900, Papers of J. C. W. Beckham, Special Reports and Studies (Goebel Incident), box 1, folder 8, bundles 8, 10–12, KDLA.

53. Fenton, *Politics in the Border States,* 44; Pearce, *Divide and Dissent,* 25.

54. Woodward, *Origins of the New South,* 377. A contemporary accusation of Goebel's campaign "precipitating civil war" appeared in *Louisville Dispatch,* November 10, 1899.

55. Proclamation, Papers of J. C. W. Beckham, Special Reports and Studies (Goebel Incident), box 1, folder 8, bundle 12 (quote), KDLA; Klotter, *Kentucky,* 206.

56. Hughes, Schaefer, and Williams, *That Kentucky Campaign,* 256; *MSA,* March 27, 1900; *Bourbon News,* March 27, 1900; *Richmond Climax,* March 28, 1900; *HMC,* March 30, 1900; *Crittenden Press,* July 19, 1900; *Hartford Herald,* September 19, 1900; *Caleb Powers, Appt., v. Commonwealth of Kentucky,* Kentucky Court of Appeals, *LRA,* 3:264.

57. Hughes, Schaefer, and Williams, *That Kentucky Campaign,* 312. This would have been the Clay County War fought between the hegemons of one county's salt-extraction industry—one Democratic, one Republican. It was an old rivalry that did not come to physical blows until the election of Kentucky's first Republican governor disrupted Clay County's political status quo. Billings and Blee, *The Road to Poverty,* 291–92.

58. *Earlington Bee,* September 20, 1900; *HGH,* October 18, 1900.

59. For the problems surrounding the characterization of Goebel's killers as "feudists," see Williams, "Henry Shapiro and the Idea of Appalachia," 353–54.

60. In John Fox Jr.'s fictionalized account of Frankfort in January 1900, published more than ten years later, Goebel's death provided an ironic twist in the plot of an imaginary feud between the Hawns and Honeycutts in an unidentified mountain county. The threat posed by "the autocrat" (an unnamed fictionalized Goebel) necessitated the two families' swearing "that they had buried the feud for a while and that they would fight like brothers for their rights." Soon after, a member of each "clan" is implicated in the governor-elect's murder. The communal conflict that had led to their initial division was subsumed by the political conflict that not only united them but prompted the Hawns and Honeycutts to engage the more modern world of the Bluegrass in a manner that bettered them with exposure to the "outside world" without stripping them of their native nobility and egalitarianism. The feud between the Hawns and Honeycutts had begun over small differences of a strictly personal nature; politics, the cause of the real-life ruptures that had been labeled as "feuds" years before, was instead treated as the force through which warring clans could be united against a common enemy worthier of their heretofore misplaced wrath. The ability of the Kentucky mountaineer to accept the progress of the outside world, rejecting communal violence while maintaining his nobler qualities, was a typical theme in Fox's portrayals of the region. The use of a Goebel figure as the unseen antagonist in a Fox novel reflected the danger that mountain Republicans saw in his candidacy but, as a literary device, represented the overly bureaucratized republic's loss of democracy that only the reinvolvement of the "pure" Anglo-Saxon yeoman could heal. In Fox's (albeit patronizing) portrayal, published years after Goebel's death, the "ignorant men" who occupied Frankfort in the winter of 1900 could be roughhewn heroes. Fox, *The Heart of the Hills,* 207. Fox was inspired to include a Goebel-like character in the novel after attending the governor-elect's funeral. York, *John Fox,* 165–66. See also Satterwhite, *Dear Appalachia,* 55–87; Ayers, *Promise of the New South,* 364–65.

61. *Hartford Herald,* October 10 (quote), 1900; Anne E. Marshall, *Creating a Confederate Kentucky,* 132.

62. *MSA,* June 28, 1898; *Lexington Herald,* September 15, 1897, August 17, 1898.

63. *SIJ,* September 17, 1897; *MSA,* September 26, 1899.

64. *NYT,* September 15, 1897.

65. McAfee, *Kentucky Politicians,* 73–76.

66. Gordon McKinney, *Southern Mountain Republicans,* 195.

67. Coates, *Stories of Kentucky Feuds,* 3.

68. Even as most Kentucky Democrats embraced free silver, it would seem that even the Democratic majority of Breathitt County favored maintaining the gold standard. *MSA,* June 2, 1896; *HVK,* June 2, 1896.

69. *Richmond Climax,* October 9, 1895.

70. *HVK*, June 23, 27, 1899; *LCJ*, February 6, 1908.

71. E. L. Noble, *Bloody Breathitt*, 1:106.

72. *Hartford Republican*, September 13, 1899; Hughes, Schaefer, and Williams, *That Kentucky Campaign*, 108.

73. *HGH*, June 19, 1899.

74. Grantham, *Southern Progressivism*, 145–49.

75. *TAPR, 1900*, 82 (quote). For other characterizations of William Goebel as an anarchist, see also *Hartford Republican*, October 5, 1900; Klotter, *William Goebel*, 68.

76. *HGH*, June 19, 1899.

77. *Lexington Herald*, July 9 (quote), 1899; *MSA*, May 21, 1901, February 19, 1908; Coulter and Connelley, *History of Kentucky*, 3:611.

78. *Lexington Herald*, August 9, 15, 1899.

79. Ibid., November 12, 1899; *NYT* (quote), November 12, 1899; *NYS*, November 12, 1899; *Hartford Republican*, November 27, 1903. *Bulldozing* was a commonly used term for voter intimidation. Summers, *Party Games*, 102.

80. *Lexington Herald*, November 12, 1899; *HVK*, January 26, 1900.

81. *NYS*, November 12, 1899.

82. These were Lexington (Fayette County), Louisville (Jefferson County), Frankfort (Woodford County), and Goebel's hometown of Covington (Kenton County). *Earlington Bee*, January 17, 1901; Hughes, Schaefer, and Williams, *That Kentucky Campaign*, 191.

83. *Washington Times*, November 10, 14, 1900.

84. *NYT*, November 10, 1900.

85. Breathitt County's fusionists were not only using the same tactic employed by Populists a few years before, but were doing so out of a similar impulse. Before it became a national movement with faraway northern plutocrats as targets, Populism's political manifestation had its beginnings in small farmers' disgust with local courthouse elites. James Turner, "Understanding the Populists," 367–68. See also Perman, *Pursuit of Unity*, 148–49, 166–69; Lester, *Up from the Mudsills of Hell*; Hahn, *A Nation under Our Feet*, 385–87; McMath, *American Populism*, 197, 203–6; Ayers, *The Promise of the New South*, 42–46, 290–305; Gordon McKinney, *Southern Mountain Republicans*, 162–66; Uzee, "The Republican Party in the Louisiana Election of 1896"; de Santis, "Republican Efforts to 'Crack' the Democratic South," 332–44; Kirwan, *Revolt of the Rednecks*, 99–100; Edmonds, *The Negro and Fusion Politics in North Carolina*; Munroe Smith, "Record of Political Events," 370; Haynes, "The New Sectionalism," 275; *LRA*, n.s., 37:886–88.

86. *Hartford Republican*, November 27, 1903; *LRA*, n.s., 37:886–88.

87. *HGH*, October 14, 1892; *MPL*, November 27, 1895, June 19, 1899; *Morse v. South et al.*, Circuit Court D of Kentucky, April 15, 1897, *The Federal Reporter*, 80:206–18; Speed, Pirtle, and Kelly, *The Union Regiments of Kentucky*, 257; *LCJ*, May 10, 1897; *MSA*, October 3, 1899; *Lexington Herald*, January 10, 1900; *MPL*, January 12, 1900.

88. E. L. Noble, *Bloody Breathitt*, 2:26; Charles C. Wells, *1890 Special Veterans' Census for Eastern Kentucky*, 222.

89. *Kentucky Union Co., &c., v. Lovely, &c.*, March 14, 1901, in *Reports of the Civil and Criminal Cases decided by the Court of Appeals of Kentucky*, 295–96; For Marcum's representation of the L&E, see *Biennial Report of the Bureau of Agriculture, Labor and Statistics of the State of Kentucky*, 45; *Lexington Herald*, November 14, 1902; E. Polk Johnson, *A History of Kentucky and Kentuckians*, 1357; U.S. Department of Agriculture Office of Experiment Stations, *Organization Lists of the Agricultural Experimental Stations*, 54; Clements, *History of the First Regiment of Infantry*, 157.

For mountain Republicans' abandonment of Civil War–era issues in favor of a more business-related identity, see John A. Williams, "Class, Section, and Culture in Nineteenth-Century West Virginia Politics," 228; Snay, "Freedom and Progress," 109–10; Gordon McKinney, *Southern Mountain Republicans*, 166–76.

90. Quoted in Lears, *Rebirth of a Nation*, 149.

91. *HGH*, May 10, 1894.

92. *Richmond Climax*, May 22, 1895; *Aikman v. Commonwealth, March 17, 1892, SWR*, vol. 18 (February 1–April 25, 1892), 937–38; *Adkins et al v. Commonwealth*, Court of Appeals of Kentucky, January 16, 1896, *SWR*, vol. 33 (December 30, 1895–March 2, 1896), 948–53.

93. Handbill: "Answer to Judge Hagins' Circular," Assorted Documents, Breathitt County Museum; *Lexington Herald*, July 9 (quote), 1899; *MSA*, May 21, 1901; Coulter and Connelley, *History of Kentucky*, 3:611.

94. *HGH*, October 17, 1901.

95. Pollard was often counsel for the Breathitt County court in higher courts. *KLR*, vol. 21, part 2 (January 1, 1903–June 15, 1903) (Frankfort: Geo. A. Lewis, 1903), 1406.

96. *HGH*, November 7, 1901.

97. Ibid., November 28, 1901; *LRA*, n.s., 37:886–89; *LEP*, May 19, 1903.

98. *KLR*, vol. 24, part 2 (January 1, 1903–June 15, 1903), 2498–2500; *MSA*, November 19, December 17, 1902; *Lancaster Central Record*, November 27, 1902; *LEP*, May 19, 1903; *BCN*, October 23, 1903.

99. *Washington Times*, August 17, 1902; *LCJ*, May ? 1903; Child, "The Boss of Breathitt," 15.

100. *HGH*, February 27, 1902; *Washington Times*, August 17, 1902; Kash, "Feud Days in Breathitt County," 344. Kash was personally acquainted with the Hargis brothers, Cox, Marcum, and most of the men involved in the conflicts of 1902 in Jackson.

101. Courtwright, *Violent Land*, 170; Ayers, *The Promise of the New South*, 256–57.

102. *HGH*, February 6, 1902.

103. For a similar change in the character of violence in a newly factoried setting, see Carlton, *Mill and Town in South Carolina*, 145–51.

104. *Hartford Republican*, June 27, 1902.

105. *MPL*, November 2, 1896; *Lexington Herald*, November 2, 3, 1896; *Richmond Climax*, November 4, 1896; *Cardwell v. Commonwealth*, Court of Appeals of Kentucky, June 23, 1898, *SWR*, vol. 46, 705–7; *Washington Times*, August 17, 1902.

106. *Spout Spring Times,* July 30, 1898; *NYT,* July 3, 1904.

107. *SIJ,* May 12, 1903; *MSA,* April 15, 1902; *MVB,* April 16, 1902; *Blue-grass Blade,* April 27, 1902; *Washington Times,* August 17, 1902.

108. Havens, Leiden, and Schmitt, *The Politics of Assassination,* 152.

109. *Lexington Herald,* April 15, 1902; *MSA,* April 15, 1902; *MVB,* April 16, 1902; *HGH,* April 17, 1902; *Lexington Leader,* July 21, 1902; *Washington Times,* August 17, 1902; *LCJ,* February 6, 1908.

110. *MSA,* April 15, 1902; *MVB,* April 16, 1902, May 9, 1903; *Blue-grass Blade,* April 27, 1902; "Telephone to Open Feud-Ridden County," 196; Child, "The Boss of Breathitt," 15; Clements, *History of the First Regiment of Infantry,* 151.

111. Kash, "Feud Days in Breathitt County," 344–45.

112. *MSA,* July 22, 29, August 5, 1902; *CDT,* July 22, 1902; *Lexington Herald,* July 23, 1902; *Maysville Bulletin,* July 23, 1902, *Paducah Sun,* July 24, 1902; *MVS,* July 25, 1902; *Hartford Republican,* July 25, 1902; *ACN,* July 30, 1902; *LEP,* May 4, 1903; Trimble, *Recollections of Breathitt,* 8.

113. *MSA,* July 22, 1902.

114. *Hargis et al. v. Parker, Judge, et al.,* Court of Appeals of Kentucky, March 10, 1905, *SWR,* vol. 85 (March 15–April 19, 1905), 705.

115. *Lexington Leader,* July 21, 1902; *LEP,* May 4, 1903.

116. *Paducah Sun,* July 24, 1902.

117. *Lexington Leader,* July 24, 1902. Democratic attacks on fusionists were nothing unfamiliar, at least elsewhere in the South, most notably 1898's White Supremacy campaign that precipitated the Wilmington Race Riot and guaranteed one-party dominance for at least a generation in North Carolina. Redding, *Making Race, Making Power,* 129–33.

118. *Lexington Leader,* July 24, 1902; *Paducah Sun,* July 24, 1902; *CDT,* July 30, 1902.

119. *Lexington Leader,* July 22, 1902.

120. For instance, the *Herald* admonished the *Sunny South* not to "prevaricate about the people of the mountains" and "stick to the truth" after it erroneously called Ben Hargis Judge Hargis's son rather than his brother; *HGH,* July 17, 1902; *Paducah Sun,* July 24, 1902. In 1902 and for years afterward, the "Hargis-Cockrell feud" was only the most common descriptive for these events. Other variations included the "Hargis-Callahan feud," the "Hargis-Marcum feud," the "Hargis-Cockrell-Marcum feud," and the "Curtis-Jett feud." See Marcosson, "The South in Fiction," 366; Green, *Towering Pines,* 91.

121. *HGH,* July 31, 1902.

122. Ibid., August 28, 1902; *Lexington Leader,* November 9, 1902.

123. Hargis attempted to have the case against Cockrell completely dismissed but, it being a criminal case, the specially appointed judge deemed a dismissal impossible. *ACN,* September 3, 1902; *HGH,* August 28 (quote), 1902.

124. *Lexington Leader,* August 27, 1902.

125. Ibid., November 14, 1902.

126. These papers were the Republican *Louisville Evening Post* and *Lexington Leader* and the Democratic *Lexington Herald,* Goebel's most vocal enemy within his own party. Kash, "Feud Days in Breathitt County," 345.

127. *Paducah Sun,* November 11, 1902; *Alexandria Gazette,* November 12, 1902; *MVB,* November 12, 1902; *HGH,* November 13, 1902; *Lexington Leader,* November 14, 1902; *Lexington Herald,* November 14, 1902; *Lancaster Central Record,* November 14, 1902; *HVK,* November 18, 1902; *Hartford Republican,* January 16, 1903. For Mose Feltner's well-documented criminal history, see *FRA,* February 25, 1893; *HGH,* February 21, 1895, May 3, 1900; *SIJ,* February 28, 1896; *MVS,* May 4, June 29, 1900; *HMC,* November 16, 1900; *MPL,* November 9, 1900, July 20, 1901.

128. *Lexington Leader,* November 14 (quote), 1902; *Lancaster Central Record,* November 14, 1902; *Berea Citizen,* November 27, 1902.

129. *Bourbon News,* November 14, 1902.

130. *Lexington Leader,* November 15, 1902.

131. Ibid., November 16, 1902. According to later court testimony, Marcum expressed the same speculations to his wife's sister. *White v. Commonwealth,* Court of Appeals of Kentucky, March 17, 1905, *SWR,* vol. 85 (March 15–April 19, 1905), 755.

132. *Lexington Leader,* November 16, 1902. See also *Berea Citizen,* November 27, 1902.

133. *HVK,* November 25, 1902; *Lancaster Central Record,* November 27, 1902.

134. *LEP,* May 4, 1903; *LCJ,* May 5, 7, 1903; *Lexington Herald,* May 5, 1903; *HGH,* May 7, 1903; *NYT,* May 5, 10, 12, 25, 31, June 5, 16, 18, 20, 28, 30, 1903.

135. *LEP,* May 5, 1903.

136. Child, "The Boss of Breathitt," 15. It would seem that Marcum's instincts were correct. Mose Feltner, Marcum's client and a suspect in an unrelated murder, said that, after being hired by Judge Hargis to kill Marcum, he had a clear opportunity to dispatch his target but hesitated because "the women were around him" and "he had his little baby in his arms." *Washington Post,* May 29, 1904. See also *LCJ,* May 4, 6, 1903.

137. *LEP,* May 8, 1903.

138. *LCJ,* May 6, 1903.

139. McClure, "The Mazes of a Kentucky Feud," 2220.

140. *SIJ,* May 12, 1903.

141. *Lexington Leader,* May 5, 1903. The *Leader* was one of few Republican Kentucky papers that freely accused specific county governments of electoral corruption. Ireland, *Little Kingdoms,* 51.

142. *MPL,* June 2, 1903.

143. Ibid., June 6, 1903.

144. "Assassination in Kentucky," 778; Keane, *Violence and Democracy,* 39.

145. *Hartford Republican,* August 21, November 27 (quote), 1903.

146. *MPL,* May 14, 1903.

147. *Lexington Morning Herald,* July 31, 1903.

148. *MPL,* June 30, 1903.

149. Instead of suggesting violence acted out for or against the legitimacy of state power, "lawlessness" denoted "a Hobbesian state in which the relations between individuals or small groups are like those between sovereign powers," a description of premodern societies most likely to experience or produce acts of violence related to "feud" or "vendetta." Vahabi, *The Political Economy of Destructive Power*, 103–5.

150. *Crittenden Press*, May 14, 1903; *Clay City Times*, May 28 (quote), 1903; *ACN*, May 13, July 29, 1903.

151. *Hartford Herald*, July 1, 1903.

152. Ibid., June 24, 1903.

153. *Larue County Herald*, quoted in *ACN*, June 10, 1903. For Republican comparisons between the investigations of Goebel's and Marcum's deaths, see *Hartford Republican*, August 21, 1903; *BCN*, March 15, 1907.

154. *ACN*, July 29, 1903.

155. *LCJ*, May 6, 1903.

156. Ibid., June 17, 1903.

157. *Lexington Herald*, May 7, 16, 1903.

158. *CDT*, May 25, 1903.

159. "As the nineteenth century drew on, the family as an institution was figured as existing, by natural decree, beyond the commodity market, beyond politics, and beyond history proper. The family thus became, at one and the same time, both the organizing figure for natural *history*, as well as its *antithesis*. McClintock, "Family Feuds," 63–64. See also Piepmeier, *Out in Public*; Said, "Secular Criticism," 231–32; Peiss, "Going Public," 817–20, 822, 826; Davidoff and Hall, *Family Fortunes*; Welter, "The Cult of True Womanhood."

160. *Richmond Climax*, September 9, 1903.

161. *Bourbon News*, May 8, 1903; *Commonwealth of Ky. vs. Curt Jett & c.*, May 28–June 19, 1903, Breathitt County Criminal Order Books and Indexes, KDLA; *Jett v. Commonwealth*, March 25, 1905, *SWR*, vol. 85 (March 15–April 19, 1905), 1179–82.

162. *CDT*, May 11, 25, 1903; *MVB*, May 26–27, 1903; *Hartford Republican*, February 26, 1904. In 1902 Fulton French collaborated with Hargis in establishing a Jackson hotel. *MSA*, July 1, 1902.

163. *CDT*, June 17, 19, 1903.

164. *LCJ*, May 10, 1903; *LEP*, May 10, 1903; *CDT*, May 7, 11, 1903.

165. *Earlington Bee*, May 28, 1903; *Annual Reports of the War Department for the Fiscal Year Ending June 30, 1903*, 330; Clements, *History of the First Regiment of Infantry*, 158.

166. Clements, *History of the First Regiment of Infantry*, 164.

167. "Comment," 1086.

168. *CDT*, June 15, 1903; *Bourbon News*, July 28, 1903.

169. *HGH*, June 25, 1903; *Lexington Herald*, February 5, 1904.

170. *CDT*, June 20, August 16, May 6, 1904. Jett was later implicated in the killing of Cockrell as well. *Jett v. Commonwealth*, filed March 25, 1905, *KLR*, vol. 27 (February–September, 1905), 603–7.

171. *MVS*, March 31, 1905; *Paducah Sun*, December 20, 1906.

172. *BCN*, May 29, 1903; *NYT*, June 21, 1903; *Richmond Climax*, July 1, 1903.

173. *MPL*, October 13, 1900; *Bourbon News*, June 5, 1903; *Hartford Republican*, August 28, 1903; *MPL*, September 15, 1903; *BCN*, June 14, 1907; McClure, "The Mazes of a Kentucky Feud," 2223–24; clipping, *St. Louis Globe-Democrat*, October 27, 1916, Appalachian Feuds Collection, box 1, series 6, Southern Appalachian Archives, HLSCA. A survey of pardons issued during Beckham's administration show a certain amount of political interest, if not prejudice. One Shepherdsville, Kentucky, "Democratic barber" received a pardon since his conviction for concealment of a deadly weapon (his straight razor) was allegedly "persecution by the Republicans instead of prosecution." However, most of these pardons made no explicit mention of political affiliation. What is indicated instead is a proliferation of pardon requests and pardon contestations originating mostly in eastern Kentucky. Of the fifty-four extant petitions sent to Governor J. C. W. Beckham in order to protest requests for pardon (with the vast majority being in reference to murder or manslaughter), twenty-nine were in regard to crimes committed east of the Bluegrass. This indicates that such crimes were well publicized and committed in a way that aroused entire communities against the accused. Many simply reflected the tenor of crime that had developed there during the early twentieth century. In one, a young man convicted for carrying a concealed weapon (probably one of the most common convictions in Kentucky jurisprudence between 1870 and 1910) claimed that he did so only because he was visiting an area of Knox County "known and regarded as a community in which the disregard for law prevails to such an extent that it has been thought foolish in him who ventured therein unarmed." Tom White's pardon can be interpreted either way. "Herbert Glenn to Gov. Beckham" (undated) and "Chadwell Hall to Governor J. C. W. Beckham" (undated), Governor's Correspondence—Contested Pardons, Papers of J. C. W. Beckham, KDLA.

174. *LEP*, May 8, 1903; *Lexington Herald*, May 11, 1903. As early as 1900, when "Redwine" was still a curse word among Kentucky Republicans (and a fair number of Democrats), Beckham supposedly issued twelve pardons to Breathitt County convicts, this out of a seven-month total of eighty-eight. Over the next three years, his apparent favoritism toward Breathitt County petitions seemed especially marked. *MPL*, August 7, 1900; *Earlington Bee*, October 11, 1900; *Hartford Republican*, October 30, 1903.

175. *Hartford Republican*, July 3, 1903.

176. *ACN*, July 8, 1903.

177. *CDT*, June 27, 1903. For a similar Beckham rebuke toward northern Republicans, see *Earlington Bee*, May 14, 1903.

178. *NYT*, September 6, 1903.

179. Because of widely publicized accounts of violence in Clay County, Bradley did eventually send the militia there. Bradley may have been somewhat aware that the renewal of hostilities in the county may have resulted from the disruption in the political status quo caused by his election as Kentucky's first Republican governor. *LCJ*, June 13, 1898; Billings and Blee, *The Road to Poverty*, 287, 291, 298–303.

180. *NYT,* January 6, 1904.

181. *Washington Post,* quoted in *Lexington Leader,* August 2, 1903.

182. *LCJ,* October 3, 1903.

183. *NYT,* September 19, 1903; Chesham, *Born to Battle,* 116.

184. *BCN,* October 23, 1903 (quote); *Hartford Republican,* November 27, 1903.

185. *BCN,* October 23, November 6, 13, 1903; *MPL,* November 19, 1903.

186. Carl Day's brother was Kentucky's former state treasurer. *Clay City Times,* May 21, 1903; *SIJ,* May 22, 1903; *Washington Times,* December 3, 1903.

For the law, see *KHJ, 1904,* 73; *Richmond Climax,* January 6, February 3, 10, 17, 24, 1904; *Berea Citizen,* February 4, 11, 1904; *Richmond Climax,* February 17, 1904; *MPL,* March 24, 1904; *MSA,* March 30, 1904; *Hartford Republican,* April 8, 1904; *BCN,* April 15, 1904; *MVB,* March 24, 30, April 5, 6, November 14, 1904; Wright, *Racial Violence in Kentucky,* 144–45; Wright, *A History of Blacks in Kentucky,* 136–48; Wright, "The Founding of Lincoln Institute," 57–70; Tapp and Klotter, *Kentucky,* 396–400, 418–25; Paul David Nelson, "Experiment in Interracial Education at Berea College," 13–27; Betty Jean Hall and Heckman, "Berea College and the Day Law," 35–52; McVey, *The Gates Open Slowly,* 153–54. All of the secondary source accounts of the Day Law have far more to say about its effects than its legislative origins.

187. *Clay City Times,* February 4, 1904; *Richmond Climax,* February 10, 1904; *Berea Citizen,* February 11, 1904; *SIJ,* March 15, 1904 (quote); Hardin, *Fifty Years of Segregation,* 12–13; Wright, *Racial Violence in Kentucky,* 144–45; Wright, *A History of Blacks in Kentucky,* 144–48.

188. Hardin, *Fifty Years of Segregation,* 12.

189. *Berea Citizen,* September 24, 1903; Norrell, *Up from History,* 244–53.

190. *Paducah Sun,* November 10, 1903; *Hartford Herald,* September 21, 1904. See also *MVB,* February 16, 1903.

191. *Richmond Climax,* February 3, 1904.

192. *KHJ, 1904,* 525.

193. *Richmond Climax,* February 3, 1904.

194. *KHJ, 1904,* 525–27; *Richmond Climax,* February 17, 24, 1904; *Nation,* February 25, 1904, 141; Klotter, *Kentucky,* 152–53.

195. *LCJ,* February 2, 1904; *MVB,* February 2, 1904; *Berea Citizen,* February 4, 1904; *Richmond Climax,* February 10, 1904.

196. Located in the foothills of Madison County, Berea College could have just as easily been termed a Bluegrass institution. Most Americans who were familiar with it placed it in the mountains, particularly because of William Frost's famous interest in the welfare of the "mountain white" and the large number of young mountaineers who made up its student body. "The Attack upon Berea College," 102–3.

197. Betty Jean Hall and Heckman, "Berea College and the Day Law," 38.

198. *Berea Citizen,* February 11, 1904.

199. Quoted in Wright, *A History of Blacks in Kentucky,* 145.

200. William G. Frost, "Berea College," 63–64.

201. Most notably Clark, *My Century in History,* 245.

202. *LCJ,* February 2, 1904; Betty Jean Hall and Heckman, "Berea College and the Day Law," 35–52.

203. *Richmond Climax,* January 6, 1904; *KHJ, 1904,* 43.

204. *MSA,* June 3, 1903; *HGH,* March 24, 1904.

205. Pierson, "Berea College and Its Mission," 418.

206. "Hostile Legislation against Berea, a Ruthless Hand Stayed by Appeal to the Constitution," *Berea Quarterly,* April 1904, 13, Berea College Vertical Files: Day Law III, HLSCA.

207. *Lexington Herald,* February 5, 1904.

208. Ibid., January 30, February 2, 4, 1904; *MSA,* February 10, 1904; *BCN,* February 12, 1904; *Berea Citizen,* March 17, 1904 (quote).

209. *AGACK, 1904* (Louisville: Geo. G. Fetter, 1904), 126–27.

210. *MPL,* March 24, 1904; *MSA,* March 9, 30, 1904; *MVB,* March 24, April 4, 5, 6, 1904; *Hartford Republican,* April 8, 1904; *Clay City Times,* April 14, 1904; *Berea Citizen,* April 14, 1904; *BCN,* April 15, 1904; *HVK,* April 15, 1904; *SIJ,* April 15, 1904; *Hartford Republican,* April 15, 1904; *FRA,* April 16, 1904; *ACN,* April 20, 1904; *Richmond Climax,* April 20, 1904; *Crittenden Press,* April 21, 1904; *AGACK, Special Session, 1905* (Louisville: George G. Fetter, 1905), 14–15.

211. In October 1904 Berea College was found to be in violation, thus beginning a four-year legal battle that concluded with the Supreme Court's upholding the Day Law. The original bill's provenance in the mountains, and persistent rumors that Day and Berea president William G. Frost had collaborated in the bill's drafting, may well have helped to prevent an arrangement that never came to be: a Republican alliance between blacks and mountaineers in Kentucky. *Nation,* November 19, 1908, 480–81; Higginbotham, "Racism and the Early American Legal Process," 16–18; Paul David Nelson, "Experiment in Interracial Education at Berea College," 24–27; Wright, *A History of Blacks in Kentucky,* 185–86; Hardin, *Fifty Years of Segregation,* 14–20, 62–65, 72–73, 85–86, 100–101, 106–7.

212. *Mrs. J.B. Marcum agst. James Hargis, February, 1904–1905,* Clark County Circuit Court Case Files, KDLA; *CDT,* February 28, 1904; *Marcum et al. v. Hargis et al.,* Court of Appeals of Kentucky, October 16, 1907, *SWR,* vol. 104 (August 28–November 27, 1907), 693–95; *Earlington Bee,* March 3, 1904; *MVS,* March 14, 1904; *Mountain Advocate,* March 4, 1904; *Hartford Republican,* March 25, 1904; *LCJ,* June 3, 1904; *ACN,* December 21, 1904; *HGH,* December 22, 29, 1904; Coulter and Connelley, *History of Kentucky,* 3:186.

213. "Notes on Important Decisions," 118–19.

214. *HVK,* January 12, 1905; *MPL,* January 28, 1908; *SIJ,* January 28, 1908; *Marcum et al. v. Hargis et al.,* Court of Appeals of Kentucky, October 16, 1907, *SWR,* vol. 104 (August 28–November 27, 1907), 694; *French v. Commonwealth,* Court of Appeals of Kentucky, November 21, 1906, *SWR,* vol. 97 (November 28, 1906–January 2, 1907),

427–33; *Herald Publishing Company, et al. v. Feltner,* decided March 17, 1914, *Kentucky Reports,* vol. 158 (March 13–May 14, 1914), 35–44; Child, "The Boss of Breathitt," 16.

215. *BCN,* November 11, 1904; *HGH,* December 8, 1904 (quote).

216. *BCN,* January 27, 1905; *Bourbon News,* January 27, 1905, February 17, March 24, 1905; *LCJ,* May 5, 1912.

217. *LCJ,* March 31, 1905.

218. *BCN,* February 17, 1905.

219. Without attempting to absolve Hargis et al. of guilt, the defense suggested that, even though Cockrell had died in Lexington, the fact that he had sustained his fatal injury in Breathitt County meant that Fayette County's bench had no jurisdiction in prosecuting the crime. *BCN,* January 27, 1905; *NYT,* March 28, 1905; *HGH,* June 8, 1905; *CDT,* May 24, 1907; *Hargis, &c. v. Parker, Judge, &c.,* filed March 10, 1905, *KLR,* vol. 27 (February–September, 1905), 441–48; *Hargis et al. v. Parker, Judge, et al.,* Court of Appeals of Kentucky, March 10, 1905, *SWR,* vol. 85 (March 15–April 19, 1905), 704–9; *Crittenden Record-Press,* May 30, 1907.

220. *MSA,* June 20, 1906; *CDT,* July 12, 1906; *BCN,* July 20, 1906. It was widely believed that key witnesses like Jett remained loyal to Hargis since "he could get any man in the penitentiary pardoned" by Governor Beckham. But although Jett was eventually paroled from prison, he was not the recipient of a pardon. *Louisville Herald,* June 8, 1908.

221. *NYT,* July 18, 1906; *CDT,* July 18, 1906; *BCN,* July 20, 1906; E. Polk Johnson, *A History of Kentucky and Kentuckians,* 2:639 (quote).

222. *Crittenden Record-Press,* May 30, 1907; *NYT,* July 20, 21, 1907; *BCN,* August 2, 1907; Child, "The Boss of Breathitt," 16–17 (quote); Chandler et al., *The South in the Building of the Nation,* 322. Elliott County proved to be an even more dramatic deviation from the general trend of Kentucky mountain Republicanism than did Breathitt County. The county was said to not even have a telegraph connection to the "outside world" as late as 1907. Before 1908, its largest Republican vote in a presidential election had been 34 percent; Shannon and McQuown, *Presidential Politics in Kentucky,* 47, 50, 55, 58, 61, 66, 72, 76, 80.

223. *CDT,* May 30, 1907; *Crittenden Record-Press,* May 30, 1907.

224. *NYT,* June 30, 1904.

225. *BCN,* May 31, 1907.

226. *Hartford Republican,* May 31, 1907.

227. Edward Callahan to J. L. "Dutch" Burton, April 19, 1905, Assorted Documents, Breathitt County Museum. Callahan's claims of his popularity in Lexington and the throngs of Democratic visitors are corroborated in *HVK,* March 21, 1905.

228. *Lexington Leader,* November 14, 1902.

229. *HMC,* February 28, 1905 (quote); *MPL,* October 17, 1905; *BCN,* October 20, 27, 1905.

230. *BCN,* November 10, 1905; *Bourbon News,* November 10, 1905; *MPL,* November 14, 1905; *Richmond Climax,* November 15, 1905; *Hartford Republican,* November 17,

1905, January 5, 1906; *NYT,* November 8, 1905, January 3, 1906; *MSA,* November 8, 22, 1905; *Cope v. Cardwell,* Court of Appeals of Kentucky, May 1, 1906, *SWR,* vol. 93 (June 27–July 25, 1906), 3–4; *LCJ,* February 6, 1908.

231. *Richmond Climax,* November 15, 1905; *MPL,* November 21, 1905; *MSA,* November 22, 1905.

232. *MSA,* November 15, 1905.

233. *MPL,* November 14, 1905.

234. *BCN,* November 10, 1905.

235. *LCJ,* October 10, 1906; *BCN,* October 12, 1906.

236. *MSA,* November 7, 1906; *BCN,* November 9, 1906; *SIJ,* November 9, 1906; *HVK,* November 10, 1906; *Official Congressional Directory, 61st Congress 2nd Session,* 39–40.

237. Breathitt County's Republican majority in this election was particularly phenomenal considering that Bryan carried the state handily in 1908. Shannon and McQuown, *Presidential Politics in Kentucky,* 80.

238. *MPL,* May 24, 1905; *Lexington Leader,* quoted in *BCN,* November 2, 1906; *BCN,* quoted in *Hartford Republican,* January 18, 1907.

239. Curiously, Democrats nominated an eastern Kentucky candidate. Republican Augustus E. Willson's opponent, Judge Samuel W. Hager of Magoffin County, was one of few mountain Democrats ever to be nominated to run for governor of Kentucky. *Berea Citizen,* March 14, 21, 1907; *Hartford Republican,* March 15, 1907; *BCN,* August 9, 1907 (quote); *MPL,* August 16, 17, 20, 31, September 14, October 26, November 4, 1907; *CDT,* November 6, 1907; Tracy Campbell, *The Politics of Despair,* 86–90; Willis, *Kentucky Democracy,* 419; Klotter, *Kentucky,* 210–12.

240. *NYT,* February 29, 1908, November 7, 1909.

241. *MSA,* August 28, 1907.

242. *BCN,* September 11, 1908.

243. *Berea Citizen,* March 5, 1908.

244. *MPL,* September 30, October 16, 1907; *Bourbon News,* October 1, 8, 1907; *HGH,* October 3, 1907; *SIJ,* October 4, 8, 1907; *Hartford Republican,* October 4, 1907.

245. *Bourbon News,* February 11, 1908.

246. *LCJ,* February 6, 8, 1908; *MPL,* February 8, 1908; *Washington Times,* February 9, 10, 1908; *NYT,* February 16, 1908; *CDT,* February 7, 1908 (quote); *FRA,* February 8, 1908; *HVK,* February 8, 11, 13, 1908; *ACN,* February 12, 19, 1908; *Breckinridge News,* February 12, 1908; *MSA,* February 12, 1908; *Clay City Times,* February 13, 1908; *Bourbon News,* February 14, 1908; *SIJ,* February 14, 1908; *MVS,* February 14, 1908; Linner, "The Human Side of Jim Hargis," 21.

247. *ACN,* February 19, 1908; *MSA,* February 19, 1908; *Earlington Bee,* February 20, 1908; *HVK,* February 20, 1908; *Berea Citizen,* February 20, March 5, 1908; *MSA,* February 26, March 4, 1908; *Clay City Times,* March 5, 1908; *HGH,* March 5, 1908; *Bourbon News,* December 24, 1908 (quote); *Hargis v. Commonwealth, December 1, 1909, Kentucky Reports,* vol. 135 (September term, 1909), 578–606.

248. *CDT,* August 26, 1908; *MVS,* September 4, 1908; *Winchester News,* December 14, 1908; *Berea Citizen,* April 29, 1909.

249. *Earlington Bee,* June 9, 1916; Kash, "Feud Days in Breathitt County," 352.

250. *Winchester News,* January 2, 1909; *HGH,* June 24, October 28, November 3, 1909; *HMC,* July 1, 1909; *Clay City Times,* June 24, November 4, 1909; *Berea Citizen,* November 4, 1909 (quote); *SIJ,* November 5, 1909; *HVK,* November 6, 1909; *NYT,* November 7, 1909; *ACN,* November 10, 1909 (quote).

251. *HVK,* July 22, 1909.

252. Fox, "On the Road to Hell-fer-Sartain," 353–55.

253. *HMC,* April 13, 1911.

254. *Hartford Republican,* May 10, 1912; "Telephone to Open Feud-Ridden County," 196. Telephone service was apparently available in Jackson in 1902 but extended to the more remote Crockettsville only a decade later.

255. *LCJ,* May 4, 5, 1912; *NYT,* May 5, 1912; *MPL,* May 6, 13, 14, October 26, 1912; *Hartford Herald,* May 8, 15, 22, 1912; *Berea Citizen,* May 9, 1912; *HMC,* May 9, 16, 1912; *HVK,* May 9, October 22, 1912; *Bourbon News,* May 10, 1912; *Hartford Republican,* May 10, 1912; *SIJ,* May 24, 1912; *Clay City Times,* October 17, 1912; *MSA,* October 23, 1912; *Berea Citizen,* October 24, 1912; *The American Library Annual, 1913,* 15.

256. *MPL,* May 14, 1912.

257. *Hartford Republican,* October 2, 1908; *BCN,* October 2, 1908.

258. *MSA,* March 5, 1913; *Lexington Herald,* March 13, 1913; *Law Notes* 16 (April 1913): 17; William M. McKinney and Greene, *Annotated Cases,* 59–64.

259. *MPL,* January 7, 1915.

260. *NYT,* September 19, 1916; clipping, *St. Louis Globe-Democrat,* October 22, 1916, Appalachian Feuds Collection, box 1, series 6, Southern Appalachian Archives, HLSCA.

261. Jett, *From Prison to Pulpit,* 17.

262. "Religion"; Donald Lee Nelson, "The Death of J. B. Marcum," 16–17.

263. *New York Tribune,* July 31, 1903.

264. Douglass, *Christian Reconstruction in the South,* 326.

265. *LCJ,* June 3, 1904.

266. Ibid.

267. *CDT,* May 10, 1903.

268. Ibid., June 5, 1905.

269. Colby, *The New International Year Book,* 401.

270. This may have been because it was his wife's lawsuit that intitiated the appeal. Although she was one of very few to announce her husband's death as a premeditated act carried out as part of a political conspiracy rather than a "feudal" action, Abrelia Marcum's litigation probably exacerbated the event's false familial significance. "Notes on Important Decisions," 118–19.

271. Lewis Franklin Johnson, *Famous Kentucky Feuds Tragedies and Trials,* 331.

272. Fox, "On the Road to Hell-fer-Sartain," 350. For Fox's role in publicizing and interpreting feud violence, see Waller, "Feuding in Appalachia," 362–63, 367–69.

273. William Dinwiddie (?), untitled manuscript, Personal Collection of Charles Hayes.

274. *BCN,* January 18, 1907.

275. Ibid., September 11, 1908.

276. William Dinwiddie [?], untitled manuscript, Personal Collection of Charles Hayes.

277. Hubac-Occhipinti, "Anarchist Terrorists of the Nineteenth Century," 117–18.

278. Ibid.; Alexander, *The Cambridge Companion to Durkheim,* 311–12; Barzun, *From Dawn to Decadence,* 695; Therborn, "'Europe' as Issues of Sociology," 22–23; Frasca, *The Rise and Fall of the Saturday Globe,* 120–21; Blanchard, *Revolutionary Sparks,* 40–41; Elwin H. Powell, *The Designs of Discord,* 72–73, 152–53, 165; Nieburg, *Political Violence,* 118–21.

279. A San Francisco anarchist used the Kentucky Republicans' purported guilt for killing Goebel to defend his party after McKinley's death: "Was any political party ever held accountable for a political murder such as the murder of Governor Goebel of Kentucky by the conspiracy of Republican politicians, or any religion held accountable for a religious murder such as the murder of President Garfield by a Christian enthusiast (Or a fanatic if you please)? Why, then, should anarchists be held accountable for the first murder by an anarchist in the United States?" Sturber, *The Anarchist Constitution,* 4.

280. Bryan, *The Commoner Condensed,* 304.

281. Watterson, "Murder Is Murder," 7.

282. *Hartford Republican,* February 2, 1900 (quote); *Cyclopedic Review of Current History* 10 (1900): 83–84; *Caleb Powers, Appt., v. Commonwealth of Kentucky,* Kentucky Court of Appeals, *LRA,* 53:260.

283. Since Goebel's position as governor-elect was not roundly recognized, his assassination can be interpreted as either "assassination by one political elite to replace another" or "assassination by the government in power to suppress political challenge," two very different motives for political murder. Kirkham, Levy, and Crotty, *Assassination and Political Violence,* 3, 6.

284. *Lexington Herald,* April 15, 1902; *Blue-grass Blade,* April 27, 1902; *New York Tribune,* April 3, 1905.

285. *Hartford Republican,* July 25, 1902; McClure, "The Mazes of a Kentucky Feud," 2219–20; "Assassination in Kentucky," 778; *Jett v. Commonwealth,* Court of Appeals of Kentucky, March 25, 1905, *SWR,* vol. 85 (March 15–April 19, 1905), 1179, 1181; *KLR,* vol. 27 (Frankfort: Geo. A. Lewis, 1905), 605.

286. William Dinwiddie (?), untitled manuscript, Personal Collection of Charles Hayes.

287. *LCJ,* May 6, 1903.

288. *NYT,* September 19, 1903; Linner, "The Human Side of Jim Hargis," 21.

289. Linner, "The Human Side of Jim Hargis," 21.

290. *Jackson Hustler*, reprinted in *HGH*, November 17, 1904.

291. Wright, *Racial Violence in Kentucky*, 327.

7. "The feudal wars of Eastern Kentucky will no doubt be utilized in coming years by writers of fiction"

1. Interviews with Edward C. Strong, July 21, 1898; and Henry Duff, July 22, 1898, *JJDD*, reel 3, pp. 2424, 2428–29.

2. The small number of historians who have addressed the cattle war have followed this logic without question. See Billings and Blee, *The Road to Poverty*, 375; Pearce, *Days of Darkness*, 124. Despite the sixty years between the two events, Billings and Blee and Pearce do not question the causal relationship between the cattle war and the Strong-Amis feud.

3. Colby, *The New International Year Book*, 406.

4. Strong Family Papers, 106, Breathitt County Public Library.

5. *NYT*, June 2, 2002.

6. *Richmond Climax*, May 22, 1889.

7. Kantrowitz, *Ben Tillman and the Reconstruction of White Supremacy*, 8–9, 273–308.

8. Blight, *Race and Reunion*, 351–54 (quote 352). See also Foster, *Ghosts of the Confederacy*, 149–59.

9. "Innumerable people use words and expressions which they have either ceased to understand or employ only because they trigger off conditioned reflexes; in this sense, words are trade-marks which are finally all the more firmly linked to the things they denote, the less their linguistic sense is grasped." Horkheimer and Adorno, "The Culture Industry," 166.

10. Dobson, "The Word *Feud*," 52.

11. Simpson and Weiner, *The Oxford English Dictionary*, 860. The anthropologist Christopher Boehm defines the blood feud as "a pattern of homicidal conflict that simultaneously involves the ideas of scorekeeping and alternating retaliation and that is theoretically interminable but generally is pacifiable through the payment of compensation for blood." *Blood Revenge*, 222.

12. Humphreys, "Law of Tenure," 7–12.

13. Jeffrey Guy Johnson, "Feud, Society, Family," 50–51.

14. Stephen Wilson, *Feuding, Conflict and Banditry*, 306–34.

15. Grutzpalk, "Blood Feud and Modernity," 130. (Grutzpalk uses "blood feud," "blood vengeance," and "vendetta" interchangeably.)

16. Ibid., 124–31.

17. Even though very recent scholarship on violence still draws a sharp distinction between "the feudistic and the political," empirical data on feud and vendetta (particularly in the Mediterranean but *not* in the United States) demonstrates a clear overlap between violence traditionally thought of as feud based and conflicts over political power,

sometimes associated with class conflict and often within the boundaries of "strong" states. The distinctions between the seemingly mutually exclusive categories of feud, warfare, and revolution are not always so well defined as some scholars have assumed. However, this has not led any of them to question the very descriptive validity of *feud* as a descriptor for the events to which it has been applied. Kalyvas, *The Logic of Violence in Civil War*, 21–25, 99, 343–46, 367 (quote), 379–81; Finley, *The Most Monstrous of Wars*, 29; Stephen Wilson, *Feuding, Conflict and Banditry*; Boehm, *Blood Revenge*; Hobsbawm, *Primitive Rebels*, 4. For works that draw a much stricter delineation between feuds and more political forms of conflict, see Warren Brown and Górecki, *Conflict in Medieval Europe*, 334; Strathern and Stewart, *Arrow Talk*, 115–27; Otterbein, *Feuding and Warfare*, 160; Blok, *Honour and Violence*, 96–100; Oscar Lewis, *Tepoztlán*, 46.

18. Jeffrey Guy Johnson, "Feud, Society, Family," 33–41; Williams, *Appalachia*, 191; Sir Walter Scott, *Tales of a Grandfather*, 45 (quote). See also Frasier, "The Book of Carlaverock," 194–200. I am grateful to John A. Williams for encouraging me to look into Sir Walter Scott's significance in the cultural construction of feuding.

19. Franklin, *The Militant South*, 193–95, 200 (quote 194).

20. The island nation of Corsica was very much on the minds of nineteenth-century literate Americans, especially those who enjoyed English translations of popular continental novels. A large part of Corsica's popularity as a literary subject among English readers was Alexander Dumas's *The Count of Monte Cristo*, in which Corsican bandits figure prominently. See also Gillies, *Palmario*; Balzac, "La Vendetta," 364–78; "The Family Feud—A French Story," 796; Brewer, *The Historical Notebook*, 997; Westengard et al.,"International Tribunals in the Light of the History of the Law," 833.

21. Gregorovius, *Wanderings in Corsica*, 21, 176–85 (quote 177).

22. "Corsican Bandits," 273.

23. Scales and Zimmer, *Power and Nation*, 289.

24. Westengard et al., "International Tribunals in the Light of the History of the Law," 833; Lydston, *The Diseases of Society*, 234; *Philadelphia Inquirer*, December 23, 1878; *NYT*, December 26, 1878.

25. *NYT*, December 26, 1878.

26. Jeffrey Guy Johnson, "Feud, Society, Family," 3.

27. "Application of the term 'feud' itself to events in the United States must be fluid because no simple criteria fit every case. 'Feud' and related labels like 'vendetta' have been used for a variety of historical conflicts that entangled personal revenge and family rivalries with material interests. As studies of particular feuds in their local contexts are beginning to show, feuds in the United States were more irregular, more complicated, and more comprehensible than traditional portrayals would indicate. Each feud arose from its own concrete sources in political, social, and economic turmoil." Jeffrey Guy Johnson, "Feud, Society, Family," 4. Although he recognizes the difficulty of applying the concept of feud in the United States as easily as in other locales, Johnson does not suggest that the word necessarily loses validity or believability in an American context

due to its being overly subjective. I submit that the word is problematic when applied uncritically to *any* historical or geographic context. *Feud* has too often been used by exogenous observers (anthropologists and journalists or, as shown in earlier chapters, missionaries and politicians) in order to fulfill the observers' expectations or goals rather than to express the actual viewpoints of "feudal" participants who may or may not consider their own use of violence (or victimhood from someone else's) to be part of a custom or institution. *Feud* is more likely a rhetorical device to make violence appear strange or illegitimate to a cosmopolitan audience or a "dominant culture" or, as demonstrated in chapter 5, to meet the needs of a dominant faction wishing to disguise its counterrevolutionary use of violence as a reciprocal response to an opponent of equal means. See Kalyvas, *The Logic of Violence in Civil War,* 39; and Waller, "Feuding in Appalachia," 370 (quote).

28. Quoted in Burstein, *The Original Knickerbocker,* 262.

29. *Message of the President of the United States Relative to the Internal Feuds among the Cherokees,* 298, Cratis D. Williams Appalachian Collection, Carol Grotnes Belk Library & Information Commons, Appalachian State University, Boone, NC.

30. "William Hudson to Col. J. Y. Dashiell, September 15, 1862," in *War of the Rebellion,* series 1, vol. 53, CSS, issue 3686 (Washington: Government Printing Office, 1898), 828.

31. Daniel, "From Blood Feud to Jury System," 97–125.

32. "A Kentucky Vendetta," 3.

33. Bruce, *Violence and Culture in the Antebellum South,* 240.

34. Richard H. King, *A Southern Renaissance,* 27.

35. Jeffrey Guy Johnson, "Feud, Society, Family," 88.

36. Wyatt-Brown, *Southern Honor,* 350–61; for the strict regimentation optimally used in a duel, see John Lyde Wilson, *The Code of Honor.*

37. Peck, *Our Country,* 298 (quote); Jeffrey Guy Johnson, "Feud, Society, Family," 173–206. Most, nearly all, accounts of Old South feuds were published at least a generation after the Civil War. DeForest, *Kate Beaumont;* Alfred Ludlow White, "A Provincial Family Feud," 1; Marion Clifford Harrison, "Social Types in Southern Prose Fiction," 31; Gossett, *Race,* 362; Carman, *Social and Economic History of the United States,* 440; Simkins and Roland, *A History of the South,* 397; Rogers and Clark, *The Croom Family and Goodwood Plantation,* 84; Cowan, *The Slave in the Swamp,* 196; Ulrich B. Phillips, *Life and Labor in the Old South,* xxxix.

38. Duclos, *Son of Sorrow,* 53–66; Hickerson, *The Falkner Feuds,* 12–18; Woodward, *The Burden of Southern History,* 271–72.

39. Burnett, *Incidents of the War,* 243–44.

40. *NYT,* January 19, 1867.

41. Jeffrey Guy Johnson, "Feud, Society, Family," 52 (quote).

42. Pettit, "Mark Twain, the Blood-Feud, and the South," 20–24; Jeffrey Guy Johnson, "Feud, Society, Family," 54–60, 135–52.

43. Twain, *Life on the Mississippi,* 194 (quote)–95. For the relationship between the supposedly factual Darnell-Watson feud and Huckleberry Finn's fictional encounter with the Grangerfords and Shepherdsons, see Budd, "The Southward Currents under Huck Finn's Raft," 222–37.

44. Billingsley, "'Standard Authors' in *Huckleberry Finn,*" 126–31; Jeffrey Guy Johnson, "Feud, Society, Family," 115–34.

45. Just as homicide in the South provided a subject for the northern press to use as a basis for regional reproach, southern newspapers used the same subjects to defend their inimitable honor-based society. Hamm, *Murder, Honor, and Law,* 48–57, 92–96.

46. The same lesson is taught in Ludwig Harder's *A Family Feud.* The novel portrays a Bavarian peasantry abused by the ramifications of a baronic family's internal battles.

47. *NYT,* October 14, 1872, quoted in Waller, "Feuding in Appalachia," 352.

48. *Savannah News,* January 30, 1883, quoted in Jeffrey Guy Johnson, "Feud, Society, Family," 70.

49. "The Stalwart Policy and the Party Policy," 138.

50. Redfield, *Homicide, North and South,* 12.

51. Ibid., 112.

52. Perman, *The Road to Redemption,* 140. Perman erroneously identifies Redfield as a correspondent for the *Cincinnati Gazette.*

53. Redfield, *Homicide, North and South,* 5.

54. Ibid., 18.

55. Summers, *The Press Gang,* 196–97, 207 (quote).

56. Kantrowitz, *Ben Tillman and the Reconstruction of White Supremacy,* 8–9, 308–9.

57. *New Orleans Picayune,* June 11, 1852; Hutton, "The Hill-Evans Feud"; Waller, "Feuding in Appalachia," 351–52.

58. James Jeffries Thompson, *A Kentucky Tragedy,* xi.

59. Ibid., iii, xii. The author went on to have a violent end of his own back in Mississippi. After returning from a stint in the Peruvian navy in 1862, Thompson wounded his father and shot his sister, brother, and stepmother to death after failing to cajole his father into giving him the family's cotton crop for an attempted blockade run to Liverpool. After he was found guilty of murder, he was lynched, but only after being given the chance to verbally repent his lust for "money, whisky and revenge." Triplett, *History, Romance and Philosophy of Great American Crimes,* 540–44.

60. The most thorough survey of feud violence's historical geography observes that the phenomenon became firmly associated with eastern Kentucky in the mid-1880s during the *New York Times*'s coverage of the Rowan County War. This may qualify as irony since Rowan County was more a foothill county than a mountain locale and far more accessible to the "outside world" than Breathitt County, where violence that earned the feud label had already been reported in the national press a few years earlier. Waller, "Feuding in Appalachia," 355–56, 373n. For a discussion of feuds being a product of the mountains and/or of the state of Kentucky, see Williams, *Appalachia,* 192.

61. Waller, "Feuding in Appalachia," 355–56, 373n; Klotter, "The Black South and White Appalachia," 837–38; Henry Shapiro, *Appalachia on Our Mind*, 29–31. Books that collected the stories of multiple feuds into one volume tended to emphasize the "mountainness" of feuds in their retelling. However, "Kentucky" was in almost every book's title, showing that either the state had not been completely eclipsed by its one troublesome region or that, by some point in the early twentieth century, the one region had come to define Kentucky as a whole despite its remaining "the Bluegrass State." See "Kentucky's Feuds"; Johnston, "Romance and Tragedy of Kentucky Feuds"; Spears, "The Story of a Kentucky Feud," 494–509; MacClintock, "The Kentucky Mountains and their Feuds: I," 1–28; MacClintock, "The Kentucky Mountains and Their Feuds: II," 171–87; Litsey, "Kentucky Feuds and Their Causes"; McClure, "The Mazes of a Kentucky Feud"; Hartley and Smyth, "The Land of Feuds," 494–509; O. O. Howard, "The Feuds in the Cumberland Mountains," 783–88; Lewis Franklin Johnson, *Famous Kentucky Tragedies and Trials*; Mutzenburg, *Kentucky's Famous Feuds and Tragedies*; Burns, *The Crucible*; Coates, *Stories of Kentucky Feuds*; Meriel Daniel Harris, "Two Famous Kentucky Feuds"; Bernice Calmes Caudill, *Pioneers of Eastern Kentucky*; Jess D. Wilson, *A Latter Day Look at Kentucky Feuds*; Pearce, *Days of Darkness*.

62. "A Kentucky Vendetta," 3.

63. Stanley later borrowed "Bloody Breathitt" in the title of a chapter in his 2010 memoir. In 1974 a Breathitt native who was one of Stanley's backup musicians was shot to death during a visit home between performances. The accused served one month of a ten-year sentence, a miscarriage of justice Stanley attributed to Bloody Breathitt's inherent qualities—as well as the defendant's immense wealth. Stanley and Dean, *Man of Constant Sorrow*, 315–24.

64. Williams, *Appalachia*, 305.

65. Jeffrey Guy Johnson, "Feud, Society, Family," 274n.

66. Wyatt-Brown, *Southern Honor*, 383.

67. Waller counts among the many misconceptions regarding the Hatfield-McCoy feud the assumption that Hatfields and McCoys were only combatants against each other while, as her research has demonstrated, men with both surnames (as well as various other surnames) took divergent sides according to their economic relationships and personal wishes rather than family loyalties. But in retrospect, many later used familial associations to explain their participation in violence. Waller, *Feud*, 78–85.

68. *LCJ*, January 31, 1900.

69. "Kinship, on the surface one of the most innocent descriptive terms one could imagine, is fraught with temporal connotations. From the early debates on 'classificatory' kinship systems to current studies of its continued importance in western society, kinship connoted 'primordial' ties and origins, hence the special strength, persistence, and meaning attributed to this type of social relation. Views of kinship relations can easily serve to measure degrees of advancement or modernization. By comparing the relative importance of kinship bonds in different societies or groups one can construct

developmental, i.e., temporal scales." Satterwhite, *Dear Appalachia*, 62; Fabian, *Time and the Other*, 75–76 (quote). See also Brantlinger, *Dark Vanishings*, 1–16, particularly 2; Fukuyama, *The Origins of Political Order*, 49–63; Abner Cohen, *Two-Dimensional Man*, 18–34; Trachtenburg *The Incorporation of America*, 35–37.

70. William G. Frost, "Our Contemporary Ancestors," 311.

71. For the most updated volume on "whiteness studies" as it pertains to Kentucky's "mountain white," see Painter, *The History of White People*, 245–46, 308. See also Williams, *Appalachia*, 199; Harkins, *Hillbilly*, 40–45; Silber, *The Romance of Reunion*, 136–58; Bederman, *Manliness and Civilization*; Anderson, *Race and Rapprochement*, 17 (quote)–25; Batteau, *The Invention of Appalachia*, 15, 57–63, 77, 81–85; Whisnant, *All That Is Native and Fine*, 87–92.

72. Semple, "The Anglo-Saxons of the Kentucky Mountains," 566.

73. Westengard et al., "International Tribunals in the Light of the History of the Law," 833.

74. Quoted in Painter, *The History of White People*, 308.

75. Emma M. Connelly, *The Story of Kentucky*, 266–67.

76. Painter, *The History of White People*, 179–81; Jeffrey Guy Johnson, "Feud, Society, Family," 201–2; Klotter, "The Black South and White Appalachia," 838–39n.

77. Shaler, *Kentucky*, 406 (quote); Henry Shapiro, *Appalachia on Our Mind*, 107–12; Whisnant, *All That Is Native and Fine*, 258–59; Blaustein, *The Thistle and the Brier*, 35.

78. Mutzenburg, *Kentucky's Famous Feuds and Tragedies*, 26; "Notable Episodes in Outlawry," 318 (quote).

79. *New International Encyclopaedia*, 500.

80. *Scribner's* 29 (1901): 563. As noted before, the assertion that "there were feuds *before* the war" in the Kentucky mountains is not supported with substantial evidence.

81. Hough, "Burns of the Mountains," 14.

82. Chandler et al., *The South in the Building of the Nation*, 302.

83. Fox, *The Heart of the Hills*, 169.

84. Kephart, *Our Southern Highlanders*, 345; John C. Campbell, *The Southern Highlander and His Homeland*, 114; Clark, *Kentucky, Land of Contrasts*, 208–9.

85. The half truth of white Appalachia's "pure" Celtic identity, and the suggestion of continuity from a premodern past therein, has sustained itself into the twenty-first century and remains a large discursive element in discussions of whiteness. Hague and Sebesta, "Neo-Confederacy, Culture, and Ethnicity," 120; Blaustein, *The Thistle and the Brier*, 19–46; Craighead, *Scotch and Irish Seeds in American Soil*; Painter, *The History of White People*, 133, 154, 179–81, 223–24; Satterwhite, *Dear Appalachia*, 68–70, 219–20, 272n; Dennis, "Events of the Month," 966.

86. James Webb, *Born Fighting*, 78–80; Vann, *Rediscovering the South's Cultural Heritage*, 46 (quote); Fischer, *Albion's Seed*, 252, 628–29, 663, 756, 767; Jordan and Kaups, *The American Backwoods Frontier*, 252.

87. Hobsbawm, "Introduction: Inventing Traditions," 6.

88. Hanna, *The Scotch-Irish or the Scot*, 61.

89. Chandler et al., *The South in the Building of the Nation*, 322.

90. Waller, *Feud*, 21.

91. Warner, "Comments on Kentucky," 263; E. L. Noble, *Bloody Breathitt*, 1:270–71.

92. Fox, *Blue Grass and Rhododendron*, 45.

93. Marcosson, "The South in Fiction," 366.

94. William Davis and Swentnor, *Bluegrass Confederate*, 251.

95. Lloyd, "A Background to Feuding," 451–52.

96. Toynbee, *A Study of History*, 149.

97. Fox, *The Heart of the Hills*, 312–13. Fox Jr. had meant for *The Heart of the Hills* to serve as a penance to eastern Kentucky for the damage he and others had inflicted on the place's image. To his regret, sales and reviews for the novel were substantial but not as good as for his past novels and short stories. York, *John Fox*, 244, 257.

98. Fox, *The Heart of the Hills*, 349. This was the only part of the book in which William Goebel was explicitly named rather than being called "the autocrat."

99. Cawein, *Poems*, 9; Rothert, *The Story of a Poet*, 154, 361.

100. Mutzenburg, *Kentucky's Famous Feuds and Tragedies*, 26. See also *NYT*, February 13, 1908; "Kentucky Tobacco War," 3.

101. Mutzenburg, *Kentucky's Famous Feuds and Tragedies*, 26–27.

102. Summers, *The Press Gang*, 59–75, 308–13; Baldasty, *The Commercialization of News in the Nineteenth Century*, 139–48.

103. Semple, "The Anglo-Saxons of the Kentucky Mountains," 618.

104. Litsey, "Kentucky Feuds and Their Causes," 287. Litsey mostly used information from the Clay County War, a scenario that fit into the feud narrative in that it did seem to be a truly horizontal conflict between elite families owing to political and economic competition allegedly spanning six decades. Still, a thorough examination of the Baker-White feud suggests that isolation and Scottish lineages had less to do with the origins of violence than Litsey suggested; see Billings and Blee, *The Road to Poverty*, 306–15.

105. McClure, "The Mazes of a Kentucky Feud," 2217.

106. John C. Campbell. *The Southern Highlander and His Homeland*, 113.

107. Harkins, *Hillbilly*, 36; Waller, *Feud*, 221–28, 248–49.

108. Waller, *Feud*, 221.

109. T. C. Crawford, *An American Vendetta;* Waller, *Feud*, 221–28.

110. Native Kentuckian D. W. Griffith produced *A Feud in the Kentucky Hills* (1912), perhaps the first motion picture treatment of the subject, as a vehicle for ingénue Mary Pickford. But it was Buster Keaton's *Our Hospitality* (1923) that brought the subject to the cinema in a more critically significant portrayal. Based loosely on of the Hatfield-McCoy feud, it provides an example of a conflation of the southern feud and the mountain feud, or perhaps evidence of the continuity, rather than rupture, between the two in the public imagination. The "Canfields" and "McKays" live deep within the mountains but, rather than being poor corn hoers, they are big-housed planters with close access to railroads

and comically huge gun collections. The origins of the feud are suitably obscured, revenge is the sole motivator, and enemy status is based purely on surname. A wedding uniting the families provides a happy ending. Family is the prime mover in all of the film's action. Perhaps the most remarkable feature of the film is that the plot is placed far back into the 1830s rather than the more accurate 1880s. The railroad, which serves as an important plot device, anachronistically reaches a setting that would not have had access to it in the time it took place. *Our Hospitality* premiered only two years after the real-life death of William "Devil Anse" Hatfield. Edward McPherson, *Buster Keaton,* 129–36; J. W. Williamson, *Hillbillyland,* 270; Schickel, *D. W. Griffith,* 179; Harkins, *Hillbilly,* 152.

111. Altina Waller shows, however, that these beginnings and endings were only peripheral to larger issues that produced the feud, not to mention that the tumultuous romance between Johnse Hatfield and Roseanna McCoy (and his eventual marriage to her cousin Nancy McCoy) was peripheral to the violence that took place between their relatives. Waller, *Feud,* 66–69, 78–85.

112. Kentucky's governor Simon Buckner and West Virginia's E. Willis Wilson came to legal blows over the extradition of members of the Hatfield family/faction to the former's state. However, since both were Democrats from different states, their conflict did not constitute a crisis of state sovereignty or intraparty conflict. Furthermore, it was Kentucky's only widely reported feud event in the 1880s that did not sanction a militia visit. Waller, *Feud,* 207–19.

113. *Williamson (WV) Daily News,* August 2, 1982, Appalachian Feuds Collection, box 1, series 6, Southern Appalachian Archives, HLSCA.

114. Waller, "Feuding in Appalachia," 370.

115. Banner, "John Ehle and Appalachian Fiction," 174; Ewen, *Social Stratification and Power in America,* 130.

116. Frierson, "The Image of the Hillbilly in Warner Bros. Cartoons of the Thirties," 86–100; Inge, "Li'l Abner, Snuffy, and Friends," 3–28; Rodger Lyle Brown, *Ghost Dancing on the Cracker Circuit,* 80–85; Harkins, *Hillbilly,* 103–40; Batteau, *The Invention of Appalachia,* 111, 131.

117. Ayers, *Vengeance and Justice,* 256. For a concise narrative of the twentieth-century origins of "pluralism" as an ideal among American intellectuals, see Menand, *The Metaphysical Club,* 377–408.

118. Penny M. Miller, *Kentucky Politics and Government,* 71.

119. Wray, *Not Quite White,* 3.

120. Anglin, "A Question of Loyalty," 111.

121. Gladwell, *Outliers,* 175. I am grateful to Lauren E. Kilgore for making me aware of this book.

122. Jeffrey Guy Johnson, "Feud, Society, Family," 3.

123. "J. K. Bailey to Governor Buckner, August 4, 1889," "Will Jennings to Governor S. B. Buckner (Wilson R. Howard cosigned), postmarked September 1, 1889," "Wilson Lewis to Governor Buckner, July 24, 1889," "T. S. Ward to Governor S. B. Buckner, July

22, 1889," "Alex A. Arthur to Governor Buckner, July 23rd, 1889," Governor's Correspondence, March–April 1889, box 2, folders 31, 34, KDLA; *HMC*, October 8, 1886; *SIJ*, August 9, 13, 1889; *Pittsburgh Dispatch*, August 7, 1889; *Richmond Climax*, September 4, 1889; *LCJ*, September 23, 1889; *AAC* 14 (1889): 487; "Commonwealth of Barbarians," 295–97; Tapp and Klotter, *Kentucky*, 395–96; Waller, *Feud*, 80.

124. Gladwell, *Outliers*, 162.

125. Ibid., 167.

126. For a concurring criticism of *Outliers*, see McNay, "Outliers and Hatred against Hillbillies."

127. Abner Cohen, *Two-Dimensional Man*, 89.

128. Deas, "Violent Exchanges," 351–53; Kalyvas, *The Logic of Violence in Civil War*, 39.

129. The novelist called Breathitt "almost the first mountain county in the State to inaugurate the terrible feud, and certainly the last to give it up." Fox, "On the Road to Hell-fer-Sartain," 350.

130. *Jackson Hustler*, April 3, 1891.

131. *HGH*, July 15, 1885.

132. Hubbard, *The Fra*, xxvii.

133. *LCJ*, May 8, 1903.

134. Kephart, *Our Southern Highlanders*, 12.

135. Furman, *The Quare Women*, 69.

136. Although the phrase "Bloody Harlan" apparently dates back to at least as early as 1909, it did not gain national currency until the 1930s. *Proceedings of the Twenty-fifth Constitutional Convention of the United Mine Workers*, 92, 169; "Kentucky Feudalism," 13–14; Tracy Campbell, *Deliver the Vote*, 206–12.

137. Marcosson, "The South in Fiction," 366.

138. *Proceedings of the Eighth Annual Conference for Education in the South*, 106.

139. *FRA*, May 13, 1905; *CDT*, February 7, 1908.

140. *Washington Post*, May 29, 1904; *CDT*, June 7, 1903. (Perhaps erroneous in many other ways as well, the *Tribune*'s account of a generations-old feud in Breathitt was notably wrong in mentioning the violent death of young bachelor Judge Burnett's imaginary wife as among the atrocities of 1878.)

141. Rolt-Wheeler, *The Boy with the U.S. Census*, 29.

142. *New York Sun*, reprinted in *Kansas City Star*, June 22, 1903.

143. *Hartford Republican*, July 25, 1902; *Lexington Leader*, November 14, 1902.

144. *LEP*, May 13, 29, 1903.

145. *Life*, July–December 1903, 8; *CDT*, June 23, 1903.

146. *American Farmer*, October 1909, 5.

147. "Discouraged," 12.

148. "An Elemental Hint," 5.

149. Beach, *The Net*, 33.

150. Hubbard, *The Fra*, xxv. The same volume also refers to Kaiser Wilhelm II's pre–World War saber rattling as "Breathitt County reasoning" (xxv–xxvii).

151. Furman, *Mothering on Perilous*.

152. Tarleton, *Bloody Ground*. Unlike most feud narratives, this novel is narrated in the present tense.

153. Fox, *A Cumberland Vendetta*; Fox, *Christmas Eve on Lonesome*; Fox, *A Mountain Europa*.

154. The song was "recovered" in Texas by a musicologist less than twenty years after Judge Hargis's death. Supposedly the Texas source singer asked that the song not be published for a number of years further. "The Murder of J. B. Markham (traditional)," Lester McFarland and Robert A. Gardner (Brunswick Balke Collender Company), 78 rpm recording, Assorted Artifacts, Breathitt County Museum; Shearin and Combs, *Syllabus of Kentucky Folk-songs*, 18–19; Combs, *Folk-songs du Midi des Etats-Unis*, 183; Mellinger, "Ballads and Songs of the Southern Highlands," 296–97; Donald Lee Nelson, "The Death of J. B. Marcum," 17–22; Wolfe, *Kentucky Country*, 8–9.

155. *Flood Control*, 2323–38; Judge Watson, *Eastern Kentucky*, 147–50; Wray, *Not Quite White*, 96–132.

156. Kidd, *Farm Security Administration Photography*; Blakey, *Hard Times and New Deal in Kentucky*, 131. Impoverished from the depletion of its timber and coal, Breathitt County was of particular interest to New Deal activists and benefited from programs like the Works Progress Administration. The county was still one of the last Democratic bastions in eastern Kentucky; the New Deal caused yet another rupture within the local party, stirring talk of a possible new "feud." See Day, *Bloody Ground*, 108–12, 148–60, 173; Lindley and Lindley, *A New Deal for Youth*, 131; Blakey, *Hard Times and New Deal in Kentucky*, 64, 68. See also Melvin et al., *Rural Poor in the Great Depression*, 27, 44, 83–84, 113–14.

157. Gooch and Keller, "Breathitt County in the Southern Appalachians," 1011–12.

158. Shackleford and Weinberg, *Our Appalachia*, 41–42.

159. Gooch and Keller, "Breathitt County in the Southern Appalachians," 1018.

160. Salstrom, *Appalachia's Path to Dependency*, 94–121. Even though New Deal programs that targeted Appalachia specifically were carried out in the interest of alleviating unemployment, Salstrom sees most of these programs as ultimately harmful, considering that they created a dependency upon monetary incomes.

161. WPA, *In the Land of Breathitt*, 54, 76.

162. "Bloody Breathitt," 19.

163. Payne, "The Hillman Case," 1011–58 (quote 1041).

164. Loyal Jones, "James Jones' Appalachian Soldier in His World War II Trilogy," 152–65.

165. James Jones, *The Thin Red Line*, 247.

166. "Poverty"; Sexton and Bellardo, *The Public Papers of Governor Louis B. Nunn*, 376–79. Howell's father, Judge Ervine Turner, and his wife, Marie, were the faces of

Democratic absolutism in Breathitt County from the Great Depression until the Great Society. Like Breathitt politicos of times past, the Turners exerted a remarkable amount of influence in Frankfort. Ellis, *A History of Education in Kentucky,* 293; Burch, "The Turner Family of Breathitt County," 401–17; Burch, *Owsley County,* 100–101; Pearce, *Divide and Dissent,* 50–51.

This followed Nunn's forwarding of the "Kentucky Un-American Activities Committee" in 1968 to defeat New Left activism in various mountain counties. Kiffmeyer, *Reformers to Radicals,* 171–72, 179–81, 201–3; Eller, *Uneven Ground,* 152–54; Whisnant, *Modernizing the Mountaineer,* 207–8.

167. Burch, "The Turner Family of Breathitt County," 404, 409n.

168. Rumsfeld, *Known and Unknown,* 128n. See also Cheney, *In My Time,* 52–53; Eller, *Uneven Ground,* 155–57; Stephen F. Hayes, *Cheney,* 58–60.

169. Coates, *Stories of Kentucky Feuds,* 3–24, 71–116.

170. Child, "The Boss of Breathitt," 15.

171. The editor's humorous speculation of the possibility that a recent deadly scuffle in Huntington, West Virginia, "may start a feud" would have been a comfort to eastern Kentuckians weary of hearing of it only in their own county. *BCN,* September 9, 1904.

172. *LCJ,* December 25, 1884.

173. Ibid., June 3, 1904.

174. *BCN,* February 17, 1905.

175. Harrison and Klotter, *A New History of Kentucky,* 346.

176. Quoted in Arthur M. Miller, "The Vote on the Evolution Bill in the Kentucky State Legislature," 317.

177. *Lexington Leader,* March 3, 1900, quoted in "Yesterday's News," 236.

178. Pilcher, *The Story of Jackson City,* 16. Jaded as he was with feuds, Pilcher once engaged in a bit of gunplay himself when a large city marshal attacked him in his own newspaper office. Pilcher fired two shots and forced the marshal to retreat. *FRA,* May 19, 1906.

179. Pilcher, *The Story of Jackson City,* 33.

180. Ibid., 49.

181. Ibid., 101.

182. Ibid., 42.

183. Ibid., 44.

184. Ibid., 58–59; Martin, "Race Cooperation," 17.

185. Pilcher, *The Story of Jackson City,* 50.

186. Ibid., 57.

187. Quoted in Bar On, *The Subject of Violence,* 44.

188. *Earlington Bee,* December 15, 1911.

189. *Richmond Climax,* April 13, 1910; clipping, *St. Louis Daily Globe-Democrat,* October 27, 1916; *Frankfort State Journal,* November 13, 1918, Appalachian Feuds Collection, box 1, series 6, Southern Appalachian Archives, HLSCA; *Bourbon News,* July 15, 1919; Jett, *From Prison to Pulpit,* 17–19, 22, 51–52, 68, 75–76.

190. Jett, *From Prison to Pulpit*, 5–8.

191. Ibid., 10, 12.

192. Ibid., 33–34.

193. Ibid., 48; "Religion."

194. Jett, *From Prison to Pulpit*, 11–12.

195. Ibid., 15–16.

196. Wireman, *Kentucky Mountain Outlaw Transformed*, 2.

197. Gooch and Keller, "Breathitt County in the Southern Appalachians," 1015.

198. Ibid., 1014.

199. Ibid., 1015.

200. "Breathitt County High School Students Give Their Thoughts about the Local Crime Situation," Appalachian Feuds Collection, Southern Appalachian Archives, box 1, series 4, HLSCA.

201. Interview with Harlan Strong, 1978, AOHP, no. 279: "Feuds in Breathitt County, Kentucky," 22.

202. Ibid., 13, 18–21.

203. Ibid., 18. Harlan Strong probably confused the deaths of Kilburn and Ben Strong with the 1929 lynching of a white man named Chester Fugate in Jackson. His confusion was probably exacerbated by the fact that Fugate was Henderson Kilburn's grandson. Unlike when Henderson Kilburn and Ben Strong were killed, Fugate's alleged murderers were tried for the crime. All eight of them were acquitted. Wright, *Racial Violence in Kentucky*, 204–5, 323; Jean Thomas, *Blue Ridge Country*, 74.

204. Brantlinger, *Dark Vanishings*, 60–67.

205. Landsberg, *Prosthetic Memory*, 3–9.

206. Kalyvas, *The Logic of Violence in Civil War*, 83, 330–63; Berkeley, *The Graves Are Not Yet Full*, 151.

207. Proposed in the late 1950s and eventually signed into law by John F. Kennedy in 1961, the ARA created opportunities for federal development initiatives in areas with high levels of poverty and unemployment. As with most other federal programs used in post–World War II Appalachia, large-scale projects were blocked by local politicians and industrialists. Whisnant, *Modernizing the Mountaineer*, 72–91.

208. Harwood, "East Kentucky's Mountain," quoted in *Area Redevelopment Act*, 650.

209. Williams, *Appalachia*, 271–72, 279–81.

Epilogue

1. Bowling, *Images of America*, 13; Trailsrus County Courthouses: Courthouses in Kentucky—Breathitt Co., http://www.trailsrus.com/courthouses/breathitt.html (viewed July 25, 2008).

2. Pilcher, *The Story of Jackson City*, 50.

3. *SIJ*, August 10, 1917 (quote); *Philadelphia Inquirer*, August 11, 1917; *Macon Telegraph*, August 15, 1917; *Dallas Morning News*, August 19, 1917; *MSA*, September 4,

1917, January 29, 1918; *Lexington Herald,* September 5, October 16, November 19, 1917; *Hartford Republican,* October 19, 1917; *Berea Citizen,* August 8, 1918; "How about It, Vermont?" 11; *Baltimore Sun,* November 22, 1917; Kilpatrick, "When Breathitt Went to Battle," 154–58; "Humor of the Law," 54; *Official Proceedings of the St. Louis Railroad Club,* 200; *Flood Control,* 2337; Clark, *The Kentucky,* 156; Schulman, *John Sherman Cooper,* 28; Frederic D. Ogden, *The Public Papers of Governor Keen Johnson,* 416.

4. Sandlin was the only native-born Kentuckian to earn the Medal of Honor in World War I. *Hartford Herald,* May 7, 1919; *New York Tribune,* December 20, 1919; *Washington Times,* December 21, 1919; Wilbanks, *America's Heroes,* 298–99; WPA, *Military History of Kentucky,* 340.

5. "Those Lawless Mountaineers."

6. *Flood Control,* 2337 (quote)–2338.

7. *Hartford Republican,* October 19, 1917.

8. Kilpatrick, "When Breathitt Went to Battle," 154.

9. Ibid., 155.

10. Hartman, "Appalachian Anxiety," 243–48.

BIBLIOGRAPHY

Primary Sources

Archival Sources

Breathitt County Museum, Jackson, KY

Assorted Artifacts
Assorted Documents

Breathitt County Public Library, Jackson, KY

Kilburn and McIntosh Family Files
Strong Family Papers

Hutchins Library Special Collections & Archives, Berea College, Berea, KY

Berea College Vertical Files: Day Law III
Founders and Founding Collection: William E. Lincoln Papers
Southern Appalachian Archives: Appalachian Feuds Collection

Kelly Library, Emory & Henry College, Emory, VA

The New York Times Oral History Project: The Appalachian Oral History Project of Alice Lloyd College, Appalachian State University, Emory and Henry College, and Lees Junior College (microfilm)

Kentucky Department of Libraries and Archives, Frankfort

Breathitt County Circuit Court Minutes
Breathitt County Circuit Court Records
Breathitt County Criminal Order Books and Indexes
Clark County Circuit Court Case Files
Governor's Correspondence
Papers of J. C. W. Beckham
Papers of Governor William Owsley

Kentucky Historical Society, Frankfort

Breathitt County Slave Schedules, 1840, 1850, 1860

Breathitt County Tax Books, 1846, 1861
Martin F. Schmidt Research Library and Special Collections
Sixth Census of the United States, 1840
Seventh Census of the United States, 1850
Eighth Census of the United States, 1860
Ninth Census of the United States, 1870

Margaret I. King Library Special Collections and Archives, University of Kentucky, Lexington

John J. Dickey Diary
The Kentucky State Gazetteer and Business Directory for 1879–1880 (microfilm reel #S92-68)
Kentucky Union Land Company Records
"Letters to the [Mt. Sterling, KY] *Sentinel-Democrat* pertaining to the Rowan County Feud and Other Matters," 1885–86
Quicksand, Kentucky, Regular Baptist Church records, 1858–98 (microfilm roll 1)
Trimble, James Green. *Recollections of Breathitt.* Jackson, KY: Jackson Times, 1915.
Samuel Wilson Collection

Personal Collection of Charles Hayes, Jackson, KY

Dinwiddie, William [?]. Untitled manuscript.

Western Reserve Historical Society Library, Cleveland, OH

"Personal Reminiscences with an Account of the Rescue of the Negro Slave," Palmer Collection

William Leonard Eury Appalachian Collection, Carol Grotnes Belk Library & Information Commons, Appalachian State University, Boone, NC

Hayes, Charles. *The Hanging of "Bad Tom" Smith and the Events Leading to His Hanging, Including a Brief Account of the French and Eversole Feud.* Jackson, KY: Breathitt County Historical Society, 1969.
Message of the President of the United States Relative to the Internal Feuds among the Cherokees, April 13, 1846 (29th Cong., 1st sess., Senate). Washington, DC: Government Printing Office, 1846.
Thompson, James Jeffries. *A Kentucky Tragedy: A History of the Feud between the Hill and Evans Parties of Garrard County, Kentucky. The Most Exciting Tragedy Ever Enacted on the Bloody Grounds of Kentucky.* Cincinnati: U. P. James, 1854.

Wilson Library, University of North Carolina, Chapel Hill

Southern Historical Collection: John Hunt Morgan Papers, 1840–70, 1890

Published Sources

Public Documents

Acts of the General Assembly of the Commonwealth of Kentucky

American Lawyer

Annual Report of the Auditor of Public Accounts of the State of Kentucky for the Fiscal Year Ending October 10, 1860. Frankfort, KY: Jno. B. Major, 1861.

Annual Report of the Auditor of the State of Kentucky for the Fiscal Year Ending October, 10, 1860. Frankfort: Jno. B. Major, 1861.

Annual Reports of the War Department for the Fiscal Year Ending June 30, 1903. Vol. 1, *Reports of the Secretary of War, Chief of Staff, Adjutant-General, Inspector-General, and Judge-Advocate-General.* Washington, DC: Government Printing Office, 1903.

Area Redevelopment Act: Hearings before a Subcommittee (No. 3) of the Committee on Banking and Currency, United States Senate (86th Cong., 1st sess. on S. 268, S. 722, and S. 1064). Washington, DC: Government Printing Office, 1959.

Central Law Journal

Congressional Globe

Congressional Serial Set

Executive Documents of the House of Representatives for the Second Session of the Forty-ninth Congress, 1886-'87. Washington, DC: Government Printing Office, 1887.

The Federal Reporter. Vol. 60 (April–May, 1894).

The Federal Reporter. Vol. 80, *Cases Argued and Determined in the Circuit Courts of Appeals and Circuit and District Courts of the United States.* Permanent ed., June–July 1897. St. Paul, MN: West, 1897.

Flood Control: Hearings before the Committee on Flood Control, House of Representatives, Seventieth Congress, First Session on the Control of the Destructive Flood Waters of the United States, January 5 to January 17, 1928, part 4, *The Mississippi River and Its Tributaries.* Washington, DC: Government Printing Office, 1928.

The General Statutes of Kentucky. Frankfort, KY: Major, Johnston, and Barrett, 1879.

House Executive Documents

Kentucky Adjutant General's Report: Confederate Kentucky Volunteers, 1861-1865. Frankfort, KY: State Journal, 1915.

Kentucky House Journal

Kentucky Law Reporter

Kentucky Public Documents

  Adjutant General's Reports

  Annual Report of the Superintendent of Public Instruction of Kentucky, for the School Year Ending December 31, 1866. Frankfort: Kentucky Yeoman Office, 1867.

  QuarterMaster General's Report

Kentucky Reports: Reports of Civil and Criminal Cases Decided by the Court of Appeals

Kentucky Senate Journal

Law Notes

Lawyers' Reports Annotated

Legislative Document No. 1: Report of the Adjutant General of Kentucky. Frankfort, KY: E. Polk Johnson, 1879.

Legislative Document No. 18: Report of the Special Committee on the Penitentiary to the Senate of Kentucky, February 26, 1880. Frankfort: Kentucky Yeoman Office, 1880.

Louisiana Affairs: Report of the Committee on That Portion of the President's Message relating to the Condition of the South—Testimony Taken by the Committee. Washington, DC: Government Printing Office, 1875.

Official Congressional Directory, 61st Congress 2nd Session, for the Use of the United States Congress. Washington, DC: Government Printing Office, 1910.

Official Report of the Proceedings and Debates in the Convention: Assembled at Frankfort, on the Eighth Day of September, 1890, to Adopt, Amend, or Change the Constitution of the State of Kentucky. Frankfort, KY: E. Polk Johnson, 1890.

Owen, David Dale. *Fourth Report of the Geological Survey in Kentucky Made during the Years 1854 to 1859*. Frankfort, KY: A. G. Hodges, 1861.

Register of Debates in Congress

Report of the Debates and Proceedings of the Convention for the Revision of the Constitution of the State of Kentucky, 1849. Frankfort, KY: A. G. Hodges, 1849.

Reports of Selected Civil and Criminal Cases Decided in the Court of Appeals of Kentucky. Vol. 5, *Containing Cases Decided at Parts of Winter Term, 1868, and Summer Term, 1869*. Louisville: John P. Morton, 1870.

Reports of the Civil and Criminal Cases Decided by the Court of Appeals of Kentucky. Vol. 110 (February 14–May 24, 1901).

Shaffner, Taliaferro P., ed. *The Kentucky State Register for the Year 1847*. Louisville: Morton and Griswold, 1847.

The Southwestern Reporter, Containing All the Current Decisions of the Supreme Courts of Missouri, Arkansas, and Tennessee, Court of Appeals of Kentucky, and Supreme Court, Court of Criminal Appeals, and Courts of Civil Appeals in Texas.

Statutes at Large and Treaties of the United States of America from December 3, 1855 to March 3, 1859 and Proclamations since 1791, Arranged in Chronological Order, Thirty-fourth Congress, Session I. Vol. 11. Boston: Little, Brown, 1863.

Testimony Taken by the Joint Select Committee to Inquire into the Condition of Affairs in the Late Insurrectionary States: South Carolina. Vol. 2. Washington, DC: Government Printing Office, 1872.

U.S. Congress Serial Set

U.S. Department of Agriculture, Office of Experiment Stations. *Organization Lists of the Agricultural Experimental Stations and Institutions with Courses in Agriculture in the United States*. Washington, DC: Government Printing Office, 1897.

U.S. War Department. *Official Army Register of the Volunteer Force of the United States Army for the Years 1861, '62, '63, '64, '65*. Part 4. Washington, DC: Government Printing Office, 1865.
The War of the Rebellion: A Compilation of the Official Records of the Union and Confederate Armies.

Newspapers and Periodicals

Abingdon Virginian
Adair County News (Columbia, KY)
Albany Argus
Alexandria (VA) *Gazette*
American Farmer
American Mercury
Annals of the American Academy of Political and Social Science
Appleton's Annual Cyclopaedia and Register of Important Events
Baltimore Sun
Berea Citizen
Big Stone Post (Big Stone Gap, VA)
Bismarck Daily Tribune
Blue-grass Blade (Lexington, KY)
Boston Daily Atlas
Boston Globe
Bourbon News (Paris, KY)
Breathitt County News (Jackson, KY)
Breckinridge News (Cloverport, KY)
Charleston (SC) *Mercury*
Chicago Daily Tribune
Chicago Inter-Ocean
Cincinnati Commercial
Cincinnati Commercial-Tribune
Cincinnati Daily Gazette
Cincinnati Enquirer
Cincinnati Press
Clay City (KY) *Times*
Cleveland Herald
Columbia (SC) *Phoenix*
Columbus (GA) *Enquirer*
Crittenden Record-Press (Marion, KY)
Cyclopedic Review of Current History
Daily Ohio Statesman (Columbus)
Dallas Morning News

Decatur (IL) *Daily News*
Earlington (KY) *Bee*
Frankfort Roundabout
Galveston News
Harper's Weekly
Hartford (KY) *Herald*
Hartford (KY) *Republican*
Hazel Green (KY) *Herald*
Hickman (KY) *Courier*
Hopkinsville Kentuckian
Independent
Jackson (KY) *Hustler*
Kansas City Journal
Kansas City Star
Kentucky [*Tri-Weekly*] *Yeoman* (Frankfort)
Knoxville Journal
Lancaster (KY) *Central Record*
Lexington Herald
Lexington Leader
Lexington Observer and Reporter
Life
Louisville Commercial
Louisville Courier-Journal
Louisville Dispatch
Louisville Evening Post
Louisville Herald
Louisville Journal
Macon (GA) *Telegraph*
Maysville (KY) *Bulletin*
Maysville (KY) *Eagle*
Maysville (KY) *Public Ledger*
McConnelsville (OH) *Conservative*
Mountain Advocate (Barbourville, KY)
Mount Vernon (KY) *Signal*
Mt. Sterling (KY) *Advocate*
Mt. Sterling (KY) *Democrat*
Mt. Sterling (KY) *Sentinel-Democrat*
Nation
National Geographic
New Hampshire Sentinel
New Orleans Picayune

New Orleans Times
New York Herald
New York Sun
New York Times
New York Tribune
Omaha Herald
Paducah Sun
Philadelphia Inquirer
Pittsburgh Dispatch
Putnam County Courier (Carmel, NY)
Raleigh News and Observer
Richmond Climax
Richmond Register
Roanoke Times
Scribner's
Semi-Weekly Interior Journal (Stanford, KY)
Spout Spring (KY) *Times*
Stewart Kentucky Herald (Lexington)
Tribune Almanac and Political Register
Wall Street Journal
Washington Herald
Washington National Republican
Washington Post
Washington Times
Western Monitor (Lexington, KY)
Wheeling (WV) *Register*
Wichita Eagle
Winchester (KY) *News*
Wisconsin Daily Patriot (Madison)
Wisconsin State Journal (Madison)

Books and Articles

Allen, James Lane. "Through Cumberland Gap on Horseback." *Harper's New Monthly Magazine*, June 1886.

Allen, William B. *Kentucky Officer's Guide and Legal Hand-book: Especially Pointing Out the Powers and Duties of County Judges, County Attorneys, Magistrates.* Louisville: J. P. Morton, 1860.

Allison, Young Ewing. *The City of Louisville and a Glimpse of Kentucky.* Louisville: Courier-Journal Job Printing, 1887.

Altsheler, Joseph Alexander. *In Circling Camps: A Romance of the Civil War.* New York: D. Appleton, 1900.

Alvord, John W., ed. *Letters from the South: Relating to the Condition of the Freedmen.* Washington, DC: Howard University Press, 1870.

"The Amazing Progress of Temperance in Kentucky." *Harper's Weekly,* March 7, 1908.

The American Library Annual, 1913. New York: Office of the Publisher's Weekly, 1913.

Anglin, Mary K. "A Question of Loyalty: National and Regional Identity in Narratives of Appalachia." *Anthropological Quarterly* 65, no. 3 (1992).

"Assassination in Kentucky." *Public Opinion,* June 18, 1903.

"The Attack upon Berea College." *Nation,* February 11, 1904.

Ayers, Edward. *Vengeance and Justice: Crime and Punishment in the 19th Century American South.* Oxford: Oxford University Press, 1984.

Balzac, Honoré de. "La Vendetta; or, the Feud." Translated by Mrs. F. A. Butler. *United States Democratic Review* 17, no. 89 (1845).

Barton, William E. "The Church Militant in the Feud Belt." *Century,* October 10, 1903.

Beach, Rex. *The Net: A Novel.* New York: Harper and Brothers, 1912.

Beard, Charles. *Readings in American Government and Politics.* New York: Macmillan, 1914.

Biennial Report of the Bureau of Agriculture, Labor and Statistics of the State of Kentucky, 1900. Frankfort, KY: Office of the Bureau, 1900.

"Bloody Breathitt." *Time,* April 8, 1940.

Brewer, E. Cobham. *The Historical Notebook with an Appendix of Battles.* London: Smith, Elder, 1891.

Brooks, Tam. "Back to Dixie, a Hard Trip." *Confederate Veteran* 30, no. 2 (1922).

Bryan, William Jennings. *The Commoner Condensed.* New York: Abbey, 1902.

Buck, Charles Neville. *The Call of the Cumberlands.* 1916. Reprint, Middlesex, UK: Echo Library, 2005.

Burnett, Alfred. *Incidents of the War: Humorous, Pathetic, and Descriptive.* Cincinnati: Rickey and Carroll, 1863.

Burns, James Anderson. *The Crucible: A Tale of the Kentucky Feuds.* Oneida, KY: Oneida Institute, 1928.

"Campaign Sketches, No. 3, by an Officer of the US Signal Corps." *Arthur's Home Magazine,* March 1865.

Campbell, John C. *The Southern Highlander and His Homeland.* New York: Russell Sage Foundation, 1921.

Carman, Harry James. *Social and Economic History of the United States.* New York: Johnson Reprint, 1968.

Caudill, Bernice Calmes. *Pioneers of Eastern Kentucky: Their Feuds and Settlements.* Danville, KY: Bluegrass, 1969.

Cawein, Madison. *Poems.* Whitefish, MT: Kessinger, 2004.

Chandler, J. A. C., et al. *The South in the Building of the Nation: A History of the Southern States Designed to Record the South's Part in the Making of the American Nation; to Portray the Character and Genius, to Chronicle the Achievements and Progress and to Illustrate the Life and Traditions of the Southern People.* Vol. 1. Richmond, VA: Southern Historical Publication Society, 1909.

Child, Richard Washburn. "The Boss of Breathitt: The Story of a Kentucky County and Its Overlord." *Collier's,* October 19, 1907.

Clark, Thomas D. *Kentucky, Land of Contrast.* New York: Harper and Row, 1968.

Clements, J. Reginald, ed. *History of the First Regiment of Infantry: The Louisville Legion and Other Military Organizations.* Louisville: Globe, 1907.

Coates, Harold. *Stories of Kentucky Feuds.* Knoxville, TN: Holmes-Durst Coal, 1942.

Colby, Frank Moore, ed. *The New International Year Book: A Compendium of the World's Progress for the Year 1909/1910.* New York: Dodd, Mead, 1910–11.

Collins, Lewis. *Historical Sketches of Kentucky Embracing Its History, Antiquities, and Natural Curiosities, Geographical, Statistical, and Geographical Descriptions.* Cincinnati: J. A. and U. P. James, 1848.

Collins, Lewis, and Richard Collins. *Collins' Historical Sketches of Kentucky.* Vols. 1–3. Covington, KY: Collins, 1878.

"Comment." *Harper's Weekly,* June 27, 1903.

"Commonwealth of Barbarians." *American Lawyer* 11 (January–December 1903).

Connelly, Emma M. *The Story of Kentucky.* Boston: D. Lothrop, 1890.

"Corsican Bandits, and Others." *Living Age,* 6th ser., 15 (July–September 1897).

Coulter, E. Merton, and William Elsey Connelley. *History of Kentucky,* 5 vols. Chicago: American Historical Society, 1922.

Craighead, James. *Scotch and Irish Seeds in American Soil: The Early History of the Scotch and Irish Churches, and Their Relations to the Presbyterian Church of America.* Philadelphia: Presbyterian Board of Publication, 1878.

Crawford, T. C. *An American Vendetta: A Story of Barbarism in the United States.* New York: Bedford, Clarke, 1889.

Crozier, E. W. *The White-Caps: A History of the Organization in Sevier County.* Knoxville, TN: Bean, Warters and Gaut, 1899.

"Crystals, News of the Week." *Pomeroy's Democrat,* May 4, 1878.

Davenport, Frederick Morgan. *Primitive Traits in Religious Revivals: A Study in Mental and Social Evolution.* New York: Macmillan, 1917.

Davie, Winston J. *Kentucky: Its Resources and Present Condition.* Frankfort: S.I.M., 1878.

Day, John F. *Bloody Ground.* Garden City, NY: Doubleday, Doran, 1941.

DeForest, John William. *Kate Beaumont.* Boston: James R. Osgood, 1872.

Dennis, Charles. "Events of the Month." *World To-day,* August 1903.

Description of a Tract of Timber, Coal, and Agricultural Land, in Breathitt County, Kentucky, Containing 67,000 Acres, with Reports on the Same from the State Geologists of Kentucky, and Others, with an Abstract of Title Appended. For Sale by J. W. Andrews. Urbana, OH: James F. Hearn, 1885.

Diary of Brigadier-General Marcus J. Wright, C.S.A.: April 23, 1861–February 26, 1863. Chapel Hill: Academic Affairs Library, University of North Carolina at Chapel Hill, 1998.

"Discouraged." *Puck,* September 16, 1903.

Doolan, Jon C. "The Court of Appeals of Kentucky." *Green Bag,* January 1900.

Douglass, Harlan Paul. *Christian Reconstruction in the South.* Cambridge, MA: Harvard University Press, 1909.

"Editorial Notes." *Missionary,* June 1890.

"An Elemental Hint." *Puck,* April 20, 1910.

"The Family Feud—A French Story." *Harper's New Monthly Magazine,* May 1853.

Fischer, David Hackett. *Albion's Seed: Four British Folkways in America.* Oxford: Oxford University Press, 1991.

Fish, Hamilton. *Tragic Deception: FDR and America's Involvement in World War II.* Greenwich, CT: Devin-Adair, 1984.

Fleming, Walter Lynwood. *Documentary History of Reconstruction: Political, Military, Social, Religious, Educational and Industrial, 1865 to the Present Time.* Vol. 2. Cleveland: Arthur H. Clark, 1907.

Forman, S. E. *Advanced Civics: The Spirit, the Form, and the Functions of the American Government.* New York: Century, 1905.

Forty-fourth Annual Report of the American Bible Society, Presented May 10, 1860. New York: American Bible Society, 1860.

Fox, John, Jr. *Blue Grass and Rhododendron: Outdoors in Old Kentucky.* New York: Charles Scribner's Sons, 1901.

———. *Christmas Eve on Lonesome and Other Stories.* New York: Charles Scribner's Sons, 1904.

———. *A Cumberland Vendetta.* New York: Grosset and Dunlap, 1900.

———. *The Heart of the Hills.* New York: A. L. Burt, 1912.

———. *A Mountain Europa: The Last Stetson.* New York: Charles Scribner's Sons, 1912.

———. "On the Road to Hell-fer-Sartain." *Scribner's,* September 1910.

———. "The Southern Mountaineer." *Scribner's,* April 1901.

Frasier, William. "The Book of Carlaverock." *Blackwood's Edinburgh Magazine,* January–June 1874.

Frost, John. *Heroes and Hunters of the West: Comprising Sketches and Adventures of Boone, Kenton, Brady, Logan, Whetzel, Fleehart, Hughes, Johnston, &c.* Philadelphia: H. C. Peck and Theo. Bliss, 1858.

Frost, William G. "Berea College." In *From Servitude to Service: Being the Old South Lectures on the History and Work of Southern Institutions for the Education of the Negro,* edited by Robert C. Ogden et al. Boston: American Unitarian Association, 1905.

———. "Our Contemporary Ancestors in the Southern Mountains." *Atlantic Monthly,* March 1899.

Furman, Lucy. *Mothering on Perilous.* New York: Macmillan, 1915.

———. *The Quare Women.* Boston: Atlantic Monthly, 1923.

General Assembly of the Knights of Labor of America, Eleventh Regular Session, Held at Minneapolis, Minnesota, October 4 to 19, 1887. Minneapolis[?]: General Assembly, 1887.

Gilbertson, Henry Stimson. *The County, the Dark Continent of the American Politics.* New York: National Short Ballot Organization, 1917.

Gillies, Robert Pierce. *Palmario; or, The Merchant of Genoa.* London: T. and W. Boone, 1839.

Gladwell, Malcolm. *Outliers: The Story of Success.* New York: Little, Brown, 2008.

Gooch, Wilbur, and Franklin J. Keller. "Breathitt County in the Southern Appalachians: Vocational Guidance in a Social Setting; The People and the Land." *Occupations,* 14, no. 9 (1936).

Goodrich, S. G. *A Pictorial Geography of the World.* Vol. 2, *The New World.* Boston: Charles D. Strong, 1856.

Gossett, Thomas F. *Race: The History of an Idea in the Making.* Dallas: Southern Methodist University Press, 1963.

Green, Harold Everett. *Towering Pines: The Life of John Fox, Jr.* Boston: Meador, 1943.

Gregorovius, Ferdinand. *Wanderings in Corsica: Its History and Its Heroes.* Vol. 1. Translated by Alexander Muir. Edinburgh: Thomas Constable, 1855.

Guerrant, Edward O. *The Galax Gatherers: The Gospel among the Highlanders.* 1910. Reprint, Knoxville: University of Tennessee Press, 2005.

Handy, Moses P. *The Official Directory of the World's Columbian Exposition, May 1st to October 30th, 1893.* Chicago: W. B. Conkey, 1893.

Haney, William Henry. *The Mountain People of Kentucky: An Account of Present Conditions with the Attitude of the People toward Improvement.* Cincinnati: Roessler Brothers, 1906.

Hanna, Charles A. *The Scotch-Irish or the Scot in North Britain, North Ireland, and North America.* Vol. 1. New York: Knickerbocker, 1902.

Harder, Ludwig. *A Family Feud.* Translated by Mrs. A. L. Wister. Philadelphia: J. B. Lippincott, 1877.

Hardy, Sallie E. Marshall. "Some Kentucky Lawyers of the Past and Present, Part II." *Green Bag,* January 1897.

Harney, Will Wallace. "A Strange Land and a Peculiar People." *Lippincott's,* October 1873.

Hartley, Davis, and Clifford Smyth. "The Land of Feuds: A Region of the United States in Which Bloodshed Is a Pastime and Cruel and Cowardly Murder Goes Unpunished—The Terrible Story of the Seven Great Kentucky Feuds." *Munsey's,* November 1903.

Harwood, Richard. "East Kentucky's Mountain Areas Make Progress in War on Sickness, Poverty, Diet." *Louisville Times,* February 18, 1959.

Haskel, Daniel, and J. Calvin Smith. *A Complete Descriptive and Statistical Gazetteer of the United States of America, Containing a Particular Description of the States, Territories, Counties, Districts, Parishes, Cities, Towns, and Villages—Mountains, Rivers, Lakes, Canals and Railroads; with an Abstract of the Census and Statistics for 1840, Exhibiting a Complete View of the Agricultural, Commercial, Manufacturing, and Literary Condition and Resources of the Country.* New York: Sherman and Smith, 1843.

"Heathen in Our Own Country." *Christian Reflector,* July 31, 1845.

"Heathen Mountaineers in Kentucky." *New York Evangelist,* December 20, 1883.

Hoffman, Charles Fenno. *A Winter in the West: By a New Yorker, in Two Volumes.* Vol. 2. New York: Harper and Brothers, 1835.

Hough, Emerson. "Burns of the Mountains: The Story of a Southern Mountaineer Who Is Remaking His Own People." *American Magazine,* Christmas 1912.

"How about It, Vermont?" *Collier's,* October 20, 1917.

Howard, O. O. "The Feuds in the Cumberland Mountains." *Independent,* April 7, 1904.

Hubbard, Elbert. *The Fra: For Philistines and Roycrofters* 14, section 2 (1914–15).

Hughes, Robert Elkin, Frederick William Schaefer, and Eustace Leroy Williams. *That Kentucky Campaign; or, The Law, the Ballot and the People in the Goebel-Taylor Contest.* Cincinnati: Robert Clarke, 1900.

"Humor of the Law." *Central Law Journal,* July 16, 1920.

Humphreys, James. "Law of Tenure." *Southern Review* 3, no. 5 (1829).

Hundley, D. R. *Social Relations in Our Southern States.* New York: Henry B. Price, 1860.

"Jackson, in the Kentucky Mountains; and Its New School Buildings." *Christian Observer,* October 13, 1897.

Jett, Curtis. *From Prison to Pulpit: Life of Curtis Jett.* Louisville: Pentecostal, 1919.

Johnson, E. Polk. *A History of Kentucky and Kentuckians: The Leaders and Representative Men in Commerce, Industry and Modern Activity.* Vols. 1–2. Chicago: Lewis, 1912.

Johnson, Lewis Franklin. *Famous Kentucky Tragedies and Trials.* Louisville: Baldwin Law Book, 1916.

Johnston, J. Stoddard "Romance and Tragedy of Kentucky Feuds, as Seen by a Writer More Than Half Century Ago." *Cosmopolitan,* September 1899.

Jones, James. *The Thin Red Line.* New York: Avon, 1975.

Jordan, Terry G., and Matti Kaups. *The American Backwoods Frontier: An Ethnic and Ecological Interpretation.* Baltimore: Johns Hopkins University Press, 1989.

Jutkins, A. J. *Handbook of Prohibition, 1885.* Chicago: 87 Washington Street, 1885.

"Kentucky Feudalism." *Time,* May 3, 1937.

Kentucky Library Commission Fourth Biennial Report, 1915–1917. Vol. 2. Frankfort, KY: State Journal, 1918.

"Kentucky's Feuds." *Public Opinion,* June 29, 1899.

"Kentucky's Political Anarchy." *Harper's Weekly,* February 10, 1900.

"Kentucky's Vendettas." *Current Literature* 26, no. 3 (1899).

"Kentucky Tobacco War." *Christian Observer,* February 19, 1908.

The Kentucky Union Railway Company. Lexington: Kentucky Union Railway, 1883.

"A Kentucky Vendetta." *Literary Digest,* July 1, 1899.

Kephart, Horace. *Our Southern Highlanders.* New York: Outing, 1913.

Kilpatrick, Lewis H. "When Breathitt Went to Battle." *Bellman,* August 10, 1918.

King, Edward. *The Great South: A Record of Journeys in Louisiana, Texas, the Indian Territory, Missouri, Arkansas, Mississippi, Alabama, Georgia, Florida, South Carolina,*

North Carolina, Kentucky, Tennessee, Virginia, West Virginia, and Maryland. Hartford, CT: American Publishing, 1875.

Kirby, James Patrick. *Selected Articles on Criminal Justice.* New York: H. W. Wilson, 1926.

Letter to the Editor from "Mugwump." *Nation,* August 22, 1889.

Levin, H., ed. *The Lawyers and Lawmakers of Kentucky.* Chicago: Lewis, 1897.

Lindley, Betty, and Ernest Lindley. *A New Deal for Youth: The Story of the National Youth Administration.* New York: Viking, 1938.

Linner, Edward S. "The Human Side of Jim Hargis." *Harper's Weekly,* February 29, 1908.

"List of Lawyers in Kentucky." *United States Monthly Law Magazine* 4 (July–December 1851).

Litsey, E. Carl. "Kentucky Feuds and Their Causes." *Frank Leslie's Popular Monthly,* January 1902.

Lloyd, A. L. "A Background to Feuding." *History Today* 2, no. 7 (1952).

"Lobbyists and Legislatures." *Nation,* March 16, 1899.

Lord, Daniel. *The Effect of Secession upon the Commercial Relations between the North and South and upon Each Section.* London: Henry Stevens, 1861.

Lydston, George Frank. *The Diseases of Society (The Vice and Crime Problem).* Philadelphia: J. B. Lippincott, 1904.

MacClintock, S. S. "The Kentucky Mountains and Their Feuds, I: The People and Their Country." *American Journal of Sociology* 7, no. 1 (1901).

———. "The Kentucky Mountains and Their Feuds, II: The Causes of Feuds." *American Journal of Sociology* 7, no. 2 (1901).

MacFarlane, James. *Coal-Regions of America: Their Topography, Geology, and Development (with a Colored Geological Map of Pennsylvania, a Railroad Map of All the Coal-Regions, and Numerous Other Maps and Illustrations).* New York: D. Appleton, 1875.

MacPherson, Col. Ernest. "The Louisville Legion." In *History of the First Regiment of Infantry: The Louisville Legion and Other Military Organizations,* edited by J. Reginald Clements. Louisville: Globe, 1907.

Manual of the Railroads of the United States. New York: H. V. and H. W. Poor, 1889.

Marcosson, Isaac F. "The South in Fiction: Kentucky and Tennessee." *Bookman: A Review of Books and Life,* December 1910.

Martin, George M. "Race Cooperation." *McClure's,* October 1922.

Matthews, Brinsley, and William Simpson Pearson. *Mōnon Ou; or, Well-nigh Reconstructed: A Political Novel.* New York: E. J. Hale and Son, 1882.

McAfee, John J. *Kentucky Politicians: Sketches of Representative Corncrackers and Other Miscellany.* Louisville: Courier-Journal Job Printing, 1886.

McClure, R. L. "The Mazes of a Kentucky Feud." *Independent,* September 17, 1903.

McKee, James L. "Invading the Kentucky Mountains." *New York Evangelist,* October 11, 1888.

McKinney, William M., and H. Noyes Greene, eds. *Annotated Cases, American and English.* San Francisco: Bancroft-Whitney, 1917.

Merrill, C. E. "The Invisible Empire." *Current,* March 28, 1885.

"Midnight Gathering of a 'Red String League,' in the Forests of North Carolina." *Frank Leslie's Illustrated,* May 9, 1868.

Miller, Arthur M. "The Vote on the Evolution Bill in the Kentucky State Legislature." *Science,* n.s., 55, no. 1421 (1922).

Miller, Penny M. *Kentucky Politics and Government: Do We Stand United?* Lincoln: University of Nebraska Press, 1994.

The Mine, Quarry and Metallurgical Record of the United States, Canada and Mexico. Chicago: Mine and Quarry News Bureau, 1897.

Moore, Frank, and Edward Everett, eds. *The Rebellion Record: A Diary of American Events.* Vol. 3. New York: G. P. Putnam, 1862.

Mutzenburg, Charles Gustavus. *Kentucky's Famous Feuds and Tragedies: Authentic History of the World Renowned Vendettas of the Dark and Bloody Ground.* New York: R. F. Fenno, 1917.

Myers, Mrs. A. A. "The Mountain Whites of the South—Extracts." *American Missionary,* January 1885.

National Almanac and Annual Record for the Year 1863. Philadelphia: George W. Childs, 1863.

Nelson, Henry Loomis. "The Kentucky 'Boss's' Desperate Campaign." *Harper's Weekly,* October 23, 1899.

New International Encyclopaedia. Vol. 8. 2nd ed. New York: Dodd, Mead, 1930.

Nineteenth Biennial Report of the Bureau of Agriculture Labor and Statistics for 1910–1911. Frankfort: Kentucky State Journal, 1912.

Ninth Report of the Railroad Commissioners of Kentucky, for the Year 1888. Frankfort, KY: Capital Office, E. Polk Johnson, 1889.

"Notable Episodes in Outlawry." Review of *Kentucky's Famous Feuds and Tragedies,* by Charles Gustavus Mutzenburg, *Nation,* September 20, 1917.

"Notes on Important Decisions." *Central Law Journal,* August 16, 1907.

"Notes on Kentucky and Tennessee." *Scribner's,* December 1874.

Official Proceedings of the St. Louis Railroad Club 30–31 (1925–27).

Ogg, Frederic Austin, and Perley Orman Ray, eds. *Introduction to American Government: The National Government.* New York: Century, 1922.

Owen, David Dale. *Fourth Report of the Kentucky Geological Survey in Kentucky Made during the Years 1858 and 1859.* Frankfort, KY: J. B. Major, 1861.

Payne, James W., Jr. "The Hillman Case: An Old Problem Revisited." *Virginia Law Review* 41, no. 8 (1955).

Peck, George. *Our Country: Its Trials and Triumph.* New York: Carlton and Porter, 1865.

Perrin, William Henry, J. H. Battle, and G. C. Kniffin. *Kentucky: A History of the State, Embracing a Concise Account of the Origin and Development of the Virginia Colony; Its Expansion Westward, and the Settlement of the Frontier beyond the Alleghanies; the Erection of Kentucky as an Independent State, and Its Subsequent Development.* Louisville: F. A. Battey, 1888.

Phillips, Christopher. "'The Chrysalis State': Slavery, Confederate Identity, and the Creation of the Border South." In *Inside the Confederate Nation: Essays in Honor of Emory Thomas,* edited by Leslie Gordon and John Inscoe. Baton Rouge: Louisiana State University Press, 2005.

Phillips, Ulrich B. *Life and Labor in the Old South.* Columbia: University of South Carolina Press, 2007.

Pierson, Delevan L. "Berea College and Its Mission." *Missionary Review of the World,* June 1904.

Pilcher, Louis. *The Story of Jackson City (Breathitt County), the Inspiration of the New Kentucky.* Lexington: Beckner, 1914.

"Poverty: Feud in the Hills." *Time,* September 12, 1969.

Powers, Caleb. *My Own Story: An Account of the Conditions in Kentucky Leading to the Assassination of William Goebel, Who Was Declared Governor of the State, and My Indictment and Conviction on the Charge of Complicity in His Murder.* Indianapolis: Bobbs-Merrill, 1905.

———. "My Own Story; of the Dramatic Campaign Preceding Kentucky's Great Political Tragedy—the Murder of Senator Goebel—and the Part I Played in the Stirring Events." *Reader Magazine,* December 1904.

Price, William T. *Without Scrip or Purse; or, "The Mountain Evangelist," George O. Barnes.* Louisville: W. T. Price, 1883.

Proceedings of the Eighth Annual Conference for Education in the South, Columbia, South Carolina, April 26–28, 1905. Atlanta: Massey Reporting, 1905.

Proceedings of the Twenty-fifth Constitutional Convention of the United Mine Workers 1 (1909).

Redfield, Horace V. *Homicide, North and South: Being a Comparative View of Crime against the Person in Several Parts of the United States.* Philadelphia: J. B. Lippincott, 1880.

"Religion: Wild Dog into Preacher." *Time,* January 26, 1931.

Report of the Special Committee on the Penitentiary to the Senate of Kentucky, February 26, 1880. Frankfort: Kentucky Yeoman Office, E. H. Porter, 1880.

Review of the Financial and Political History of the State of Kentucky for the Past Twenty-eight Years under Democratic Government: And a Comparative Statement Contrasting Kentucky with the Government of Other States. Louisville: Courier-Journal, 1895.

Richardson, Albert Deane, and Benjamin Russel Hanby. *The Secret Service, the Field, the Dungeon, and the Escape.* Hartford, CT: American Publishing, 1866.

Ripley, George, and Charles Dana, eds. *The New American Cyclopaedia: A Popular Dictionary of General Knowledge.* Vol. 3. New York: D. Appleton, 1859.

Robertson, George. *Scrap Book on Law and Politics, Men and Times.* Lexington: A. W. Elder, 1855.

Rogers, William, and Erica Clark. *The Croom Family and Goodwood Plantation: Land, Litigation and Southern Lives.* Athens: University of Georgia Press, 1999.

Rolt-Wheeler, Francis. *The Boy with the U.S. Census*. Boston: Lothrop, Lee and Shepard, 1911.

Rumsfeld, Donald. *Known and Unknown: A Memoir*. New York: Penguin, 2011.

Scott, Sir Walter, Bart. *Tales of a Grandfather*. Edinburgh: Adam and Charles Black, 1868.

Semple, Ellen Churchill. "The Anglo-Saxons of the Kentucky Mountains: A Study in Anthropogeography." *Bulletin of the American Geographical Society* 42, no. 8 (1910).

Shaler, Nathaniel Southgate. *Kentucky, a Pioneer Commonwealth*. Boston: Houghton, Mifflin, 1886.

Simkins, Francis B., and Charles Roland. *A History of the South*. 4th ed. New York: Knopf, 1972.

Smith, Munroe. "Record of Political Events." *Political Science Quarterly* 14, no. 2 (1899).

Smith, Zachariah Frederick. *The History of Kentucky: From Its Earliest Discovery and Settlement, to the Present Date, Embracing Its Prehistoric and Aboriginal Periods*. Louisville: Courier-Journal, 1886.

Sneed, William C. *A Report on the History and Mode of Management of the Kentucky Penitentiary from Its Origin, in 1798, to March 1, 1860*. Frankfort, KY: Jno. B. Major, 1860.

"Southern Aids to the North." *Continental Monthly: Devoted to Literature and National Policy*, March 1862.

Spaulding, Arthur W. *The Men of the Mountains: The Story of the Southern Mountaineer and His Kin of the Piedmont; with an Account of Some of the Agencies of Progress among Them*. Nashville: Southern Publishing, 1915.

Spears, John R. "The Story of a Kentucky Feud." *Munsey's*, June 1901.

"The Stalwart Policy and the Party Policy." *Nation*, August 28, 1879.

Stanley, Ralph, and Eddie Dean. *Man of Constant Sorrow: My Life and Times*. New York: Gotham Books, 2010.

Stewart, Cora Wilson. "The Breathitt County Vendetta." *Wide World*, May 1904.

Storke, Elliot G. *A Complete History of the Great American Rebellion, Embracing Its Causes, Events and Consequences, with Biographical Sketches and Portraits of Its Principal Actors*. Auburn, NY: Auburn, 1865.

Storke, Elliot G., and L. P. Brockett. *A Complete History of the Great American Rebellion, Embracing Its Causes, Events and Consequences, with Biographical Sketches and Portraits of Its Principal Actors*. Vol. 2. Auburn, NY: Auburn, 1865.

Sturber, D. I. *The Anarchist Constitution*. San Francisco: Radical, 1903.

Tarleton, Fiswoode. *Bloody Ground: A Cycle of the Southern Hills*. New York: Lincoln Mac Veagh—Dial Press, 1929.

"Telephone to Open Feud-Ridden County." *Telephony*, September 1905.

Testimony Taken by the Joint Select Committee to Inquire into the Condition of Affairs in the Late Insurrectionary States: North Carolina. Washington, DC: Government Printing Office, 1872.

Thomas, Jean. *Blue Ridge Country*. New York: Duell, Sloan and Pearce, 1942.

Thompson, G. A. *The Geographical and Historical Dictionary of America and the West*

Indies, Containing an Entire Translation of the Spanish Work of Colonel Don Antonio de Alcedo. Vol. 5. London: Carpenter and Son, 1815.

"Those Lawless Mountaineers." *Christian Science Monitor,* August 2, 1917.

"The Timber Boom." *Scientific American,* May 4, 1895.

Tomes, Robert, and Benjamin Smith. *The War with the South: A History of the Late Rebellion, with Biographical Sketches of Leading Statesmen and Distinguished Naval and Military Commanders, etc.* Vol. 3. New York: Virtue and Yorston, 1864.

Toynbee, Arnold. *A Study of History.* Abridgement of vols. 1–6 by D. C. Somervell. New York: Oxford University Press, 1947.

Triplett, Frank. *History, Romance and Philosophy of Great American Crimes and Criminals (with Personal Portraits, Biographical Sketches, Legal Notes of Celebrated Trials, and Philosophical Disquisition concerning the Causes, Prevalence and Prevention of Crime).* New York: N. D. Thompson, 1884.

Twain, Mark. *Life on the Mississippi.* New York: Penguin Classics, 1984.

Vanatta, Hugh R. "On the Trail of a Mystery." *Argosy All-Story Weekly* 32, no. 1 (1899).

Vann, Barry. *Rediscovering the South's Cultural Heritage.* Johnson City, TN: Overmountain, 2004.

The Virginias 5, no. 2 (1884).

Warner, Charles Dudley. "Comments on Kentucky." *Harper's New Monthly Magazine,* January 1889.

———. *Studies in the South and West with Comments on Canada.* New York: Harper and Brothers, Franklin Square, 1889.

Watterson, Henry. "Murder Is Murder." *Courier-Journal Almanac for 1902,* vol. V (January 1902).

Webb, James. *Born Fighting: How the Scots-Irish Shaped America.* New York: Broadway Books, 2005.

Westengard, Jens Iverson, Joseph H. Beale, Porter E. Sargent, a Siamese Student, and John Raeburn Green. "International Tribunals in the Light of the History of the Law." *Harvard Law Review* 32 (1918–19).

Wheatley, R. "Correspondence: Religious and Civil Matters in Kentucky." *Zion's Herald,* January 28, 1875.

White, Alfred Ludlow. "A Provincial Family Feud." *Short Stories: A Magazine of Select Fiction,* January–April 1892.

Wilson, Jess D. *A Latter Day Look at Kentucky Feuds.* Manchester, KY: Possum Trot University Press, 1999.

Wilson, John Lyde. *The Code of Honor; or, Rules for the Government of Principals and Seconds in Duelling.* Charleston: J. Phinney, 1858.

Wilson, Thos. L. *Sufferings Endured for a Free Government; or, A History of the Cruelties and Atrocities of the Rebellion.* Philadelphia: Smith and Peters, 1865.

Wines, E. C., and Theodore W. Dwight. *Report on the Prisons and Reformatories of the United States and Canada, Made to the Legislature of New York, January, 1867.* Albany: Van Benthuysen and Sons, 1867.

Wireman, Charles Little. *Kentucky Mountain Outlaw Transformed.* Intercession City, FL: Intercession, 1950.

"Yesterday's News." *Register of the Kentucky Historical Society* 95, no. 3 (1997).

Secondary Sources

Unpublished Theses, Dissertations, and Monographs

Astor, Aaron. "Rebels on the Border: Civil War, Emancipation and the Reconstruction of Kentucky and Missouri." Unpublished manuscript in author's possession.

Bland, Gaye. "Populism in Kentucky, 1887–1896." PhD diss., University of Kentucky, 1979.

Collins, Ernest. "Political Behavior in Breathitt, Knott, Perry and Leslie Counties." MA thesis, University of Kentucky, 1940.

Conti, Eugene A., Jr. "Mountain Metamorphoses: Culture and Development in East Kentucky." PhD diss., Duke University, 1978.

Coulter, E. Merton. "Some Reasons for Kentucky's Position in the Civil War." MA thesis, University of Wisconsin, 1915.

Crawford, Robert Gunn. "A History of the Kentucky Penitentiary System, 1856–1937." PhD diss., University of Kentucky, 1955.

Harris, Meriel Daniel. "Two Famous Kentucky Feuds." MA thesis, University of Kentucky, 1940.

Harrison, Marion Clifford. "Social Types in Southern Prose Fiction." PhD diss., University of Virginia, 1921.

Hutton, T. R. C. "The Hill-Evans Feud: Extralegal Violence in Antebellum Kentucky." MA thesis, Appalachian State University, 2002.

Johnson, Jeffrey Guy. "Feud, Society, Family: Feud Narratives in the United States, 1865–1910." PhD diss., Harvard University, 2001.

Lewis, John Sherwood. "Becoming Appalachia: The Emergence of an American Subculture, 1840–1860." PhD diss., University of Kentucky, 2000.

Owen, Thomas Louis. "The Formative Years of Kentucky's Republican Party, 1864–1871." PhD diss., University of Kentucky, 1981.

Prichard, Edward F., Jr. "Popular Political Movements in Kentucky, 1875–1900." Senior thesis, Princeton University, 1935.

Pudup, Mary Beth. "Land before Coal: Class and Regional Development in Southeast Kentucky." PhD diss., University of California, Berkeley, 1987.

Rhyne, J. Michael. "Rehearsal for Redemption: The Politics of Post-emancipation Violence in Kentucky's Bluegrass Region." PhD diss., University of Cincinnati, 2006.

Rice, Kelly. "History of Education in Breathitt County, Kentucky." MA thesis, University of Kentucky, 1933.

Sullivan, James P. "Louisville and Her Southern Alliance." PhD diss., University of Kentucky, 1965.

Tapp, Hambleton. "Three Decades of Kentucky Politics, 1870–1900." PhD diss., University of Kentucky, 1950.

Volz, Harry August. "Party, State and Nation: Kentucky and the Coming of the American Civil War." PhD diss., University of Virginia, 1982.

Webster, Gerald R. "The Spatial Reorganization of the Local State: The Case of County Boundaries in Kentucky." PhD diss., University of Kentucky, 1984.

Books, Articles, and Presented Research

Alexander, Jeffrey C. *The Cambridge Companion to Durkheim.* Cambridge: Cambridge University Press, 2005.

Almond, Gabriel A. "Comparative Political Systems." *Journal of Politics* 18, no. 3 (1956).

Almond, Gabriel, and Sidney Verba. *The Civic Culture: Political Attitudes and Democracy in Five Nations.* Princeton, NJ: Princeton University Press, 1963.

America at the Polls: A Handbook of American Presidential Election Statistics. Washington, DC: Congressional Quarterly, 1920–56.

Anderson, Stuart. *Race and Rapprochement: Anglo-Saxonism and Anglo-American Relations, 1894–1904.* East Brunswick, NJ: Associated University Presses, 1981.

Apel, Dora. *Imagery of Lynching: Black Men, White Women and the Mob.* New Brunswick, NJ: Rutgers University Press, 2004.

Arnold, Thomas Clay. "Rethinking Moral Economy." *American Political Science Review* 95, no. 1 (2001).

Aron, Stephen. *How the West Was Lost: The Transformation of Kentucky from Daniel Boone to Henry Clay.* Baltimore: Johns Hopkins University Press, 1996.

———. "Pioneers and Profiteers: Land Speculation and the Homestead Ethic in Frontier Kentucky." *Western Historical Quarterly* 23, no. 2 (1992).

Ash, Stephen. *When the Yankees Came: Conflict and Chaos in the Occupied South, 1861–1865.* Chapel Hill: University of North Carolina Press, 1995.

Auman, William T., and David D. Scarboro. "The Heroes of America in Civil War North Carolina." *North Carolina Historical Review* 58 (October 1981).

Ayers, Edward. *The Promise of the New South: Life after Reconstruction.* 15th anniversary ed. Oxford: Oxford University Press, 2007.

———. *Vengeance and Justice: Crime and Punishment in the 19th Century American South.* Oxford: Oxford University Press, 1984.

Baggett, James Alex. *The Scalawags: Southern Dissenters in the Civil War and Reconstruction.* Baton Rouge: Louisiana State University Press, 2003.

Bailey, Rebecca J. *Matewan before the Massacre: Politics and Coal, the Roots of Conflict in Mingo County, 1793–1920.* Charleston: West Virginia Press, 2008.

Baird, Nancy Disher. *Luke Pryor Blackburn: Physician, Governor, Reformer.* Lexington: University Press of Kentucky, 1979.

Baker, Bruce E. *This Mob Will Surely Take My Life: Lynchings in the Carolinas, 1871–1947.* London: Hambledon Continuum, 2009.

Baldasty, Gerald J. *The Commercialization of News in the Nineteenth Century.* Madison: University of Wisconsin Press, 1992.

Banker, Mark T. *Appalachians All: East Tennesseans and the Elusive History of an American Region.* Knoxville: University of Tennessee Press, 2010.

Banks, Alan. "The Emergence of a Capitalistic Labor Market in Eastern Kentucky." *Appalachian Journal* 7, no. 3 (1980).

Banner, Leslie. "John Ehle and Appalachian Fiction." In *An American Vein: Critical Readings in Appalachian Literature,* edited by Danny L. Miller, Sharon Hatfield, and Gurney Norman. Athens: Ohio University Press, 2005.

Barnes, Kenneth. *Who Killed John Clayton? Political Violence and the Emergence of the New South, 1861–1893.* Durham, NC: Duke University Press, 1998.

Barnett, Todd H. "Virginians Moving West: The Early Evolution of Slavery in the Bluegrass." *Filson Club Historical Quarterly* 73, no. 3 (1999).

Barney, Sandra Lee. *Authorized to Heal: Gender, Class, and the Transformation of Medicine in Appalachia, 1880–1930.* Chapel Hill: University of North Carolina Press, 2000.

Barney, William. *The Road to Secession: A New Perspective on the Old South.* New York: Praeger, 1972.

Bar On, Bat-Ami. *The Subject of Violence: Arendtian Exercises in Understanding.* Lanham, MD: Rowman and Littlefield, 2002.

Barzun, Jacques. *From Dawn to Decadence: 500 Years of Western Cultural Life, 1500 to the Present.* New York: Harper-Collins, 2001.

Batteau, Alan. *The Invention of Appalachia.* Tucson: University of Arizona Press, 1990.

———. "Mosbys and Broomsedge: The Semantics of Class in Appalachian Kinship Systems." *American Ethnologist* 9, no. 3 (1982).

Baudrillard, Jean. *The Transparency of Evil: Essays on Extreme Phenomena.* Translated by James Benedict. New York: Verso, 1993.

Beardsworth, Richard. *Derrida and the Political.* New York: Routledge, 1996.

Bearman, Peter S. "Desertion as Localism: Army Unit Solidarity and Group Norms in the U.S. Civil War." *Social Forces* 70, no. 2 (1991).

Bederman, Gail. *Manliness and Civilization: A Cultural History of Gender and Race in the United States, 1880–1917.* Chicago: University of Chicago Press, 1995.

Belue, Ted Franklin. *The Hunters of Kentucky: A Narrative History of America's First Far West, 1750–1792.* Mechanicsburg, PA: Stackpole Books, 2011.

Bensel, Richard Franklin. *The American Ballot Box in the Mid-Nineteenth Century.* Cambridge: Cambridge University Press, 2004.

———. *Yankee Leviathan: The Origins of Central State Authority in America, 1859–1877.* Cambridge: Cambridge University Press, 1990.

Berkeley, Bill. *The Graves Are Not Yet Full: Race, Tribe, and Power in the Heart of Africa.* New York: Basic Books, 2001.

Berlin, Ira, Barbara J. Fields, Steven F. Miller, Joseph P. Reidy, and Leslie Rowland. "The Destruction of Slavery, 1861–1865." In *Slaves No More: Three Essays on Emancipation and the Civil War.* Cambridge: Cambridge University Press, 1992.

Billings, Dwight, and Kathleen Blee. *The Road to Poverty: The Making of Wealth and Hardship in Appalachia.* Cambridge: Cambridge University Press, 2000.

———. "Where 'Bloodshed Is a Pastime': Mountain Feuds and Appalachian Stereotyping." In *Confronting Appalachian Stereotypes: Backtalk from an American Region,* edited by Dwight Billings, Gurney Norman, and Katherine Ledford. Lexington: University Press of Kentucky, 1999.

Billings, Dwight, Gurney Norman, and Katherine Ledford, eds. *Confronting Appalachian Stereotypes: Backtalk from an American Region.* Lexington: University Press of Kentucky, 1999.

Billings, Dwight, Mary Beth Pudup, and Altina Waller. "Taking Exception with Exceptionalism: The Emergence and Transformation of Historical Studies of Appalachia." In *Appalachia in the Making: The Mountain South in the Nineteenth Century,* edited by Mary Beth Pudup, Dwight Billings, and Altina Waller. Chapel Hill: University of North Carolina Press, 1995.

Billingsley, Dale B. "'Standard Authors' in *Huckleberry Finn." Journal of Narrative Technique* 9, no. 2 (1979).

Birchfield, Martha J. "Beckham County: A Political Folly." *Filson Club Historical Quarterly* 64, no. 1 (1990).

Black-Michaud, Jacob. *Cohesive Force: Feud in the Mediterranean and the Middle East.* New York: St. Martin's, 1975.

Blakey, George T. *Hard Times and New Deal in Kentucky, 1929–1939.* Lexington: University Press of Kentucky, 1986.

Blanchard, Margaret A. *Revolutionary Sparks: Freedom of Expression in Modern America.* New York: Oxford University Press, 1992.

Blaustein, Richard. *The Thistle and the Brier: Historical Links and Cultural Parallels between Scotland and Appalachia.* Jefferson, NC: McFarland, 2003.

Blethen, H. Tyler, and Curtis Wood. "The Appalachian Frontier and the Southern Frontier: A Comparative Perspective." *Journal of the Appalachian Studies Association* 3 (1991).

Blight, David. *Race and Reunion: The Civil War in American Memory.* Cambridge, MA: Harvard University Press, 2002.

Blok, Anton. *Honour and Violence.* Cambridge: Polity, 2001.

Bloom, Jack. *Class, Race, and the Civil Rights Movement: The Changing Political Economy of Southern Racism.* Bloomington: University of Indiana Press, 1987.

Boehm, Christopher. *Blood Revenge: The Anthropology of Feuding in Montenegro and Other Tribal Societies.* Lawrence: University Press of Kansas, 1984.

Bolin, James Duane. *Bossism and Reform in a Southern City: Lexington, Kentucky, 1880–1940.* Lexington: University Press of Kentucky, 2000.

Bolton, S. Charles. *Territorial Ambition: Land and Society in Arkansas, 1800–1840.* Fayetteville: University of Arkansas Press, 1993.

Bowling, Stephen D. *Images of America: Breathitt County.* Charleston, S.C.: Arcadia, 2010.

Bowman, Shearer Davis. "Kentucky's 'Athens of the West' Viewed in a 'Distant Mirror.'" In *Bluegrass Renaissance: The History and Culture of Central Kentucky, 1792–1852,* edited by James C. Klotter and Daniel Rowland. Lexington: University Press of Kentucky, 2012.

Brandt, Nat. *The Town That Started the Civil War.* Syracuse, NY: Syracuse University Press, 1990.

Brantlinger, Patrick. *Dark Vanishings: Discourse on the Extinction of Primitive Races.* Ithaca, NY: Cornell University Press, 2003.

Brockman, William Everett. *History of the Hume, Kennedy and Brockman Families in Three Parts.* Washington, DC: Chas. H. Potter, 1916.

Brown, Cynthia, and Farhad Karim, eds. *Playing the "Communal Card": Communal Violence and Human Rights.* New York: Human Rights Watch, 1995.

Brown, David S. *Richard Hofstadter: An Intellectual Biography.* Chicago: University of Chicago Press, 2006.

Brown, James S. *Beech Creek: A Study of a Kentucky Mountain Neighborhood.* Berea, KY: Berea College Press, 1988.

Brown, R. Ben. "Free Men and Free Pigs: Closing the Southern Range and the American Property Tradition." *Radical History Review* 2010, no. 108 (2010).

Brown, Richard Maxwell. *Strain of Violence: Historical Studies of American Violence and Vigilantism.* Oxford: Oxford University Press, 1975.

Brown, Rodger Lyle. *Ghost Dancing on the Cracker Circuit: The Culture of Festivals in the American South.* Jackson: University of Mississippi Press, 1997.

Brown, Thomas J. "The Roots of Bluegrass Insurgency: An Analysis of the Populist Movement in Kentucky." *Register of the Kentucky Historical Society* 78, no. 3 (1980).

Brown, Warren, and Piotr Górecki. *Conflict in Medieval Europe: Changing Perspectives on Society and Culture.* Burlington, VT: Ashgate, 2003.

Brown, Wendy. *Regulating Aversion: Tolerance in the Age of Identity and Empire.* West Orange, NJ: Princeton University Press, 2006.

Bruce, Dickson. *Violence and Culture in the Antebellum South.* Austin: University of Texas Press, 1979.

Brundage, W. Fitzhugh. *Lynching in the New South: Georgia and Virginia, 1880–1930.* Urbana: University of Illinois Press, 1993.

Buck, Pem Davidson. *Worked to the Bone: Race, Class, Power, and Privilege in Kentucky.* New York: Monthly Review, 2001.

Budd, Louis J. "The Southward Currents under Huck Finn's Raft." *Mississippi Valley Historical Review* 46, no. 2 (1959).

Bull, Jacqueline. "Writings on Kentucky History, 1958." *Register of the Kentucky Historical Society* 58, no. 3 (1960).

Burch, John R. *Owsley County, Kentucky, and the Perpetuation of Poverty.* Jefferson, NC: McFarland, 2007.

———. "The Turner Family of Breathitt County, Kentucky, and the War on Poverty." *Register of the Kentucky Historical Society* 107, no. 3 (2009).

Burckel, Nicholas. "From Beckham to McCreary: The Progressive Record of Kentucky Governors." *Register of the Kentucky Historical Society* 76, no. 4 (1978).

Burstein, Andrew. *The Original Knickerbocker: The Life of Washington Irving.* New York: Basic Books, 2007.

Burton, Orville Vernon. *In My Father's House Are Many Mansions: Family and Community in Edgefield, South Carolina.* Chapel Hill: University of North Carolina Press, 1987.

Callahan, Richard J., Jr. *Work and Faith in the Kentucky Coal Fields: Subject to Dust.* Bloomington: Indiana University Press, 2009.

Campbell, Tracy. *Deliver the Vote: A History of Election Fraud, an American Tradition—1742–2004.* New York: Carroll and Graf, 2005.

———. *The Politics of Despair: Power and Resistance in the Tobacco Wars.* Lexington: University Press of Kentucky, 2005.

Carlton, David L. *Mill and Town in South Carolina, 1880–1920.* Baton Rouge: Louisiana State University Press, 1982.

Cash, W. J. *The Mind of the South.* New York: Vintage Books, 1969.

Caudill, Harry. *Their's Be the Power: The Moguls of Eastern Kentucky.* Urbana: University of Illinois Press, 1983.

Chapman, Conrad Wise. *Ten Months in the "Orphan Brigade": Conrad Wise Chapman's Civil War Memoir.* Kent, OH: Kent State University Press, 1999.

Cheney, Dick. *In My Time: A Personal and Political Memoir.* New York: Simon and Schuster, 2011.

Chesham, Sallie. *Born to Battle: The Salvation Army in America.* Chicago: Rand-McNally, 1965.

Ching, Barbara, and Gerald W. Creed. "Recognizing Rusticity: Identity and the Power of Place." In *Knowing Your Place: Rural Identity and Cultural Hierarchy,* edited by Barbara Ching and Gerald W. Creed. New York: Routledge, 1997.

Clark, Thomas D. *Agrarian Kentucky.* Lexington: University Press of Kentucky, 1977.

———. *The Kentucky.* Bicentennial ed. Lexington: University Press of Kentucky, 1992.

———. *My Century in History: Memoirs.* Lexington: University Press of Kentucky, 2006.

———. "The People, William Goebel, and the Kentucky Railroads." *Journal of Southern History* 5, no. 1 (1939).

Clements, J. Reginald, ed. *History of the First Regiment of Infantry: The Louisville Legion and Other Military Organizations.* Louisville: Globe, 1907.

Cohen, Abner. *Two-Dimensional Man: An Essay on the Anthropology of Power and Symbolism in Complex Society.* Berkeley: University of California Press, 1974.

Cohen, Stanley. "Crime and Politics: Spot the Difference." In *Law, Society, and Economy,* edited by Richard Rawlings. Oxford: Oxford University Press, 1997.

Combs, Joseph Henry. *Folk-songs du Midi des États-Unis.* Paris: Presses Universitaires de France, 1925.

Congleton, Betty Carolyn. "The Jackson Academy and the Quest for Presbyterian Ascendency in Breathitt County." *Register of the Kentucky Historical Society* 91, no. 2 (1993).

Connelly, Thomas. "Neo-Confederatism or Power Vacuum: Post War Kentucky Politics Reappraised." *Register of the Kentucky Historical Society* 64 (October 1966).

Conteh-Morgan, Earl. *Collective Political Violence: An Introduction to the Theories and Cases of Violent Conflicts.* New York: Routledge, 2003.

Conti, Eugene A., Jr. "The Cultural Role of Local Elites in the Kentucky Mountains: A Retrospective Analysis." *Appalachian Journal* 7, nos. 1–2 (1979–80).

Cooling, B. Franklin. "After the Horror: Kentucky in Reconstruction." In *Sister States, Enemy States: The Civil War in Kentucky and Tennessee,* edited by Kent T. Dollar, Larry H. Whiteaker, and W. Calvin Dickinson. Lexington: University Press of Kentucky, 2009.

——. "A People's War: Partisan Conflict in Tennessee and Kentucky." In *Guerrillas, Unionists, and Violence on the Confederate Home Front,* edited by Daniel E. Sutherland. Fayetteville: University of Arkansas Press, 1999.

Copeland, James E. "Where Were the Kentucky Unionists and Secessionists?" *Register of the Kentucky Historical Society* 71, no. 4 (1973).

Coulter, E. Merton. *The Civil War and Readjustment in Kentucky.* Chapel Hill: University of North Carolina Press, 1926.

——. "Early Frontier Democracy in the First Kentucky Constitution." *Political Science Quarterly* 39, no. 4 (1924).

Coulter, E. Merton, and William Elsey Connelley. *History of Kentucky.* Vols. 2–4. Chicago: American Historical Society, 1922.

Courtwright, David T. *Violent Land: Single Men and Social Disorder from the Frontier to the Inner City.* Cambridge, MA: Harvard University Press, 1996.

Cowan, William Tynes. *The Slave in the Swamp: Disrupting the Planter Narrative.* New York: Routledge, 2005.

Crane, J. Michael. "'The Rebels Are Bold, Defiant, and Unscrupulous in Their Dementions of All Men': Social Violence in Daviess County, Kentucky, 1861–1868." *Ohio Valley History* 2, no. 1 (2002).

Crawford, Beverly. "The Causes of Cultural Conflict: An Institutional Approach." In *The Myth of "Ethnic Conflict": Politics, Economics, and "Cultural" Violence,* edited by Beverly Crawford and Ronnie D. Lipschutz. Berkeley: International and Area Studies, University of California Press, 1998.

Crawford, Martin. *Ashe County's Civil War: Community and Society in the Appalachian South.* Charlottesville: University Press of Virginia, 2001.

Crofts, Daniel W. *Reluctant Confederates: Upper South Unionists in the Secession Crisis.* Chapel Hill: University of North Carolina Press, 1989.

Cunningham, Rodger. "Appalachian Studies among the Posts." *Journal of Appalachian Studies* 9, no. 2 (2003).

Current, Richard Nelson. *Lincoln's Loyalists: Union Soldiers from the Confederacy.* Boston: Northeastern University Press, 1992.

Curry, Richard O., ed. *Radicalism, Racism, and Party Realignment: The Border States during Reconstruction.* Baltimore: Johns Hopkins University Press, 1969.

Dacus, J. A. *Annals of the Great Strikes in the United States: A Reliable History and Graphic Description of the Causes and Thrilling Events of the Labor Strikes and Riots of 1877.* Chicago: L. T. Palmer, 1877.

Dahl, Robert Alan. *Political Oppositions in Western Democracies.* New Haven, CT: Yale University Press, 1969.

Dallam, Peter Frances, ed. *A Union Woman in Civil War Kentucky: The Diary of Frances Peter.* Lexington: University Press of Kentucky, 2000.

Dalton, C. David. "Brig. General Humphrey Marshall." In *Kentuckians in Gray: Confederate Generals and Field Officers of the Bluegrass State,* edited by Bruce S. Allardice and Lawrence Lee Hewitt. Lexington: University Press of Kentucky, 2008.

Daniel, Michelle. "From Blood Feud to Jury System: The Metamorphosis of Cherokee Law from 1750 to 1840." *American Indian Quarterly* 11, no. 2 (1987).

Das, Veena. "Sexual Violence, Discursive Formations, and the State." In *States of Violence,* edited by Fernando Coronil and Julie Skurski. Ann Arbor: University of Michigan Press, 2006.

Davidoff, Leonore, and Catherine Hall. *Family Fortunes: Men and Women of the English Working Class, 1780–1850.* London: Hutchison, 1987.

Davis, D. H. "Urban Development in the Kentucky Mountains." *Annals of the Association of American Geographers* 15, no. 2 (1925).

Davis, William, and Meredith Swentnor, eds. *Bluegrass Confederate: The Headquarters Diary of Edward O. Guerrant.* Baton Rouge: Louisiana State University Press, 1999.

Davison, Charlotte. *Davi(d)son: The First Ten—The Second Ten and Many Allied Families.* N.p., 1985.

Deas, Malcolm. "Violent Exchanges: Reflections on Political Violence in Colombia." In *The Legitimization of Violence,* edited by David Apter. Chippenham, UK: Antony Rowe, 1997.

Decker, Elmer, and Lois M. Jones. *Knox County Kentucky History.* Lexington: L. Jones, 2002.

Degler, Carl. *The Other South: Southern Dissenters in the Nineteenth Century.* New York: Harper and Row, 1974.

DenBoer, Gordon, and John H. Long, eds. *Kentucky: Atlas of Historical County Boundaries.* New York: Charles Scribner's Sons, 1995.

de Santis, Vincent P. "Republican Efforts to 'Crack' the Democratic South." *Review of Politics* 14, no. 2 (1952).

Dobson, E. J. "The Word *Feud.*" *Review of English Studies* 7, no. 25 (1956).

Dollar, Kent T., Larry H. Whiteaker, and W. Calvin Dickinson, eds. *Sister States, Enemy States: The Civil War in Kentucky and Tennessee.* Lexington: University Press of Kentucky, 2009.

Drake, Michael S. *Problematics of Military Power: Government, Discipline and the Subject of Violence*. New York: Routledge, 2002.

Drake, Richard B. *A History of Appalachia*. Lexington: University Press of Kentucky, 2001.

Dray, Philip. *At the Hands of Persons Unknown: The Lynching of Black America*. New York: Random House, 2003.

Dubois, W. E. B. *Black Reconstruction in America*. New York: S. A. Russell, 1935.

Duclos, Donald Phillip. *Son of Sorrow: The Life, Works and Influence of Colonel William Falkner, 1825–1889*. San Francisco: International Scholars, 1998.

Dunaway, Wilma. *The African-American Family in Slavery and Emancipation*. Cambridge: Cambridge University Press, 2003.

———. *The First American Frontier: Transition to Capitalism in Southern Appalachia, 1700–1860*. Chapel Hill: University of North Carolina Press, 1996.

———. *Slavery in the American Mountain South*. Cambridge: Cambridge University Press, 2003.

———. "Speculators and Settler Capitalists: Unthinking the Mythology about Appalachian Landholding, 1790–1860." In *Appalachia in the Making: The Mountain South in the Nineteenth Century*, edited by Mary Beth Pudup, Dwight Billings, and Altina Waller. Chapel Hill: University of North Carolina Press, 1995.

Dunn, Durwood. *Cades Cove: The Life and Death of a Southern Appalachian Community, 1818–1937*. Knoxville: University of Tennessee Press, 1988.

Dupre, Daniel. "Ambivalent Capitalists on the Cotton Frontier: Settlement and Development in the Tennessee Valley of Alabama." *Journal of Southern History* 56, no. 2 (1990).

Durrill, Wayne K. "Political Legitimacy and Local Courts: 'Politicks at such a rage' in a Southern Community during Reconstruction." *Journal of Southern History* 70, no. 3 (2004).

———. *War of Another Kind: A Southern Community in the Great Rebellion*. New York: Oxford University Press, 1990.

Eckstein, Harry. "A Culturalist Theory of Political Change." *American Political Science Review* 82, no. 3 (1988).

———. "Theoretical Approaches to Explaining Collective Political Violence." In *Handbook of Political Conflict: Theory and Research*, edited by Ted Robert Gurr. New York: Free Press, 1980.

Edmonds, Helen G. *The Negro and Fusion Politics in North Carolina, 1894–1901*. Chapel Hill: University of North Carolina Press, 1951.

Edwards, Laura F. "The People's Sovereignty and the Law: Defining Gender, Race, and Class Differences in the Antebellum South." In *Beyond Black and White: Race, Ethnicity, and Gender in the U.S. South and Southwest*, edited by Stephanie Cole, Alison Marie Parker, and Laura F. Edwards. College Station: Texas A&M Press, 2004.

Eller, Ronald. *Uneven Ground: Appalachia since 1945*. Lexington: University Press of Kentucky, 2008.

Ellis, William E. "The Bingham Family: From the Old South to the New South and Beyond." *Filson Club Historical Quarterly* 61, no. 1 (1987).

———. *A History of Education in Kentucky.* Lexington: University Press of Kentucky, 2011.

———. *The Kentucky River.* Lexington: University Press of Kentucky, 2000.

Escott, Paul. *Many Excellent People: Power and Privilege in North Carolina, 1850–1900.* Chapel Hill: University of North Carolina Press, 1984.

Ewen, Lynda Ann. *Social Stratification and Power in America: A View from Below.* Lanham, MD: General Hall, 1998.

Fabian, Johannes. *Time and the Other: How Anthropology Makes Its Object.* New York: Columbia University Press, 1983.

Fairbank, Calvin. *Rev. Calvin Fairbank during Slavery Times.* Chicago: Patriotic, 1890.

Fairclough, Adam. "'Scalawags,' Southern Honor, and the Lost Cause: Explaining the Fatal Encounter of James H. Cosgrove and Edward L. Pierson." *Journal of Southern History* 77, no. 4 (2011).

Faust, Drew Gilpin. *The Creation of Confederate Nationalism: Ideology and Identity in the Civil War South.* Baton Rouge: Louisiana State University Press, 1988.

Fearon, James D., and David D. Laitin. "Ethnicity, Insurgency, and Civil War." *American Political Science Review* 97, no. 1 (2003).

Feldman, Allen. *Formations of Violence: The Narrative of the Body and Political Terror in Northern Ireland.* Chicago: University of Chicago Press, 1991.

Feller, Daniel. *The Jacksonian Promise: America, 1815–1840.* Baltimore: Johns Hopkins University Press, 1995.

———. *The Public Lands in Jacksonian Politics.* London: University of Wisconsin Press, 1984.

Fellman, Michael. *Inside War: The Guerrilla Conflict in Missouri during the American Civil War.* Oxford: Oxford University Press, 1989.

Fenton, John H. *Politics in the Border States.* New Orleans: Hauser, 1957.

Finley, Milton. *The Most Monstrous of Wars: The Napoleonic Guerilla War in Southern Italy, 1806–1811.* Columbia: University of South Carolina Press, 1994.

Fitzgerald, Michael W. "Extralegal Violence and the Planter Class: The Ku Klux Klan in the Alabama Black Belt during Reconstruction." In *Local Matters: Race, Crime, and Justice in the Nineteenth-Century South,* edited by Christopher Waldrep and Donald G. Nieman. Athens: University of Georgia Press, 2001.

———. *The Union League Movement in the Deep South: Politics and Agricultural Change during Reconstruction.* Baton Rouge: Louisiana State University Press, 1989.

Foner, Eric. *Reconstruction: America's Unfinished Revolution, 1863–1877.* New York: Harper and Row, 1988.

Foote, Shelby. *The Civil War: A Narrative.* Vol. 3, *Red River to Appomattox.* New York: Random House, 1974.

———. "The Education of Richard Hofstadter." *Nation,* May 4, 1992.

Ford, Lacy K. *Deliver Us from Evil: The Slavery Question in the Old South.* Oxford: Oxford University Press, 2009.

———. "Origins of the Edgefield Tradition: The Late Antebellum Experience and the Roots of Political Insurgency." *South Carolina Historical Magazine* 98, no. 4 (1997).

———. Review of *Feud: Hatfields, McCoys, and Social Change in Appalachia, 1860–1900*, by Altina Waller. *Journal of Southern History* 55, no. 4 (1989).

Formisano, Ronald P. "The Concept of Political Culture." *Journal of Interdisciplinary History* 31, no. 3 (2001).

Foster, Gaines M. *Ghosts of the Confederacy: Defeat, The Lost Cause and the Emergence of the New South*. New York: Oxford University Press, 1987.

Foucault, Michel. *Discipline and Punish: The Birth of the Prison*. Translated by Alan Sheridan. New York: Vintage Books, 1977.

Fowler, John D. *Mountaineers in Gray: The Story of the Nineteenth Tennessee Volunteer Infantry Regiment, C.S.A.* Knoxville: University of Tennessee Press, 2004.

Franklin, John Hope. *The Militant South, 1800–1861*. Cambridge, MA: Harvard University Press, 1956.

Frasca, Ralph. *The Rise and Fall of the Saturday Globe*. Selinsgrove, PA: Susquehanna University Press, 1992.

Freehling, William W. *The South vs. the South: How Anti-Confederate Southerners Shaped the Civil War*. Oxford: Oxford University Press, 2001.

Friedman, Lawrence. *The White Savage: Racial Fantasies in the Postbellum South*. Englewood Cliffs, NJ: Prentice-Hall, 1970.

Friend, Craig Thomas. *Along the Maysville Road: The Early American Republic in the Trans-Appalachian West*. Knoxville: University of Tennessee Press, 2005.

———. *Kentucke's Frontiers*. Bloomington: Indiana University Press, 2010.

Frierson, Michael. "The Image of the Hillbilly in Warner Bros. Cartoons of the Thirties." In *Reading the Rabbit: Explorations in Warner Bros. Animation*, edited by Kevin S. Sandler. New Brunswick, NJ: Rutgers University Press, 1998.

Fukuyama, Francis. *The Origins of Political Order: From Prehuman Times to the French Revolution*. New York: Farrar, Straus and Giroux, 2011.

Gastil, Raymond D. "Homicide and a Regional Culture of Violence." *American Sociological Review* 36, no. 3 (1971).

Gaston, Paul M. *The New South Creed: A Study in Southern Mythmaking*. New York: Knopf, 1970.

Gates, Paul W. "Tenants of the Log Cabin." *Mississippi Valley Historical Review* 49, no. 1 (1962).

Geiger, Mark W. *Financial Fraud and Guerilla Violence in Missouri's Civil War, 1861–1865*. New Haven, CT: Yale University Press, 2010.

Gordon, Leslie, and John Inscoe, eds. *Inside the Confederate Nation: Essays in Honor of Emory Thomas*. Baton Rouge: Louisiana State University Press, 2005.

Gorn, Elliot J. "'Gouge and Bite, Pull Hair and Scratch': The Social Significance of Fighting in the Southern Backcountry." *American Historical Review* 90, no. 1 (1985).

Gosse, Phillip. *The History of Piracy*. New York: Tudor, 1946.

Graham, Hugh Davis, and Ted Gurr, eds. *Violence in America: Historical and Comparative Perspectives.* Beverly Hills, CA: Sage, 1979.

Graham, Hugh, Stephen Paul Mahinka, and Dean W. Rudoy, eds. *Violence: The Crisis of American Confidence.* Baltimore: Johns Hopkins University Press, 1971.

Grantham, Dewey W. *The Life and Death of the Solid South: A Political History.* Lexington: University Press of Kentucky, 1992.

———. *Southern Progressivism: The Reconciliation of Progress and Tradition.* Knoxville: University of Tennessee Press, 1983.

Groce, W. Todd. *Mountain Rebels: East Tennessee Confederates and the Civil War, 1860–1870.* Knoxville: University of Tennessee Press, 1999.

Grutzpalk, Jonas. "Blood Feud and Modernity: Max Weber's and Emile Durkheim's Theories." *Journal of Classical Sociology* 2, no. 2 (2002).

Gudridge, Patrick O. "Privileges and Permissions: The Civil Rights Act of 1875." *Law and Philosophy* 8, no. 1 (1989).

Gurr, Ted Robert. *Violence in America: Protest, Rebellion, Reform.* Vol. 2. Newbury Park, CA: Sage, 1989.

———. *Why Men Rebel.* Princeton, NJ: Princeton University Press, 1970.

Hackney, Sheldon. "Southern Violence." *American Historical Review* 74, no. 3 (1969).

———. "Southern Violence." In *Violence in America: Historical and Comparative Perspectives,* edited by Hugh Davis Graham and Ted Gurr. Beverly Hills, CA: Sage, 1979.

Hague, Euan, and Edward H. Sebesta. "Neo-Confederacy, Culture, and Ethnicity: A White Anglo-Celtic Southern People." In *Neo-Confederacy: A Critical Introduction,* edited by Euan Hague, Heidi Beirich, and Edward H. Sebesta. Austin: University of Texas Press, 2008.

Hahn, Steven. "Hunting, Fishing and Foraging: Common Rights and Class Relations in the Postbellum South." *Radical History Review* 26 (October 1982).

———. *A Nation under Our Feet: Black Political Struggles in the Rural South, from Slavery to the Great Migration.* Cambridge, MA: Belknap Press of Harvard University Press, 2003.

———. *The Roots of Southern Populism: Yeoman Farmers and the Transformation of the Georgia Upcountry, 1850–1890.* Oxford: Oxford University Press, 1983.

———. "The Yeomanry of the Nonplantation South: Upper Piedmont Georgia, 1850–1860." In *Class, Conflict and Consensus: Antebellum Southern Community Studies,* edited by Orville Vernon Burton and Robert C. McMath. Westport, CT: Greenwood, 1982.

Hall, Betty Jean, and Richard Allen Heckman. "Berea College and the Day Law." *Register of the Kentucky Historical Society* 66, no. 1 (1968).

Hall, Jacquelyn Dowd. *Revolt against Chivalry: Jessie Daniel Ames and the Women's Campaign against Lynching.* New York: Columbia University Press, 1979.

Hall, Susan G. *Appalachian Ohio and the Civil War, 1862–1863.* Jefferson, NC: McFarland, 2000.

Hamm, Randall Hall. *Murder, Honor, and Law: Four Virginia Homicides from Reconstruction to the Great Depression.* Charlottesville: University of Virginia Press, 2003.

Hardin, John A. *Fifty Years of Segregation: Black Higher Education in Kentucky, 1904–1954.* Lexington: University Press of Kentucky, 1997.

Harkins, Anthony. *Hillbilly: A Cultural History of an American Icon.* New York: Oxford University Press, 2005.

Harpine, William D. *From the Front Porch to the Front Page: McKinley and Bryan in the 1896 Campaign.* College Station: Texas A&M Press, 2006.

Harris, Trudier. *Exorcising Blackness: Historical and Literary Lynching and Burning Rituals.* Bloomington: Indiana University Press, 1984.

Harrison, Lowell H. *The Antislavery Movement in Kentucky.* Lexington: University Press of Kentucky, 1978.

———. *The Civil War in Kentucky.* Lexington: University Press of Kentucky, 1975.

———. "The Government of Confederate Kentucky." In *The Civil War in Kentucky: Battle for the Bluegrass State,* edited by Kent Masterson Brown. Mason City, IA: Savas, 2000.

———, ed. *Kentucky's Governors, 1792–1985.* Lexington: University Press of Kentucky, 1985.

———. "Taylor, William Sylvester." In *The Kentucky Encyclopedia,* edited by John E. Kleber, Thomas Dionysius Clark, and Lowell H. Harrison. Lexington: University Press of Kentucky, 1992.

Harrison, Lowell Hayes, and James C. Klotter. *A New History of Kentucky.* Lexington: University Press of Kentucky, 1997.

Harrold, Stanley. *Border War: Fighting over Slavery before the Civil War.* Chapel Hill: University of North Carolina Press, 2010.

———. "Violence and Nonviolence in Kentucky Abolitionism." *Journal of Southern History* 57, no. 1 (1991).

Hartman, Ian C. "Appalachian Anxiety: Race, Gender, and the Paradox of 'Purity' in an Age of Empire, 1873–1901." *American Nineteenth Century History* 13, no. 2 (2012).

Havens, Murray Clark, Carl Leiden, and Karl M. Schmitt. *The Politics of Assassination.* Englewood Cliffs, NJ: Prentice Hall, 1970.

Hayes, Stephen F. *Cheney: The Untold Story of America's Most Powerful and Controversial Vice President.* New York: Harper Collins, 2007.

Haynes, Frederick Emory. "The New Sectionalism." *Quarterly Journal of Economics* 10, no. 3 (1896).

Heidbuchel, Esther. *The West Papua Conflict in Indonesia.* Wettenberg: Johannes Herrmann J&J-Verlag, 2007.

Herr, Kincaid. *Louisville and Nashville Railroad, 1850–1963.* Lexington: University Press of Kentucky, 2000.

Hickerson, Thomas Felix. *The Falkner Feuds: The Fatal Feuds of W. C. Falkner.* Chapel Hill, NC: Colonial, 1964.

Higginbotham, Aloyisus Leon. "Racism and the Early American Legal Process, 1619–

1896." In "Blacks and the Law," special issue, *Annals of the American Academy of Political and Social Science* 407 (May 1973).

———. *Shades of Freedom: Racial Politics and Presumptions of the American Legal Process*. Oxford: Oxford University Press, 1998.

Hobsbawm, Eric. "Introduction: Inventing Traditions." In *The Invention of Tradition*, edited by Eric Hobsbawm and Terence Ranger. London: Cambridge University Press, 1983.

———. *Primitive Rebels: Studies in Archaic Forms of Social Movement in the 19th and 20th Centuries*. New York: Norton, 1959.

Hoffer, Williamjames H. *The Caning of Charles Sumner: Honor, Idealism, and the Origins of the Civil War*. Baltimore: Johns Hopkins University Press, 2010.

Hoffman, Steven J. "Looking North: A Mid-South Perspective on the Great Strike." In *The Great Strikes of 1877*, edited by David O. Stowell. Champaign: University of Illinois Press, 2008.

Hofstadter, Richard. "Reflections on Violence in the United States." In *American Violence: A Documentary History*, edited by Richard Hofstadter and Michael Wallace. New York: Knopf, 1970.

Hollingsworth, Randolph. "'Mrs. Boone, I presume?' In Search of the Idea of Womanhood in Kentucky's Early Years." In *Bluegrass Renaissance: The History and Culture of Central Kentucky, 1792–1852*, edited by James C. Klotter and Daniel Rowland. Lexington: University Press of Kentucky, 2012.

Holmes, William F. "Moonshining and Collective Violence, 1889–1895." *Journal of American History* 67, no. 3 (1980).

———. "Whitecapping: Agrarian Violence in Mississippi, 1902–1906." *Journal of Southern History* 35, no. 2 (1969).

Holt, Michael. *The Rise and Fall of the American Whig Party: Jacksonian Politics and the Onset of the Civil War*. New York: Oxford University Press, 1999.

Honey, Michael K. "The War within the Confederacy: White Unionists of North Carolina." Special issue, *Prologue* 26 (1994).

Hood, James Larry. "For the Union: Kentucky's Unconditional Unionist Congressmen and the Development of the Republican Party in Kentucky, 1863–1865." *Register of the Kentucky Historical Society* 76, no. 3 (1978).

Horkheimer, Max, and Theodor W. Adorno. "The Culture Industry: Enlightenment as Mass Deception." In *Dialectic of Enlightenment*, translated by John Cumming. New York: Continuum, 1994.

Howard, Victor B. *Black Liberation in Kentucky: Emancipation and Freedom, 1862–1884*. Lexington: University Press of Kentucky, 1983.

Hower, James C. "'Uncertain and Treacherous': The Cannel Coal Industry in Kentucky." *Nonrenewable Resources* 4, no. 4 (1995).

Hsiung, David C. *Two Worlds in the Tennessee Mountains: Exploring the Origins of Appalachian Stereotypes*. Lexington: University Press of Kentucky, 1997.

Hubac-Occhipinti, Olivier. "Anarchist Terrorists of the Nineteenth Century." In *The History of Terrorism from Antiquity to Al Qaeda,* edited by Gerard Chaliand and Arnaud Blin, translated by Edward Schneider, Kathryn Pulver, and Jesse Browner. Berkeley: University of California Press, 2007.

Hubbs, G. Ward. *Guarding Greensboro: A Confederate Company in the Making of a Southern Community.* Athens: University of Georgia Press, 2003.

Huddle, Mark A. "Soul Winner: Edward O. Guerrant, the Kentucky Home Missions, and the 'Discovery' of Appalachia." *Ohio Valley History* 5, no. 4 (2005).

Hudson, John G. H. "Feud, Vengeance and Violence in England from the Tenth to the Twelfth Centuries." In *Feud, Violence and Practice: Essays in Honor of Stephen D. White,* edited by Belle S. Tuten and Tracey L. Billado. Farnham, UK: Ashgate, 2010.

Hume, Edgar Erskine. "The Hume Genealogy; Being an Account of the Francis Hume Branch of the Wedderburn Humes of Scotland, Virginia and Kentucky." *Register of the Kentucky Historical Society* 12, no. 34 (1914).

Hurst, J. C., comp. *Hursts of Shenandoah; Also Keyser-Landsaw.* Lexington: Hurst, n.d.

Hyman, Michael R. *The Anti-Redeemers: Hill-Country Political Dissenters in the Lower South from Redemption to Populism.* Baton Rouge: Louisiana State University Press, 1990.

Ifill, Sherrilyn A. *On the Courthouse Lawn: Confronting the Legacy of Lynching in the Twenty-first Century.* New York: Beacon, 2007.

Inge, M. Thomas. "Li'l Abner, Snuffy, and Friends: The Appalachian South in the American Comic Strip." In *Comics and the U.S. South,* edited by Brannon Costello and Qiana J. Whitted. Jackson: University of Mississippi Press, 2012.

Ingmire, Francis Terry, ed. *Breathitt County, Kentucky Death Records, 1852–1858, 1874–1878.* St. Louis: Ingmire, 1983.

Inscoe, John C. Introduction to *Enemies of the Country: New Perspectives on Unionists in the Civil War South,* edited by John C. Inscoe and Robert C. Kenzer. Athens: University of Georgia Press, 2001.

———. *Mountain Masters: Slavery and the Sectional Crisis in Western North Carolina.* Knoxville: University of Tennessee, 1989.

———. "The Racial 'Innocence' of Appalachia: William Faulkner and the Mountain South." In *Confronting Appalachian Stereotypes: Backtalk from an American Region,* edited by Dwight B. Billings et al. Lexington: University Press of Kentucky, 1999.

Inscoe, John C., and Robert C. Kenzer, eds. *Enemies of the Country: New Perspectives on Unionists in the Civil War South.* Athens: University of Georgia Press, 2001.

Inscoe, John C., and Gordon B. McKinney. *The Heart of Confederate Appalachia: Western North Carolina in the Civil War.* Chapel Hill: University of North Carolina Press, 2000.

Ireland, Robert. "Aristocrats All: The Politics of County Government in Ante-bellum Kentucky." *Review of Politics* 32, no. 3 (1970).

———. *The County Courts in Antebellum Kentucky.* Lexington: University Press of Kentucky, 1972.

———. "Homicide in Nineteenth Century Kentucky." *Register of the Kentucky Historical Society* 81, no. 2 (1983).

———. *The Kentucky State Constitution: A Reference Guide.* Greenwood, CT: Greenwood, 1999.

———. *Little Kingdoms: The Counties of Kentucky, 1850–1891.* Lexington: University Press of Kentucky, 1977.

———. "The Place of the Justice of the Peace in the Legislature and Party System of Kentucky, 1792–1850." *American Journal of Legal History* 13, no. 3 (1969).

Jackman, John S. *Diary of a Confederate Soldier: John S. Jackman of the Orphan Brigade,* Edited by William C. Davis. Columbia: University of South Carolina Press, 1997.

Jenkins, Sally, and John Stauffer. *The State of Jones: The Small Southern County That Seceded from the Confederacy.* New York: Doubleday, 2009.

Jillson, Willard, ed. *The Kentucky Land Grants: A Systematic Index to All of the Land Grants Recorded in the State Land Office at Frankfort, Kentucky, 1782–1924.* Louisville: Standard, 1925.

———. *Old Kentucky Entries and Deeds: A Complete Index to All of the Earliest Land Entries, Military Warrants, Deeds and Wills of the Commonwealth of Kentucky.* Louisville: Standard, 1926.

Johnson, Chalmers. *Revolutionary Change.* Stanford, CA: Stanford University Press, 1982.

Johnson, E. Polk. *A History of Kentucky and Kentuckians: The Leaders and Representative Men in Commerce, Industry and Modern Activity.* Vol. 1. Chicago: Lewis, 1912.

Jones, Loyal. "James Jones' Appalachian Soldier in His World War II Trilogy." *Journal of the Appalachian Studies Association* 3 (1991).

Kalyvas, Stathis. *The Logic of Violence in Civil War.* Cambridge: Cambridge University Press, 2006.

Kantrowitz, Stephen. *Ben Tillman and the Reconstruction of White Supremacy.* Chapel Hill: University of North Carolina Press, 2000.

Kash, Kelly. "Feud Days in Breathitt County." *Filson Club Historical Quarterly* 28, no. 4 (1954).

Kaufman-Osborn, Timothy V. "Capital Punishment as Legal Lynching?" In *From Lynch Mob to the Killing State: Race and the Death Penalty in America,* edited by Charles J. Ogletree Jr. and Austin Sarat. New York: New York University Press, 2006.

Kaur, Ravinder. "Mythology of Communal Violence: An Introduction." In *Religion, Violence and Political Mobilisation in South Asia,* edited by Ravinder Kaur. New Delhi: Sage, 2005.

Keane, John. *Violence and Democracy.* Cambridge: Cambridge University Press, 1994.

Khan, Furrukh A. "Speaking Violence: Pakistani Women's Narratives of Partition." In *Gender, Conflict and Migration,* edited by Navnita Chadha Behera. London: Sage, 2006.

Kidd, Stuart. *Farm Security Administration Photography, the Rural South, and the Dynamics of Image-Making, 1935–1943.* Lewiston, NY: Edwin Meller Press, 2004.

Kiffmeyer, Thomas. *Reformers to Radicals: The Appalachian Volunteers and the War on Poverty.* Lexington: University Press of Kentucky, 2008.

Kilcullen, David. *The Accidental Guerrilla: Fighting Small Wars in the Midst of a Big One.* London: Oxford University Press, 2009.

Kincaid, Robert L. "Lincoln Allegiance in the Southern Appalachians." In "Lincoln Sesquicentennial," special issue, *Journal of the Illinois Historical Society* 52, no. 1 (1959).

King, Richard H. *A Southern Renaissance: The Cultural Awakening of the American South, 1930–1955.* Oxford: Oxford University Press, 1980.

Kinkead, Elizabeth Shelby. *A History of Kentucky.* New York: American Book, 1915.

Kirkham, James F., Sheldon G. Levy, and William J. Crotty. *Assassination and Political Violence: A Report to the National Commission on the Causes and Prevention of Violence.* New York: Praeger, 1970.

Kirwan, Albert D., ed. *Johnny Green of the Orphan Brigade: The Journal of a Confederate Soldier.* Lexington: University of Kentucky Press, 1956.

———. *Revolt of the Rednecks: Mississippi Politics, 1876–1925.* Lexington: University of Kentucky Press, 1951.

Kleber, John E., Thomas Dionysius Clark, and Lowell H. Harrison, eds. *The Kentucky Encyclopedia.* Lexington: University Press of Kentucky, 1992.

Klein, Maury. *History of the Louisville and Nashville Railroad.* New York: Macmillan, 1972.

Klotter, James C. "The Black South and White Appalachia." *Journal of American History* 66, no. 2 (1980).

———. "Central Kentucky's 'Athens of the West' Image in the Nation and History." In *Bluegrass Renaissance: The History and Culture of Central Kentucky, 1792–1852,* edited by James C. Klotter and Daniel Rowland. Lexington: University Press of Kentucky, 2012.

———. "Feuds in Appalachia: An Overview." *Filson Club Historical Quarterly* 56, no. 3 (1982).

———. *Kentucky: Portrait in Paradox, 1900–1950.* Frankfort: Kentucky Historical Society, 1996.

———. *William Goebel: The Politics of Wrath.* Lexington: University Press of Kentucky, 1977.

Klotter, James C., and Freda C. Klotter. *A Concise History of Kentucky.* Lexington: University Press of Kentucky, 2008.

Klotter, James C., and Daniel Rowland, eds. *Bluegrass Renaissance: The History and Culture of Central Kentucky, 1792–1852.* Lexington: University Press of Kentucky, 2012.

Kulikoff, Allen. *The Agrarian Origins of American Capitalism.* Charlottesville: University Press of Virginia, 1992.

Laitin, David D. *Nations, States, and Violence.* Oxford: Oxford University Press, 2007.

Lamley, Harry J. "Lineage Feuding in Southern Fujian and Eastern Guangdong under Qing Rule." In *Violence in China: Essays in Culture and Counterculture,* edited by

Jonathan Neaman Lipman and Steven Harrell. Albany: State University of New York Press, 1990.

Landsberg, Alison. *Prosthetic Memory: The Transformation of American Remembrance in the Age of Mass Culture.* New York: Columbia University Press, 1994.

Lane, Charles. *The Day Freedom Died: The Colfax Massacre, the Supreme Court, and the Betrayal of Reconstruction.* New York: Macmillan, 2008.

Laver, Harry S. *Citizens More Than Soldiers: The Kentucky Militia and Society in the Early Republic.* Lincoln: University of Nebraska Press, 2007.

Lears, Jackson. *Rebirth of a Nation: The Making of Modern America, 1877–1920.* New York: Harper Collins, 2009.

Lee, Wayne. *Crowds and Soldiers in Revolutionary North Carolina: The Culture of Violence in Riot and War.* Gainesville: University Press of Florida, 2001.

Lemann, Nicholas. *Redemption: The Last Battle of the Civil War.* New York: Farrar, Straus and Giroux, 2006.

Lester, Connie L. *Up from the Mudsills of Hell: The Farmers' Alliance, Populism, and Progressive Agriculture in Tennessee, 1870–1915.* Athens: University of Georgia Press, 2006.

Lewis, Oscar. *Tepoztlán, Village in Mexico.* New York: Holt, 1960.

Lewis, Patrick A. "The Democratic Partisan Militia and the Black Peril: The Kentucky Militia, Racial Violence, and the Fifteenth Amendment, 1870–1873." *Civil War History* 56, no. 2 (2010).

Lewis, Ronald. *Transforming the Appalachian Countryside: Railroads, Deforestation and Social Change in West Virginia, 1880–1920.* Chapel Hill: University of North Carolina Press, 1998.

Link, William A. *The Paradox of Southern Progressivism, 1880–1930.* Chapel Hill: University of North Carolina Press, 1992.

Lucas, Marion B. *A History of Blacks in Kentucky.* Vol. 1. Frankfort: Kentucky Historical Society, 1992.

Luntz, Benjamin F. *Forgotten Turmoil: The Southeastern Kentucky Ku Klux Klan.* Philadelphia: Xlibris, 2006.

MacGregor, Felipe E., S.J., and Marcial Rubio Correa. "Rejoinder to the Theory of Structural Violence." In *The Culture of Violence,* edited by Kumar Rupesinghe and Marcial Rubio Correa. Tokyo: United Nations University Press, 1994.

Mackey, Robert. *The Uncivil War: Irregular Warfare in the Upper South, 1861–1865.* Norman: University of Oklahoma Press, 2004.

Mackey, Thomas C. "Not a Pariah, but a Keystone: Kentucky and Secession." In *Sister States, Enemy States: The Civil War in Kentucky and Tennessee,* edited by Kent T. Dollar, Larry H. Whiteaker, and W. Calvin Dickinson. Lexington: University Press of Kentucky, 2009.

Madison, James H. *A Lynching in the Heartland: Race and Memory in America.* New York: Palgrave Macmillan, 2001.

Mallon, Florencia E. *Peasant and Nation: The Making of Postcolonial Mexico and Peru.* Berkeley: University of California Press, 1995.

Mamdani, Mahmood. "Making Sense of Political Violence in Postcolonial Africa." In *War and Peace in the 20th Century and Beyond: Proceedings of the Nobel Centennial Symposium,* edited by Geir Lundestad and Olav Njolstad. River Edge, NJ: World Scientific, 2003.

Markovitz, Jonathan. *Legacies of Lynching: Racial Violence and Memory.* Minneapolis: University of Minnesota Press, 2004.

Marshall, Anne E. *Creating a Confederate Kentucky: The Lost Cause and Civil War Memory in a Border State.* Chapel Hill: University of North Carolina Press, 2010.

———. "'The Rebel Spirit in Kentucky': The Politics of Readjustment in a Border State, 1865–1868." In *The Great Task Remaining before Us: Reconstruction as America's Continuing Civil War,* edited by Paul Cimbala and Randall M. Miller. New York: Fordham University Press, 2010.

Mathias, Frank, ed. *Incidents and Experiences in the Life of Thomas W. Parsons, from 1826 to 1900.* Lexington: University Press of Kentucky, 1975.

———. "Kentucky's Third Constitution: A Restriction of Majority Rule." *Register of the Kentucky Historical Society* 75, no. 1 (1977).

Mathias, Frank, and Jasper B. Shannon. "Gubernatorial Politics in Kentucky." *Register of the Kentucky Historical Society* 88, no. 3 (1990).

Matthews, Gary R. "Beleaguered Loyalties: Kentucky Unionism." In *Sister States, Enemy States: The Civil War in Kentucky and Tennessee,* edited by Kent T. Dollar, Larry H. Whiteaker, and W. Calvin Dickinson. Lexington: University Press of Kentucky, 2009.

Matthews, Gary Robert, and James A. Ramage. *Basil Wilson Duke, CSA: The Right Man in the Right Place.* Lexington: University Press of Kentucky, 2005.

McAdams, Dan P. "Redemptive Narratives in the Life and the Presidency of George W. Bush." In *The Leader: Psychological Essays,* edited by Charles B. Strozier, Daniel Offer, and Oliger Abdyli. 2nd ed. New York: Springer, 2011.

McAllister, James G., and Grace Owings Guerrant. *Edward O. Guerrant: Apostle to the Southern Highlanders.* Richmond, VA: Richmond Press, 1950.

McCauley, Deborah V. *Appalachian Mountain Religion: A History.* Urbana: University of Illinois Press, 1995.

McClintock, Anne. "Family Feuds: Gender, Nationalism and the Family." *Feminist Review,* no. 44 (Summer 1993).

McCurry, Stephanie. *Confederate Reckoning: Power and Politics in the Civil War South.* Cambridge, MA: Harvard University Press, 2010.

McFaul, John. *The Politics of Jacksonian Finance.* Ithaca, NY: Cornell University Press, 1972.

McKenzie, Robert Tracy. *Lincolnites and Rebels: A Divided Town in the American Civil War.* Oxford: Oxford University Press, 2006.

McKinney, Gordon. "The Civil War and Reconstruction." In *High Mountains Rising:*

Appalachia in Time and Place, edited by Richard A. Straw and H. Tyler Blethen. Urbana: University of Illinois Press, 2004.

———. "Industrialization and Violence in Appalachia in the 1890's." In *An Appalachian Symposium,* edited by Joel W. Williamson. Boone, NC: Appalachian Consortium, 1977.

———. *Southern Mountain Republicans, 1865–1900: Politics and the Appalachian Community.* Chapel Hill: University of North Carolina Press, 1978.

McKnight, Brian D. *The Civil War in Appalachian Kentucky and Virginia.* Lexington: University Press of Kentucky, 2006.

———. *Contested Borderland: The Civil War in Appalachian Kentucky and Virginia.* Lexington: University Press of Kentucky, 2006.

McMath, Robert C., Jr. *American Populism: A Social History, 1877–1898.* New York: Hill and Wang, 1993.

———. "Community, Region, and Hegemony in the Nineteenth-Century South." In *Toward a New South? Studies in Post–Civil War Southern Communities,* edited by Orville Vernon Burton and Robert C. McMath Jr. Westport, CT: Greenwood, 1982.

McNay, Don. "Outliers and Hatred against Hillbillies." *Richmond* (KY) *Register,* December 6, 2008.

McPherson, Edward. *Buster Keaton: Tempest in a Flat Hat.* New York: Newmarket, 2004.

McPherson, James. "Abolitionists and the Civil Rights Act of 1875." *Journal of American History* 52, no. 3 (1965).

———. *For Cause and Comrades: Why Men Fought in the Civil War.* Oxford: Oxford University Press, 1997.

McVey, Frank L. *The Gates Open Slowly: A History of Education in Kentucky.* Lexington: University of Kentucky Press, 1949.

Mellinger, E. Henry. "Ballads and Songs of the Southern Highlands." *American Folklore* 42, no. 165 (1929).

Melvin, G., Bruce Lee Melvin, John Nye Webb, and Carle Clark Zimmerman. *Rural Poor in the Great Depression: Three Studies.* Salem, NH: Ayer, 1971.

Menand, Louis. *The Metaphysical Club: A Story of Ideas in America.* New York: Farrar, Strauss and Giroux, 2001.

Mendel, Arthur P., ed. *Essential Works of Marxism.* New York: Bantam Books, 1961.

Menzel, Donald C. Introduction to *The American County,* edited by Donald C. Menzel. Tuscaloosa: University of Alabama Press, 1996.

Miller, Penny M. *Kentucky Politics and Government: Do We Stand United?* Lincoln: University of Nebraska Press, 1994.

Miller, William Ian. *Bloodtaking and Peacemaking: Feud, Law, and Society in Saga Iceland.* Chicago: University of Chicago Press, 1990.

Mitchell, Robert D., ed. *Appalachian Frontiers: Settlement, Society, and Development in the Preindustrial Era.* Lexington: University Press of Kentucky, 1991.

Mitchell, S. A. "The Return of Halley's Comet." *American Review of Reviews,* April 1910.

Moore, John Hammond. *Carnival of Blood: Dueling, Lynching, and Murder in South Carolina, 1880–1920.* Columbia: University of South Carolina, 2006.

Moore, Tyrel G. "Economic Development in Appalachian Kentucky." In *Appalachian Frontiers: Settlement, Society, and Development in the Preindustrial Era,* edited by Robert D. Mitchell. Lexington: University Press of Kentucky, 1991.

Mosgrove, George Dallas. *Kentucky Cavaliers in Dixie: Reminiscences of a Confederate Cavalryman.* Jackson, TN: McCowart-Mercer, 1957.

Nelson, Donald Lee. "The Death of J. B. Marcum." *JEMF Quarterly* 11 (part 1), no. 37 (1975).

Nelson, Paul David. "Experiment in Interracial Education at Berea College, 1858–1908." *Journal of Negro History* 59, no. 1 (1974).

Nelson, Scott Reynolds. *Iron Confederacies: Southern Railways, Klan Violence and Reconstruction.* Chapel Hill: University of North Carolina Press, 1999.

———. "Red Strings and Half Brothers: Civil Wars in Alamance County, North Carolina, 1861–1871." In *Enemies of the Country: New Perspectives on Unionists in the Civil War South,* edited by John C. Inscoe and Robert C. Kenzer. Athens: University of Georgia Press, 2001.

Nieburg, H. L. *Political Violence: The Behavioral Process.* New York: St. Martin's, 1969.

Nieman, Donald. *Black Freedom/White Violence, 1865–1900.* New York: Garland, 1994.

Nirenburg, David. *Communities of Violence: Persecution of Minorities in the Middle Ages.* Princeton, NJ: Princeton University Press, 1996.

Nisbett, Richard, and Dov Cohen. *Culture of Honor: The Psychology of Violence in the South.* New York: Westview, 1996.

Noble, E. L. *Bloody Breathitt.* Vols. 1–3. Jackson, KY: Jackson Times, 1936.

Noble, George Washington. *Behold He Cometh in the Clouds: A Religious Treatise from Inspiration and Illumination with Life and Adventures of the Author.* Hazel Green, KY: Spencer Cooper, 1912.

Noe, Kenneth. "'Deadening Color and Colder Horror': Rebecca Harding Davis and the Myth of Unionist Appalachia." In *Confronting Appalachian Stereotypes: Backtalk from an American Region,* edited by Dwight B. Billings et al. Lexington: University Press of Kentucky, 1999.

———. "Red String Scare: Civil War Southwest Virginia and the Heroes of America." *North Carolina Historical Review* 69, no. 3 (1992).

Noe, Kenneth, and Shannon H. Wilson, eds. *The Civil War in Appalachia: Collected Essays.* Knoxville: University of Tennessee Press, 1997.

Norrell, Robert J. *Up from History: The Life of Booker T. Washington.* Cambridge, MA: Harvard University Press, 2009.

Oakes, James. *The Ruling Race: A History of American Slaveholders.* New York: Knopf, 1982.

O'Brien, Sean Michael. *Mountain Partisans: Guerrilla Warfare in the Southern Appalachians, 1861–1865.* Westport, CT: Praeger, 1999.

Ogden, Frederic D., ed. *The Public Papers of Governor Keen Johnson, 1939–1943.* Lexington: University Press of Kentucky, 1982.

Ogden, Suzanne. "Inoculation against Terrorism in China: What's in the Dosage?" In *Democratic Development and Political Terrorism: The Global Perspective,* edited by William J. Crotty. Boston: Northeastern University Press, 2005.

Oliver, Stuart. "The Thames Embankment and the Disciplining of Nature in Modernity." *Geographical Journal* 166, no. 3 (2000).

Orend, Brian. *War and International Justice: A Kantian Perspective.* Waterloo, Ontario: Wilfrid Laurier University Press, 2000.

Orwell, George. "Politics and the English Language." In *A Collection of Essays.* New York: Doubleday, 1954.

Osthaus, Carl R. *Partisans of the Southern Press: Editorial Spokesmen of the Nineteenth Century.* Lexington: University Press of Kentucky, 1994.

Otterbein, Keith. *Feuding and Warfare: Selected Works of Keith F. Otterbein.* Langhorne, PA: Gordon and Breach, 1994.

Otto, John Solomon. "The Decline of Forest Farming in Southern Appalachia." *Journal of Forest History* 27, no. 1 (1983).

Owens, Patricia. "Distinctions, Distinctions: 'Public' and 'Private' Force?" In *Mercenaries, Pirates, Bandits and Empires: Private Violence in Historical Context,* edited by Alejandro Colás and Bryan Mabee. New York: Columbia University Press, 2010.

Owings, Elizabeth S. *The Amis Family and Their Known Descendants.* Clinton, MS: E. S. Owings, 1996.

Owsley, Frank. *Plain Folk of the Old South.* Baton Rouge: Louisiana State University Press, 1949.

Painter, Nell I. *The History of White People.* New York: Norton, 2010.

Palmer, Bryan D. "Discordant Music: Charivaris and Whitecapping in Nineteenth-Century North America." *Labour/Le travail* 3 (1978).

Paludan, Phillip. *A People's Contest: The Union and Civil War, 1861–1865.* 2nd ed. Lawrence: University Press of Kansas, 1996.

———. *Victims: A True Story of the Civil War.* Knoxville: University of Tennessee Press, 1981.

Pandey, Gyanendra. *Routine Violence: Nations, Fragments, Histories.* Stanford, CA: Stanford University Press, 2006.

Parsons, Elaine Frantz. "Klan Skepticism and Denial in Reconstruction-Era Public Discourse." *Journal of Southern History* 77, no. 1 (2011).

Payne, James W., Jr. "The Hillman Case: An Old Problem Revisited." *Virginia Law Review* 41, no. 8 (1955).

Pearce, John Ed. *Days of Darkness: The Feuds of Eastern Kentucky.* Lexington: University Press of Kentucky, 1994.

———. *Divide and Dissent: Kentucky Politics, 1930–1963.* Lexington: University Press of Kentucky, 1987.

Peiss, Kathy. "Going Public: Women in Nineteenth-Century Cultural History." *American Literary History* 3, no. 4 (1991).

Peluso, Nancy Lee, and Peter Vandergeest. "Genealogies of the Political Forest and Customary Rights in Indonesia, Malaysia, and Thailand." *Journal of Asian Studies* 60, no. 3 (2001).

Perkins, Elizabeth A. *Border Life: Experience and Memory in the Revolutionary Ohio Valley.* Chapel Hill: University of North Carolina Press, 1998.

Perman, Michael. *Pursuit of Unity: A Political History of the American South.* Chapel Hill: University of North Carolina Press, 2009.

———. *The Road to Redemption: Southern Politics, 1869–1879.* Chapel Hill: University of North Carolina Press, 1984.

Perry, Robert. *Jack May's War: Colonel Andrew Jackson May and the Civil War in Eastern Kentucky.* Johnson City, TN: Overmountain, 1998.

Pettit, Arthur G. "Mark Twain, the Blood-Feud, and the South." *Southern Literary Journal* 4, no. 1 (1971).

Picht, Douglas R. "The American Squatter and Federal Land Policy." *Journal of the West* 14, no. 3 (1975).

Piepmeier, Alison. *Out in Public: Configurations of Women's Bodies in Nineteenth-Century America.* Chapel Hill: University of North Carolina Press, 2004.

Pinker, Steven. *The Better Angels of Our Nature: Why Violence Has Declined.* New York: Viking, 2011.

Pocock, J. G. A. *The Machiavellian Moment: Florentine Political Thought and the Atlantic Republican Tradition.* Princeton, NJ: Princeton University Press, 1975.

Portelli, Alessandro. *They Say in Harlan County: An Oral History.* Oxford: Oxford University Press, 2010.

Powell, Elwin H. *The Designs of Discord: Studies in Anomie.* New Brunswick, NJ: Transaction, 1988.

Powell, Levi W. *Who Are These Mountain People?* New York: Exposition, 1966.

Preston, John David. *The Civil War in the Big Sandy Valley of Kentucky.* Baltimore: Gateway, 1984.

Przybyszewski, Linda. "The Dissents of John Marshall Harlan I." *Journal of Supreme Court History* 32, no. 2 (August 20, 2007).

Pudup, Mary Beth, Dwight Billings, and Altina Waller, eds. *Appalachia in the Making: The Mountain South in the Nineteenth Century.* Chapel Hill: University of North Carolina Press, 1995.

Quisenberry, Anderson Chenault. *Kentucky in the War of 1812.* Baltimore: Genealogical, 1996.

Rable, George. *But There Was No Peace: The Role of Violence in the Politics of Reconstruction.* Athens: University of Georgia Press, 1984.

Ramage, James A. "The Green River Pioneers: Squatters, Soldiers, and Speculators." *Register of the Kentucky Historical Society* 75, no. 3 (1977).

Ramage, James A., and Andrea S. Watkins. *Kentucky Rising: Democracy, Slavery, and Culture from the Early Republic to the Civil War.* Lexington: University Press of Kentucky, 2011.

Ramsey, Thomas R., Jr. *The Raid: East Tennessee, Western North Carolina, Southwest Virginia.* Kingsport, TN: Kingsport Press, 1973.

Redding, Kent. *Making Race, Making Power: North Carolina's Road to Disfranchisement.* Urbana: University of Illinois Press, 2003.

Rhyne, J. Michael. "'We Are Mobed and Beat': Regulator Violence against Free Black Households in Kentucky's Bluegrass Region, 1865–1867." *Ohio Valley History* 2, no. 1 (2002).

Richardson, Heather Cox. *West from Appomattox: The Reconstruction of America after the Civil War.* New Haven, CT: Yale University Press, 2007.

Robbins, Roy M. "Preemption—A Frontier Triumph." *Mississippi Valley Historical Review* 18, no. 3 (1931).

Robertson, James Rood, ed. *Petitions of the Early Inhabitants of Kentucky to the General Assembly of Virginia, 1769–1792.* Louisville: John P. Morton, 1914.

Rockenbach, Stephen. "'The Weeds and the Flowers Are Closely Mixed': Allegiance, Law, and White Supremacy in Kentucky's Bluegrass Region, 1861–1865." Paper presented at the Southern Historical Association, Atlanta, November 4, 2005.

Rolff, James Robert. *Strong Family of Virginia and Other Southern States.* Oak Forest, IL: J. R. Rolff, 1982.

Rossiter, Clinton. *Parties and Politics in America.* Ithaca, NY: Cornell University Press, 1964.

Rothert, Otto Arthur. *The Story of a Poet: Madison Cawein.* Louisville: J .P. Morton, 1921.

Rubenstein, Richard. *Rebels in Eden: Mass Political Violence in the United States.* Boston: Little, Brown, 1970.

Rumsfeld, Donald. *Known and Unknown: A Memoir.* New York: Penguin, 2011.

Said, Edward. "Secular Criticism." In *The Edward Said Reader,* edited by Moustafa Bayoumi and Andrew Rubin. New York: Vintage Books, 2000.

Salstrom, Paul. "The Agricultural Origins of Economic Dependency." In *Appalachian Frontiers: Settlement, Society, and Development in the Preindustrial Era,* edited by Robert D. Mitchell. Lexington: University Press of Kentucky, 1991.

———. *Appalachia's Path to Dependency: Rethinking a Region's Economic History, 1730–1940.* Lexington: University Press of Kentucky, 1997.

Sarris, Jonathan. *A Separate Civil War: Communities in Conflict in the Mountain South.* Charlottesville: University of Virginia Press, 2006.

Satterwhite, Emily. *Dear Appalachia: Readers, Identity, and Popular Fiction since 1878.* Lexington: University Press of Kentucky, 2011.

Savenije, Wim, and Chris Van der Borgh. "Youth Gangs, Social Exclusion and the Transformation of Violence in El Salvador." In *Armed Actors: Organised Violence and State Failure in Latin America,* edited by Kees Koonings and Dirk Kruijt. London: Zed Books, 2004.

Scales, Len, and Oliver Zimmer. *Power and Nation in European History.* Cambridge: Cambridge University Press, 2005.

Scalf, Henry P. *Kentucky's Last Frontier.* Johnson City, TN: Overmountain, 1966.

Schickel, Richard. *D. W. Griffith: An American Life.* New York: Simon and Schuster, 1984.

Schlichte, Klaus. "State Formation and the Economy of Intra-state Wars." In *Shadow Globalization, Ethnic Conflicts and New Wars: A Political Economy of Intra-state War,* edited by Dietrich Jung. New York: Routledge, 2003.

Schmidt, Stefen W., Laura Guasti, Carl H. Lande, and James C. Scott, eds. *Friends, Followers and Factions: A Reader in Political Clientelism.* Berkeley: University of California Press, 1977.

Schoenbachler, Matthew G. *Murder and Madness: The Myth of the Kentucky Tragedy.* Lexington: University Press of Kentucky, 2009.

Schulman, Robert. *John Sherman Cooper: The Global Kentuckian.* Lexington: University Press of Kentucky, 2004.

Schulte-Bockholt, Alfredo. *The Politics of Organized Crime and the Organized Crime of Politics: A Study in Criminal Power.* Oxford: Lexington, 2006.

Scott, James C. "Corruption, Machine Politics and Political Change." *American Political Science Review* 63, no. 4 (1969).

———. *Domination and the Arts of Resistance: Hidden Transcripts.* New Haven, CT: Yale University Press, 1990.

———. "Protest and Profanation: Agrarian Revolt and the Little Tradition, Part II." *Theory and Society* 4, no. 2 (1977).

———. *Seeing Like a State: How Certain Schemes to Improve the Human Condition Have Failed.* New Haven, CT: Yale University Press, 1998.

———. *Weapons of the Weak: Everyday Forms of Peasant Resistance.* New Haven, CT: Yale University Press, 1985.

Severance, Benjamin. *Tennessee's Radical Army: The State Guard and Its Role in Reconstruction, 1867–1869.* Knoxville: University of Tennessee Press, 2005.

Sexton, Robert F., and Lewis Bellardo, eds. *The Public Papers of Governor Louis B. Nunn, 1967–1971.* Lexington: University Press of Kentucky, 1975.

Shackleford, Laurel, and Bill Weinberg, eds. *Our Appalachia.* Lexington: University Press of Kentucky, 1988.

Shaffer, John W. *Clash of Loyalties: A Border County in the Civil War.* Morgantown: West Virginia University Press, 2003.

Shannon, Jasper B., and Ruth McQuown. *Presidential Politics in Kentucky, 1824–1948.* Lexington: Bureau of Government Research, College of Arts and Sciences, University of Kentucky, 1950.

Shapiro, Henry. *Appalachia on Our Mind: The Southern Mountains and Mountaineers in the American Consciousness, 1870–1920.* Chapel Hill: University of North Carolina Press, 1978.

Shapiro, Herbert. *White Violence and Black Response: From Reconstruction to Montgomery.* Amherst: University of Massachusetts Press, 1988.

Shapiro, Karin A. *A New South Rebellion: The Battle against Convict Labor in the Tennessee Coalfields, 1871–1896.* Chapel Hill: University of North Carolina Press, 1998.

Sharfstein, Daniel. *The Invisible Line: Three American Families and the Secret Journey from Black to White.* New York: Penguin, 2011.

Shearin, Hubert G., and Joseph Henry Combs. *Syllabus of Kentucky Folk-songs.* Lexington: Transylvania, 1911.

Short, James F., and Marvin E. Wolfgang, eds. *Collective Violence.* Philadelphia: American Academy of Political and Social Science, 1972.

Shortridge, Wilson Porter. "Kentucky Neutrality in 1861." *Mississippi Valley Historical Review* 9, no. 4 (1923).

Silber, Nina. *The Romance of Reunion: Northerners and the South, 1865–1900.* Chapel Hill: University of North Carolina Press, 1993.

Simkins, Francis Butler. *The South, Old and New: A History, 1820–1947.* New York: Knopf, 1947.

Simon, John Y. "Lincoln, Grant, and Kentucky in 1861." In *The Civil War in Kentucky: Battle for the Bluegrass State,* edited by Kent Masterson Brown. Mason City, IA: Savas, 2000.

Simpson, J. A., and E. S. C. Weiner, eds. *The Oxford English Dictionary.* 2nd ed. Oxford: Clarendon, 1989.

Singh, V. V. *Communal Violence.* Jaipur: Rawat, 1993.

Skolnick, Jerome. *The Politics of Protest.* New York: Ballantine Books, 1969.

Slap, Andrew L. "Introduction: Appalachia, 1865–1900." In *Reconstructing Appalachia: The Civil War's Aftermath,* edited by Andrew L. Slap. Lexington: University Press of Kentucky, 2010.

Slotkin, Richard. *Regeneration through Violence: The Mythology of the American Frontier.* Middletown, CT: Wesleyan University Press, 1973.

Smallwood, James A. *The Feud That Wasn't: The Taylor Ring, Bill Sutton, John Wesley Hardin, and Violence in Texas.* College Station: Texas A&M University Press, 2008.

Smiley, David L. *The Lion of White Hall: The Life of Cassius M. Clay.* Madison: University of Wisconsin Press, 1962.

Smith, Albert C. "'Southern Violence' Reconsidered: Arson as Protest in Black-Belt Georgia, 1865–1910." *Journal of Southern History* 51, no. 4 (1985).

Smith, Carl S. *Urban Disorder and the Shape of Belief: The Great Chicago Fire, the Haymarket Bomb, and the Model Town of Pullman.* Chicago: University of Chicago Press, 1995.

Smith, Edward C. *The Borderland in the Civil War.* New York: Macmillan, 1927.

Smith, Gerald L. "Slavery and Abolition in Kentucky: 'Patter-rollers' were everywhere.'" In *Bluegrass Renaissance: The History and Culture of Central Kentucky, 1792–1852,* edited by James C. Klotter and Daniel Rowland. Lexington: University Press of Kentucky, 2012.

Snay, Mitchell. "Freedom and Progress: The Dilemma of Southern Republican Thought during Radical Reconstruction." *American Nineteenth Century History* 5, no. 1 (2004).

Sparks, John. *Raccoon John Smith: Frontier Kentucky's Most Famous Preacher.* Lexington: University Press of Kentucky, 2005.

Speed, Thomas, Alfred Pirtle, and Robert Morrow Kelly. *The Union Regiments of Kentucky.* Louisville: Courier-Journal, 1897.

Spencer, Manual Ray. *The Descendants of Joseph Spencer.* N.p.: M. R. Spencer, 1996.

Sprague, Stuart Seely. "The Kentucky Pocket Plantation: Sources and Research Strategies, Mason County as a Case Study." *Filson Club Historical Quarterly* 71, no. 1 (1997).

Stealey, Orlando Oscar. *Twenty Years in the Press Gallery.* New York: Publishers Printing, 1906.

Stickles, Arndt M. *Simon Bolivar Buckner: Borderland Knight.* Chapel Hill: University of North Carolina Press, 1940.

Stiles, T. J. *Jesse James: Last Rebel of the Civil War.* New York: Vintage Books, 2003.

Stoddard, Johnston J., ed. *First Explorations of Kentucky: Doctor Thomas Walker's Journal of an Exploration of Kentucky in 1750, Being the First Record of a White Man's Visit to the Interior of That Territory, Now First Published Entire, with Notes and Biographical Sketch; Also Colonel Christopher Gist's Journal of a Tour through Ohio And Kentucky in 1751, with Notes and Sketch.* Louisville: John P. Morton, 1898.

Storey, Margaret M. "'I'd Rather Go to Hell': White Unionists, Slaves, and Federal Counter-insurgency in Civil War Alabama." *North & South* 7, no. 6 (2004).

———. *Loyalty and Loss: Alabama's Unionists in the Civil War and Reconstruction.* Baton Rouge: Louisiana State University Press, 2004.

Strathern, Andrew, and Pamela J. Stewart. *Arrow Talk: Transaction, Transition, and Contradiction in New Guinea Highlands History.* Kent, OH: Kent State University Press, 2000.

Straw, Richard A., and H. Tyler Blethen, eds. *High Mountains Rising: Appalachia in Time and Place.* Urbana: University of Illinois Press, 2004.

Summers, Mark Wahlgren. *Party Games: Getting, Keeping and Using Power in Gilded Age Politics.* Chapel Hill: University of North Carolina Press, 2004.

———. *The Press Gang: Newspapers and Politics, 1865–1878.* Chapel Hill: University of North Carolina Press, 1994.

Sumner, Charles. *Charles Sumner: His Complete Works; with Introduction by George Frisbie Hoar.* Boston: Lee and Shepard, 1900.

Sutherland, Daniel E. *A Savage Conflict: The Decisive Role of Guerillas in the American Civil War.* Chapel Hill: University of North Carolina Press, 2009.

Sydnor, Charles S. *The Development of Southern Sectionalism, 1819–1848.* Baton Rouge: Louisiana State University Press, 1948.

Tallant, Harold D. *Evil Necessity: Slavery and Political Culture in Antebellum Kentucky.* Lexington: University Press of Kentucky, 2003.

Tapp, Hambleton, and James Klotter. *Kentucky: Decades of Discord, 1865–1900.* Frankfort: Kentucky Historical Society, 1977.

Thelen, David. *Paths of Resistance: Tradition and Dignity in Industrializing Missouri.* Oxford: Oxford University Press, 1986.

Therborn, Goran. "'Europe' as Issues of Sociology." In *European Societies: Fusion or Fission?* edited by Thomas P. Boje, Bart van Steenbergen, and Sylvia Walby. New York: Routledge, 1999.

Thomas, Elaine. "Muting Inter-ethnic Conflict in Post-imperial Britain: The Success and Limits of a Liberal Political Approach." In *The Myth of "Ethnic Conflict": Politics, Economics, and "Cultural" Violence,* edited by Beverly Crawford and Ronnie D. Lipschutz. Berkeley: International and Area Studies, University of California Press, 1998.

Thompson, E. P. *Making of the English Working Class.* New York: Vintage Books, 1966.

———. "The Moral Economy of the English Crowd in the Eighteenth Century." *Past and Present,* no. 50 (February 1971).

———. *Whigs and Hunters: The Origin of the Black Act.* New York: Pantheon Books, 1975.

Thompson, Ed Porter. *History of the First Kentucky Brigade.* Cincinnati: Caxton, 1868.

———. *History of the Orphan Brigade.* Louisville: Lewis N. Thompson, 1898.

Thompson, Lawrence Sidney. *Kentucky Tradition.* North Haven, CT: Shoe String, 1956.

Thorpe, Francis Newton. *The Constitutional History of the United States.* Vol. 3, *1861–1895.* Chicago: Callaghan, 1901.

Tilly, Charles. *The Politics of Collective Violence.* Cambridge: Cambridge University Press, 2003.

Torgovnick, Marianna. *Gone Primitive: Savage Intellects, Modern Lives.* Chicago: University of Chicago Press, 1990.

Trachtenburg, Alan. *The Incorporation of America: Culture and Society in the Gilded Age.* New York: Hill and Wang, 1982.

Trelease, Allen. *White Terror: The Ku Klux Klan Conspiracy and Southern Reconstruction.* Baton Rouge: Louisiana State University Press, 1971.

———. "Who Were the Scalawags?" *Journal of Southern History* 29, no. 4 (1963).

Trotter, William R. *Bushwhackers: The Civil War in North Carolina (The Mountains).* Winston-Salem, NC: J. F. Blair, 1991.

Turner, James. "Understanding the Populists." *Journal of American History* 67, no. 2 (1980).

Turner, Wallace B. "Kentucky Politics in the 1850's." *Register of the Kentucky Historical Society* 56, no. 2 (1958).

The Union Army: A History of Military Affairs in the Loyal States, 1861–1865—Records of the Regiments in the Union Army—Cyclopedia of Battles—Memoirs of Commanders and Soldiers. Vol. 4. Madison, WI: Federal Publishing, 1908.

Uzee, Phillip D. "The Republican Party in the Louisiana Election of 1896." *Louisiana History* 2, no. 3 (1961).

Vahabi, Mehrad. *The Political Economy of Destructive Power.* Northhampton, UK: Edward Elgar, 2004.

Vandal, Gilles. *Rethinking Southern Violence: Homicides in Post–Civil War Louisiana, 1866–1884.* Columbus: Ohio State University Press, 2000.

Van Noppen, Ina Woestemeyer. *The South: A Documentary History.* Princeton, NJ: Van Nostrand, 1958.

Van Young, Eric. *The Other Rebellion: Popular Violence, Ideology, and the Mexican Struggle for Independence, 1810–1821.* Stanford, CA: Stanford University Press, 2001.

Verhoeff, Mary. *The Kentucky Mountains: Transportation and Commerce, 1750 to 1911; A Study in the Economic History of a Coal Field.* Louisville: John P. Morton, 1911.

———. *The Kentucky River Navigation.* Louisville: John P. Morton, 1917.

Wade, Wyn Craig. *The Fiery Cross: The Ku Klux Klan in America.* New York: Simon and Schuster, 1987.

Walden, Geoffrey R. *Remembering Kentucky's Confederates.* Charleston, S.C.: Arcadia, 2008.

Waldrep, Christopher. "Rank and File Voters and the Coming of the Civil War: Caldwell County, Kentucky as Test Case." *Civil War History* 35, no. 1 (1989).

———. "Word and Deed: The Language of Lynching, 1820–1953." In *Lethal Imagination: Violence and Brutality in American History,* edited by Michael A. Belleiles. New York: New York University Press, 1999.

Waldrep, Christopher, and Donald G. Nieman, eds. *Local Matters: Race, Crime, and Justice in the Nineteenth-Century South.* Athens: University of Georgia Press, 2001.

Waldstreicher, David. "Rites of Rebellion, Rites of Assent: Celebrations, Print Culture, and the Origins of American Nationalism." *Journal of American History* 82, no. 1 (1995).

Wall, Maryjean. "'A richer land never seen yet': Horse Country and the 'Athens of the West.'" In *Bluegrass Renaissance: The History and Culture of Central Kentucky, 1792–1852,* edited by James C. Klotter and Daniel Rowland. Lexington: University Press of Kentucky, 2012.

Waller, Altina. *Feud: Hatfields, McCoys, and Social Change in Appalachia, 1860–1900.* Chapel Hill: University of North Carolina Press, 1988.

———. "Feuding in Appalachia: Evolution of a Cultural Stereotype." In *Appalachia in the Making: The Mountain South in the Nineteenth Century,* edited by Mary Beth Pudup, Dwight Billings, and Altina Waller. Chapel Hill: University of North Carolina Press, 1995.

Walpole, Matthew. "The Closing of the Open Range in Watauga County, N.C." *Appalachian Journal* 16, no. 4 (1989).

Warren, Mervyn A. *King Came Preaching: The Pulpit Power of Martin Luther King, Jr.* Downers Grover, IL: Intervarsity, 2001.

Watlington, Patricia. *The Partisan Spirit: Kentucky Politics, 1779–1792.* New York: Atheneum, 1972.

Watson, Harry. *Jacksonian Politics and Community Conflict: The Emergence of the Second Party System in Cumberland County, North Carolina.* Chapel Hill: University of North Carolina Press, 1981.

Watson, Judge. *Eastern Kentucky, Economic and Cultural, 1900–1962.* Lakeland, FL: J. Watson, 1993.

Weaver, Bill L. "Louisville's Labor Disturbance, July, 1877." *Filson Club Historical Quarterly* 48, no. 2 (1974).

Webb, Ross. *Kentucky in the Reconstruction Era.* Lexington: University Press of Kentucky, 1979.

———. "Kentucky: Pariah among the Elect." In *Radicalism, Racism, and Party Realignment: The Border States during Reconstruction,* edited by Richard O. Curry. Baltimore: Johns Hopkins University Press, 1969.

Webb, Samuel. "From Independents to Populists to Progressive Republicans: The Case of Chilton County, Alabama, 1880–1920." *Journal of Southern History* 59, no. 4 (1993).

———. *Two-Party Politics in the One-Party South: Alabama's Hill Country, 1874–1920.* Tuscaloosa: University of Alabama Press, 1997.

Weber, Eugen. *Peasants into Frenchmen: The Modernization of Rural France.* Stanford, CA: Stanford University Press, 1976.

Weber, Max. *From Max Weber: Essays in Sociology.* Edited by H. H. Gerth and C. Wright Mills. New York: Routledge, 2001.

Wells, Charles C., ed. *1890 Special Veterans' Census for Eastern Kentucky.* Baltimore: Gateway, 2000.

Wells, John Britton. *10th Kentucky Cavalry, CSA: May's, Trimble's, Diamond's "Yankee Chasers."* Baltimore: Gateway, 1996.

Welter, Barbara. "The Cult of True Womanhood: 1820–1860." *American Quarterly* 18, no. 2 (1966).

Whisnant, David. *All That Is Native and Fine: The Politics of Culture in an American Region.* Chapel Hill: University of North Carolina Press, 1983.

———. *Modernizing the Mountaineer: People, Power, and Planning in Appalachia.* Rev. ed. Knoxville: University of Tennessee Press, 1994.

White, Hayden. *Metahistory: The Historical Imagination in Nineteenth-Century Europe.* Baltimore: Johns Hopkins University Press, 1973.

Wickham-Crowley, Timothy P. "Terror and Guerrilla Warfare in Latin America, 1956–1970." *Comparative Studies in Society and History* 32, no. 2 (1990).

Wiebe, Robert. *The Search for Order, 1877–1920.* New York: Hill and Wang, 1967.

Wiese, Robert. *Grasping at Independence: Debt, Male Authority, and Mineral Rights in Appalachian Kentucky, 1850–1915.* Knoxville: University of Tennessee Press, 2001.

Wilbanks, James H. *America's Heroes: Medal of Honor Recipients from the Civil War to Afghanistan.* Santa Barbara, CA: ABC-CLIO, 2011.

Wilder, Minnie S., ed. *Kentucky Soldiers of the War of 1812, with an Added Index.* Baltimore: Genealogical Publishing, 1969.

Williams, John A. *Appalachia: A History.* Chapel Hill: University of North Carolina Press, 2002.

———. "Class, Section, and Culture in Nineteenth-Century West Virginia Politics." In *Appalachia in the Making: The Mountain South in the Nineteenth Century,* edited by

Mary Beth Pudup, Dwight Billings, and Altina Waller. Chapel Hill: University of North Carolina Press, 1995.

———. "Henry Shapiro and the Idea of Appalachia: A Review/Essay." *Appalachian Journal* 5, no. 3 (1978).

Williamson, J. W. *Hillbillyland: What the Movies Did to the Mountains and What the Mountains Did to the Movies.* Chapel Hill: University of North Carolina Press, 1995.

Williamson, Joel. *The Crucible of Race: Black-White Relations in the American South since Emancipation.* New York: Oxford University Press, 1984.

Willis, George L. *Kentucky Democracy: A History of the Party and Its Representative Members, Past and Present.* Vol. 1. Louisville: Democratic Historical Society, 1935.

Wilson, Jess D. *The Sugar Pond and the Fritter Tree.* Berea, KY: Kentucke Imprints, 1981.

———. *When They Hanged the Fiddler and Other Stories from "It Happened Here": Including Some Unpublished Works by the Author.* Berea, KY: Kentucke Imprints, 1978.

Wilson, Stephen. *Feuding, Conflict and Banditry.* Cambridge: Cambridge University Press, 1988.

Wiltz, John E. "The 1895 Election: A Watershed in Kentucky Politics." *Filson Club Historical Quarterly* 37, no. 2 (1963).

Wireman, Charles Little. *Kentucky Mountain Outlaw Transformed.* Intercession City, FL: Intercession, 1950.

Wolfe, Charles K. *Kentucky Country: Folk and Country Music of Kentucky.* Lexington: University Press of Kentucky, 1982.

Wood, Amy Louise. *Lynching and Spectacle: Witnessing Racial Violence in America, 1890–1940.* Chapel Hill: University of North Carolina Press, 2009.

Wood, Gordon. "Interests and Disinterestedness in the Making of the Constitution." In *Beyond Confederation: Origins of the Constitution and American National Identity,* edited by Richard Beeman, Stephen Botein, and Edward C. Carter. Chapel Hill: University of North Carolina Press, 1987.

Wood, Norman Barton. *The White Side of a Black Subject: A Vindication of the Afro-American Race, from the Landing of Slaves at St. Augustine, Florida, in 1565, to the Present Time.* Chicago: American Publishing, 1897.

Woodson, Mary Willis. "My Recollections of Frankfort." *Register of the Kentucky Historical Society* 61, no. 3 (1963).

Woodward, C. Vann. *The Burden of Southern History.* 3rd ed. Baton Rouge: Louisiana State University Press, 1993.

———. *Origins of the New South, 1877–1913.* Baton Rouge: Louisiana State University Press, 1951.

Wooster, Ralph A. *Politicians, Planters and Plain Folk: Courthouse and Statehouse in the Upper South.* Knoxville: University of Tennessee Press, 1975.

———. *The Secession Conventions of the South.* Princeton, NJ: Princeton University Press, 1962.

Workers of the Writers' Program of the Works Projects Administration in the State of Kentucky. *In the Land of Breathitt*. Northport, NY: Bacon, Percy and Daggett, 1941.

———. *Military History of Kentucky, Chronologically Arranged*. Frankfort, KY: State Journal, 1939.

Wray, Matt. *Not Quite White: White Trash and the Boundaries of Whiteness*. Durham, NC: Duke University Press, 2006.

Wright, George C. "The Founding of Lincoln Institute." *Filson Club Historical Quarterly* 49, no. 1 (1975).

———. *A History of Blacks in Kentucky*. Vol. 2, *In Pursuit of Equality, 1890–1980*. Frankfort: Kentucky Historical Society, 1992.

———. *Racial Violence in Kentucky, 1865–1940: Lynchings, Mob Rule, and "Legal Lynchings."* Baton Rouge: Louisiana State University Press, 1996.

Wyatt-Brown, Bertram. "The Civil Rights Act of 1875." *Western Historical Quarterly* 18, no. 4 (1965).

———. *Honor and Violence in the Old South*. Oxford: Oxford University Press, 1986.

———. *Southern Honor: Ethics and Behavior in the Old South*. 25th anniversary ed. Oxford: Oxford University Press, 2007.

"Yesterday's News." *Register of the Kentucky Historical Society* 95, no. 3 (1997).

York, Bill. *John Fox, Jr.: Appalachian Author*. Jefferson, NC: McFarland, 2003.

Young, Lot D. *Reminiscences of a Soldier of the Orphan Brigade*. Chapel Hill: Academic Affairs Library, University of North Carolina at Chapel Hill, 1998.

Zuczek, Richard. *State of Rebellion: Reconstruction in South Carolina*. Columbia: University of South Carolina Press, 1996.

Electronic Sources

Interview with William Haddix, 1938. Federal Writers' Project (interviewer: Margaret Bishop), http://www.breathittcounty.com/BreathittWeb2/THaddix.html (viewed December 19, 2008).

Lineage of Edward Callahan and Mahala Brock. http://kykinfolk.com/breathitt/databases/edwardcallahan_mahalabrock/d1.htm (viewed March 1, 2011).

Orend, Brian. "War." In *The Stanford Encyclopedia of Philosophy (Fall 2008 Edition)*, edited by Edward N. Zalta. http://plato.stanford.edu/entries/war/ (viewed April 30, 2012).

Spencer, Herbert W. "Captain Bill's January Raid," 1961. http://www.artontherocks.net/genes/tree/np77.htm (viewed November 20, 2006).

Tobin, Jonathan S. "Why Nothing Can Be Done about Shootings." *Commentary*, July 22, 2012. http://www.commentarymagazine.com/2012/07/22/why-nothing-can-be-done-about-shootings-aurora-gun-control/ (viewed July 23, 2012).

Trailsrus County Courthouses: Courthouses in Kentucky—Breathitt Co. http://www.trailsrus.com/courthouses/breathitt.html (viewed July 25, 2008).

INDEX

Coulter, E. Merton, 68, 81, 282n129,
299n172, 300n3, 301n10
Cox, Braxton, 171; killing of, 172–76,
179, 181, 183, 192, 193, 197, 199,
201, 203–4, 205, 340n100
Crawford, Matt, 199
Crawford, T. C., 229–30, 233
Crittenden, John J., 39, 299n174
Crockettsville, KY: Callahan home in,
145, 163, 165, 196–97; as polling
place, 84–87; telephone service in,
349n254; as Unionist mustering
ground, 52–54

Davis, Jefferson, 39
Day, Carl, 187–90, 345n186
Democratic Party: and Breathitt
County, 26, 27, 48, 52, 65–66, 102–
3, 109, 150, 162–63, 170, 179–80,
192–93, 241, 278n99, 283n146; in
Civil War, 48, 52, 278n99; and Jim
Crow legislation, 187–90, 345n186;
Kentucky politicians in, 132, 154,
179–80, 192, 320n70; and Ku Klux
Klan, 79–80, 261n12, 304n49; and
Republicans' views of, 81, 82, 97,
185
depoliticization of violence, 6; and
Civil War, 39, 41, 66, 68, 82;
in eastern Kentucky, 105, 106,
127–28, 150, 195, 205–6, 249,
314n204, 314n206; feud used for,
78, 85–87, 90, 91, 127–28, 150,
195, 216–17; and hierarchies of
time and space, 221–22, 231–32,
249–50, 264n24; and Ku Klux Klan,
80; during Reconstruction, 74, 78,
79, 85–87, 90–91, 97, 127–28, 150;
and William Strong, 105, 150, 249,
293n90; and war memory, 101,
324n110

Dickey, James Jay: antispeculation
screeds, 134–35; on Breathitt
County, 121–23, 124–26; on
economic success, 124–25, 235–36;
and Guerrant, 118–19; Hatfield-
McCoy feud, reports, 235; Jackson,
arrives in, 118; and *Jackson
Hustler,* 123–24; on law and order,
140; lynching, witnesses, 109; on
prohibition, 137, 141; on railroad,
133–34; and William Strong,
207–10
Donati's Comet, sighting, 37, 285n1
Durkheim, Émile, 210

Edgefield, SC ("bloody Edgefield"), 5,
74, 264n20
Ehrlichman, John, 243
Elliott County, KY, 192, 347n222
Estill County, KY, 21, 27, 45, 52, 59, 89,
269n6, 307n106
Eversole, John, 52, 54, 55, 58, 59, 66
Eversole, Joseph, 52, 54, 58, 61, 66
Eversole Joseph (the younger), 129,
168
Eversole, William, 52, 54, 58
execution, 138–40, 144, 168–70

Fairbank, Calvin, 27, 42
Falkner, William C., 214
Farm Security Administration, 241
Federal Writers' Project. *See* Works
Progress Administration
Fee, John G. (founder of Berea
College), 32, 77
Feltner, Mose, 176, 200–201, 342n136;
death, 197
feud, 1–2, 4, 6–9, 210–35; and Civil
War, 39, 66, 67–68, 70–71, 74, 78;
and depoliticization of violence, 6,
39, 78, 81, 85–87, 90, 91, 110,

NEW DIRECTIONS IN SOUTHERN HISTORY

SERIES EDITORS
Michele Gillespie, Wake Forest University
William A. Link, University of Florida

Cultivating Race: The Expansion of Slavery in Georgia, 1750–1860
Watson W. Jennison

Remembering the Battle of the Crater: War as Murder
Kevin M. Levin

The View from the Ground: Experiences of Civil War Soldiers
edited by Aaron Sheehan-Dean

Reconstructing Appalachia: The Civil War's Aftermath
edited by Andrew L. Slap

Blood in the Hills: A History of Violence in Appalachia
edited by Bruce E. Stewart

Moonshiners and Prohibitionists: The Battle over Alcohol in Southern Appalachia
Bruce E. Stewart

Southern Farmers and Their Stories: Memory and Meaning in Oral History
Melissa Walker

Law and Society in the South: A History of North Carolina Court Cases
John W. Wertheimer

Family or Freedom: People of Color in the Antebellum South
Emily West

CPSIA information can be obtained at www.ICGtesting.com
Printed in the USA
BVOW07*0054230713

326607BV00001B/1/P